Studies in Modern Capitalism · Études sur le capitalisme moderne

The Ottoman Empire and the World-Economy

Studies in modern capitalism · Études sur le capitalisme moderne

This series is devoted to an attempt to comprehend capitalism as a world-system. It will include monographs, collections of essays and colloquia around specific themes, written by historians and social scientists united by a common concern for the study of large-scale long-term social structure and social change.

The series is a joint enterprise of the Maison des Sciences de l'Homme in Paris and the Fernand Braudel Center for the Study of Economies, Historical Systems, and Civilizations at the State University of New York at Binghamton.

Other books in the series

Maurice Aymard (ed.): *Dutch capitalism and world capitalism/Capitalisme hollandaise et capitalisme mondial*
Iván T. Berend, György Ráni: *The European periphery and industrialization, 1780–1914*
Pierre Bourdieu: *Algeria 1960*
Andre Gunder Frank: *Mexican agriculture 1521–1630: transformation of the mode of production*
Folker Fröbel, Jürgen Heinrichs, Otto Kreye: *The new international division of labour: structural unemployment in industrialized countries and industrialization in developing countries*
Çağlar Keyder: *The definition of a peripheral economy: Turkey 1923–1929*
Peter Kriedte, Hans Medick, Jürgen Schlumbohm: *Industrialization before industrialization: rural industry in the genesis of capitalism*
Bruce McGowan: *Economic life in Ottoman Europe: taxation, trade and the struggle for the land, 1660–1800*
Ernest Mandel: *Long waves of capitalist development: the Marxist interpretation*
Michel Morineau: *Ces incroyables gazettes et fabuleux métaux: les retours des trésors américains, d'après les gazettes hollandaises (16e–18e siècles)*
Henri H. Stahl: *Traditional Romanian village communities: the transition from the communal to the capitalist mode of production in the Danube region*
Immanuel Wallerstein: *The capitalist world-economy: essays*
Immanuel Wallerstein: *The politics of the world-economy: the states, the movements and the civilizations*
Antoni Mączak, Henryk Samsonowicz and Peter Burke (eds.): *East-central Europe in transition: from the fourteenth to the seventeenth century*
Lucette Valensi: *Tunisian peasants in the eighteenth and nineteenth centuries*

The Ottoman Empire and the World-Economy

Edited by
HURİ İSLAMOĞLU-İNAN

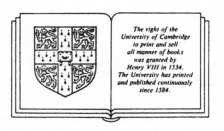

The right of the University of Cambridge to print and sell all manner of books was granted by Henry VIII in 1534. The University has printed and published continuously since 1584.

Cambridge University Press
Cambridge
New York Port Chester Melbourne Sydney

& Éditions de la Maison des Sciences de l'Homme
Paris

PUBLISHED BY THE PRESS SYNDICATE OF THE UNIVERSITY OF CAMBRIDGE
The Pitt Building, Trumpington Street, Cambridge, United Kingdom
and Editions de la Maison des Sciences de l'Homme
54 Boulevard Raspail, 75270 Paris Cedex 06

CAMBRIDGE UNIVERSITY PRESS
The Edinburgh Building, Cambridge CB2 2RU, UK
40 West 20th Street, New York NY 10011–4211, USA
477 Williamstown Road, Port Melbourne, VIC 3207, Australia
Ruiz de Alarcón 13, 28014 Madrid, Spain
Dock House, The Waterfront, Cape Town 8001, South Africa

http://www.cambridge.org

First published 1987
Reprinted 1990
First paperback edition 2002

A catalogue record for this book is available from the British Library

Library of Congress Cataloguing in Publication data
The Ottoman Empire and the world-economy.
(Studies in modern capitalism = Études sur le
capitalisme moderne)
Includes index.
1. Turkey – Economic conditions. 2. Turkey – Foreign
economic relations. 3. Agriculture – Economic aspects –
Turkey – History. 4. Turkey – Industries – History.
5. Labor supply – Turkey – History. 6. Turkey – History –
Ottoman Empire, 1288–1918. I. Islamoğlu-İnan, Huri,
1947– . II. Series: Studies in modern capitalism.
HC492.088 1987 330.9561'01 87-17544

ISBN 0 521 32423 8 hardback
ISBN 2 7351 0 161 4 (France only)
ISBN 0 521 52607 8 paperback

Contents

Illustrations

Tables

Acknowledgements

A number of the articles in this volume have already appeared separately. We are grateful to the editors of these publications for their kind cooperation in granting permission to publish here.

Peter Gran, 'Late-eighteenth-early-nineteenth-century Egypt: merchant capitalism or modern capitalism?', in Robert Mantran (ed.), *L'Égypte au XIXe siècle: rupture et continuité* (Paris, CNRS, 1982).

Huri İslamoğlu and Çağlar Keyder, 'Agenda for Ottoman history', *Review*, I, 1 (1977), 31–55.

Alan R. Richards, 'Primitive accumulation in Egypt, 1789–1882', *Review*, I, 2 (1977), 3–49.

Murat Çizakça, 'Price history and the Bursa silk industry: a study in Ottoman industrial decline, 1550–1650', *The Journal of Economic History*, XL, 3 (1980), 533–50.

Suraiya Faroqhi, 'Notes on the production of cotton and cotton cloths in sixteenth- and seventeenth-century Anatolia', *The Journal of European Economic History*, VIII, 2 (1979), 405–17.

Donald Quataert, 'The silk industry of Bursa, 1880–1914', *Collection Turcica*, III, *Contribution à l'histoire économique et sociale de l'Empire ottoman* (Paris, Association pour le Développement des Études Turques, 1984), pp. 481–503.

Donald Quataert, 'A provisional report concerning the impact of European capital on Ottoman port workers, 1880–1909', in *Économie et sociétés dans l'empire Ottoman* (Paris, CNRS, 1983), pp. 459–70.

Note: The transliteration system used by each individual contributor has been retained.

Introduction: 'Oriental despotism' in world-system perspective

HURİ İSLAMOĞLU-İNAN

Central to the establishment of Western domination over the 'East' is the writing of the history of the 'East' in terms of Western hegemony. This practice is particularly manifest and developed in the case of the Ottoman Empire, which encompassed large areas of the Middle East, North Africa, and the Balkans for nearly four centuries until the outbreak of the First World War. The Ottoman territories, because of their proximity to and long-standing military, diplomatic, commercial and cultural contacts with Western Europe, felt the tremors of European expansion more immediately and intimately than other 'Eastern' world regions. In the late eighteenth and nineteenth centuries, at the 'historical moment' of direct European penetration of Ottoman lands, there developed a body of beliefs – assumptions about the history and the social structure of the Ottoman Empire.[1] Part of the European *Weltanschaung* formulated by the Enlightenment writers and by Hegel, this discourse is premised on an essential duality or oppositionality in the historical developments of the East and the West.[2] As such, the West is viewed as the privileged domain of world-history characterized by change and development, and the East as the non-privileged, unchanging therefore the *ahistorical* domain. On the one hand, this notion embodies a Western self-definition that requires conceptualizing the 'Other' (the East) as its opposite or as a contrastive backdrop to its own development whereby the history of the East becomes that of the West in negation.[3] In practice, it has served as the ideology of Western domination that was conceived as the primary stimulus to change in the otherwise stagnant East. On the other hand, implicit in this dualistic conception of world history is a mode of analysis that is ahistorical. The East and the West are conceived as ideal-type societies locked in their respective cultural and geo-political specificities. In this context, 'historical' analysis is one of contrasting ideal types: dynamic, rational, democratic West versus static, irrational, authoritarian (despotic) East.[4]

This European world-view finds its concrete expression in the nineteenth-century Orientalist tradition of studying art, history, literature and religion, in the Marxian concept of the Asiatic Mode of Production (AMP) as well as in the developmentalist literature in social sciences of the post-World War II period. In the past two decades the fundamental assumptions of these perspectives on the Ottoman Empire are questioned by an increasing number of scholars.[5] In essence, such questioning represents no less than an attempt at 'decolonizing' Ottoman history, dissociating it from the self-image of the West and restoring the Ottoman Empire its place in world history. It means the rewriting of Ottoman history.

The essays in this volume are a part of this attempt at rewriting Ottoman history. In doing this, first, they attempt a new conceptualization of Ottoman history and society that primarily derives from the world-system perspective formulated by I. Wallerstein.[6] What the world-system perspective does is to challenge the ahistorical and dichotomous views of world history and seeks to place the historical development of the Ottoman Empire in the context of a 'singular transformation' process – that of the European world-capitalist system. As such, this perspective rejects the notion of culturally or geo-politically determined ideal types in explaining the historical development of different world regions. Instead it explains the differential development of the Ottoman and the Western European societies in terms of the 'fluctuating reality' of the world-capitalist system as it expanded to include the Ottoman territories after the sixteenth century. This process termed 'incorporation' describes the transformation of Ottoman structures after they came in contact with world-economic forces. How individual authors conceptualize the transformation of the Ottoman society incumbent on 'incorporation', I will discuss later. Parallel to its conceptual emphasis, the volume includes a significant body of micro-historical research on social-economic structures and trends. This trend in Ottoman historical writing reveals the influence of the *Annales* school of historians, most notably of F. Braudel, and is pioneered in the works of Ömer L. Barkan and Halil İnalcık.[7] It stands in sharp contrast, however, to the conventional studies of the Ottoman Empire that focus on political–military–cultural institutions.

The organization of the volume reflects, to a degree, its dual focus on conceptualization and empirical research. The first part includes general theoretical discussions about the Ottoman social structure, its internal dynamics and its transformation under the impact of global economic developments. The remaining three parts consist of case studies on agrarian, industrial and commercial structures and their transformation in different areas at different time periods. The distinction between the 'theoretical' and the 'concrete', however, is more for organizational purposes than real. The case studies either directly address themselves to theoretical problems or provide 'facts' that inform the general interpretative schemes, suggesting new avenues of conceptualization. Conceptual models, in turn, serve to place the specific research in the context of the 'larger picture' and define new research problems. Before attempting a discussion of individual contributions, a few remarks are in order on the prevailing conceptions of the Ottoman Empire since the critique of these approaches provide a starting point for new conceptualizations presented in this volume.

Ahistorical conceptions of Ottoman history

For the nineteenth-century Orientalist tradition,[8] 'Islamic' civilization, of which the Ottoman Empire was a part, constituted the object of study. This civilizational unit was then defined in cultural essentialist terms. Not only was a highly heterogeneous entity, the 'Islamic' world, made uniform by the existence of an Islamic *geist*; diverse institutions or cultural expressions were assumed to be concrete manifestations of this primary cultural essence. Initially focusing on the philological deciphering of such cultural forms as literary, philosophical, religious, and legal texts, the Orientalists viewed the history of the 'Islamic' civilization as one of 'decline' or 'stagnation' following a 'golden age' in the classical period between the ninth and the twelfth centuries. While decline was explained in terms of a flaw in the Islamic cultural essence, the rise of the Ottoman Empire constituted an anomaly in this unilinear downward path of 'decline'.[9] To accommodate it, on the one hand, the Orientalist emphasis shifted from a textual to an institutional mode of analysis; on the other hand, the cultural entity of the 'Islamic' civilization had to be juxtaposed with another nineteenth-century intellectual construct, that of 'Oriental despotism'.

The analysis of Ottoman 'despotism' as an antithesis to European monarchy was very much part of the European political discourse since the Renaissance. Beginning with the Enlightenment thinkers, especially with Montesquieu, however, the notion of 'despotism' acquired a more general denotation. It came to describe all Asian polities including that of the Ottoman Empire whereby geographical determinants of social-political structures were emphasized.[10] At the same time, the contrasting of political structures, the relationships between the state and society in the East and the West became an indispensable intellectual exercise in the late eighteenth and the nineteenth centuries.[11] This was also the theoretical context in which the notion of the AMP was formulated by Marx and Engels. The story of the AMP is familiar and need not concern us here.[12] Moreover, the AMP was not a theoretical model generated solely for the analysis of the Ottoman Empire. What needs to be stressed, however, is that the AMP embodies the central assumption of 'Oriental despotism' – that of the existence of a gap between a mammoth state and an unintegrated social structure. Hence, in Marx and Engels' formulations of the AMP, the defining feature of Asian society was the absence of intermediary structures of classes (i.e., landed aristocracy, merchant class) between the hydraulic state and the undifferentiated agrarian base. This meant the absence of any limits to the authority of the state; it meant the absence of 'civil society' and the preponderance of the state. It was explained in terms of Asian geography (climatic aridity) or of the cellular organization of society in self-sufficient village communities. The Asian society without classes and therefore without class conflict was then assumed to be stationary, without history. As such, change could come to the East only from without, more precisely, through Western intervention.

That the AMP is theoretically inadequate and empirically inaccurate is amply demonstrated.[13] Yet, the assumptions of the AMP about the stationariness of the East and its despotic political structure rooted in geography and agrarian social structure are carried over to the post-World War II analyses of Asian societies – those of Soviet Russia and China, as well as the former Ottoman territories of the Middle East and North Africa.[14] In these analyses the AMP serves at times rather too explicitly the ideological function of underlining the superiority of the West *vis-à-vis* the East. On the one hand, this takes the form of cold-war rhetoric, pure and simple.[15] On the other hand, it serves to legitimate Western colonial penetration of non-Western areas by stressing the beneficial effects of such penetration in the development process. Shlomo Avineri's study of Arab society provides an excellent example of the latter case.[16] Avineri traces the despotic militarism of the contemporary Arab elites and the social-economic underdevelopment of Arab societies to their allegedly stagnant and classless origins under Ottoman despotism. He then proceeds to show how direct Israeli colonization of Palestine has helped to eradicate the past relics of the AMP and to launch this region on the road to modernity.

Orientalist descriptions of Islamic polity and society closely approximate to the conceptions of 'Oriental despotism' that dominated the Enlightenment and the nineteenth-century European intellectual discourse. True to their culturalist orientation, however, Orientalists explain the phenomenon of Oriental despotism in terms of Islamic cultural properties and *not* in terms of geography or social-economic structures. Thus, in this conception Islamic society is viewed as a cellular structure in which village communities, tribes, guilds, ethnic and religious groupings constitute separate and autonomous units that are integrated only on the level of religious ideology and institutions. 'Oriental despotism' or the political structure is then superimposed by force on the society and, as such, it is external to the society's integration.[17] Underlying this conception of the relations between the repressive state and the 'atomistic society' is the assumption that the Islamic society lacked a notion of 'political domination based on general consent'.[18] On the one hand, the rule of the despot was uncontested by different social groupings whose rights and interests were not embodied in a rational body of law and who therefore could not claim a legitimate political existence nor bring about political changes in the existing legal framework. On the other hand, the ruler required no legitimation in the eyes of his subjects who were excluded from the polity. His authority lay in the sheer exercise of force and in the flawed Islamic political theory that recognized the legitimacy of the *de facto* ruler. Once again state and society relations thus defined read the absence of civil society. They also mean the absence of liberalism, humanism, and parliamentarism in Islamic society.[19] These absences rooted in Islamic cultural traits (in law, moral code and customs) in turn explain the political and social stagnation of the society, its political instability and disorder as witnessed in the circulation of dynasties and in sporadic revolts, and, finally, in the indifference of the populace to the upheavals on the level of the polity. In describing this story, Orientalist research focuses on the study of repressive political institutions (army, bureaucracy) and on religious-cultural institutions (Islamic law, the religious scholars, *sufi* orders) that legitimate this repression. The 'decline' or the 'stagnation' of the Islamic Ottoman society is then traced in the history of individual institutions.[20] Thus, the 'golden age–decline', problematic is recast in the framework of 'Oriental despotism' whereby the Ottoman golden age in the sixteenth century characterized by institutional flourishing was followed by a period of institutional decline owing to a flawed cultural essence or to Islam.[21]

Finally, what needs to be stressed is the ideological function of the culturalist view of 'Oriental despotism'. To begin with, the assumption that the Islamic political theory recognized the legitimacy of effective *de facto* rulers served to legitimate Western colonial rule as long as it was more efficient than the 'corrupt' pre-colonial one. Second and most importantly, the assumption of the absence of structural links between the state and the society supplied the ideological argument that the overthrow of the 'despotic' state and its replacement by a more humane colonial state would in no way impair the functioning of the Islamic society.[22]

Culturalist and 'stagnationist' assumptions of nineteenth-century Orientalism are recast in the developmentalist (modernizationist) literature of the post-World War II period.[23] Central to the developmentalist approach is the Weberian characterization of Islamic society.[24] Weber, like Marx before him, sought to explain why rational capitalism did not develop in Islamic society. In doing so, he concentrated on the absence of urban commercial classes which he attributed to the specific character of the Islamic ideological-political structures – Islamic ethics, law and despotism. This 'cultural essentialism' in Weberian garb takes the form of a dichotomous conception of tradition versus modernity in the modernization literature. Modernizationists take the individual nation-states that came into existence after the dissolution of the Ottoman rule in the Middle East and North Africa, and not the Islamic civilization, as their unit of analysis. But, in explaining the economic and the political 'underdevelopment' of these basically political units, they stress the essential Islamic cultural properties (traditionalism) embodied in the attitudes and briefs of individuals and in institutions which inhibit the development of modern (Western) attitudes and institutions. Of the latter, secularist-nationalist world-view, entrepreneurial spirit, and parliamentary democracy are signalled out. 'Modernization' ('Westernization'), on the other hand, is viewed as the end-state of development and, to achieve it, institutions and attitudes are to be refashioned or 'reformed' after Western models. In the implementation of 'reforms' modernizationists stress the centrality of Western-educated bureaucratic-military elites. More importantly, the theory provides legitimation for the use of force by these elites in the name of an 'ultimate good', that of modernization. Finally, this model of transformation from above is justified in terms of the 'history' (rather the 'non-history') of Islamic society which, not having a bourgeoisie, experienced no political reorganization or revolutions from below and therefore can generate neither indigenous nationalisms nor parliamentary democracies.

One widespread reaction to the prevailing conceptions of Ottoman history and society has been to reject the alleged essential oppositionality in the historical developments of the Ottoman Empire and the West. Instead, these critics argue for the generalisability of the Western historical experience to the entire globe, in general, and to the Ottoman Empire in particular. The argument takes several forms. The first is the orthodox Marxist stance, which tends towards a position of quasi-universal feudalism in describing the Ottoman social structure. This view posits a unilinear model of historical development that sees in history a pre-ordained course along the stages of feudalism–capitalism–socialism which every society, each in its own pace, must take. By obscuring the specificity of development paths in different world regions under the undifferentiated rubric of feudalism, this approach, however, falls into the trap of 'ahistoricism' that plagues the modernizationists: 'ideal stages' take the place of Weberian ideal types.[25] A second criticism of the conventional views is one that generalizes the development of capitalism to the Ottoman ('Islamic') society. Inspired by the work of Maxime Rodinson,[26] this approach seeks to demonstrate that the capitalist sector (defined in terms of the existence of merchant and financial capital) was an integral part of Islamic societies throughout their history and that Islam as a culture system was not antithetical to capitalist development. This Rodinsonian view bears much too strongly the marks of reaction to the Weberian–modernizationist paradigm and to the Euro-centric conceptions of 'Islamic' history. This reactive posture then results in the search for 'capitalist' characteristics in lieu of those assumed by the Weberian lore as hindering capitalist development.[27] To begin with, by defining capitalism in terms of the mere presence of capital (merchant and finance), this approach renders capitalism an ahistorical category that can be spotted in nearly all societies one cares to look into. In the second place, this view does not question the validity of the ahistorical category of 'Islamic civilization' as the unit of analysis. As such, Rodinson seeks to refute prevailing conceptions of 'Islamic' history and society on their own terms without questioning the ideological function of their formulations or without leaving the conceptual domain they defined.[28]

In brief, what is primarily wrong with the AMP, nineteenth-century Orientalist and modernizationist conceptions of Ottoman ('Islamic') society is that they are ahistorical. The 'history' of the Ottoman Empire is explained in terms of essential (internal) therefore unchanging and ahistorical properties – culture or geography. Conceptions of cellular social structure underlie the stationariness, the ahistorical character of the Ottoman Empire. Historical development then becomes a function of Western penetration, to which is attached a positive value. As such, these conceptions cannot provide accurate analyses of the historical transformation, of the internal dynamic of the Ottoman Empire in the period both prior to and after Western penetration. Ultimately, their primary concern remains with Western development and in showing how and why the Ottoman Empire departed from the Western pattern. Hence, such questions as why capitalism did not develop or why liberal thought did not flourish in Ottoman lands are central to these discussions; these approaches serve to highlight the uniqueness (or the specific dynamic) of Western development as it is brought into focus through contrasting it with its opposite in the East.[29] More importantly, they fulfil an ideological function, that of underlining the superiority of the West *vis-à-vis* the Ottoman Empire, and therefore wittingly or unwittingly help to justify Western domination in the particular moments of encounter between the West and the Ottoman Empire (or the former Ottoman territories). On the other hand, the critiques of Orientalism, the modernization theory and of the AMP tend either to dismiss the specificity of Ottoman historical development in an attempt to fit it in the theoretical grid of a universal feudalism *or* repeat the ideological assumptions of their opponents in the midst of empirical bickerings over absences or presences of capitalistic or liberal traits. The world-system perspective seeks to move away from the essentially *ahistorical*[30] and *ideological* conceptions of Ottoman history (and from the approach of the latter's critiques) towards new categories of analysis.

Ottoman Empire and the world-system perspective

Articles in Part I of this volume by Wallerstein, Decdeli and Kasaba and by İslamoğlu and Keyder are general formulations of the world-system perspective as it is applied to the study of Ottoman history and social structure. In general terms, the world-system perspective explains the differential development of Western Europe and the Ottoman Empire in terms of the historical development of the European world-economy beginning in the sixteenth century. In doing so, it stresses the historicity of both the 'underdevelopment' of the Ottoman territories and the capitalist 'development' in Western Europe. Hence, the central question is no longer one of why capitalism did not develop in the Ottoman lands or 'why can't they be like us?'; but how capitalist world-economy, once it developed in Europe, affected the development of other world regions. More precisely, the world-system perspective[31] seeks to delineate the transformation patterns in the different zones of the world-economy as it expanded through trade and brought about an ever more efficient organization of production through an ever-increasing regional specialization. The three zones of specialization are the core, semi-periphery and the periphery. The trade-induced division of labour between these regions was then matched by the development of different modes of labour organization in the different zones (i.e., free wage labour in the core, share-cropping in the semi-periphery, 'coerced' cash-crop labour in the periphery) and by the differential strength of state structures (strong in the core and weak in the periphery). What this means is that not every region flourished or developed on an equal footing. On the other hand, the differential development of production systems, labour organizations and of state structures ensured the flow of surplus from the periphery to the core and the maximization of profits in the system, thus giving rise to accumulation of capital in the core and to 'underdevelopment' in the periphery. In this sense, no world region can be said to have been the innately 'privileged' domain of world-history nor is any region innately non-privileged. Moreover, given the specific nature of the world-capitalist development characterized by the 'unequal' development of different regions, one cannot talk about the beneficial effects of Western penetration (colonial or commercial) on non-Western regions. Thus, for instance, it is suggested that the unintegrated social structure and the 'backward' or 'underdeveloped' features such as stagnating peasant economies, enslaved or exploited rural labour, declining imperial commerce and the relative absence of an indigenous (Muslim) merchant class as well as the tenacious hold of religious ideology or 'traditionalism' and a 'weak' authoritarian state structure – that the nineteenth-century writers of the Ottoman Empire observed and their twentieth-century counterparts continue to unearth – were not after all innate to Ottoman or Islamic society. Instead, it is argued, these were 'transformed' structures of a society that was undergoing profound structural changes under the impact of Western penetration. Nor is there the possibility for non-Western areas to replicate the Western model of development or Western institutions. The so-called 'modern' institutions are peripheral structures that emerged under the impact of Western penetration and as such serve to reproduce the area's 'underdevelopment'.

The world-system perspective also stresses the 'historicity' of regions prior to their confrontation with the European world-economy. That is, it seeks to delineate their internal dynamic. In doing so, it differs from the Orientalist and modernizationist approaches in the choice of unit of analysis. Instead of the cultural unit of the 'Islamic' civilization, İslamoğlu and Keyder and Wallerstein, Decdeli and Kasaba take as their object of study the social system of the 'redistributive world empire' defined in terms of its internal division of labour or its mode of integration. Hence, in contrast to 'cellular' conceptions of the Ottoman social structure in which discrete parts reproduce their own stagnation, the Ottoman world-empire describes an integrated whole. It is characterized by political determination of the economic division of labour whereby the controls of the central state over the production, appropriation, and distribution of the surplus serve to integrate the different economic practices (agrarian economy of peasants, urban craft production, and trade). In identifying the mechanisms of integration, the world-system approach points to the extraction of surplus in the form of taxes and to the organization of trade and markets by the state. İslamoğlu and Keyder also employ the theoretical construct of the AMP in describing the Ottoman totality. In doing this, they attempt to avoid the main theoretical problem of the conventional AMP formulations – that of explaining the existence of a highly developed state structure in a classless society – by defining the state as the surplus-receiving class and by making the state the locus of both the intra-class conflicts among various claimants to the surplus and the inter-class conflict between the merchants and the recipients of the surplus. The article by İslamoğlu-İnan on agrarian class relations in Ottoman Anatolia included in Part II, however, contests this class reductionist view of the state that defines the state and its relationship to society simply in terms of the state's role as the extractor of surplus. Instead she argues that the basis of state power lay outside the surplus extraction process and in the political-juridical structures that constituted the basis for the legitimation of that power. Hence, through its political and legal practices, the state intervened in the economy and society and in the social class relations. This analysis seeks to refute the conventional 'Oriental despotism' thesis that views the 'gap' between the political structure and the society and the absence of intermediary structures, except for those mechanisms essential for the tribute collection, as the defining features of Asian society and that poses political power in Asia as absolute and arbitrary and therefore devoid of any legitimating principle. Finally, Sunar's article in Part I describes the internal structure of the Ottoman system as redistributive-patrimonial based on the domestic mode of production of peasantş in which both exchange and production were state institutions. Viewing the society as an institution of the state, Sunar, unlike İslamoğlu and Keyder, does not attribute the integration of the Ottoman system to a class dynamic; instead he focuses on the dynamics of the state structure and stresses the vertical integration of social-economic units into that structure, whereby power and status and not economic class describe the system of social stratification.

Central to İslamoğlu and Keyder's conception of the internal dynamic of the Ottoman structure is the role of merchant capital and of internal trade.[32] Empirical research also points to the primacy of trade and markets inside the Ottoman 'world-empire'. İslamoğlu-İnan's research shows that the collection of taxes in kind required an extensive network of urban and rural markets that served the recipients of revenues, who converted either part or the whole of the product tax into cash in these markets. In fact, she argues that surpluses appropriated in the form of taxes constituted the larger part of the marketed surpluses and therefore were the primary determinants of commercial activity within the Empire. Hence, the market involvement of the peasant economy was to a large degree mediated through the mechanism of taxation. Faroqhi's study of cotton and cotton-cloth production in sixteenth-century Anatolia shows that merchant capital directly penetrated the rural economy, providing the intermediary link between that economy and the larger society. On the one hand, Faroqhi argues that rural cotton manufacturing was carried out in close connection with the market. On the other hand, she shows that, contrary to the conceptions of autarchic village units embodying a unity of handicrafts and agriculture,[33] rural craft production was organized along the lines of a putting-out system in which the merchants provided the raw materials and purchased the finished products destined for larger markets beyond the locale of production. At the same time, the merchant class constituted an intermediary structure between the state and the larger society. The central state and its institutions was a major market for the products of both the agrarian economy and the rural and urban craftsmen. More importantly, as Faroqhi shows elsewhere,[34] the central state, through its controls over trade and markets, ensured the flow of goods to designated markets for the provisioning of towns and of those areas where certain goods were not produced. As such, the only mode of state intervention in the society was not through taxation. The state intervened to regulate the circulation of goods within the Empire and this presupposed the existence of a highly complex organization of trade and markets. Hence, on the basis of recent research, it can be argued that, contrary to Weberian formulations and those of their opponents, the problem is not one of the absence or presence of merchant capital or commercial development but that of how these were integrated into the system. In the Ottoman system such integration took place via the political controls of the central state.

Most importantly, however, the world-system perspective seeks to show how trade and market structures of the Ottoman Empire were transformed with the expansion of European trade after the sixteenth century. This process, which signalled the eventual dissolution of the Ottoman world-empire, describes its 'incorporation' into the European capitalist system (İslamoğlu and Keyder, Wallerstein, Decdeli and Kasaba). This meant the transformation of the Ottoman Empire into a raw-material-producing region, i.e., periphery, for the European core markets in exchange for manufactured goods. It also meant the disruption of the political unity of the Empire – that is the undermining of its integrative principle that focused on the state's ability to direct the flow of goods inside the world-empire. In more concrete terms, the increased demand for

Ottoman agricultural goods and the consequent high prices of these goods in the European markets attracted the Ottoman merchant capital to these markets and therefore made possible its escape from state controls. As a result, merchant capital was increasingly integrated into the economic division of labour of the European market; internal trade and market networks declined relative to foreign trade (Genç) and trade shifted from inland centres to coastal towns; the indigenous and predominantly Muslim merchant classes were dealt a blow as foreign merchants or their agents – the Christian minorities – gained precedence (Richards).[35] (Hence, it was not so much Islamic ideology as the changes in the structure of trade resulting from the rise of the world-economy that led to the withdrawal of Muslims from commercial activities.) Subsequently, world-empire ceases to be a valid unit of analysis; instead the world-capitalist economy that is integrated via the market becomes the proper object of study. Hence, a new periodization is introduced whereby the history of the Ottoman Empire after the sixteenth century is not one of continual decline to be shaken by the sudden Western penetration in the nineteenth century. Its history after the sixteenth century is one of its 'incorporation' into the world-system or of 'peripheralization'.

It is in this context of 'peripheralization', or of the transformation in trade and market structures, that the world-system perspective seeks to explain the transformations in the Ottoman agrarian economy and society, in craft production as well as in the state structure. It is thus argued that commodity production for European markets led to the stagnation of the rural economy of independent peasant producers, and commercial production increasingly took place on large estates worked by enserfed peasants ('coerced cash-crop labour') or under exploitative share-cropping arrangements. At the same time, peripheralization signalled de-industrialization or the undermining of Ottoman handicraft industries as cheap European factory-made goods invaded the Ottoman market. Finally, peripheralization meant the 'weakening' of the Ottoman centralized state with the decline in the state's ability to control the production, distribution, and appropriation of economic surpluses, and the rise of rival political nodules (*ayans*, *derebeys*) that competed for these surpluses (feudalization). The outcome of this development was the rise, in the nineteenth century, of a 'new' centralized state (the Tanzimat state) that sought to fashion its institutions (as well as its ideology or self-conception) after Western models, so as to make possible its functioning as part of the world inter-state system and to respond to global economic processes. In short, the peripheral structure of the Ottoman Empire was one in which the internal integration of the system, its political rationality, was undermined. It was characterized by the appearance of disarticulated structures such as the 'weak' state and the 'foreign' or minority merchants – which, in turn, were integrated into the larger totality of the European capitalist economy.

World-system approach to the study of Ottoman history re-evaluated

The world-system perspective is, however, criticized for its one-sided and 'economistic' approach to peripheral transformation, that is, for assigning potency and causality to changes in European trade structure in bringing about social-economic as well as political changes in the periphery.[36] It is argued that, while the world-system approach is successful in rejecting the cultural essentialist and therefore the ahistorical stance of the modernization theory, it nevertheless fails to explain the specific local (regional) histories and class relations in pre-capitalist societies, and therefore it cannot account for the diverse development patterns in the periphery.[37] Instead it posits a picture of world-capitalist development in which the periphery is a passive recipient of the impulses from the core, and its transformation proceeds along the lines dictated by the exigencies of its location (status) in the world-economic division of labour. On the other hand, explaining the specific development paths in different world regions requires that non-economic structures – state, kinship, religion, law – are taken into account.[38]

Research on social-economic change in pre-capitalist societies suggests that these non-economic practices enter the constitutive structure of class relations and make possible the extraction of surplus. Hence, it is argued that the superstructures are the dominant practices in pre-capitalist society; as such, they prove to be resilient to economic impulses and, more importantly, they shape the extent and the manner in which the economic factors, including the expansion of world trade, affected changes in production systems, social relations of production, and in class or power structures.[39]

Recent research on Ottoman history draws attention to the criticism of the one-sidedness and the 'economism' of the world-system approach. In fact, it points to an urgent need for a theoretical juxtaposition of the two influential social science perspectives of the past decade – those of Immanuel Wallerstein and Barrington Moore.[40] First, studies of the internal dynamic of the Ottoman society point to the presence of specific patterns of transformation at different time periods in different regions during the 'incorporation' process. These patterns do not always conform to those predicted in the general formulations of the world-system perspective; nor are they always best suited to the maximization of profits in the world-economy. When they do conform to these patterns, it is because of the specific configuration of historically evolved structures in that region and *not* because of unmediated responses to outside economic stimuli. The emphasis on the specificity of development paths in different regions need not, however, signal a narrow parochialism inherent in regional histories or a reversion to essentialist explanations of the development process. Instead, what is to be emphasized is the two-sidedness of the incorporation process and how the specific structures in a given region were responsible for moulding the particular kind of 'peripheral' transformation that came about once the area was subjected to the influence of global economic processes. Put differently, what is called for is a re-definition of 'incorporation' as a complex combination of global economic developments and locally specified systems of class interactions and power structures.[41]

In this volume Peter Gran's article represents a criticism of the one-sidedness of the world-system perspective. Gran argues for an acentric global system in which participation of individual areas was not determined so much by their structural positions, either as core or periphery, but by the internal dynamic specific to these areas. Studying eighteenth-century Egyptian history, Gran describes this 'internal dynamic' in terms of the indigenous capitalist development of the Egyptian political economy resulting from its integration with that of southern France through the wheat trade. In this context, he underlines the 'capitalist' character of the Egyptian merchant class – by virtue of its participation in the global capitalist market, of its autonomy from the state structure, and finally, of its utilitarian ideology. Put differently, Gran argues that Egypt during this period was not simply the *tabula rasa* upon which the European economic and also cultural superiority were imposed; it participated in the world-market with its own structures, opened up or resisted European commerce, responding to the dictates of its own internal dynamic. As such, Egypt was an active partner in its relations with Europe and was central (and not peripheral) to the development of global capitalism. But, according to Gran, Egyptian capitalist dynamic was interrupted as the indigenous (capitalist) commercial class was undermined by the rise of 'state commercial capitalism' under Mehmet Ali – a development which Gran equates with 'peripheralization'.

Gran's analysis reflects the Rodinsonian tradition of stressing the indigenous 'capitalist' development of 'Islamic' societies based on their commercial development. Stressing the context of 'global capitalism', however, Gran also challenges the narrowly political and Euro-centric periodization of Egyptian history favoured by modernizationists, who take 1798, the year of the French invasion, as the beginning of 'modern' Egyptian history. Gran shows that neither the French invasion nor the rise of Mehmet Ali constituted an eruption *sui generis*; these developments were part of the transformation of Egyptian society which had been interacting with Europe long before 1798.

Articles in Part II by Pamuk and Kurmuş on Ottoman agriculture in nineteenth-century Anatolia point to the role of Ottoman internal structures in determining the course of agrarian transformation. In this context, they question the thesis of the tendency towards the formation of commercial estates (*çiftlik*) worked by 'coerced cash-crop labour' or 'share-cropping' in response to increased European demand. Pamuk's research shows that small peasant holdings predominated especially in Anatolia, and commercial production for export markets took place in that context. Moreover, Pamuk suggests that the power of *ayans* (local notables) did not derive from large-scale commercial ventures on *çiftliks* but was in the main based on their ability to appropriate surplus in the form of taxes (that were formerly due to the central state) and their marketing of these surpluses. To the extent changes did take place in the organization of production and in social relations of production, the nature of such changes was determined by the historically evolved class structures in the different regions of Anatolia and Thrace. This analysis thus underlines the regional variations in the responses of agrarian structures to increased commodity production. On the other hand, Pamuk stresses the role of the state – that never lost its formal independence – in the preservation of the free-holding peasantry. In doing so, the state not only sought to maintain its fiscal base but also to counteract the rise of a landed class that could challenge its authority. Similarly, Kurmuş shows that, despite increased European demand for Ottoman raw cotton (especially in the cotton famine during the American civil war) and the British attempts to increase cotton exports from western Anatolia, there was neither a shift to mono-crop production nor any significant changes in the peasant organization of production. In explaining this, Kurmuş points to the reluctance of the Ottoman government to support British attempts to increase cotton growing and therefore to transform the existing agrarian structures. What is significant is that the government's reluctance to encourage agricultural production for export was confined to areas where peasant production predominated. Western Anatolia was one such region. In the formerly uncultivated areas such as Adana, however, the Ottoman government was more cooperative (Pamuk).

The essay by McGowan also questions the thesis of the causal relationship between commercialization of agricultural production and the rise of large estates (*çiftliks*) and the enserfment of peasantry. He argues that in Ottoman Croatia and Slovania during the eighteenth century, the *çiftliks* never really developed into large estates but consisted of several holdings cultivated by peasant households from which the janissaries or tax-farmers extracted surplus in the form of product tax which they, in turn, marketed. As such, McGowan seeks to show, market demand for agricultural goods and the generalization of tax-farming did not necessarily entail the disruption of peasant organization of production. He stresses elsewhere that, while the tax-farmers might have squeezed more surplus from peasant producers as market demand expanded, because the tax-farmers operated within the administrative-juridical framework of the state, the increased exploitation of the peasantry did not result in the alienation of peasant holdings or in 'enserfment'.[42] Conversely, McGowan shows that in the Middle Danube during the seventeenth and the eighteenth centuries enserfment of peasantry did take place without the expansion of export trade and as a result of changes in power relations between the peasants and the landlords following the end of Ottoman rule.

Similarly, İslamoğlu-İnan, studying the commercialization trends in Ottoman agriculture in sixteenth-century north-central Anatolia prior to the 'incorporation' of this region into the world market, shows that commercial production in response to increased domestic market demand did not result in the destruction of the peasant household economy. In explaining why commercial farms did not develop or why peasants were not ousted from their lands, she stresses the role of political-juridical structures of the state – which intervened in the production, appropriation, and the distribution of agrarian surpluses – in maintaining the integrity of peasant holdings and in limiting the marketed surpluses to those collected in the form of taxes.

Thus, the studies on Ottoman agriculture both prior to and after the incorporation into the world-market point to the role of non-economic structures, most notably that of the Ottoman state, in determining the course of agrarian transformation. Of course, this warrants a discussion of the specific character of the Ottoman state and the modalities of its transformation. Sunar's essay addresses itself to this problem, especially for the period when the Ottoman economy was increasingly integrated into world-economic division of labour. Sunar stresses the relative autonomy of the Ottoman state from the landowning class (or the *ayans*), on the one hand, and on the other, the political-juridical dependence of the *ayans* on the state while they were increasingly becoming independent economically. As such, the *ayans* did not control the state nor could they consolidate land and labour entirely. Sunar also argues that the competitive matrix of the international state system in the nineteenth century provided the space in which the state could act. At the same time, institutional innovations incumbent on the restructuration of the 'old' state as a unit within an inter-state system served to strengthen it *vis-à-vis* the *ayans*. Thus, the 'peripheral' transformation of the Ottoman state structure – given the historically evolved class relations in the Empire – resulted in the consolidation of a bureaucracy that allied itself with the merchant class against the landlords. While the state through its free-trade policies and legal-administrative reforms served to legitimate and facilitate the 'peripheralization' process (thereby securing a portion of trading surplus), it also employed its newly gained strength against the *ayans* and for preserving free-holding peasants that constituted its fiscal base. According to Sunar, it is largely this specificity of the 'weakening' of the Ottoman state structure in which the state remained differentiated from a landowning class completely dependent on world trade that accounts for the Ottoman Empire managing to retain its political independence.

Alan Richards' study of the transformation of agrarian structures in nineteenth-century Egypt reveals a very different picture of 'peripheral' transformation than the one in Ottoman mainlands. This primarily focuses on the difference in the nature of the Egyptian and Ottoman state structures. Richards shows that, in Egypt, Mehmet Ali after severing ties with the Ottoman

Empire sought to establish a 'world empire'. But his was a 'world empire' that largely depended on state monopolies over export trade and, as such, its survival was premised on Egypt's integration into the world market as an exporter of cotton. Thus, the state directly intervened in the agricultural production process to make possible large-scale production of cotton for the European market. The outcome was the undermining of the peasant subsistence economy allowing a new class of landowners to expropriate peasant holdings and to form large commercial estates, employing the peasants as share-croppers, coerced cash-crop labour or as wage labourers. Later, Richards argues, the landowning class, allied with Christian merchants, came to control the state apparatus, and the struggles for power among different groups of landowners largely describe the history of Egypt in the nineteenth century. What this analysis suggests is that the Egyptian state, increasingly identified with the interests of the landowning class at the expense of the peasantry, lacked the relative autonomy that Sunar ascribes to the Ottoman state. This led, according to Richards, to the loss of legitimacy of the state (especially when Christian merchants assumed the role of tax-collectors) in the eyes of the large rural masses. The upshot of this development was the peasant uprisings that finally triggered direct colonial intervention by the British. On the other hand, the relative absence of peasant revolts in Ottoman Anatolia, for instance, suggests that the reluctance of the Ottoman state to intervene in the transformation of rural structures on the side of landowners, foreign or native, stemmed at least partly from its concern for legitimacy and not only from fiscal considerations.

Another facet of peripheral development, according to the general formulations of the world-system perspective, was the decline in Ottoman handicraft industries and the stagnation of trade inside the world-empire. This took place as the production of agricultural commodities were increasingly directed towards external markets and away from internal ones, on the one hand, and as the imports of manufactured goods undermined the internal demand for domestic manufactures, on the other.

Essays by Genç, İnalcık, and Çizakça study the impact of European imports on Ottoman textile industries and on domestic trade in textiles. Genç, on the basis of data on customs tax-farms, shows that the beginning of decline in Ottoman textile industries and stagnation of domestic trade in 1760 and 1770 coincided with the rise in European imports in this period. İnalcık, however, concentrating on imports of British cotton goods, shows that these goods, except for cotton yarn, did not penetrate the Ottoman mass markets until the mid nineteenth century. British exports to the Ottoman Empire in the eighteenth century consisted largely of imitations of fine Indian cotton goods which were used primarily by the Ottoman upper classes. He thus argues that the locally produced cotton cloths dominated the larger Ottoman market well into the nineteenth century, while the British imports displaced the original Indian cotton goods in the limited market for luxury goods. The domestic cotton-weaving enterprises İnalcık refers to were primarily cottage industries outside the guild structures. Employing cheap female or child labour, these industries were able to keep the prices below levels that the British factory-made clothes could possibly compete with. At the same time rural weavers were increasingly cut off from markets beyond the locale of production and the large urban markets were supplied by European imports. İnalcık's study suggests a possible 'involution' of the Ottoman proto-industrial process. Hence, it appears that it was only in the latter part of the nineteenth century that the Ottoman countryside witnessed a 'union of crafts and agriculture' that the AMP formulations frequently ascribe to it.

But, if Ottoman cotton-cloth production proved resilient in the face of competition from British manufactures, Çizakça's essay indicates that the same was not true in the case of silk-cloth production. Studying the Bursa silk industry that produced for Ottoman upper classes and for European markets, Çizakça shows that in the period between 1550 and 1650 the increased European production of silk cloths, on the one hand, and the imports of British broadcloth, on the other hand, resulted in a decline in the demand for Bursa manufactures both in the domestic and the foreign markets. This, coupled with the rise in the price of raw silk under the impact of increased demand of European industries and the price revolution, rendered the production of silk cloth unprofitable for Bursa manufacturers, who then turned to the production of raw silk for export. Çizakça thus seeks to explain the absence of technological innovations in the Bursa silk industry during this period in terms of its market responsiveness, of the forces of supply and demand that rendered it unprofitable for Ottoman silk manufacturers to invest in new technologies. He further stresses this 'market responsiveness' by pointing to the revival of the Bursa industry in the late seventeenth and the eighteenth centuries when the European and domestic demand patterns were reversed; finally, he points to the definitive decline of Bursa silk manufactures ('de-industrialization') with the increased European demand for raw silk in the nineteenth century.

Quataert's article on raw-silk production in Bursa in response to the demand of European industries in the nineteenth century stresses the changes in the organization of production and social relations of production as European capital and technology intervened to increase production and efficiency. In doing so, Quataert describes the peripheral transformation of silk production in the Ottoman Empire – a process also studied by Owen in relation to Mount Lebanon. In fact, these two studies show how the specific configuration of social and political structures in the two different Ottoman regions shaped the pattern of their respective peripheral developments. Owen describes the opening of Mount Lebanon to European merchant capital after 1861 when this area was alienated from the Ottoman state structure. As a result, at the instigation of European merchants, silk-reeling factories were established to meet the increased demand of European factories for raw silk. Owen stresses the fact that

European merchants did not seek to transform either the techniques or the social and economic relations of production. Instead they relied on local social and economic structures and were content to reap the profits from export trade. Hence, small-scale factories were located in villages where they were staffed by peasant women, while cocoon production was undertaken by peasant households under share-cropping arrangements. This pattern of development stands in sharp contrast to the one in Bursa where the Public Debt Administration (PDA) intervened at all stages of production, introducing new technologies (steam-powered mills), and organizing production in large-scale urban reeling factories that employed wage labour. In this context, Quataert draws attention to the fact that, unlike merchant capital which was primarily interested in trading profits, PDA had assumed the revenue-collection function of the Ottoman state and was interested in increasing the silk tithe. In performing the latter task, PDA had the backing of the Ottoman state. This factor may explain the relative success of the Bursa enterprise in transforming the entire structure of production, especially if one considers the failure of British attempts at modernizing cotton production in western Anatolia in the absence of state cooperation (Kurmuş). Finally, Quataert's essay points to a number of problems that the transformation of Bursa silk production posed for the Ottoman state. Unlike the case of agriculture, where the state could exercise its relative autonomy to prevent direct intervention by European merchant capital and its representatives – Christian minority merchants – in the production process, in the case of silk production, Armenians, Greeks and also Europeans came to dominate all levels of production at the expense of Muslims. This development, Quataert suggests, had the effect of impairing the legitimacy of the Ottoman state in the eyes of the Muslim population.

The picture of the Ottoman state caught between the requirements of its own legitimacy and those of its new role in the European inter-state system incumbent on its 'peripheralization' also provides the leitmotif of Quataert's study of Istanbul port workers. Quataert shows that European intervention in the building and administration of ports in Istanbul during the period 1888–1909 brought the Ottoman port workers in direct conflict with foreign investors, whose demands for establishing wage rates and for rationalizing the work force they resisted. In this confrontation, the Ottoman state lent its implicit support to the workers through bureaucratic foot-dragging in implementing the demands of the European company. In doing so, the Ottoman state was expressing its own resistance to European penetration, on the one hand, and seeking to retain its legitimacy in the eyes of the workers, on the other. Hence, Quataert's study is suggestive of two structural specificities of the Ottoman 'peripheralization'. First, is the 'resistance space' that the absence of direct colonization allowed the Ottoman central bureaucracy. Second, is the emergence of a dualistic legal framework: one, the 'new' legality that regulated the relationship between European capital and the Ottoman state; the other, the 'old' legality that regulated the relationship between the state and the various groups through the mediations of specific institutions (in the present context between the port workers and the state through the mediation of guilds). Quataert's analysis points to a contradiction between these two legalities – a contradiction inherent in the 'weakening' of the Ottoman state structure.

Finally, Faroqhi's essay on Ottoman–Venetian political and commercial relations raises a number of important questions about the nature of Ottoman state power and the mechanisms of its legitimation in the sixteenth and the seventeenth centuries – in the period prior to the Empire's 'incorporation' into the world-system. Most importantly, Faroqhi seeks to refute the prevailing assumptions about Ottoman centralization and the explanations of Ottoman 'decline' that centre around the central state's inability to impose its authority on the provincial administrators. Central to this thesis is the increased participation of provincial administrators in contraband trade with foreign merchants. Faroqhi argues that the organization of state power at a number of different levels allowed the local administrators a degree of autonomy in their dealings with foreign merchants. At the same time, Faroqhi points to a contradiction between this practice, which stressed peaceful relations with foreigners, and the ideology of the state which focused on the *gazi* principle or expansion into the new territories by means of Holy War. This contradiction, Faroqhi argues, allowed the state a certain degree of flexibility in its functioning.

Some perspectives for future research

Lastly, a few remarks are in order on the implications of the present volume for future research on Ottoman history. Most importantly, despite the fact that the individual articles concentrate on the study of social-economic structures and that their explanations of Ottoman transformation are essentially 'economistic', these studies point to the inadequacy of our knowledge of the nature of state power, the mechanisms of its legitimation. This, in turn, constitutes a major gap in our understanding of the Ottoman system in which the state was the dominant structure that served to integrate the society and the economy. Of course, the world-system perspective is by no means insensitive to this point. Yet, in viewing the 'weakening' of the 'old' state as a necessary outcome of the incorporation process, this approach simply concentrates on the changes in the state apparatus (army, bureaucracy, etc.) to facilitate the operations of the world-economy (Wallerstein, Decdeli and Kasaba). As a result, the emphasis is on the latter process, that of the unhindered flow of factors of production in the world-market. On the other hand, studies that focus on the internal dynamic of the Ottoman state structure suggest that it was this dynamic that determined the specific mode of 'peripheralization' (Sunar) and point to the complexity of the transformation process which revealed contradictions which frequently blocked the smooth functioning of the world system. This blocking was, however, more than a mere resistance on the part of the pre-capitalist state. In the process, the basis of legitimacy of state power – its organizing principle – was undermined, transforming it into a hybrid structure torn between the preservation of its right to rule and the requirements of its role in the inter-state system. It is in this context that the 'weakening' of the Ottoman state structure remains to be further specified and conceptualized.

In this regard, what needs to be stressed is the theoretical inadequacy of the concept of 'Oriental despotism' that insidiously creeps into the analyses of the Ottoman state structure (e.g. İslamoğlu and Keyder). Central to 'Oriental despotism' is the assumption of the absence of the separation and therefore of the contradiction between the political society (state) and the civil society. Thus, in contrast to European feudalism, in Eastern despotism the 'state is everything' and civil society is primordial or absent. On the other hand, given the identification of the state with coercion, what characterized the relationship between the state and the society was domination without any intermediate structures that had an existence independent of the central state.[43]

An alternative way of looking at this problem is one that does not take the state as simply the site of 'coercion' but defines it as a combination of coercion and hegemony (or consent).[44] Central to this conception is the assumption that state power requires consensus that both encompasses and conceals coercion. This consensus, in turn, depends on the effectiveness of the ideological-political practices that legitimate state power. At the same time, this approach admits the presence of classes or groups that have independent existences from the state. It is argued that the class that held state power had to reconcile its interests with those of other groups through the forging of ideological unity between the different groups.

Viewed in this perspective, the Ottoman ruling class of central 'bureaucrats' can be described as a 'hegemonic' class that was able to reconcile the interests of different groups within the society – merchants, artisans, peasants, tribal groupings, pre-Ottoman ruling groups.[45] The 'hegemonic' ideology had, however, a dual focus. First, was that of Islamic precepts embodied in the *Şeriat* (Islamic Law); these provided the organizing principles (or ideology) of social life. In this respect, principles regulating family relations (marriage, divorce, inheritance), organization of urban life around *vakıf*s (pious endowments), the crafts guilds as well as the *tarikat*s or mystical orders (that involved the organization of rural as well as urban life) deserve special attention. The second focus of the 'hegemonic' ideology was the Sultanic law (or *örf*); its basic premise was that the ruler was responsible for the welfare of its subjects.[46] *Örf* provided the organizing principle for the relationship between the rulers and the other groups in the society. But the consent to the rulers was mediated through institutions, e.g., *tarikat*s (mystical confraternities), guilds and *medrese*s (institutions of higher learning), organized around the Islamic ideology. This conceptualization, in turn, need not assume a vertical integration of the society.

What needs to be stressed and specified is how different institutions cut through class lines or affect the lives of individuals from different social groups, unifying them in a social entity.

The linchpin of this complex ideological matrix was the *ulema* (religious scholars). First, the *ulema* in their capacity as judicial functionaries were responsible for mediating the relationship between the ruling class and the other social groups through the application of the *örf* principles. Secondly, they mediated the relationships within the society in their capacity as *vakıf* administrators, as judges responsible for the application of family law. Finally, the role of the *ulema* in mediating the hegemonic ideology through the educational system has to be underlined. Thus, the picture is one in which the *ulema* can be characterized as 'organic intellectuals' whose activities were directed towards the reproduction of dominant social relations. At the same time, the *ulema* were integrated with the merchant and landowning classes, the interests of whom were reconciled with those of the ruling class. The ideological unity that made possible this reconciliation was to a great extent the result of the *ulema*'s intellectual activities.[47]

Peripheralization signalled the undermining of this scheme of legitimation of state power. First, centralization measures in the form of reforms in the army and the administration, enacted to fulfil the requirements of economic integration into the world-market, heralded the formation of a new ruling class of bureaucrats. This class was characterized by its inability to reconcile its interests with those of other classes in the society. This was primarily because its very existence came to depend increasingly on global linkages and interests often in contradiction with the interests of indigenous classes. The alliance of the central bureaucracy with 'foreign' merchants or their minority agents is a case in point. Concomitant with this development was the undermining of the universalistic world-view (hegemonic ideology) that forged the interests of different groups. The new role of the central bureaucracy as an agent in facilitating the operations of the world-economy meant the adoption of Western principles in organizing the state and its relationship with the society.[48] These principles, however, came into conflict with the old organizational principle that focused on the role of the sultan as the protector of his subjects. For instance, in order to meet the expenses incurred by the adoption of new reform measures, the central state resorted to more coercive means of surplus extraction (or taxation).[49] Put differently, the concern of the central bureaucracy to legitimate itself within the inter-state system often came into conflict with its concern to legitimate itself inside the Empire (Quataert). In the event that the ruling class which held state power was unable to reconcile this conflict, it resorted to 'coercion'. Hence, it is in this context one could talk about rule without consent or Ottoman 'despotism' that the nineteenth-century writers were so keen in observing. Again, in this historical context one could view the 'weakening' of the Ottoman state structure incumbent on the 'peripheralization' process in terms of the undermining of the hegemony of the Ottoman ruling class and of its alienation from other classes.

Another aspect of the disruption of hegemony or rupture of political-ideological mediation between the state and the society was the withdrawal of different social groups into institutions organized around Islamic precepts. At the same time, increasingly, and especially with the adoption of Western institutions (such as schools, court system), the role of Islamic institutions in mediating the 'consent' of the society to the exercise of political authority was impaired.[50] Hence, it can be argued that the severing of the channels of communication between the state and the social forces and the 'weakening' of the latter was part of a historical process; and the 'weakness' or the absence of 'civil society' was not an inherent feature of Ottoman society.[51] To elaborate further, just as the state was losing its legitimacy in the eyes of the ruled, the latter were losing their status as legitimate subjects in the eyes of the new bureaucrats. To this new class the rest of the society came to represent the 'traditional masses' that were to be reformed and hauled into the modern world. The reaction of the society seems to have been one of involution. Classes that were not integrated into the 'peripheral' structure – most important among them were the artisans, urban lower-middle classes, lower bureaucrats – emerged as discrete units that came to express their resistance to the new order in terms of Islamic ideology.[52] The outcome of this development appears to have been the rigidification of Islam as it increasingly represented a defensive posture with its face turned towards an idealized past and no longer a medium for interpreting the present or perceiving the future. In this sense traditionalism[53] was the result of a historical process whereby the hegemonic structure of the Ottoman society was undermined and it was *not*, as assumed by modernizationists, an inherent feature of the society. In other words, 'traditionalism' was an expression by the society of the need to preserve its identity in an alien modern world.

Finally, another facet of 'traditionalization' needs to be pointed out. The state-builders during the reform period (1830–76) sought legitimation in Western culture. In this sense this period witnessed a disruption of the 'ideological unity' of the Ottoman society. On the one hand, this manifested itself in the inability of the new bureaucratic class to become hegemonic. On the other hand, it meant the emergence of a dichotomous structure of culture, a pattern that was reflected in the existence of two types of intellectuals – the traditional or the *ulema*, and the 'modern' or the bureaucrats educated in state schools.[54] Under Abdulhamid II (1876–1908), however, pan-Islamism represented the adoption of a defensive posture on the part of the ruling class – centred around the court – and certain *ulema* groups at the expense of 'Westernized' elites.[55] Hence, just as the society was 'traditionalizing' to protect itself from the onslaught of the 'Westernizing' Tanzimat state, under Abdulhamid the state structure was 'traditionalizing' to preserve itself in the face of European expansion. In the process, the state was becoming increasingly more rigid and oppressive inside the Empire. One explanation for this may be that Islamic ideology could not provide the ideological unity among different classes in a society the social-political cohesion of which was undermined through the integration of its principal classes (bureaucracy and merchants) into the European world-system.

To summarize, this alternative conception of the Ottoman state, its relation to society, the mechanisms of its legitimation and the transformation of these structures under the impact of global economic developments calls for a 'total' history of the Ottoman Empire. Such a history is to go beyond the mere study of the transformation of social-economic structures in response to changes in trade-market structures as the Ottoman Empire was incorporated into the world capitalist economy. It should seek to delineate the specific political-ideological practices and to view them in the context of the social-economic dynamic. Among the former, the study of the nature of state power, the legal system (both the *Şeriat* and the *örf*), the parameters of legitimation of state power, different forms of property, and of the intermediary structures such as the *vakıf*s, *medrese*s, *tarikat*s that mediated the relationship between the state and the larger society – are of particular importance. This means, first, an attempt to free the writing of Ottoman history from the constricting specialization of different disciplines, of different histories – in short, a history without compartments.

Secondly, the 'total' history approach brings into focus the specificity of the Ottoman historical development. Recent studies of agrarian structures, crafts production and trade included in this volume point to the centrality of non-economic factors, most importantly of the state structure, in determining the specific mode of Ottoman peripheral transformation. On the other hand, the focus on specific historical development is not for the purpose of delineating the specificity of Ottoman stagnation whereby the study of Ottoman history (rather non-history) provides a contrastive backdrop to the unique dynamism of Western history.[56] Instead, what is underlined is the specific internal dynamic of Ottoman society and the mechanisms through which this dynamic was transformed and undermined in the course of its 'peripheralization'. In this context, it should be noted that 'peripheralization' was by no means a unilinear process with necessarily predictable outcomes. It is possible to locate the modalities of resistance to the patterns of transformation dictated by the exigencies of the world-market. Given the context of the historically evolved structure of the Ottoman Empire, such resistance focused on the state, which sought to maintain its existence and in the process was transformed itself. Now this transformation was in the direction of the rise of new bureaucratic elites increasingly alienated from the society; it meant a pattern of 'revolutions from above'[57] and the undermining of the institutions of civil society as the intermediary structures between the state and the society were swept aside in the name of modernization policies. As such, a cursory glance at these developments reveal a picture that closely approximates to the much-favoured descriptions of

'Oriental despotism'. Yet, to emphasize the *historicity* of these developments in the context of the history of the world-capitalist system, constitutes a conceptual break with those theorizations that identify them as essential features.

At the same time, the emphasis on *historicity* and *specificity* means the delineation of contradictions in the transformation process as old structures encountered new ones. Admittedly, to pursue such a course of analysis is more difficult than to assume a model in which the 'good' forces of modernity did, or at least should, sweep aside the 'bad' or the 'traditional'. But this is a hardship which the historians of the Ottoman Empire, as well as those of other regions in the world periphery, should expect to endure. What is at stake is not merely a debate on historical methodology but a way of looking at the present and of evaluating the possibilities for future political action.

Part I

Theoretical approaches

1 ❧ Late-eighteenth- early-nineteenth-century Egypt: merchant capitalism or modern capitalism?*

PETER GRAN

Among the great advances within Egyptian historical studies of the past decade have been those made in the area of Egyptian commercial and artisanal history; our new knowledge renders an important part of the older conceptual vocabulary used in this field obsolete. In particular the term merchant capital, a term originally used to describe pre-modern European commerce, is by now an imprecise concept to use to describe Arab and Egyptian commercial production of the late eighteenth and early nineteenth century. This essay explores the various ramifications of its usage and proceeds to argue in favour of abandoning it for modern capitalism. For modern capitalism, given what we now know, can better be defined as a global and not as a national phenomenon.[1]

The idea of merchant capital arose in social science thought as a contrast to modern capital; it conveyed the idea of the circulation of luxury goods where modern capital contained the idea of the production of necessities. Its value lay in the explanation, which was true for Europe, as to why at various times merchant capital did not lead to modern capitalism but sometimes stood as an obstacle to it. When merchant capital is applied to the study of Egypt and the Arab world of the eighteenth century, scholars have frequently exaggerated the feature which the Arab case shared with Europe, notably the relation of elite merchants with rulers, and the interest of rulers in procuring luxuries. In the process, the role of artisans and nomads is devalued and the production side of the urban economy gets lost sight of. Furthermore the focus on elite merchants and their relation to the rulers of states introduces the state as an important factor, which it was in Europe and at certain times in Middle Eastern history but not in the period under discussion. Among the drawbacks of trying to study Egyptian commerce and production in a national framework is that one is predisposed to play down the importance of historic regions and hinterlands in which there were many centres of production and distribution. This is not

*I take this opportunity to thank Daniel Goodwin, Talad Asad and Rifaat Abou El-Hajj for their comments.

always obvious to the researcher because the various state archives and chronicles usually emphasize the *tujjār* (merchants) of Cairo and more vaguely its artisanal set-ups, thereby legitimating for the historian his/her original decision to use the concept of merchant capital and to stress the role of Cairenes. And of course historians attempt to use the categories which they find so as not to violate their material by imposing anachronistic concepts on it. But as a result of adhering literally to the word 'merchant' more than to an implied dynamics of the context, it is difficult for scholars to establish a point which their sources were interested in blurring or covering up. An example explored in some depth in the second half of this essay is the question of the economic bases which one might infer for the Napoleonic invasion of Egypt in 1798. It is quite a germane example as it highlights what a difference the approach to the material makes for the type of conclusion reached. In this important instance, the original French writers served to contribute further to the mystification of the Egyptian commercial industrial economy by subordinating it in their accounts, thereby perpetuating in subsequent historical literature the image that it was traditional and fading like the old Egyptian state itself and of no importance to Europe. The result was that the Egyptian merchant, artisan, and nomad appeared to be stuck in some rut and to have no relation to modern capitalism, which was mainly to be found in far-off Europe.

Before proceeding it would be helpful to probe somewhat more deeply into the concept of merchant capital as it is commonly used. Merchant capitalists differed from modern capitalists in that they did not seek to re-invest in trade or production but in land, preferring an extractive relation to productive processes as a matter of course. Socially, merchants intermarried with the rulers where possible and existed in a complex complementary relation to them, unlike the relation of merchants to rulers in the early modern West. Marx in *Capital* spoke of the necessity of destroying merchant capital for modern capitalism to arise. In *Grundrisse*, this dichotomy of modern and medieval breaks down, but without an adequate restatement of the nature of production and distribution.[2]

The use of the term 'merchant' capital one could argue obscures the most important aspects of what is going on. It implies a close link between the ruler or the state and the 'merchants'. However in the late eighteenth century the state was weak; the regions of Egypt had strong identity, and the most important aspect about the 'merchants' was not their relation with a ruler like the Ottoman Pasha but rather their dealings with the artisans and their various struggles to control the market and commodity production. In this context, the imposition of a retrospective national history, i.e., a Western model of history in which the state is the central reality and taken for granted, trivializes the 'merchant' by reducing him to his relation to the ruler and to trade statistics. Merchant capitalism or, as I would claim, the capitalism of this period has two crucial anti-state orientations which a Western-centred nation-building model of history would miss. The first is the role of merchants in maintaining *inter-regional* economies such as the Egyptian Delta and the Marseilles region of France, both of which areas were holding out for greater autonomy *vis à vis* Paris and Cairo. The second is the role of merchants in trading with and/or struggling with or against other merchants in hinterland regions of the state, such as in the case of Egypt, Sudan, Libya, or Yemen.

Yet to make a hypothesis about some historical process which goes against the writing of Western national history is difficult. It has been the convention of the historians of modern history, students of the period 1550 to the present, to organize their discipline around states and around the idea of the uniqueness of the states of the West. By this, it is commonly meant the steady development of a handful of countries of north-west Europe, including ultimately America. The idea of the rise of the West had utility for all the different parts of the discipline. For economic historians, it permitted a focus on the countries progressing toward industrialization and thereafter dominating international trade. For social historians, the distinctive social structure of these countries with their large working classes was a clear domain of work. For cultural and intellectual historians, the rise of the West was also appropriate. For some, this meant Protestantism, or the work ethic, for others the rise of positivism, realism or utilitarianism, but for all, the philosophical and cultural trends which dominated the West appeared to distinguish the West from the rest of the world. For historians of the non-West, and among them Orientalists, the uniqueness of the West has served as a principle of organization, although with results which now are increasingly perceived as being unsatisfactory. This will bring us presently to the topic of what alternatives there are to formulating the role of the third world, if one abandons the model based on the uniqueness of the West, understood as nation states.

By accepting the assumption of the uniqueness of the West, Orientalists found themselves with a ready-made frame which predefined a wide range of problems which they were called on to address. The great period of their study was to be the medieval era, especially that part which fed into the West through translation movements. The later so-called post-classical period was defined by its limited achievements and eventual decline. The uniqueness of the West appears to preclude ideas of the simultaneous rise of countries of the non-West. Thus non-Western economic activity, trade and production in particular, has never been seen as anything but part of declining tradition. Only contact with the modern West could possibly, according to historical theory, usher in a new age for countries which had logically to be defined as being in stasis for centuries. The Marxist historical tradition, like the Anglo-American modernization school, follows this same broad outline. In Marxism, the concept of the outward-radiating enlightenment of the West is replaced by the impact of modern capitalism on pre-capitalist structures. The unique and fairly static Orient of the Marxist Asiatic mode of production or feudalism finally gives way to capitalism. The heuristic value of Orientalism for the formation of Western self-identity is quite obvious; the Orient is the background, for, if the self is marked by rationalism, science and progress, some place must logically be other. The Orient and the Oriental is that other.[3] Not surprisingly, study of the cultural or material life of later Arabic history can scarcely be said to have ever been systematically undertaken. Most of the materials which such a study would require, by which I mean the manuscripts dispersed in the private libraries of the East, have never been assembled much less utilized.[4] Does this non-testing of the central assumption of Oriental stagnation over a long period of time point to some inner scholarly doubts, covered by the very selective documentation used in standard books of later Arabic history? Doubt is perhaps too strong. Most writers have accepted at face value the statements of the Savants of Napoleon who came to Egypt in 1798. Until now only a few critics of Orientalism treat the great book, *Description de l'Égypte*, as colonial ideology (or image formation); most scholars treat it as a work of science. Furthermore, the modern Arab scholarly community has corroborated the findings of Western scholars and has itself shown over a long period of time – the colonial era to be precise – a predilection for the medieval period. Given the general ethos of Western culture, no one would undertake a criticism of the taste of precisely that segment of the Arab intelligentsia most familiar with Western scholarly methods and categories of thought. Since the late 1960s, however, there have been changes both in the West and in the Arab world which permit a deep re-evaluation of all the intellectual production of the previous era of colonial domination.

Indeed, when one turns now to review what has been learned about the history of inter-Arab commerce, a quick glance at standard works raises serious methodological questions, if nothing else. How adequate is the basic term 'merchant' for the roles played by individuals known in Arabic as *tujjār*? How viable is it to talk about trade history and merchants, leaving out the numerically most important part of the commercial sector, the artisans and the tribes? One can only conclude that the stress on elite merchants and their institutions best fits into the writing of state history.

The commercial sector in late-eighteenth-century Egypt as capitalism

The recent monographs on trade and industry in Egypt in the eighteenth and early nineteenth century show that the merchants had a complex relation of dominance over artisans who produced commodities, as they had complex relations of dominance over a chain of tribal affiliates who moved goods and procured crucial products like slaves. 'Merchants', it is clear, sold not only luxury products but everyday commodities, and commodities important for the international economy as well. 'Merchants' had a managerial and administrative function in relation to guild labour and day labour which blurred the traditional distinction between merchant and industrialist. Add to this the historical situation in late-eighteenth-century Egypt of a growing urban day-labour force and of the monetarization of the Delta economy; the result was that the 'merchants' engaged in some fairly modern labour-relations activities. The interest of the 'merchants' in conservative mass-oriented *ṣūfī* orders like the revived Khalwatiya will find counterparts in the modern labour history of many lands.

The commercial sector of the Arab world from the late medieval period until the nineteenth century was composed of a number of well-known elements. Often these have been studied in isolation from each other and the systematic character has thereby been obscured. What follows is a schematic portrayal emphasizing their systemic character. The most visible parts of the commercial sector are the partners of the principal *wakālāt* (trade houses). They are generally wealthy and, as a result, many of their transactions are recorded in the Sharīᶜah court archives and their wills can be found in the Ministry of Awqāf. The main partners of these larger trade houses had multiple dealings with smaller merchants who did the local retail trade, owned shops, or engaged in hawking. The rich merchants procured large quantities of the materials sought in the various markets by advancing the capital and then kept these materials in their warehouses, to sell when it was most profitable. The main partners also engaged in entrepôt trade; in many instances, as in the case of the Cairo merchants, they profited from the location of Cairo connecting Africa and the Arab Near East. Cairo merchants also invested in capitalist agriculture. It is clear their decision to buy into the Delta and not to deal with the rebellious Cairo labour market of the 1790s was a major factor in the decline of production in Cairo. In analysing the range of activities involved in this tableau, it is not clear that the term 'merchant' is at all appropriate. During the era when some of the great houses made their fortunes from the distribution of Yemeni coffee, the role of distribution and transhipment was obviously very prominent, but never to the exclusion of the other activities mentioned. By the middle of the eighteenth century, new sources of coffee on a world scale reduced the importance of the Yemeni source and consequently the Cairo market in the coffee trade. Rather, the merchants of the Cairo *wakālāt* were engaged in production of commodities until the rate of return in land attracted them. Under nineteenth-century conditions, the structure of the commercial sector changed appreciably following the influx of massive quantities of cheap Western industrial goods. Under these nineteenth-century conditions, a number of foreign merchant houses arose in Alexandria and Cairo and facilitated the importation of increasing quantities of foreign goods. This did not however destroy the indigenous production structures which continued into the twentieth century and until today, with certain mutations. Thus, one cannot distinguish for the Arab world a pure distributive sector apart from production. The merchant house's role in financing the artisanal production of commodities, through procurement of raw goods, through its ultimate power of veto, i.e., refusal to buy what is produced, and through its role in paying for labour by virtue of brokerage relationship between producer and consumer, involves it intimately in the production circuit. As noted before, it was a matter of grave concern to the rich merchants in the conservative *ṣūfī ṭuruq* (mystical confraternities) that the guilds were breaking down and that radical social organizations were springing up, some of a religious character, some closer to banditry. The rich merchants attempted to deal with the incipient labour rebellion through sponsoring the revival in this period of mystical confraternities.[5] Their efforts appear to have broken down in the 1790s when the level of violence was such that Cairo became increasingly impossible to use as a work place. By that time as well, agrarian capitalism was developing and its primary locus was the Delta rice fields. The advantages to the merchant-producers of the eighteenth century of maintaining guilds, *ṭuruq*, the residential *ḥāra* (quarter) system, as well as state apparatus like the market inspectorate, were obviously that they served as a buffer between themselves and the masses.

However, at the end of the eighteenth century, as guild bonds weakened and as the number of day-wage workers increased, class conflict came into the open. One particularly inflammatory area of conflict was over the sale of drinking water. With the breakdown of the Cairo aquaduct, the water carriers had to draw the water from much further away, and by hand or with the help of animals. For their extra hardship they received no additional recompense, so that a large number of people were engaged in this frustrating manual labour under bad conditions. At the same time pure water was available to the rich for a fee. Certain merchants were apparently engaged in selling to the rich. The water-carrier guild was thus losing its main market, as it was obliged by law to give water free to the poor. Water carriers were politically active among the very radical *bayyūmīya ṣūfī* (mystical confraternity of bayyūmīya) order at the end of the eighteenth century. This class conflict in Cairo, as in other parts of the periphery of the world-market (the traditional raw-goods-producing regions of the third world), proceeded according to a different rhythm than was the case in industrial countries like England, and perhaps has gone unnoticed for that reason. The artisans belonged to a larger society which had not been totally uprooted from the land. In many instances they could withhold their labour without fear of starving. They could also exploit political and economic rivalries which existed among the property-owning class with which they were linked in a variety of ways. They could and did help to propel the ever-sharpening conflicts of the mamluk beys against each other in the 1790s, aligning themselves with different houses, each of which hoped to control the choice land and the most valuable trade routes. Class conflict also can be found in religious discourse. It took the form of arguments about true Islam; the orthodox *ṣūfīs* argued with the radical *ṣūfīs*.[6] Only with the rise of a strong central state could the work force be controlled. It is well known that even Muḥammad ʿAlī met continuing resistance. There was industrial sabotage in the 1820s. The level of productivity was so low that one suspects some idea of work slow-down must have been at play. In sum, the roles of distribution and production were often interpenetrating ones and the fate of either or both depended concretely on the labour struggle. In the late 1790s, the urban labourers clearly had the upper hand, guild structure was smashed and urban consumption of goods disrupted. In the last section, I will argue that this upset the French economy and helped precipitate the French invasion of Egypt in 1798.

If the Cairo *tujjār* so clearly exceeded the conventional bounds of merchant capital in range and scope of their traditional activities, why has this not been felt in the formulations of the economic models of world history? Local nationalisms do not usually obtrude. A survey of existing theories shows that for the period of the Industrial Revolution the emphasis has been either on the development of capitalism as self-contained in one or at most a few countries or in picturing a European-centred international division of labour. In either case the production of the European countries affects what takes place on the periphery, often distribution, and not the other way around. The main dynamics of the third world countries in these models are the dynamics between them and Europe; internal dynamics like local production are not granted a very important position.

A closer look at France and Egypt and their relationships at the end of the eighteenth century does not accommodate standard models. Both countries are largely pre-capitalist; France was industrializing. The principal crisis in the development of capital at this point lay in the sphere of distribution, more than production. The peasants of the French south were producing food but would not market it at the prices offered to them.[7] The Egyptian peasants were producing food stuff; there was an intense struggle over who was to market it and where it was to go. The Ottoman law in Egypt insisted that sale of foodstuffs to Europe were forbidden and they were to go to İstanbul. Europeans wanted to buy them desperately; however, after 1794, as a result of the French law forbidding the export of bullion, they lacked the credit to do so. Ultimately there was the invasion. The activities of the *tujjār* clearly were shaking the larger capitalist system.

The dual nature of modern capitalism

Another type of model is called for which places its emphasis less on centre-periphery, industrial–non-industrial, and more on the dual system of production which distinguishes capitalism from systems which have preceded it. The capitalist ruling class, through production and distribution, proceeds to extract maximum surplus value and to reproduce and expand its power through the maintenance of alternative types of economic orientations which simultaneously exist everywhere: the system of wage predominance and the unwaged domain, archetypically the factory and the home. The Western capitalist and the Eastern capitalist of the late eighteenth century go back and forth between roles every day of their lives, as do their labourers. Both Eastern and Western capitalists are capable of intermixing aspects of the opposing system when it contributes to discipline and output. Children are given cash allowances, women are allowed to earn supplementary incomes or in the 'factory' sector, non-economic forms of coercion like moral suasion or religion are employed. Historical explanations can perhaps account for why one region eventually came to dominate commodity production for a certain period, but this has to do with labour struggle not capitalism *per se*.[8]

The most common objection to the idea of capitalism which I have outlined is that pre-capitalist forms or relationships should be considered an enduring part of capitalism. Recently, however, a theoretical writer has begun to espouse this new view on a limited scale. Pierre-Philippe Rey argues that the period of the Industrial Revolution was a transitional period in which the Western capitalists made use of pre-capitalist structures while capitalism was expanding.[9] In the Egyptian context Rey might point to the temporary eighteeenth-century role of the *dallāla* (middle man) who entered the homes of the rich and brought about the shift in consumer taste to French drapes and other European commodities. The *dallāla* started a revolution of re-socialization of the upper classes toward Europe away from Egyptian artisanal luxury production. For Rey, then, the development of capitalism while making use of the *dallāla* is still a great linear progression from one centre. That capitalism has now or recently reached areas where little exchange value was previously produced I have no doubt, but to claim that these regions are now integrated into the world-market, the linear fulfilment, ignores what happens to the majority of the people in these various regions. For example, many leave Upper Egypt and arrive in the *bidonvilles* of Old Cairo, to live a hand-to-mouth existence. These form a separate culture from factory workers and can only with difficulty be seen as a traditional capitalist reserve industrial army. Many stay in Upper Egypt, participating in the cash economy during some part of the year but remaining generally in the orbit of use-value. Women are noticeable in the latter category. I would therefore make a periodization for Egypt that the first half of the nineteenth century was the period of capitalist state formation and of resistance to it, that is, exchange value became more general. The resistance came from the hinterland as well, compelling Egypt to conquer the Sudan. After 1860, capitalist relations of production began to spread rapidly into new regions and this was expedited by the increasing profitability of Upper Egypt with the introduction of perennial irrigation there in the colonial period. By World War I, or shortly after, this process slowed down. By the interwar period, Dr Wendell Cleland observed, there was a dangerous growth in the Egyptian population and particularly in the cities, suggesting a spread of use-value. The growth of the slums permitted some capitalists to develop a number of small production units (the *warsha*) in places like Būlāq, and cottage industry elsewhere. The workshop owners favoured the employment of children, older people and of temporary workers; the workshop economy was based on profiting by avoiding the formation of a classical capitalist working class. Such a class in Egypt would have been too big and strong for the government to handle. The last thirty years has seen the growth in the numbers of workshops, a return to cottage industry and a huge mushrooming of the urban population. In the same period the government has increasingly relied on religion, a non-economic form of coercion, to maintain discipline over the masses. Thus anti-clericalism of the liberal age gave way in Egypt to a renewed reliance on the *ʿulamāʾ* and *ṣūfīs*. While religion has generally been making a revival, this was not a linear development either. During the period when Nāṣir hoped to base his state on the industrial worker, Islam and other state ideologies were interpreted in an increasingly secular and leftist way.[10] By 1961 this was not possible and a strong reformation of religion proceeded with state blessing. In sum, neither the economic nor cultural forms of a limited petty-commodity production lead one to support Rey's assumption that capitalism, *à la* classical theory, is on the way and that the use of pre-capitalist forms is a passing strategy of the market.[11] Rey like most theorists of modern history assumes that the West is the centre of history. Despite his weaknesses, Rey is not without interest because he is among the first to acknowledge the role of pre-capitalist forms for the modern world-market. He thereby breaks to a degree with the 'uniqueness of the West' idea.

The acentric character of modern capitalism and the transformation problem

If we define capitalism as an acentric world system, our first task will be to investigate how the system as a whole progressed through the great watersheds like the Industrial Revolution, which can no longer be accepted as a matter of local pride on the part of the British and French. We need a systematic study of value maximization which involves much of the world. It will require the ability to weigh or evaluate critically the contribution of different sub-structures of the world-market in new ways. The old basis for evaluating the role of different parts of the world was to evaluate the nature and quantity of the work which they perform in reproducing themselves and the larger global economy; here we return to the idea of Marx, Ricardo and J. S. Mill of a labour theory of value. As the term 'labour theory of value' suggests, this theory attempts to link value to required labour inputs. This theory was in vogue among economists throughout Western Europe until 1870, when it was held to be too complicated to apply and hence not fruitful.[12] Among the problems with this theory, which later came to be known as the transformation problem, was the difficulty of calculating the value of congealed labour in a machine or machine made good *vis-à-vis* a raw good produced somewhere else without a machine. The genesis and development of the machine reproduced in various commodities has led some commentators to find the application of the labour theory of value to be weighted heavily toward Western economies. The worker might make a product ten times as fast with his machine and still be doing more work than the worker elsewhere who did not have a machine or such a good machine. The costs of distribution are likewise mystified. It is to be noted that, by 1870, much of the primary goods production had been shifted to the colonial world and that some of the early critics of colonialism were arguing that the economic benefits which the West received from the colonies far outstripped what they were conferring on the colonies, a criticism many found to be embarrassing.

A solution to the classic transformation problem suggests itself if one first adopts an appropriate base point in time from which to make comparative measurements over time of national outputs: secondly, if price and cost are simultaneously analysed so that the labour theory includes distribution. The solution to transformation problems in economics would seem logically to come not only from the congeries of data within economics but also from a guiding theory of history. One can count the congealed labour for each machine once and not for each machine-made product. In other words, we have to question the cumulativeness implied by the rise in the organic composition of capital, even its computation in a national framework. In the middle of the sixteenth century, relative military parity of Europe and the Ottomans was financed by x amounts of raw wool and other products for x amounts of cannon and other finished products. By the eighteenth century the volume of trade in every category increased substantially, but the rate of raw goods exported for requisite finished goods increased; if the ruling classes in the Ottoman Empire had opted for the same level of military parity which they enjoyed in the mid sixteenth century, then the volume would have been even greater. It is the change in the rate or ratio of finished to raw goods over two centuries which constitutes a well-known if not acknowledged contribution of the Ottoman Empire to the Industrial Revolution, but what of the unwaged or of the waged services of distribution of goods in the Empire?

Egypt and Algeria as part of French capitalism: the need for a historiographical rupture – problems of sources as well as of theory

To move from the general argument to the particular case,[13] one must usually expect to encounter a number of simplifications, often to the point where the individual case is made to bear an intolerable burden, so far-reaching is the argument. But it makes more concrete what has been said about relying on merchant capital as a discrete phenomenon in the eighteenth century. In arguing that the Napoleonic invasion of Egypt was an incident in the history of a larger capitalism, I have claimed that France was industrializing despite internal and external opposition. The Seven Years' War created severe limitations for France with the loss of her New World Colonies, meaning a loss of access to many sources of raw goods and markets, and as a consequence France's Mediterranean policy at the end of the eighteenth century and in the first third of the nineteenth was an important outgrowth of her domestic needs. Agriculture in the French south in this period was stagnant, and the food riots of Marseilles in the early 1790s point to this fact. Not surprisingly in this period there was a tremendous interest in the minds of French consuls and merchants in the possibility of taking over what they saw were rich agricultural lands of Egypt, later those of Algeria. When Napoleon landed in Egypt, he showed particular interest in this fertile Delta land and in the trade routes which would bring from the hinterland new riches. A number of parallels exist in the events leading to the invasion of Algeria in 1830.

My interest here is not so much in the details, or simply in revisionary historiography, but to point to a fundamental obstacle preventing many historians from integrating the kinds of historical experiences recounted here, and that obstacle stems from a restricted notion of the use of documentary evidence. Napoleon and other French government officials never acknowledged, in my reading, that economic problems in the French south were really motivating them. As is well known, the official reasons given were of a political and cultural sort. The invasion was said to be aimed at striking at the British in India, interest in ancient Egypt, possible interest in a colony, etc. The official political writings did not mention the protracted commercial negotiations of the 1790s between France and Egypt in which it was obvious that France's policy of forbidding the export of bullion to pay for imports had totally tied the hands of French merchants in Egypt, who burned up their credit. The official reasons do not indicate the logic of the timing, and, assuming the truthfulness of the declared motives, do not explain why the expedition was abandoned so rapidly. More seriously, they give no explanation for Napoleon risking his life and that of his army to sail through British controlled waters to get to Egypt. The chances of getting caught at sea were fairly high. If all such evidence is considered secondary (non-archival), and the logic of the structure of the events is devalued, then I confront an epistemological problem. Napoleon and the French ruling class would never frankly discuss their situation in my terms;[14] they would never acknowledge that the political economy of the Egyptian Delta could be part of the history of the south of France.[15] Even when we know that the options for procuring food were few, in effect we are forced to accept official propaganda that the peasants of Provence were prosperous and that if France depended on them they could be forced against their wills to market their food produce. Thus, even in the face of conventional methodology, we must claim that Egypt was more than a 'foreign' option separated in the archives from domestic ones.[16]

Let us proceed then if necessary in the spirit of Foucault while searching for a way back to more conventional historiography. It was in the interests of Paris to govern or administer the south; the Marseilles merchants resisted, trying to keep the south dependent on the export trade which was in their hands. Thus the French regional struggle produced interesting convergences and divergences between the south and the north; in large measure, it accounts for the peculiar rhythm of French policy at least until the July Monarchy, when a national market gave the north decisive control over the country. Thus in 1798 and in 1830 both the north and the south had Mediterranean interests; the north alone wanted to create a colony which would provide a stable source of grain.[17] The merchants of Marseilles were interested in French expansion in the Mediterranean as they would be primary beneficiaries but they were not interested in losing their power *vis-à-vis* Paris. How better can one explain the conflicts and irresolution in policy, the lack of commitment of the French government to the invasion of Egypt when it encountered difficulties and the analogous problem all through the July Monarchy over the administration of Algeria?[18] A number of well-known monographs exist but make totally different points. They portray the conflicts as personality issues between Napoleon and Menou, or governors and settlers, as the documents of course state.

How can one make an argument within the framework of traditional historiography which would show these developments? The long history of French commercial frustration in Egypt and of Marseilles merchants à la Sismondi is a part of commercial and not political history. The idea that there was any link between economics and politics in the fact of the famous merchant, Magellon, the senior French merchant in Egypt, coming home to live in Paris and lobbying for a French invasion can be dismissed on traditional methodological grounds. Magellon's well-known *Memoir* to Talleyrand about the utility of an invasion is strictly speaking outside the political sphere. Indeed, one must argue that the political class does not respond to interest groups in a one-to-one fashion. One would think this was not in their interest and yet this is what is expected by a good number of contemporary historians, 'Little Englanders', and the like. A politician like Talleyrand became a statesman, one would think, by disguising the rather particularistic nature of interests, by giving them a general character and thereby broadening the potential appeal of his projects. Politicians in France who represented only one interest and were known to speak in its defence were of a lesser order. The colon (settler) lobby is such a case. The political sphere is thus not the place where one can expect to discover Napoleon's motives. Even if in a chance remark he should mention the riches of Egypt, such comments are rhetoric.[19]

We agree in a theoretical sense that the invasion was not caused simply by food riots. Food riots were suppressed by the Revolution, but this in turn had certain political consequences which perhaps made life difficult for the Jacobins in Marseilles. The invasion itself was a political and military event; it required translation of one sort of reality into another. Yet the food supply remains a crucial question. When one reads Paul Masson, or Gaston Rambert, or others who have worked in the Archives of the Marseilles Chamber of Commerce, one is given a clear exposé of trade history. Grain imports are recorded each year from dozens of countries, even after the limitations from the loss of the Seven Years' War which was naturally bad for Marseilles. Unfortunately, the impression one receives from reading the tables and charts is that there was an external market which could be taken for granted and that the complaints of particular consuls or merchants here or there were simply the complaints of individuals, as the market existed independently of them. But on close examination of the 1790s we find a wartime situation for France, so that a good proportion of French farmers were in the army; Egypt had been an important source for more than a century up through the early 1790s; only then had exports to France deteriorated, so that it was against a considerable background and not just the events of the moment that Magellon spoke.

A final thought about sources and the way they are used. French political sources allege many reasons for Napoleon's invasion of Egypt. The reasons given may not be wrong. When Talleyrand spoke of Napoleon's ambitiousness, one cannot doubt him. His claim that the Directory feared Napoleon and let him undertake a dangerous mission on the chance that he might be killed may also be true. Perhaps it is best to understand the Directory as being central to ruling circles. Napoleon was simply powerful and dangerous and drawn to the Orient. Logically the Directory would try to get rid of him with an Eastern campaign. At the same time, the Directory may not have wanted to advertise either the food problems or the clout of Marseilles in the political process and so simply did not broadcast it. In a complicated wartime situation, much of what it did was probably presented to the public under one guise or another and not for what it was. Clearly there is no one-to-one fit between politics and policy. If there were, there would be no need for political history. But, in stressing the legitimate and important role of political history, it is important to emphasize that historians can easily trivialize this subject by reducing it to the declared motivation of individual actors.

This essay began by asserting that the conventional characterization of Arab merchants, in this case Egyptians, between 1760 and 1860 as merchant capital and thus pre-capitalist is misleading. The roles which they played in guiding production internally and in struggling along with other merchants for their share of profit on the world-market simply cannot be integrated into the traditional concept. The alternative proposed was that they were capitalists participating in the world-market of their period which was going through the great watershed of the Industrial Revolution. This point was argued in several ways: historically in terms of the south of France's dependence on Egyptian food stuff, theoretically that the older formulations were so constructed that capitalism only dealt with wage-labour production in a single country leaving out the home, the non-waged sector, and the role of international distribution. A more adequate formulation must be global but acentric and elaborate the two contradictory moments, which under capitalism are played off against each other; the one is the waged system and the other the non-waged. The essay concluded with practical problems of utilizing conventional historical sources to write a kind of history which is non-national, that is how to write world-history from archives each of which is essentially national. It is suggested that only by an epistemological rupture with the literal apprehending of what are usually termed primary and hence true sources can one hope to make a fuller and deeper use of them.

The impact of textual deconstruction in Middle East historiography has the same potentialities as it does elsewhere for undermining conventional conclusions, as well as for calling into question the handling of sources. It also holds out the possibility for scholars, who wish to get beyond the rigid patterns which have held sway over the past century. The example developed here is that of Egyptian history. A rereading of various sources already familiar reveals it to be a modern rival capitalist competing with France. Egypt does not have to be subsumed into an Orient, decodable only by a specialist. In the long run, I believe scholars who are sceptical about changing methodology might none the less find the place of Egypt or the Middle East more generally in the history of world capitalism an important subject to pursue. If the way to break into it involved some changes in approach these also might come to be accepted. However, at the present time, other fields of scholarship, two in particular, lead the way in seizing the new opportunities; one is feminist studies and the other is peasant studies. Both required a quite formidable conceptual reorganization of the nature of history. What is involved here seems on the face of it to be of a much lesser order. Simply, can we get beyond the economic model of core and periphery and speak about the political struggles uniting – thereby also dividing – parts of cores and parts of peripheries? Would this not be a plausible approach to studying the era before the great centralization of power in the nation-state framework took place? Would a global history built from the sum of local and national archival sources not be facilitated by a more explicit discussion of assumptions in using texts and archives as part and parcel of a study which makes use of them. In sum, I believe that we historians might do well to imitate the anthropologists who spend part of their time reflecting on the nature of the ethnographic encounter while they try at the same time to do ethnography.

2 Agenda for Ottoman history

HURİ İSLAMOĞLU AND ÇAĞLAR KEYDER

In this article we propose a new reading (and writing) of Ottoman history. This reading derives from certain concepts and theoretical constructions which form the basis of an emerging paradigm in social sciences.[1] We hope that the proposed reading will provide the conceptual framework in which new research problems may be defined.

The ancestry of the new paradigm is diverse: L. Althusser and E. Balibar for the morphology of mode of production, A. G. Frank for the concepts of core and periphery, I. Wallerstein for the definition of world-empire and world-economy as proper units of study.[2] Within this paradigm Ottoman history should describe the transition from world-empire (in which the Asiatic mode of production was dominant) to a peripheral status in the capitalist world-economy. The following account advances our proposed reading. First, however, we attempt a characterization and critique of the present literature.

Critique of the present paradigm

In order to evaluate the theoretical limitations of Ottoman historians it is essential to set forth the implicit assumptions underlying their work. Though not articulated as such, these assumptions are shared by Ottomanists and are implicit in their research to an extent that the claim that they are working within a single paradigm is justified. To demonstrate the common assumptions of this paradigm we have chosen three representative works on Ottoman history – H. İnalcık, *The Ottoman Empire*; Gibb and Bowen, *Islamic society and the West*; and B. Lewis *The emergence of modern Turkey*.[3] Each of these books has the status of standard text for one of the two periods which provide the temporal framework in constructing the history of the Empire. The first two deal with the 'golden age' and the beginnings of decline, while the latter's primary concern is with the age of reform and 'Westernization'.[4]

Within this periodization, which reflects the assumptions of the paradigm, the object of study emerges as a summation of an unintegrated set of institutions. In all three of these works the analysis assumes that each institution had its own space of existence and therefore its own history; that each institution evolved according to its own 'idea' and degenerated when it ceased to conform to that 'idea'. Institutions experienced decline as the result not of factors inherent in themselves but of external factors, such as population growth, an unprecedented rise in prices, changes in the structure of trade, or the growing military and economic power of the West. This does not mean, however, that in these works each institution receives an equal amount of attention. There are privileged institutions such as the land system or the central bureaucracy, and the history of the Empire is traced through their individual histories. This history, in turn, is structured in terms of a golden age versus a period of decline, the contours of which follow the temporality of the privileged institution. Thus the composite institutional 'flowerings' and 'declines' signify the periods of golden age and decline for the system as a whole. Reforming of institutions, however, is not seen as the resurrection of their former selves but as the substitution of new institutions that fulfil the functions of the decaying ones. It is thus argued that what in fact occurred was an external refashioning of institutions to meet new requirements under the modernizing influence of the West.

History constructed in this way, as a unilinear progression from golden age to decline and then to refashioning on Western models, stems from an analysis of Ottoman society in terms of a particular world-view. This view is characterized by its faithful adherence to the 'idea' of Near Eastern society.

İnalcık's history is structured on the 'idea' of Near Eastern society as projected through juristic texts. This 'idea', taken for its 'real' referrent, embodies the assumption that the philological decipherment of these texts will lead to the unveiling of the 'actual' society itself. Thus the totality becomes one which is ideologically defined: the society is the ideal it holds of itself, and its history is the reading of texts unfolding this ideal.[5] The 'idea' posits a view of society divided into two functionally determined groups. The rulers, personified in the absolute sovereign, constituted a 'military' class comprising all groups which serve and represent the absolute ruler in the performance of his function of establishing 'public order' and dispensing 'justice and protection' to the ruled. The second group, the subjects (*reaya*), consisted of the tillers of soil, craftsmen, and merchants.[6] They constituted a class whose surplus in the form of taxes was channelled to meet the requirements of the rulers. Thus the relations between the rulers and the ruled were characterized by reciprocity and circularity. The ruled owed absolute obedience to the sovereign and were required to pay taxes to maintain his might and authority so that the absolute sovereign might protect them against abuses, form armies, and institute an administrative apparatus to maintain public order. This apparatus existed in order to enable the class of rulers to establish control over the sources of revenue in the form of taxes, thus ensuring the prosperity of the state.[7] The class structure so defined rested on an 'idea' of state which is equated with the absolute authority of the sovereign and which regarded justice and maintenance of public order as essential for its endurance.[8] Given this ideological structure of the state, its specific functions are posited in terms of the global one of perpetuating the eternal order and of protecting the interests of the subject population. Consequently the institutions through which these functions were fulfilled are viewed as emanations from the ideological essence of the state.[9] Thus İnalcık in his analysis of the specific Ottoman institutions such as those of the palace, central bureaucracy, provincial administration, and the *tımar* system is not concerned with the changing functions or the evolution of the real workings of these institutions but the evolution of the state ideology as reflected in each institution. His problem is to provide an explanation for the coherence of the totality. While the institutions directly embodied the state ideology, the economic life especially in the cities (which İnalcık calls the 'social and economic life') was relatively independent of such direct control. However, there too, the state's ideological self-conception was concretized because the organization of urban economic life followed the principle of the Islamic ideal (for example, the guild system). Thus the integration of vertical elements, the institutions, and the horizontal 'social and economic life' was assured through the mediation of ideology.

Given this ideological functioning of the society the decline of the system cannot be sought in its internal dynamic but is explained in terms of external factors. In İnalcık's history, these external factors were the price inflation of the late sixteenth century, and the changes in the structure of trade which resulted in the weakening of the state's control over the economy, thus rendering it unable to fulfil its ideological function. Confronted with the economic and political superiority of the West, beginning at the end of sixteenth century; the Ottomans became aware that these institutions had 'outlived their usefulness and that they were ill-suited to the new era'.[10] Thus adaptation to new conditions required compromising the ideological purity of the institutions, thereby signalling their decline. According to İnalcık, Ottoman history from the seventeenth century on is the history of this decline.

Gibb and Bowen's history, like that of İnalcık, adheres to the institutional mode of analysis. They, too, are faced with the problem of providing an explanation for the coherence of an unintegrated set of institutions.[11] Consistent with the choice of their unit of analysis – that of civilization with an Islamic essence – they assign the role of cementing the totality to religious ideology, i.e., Islam. In so doing they operate within the confines of nineteenth-century historical tradition musing on the rise and fall of civilizations. Given this perspective of atomized civilizations, Gibb and Bowen assume that the Islamic society lived in 'isolation' until its first real contact with the West in the form of the Napoleonic invasion. Therefore its decline can be explained in terms of the 'diminution in the strength of the Islamic spirit'. This concept of decline also characterizes the Orientalist paradigm, which views the history of Islamic societies as one of continual decline after a high point in the early medieval period. Although the Orientalist paradigm admits an arrest in this unilinear path of decline occasioned by the formation of the Ottoman Empire, Gibb and Bowen prefer to ignore this anomaly and concentrate their meticulous attentions on the golden age of high civilization. This very anomaly, however, constitutes the object of their history. Hence, in order to explain the functioning of Ottoman society, they are forced to employ a set of assumptions outside the Orientalist paradigm – those of 'Oriental despotism'.[12]

These assumptions are the rigid division of the society into the rulers and the ruled. The former were segregated from the latter and locked up in the grid of institutions through which they exercised their absolute rule over the ruled. The ruled were divided into atomized autonomies of villages, tribes, quarters, and guilds, and were not integrated except for economic and religious links between them. This society was characterized by 'stasis'.

Given these assumptions, however, Gibb and Bowen are unable to carry out their proposed objective of studying the internal dynamic of Ottoman society. Instead their analysis remains static. First, in such a scheme the groups within the 'ruling institutions', i.e., bureaucrats, soldiers, *ulema*, are not conceived as having interests specific to each group; rather, they are viewed as undifferentiated parts of the central administration. Thus relations among these groups were characterized by perfect harmony. Secondly, assuming a rigid segregation of the rulers from the ruled, Gibb and Bowen ignore the role of the bureaucrats in articulating the system by acting as intermediaries between the central administration and the local groups. Thirdly, by assuming that the performance of tasks required for the maintenance of the central administration (such as tax-collection) was limited to the members of the ruling institution, they ignore the utilization by the central government of local notables for social control.[13] Similarly, Gibb and Bowen do not admit the integration of ruled within the system through the mechanism of internal market networks and internal trade. Thus operating within the confines of a set of unarticulated 'autonomies', Gibb and Bowen fail to explain the functioning of the Ottoman society and are unable to locate its potential dynamic which is to be sought in the complex patterns of articulation between the various groups.

Furthermore, given the specific nature of their totality, when confronted with the problem of how the society is held together, they have no other recourse but to turn to yet another institution, the religious institution, to which they assign the function of providing the ideological network to hold together the separate groups within the society.

By juxtaposing the assumptions of Oriental despotism and of the Orientalist paradigm, they draw a picture of a society in 'stasis' and 'isolated' in its civilizational specificity. Changes are to be explained in terms of external factors. Operating in a world of cultural history, Gibb and Bowen locate this external factor in the Napoleonic invasion and the consequent transmission of the ideas of the French Revolution into the Ottoman society. Of these ideas, secularism and liberty are assumed to have had a key role in affecting the transformation of a society with an Islamic essence and despotic form of government.[14] In so doing, they totally ignore the pattern of relations that existed between the Ottoman society and the West on the level of the economy, and the integration of this society into the world-economy beginning in the sixteenth century. As we shall see, this shortcoming is one of the features of Lewis' book as well.

While, for İnalcık and for Gibb and Bowen, the Ottoman Empire in its golden age was the privileged realm of analysis, Lewis' book shifts the emphasis to the period of decline and Westernization. Accordingly, his implicit conceptual apparatus borrows from a different theoretical framework, that of modernization literature.[15] Writing in the 1950s, it was quite natural that he proceeded as he did, first by identifying the external causes of decline of the Empire, and then by supplying the stages of borrowing from the 'Western tradition'. For Lewis, the water-shed in Ottoman history is Autumn 1793, when Selim III wrote to Paris to mail-order technicians and recruits.

The nineteenth century witnessed further efforts to fill up the gap created by the persistent decline in the institutions of the Empire. This process gradually allowed for the adaptation of European institutions, as well as the Occidental world-view. The mechanisms of transmission were specified, and the 'impact of the West' gauged. However, ideological borrowings soon overtook the actual process of institutional modernization which created a conflict between reformists and reactionaries.[16] Finally, the short-lived revolution of the Young Turks achieved the culmination of its 1789-vintage ideas in the formation of the Turkish Republic.

This model of institutional borrowings embodies an entire body of literature which concentrated on the military and administrative reforms beginning with Selim III and including the Tanzimat and post-Tanzimat attempts.[17] The common strand in this literature is its author's concentration on particular elements of the superstructure.

Of course, Lewis did not intend to write an economic history. But his book exemplifies the exclusively political and ideological emphasis found in most of modernization literature. While the discussion of economic integration into capitalism is minimal, institutional and legal reforms occupy the front lines. Thus, theorization of the impact of capitalist penetration is absent, and therefore no argument can be advanced regarding the relationships between, for example, new jurisdictions and requirements of merchant capital. In addition, since this articulation with the capitalist world-economy is not theorized, the case of the country in question is treated in a vacuum without any regard to its structural position inside the world-economy. Hence each case-country replicates the paradigmatic development of an earlier case. For Lewis, the political development of France serves as the model. The distorted reflection of the bourgeois model in the peripheral mirror is miraculously uprighted through the good graces of modernization optics. It is, of course, the specificity of this distortion that we wish to capture through the concept of 'peripheralization'.

The Ottoman social formation

We conclude from this analysis of the present dominant paradigm in Ottoman history that a new definition of the object of study is in order, since the present paradigm is characterized by an inability to integrate – both in structure and in time – its various areas of concentration. Its problematic confines it to a dichotomous temporalization of Ottoman history, consonant with the implicit theorizations underpinning historical reseach. A hybrid institutionalist functionalism on the one hand, and a crude modernization perspective on the other provide the framework for most present research in Ottoman history. Our attempt in the following section will be to advance a totalizing framework, seeking to integrate both the diverse elements of the structure into an intelligible whole, and to bring together the two disjointed temporalities of the sixteenth and the nineteenth centuries by means of a periodization centred on the concept of peripheralization.

This totality is the theoretical construct of 'social formation' through which the Ottoman Empire will be studied. The Ottoman social formation was characterized by a dominant Asiatic mode of production,[18] in which the control of the central authority over the production and appropriation of surplus constituted the crucial mechanism of reproduction. The articulated whole was reproduced according to the requirements of this mode, but it also incorporated forms of petty commodity production, and, of course, merchant capital. In its later stages, the social formation contained 'feudalized' areas as well, which, however, remained subordinate to the division of labour imposed by the ruling class, concretized in the state. We shall now discuss how these different economic practices were integrated through the political control of the state.

The Asiatic mode of production is characterized by independent peasant production in which the peasants do not form autonomous units but constitute components of a larger unit, the limits of which are defined by the extent of the authority of the state. The peasant producer is integrated into the larger unit through the delivery of his surplus in the form of taxes to the state, and through the ideological-juridical apparatus that provides the matrix for the state's extraction of agricultural surplus. Thus, this integration ensures a political determination of the division of labour within the system.

The ideology of the ruling class focused on the state was consonant with this political control over the economy. Thus the peasants came to believe (the belief being reinforced by juridical practice) that all land belonged to the sultan; and that the state, in order to preserve the eternal order, did not permit accumulation of land. In the cities, a similar ideological function was served by the *hisba* (surveillance of public morals) regulating guild practices. Even mercantile activity was covered in ideological prescriptions: *riba*, speculative profiteering, was prohibited, although merchants as a class received protection and privileges owing to their contribution in 'increasing the wealth of the land'.

The state is not confined to the political instance; it is the dominant vertical element that integrates the system in the Asiatic mode of production, cutting through the economic, political, and ideological levels. By means of its administrative apparatus, it controls tax revenues and therefore the production of agricultural surplus.[19] In the original conception of the Ottoman Empire, this function of the state was performed through the institution of *tımar*.[20] *Tımar* was the generic term accorded to a system of land grants distributed for the purpose of supporting a provincial army. The beneficiaries of the grants were state officials empowered to collect the traditional product-tax of *öşr*,[21] in the area designated as their *tımar*. These grantees (*sipahis*), in exchange for the privilege of collecting taxes, had to support and deliver during time of war a specified number of mounted soldiers. In addition, they functioned as the administrative cadre representing the central authority in the smallest villages. Together with the *kadı*, the judiciary representative who was empowered to apply the edicts of the *şeriat* and the Sultanic law, the *sipahis* formed a bureaucratic layer, locally reproducing the political and ideological functions of the state.

The *sipahi* collected the traditional tax in kind, which necessitated the prestation of corvée labour from the peasants when the product which was due to the *sipahi* was carried to the nearest market. The *sipahi*, in order to fulfil his obligations of provisioning the mounted soldiers with horses and arms, was in need of cash, which he obtained through selling the surplus product. *Sipahis* were accorded tax-collection rights for a specified period. Although the office was often extended from father to son, the *kadı*, who was answerable only to Istanbul, acted as a check on the possible abuses of the *sipahi*.[22] The *tımar* system, however, ceased to be operative after the sixteenth century. We shall later discuss the reasons for its demise and the system of tax-farming which replaced it.

The integration of urban crafts and trade into the social formation was also effected through state control. This control translated into a determination of the economic division of labour which ensured the delivery of surplus to the seat of its utilization in the required product-form.

In the Ottoman social formation, urban craft production was undertaken by guilds under strict state regulations (*hisba*).[23] The state controlled the production process, that is, allocation of raw materials; quantity and quality of the goods produced; and it also fixed prices. This supervision of urban production was in part achieved through the mechanism of the state's control over internal trade. The state directed the movement of raw materials and enacted prohibitions on their export in order to assure that the guilds were supplied with the raw materials they required. Manufactures, on the other hand, were sold at authorized markets. The state's control over input and output prices, as well as over the scale of production, meant that capital accumulation within the guild structure was effectively prevented. It also meant that the state, both through the taxation of manufactures sold in the markets, and through its position as the chief purchaser of artisanal production, laid claim on the surplus during the process of circulation.

Although trade in general was not subject to *hisba* regulations which governed the guilds, the state imposed strict controls over internal and external trade. Internal trade which ensured the functioning of a highly monetized economy with a developed division of labour was organized through a system of regional and inter-regional markets. These markets were established with the state's official sanction and their location was administratively determined.[24] The regional markets were weekly markets formed in villages and small towns. They served multiple functions. State officials who received their salaries in the form of taxes in kind converted a portion of their revenues into cash; peasants sold part of their produce in order to obtain money required for the payment of certain taxes; urban guilds as well as rural craftsmen purchased their raw materials and foodstuffs, and sold their manufactures. There were also urban markets where guilds could purchase their raw materials. Other markets were formed on trade and army routes to meet the requirements of long-distance caravans and troops. Inter-regional markets (fairs) held annually or bi-annually, especially in the Balkan provinces of the Empire, provided a site for the exchange of goods from the more distant regions of the Empire. The state promoted all these markets, ensured the safety of merchants and their wares along the trade routes and in the market places, and it closely supervised the business transactions.[25] Markets were also a major source of revenue in the form of market taxes (*bac pazar*) determined in proportion to business transacted. These revenues either accrued to the state officials who were the recipients of land-grants or were farmed out to officials who competed strenuously for these privileges. In addition to market taxes, internal trade provided the state with revenues in the form of customs dues, which were farmed out to state officials and to great merchants.[26] The Ottomans, consistent with their policy of promoting internal trade, abolished most of the customs (*octroi*) in Anatolia and the Balkans pre-dating the Ottoman rule. However, they established some major customs such as those in Istanbul and Diyarbakır both as sources of revenue and as means of controlling the movement of goods.

The concern for the direction of the movement of goods was a prime consideration in the state's control over internal trade. In addition to supervision of markets, this control was effected through the granting of concessions to merchants. The sale of these concessions, of course, provided the state with revenue. More significantly, however, the state, by limiting the right to purchase goods from local markets to officially sanctioned merchants, ensured the movement of these goods towards the major cities, especially to Istanbul. Thus the satisfactory provisioning of Istanbul was assured through the state's control over internal trade.[27] However, in the late sixteenth century, with the rise in the prices of grain and raw materials in Western Europe, the state found it more and more difficult to exercise a control over merchants who preferred to sell these commodities in more profitable markets. Contraband trade carried the day. This crisis whereby the state was unable to control the movement of goods is well attested to by the increasing numbers of government edicts prohibiting contraband and by the attempts to enforce the prohibition on exports.[28]

We have seen that the state's control over internal trade achieved a number of systemic functions at once. First, the extent of mercantile activity and therefore mercantile accumulation was thus controlled. Secondly, through restrictions, sanctions, and prohibitions, the flow of commodities inside the Ottoman world-empire was regulated. This assured a certain division of labour designed to provide the surplus-receiving class with the commodities they required for their consumption. In the written law of the Empire, this last designation was reflected in the formulation of 'the necessity of provisioning Istanbul'. Thirdly, and this is the most important function from the point of view of the articulation of the social formation, internal trade provided the link between the Asiatic mode of production (with its peasant producers and tax-collecting state officials) and petty commodity production in the urban guilds. Thus merchant capital supplied the concrete form of articulation which was ultimately effected at the political level by the state.

Given this crucial location of internal trade, it follows that the weakening of political control over its functioning would threaten a disarticulation of the system. In other words, the reproduction of the system would no longer be guaranteed. In fact, as we shall later discuss, this tendency to disarticulation asserts itself when internal trade escapes administrative control (a process which started through the incentives offered to contraband trade during the price inflation), and gradually articulates with external trade. This development is also the story of the peripheralization of the Ottoman world-empire.

External trade in the Ottoman social formation was by no means limited to luxury items but included the raw materials essential for the guilds as well as foodstuffs. Here, too, the state's control achieved systemic functions, similar to the ones we have discussed for internal trade. This control was effected through the sale of concessions which gave merchants the right to trade in essential commodities. This mechanism, in turn, served to provide the state with the money it always required. In fact, merchant capital was integrated into the system as money capital through the role of commercial concessions as well as tax-farming and usury operations. Merchants as bankers were the state's chief creditors, and as tax-farmers they advanced considerable sums to the state.[29]

The Ottoman state, from its inception in the fourteenth century, sought to establish control over international trade routes. This consideration, in fact, largely determined the pattern of Ottoman territorial expansion.[30] During the sixteenth century the Ottoman state monopolized the silk and spice trades and Bursa became an entrepôt for East–West trade, where silk from Iran and spices and dyes from India were exchanged for European woollens. Akkerman, Kilia, Kaffa on the Black Sea were entrepôts for Northern trade with Poland, Russia, and Crimea. Here the products of the East and of Anatolia via Bursa and Istanbul, as well as Mediterranean foodstuffs, were exchanged for the wheat, furs, and iron goods of the North.[31] Italian cities – Venice, Genoa, Florence – were intermediaries in the trade with Western Europe. The control of this trade shifted amongst these states depending on their political standings with the Ottoman government. In the sixteenth century, Ragusa gradually acquired a monopoly position. Venice, however, despite the loss of its supremacy in the Levant, continued to be active in spice and silk trades until the seventeenth century.[32] In fact, the Portuguese discovery of the sea route around the Cape, and the consequent attempt to divert the spice trade to this new route, did not significantly change the volume of trade conducted along the traditional routes.[33] Although Ottoman–Persian wars and social upheavals in Anatolia in the late sixteenth century might have had adverse effects on the traffic along the land route, Alexandria and Aleppo continued to supply Europe with spices. Only after the entry of the English and the Dutch into the Indian Ocean in the later part of the seventeenth century was the spice trade diverted from the Ottoman territories.[34]

Transit trade in silk experienced a similar fate. With the disruption of the silk route through eastern Anatolia at the end of the sixteenth century, Bursa ceased to be the major entrepôt for this trade. This coincided with the entry of the English, French, and the Dutch into Levant trade and the displacement of Venice as Europe's chief supplier of silk via Aleppo. For a brief interval until the mid seventeenth century, European merchants in Aleppo and İzmir turned to Syrian silk. But, when they established their hegemony in the Indian Ocean, the Dutch and the English came to supply Europe with silks of Persia, Bengal and China.[35]

This development, in turn, was to have multiple repercussions for the Ottoman system. First, it signalled the loss of a significant source of revenue for the state in the form of customs dues from the transit trade. Secondly, it resulted in the decline of such cities as Bursa and Aleppo as centres for trade and industry. Thirdly, the shift in trade routes signified the rise of the Atlantic economy and a new mode of commercialization which, as we shall discuss later, was to undermine the system.

The active participation of the English, French, and the Dutch in Levant trade, beginning in the latter half of the sixteenth century, can be characterized as a transitional stage in the articulation of the Ottoman system with the world-economy. This trade included such items as silk and spices as well as staples for rising European industries such as cotton and wool. In the 1580s, the Ottoman government granted trading privileges to the English who imported mohair-yarn cotton, and silk, and sold woollen broadcloth, tin, and steel. In the last quarter of the seventeenth century, England was the largest trader in the Levant, until it was overtaken by France who reigned supreme until the end of the eighteenth century.[36] On the Ottoman side, this is attested to by the increase in the trade with France which consisted of exports of cotton and cotton thread and imports of cloth. During this time İzmir and Selanik emerged as major ports. The same period also witnessed a significant increase in cotton exports to Central Europe over the land route.[37]

The increase in external trade, however, was not limited to cotton exports. Beginning in the late sixteenth century, with the rising demand for raw materials and grains and the consequent price inflation in Western Europe, these commodities found their way into European markets not through the regular channels of external trade controlled by the state, but by means of an increasing volume of contraband operations. This period also witnessed a significant growth in population. The Ottoman state, faced with an increased demand for raw materials and for grains in cities, imposed strict prohibitions on exports. In so doing, it provided additional incentive for contraband. The result was a weakening of the state's control over external trade, a development with multiple repercussions for the system. It meant shortages in grains and raw materials essential for the guilds, which resulted in high prices for these commodities, an inflationary trend further aggravated by the influx of European silver. Guild production was threatened with competition from cheap European manufacturers. The palace as the major purchaser of foodstuffs found itself faced with ever-increasing expenditures.

The increase in illegal exports was achieved through the penetration of merchant capital inside the agricultural sector. Even state officials who held land grants engaged in the smuggling of their produce. The volume of such trade and the consequent development of commodity production in the Empire depended, to a large measure, on the dynamics of the growing capitalist economy outside its borders. But the crucial point was that the change in the structure of trade resulted in the eventual integration of the Ottoman system into the world-economy as a supplier of raw materials and importer of manufactures, that is, its peripheralization.

As can be seen in this historical digression, external trade may not be analysed as a factor inside the system dominated by the political rationality of the state. The volatility of external trade owing to shifts outside the domain of control of the Ottoman state was the principal variable undermining this rationality. Given its geographical situation, the Ottoman Empire could not remain impervious to developments in the privileged domain of 'hot' history: Western Europe.

Contradictions within the social formation

The Ottoman social formation, as we have described it, contained certain contradictions which became manifest conjuncturally. These contradictions, some of which we have already mentioned, were inherent in the normal functioning of the social formation. In ideological readings of Ottoman history, external factors became the disrupters of the harmonious equilibrium that had emanated from the palace to the farthest reaches of the Empire. In the approach proposed here, external factors are comprehensible only through their mobilization of contradictions existing latently within the social formation. Thus, for example, shifts in the structural position of the Ottoman Empire *vis-à-vis* the world-economy became disruptive because of the prior existence of merchant capital within the system.

Since we presented the social formation as an articulation with the Asiatic mode of production in dominance, we can immediately identify two separate loci of contradictions: those embedded in the Asiatic mode of production, and those resulting from its articulation into the social formation.

It was mentioned above that the production process in the Asiatic mode of production does not create conflict or a confrontation between the producers and the appropriators or surplus. The individual peasant comes into contact only with the tax-collector, who acts in the name of the central authority, only after the production process, which he carried out as a free peasant.[38] In this way the Asiatic mode of production is distinguished from the slave, feudal, or capitalist modes of production; class conflict is not graspable in the production experience. For this reason its principal dynamic is to be found in intra-class and not inter-class conflict. In this analysis, class will refer to those groups with a claim on the output through a determinate position in the social structure.

In the Ottoman social formation, only state officials had a claim on the surplus. This surplus-receiving class consisted of various factions corresponding to diverse functions in the state. These factions were those of *tımar*-holders, market inspectors, and tax-farmers, all of whom perform the function of revenue collection; and of *ulema*, judges, and bureaucrats in Istanbul, who performed the ideological, legal, and administrative functions of the state. Various stratifications inside the surplus-receiving class were possible depending on the specific conjuncture: for example, between the *ulema* and the bureaucracy, or between the military and the palace.[39] In fact, from the seventeenth century until the abolition of the Janissary Corps in 1826, the military was effectively independent of the control of the central authority, which permitted the janissaries to gain control over certain sources of revenue.[40] There is, however, another conflict over revenue which is more permanent and structural. It results from the institutionalization of tax-collection. The central authority requires local representation both for tax-collecting and purposes of ideological-political legitimation. Yet the authority vested in local representatives threatened to grow at the expense of the palace. Stronger local representation created a potential threat. Thus, this intra-class conflict worked as a centrifugal force, tending to create local potentates who declared relative independence from the central authority.

Whenever the process of separation from the central authority was complete, a new unit was formed duplicating the larger unit. In the eighteenth century, for example, the *ayans*, gaining relative independence from the Porte, substituted their local authorities for those of the sultan, and otherwise replicated all the functions vested in the central authority.[41] Not all *ayans*, of course, attained such autonomy. Most smaller *ayans* could do no more than cut into the surplus destined for Istanbul; they formed tributary arrangements with the palace, merely increasing their shares out of the revenue. In such situations, the political and ideological institutions remained dependent on the central authority; the *kadis* and municipal administrators were appointed by the palace. The *ayans* merely increased their share-out of the surplus without altering the reproduction of the system. This development of the smaller *ayans* is perhaps closer to what has been termed 'feudalization'. Here, there is a parcellization at the economic level without a break-off from the larger political-ideological nexus of the state. It should be remembered, however, that this 'feudalization', or rather the localization of power, did not indicate a transition to feudalism. The local potentates remained politically subordinate to the central authority, and the division of labour inside the Empire was not significantly disrupted, unless 'feudalization' coincided with commercialization.

The immediate translation of these developments inside the relations characterizing the Asiatic mode of production was a relative decline in the revenue collected by the central authority. The state depended on an efficient extraction of the surplus, not only because of its budgetary needs, but also because this prevented the rise of rival centres of power which required surplus for the process of institutionalizing their authority. Therefore, the relative decline in revenue doubly threatened the nodal position of the state in the reproduction of the social formation. A revenue crisis meant that the political-ideological (and of course disciplinary) functions of the state could not be performed effectively; and it also signalled the rise of competing power structures.

We are not claiming that, historically, the main cause of revenue crises was the local usurpation of surplus. In fact, from the late sixteenth century on, revenue crises in the Ottoman state became endemic, and measures designed to fight the deficitary tendency seemed to dominate the policies of the Porte. The immediate causes of the late-sixteenth-century development were the growing military expenses, the population increase in Anatolia, and the price inflation. We will analyse the impact of these 'mobilizing' factors at the end of this section.

It was mentioned above that the reproduction of the Ottoman social formation involved a political control over the division of labour which could only be implemented by limiting the degree of functioning of merchant capital. The existence of merchant capital naturally entailed the production of commodities for the market. In fact it was through the close state supervision of the market that merchant capital could be kept within politically desirable bounds. However, the success of this political control, and consequently the successful reproduction of the social formation, required that the state as the locus of institutions enabling political control remain powerful *vis-à-vis* merchant capital. The tendency inherent in merchant capital is for its extended reproduction through incorporating a greater proportion of economic activity inside the sphere of commodity production. It was this tendency which threatened the reproduction of the Ottoman social formation. In effect, this potential contradiction between the existence of commodity production and the political rationality of the Ottoman social formation took its toll when merchant capital inside the Empire was integrated into the circuit of capital's valorization in the world-capitalist economy. It was then that merchant capital expanded into areas formerly closed to commodity production. As we shall show later, the peripheral transformation that this expansion entailed could only effect certain evolutions in the forces of production. Proto-industrialization, for example, because of its potential competition with manufactured imports, would not be one of the evolving organizational forms. As Tilly and Tilly remarked in a survey of European historiography, the absence of such proto-industrial activity is one of the differentiating factors characterizing today's periphery.[42] The causes of this absence are, of course, to be looked for in the process of the destruction of crafts during the phase of their competition with manufactured imports. On the other hand, petty commodity production in individual farms and feudalized cash-crop production were forms that readily articulated with merchant capital.

We have dealt theoretically with two of the possible contradictions inside the social formation as we have defined it. Although other contradictions may be specified, it can be asserted that their outcomes as well will collapse into the categorization adopted above: tendencies either toward the parcellization of economic and political control, or toward the expansion of the realm of the market and consequently the weakening of political control over the economy.

It is, however, impossible to observe these tendencies in isolation from counteracting forces and from external factors which create the conditions for the tendencies to assert themselves in the historical-concrete space. We shall, therefore, analyse two such external factors which have been utilized by Ottomanists to explain either adaptations or decline of institutions in the Empire, and attempt to show their workings through the structure of contradictions inherent in the social formation. These factors which are of varying degrees of exogeneity all fall inside the same time period. The price inflation showed its effects at the end of the sixteenth century; population increase and the shift in the trade routes occurred roughly within the same time period. Hence it would be difficult to separate the effects of these factors in order to deal with each individually. For the purposes of exposition this less-than-ideal method will be adopted. We shall concentrate on population and prices; shifts in trade routes have been discussed above and will be touched upon in the context of price inflation.

The population growth that the Ottoman Empire witnessed during the later sixteenth century was characterized by a market increase in the numbers of non-producers relative to producers and an increase in urban population relative to rural population.[43] The dynamics of this process is to be sought in the pattern of responses to demographic change which characterizes pre-capitalist formations. Given the inelasticity of agricultural production, despite an initial phase of extension of arable lands, these economies were unable to support an increasing population. The subsistence crisis first manifested itself in the rural sector and forced the flight of population into urban areas where the army and other administrative institutions, as well as towns themselves, were privileged recipients of the limited food supplies.[44]

In the Ottoman Empire a large number of the rural uprooted population found their way to Istanbul and other cities, or joined religious schools (*medreses*). The vagrancy of the new urbanites created problems, often solved through employment by the state. *Medreses* also created problems because the endowments of these pious foundations, already reduced under the impact of price inflation, fell behind the requirements of an expanded student body. Sometimes, the apprentice *ulema* took to extorting food from the peasants, and sometimes the *medrese* administration attempted to expand their tax base at the expense of the peasants.

Population growth was thus translated into an intensified struggle for tax revenues among the factions of the surplus-receiving class. This struggle became most pronounced at the juncture where the system's inherent conflictual tendency was located, that is, in the struggle between the central government and provincial adminstrations. The increasing population swelled the ranks of the central army, the janissaries, and of the palace employees, thus exerting a pressure on the existing state revenues. The central government, in order to meet its increased expenditures, was compelled to seek additional sources of revenue in the form of extraordinary taxes (*avariz*)[45] and through the sale of tax farms. The provincial administrators, especially those in Anatolia, on the other hand, found themselves surrounded with inflated entourages when the rural unemployed gravitated towards the occupation of irregular soldiers (*levend*).[46] Thus, unable to meet their requirements with the revenues allotted to them by the state, provincial administrators resorted to banditry in the countryside. No longer supplying the central government with mounted soldiers, they deprived the state of its share of tax revenues. Moreover, their extortions in the countryside forced peasant flights, resulting in upheavals and a decline in agricultural production.

The loss of control by the central administration over the sources of revenue, and its appropriation by provincial administrators and the *ulema* in religious schools, were concretized in the Celali[47] uprisings – a prelude to the system's 'feudalization' in Anatolia.

A rise in the number of urban-dwellers accompanied population growth. Existing towns became larger, and some villages developed into towns. This urbanization, however, was not entirely caused by demographic pressure. At least in its initial phases, population increase had resulted in an increase in the volume of output and of the marketed surplus. Local markets and regional trade had expanded both as a result of increased town population and increased commodity production in agriculture. Together with the weakening control of the central authority on provincial administration, this development could have led to a complete escape of merchant capital from under the political control of the state. However, the devastation in the countryside following the Celali uprisings, peasant flights, and re-nomadization checked the tendency towards the full monetization of agricultural production.

Another development of the sixteenth century, partly caused by population growth, and partly reflecting a world-wide tendency, was the price inflation. The change in the structure of trade which resulted in the increasing activity of merchant capital, concretized in contraband trade, meant the flooding of the Ottoman market with Spanish *real*.[48] The widespread usage of *real* without being converted into Ottoman currency (*akçe*) signalled the abandonment of the Ottoman system to the movements of world prices. Thus the state lost control over its currency in that it no longer had a monopoly over issuing coins, and could not debase a currency which it had not minted. Thus it was deprived of one of the traditional measures utilized to counteract declining revenue. With the weakening of its controls over external trade and an increase in contraband in response to European demand, the state could not fulfil its systemic function of fixing the prices within the world-empire. The forming of prices outside the world-empire and the consequent divergence between decreed prices and world prices was another factor contributing to the liberation of merchant capital.

At the same time, the increase in prices, to which contraband contributed, meant that state expenditures in money terms had to increase as well, while certain taxes, which were customarily assessed at 30–40 year intervals,[49] declined in real terms.

The revenue crisis beginning in the sixteenth century was exacerbated through increases in expenditures. The most important increase was in the requirements of the military. Changes in the technology of war shifted the balance from mounted to foot soldiers, necessitating the maintenance of a permanently stationed army. Thus the palace had to house and feed (and pay a salary to) a growing number of janissaries. These janissaries were mostly stationed in Istanbul and it was therefore of crucial importance that they received their salaries promptly.[50] The development away from mounted soldiers also confirmed the outmodedness of the *tımar* system as a mode of revenue extraction. Tax revenue was now required in money form, and not as use-specific cavalry.

The new mode of revenue collection which came to dominate the fiscal system was tax-farming. The practice of tax-farming, i.e., farming out of specified revenues to the highest bidder, had been an integral part of the Ottoman tax system since its inception. This system (*iltizam*) had always been the main source of liquid funds for the central authority. It had, however, been confined to certain sources of revenue such as customs dues, the poll-tax levied on non-Muslims, and the sheep-tax. Beginning in the seventeenth century the *iltizam* system was applied to the traditional agricultural tax of *öşr* as well. Revenues on imperial domains, on *vakıf* (pious foundation) estates, on former *tımar* land, were all farmed out.[51]

In the sixteenth century, when only certain revenues were farmed out, great Jewish merchants of Istanbul served as creditors to the state and thereby found a domain of valorization where merchant capital and money capital were interchangeable. They could lend the palace money accumulated in trade and thus obtain the privilege of further trade, while at the same time earning interest on their loans.

The tax-farming system, so advantageous to the possessors of liquid funds, proved to be well-suited to an environment characterized by money fortunes accumulated during the inflationary period.[52] Thus the money revenue requirements of the state coincided with the demands of the newly rich, some of whom were themselves highly placed bureaucrats, janissaries, and *ulema*. Thus merchants were no longer the sole purchasers of tax-farms. By the end of the seventeenth century, tax-farming had rapidly spread, and had begun to cause worries in that the tax-farmers pursuing short-term maximization abused their granted sources of revenue. As a measure to counteract this possibility, a new system was devised in 1695, whereby tax-farms were granted on a life-time basis (*malikane*), and the grantee acquired the right to manage his farm independently of state supervision, as well as the right to sell his expected revenue.[53]

The tax-farmer's main function was to provide the state with money. Therefore his contractual relationship with the state was defined in strictly pecuniary terms. In this relationship, the state was the recipient of money capital which was advanced prior to the collection of taxes. Hence during the process of realization of interest, the tax-farmer, unlike the *sipahi*, had no obligation to perpetuate the ideological-political relationship between the direct producer and the state. His concern was the maximization of returns on capital advanced. Although legally bound by the traditional rates of taxation, he sought constantly to transgress these bounds, and frequently did so, especially if he held an adminstrative position as well.

Tax-farmers provided the state with loans and obtained the right to collect the taxes, but they also introduced a new relation in agriculture: usury.[54] Usury never developed to an extent sufficient to destroy small property. Yet it was a means to increase exploitation, and to bind peasants to feudalized units of production, for instance as share-croppers. Usury served to accelerate both capital accumulation and the destruction of the free state of the peasantry.

Both of these developments undermined the reproduction of the system which depended on the maintenance of small property in the countryside.[55] Money capital, like merchant capital, may articulate with all forms of pre-capitalist production.[56] Again like merchant capital, it also destroys the basis of the political reproduction of the system. It does this in two ways: by mediating the rise of *ayans*, and by accelerating commercialization.

Tax-farmers were legally (and literally) accountable to the central authority. While they were guaranteed military aid by local administrators to deal with reluctant tax-payers, they also had to present their financial accounts to be controlled by the bureaucrats. Of course, this checking mechanism could not operate when the tax-farmer and his auditor were the same person, or when the local administrator was also the tax-farmer. Through such identities, tax-farming was closely linked to the development of local potentates.

By the early eighteenth century, certain tax-farmers of local origin had transformed themselves into local potentates, or *ayans*. They had earlier been merchants, moneychangers, or provincial *ulema*, and had received tax-farms as sub-contractors to Istanbul merchants or high officials. These enriched sub-contractors were usually the local representatives of governors as well (*mütesellim*). Thus they could add political authority to economic accumulation and as such became known as *ayans*.[57]

On the other hand, the more important *ayans*, who created troubles during the eighteenth century, were provincial officials originally appointed by the Porte.[58] Taking advantage of a weak central authority, they sought to establish themselves permanently as governors. The mechanism whereby they could purchase tax-farms for the entire area under their administrative authority also allowed them to build up a client group of locally powerful sub-contracting tax-farmers. Thus tax-farming was important both as a device for economic enrichment and as a mechanism for building up political authority.

Another development which was accelerated by tax-farming was the emergence of commercial estates (*çiftlik*) in the eighteenth century. The onset of tax-farming had already broken the ideological reciprocity between the producer and the state, allowing for an intensified exploitation of the peasant. This potential, together with a growing European demand for wheat, maize, cotton, and tobacco, incited tax-farmers and especially *malikane* holders to produce commercially for the market on an expanded scale.[59] Large *çiftliks* were established in the Balkans, in Thrace (supplying the Istanbul market), and in western Anatolia, where İzmir developed from a small coastal town to a major port of export trade within a century.[60]

Çiftliks were examples of commercial farming where enserfed peasantry or share-croppers were employed. Aside from the novelty of the labour organization, *çiftlik*s also altered the traditional crop pattern. Cash-crops replaced subsistence grains. Owners of *çiftlik*s accumulated commercial profits obtained through selling these crops to European merchants directly. These sales were carried out illegally, since administered prices inside the empire were always lower than prices obtainable in export markets. The eighteenth-century fairs in the Balkans, and similar developments in Anatolia during the latter half of the eighteenth and early nineteenth centuries, must be interpreted in this context.

From the point of view of the peasants, most of whom were under debt bondage, the *çiftlik* system meant a serious deterioration in their status. There was an obvious increase in the rate of exploitation in economic terms.[61] Most of the taxes payable to the state did not cease and the dues demanded by the *çiftlik*-holders comprised half of the produce after the payment of *öşr*, in addition to labour services required of the peasant. Moreover, peasants under the *çiftlik* system lost security of tenure. Many Balkan *çiftlik*s were minor fortifications guarded by armed men (*kırcalıs*) who were instrumental in forcing peasant flights, thus making available more land for commercial production.

From the point of view of the political system, the rise of the *çiftlik* was the most disruptive development. Commercialization of production and, more importantly, change in the status of the peasantry, both of which the *çiftlik* entailed, are necessary components in a process of peripheralization. With the *çiftlik* organization, integration of the Ottoman system into the capitalist world-economy attained an irreversible momentum. In the early nineteenth century, the process of development of *ayan*s was reversed through a wave of centralizations, but the growth of commercial agriculture continued without such reversals.

Peripheralization and the colonial state

Thus far, we have discussed isolated strands in the development of the Ottoman social formation, leading to its dissolution as a world-empire. As production became commodity production and as these commodities began to enter the circuit of industrial capital in its valorization process, peripheralization asserted itself. Becoming a periphery is identical with entering the world division of labour and thus ceasing to be a self-contained unit of reproduction.

The isolated strands of tax-farming, contraband trade, price and population movements gain significance when they are analysed as contributing to such an integration into the circuit of world capital. It must first be mentioned that the timing of this integration varied from one specific region to another. The Balkans became integrated into the European economy beginning in the eighteenth century. For Egypt and the Levant, the process gained momentum during the first quarter of the nineteenth century. In Anatolia, the volume of trade increased significantly beginning in the 1830s. Of course, exact dates are impossible to determine for this process, the commencement of which, as we showed above, can be traced back to the sixteenth century.

Nor is it possible to describe a single mode of peripheralization. Again depending on the region, various forms emerged: commercial *çiftliks* in the Balkans, large cotton estates in Egypt,[62] petty commodity production in peasant farms in western Anatolia. Labour organization ranged from share-cropping to family units working on their own lands, via wage labour in capitalist farms. While foodstuffs and raw materials were the major export commodities, hand-woven carpets in western Anatolia also became a peripheral product.

Trade was organized by foreign trading companies and merchants stationed in a few cities (Selanik, Istanbul, İzmir, Beirut, Alexandria). Merchant capital of foreign origin entered into a division of labour with native capital, in this case with ethnic minorities. It was the Jews, the Greeks, and the Armenians, who acted as intermediaries between British, French, Italian, and German merchants and the actual producers.[63]

External trade of the Ottoman Empire increased in the first three decades of the nineteenth century, especially after the advent of steam-freighters in the eastern Mediterranean.[64] Growing imports of European manufacturers meant a decline in guild production and rural crafts, while raw materials were now channelled to export markets.[65] After the 1838 trade treaties with core countries and with the beginnings of railroad construction, penetration of merchant capital into even the most resistant region of the Empire, Anatolia, was accelerated.[66] Foreign and local merchant capital was articulated inside the legal framework through judiciary reforms. There were also attempts by foreign capital to set up capitalist farms in the İzmir region, although these remained insignificant.[67]

The history of foreign capital, public debt, and trade in the second half of the nineteenth century is typical of a peripheralization process, and is too well known to repeat here.[68] We will, however, briefly discuss the attendant changes at the political level.

These developments in economic integration were not automatically reflected at the political level. There was, in the initial stages, considerable dislocation between the new economic orientation of the Empire and the old form of state appropriate to the Asiatic mode of production. This created contradictions which became manifest as the legal and political requirements of merchant capital clashed with the existing institutions. If we define a 'colonial state' as that form of state in the periphery which primarily serves the needs of merchant capital, the transformations in the politics of the nineteenth-century Ottoman Empire may be interpreted as the transition from a state mechanism of the Asiatic type to a colonial state. 'Modernization' and 'reform' of the Ottoman Empire should be evaluated within such a perspective.

It should not be forgotten, however, that this transformation did not occur simply at the instigation of merchant capital or, more precisely, at the instigation of the core states serving merchant capital. It also conformed to the economic requirements of the bureaucratic class and to the ideological inspirations of a ruling class closely articulated with 'Western-modern' ideas.[69]

With the transformation of the state into a colonial state, the Ottoman system lost its specificity. It was now characterized by the dominance of the capitalist mode of production both at the economic and the political levels. Therefore, it was no longer a proper unit of study. Its subsequent history could be analysed only within the dynamics of the world-capitalist system as an integral, albeit functionally differentiated, component of this system.

3 ❧ State and economy in the Ottoman Empire*

İLKAY SUNAR

The object of this paper is to examine the organization of economic activity in the Ottoman Empire, both in its traditional form and in its later transformation. Let me state at the outset the argument of the paper as well: Economic life in the Ottoman Empire was organized as a redistributive system by a patrimonial state;[1] the transformation of this system was neither the consequence of a dynamic inscribed into the system nor the simple outcome of a direct impulse transmitted from outside; rather, it was the interaction of internal and external forces which determined the process of such transformation. The primary shock to the Ottoman system was provided from outside, but the response to the shock was mediated by the domestic patrimonial structure. In order to account for Ottoman transformation, therefore, we need to specify both the nature of international developments and the type of internal economic organization upon which such developments impinged.

It is necessary to specify first the nature of external developments, for, in the absence of their impact, the conservatism inherent in the structure of Ottoman order would have been never overcome. By the conservatism of the Ottoman order, however, I do not mean that it was necessarily a static or stable order. On the contrary, within the Ottoman order there were conflicts, especially over political power and the control of land and labour. But these were characteristically patrimonial conflicts that tended to upset political authority, or at worst to fragment society into patrimonial segments that were structurally alike, rather than revolutions intended to transform the overall structure of society. These conflicts might exhaust or impoverish society, but they had no tendency to transform it. This is why the prime mover of Ottoman transformation must be located outside the patrimonial-redistributive structure, specifically, in the developments in Western Europe of the sixteenth century.

What we find in Western Europe in the first half of the sixteenth century is the emergence of a new kind of economic order that was coordinated into a European-wide, interdependent division of labour through an inter-state market system in which economic exchange and the production for it by

*This is a revised version of an earlier essay: 'Antropologie politique et économique: L'Empire ottomane et sa transformation', *Annales, ESC*, XXXV, 3–4 (May–August 1980), 551–79. This essay was initially written as a paper for a conference on the Ottoman Empire and North Africa, held in Istanbul, Turkey, on May 21–25, 1975, sponsored by the Social Science Research Council of New York.

different regions were oriented to maximum profits. In other words, what we find at this time in Europe is the development and diffusion of market economics beginning to operate on a European-wide basis.

In one striking aspect, the emergent European-wide economy and the Ottoman Empire were similar: both were 'worlds' constituted of a single division of labour and multiple cultural communities – one was a world-economy, the other a world-empire.[2] The crucial difference was the existence of a common political structure in one and its lack in the other. The European world-economy was a complex of multiple polities and cultures linked together through the institution of the market; the Ottoman Empire, on the other hand, lacked the integrative market but held together as a redistributive system under the supervision of a supreme state.

As these worlds came to interact under conditions altered largely by the development of the European market economy, the result was not the formation of a new and larger redistributive world-empire, but the dissolution of the Ottoman redistributive system. From mid sixteenth century onwards, the political economy of the Empire, subject to the dynamics of the European world market and the exigencies of the Ottoman state, evolved gradually into a complex socio-economic formation which occupied in the network of world-market a peripheral status until its demise in the twentieth century.

In regarding the Ottoman economic transformation as a process of articulation with the European market system, I am not suggesting that prior to the emergence of that system the Ottoman economy was a world sealed off from the outside. What is suggested is that not every interaction is of the kind which leads towards dissolution, or towards interdependence with another economy to constitute in the end a single system.[3] Economic exchange was certainly a significant aspect of Ottoman relations with the outside world before the emergence of the European market system. In fact, external trade, carried on by a large group of merchants specializing primarily in long-distance and transit trade, constituted an important source of revenue for the Ottoman state. But such trade did not disrupt the basic organization of economic life, for it was administered by the state and largely catered to its demands for luxury goods. To put it in Karl Polanyi's language, this was an administered form of trade utilizing 'ports of trade' external to the organization of production instead of a 'market trade' organically bound to productive activity.[4] Since transit trade as well as exports and imports were not means for supplying an anonymous market with essential goods but a matter of providing riches for the state under luxury trade, the cycle of external exchange took place primarily through the medium of the state, and thus remained without a determining effect on the methods and purposes of production.

What, therefore, needs to be explored in the following pages is a two-sided dynamic, which informed the new type of interaction: an increasing demand for Ottoman primary goods stimulated by an expanding European market on the one hand, and a less administered form of external trade engendered by the revenue concerns of an anxious Ottoman state on the other.

Economic organization of the Ottoman Empire

If economic exchange, in the form of transit trade, was an important aspect of traditional Ottoman relations with the outside world, it was also, in the form of market exchange, a significant source of internal economic activity. However, while market exchange was becoming *the regulative principle* of economic activity in sixteenth-century Western Europe, in the Ottoman Empire it remained simply *a form of transaction* that was neither co-extensive with economic organization nor a principal mode of social integration. In the Ottoman Empire, market exchange was in reality market-place exchange where buying and selling were oriented to livelihood. That is to say, exchange and the production for it were for use and not for profit, or, more accurately, market-place exchange assumed not merely production for use but production for use-value: the manufacture of commodities for sale in the market in order to obtain money for the purchase of other commodities. In sum, it was commodity–money–commodity relations which pervaded market relations; or, to call it by its name, it was simple commodity production that was prevalent.

We are, as you see, coming to the essential feature of Ottoman economics, for the production of use-values is a characteristic of peasant economies in which peasants relate to exchange with an interest in consumption, and so to production with an interest in livelihood. And, to define a peasant economy simply: it exists where most production takes place in agriculture, and where the dominant and most widespread unit of production is the peasant household. Clearly, there may be units of production other than the household; in a peasant economy, the household is not the only unit of production, it is simply the dominant one.[5]

A peasant economy, then, is by nature a function of domestic production. In a stimulating essay, Marshall Sahlins suggests that under-production (relative to existing possibilities) is the characterizing feature of all economies (i.e., primitive and peasant) organized by domestic groups.[6] This is because nothing within the organization of the household pushes it to produce above its subsistence needs. Furthermore, since any given family over time and certain families at any given time are bound to fail to produce for their livelihood, unless the 'domestic economy is forced beyond itself' to produce surplus above its subsistence needs, 'the entire economy does not survive'. However, it never really happens that the 'household manages the economy, for by itself the domestic stranglehold on production could only arrange for the expiration of society'. Clearly, we have here the suggestion that peasant economic activity characterized by domestic production does not have a built-in stimulus for surplus production, and that in fact such activity is not capable of shifting by itself into a self-sustaining, institutional process. The stimulus to production as well as the means for the overall organization of domestic groups must be supplied from outside if society is to survive. Not only does the domestic household need to be made to work over and above its subsistence needs, but also its relations with the outside world need to be institutionalized. Sahlins claims that the peasant household transcends itself and connects with the outside world only under obligations laid upon it by kinship ties, religious beliefs and political pressures. Ultimately, surplus production and the organization of its distribution are simultaneous functions of the stimulus provided to the economy by the specific structures of kinship, religion and political power.[7]

Needless to say, the fact that the processes of production, distribution and exchange are organized into a coordinated effort through non-market means holds true for all pre-market systems. In the Ottoman Empire, such organization was a function of the redistributive state. This was in contrast to the emerging European market in which coordination of economic activity (and division of labour) were beginning to be achieved through a competitive process where there were few or no restrictions on the mobility of capital and labour. The crucial feature of Ottoman organization was that it was a system of production for use in which the hierarchical division of labour, as well as the methods and purposes of production were structured by the state.[8] This was also in contrast to European feudalism where domestic underproduction was overcome by local (manorial) organization, and where the production of surplus was stimulated and appropriated by the lord who had direct and personal control over serf-tenants who worked the land on his estate or manor. In the Ottoman Empire, under a redistributive patrimonial system, the production of surplus was stimulated and appropriated by the state elite, which used its control over the state machinery to tax the peasants who, in turn, had direct access to productive resources.

Such a view of Ottoman economic organization means that models of Ottoman economy built after the manorial system (feudalism) are fundamentally misleading, for what is taken to correspond to the manor, the *tımar* (benefice holding), unlike the manor was not a system or unit of production but rather a political-administrative institution designed to incorporate the peasant household into the larger world of the imperial state. As the *tımar* holder, the *sipahi* was not, like a feudal lord, directly involved in the process of household production, and with a labour force of his own – he was more like a military figure in charge of an administrative institution that was confined in function to the collection of taxes and the provision of troops in times of war. Furthermore, unlike the feudal lord, the *sipahi* had no claims of ownership either over the land or the *raiyya* (peasant). Theoretically, all the land and the people 'belonged' to God and were in the trust of the padişah. The real privilege of the use of land, however, resided in the household. The form of land 'ownership' by the state was more inclusive than exclusive, such that no household was in the normal course of things excluded from access to the means of its own survival. The investment of 'ownership' in the state gave the peasantry something of a permanent guarantee of livelihood. Thus the *tımar* was not a unit of ownership interposed between the family and its means of production; rather, it was a political institution superposed onto the family, which retained the primary relation to productive resources.

In sum, it was the state, as the linchpin of the redistributive mechanism, the pervasive network of patron-client relations, and the over-arching political-administrative system, which provided for the provisioning of society through the movement of goods from the producers to the political centre and from the centre to the populace. In this scheme of things, where distributors were the rulers and the producers the ruled, the order of stratification was ratified and maintained by the state, resting on the principle 'from each according to his status obligations in the system, to each according to his rights in the system', and justified by the 'circle of equity'.[9] The obligations of the state, on the other hand, were formulated as the dispensation of justice (*adâlet*) and the administration of welfare (*hisba*).

In agriculture, it was the *sipahi*, as the administrative agent, who mediated between the state and the peasantry and served as the nexus of exchange. In industry, it was the corporative structure of guilds which bound the town craftsmen to the ruling centre.[10] In trade, it was the merchants who were the clients of the state: the state provided the security of trade and granted them monopolies; the merchants, in return, gave loans to the state, assisted the regime in taxation, ensured a steady revenue from custom charges, and supplied the patrimonial elite with luxury goods.[11] The consequent concentration of surplus at the centre, on the other hand, served to maintain the state apparatus and general welfare. Thus, in the Ottoman Empire, while economic activity was a function of the state, it also functioned to maintain the state.

As suggested above, in the scheme of Ottoman order, exchange and the production for it were not organized for the free sale of commodities in a market for maximum profit. Instead, economic activity was organized and coordinated by the state as a system for use.[12] Internal production and exchange were ensconced in state institutions, and while external exchange was, in the form of transit trade in luxuries, an important source of capital accumulation and revenue, it was also regulated and controlled by the state, and hence deprived of its possible transforming effects on the state-administered mode of domestic production. There was, as a consequence, a strong tendency for production to move in customary ways and to settle into a conservative pattern.

This is why I have suggested at the beginning that we must seek the prime mover of Ottoman economic transformation in the dynamics of the external environment, particularly in the development of the European market economic system, for such a development entailed two significant alterations in the external circumstances of the Empire which, in turn, had crucial implications for its survival. One was the re-routing of trade routes, and the other was the flow of enormous quantities of silver and gold from the Americas and the consequent price revolution. The structure of needs, motivations, and capabilities which thrust Europeans on the requisite overseas ventures of these developments constitutes the fascinating story of the 'origins of capitalism'.[13] From the point of view of our concerns here, it will have to suffice to say that the circumnavigation of trade routes and the price revolution consequent on the flow of cheap metals, particularly silver, produced severe financial problems for the Ottoman state.[14]

Our thesis is that the attempts of the Ottomans to adjust to these external alterations, which produced a sharp revenue squeeze for the state, in conjunction with the expansion of the European market economy, set in motion a new process of interaction with the outside that can best be described as the incorporation of the redistributive world-empire into the capitalist world-market. And it is suggested that this incorporation and the simultaneous transformation of the Ottoman economy, in turn, can best be studied as a long-term *dissolution* process in which the Ottoman economy ceased to be redistributive without becoming a capitalist market economy. The emerging, articulated structure of the Empire was specific without being self-complete: as an articulated combination of redistributive patrimonialism and the world-market economy it was a specific structure, but once it began to reproduce itself in conjunction with the world-system, it was not a self-complete whole.[15] Thus, it might be best to designate this new structure as a peripheral formation, meaning that it possesses a specificity of its own without being a self-contained unit. The unit that was self-contained and within which the peripheral formation operated was, of course, the world-system. In sum, the point is that the redistributive Empire and the European market system were articulated in such a way as to constitute a specific structure that cannot be conceptualized apart from the world-system; and hence, if there are stages, crucial turning-points, or watersheds in Ottoman history, after the seventeenth century, they too cannot be understood solely as internal affairs severed from the turns and twists of the world-system as a whole.

There were essentially two crucial turning-points in the development of the world-market system: the commercialization of agriculture in the sixteenth century and the development of industrial capitalism in the nineteenth century. Both developments had significant impact throughout the world-system, including the Ottoman Empire. The commercialization of agriculture and industrialization were essentially processes internal to the world-system with, however, differential impact in different regions of the system.[16] Below, I shall attempt to view the transformation of the redistributive structure of the Empire with reference to these two crucial stages of the world-market system, and with all the linkages and shared and contradictory interests which such incorporation/transformation involved.

Dissolution of traditional economy

During the seventeenth and eighteenth centuries, the Ottoman economy simultaneously underwent incorporation into the world-market system and the commercialization of its agriculture.[17] The whole process was set in motion by the fiscal crises which followed upon the circumnavigation of trade routes and the impact of the price revolution. The consequent squeeze on state revenues reached such proportions that the Ottoman state felt compelled to undertake defensive measures in response. The initial attempt of the Ottoman state was to try to restore the financial health of the Empire through a series of protracted but spasmodic wars fought to break out of the European noose around her trade. When these attempts failed, the result was not only further decline in trade but also financial exhaustion, which along with runaway inflation played havoc with the imperial fiscal structure. At this point, the options left to the state were not many: either to tap more internal resources and/or to cooperate with the European powers (particularly the Dutch and English). The Ottoman state elite decided to do both, namely, to extend tax-farming in order to extract more surplus out of agriculture, and to allow capitulary grants to foreign merchants in order to revitalize her trade. The outcome of these measures was less administered, a sort of *laissez-faire* type of trade policy by which Ottoman primary goods began to be exchanged for manufactured European products.[18]

These policy measures were not, however, unfamiliar to Ottoman practice; on the contrary, they were both an expression of the monopoly-patronage (*mukataa*) system by which certain economic concessions, in return for a specified sum, would be eased to interested contractors. The granting of trade privileges to foreign merchants was as old as the Empire: as residents of *mustamin* communities, foreign merchants were granted *aman* (protection) by an imperial *ahdname* (promise) by which their safety of passage through Ottoman lands and seas was guaranteed by the Ottoman state.[19] When the state began to seek additional revenue to boost its declining fortunes, these protections traditionally granted for residence in ports of trade and for safety of passage were enlarged to include the privileges of export and import within the Empire.[20] Tax-farming was also a customary practice, although its origins remain somewhat obscure. However, what had been a limited practice became, after the mid sixteenth century, widespread in agriculture. The state expected to generate funds by leasing land to the highest bidder, while the tax-farmer, given the opportunities for exporting staple goods, found such land to be an attractive source of income.

Clearly, the state, the tax-farmers, the foreign merchants and the whole string of intermediaries and their hangers-on – all benefited from the commercialization of agriculture and its outward orientation. Together, they also formed an alliance of interests that was imposed upon the peasant household. When tax-farming became the dominant practice, what emerged to replace the *timar* was a system of estates organized as a system of exchange and production for the world market. And, as these estates encroached upon the domestic economy, the household was converted into a labour force coerced to produce cash crops for export.[21] The end result, however, was not only the destruction of the domestically based and *tımar*-organized agricultural production, but also a significant decline in the autonomous and formative powers of the state itself. Let us now view these changes and their ramifications in somewhat more detail.

First, as far as the destruction of the *tımar* system was concerned, from the state's viewpoint there were reasons to believe that the system had lost its original significance anyway.[22] For one thing, the conditions of war had so changed that the essential role of the Ottoman cavalry was seriously compromised; the burden of war was borne more by the janissaries (the standing army) than the cavalry. For another, since the military burden fell on the janissaries, the effect was that more salaries had to be paid out of the fragile central treasury. Hence, given the financial problems of the state, tax-farming was an attractive alternative by which the state could generate the funds it so desperately needed. It was true, however, that while tax-farming provided the state with an immediate source of revenue, in the long run it led to the erosion of its tax base, since the flow of taxes upward to the centre became increasingly subject to the interference of the tax-farmers. As we shall see, the long-run effect, or the unintended consequences of the state's action, later came back to haunt the state itself.

Second, the inflow of cheap silver and the consequent price revolution, the runaway inflation, hit especially hard those groups in the Empire that were largely dependent on money transactions for their livelihood. The traditional problem of the economy had been shortage of specie; with the inflow of silver, the problem was reversed: speculation, counterfeiting, smuggling, and usury became rampant. As a response, the state devalued and debased the currency. The result was a terrible squeeze on fixed incomes, and lowered value for primary goods which were then exported, smuggled out in great quantities, leaving the local crafts industry with a shortage of material for its own uses. Hence, what we witness in the Empire during the seventeenth century is great pressure on fixed incomes and stagnation of crafts industry, along with increasing export commerce.

Third, the impact of commercialization on the peasantry was twofold: it led, on the one hand, to increases in labour services and, on the other, to the abandonment of their lands when they could not pay money-rent. Large numbers of peasants either migrated to the cities or became fodder for rebel armies. Rebellions appear to have lasted throughout the seventeenth century, and seem largely to have been acts of plunder against the tax-farmers, organized by former military gentry (*sipahis*), and in fact, by the provincial governors, who went so far as to challenge the authority of the state.[23] These rebellions were finally defused, but in the meantime their impact on the social structure was considerable. Peasants flocking to the cities in great numbers could not be absorbed by a stagnating industry, well guarded by its monopoly status. Since they could not burst in upon the guild system, they filled the ranks of the military and the religious schools. As a result, there was considerable discontent among both the students of religion and the janissaries. The number of janissaries, for instance, rose from around 40,000 to 100,000 between the mid sixteenth century and the turn of the century.[24] It is no wonder that Koçi Bey complained about the degeneration in the standing army: by the seventeenth century, the once formidable Ottoman military machine had indeed become corrupt and demoralized.

Fourth, the commercialization of agriculture had considerable impact on the patrimonial hierarchy as well. A major complaint of Koçi Bey was, in fact, the corruption prevalent among the patrimonial elite. Here the problem is better understood if we ask the question about the new landholders, the tax-farmers who came in to fill the place of the former *sipahis*. Who were they? It appears that there were three possible sources of significant wealth which could have afforded to bid for land: merchants (usurers included), local notables, and highly placed patrimonial bureaucrats. The high-level bureaucrats were benefice holders as well, but they were in perpetual discomfort owing to the sultan's frequent practice of confiscation (*müsadere*) of bureaucratic wealth, particularly in times of financial troubles. Hence, when the commercialization of agriculture made land an attractive source of income, not only merchants and local notables but also the bureaucratic elite were among those who acquired land. It was this transformation of the patrimonial bureaucrats that Koçi Bey was decrying. Traditionally, the political elite had been socially detached; in the seventeenth century, however, they began to acquire social interests that were in conflict with their patrimonial functions. Soon they ceased to be the Platonic guardians of the state; their political power became more a means of acquisition of social wealth and less an instrument of justice.

Ottoman developments in the seventeenth and eighteenth centuries were largely the function of changes which came about in the organization of Ottoman agriculture, namely, the dissolution of the *tımar* system and the concomitant shift from a system of production for internal use to a system of production for the world-market. Such changes entailed also the formation of large estates, that were classified according to their fiscal status. Tax-farms leased out by the state for one or two years were called *iltizam*; the *iltizam*, however, were soon replaced by the *malikane*, estates that were contracted for a lifetime. There were also, of course, the *vakıf* lands, nominally corporate religious estates endowed by the pious, but, by the eighteenth century, ultimately used as the property of those who held them.

The emergence of these estates generated a whole new network of relations and institutions which permeated and substantially changed the structure of Ottoman patrimonialism. In the traditional Ottoman setting, agricultural communities, vertically integrated into state institutions, had been cloisters of political and cultural conservatism with little or no tendency toward the development of class differences. The transition to cash-crop production changed this tranquil view: household labour became differentiated into such forms as share-cropping, tenancy, hired labour, etc., when instead of the *sipahi* superposed on to the domestic economy, the estate holder was interposed between the household and its means of production.[25] Also, the state was able to exercise less control over the class of estate holders than it had been over the *sipahis*; although the estate holders were formally subject to state control, they began to be increasingly autonomous elements by way of their articulation with the world-market. In sum, as surplus production as well as the organization of exchange became less state functions and more matters of production and exchange for the world-market, the whole basis of stratification in the Ottoman Empire began to be compromised: superimposed on to a stratification system based on association with the state, there began to emerge an embryonic class system based on association with the world-market.

It was this emerging network of market-based relations, and the relative autonomy which it entailed for the estate holders, which, I suggest, culminated in the rise of the *ayans* in contravention of state power at the beginning of the nineteenth century. In 1808, when the state was essentially forced to recognize the power of the *ayans* through an agreement, what we witness, in Perry Anderson's terminology, is the parcellization of sovereignty[26] – not, however, as a consequence of vertical allocators of sovereignty, which characterized Western feudalism, but as a consequence of vertical disassociation that was a function of the horizontal integration of the estate system with the world-market. Ironically, therefore, 1808 marks the point in Ottoman history when the customary preoccupation of the state with immediate financial concerns caught up with it politically: the cumulative effects of revenue concerns gave rise to a constellation of social groups which in time came to challenge the patrimonial power of the state.

Some have deduced from these changes the development of feudalism in the Ottoman Empire, while others have been quick to see in these changes the development of capitalism.[27] Neither of these views appears however, on close investigation, to be valid. Those who claim that the changes which the Ottoman Empire underwent in the seventeenth and eighteenth centuries add up to feudalism appear to base their arguments on the shift from the *tımar* system to estate economics, the rise of the *ayans*, and the emergence of repressed labour. It is true, of course, that the functions of the state, in the period under discussion, were increasingly disintegrated in a vertical movement downward toward *ayan*ship, at the level of which political and economic relations were integrated. Nonetheless, three major types of evidence stand against the argument of feudalism. First, the estate holders never reached the kind of political, social, and juridical autonomy that feudal lords enjoyed in Western Europe, nor were they ever able to appropriate the state apparatus for their own use. The state continued to hold power over the estates, minimally by its juridical monopoly over land and labour, and maximally through political and military intervention. Second, feudalism was essentially a social system for use, whereas generalized commodity (market) production became increasingly prevalent in Ottoman agriculture during the seventeenth and eighteenth centuries. To be sure, it was a disarticulated form of market production because of the peripheralization of economic activity, but the point remains that generalized commodity production is in principle incompatible with feudalism. And third, unlike a feudal economy, the peripheral mode was not one of simple reproduction; it was a system of extended reproduction which, however, began to take place in articulation with the centres of the world-system.

As for the argument that it was capitalism which developed in the Ottoman Empire after its incorporation into the world-system, it is based largely on the assumption that since the world-system was capitalist so must have been the Ottoman economy which constituted a part of it. This is an unfortunate conclusion that can be drawn from the works of André Gunder Frank and Immanuel Wallerstein, if the world-system is treated as a totality of which the various regions, or states, are parts without specificities of their own. This would then obscure the structural differentiation of regions, their specificity, and their relative autonomy. It is precisely because we need to grasp conceptually the specificity of the Ottoman economic structure (which lacked free wage labour) that we propose a third category: the peripheral formation, which in the Ottoman case was an articulated combination of capitalist market and redistributive patrimonialism, and which cannot be understood apart from the conceptual framework of the world-system. In refusing the arguments of both feudalism and capitalism, I submit that neither the actions of the state nor the behaviour of the commercialized social groups can be explained wholly by a capitalist rationality or a patrimonial logic, but by a peculiar combination of the two.

In the case of the commercialized groups, we find the distinctive traits of Ottoman peripheralism. They lacked capital and tended to monopolize the best land, while they continued to rely on traditional technology. The peasant smallholdings, which continued to be widespread, are relevant in this context: they were a source of cheap labour for the estates. The estate holder made up for the low capital intensity of investment with high intensity of labour. Why, it may be asked at this point, was there no reinvestment in land? Three major reasons, I believe, account for this lack, and for the low organic composition of capital. First, the Ottoman economy as a periphery possessed by nature a process of extended reproduction wherein surplus labour extracted from the peripheral agriculture went partially to support capital accumulation at the centre. Second, the estate holders, who generally resided in the cities and leased their tax-farming privileges to a third party, were, in their life-style, imitative of the patrimonial elite. Far from being an anxious lot driven to enlarge production in order to procure salvation through worldly success, they were generous rather than frugal, consumptive instead of productive, and dependent instead of independent.[28] In short, they were interested more in easy profits and less in developing a standpoint from which they could oppose the patrimonial ethos. Their privileges were essentially derived from the state; thus, they were economically influential but politically dependent. The third reason for the low organic composition of capital was the patrimonial style of spending by the state of revenues which it was capable of extracting from the populace. The concerns of the state continued to be patrimonial in substance: the provision of funds for the central treasury instead of reinvestment, continued habits of lavish consumption and military expenditures instead of savings, and continued reliance on war for purposes of land and labour annexation instead of an entrepreneurial drive for capital accumulation and economic development. In sum, neither the state nor the commercialized groups perceived each other as potential partners in development. On the one hand, they were dependent on each other – the state financially, the commercial groups politically – on the other, they viewed each other with growing suspicion. The outcome was the creation of a field of tension that kept the economy stagnant and open to foreign penetration.

At the end of the eighteenth century, then, we have the increasing separation of the economy from the state; and yet, the state continued to be the dominant structure. The class of landholders in the Ottoman Empire never congealed into a kind of counterpart to Western aristocracy which controlled the state apparatus on its own behalf. Land and labour were never entirely consolidated under *ayan* control, since they remained always subject to the intervention of the state. The relationship between the state and the landholders was either a matter of collusion or a mater of tension, depending on the conjuncture of events and forces. In the event of collusion, the state shared an interest with the estate holders in deriving revenue from peripheral articulation; in the event of tension, it was the relative autonomy of the state and/or the landholders that was at stake.

The tensions of interdependence

We have so far underlined the interdependence of the various groups in the peripheral Ottoman formation. This interdependent articulation, composed of various elements, would have reproduced itself indefinitely if it had not concealed tensions at some levels. There were signs, of course, that Ottoman agriculture was structurally entrenched in the cash nexus which linked the Ottoman economy to the European world-market. The introduction of new crops such as cotton and maize, the promotion of free exchange of grain by the *malikane* and *çiftlik* holders, the near disappearance of Muslim transit merchants and the expansion of resident foreign merchants and local minority agents, the depopulation of the hinterland, and the uneven commercialization of the different regions of the Empire were all signs of a peripheral economy. Various parties shared an interest in this arrangement. The primary needs of the core states, the profits of the estate holders, intermediary minorities, foreign merchants, and, indeed, the very revenue needs of the Ottoman state were at the foundation of the peripheral economy. These groups, I have suggested, composed the interest structure constitutive of peripheralization, but there were contradictory tensions nevertheless. We must now focus on them.

The peasants had been the immediate losers. For them, the commercialization of agriculture and the concomitant emergence of the estate system meant a 'transition from a social and economic structure founded upon a system of moderate land rent and few services to one of excessive land rent and exaggerated services'.[29] When the peasant household was in dire need, when it could not meet its rent dues or taxes, the estate holder extended loans to it. But, when the peasant was unable to repay the loan, the repayment would be required at harvest time in specified quantities of commodities, such as silk, olive oil, cotton, or grain. If the peasant was unable to pay this burdensome debt, then his land would be appropriated by his creditor. When the household thus lost the control of its land, it was reduced to mere labour readily available for the estates as share-cropper, tenant, or hired labour. Since the estates tended to monopolize the best land, it would be fair to assume that a large portion of the remaining households held land barely adequate for their subsistence, and, hence, were forced on occasion to work on the estates. Although there is hardly any information on these matters, others probably survived as subsistence units outside the parameters of the peripheral economy. In general, however, what we do see is the increasing differentiation of labour relations, and the embryonic development of class differences, although political and economic relations continued to be integrated at each level of the peripheral formation.

A level of tension which cut across the emerging class differences was the uneven development of the hinterland and the coastal areas. The linkage of the Ottoman economy with the European world-market had transformed the regional and urban structure of the Empire as well as its social organization. In the traditional Ottoman setting, cities had been located inland, largely owing to the flow of pilgrim and transit traffic through Ottoman lands. But, as this traffic declined and the nature of external trade underwent transformation, the structure, locale, and size of Ottoman towns began to change also. When the Ottoman economy opened outward towards the West, the whole alignment of towns shifted toward the coasts, particularly in the Balkans close to Western access. The western regions of the Empire in general and the coastal cities in particular prospered while interior towns declined and decayed.[30] Anatolia, particularly eastern Anatolia, remained up to the nineteenth century the least touched by the commercial spirit radiating from Europe: hence, eastern regions of the Empire were among the victims of peripheralism as well.

Yet another unhappy group in the peripheral economy was, ironically, the Orthodox merchants of the Balkans. They were displeased not because they had grown poorer but because they could not retain all that they gained: they were still the *reaya* of the Empire, subject to her discriminatory taxes. These merchants had emerged as the middlemen between the Muslim landholders and the European merchants. Thus, while they had their shared interests in peripheral integration, they were restricted in their economic and social mobility by the Muslim monopoly on land and the burdensome Ottoman taxes. As one Bulgarian described it,

Compared with the life of the Turks, our life was patently on a higher level. Take livelihoods. For the Bulgarians, these were so varied – there were indeed hardly any manufacture or fields of commerce in which they did not deal. As for the Turks, their agriculture was all they knew. And our leading people, our merchants and chorbajii [village notables] – how much higher they stood in alertness of spirit, in national consciousness as well as in monetary wealth than the Turkish leading folk. Yet for all this, we Bulgarians felt a subconscious fear of the Turks . . . The fear of all our folk for the Turks arose from the fact that although we lived in the villages unoppressed by them, we felt nevertheless that they were the masters . . . Turkish was the whole power. Turkish was the kingdom. And we Bulgarians were their subjects.[31]

It is not surprising that, as some of the leading people, the merchants became the leaders of the nationalist-separatist movements of the Balkans, and drew their support from the peasantry.[32] Whereas the landholders were mostly of Muslim origin, the peasants, like the merchants, were Orthodox Christians.

Then, of course, there was the contradictory development of interests between the Ottoman state and the elite class of Muslim landholders. We are referring primarily to the *ayans*, who derived their power largely from the commercialization of agriculture and the evolution of land tenure. As we noted above, by the end of the eighteenth century, the *ayans* had grown into powerful *derebeys* in control of considerable land and labour, equipped with armies of their own, capable of challenging the authority of the state, and intent on establishing sovereignties all their own.[33] The initial response of the state to this growing force was to attempt to bring it under control through centralizing measures. These efforts, however, were promptly stopped when the state was forced to sign a covenant with the *ayans* in 1808. This agreement legitimized in effect the status of the *ayans* and extended to them the kind of immunities which had been hitherto enjoyed by the foreign and minority merchants. It also forecast the later conflicts that were bound to occur between the *ayans* and the state.

And finally, there was the tension between the Ottoman state and other states of the world-economy. The incorporation of Ottoman economics into the world-system was of interest to both the European states and the Ottoman state – since the former secured primary goods while the latter financed its depleted treasury. But the interests of the European powers and the Ottoman state were neither identical nor permanent. After all, the incorporated status of the Ottoman economy had weakend the Ottoman state, and subordinated the once-mighty Empire to a peripheral status in the world-system. It is, therefore, significant to know what exactly the role of the states was in the world-economy. This is a particularly pertinent question since the states of the world-system were not simply passive objects subject to the free operation of the world-system; on the contrary, they actively intervened in market operations, and their structural positions changed over time, relatively independently of the class structure of their respective societies. When we enter the nineteenth century, the position of the Ottoman state, and the changes which it underwent, cannot be understood merely in terms of its relations to the internal forces discussed above, but also in terms of its pattern of interaction with the other states of the world-system.

When we observe the Near Eastern theatre at the beginning of the nineteenth century, the main actors are the Ottoman state, Great Britain, Russia, France, and Austria. The politics of the European powers toward the Ottoman Empire differed considerably from each other; each had competitive policies with regard to what had then become the 'Eastern Question'.[34] The Eastern Question was, in fact, born out of these conflicting interests of the European states when the world-economy entered the period of industrial capitalism. The peculiar characteristic of this period at the beginning of the nineteenth century was the rapid industrialization of England and her increasing commercial-industrial supremacy, which stimulated political, military, and economic competition throughout the European world-system.

In the Near East, among the main contenders for power was Russia. Her objective was to maintain control of the straits which controlled her access to the Mediterranean. She could achieve her diplomatic objectives either by the defeat and partition of the Empire, or by a virtual protectorate over a weak and subservient Ottoman state. Thus, in the nineteenth century, while Russian strategy shifted from one policy to the other depending on the conjuncture of forces, it was a constant source of pressure and threat to the Ottoman state. On the Western European front of the Empire, while Britain was contending for supremacy in the world-market, France was following behind England, but still intent on breaking the imminent British hegemony. Napoleon's expedition to Egypt in 1798 had failed, just as the strategy of continental blockade was to fail later; and yet, France would make one last attempt by backing Mehmet Ali in Egypt against the sultan in the 1830s. The threat of Mehmet Ali, however, initially forced the sultan to conclude a treaty of friendship with Russia in 1833, which put Britain on the alert, and eventually formed the basis of an Anglo-Ottoman alliance. Only two decades later, of course, Britain and France would join together to draw the Ottoman Empire into the Crimean War against Russia.

In sum, then, the pressure of the foreign states in combination with the emergent Balkan nationalist movements and the growing power of the *ayans* put enormous strain on the Ottoman state and threatened her with military, administrative, and financial collapse. The Ottoman state, however, survived throughout the nineteenth century. How was this possible? To put it succinctly, the Ottoman state survived because a series of institutional innovations were undertaken and designed to serve as props for its revival. And yet, inscribed into these very innovations was the price of survival: the underdevelopment of the Ottoman economy. This was the grand paradox of the Ottoman Empire reflected in its overall structure in the nineteenth century. In essence, the Ottoman order became a hybrid composition whose surface modernization again and again betrayed an underlying process of underdevelopment. It is crucial, therefore, to focus on these innovations in order to understand the paradoxical developments of the nineteenth century. This we must do by situating the forces behind the developments themselves.

The paradox of peripheralism

Among the great advocates and supporters of reforms in the Ottoman Empire was Great Britain. In the face of Russian encroachments and the treaty of 1833, which gave Russia virtual protectoral control over the Empire, the obvious policy for Britain was to shore up the Ottomans against Russia at all costs. 'The preservation of the territorial integrity of the Ottoman Empire': this was the policy of the British in the Near East until the end of the 1870s, despite its inconsistencies and shifting sympathies and support of Balkan nationalisms. This is also the policy that has divided students of nineteenth-century Ottoman Empire: taking seriously the claim of the English that they were the true architects of the Reform Period (Tanzimat, 1839–76), some have hailed the English as the true precursors of Turkish modernization, while others have condemned the English as imperialists solely responsible for Ottoman underdevelopment and collapse. Thus both positions rely on the same assumption of British supremacy but focus on the two different aspects of its outcome: modernization, on the one hand, and underdevelopment, on the other. In our view, the period of reforms and the attendant process of underdevelopment cannot be understood by external pressures alone; although primacy must be granted to the international state system, and although the parameters of nineteenth-century Ottoman developments were drawn by external constraints, the fact still remains that the competitive matrix of the international (world-) system allowed the Ottoman state a *relative* autonomy which, in turn, allowed her to seek alliances that were to her own benefit. If British support for the Ottoman state was vital so was Ottoman survival for British interests. Hence, it seems to me to be erroneous to view these reforms as stemming from a single source; instead, the innovations appear to me to be the condensed outcome of a conjuncture overdetermined by the particular position of the Ottoman state *vis-à-vis* the external international system *and* the internal structure of social classes.

The prevention of military and administrative collapse required measures for centralization and rationalization of authority in general, and a modernized army, a reformed bureaucracy, and a uniform tax system in particular.[35] The transformation of the tax system was particularly crucial since it provided the financial basis for military and administrative reforms. But an attempt to increase the tax flows upward towards the state was subject to the resistance of the *ayans* which, as we have noted, had grown especially strong at the beginning of the nineteenth century. And yet, these *derebeys* and *ayans* were never able to penetrate the state apparatus so as to use it to their own benefit. The state bureaucracy remained relatively independent and differentiated from the landed powers. It was this differentiation from the *ayans* in combination with the competitive milieu of the international state system which, at the beginning of the nineteenth century, provided Mahmud II with the relative autonomy required to launch a series of reforms designed to break the power of the *ayans* and to consolidate central power through the creation of a modernized standing army and a rationalized bureaucracy. His large-scale attacks on the *ayans* deprived them of some of their 'national' power; he succeeded in fractionalizing them into smaller powers deprived of their military might, although he could not eliminate them altogether. The *ayans* and their descendants continued as a class of landholders always related to the world-economy through trade.

The successful attempts of Mahmud II were significant, but so were his failures, for together they reveal the possibilities for reform as well as its difficulties. Mahmud II was successful in eliminating the military power of the *ayans* and in initiating military and administrative reforms. But he failed to provide an adequate tax basis for a sustained process of innovations on the one hand, and to pay simultaneously for wars and court and cultural life on the other. The fundamental thrust of his policy was to eliminate the landholding class in order to tap the peasant household directly. But the sheer magnitude of bureaucratic officialdom required to channel taxes directly to the state would alone have made this job enormously difficult, not to mention the resistance of the local powers and notables to the upward mobilization of increased resources. Hence, when Mahmud II failed in his policy directed towards the restoration of the domestic mode of production, state functions had to rely on landholders and notables organized in their private capacities, or else on semi-bureaucratic organizations that were largely run by the very same local groups.

The period of Tanzimat was an attempt to overcome these difficulties,[36] namely, the resistance of the landholding groups and the nationalist movements of the Balkans, on the one hand, and the obstacles to reform posed within the bureaucracy by provincial governors (*paşas*) and other high-ranking officials who were poorly paid, and, therefore, allowed or forced to engage in corruption by withholding revenue from the state, on the other. The foreign pressures continued as well; Britain, however, now appeared as the patron saint of the Ottoman sultan. The political strategy of the Tanzimat was simple: to promote a secular universalist politics designed to strengthen central authority. Such universalism, it was thought, would benefit all and harm none: it would serve the preservation of the Ottoman state by appeasing nationalist movements, it would integrate the local powers into the state apparatus through measures of democratization (e.g. establishment of provincial consultative assemblies (*meclis*)), and it would promote uniformity and rationalization through the codification of laws, the establishment of formal equality for all citizens, and the recognition of private property.[37] The crucial question of revenue crisis would be solved by a combined effort of eliminating the landholders when possible, collaborating with them if necessary, and ultimately by short-circuiting them through alliance with merchant capital. Throughout the Tanzimat, in shifting proportions, this mixture of policy was applied, however, with adverse effects in each case.

The efforts towards the elimination of the landholding class and the corrupt *paşas* were of no consequence: they were too well established in the peripheral economy and the fiscal practices of the Ottoman state. Each attempt towards the consolidation of peasant holdings had contradictory results: for one thing, the state demands on the peasantry for increased taxation with no service returns made the landholder appear more sympathetic to the peasantry, since these landholders performed at least minimal social services in return for their exploitation. Another effort in the same direction was the land code of 1858, planned to reinforce peasant holdings by granting them direct title to the land.[38] The outcome, again, was not the elimination of the intermediary groups between the household and the state but the consolidation of land under the ownership of *ayan* and *eşraf*. And yet another attempt had adverse effects as well: the establishment of provincial consultative assemblies was designed to incorporate the local powers into the administrative structure, and to use them as non-bureaucratic tax-collection agents.[39] But, in practice, these assemblies proved to be power bases for the local groups, used to consolidate their resistance against central authority.

In comparison to its changing policy towards the landholding class, the more constant state policy during the Tanzimat was its somewhat reluctant but inevitable reliance on the merchant class. This reliance/alliance was designed to bypass the landholding class in order to provide increasing revenue for the state, and, in the meantime, to win the support of the orthodox merchants and the British. The adverse consequences of this alliance, however, were more far reaching than those directly practised upon the landholding classes: it eliminated the Muslim merchant class, destroyed Ottoman crafts industry, fuelled nationalist aspirations, and, most fundamentally, reproduced peripheral relations at a more intensified level of integration, subjecting the economy to increasing disarticulation, surplus outflows, and contracting state revenues.[40]

From the viewpoint of the state, alliance with the merchants, more accurately, with *minority* merchants, had the following advantages: (1) a stimulated trade with Western Europe in general and the British in particular would subject the peasantry to increasing commercialization and thereby generate money-rent for the state; (2) it would afford the state increasing revenue through taxation of increasing volume of trade; (3) encouragement of minorities and foreigners to deal in trade would protect the state against the threat of a growing rentier class of landholders since minorities and foreigners had no access to land; (4) the accumulated minority merchant capital, since it could not be directly invested in land, would provide the state with the needed loans and credits, thus serving a much needed banking function for the state; (5) the policy of increasing commercialization would satisfy both British and minority interests, winning their support for the state.

It is in the light of these calculations based on the relationship of the state to the internal and external forces that we should interpret the free-trade policy of the Tanzimat. To be sure, British and minority capital had much to gain from free-trade policy, but so had the Ottoman state. The Anglo-Ottoman treaty of free commerce signed in 1838 was, from the viewpoint of the state, to serve a twofold purpose: first, it would result in increasing taxation for the state by imposition of duties on imports (5 per cent), exports (12 per cent), and transit trade (3 per cent).[41] It is true that British, and later European, merchants would have free access to purchases and sales anywhere in the Empire by the removal of monopolies but the removal of monopolies was not much of a loss: they had been reduced to a few items anyway, and the state had more to gain from the new duties than it did by farming out these monopolies. The second gain the Ottomans expected from the 1838 treaty was more immediate and political in essence: the breakdown of trade monopolies in Egypt, much more consolidated and widespread there than in the Empire, would help undermine Mehmet Ali both fiscally and politically – the latter, of course, being partly dependent on British political and military support for the Ottoman sultan.

Once again, it is true that Mehmet Ali's power was sapped and eventually destroyed, but the same consequences were visited upon the Ottoman Empire: conjunctural calculations of advantage had adverse structural results, which we must now examine.

The growing dominance of merchant capital brought about a rapidly increasing change in the pattern of production and consumption. In the nineteenth century, the merchants imposed upon the pattern of production and consumption the imperatives of world industrialism: they were interested in selling (exporting) primary agricultural goods at the same time that they were interested in buying (importing) manufactured commodities. This process disassociated, of course, the structure of production and consumption, as a result of which the agricultural population produced goods it could not use and used goods it could not produce. In short, as production became dependent on the demands of the industrial world, market consumption became subordinate to imported commodities.

In the meantime, as industrial imports entered the Empire freely and altered the consumption patterns of the population, they created an increasing market for imports which could undersell home production and undermine what remained of industrial organization.[42] The decline of industry, on the other hand, doubled back on agriculture: in the absence of urban, industrial demand for labour, peasants were trapped in agriculture, and served as a cheap source of labour for the landholders, who could intensify labour services without any need for the improvement of agricultural productivity: labour was cheap, technological innovations expensive. In fact, the landholder was himself trapped in agriculture. His unwillingness to invest in industry might have been partly due to his patrimonial outlook, but it was in perfect accord with the structural constraints within which he found himself: industry, subject to decline in the face of European competition, was of necessity out of reach. Hence, in the absence of industrial opportunities, and with the availability of cheap labour and the risks attendant on capitalization of land, the landholding class preferred to enlarge their holdings, to serve as moneylenders, and to put on a lavish display of new habits of consumption. The frst two activities were profitable without requiring any extra effort to improve conditions; the latter conferred status.

Although the constraints on the landowning class were real in so far as the lack of industrial opportunities were concerned, their inclinations towards making easy profits, without transforming the social organization of agricultural production, was not atypical. In fact, not only landowners but merchants and the state were all competitors for peasant surplus; and, none, it must be added, was interested in transforming the social relations of production in agriculture. The differences among them could be reduced to the following: the state was interested in preserving and extending the freeholding peasantry for taxation purposes,[43] while the landowner was interested in keeping them subordinate to himself. To the merchant it did not matter much whom he dealt with as long as he could rely on somebody to supply him with goods and provide him a market for his sales. Now, it so happened that he could not rely on the peasant household: the increasing revenue demands of the state forced the peasantry to work as share-croppers for the landowners, who could supply the peasant with the money credits to pay his taxes and provide him with social services as well. This is why the peasant grievances in the nineteenth century were more often directed against the state rather than the landlords – the peasantry preferred the patronage of the landlord to that of the state. The result was that labour and land came increasingly under landlord control in contravention of state power and resources.

I have said that the merchant class shared with the landlords and the state a conserving attitude toward the social *relations* of production, although the merchants exercised a transformative function on the *patterns* of production and consumption. This conservative attitude is at bottom a reflection of the merchants' inability to transform the social organization of production without reliance on some other force. Since merchants exist as circulatory capital between separated realms of production, they cannot transform premises they do not control. However, merchants are no less interested than anybody else in becoming rentier landlords.[44] It was this outlet that was closed to the merchant class in the Ottoman Empire since landownership was a monopoly of the Muslims. As a result, merchant capital, penned up in circulation, served several functions: it was a surrogate banking institution for the state, which became heavily dependent on the *sarraf* for loans in the nineteenth century. Merchant capital was also the money behind tax-farmers, corrupt *pashas*, and *mukataa* (monopoly) holders. Nevertheless, the growing group of merchants, particularly in the Balkans, was increasingly frustrated by the discrepancy between its wealth and its lack of political power and social prestige. It comes as no surprise, therefore, to find the merchants agitating the Christian *reaya* against the Muslim landowners in the Balkans, and leading the nationalist movements against the state. In short, free-trade policy, by increasing merchant capital and shutting off landed wealth, served to fuel nationalist aspirations no less than the ethnic discrimination to which merchants were subject and the protection which they received from the foreign powers.

Finally, we must briefly mention the adverse consequences of increasing export production on the structure of the Ottoman economy, on the one hand, and the adverse consequences of growing import demands on the magnitude of state revenues, on the other. Increasing commodity production for export simply deepened the disarticulated structure of Ottoman economics – segments more and more disassociated from each other were increasingly bound up with the external market: urban centres shifted towards the coastal areas, particularly in Syria, Palestine, and Anatolia, the construction of transportation (railways) and communication lines involved ever more regions directly in export production, and as more and more labour and land were involved in export production less of them remained outside the parameters of the world market. Increasing import demands, on the other hand, resulted in a severe imbalance of exports and imports, and in an equally severe balance-of-payments problem.[45] The state bureaucracy attempted to cope with these problems (reinforced by a flimsy treasure drained of resources by nationalist separations, wars, etc.) by borrowing from the European states. The outcome, however, was disastrous: caught in an increasing spiral of debts,[46] the Ottoman state was eventually overwhelmed by financial troubles, and, finally, subordinated to the control of the creditor nations, which further undermined the tax bases of the Ottoman state by appropriating an important portion of the surplus directly from the population.[47]

This was, in brief, the peripheral structure of Ottoman society at the end of the nineteenth century. It was a structure disarticulated, subject to outflow of value, and essentially pre-capitalist in its social relations of productive activity. I have tried to show above that this structure was reproduced and intensified as an apparently paradoxical consequence of Tanzimat reforms. I have also tried to contend that the surface modernization of the Ottoman state underwritten by a process of underdevelopment is best understood as the outcome of the balance (articulation) of internal and external forces. In this respect, the international state system was the determinant factor while the Ottoman state played the dominant role. That is to say, the international environment constituted the matrix within which the Ottoman state could act. The calculations of the state had to be made within the parameters of this matrix.

Conclusion: the Turkish revolution

At the end of the nineteenth century the Ottoman state collapsed financially; at the beginning of the twentieth century it was incapacitated militarily and administratively as well. Under extreme pressure from external states, the Ottoman Empire was dismembered, led into World War I, reduced ethnically to the Turkish population and geographically to Asia Minor, and, finally, was threatened with total colonization. And yet, from the remains of the Empire emerged the Turkish Republic. This transition from Empire to Republic deserves a brief concluding note, for it is important, I believe, for the light it sheds on the specific meaning of the Turkish revolution by illuminating the continuities and breaks with the past.

The causes of the Turkish revolution are familiar since they inhere in the collapse of the Ottoman Empire which we have examined above. Most succinctly stated, the Ottoman Empire collapsed because the state failed to mobilize sufficient resources and men to promote political unity and economic development in the face of internal resistance and external pressure. The dynamics of the Turkish revolution, on the other hand, were shaped by the specific structure of the Ottoman Empire as a peripheral agrarian bureaucratic state: only the state bureaucracy and the military were significantly differentiated from vested economic interests and sufficiently organized to lead a resistance movement against foreign invasions, and to launch an 'elite revolution' in the name of national unity and welfare. To put it differently, no group other than the bureaucracy possessed in the Empire sufficient structural space for the political autonomy required to organize collective action against external threat, or for internal change. The Turkish revolution, therefore, was a 'revolution from above' conceived and executed by the cooperation of the civil and military bureaucrats.[48] In short, when the incapacitation of central administrative and military organization was coupled with the nationalist response of a statist marginal elite group of bureaucrats, the result was a rebirth: in 1923 the Turkish Republic was founded.

The outcome of the Turkish revolution is not as clearly specifiable as its causes, dynamics, and the military success of its resistance phase. In fact, it has been somewhat puzzling, and has posed the question of whether it was a revolution at all. Although military success was assured and political independence was established, the Turkish revolution involved no peasant insurrection, bourgeois conspiracy, violent upheavals, or significant shifts in the balance of political and social forces.[49] The state continued to be an apparatus dominated by the bureaucracy; the struggles for the appropriation of state institutions had not been conflicts inter-class in nature but at most intra-bureaucratic, between a younger, marginal group of state-employed (or oriented) elites and an older generation of more established bureaucrats. Moreover, in their response to the problematics of social control, the younger generation of bureaucrats was not much different from its reformist predecessors of the nineteenth century: they too sought to extend and rationalize state power on the one hand, and relied on the social elites on the other.

It is futile, in short, to seek a revolutionary transformation in the establishment of the Republic when our perspective is determined by the image of 'social revolutions' – revolutions that are conceived to be born and bred in the bosom of society by a dynamic class that is bent on liberating itself (and the rest of society) from an inhibiting state apparatus dominated by a moribund ruling class. Judged in these terms, the Turkish revolution was, indeed, no revolution at all – it involved neither cataclysmic class struggles nor a class transfer of state power. But this is another way of saying that the Turkish revolution was not a social revolution – and, true enough, it was not in the realignment of class forces but in the practice, by a revolutionary elite, or a new conception of the *origins* and *ends* of state power that a radical break was made in Turkey with the Ottoman past. In essence, and at its most profound level, the Turkish revolution was an ideological revolution informed by a new paradigm of legitimacy established by reference to the sources and aims of state power.[50]

'All theories of legitimacy take the form of establishing a principle which, while it resides outside of power and is independent of it, locates or embeds power in a realm of things beyond the wills of the holders of power: the legitimacy of power stems from its *origin*.'[51] In the Ottoman Empire, the legitimacy of state power rested on a pre-established divine order. Social order was, in turn, conceived to issue from this larger order of being, and assumed to be constituted by the intermediary function of the state. The state institutions, suffused with a religious quality, permeated society so as to establish and maintain a social structure viewed to be a faithful reflection or representation of the true order of things. The true order of things was essentially revealed in religion, and further discoveries of this pattern were possible through theological methods grounded in religious epistemology. Thus, the authority of the state was justified on the grounds that it rested on the true knowledge of things, untinged by man's cognitive apparatus and independent of his desires and opinions.

With the founding of the Republic, this religious cosmology was exchanged for a nationalist ontology and a positivist epistemology.[52] Social order was no longer thought to issue from a religious order but from a configuration of national values discovered by expert knowledge. Thus, state power derived its legitimacy from a national order that existed beyond the will of the holders of power but was subject for its discovery to the expertise of the state. The state was, at one and the same time, the discoverer of nationalist morality, its guardian, and its disseminator as well.

There were those, of course, who insisted that political authority must originate in 'democratic consent',[53] but most among the revolutionary elite knew better: to consent to the principle of democratic consent would have meant to succumb to the dominant value system prevalent among the people, and the dominant value system among the people was not nationalist but religious. Hence, the state had to rely on state-party institutions and the local elites: the former served as ideological apparatuses designed to disseminate a nationalist culture among the people, while the latter were to serve as partners in social control. (The local elites, of course, were double-faced: the face turned to the peasantry was religious and the face turned to the state was secular and nationalist – so long as they did well under bureaucratic administration.) Moreover, where the principle of democratic consent would have imposed restrictions upon the revolutionary elite, intent on ideological transformation, the transcendent principle of national order (interest) released them of such restrictions. In the end, therefore, while the regulative principle of order was transferred from religion to nationalism the regulative apparatus remained the state, the same as in the past.

Arguments about democratic consent were off the point at another level: in so far as the people were concerned the test of legitimacy for them was not power's origin but its end. And, from this point of view, the declared aim of the state was the 'progress and happiness' of all the people, which fundamentally meant economic development and welfare for all. Whereas the fundamental aim of the Ottoman state had been fiscalism and the maintenance of the order of stratification, the primary purpose of the Republican state was to increase production and consumption, a kind of material plenty now defined as constitutive of a modern mood called happiness.

A new purpose demands a new paradigm, and so, the state bureaucracy adopted for economic development a model of 'national economics', best described and defined by the founding father of the Republic, Mustafa Kemal Atatürk, himself:

> The end of Etatist policy, while it recognizes private initiative and action as the main basis of the economy, is to bring the Nation in the shortest possible time to an adequate level of prosperity and material welfare, and in order to achieve this, to ask the State to concern itself with those affairs where this is required by the high interests of the Nation, especially in the economic field.[54]

In the conceptions and practice of the revolutionary elite the model of national economics emerged as a mixture of etatism and market economics. It was neither a fully grown etatism nor an independent market economy but a hybrid system that has been best described as 'state capitalism'.

Here again, as in nationalism, the state was the instrument of a new order, an apparatus designed to make new pathways in social and economic relations. As nationalism could not be relied upon to hold society together and/or to spur development, so neither could market economics be expected to resolve the revolutionary problems of unity and progress: social relations were embedded neither in nationalism nor in the dynamics of a capitalist market. Nationalism was not a widespread sentiment but an elite vision, and market rationality was not sufficiently widespread to constitute a mode of organization equal to a general order, nor a source for sustained stimulus to surplus production.

The revolutionary ideology, then, relied on the state for the realization of a modern society in Turkey. The modern society itself, however, was ultimately conceived in apolitical terms: the two fundamental underpinnings of modern society, integration and development, were regarded as extra-state functions. National values, once discovered, were relied upon to generate unity while the self-steering mechanism of the market would provide development – in either case, there was little or no need for political guidance once the initial, instrumental role of the state had been completed. In the new republican paradigm, therefore, the state was reduced to the status of a superstructure, in contrast to the Ottoman order in which the state was the precondition of both wealth and coherence.

Of these two supporting bases of modernity, nationalism has proved to be the basis of identity defined in reference to the Ottoman past. The market rationality and the principle of possessive individualism, on the other hand, have proved to be the dominant determinants of economic action. The core institution of the system, in other words, has shifted from the nationalist state to the economy as market, and the horizontal (class) system of stratification based on association with the market has sharply cut into and dominated the vertical (status) system of stratification based on association with the state. Such shifts, I have tried to suggest, were inherent in the conception of social order and progress formulated at the beginning of the Republic. In actual fact, it was in the 1950s that the culmination of the original formulation occurred when the gradual transfer of state power, from bureaucratic to entrepreneurial control, made possible, for the first time in Turkish history, the relatively free development of market economics and market society.[55]

4 The incorporation of the Ottoman Empire into the world-economy

IMMANUEL WALLERSTEIN, HALE DECDELİ AND REŞAT KASABA

The history of the world prior to *c.* 1500 (and since the Neolithic Revolution) is one of the co-existence on the planet of multiple social systems, which took three major forms: world-empires, world-economies, and what may be called mini-systems.[1] The important thing to note is that, in this long stretch of history, world-empires were the 'strong' form. They expanded, and incorporated within them what had been world-economies and mini-systems. They reached the limits of their possibilities of expansion. They contracted and, in the areas which they no longer controlled, there was space in which new world-economies and mini-systems could grow up. World-empires were relatively long-lasting whereas individual world-economies or mini-systems tended to be relatively unstable and short-lived (let us say up to 100–150 years).

What changed *c.* 1500 is that there grew up in Europe a new world-economy which, for the first time in history, was able to consolidate itself, and develop fully the capitalist mode of production and the inter-state system which is the structural correlate of a world-economy.

This meant that, suddenly, this world-economy had become the 'strong' form. From then on, it would be the capitalist world-economy that would expand by virtue of its internal dynamic. As it expanded, regularly but discontinuously, it incorporated the world-empires and mini-systems it found at its edges, until by the twentieth century it had incorporated the whole globe, and created an historically new situation, the existence of a singular world-system (as opposed to the previous situation of multiple coexisting world-systems).

About 1500, the Ottoman Empire was a world-empire, still in its expanding phase. It bordered, as we know, the new European world-economy, and indeed had many modes of contact – diplomatic, military, trade. It is the thesis of this paper that, at some point in time, the capitalist world-economy expanded and 'incorporated' the Ottoman world-empire. We say 'at some point in time', since the point of time is a matter of scholarly debate which is not yet resolved.[2] It should also be noted that various parts of the Ottoman Empire – Rumelia,

Anatolia, Syria, etc. – may be said to have been 'incorporated' into the capitalist world-economy at different points in time.

What we mean by incorporation is that the production processes of the region became part of the integrated division of labour of the capitalist world-economy, responding to the imperatives of the drive for accumulation of capital. This often required changes in the property structure and the social relations of production. It normally involved new pressures on the labour force to ensure that labour power was available for those enterprises which were the most profitable in terms of the world-economy. Hence 'peripheralization' involved in most cases an increase in the social coercion of labour.

Furthermore, peripheralization necessarily required, whenever a world-empire was incorporated, a relative diminution of the ability of the state structure to interfere with the flows of the factors of production within the boundaries of the world-economy. It required restructuring the state machinery as a state that operated within an inter-state system (as opposed to a self-centred and self-responsive world-empire).

What we shall do in this paper is discuss, with particular reference to the Ottoman Empire, this process of incorporation – outlining the mechanisms of 'peripheralization', and describing the resulting peripheral structure of the incorporated Ottoman state (no longer a world-empire). We shall then point out how this perspective on late Ottoman history differs from that of others and what may be illuminated by using this perspective.

We start by a brief and familiar description of the structure of the Ottoman Empire in the period *c.* 1300–1600, when it was clearly and unambiguously an economically autonomous world-empire. The main production activities, as in all world-empires, were agriculture and urban crafts. A large portion of the surplus of both activities was subject to tribute mechanisms which directed the flow towards the political centre, from whence it was re-allocated. This re-allocation was effectuated through the formal bureaucracy, whose political control of the economy was reinforced by the religious ideology. In this way, the boundaries of the 'political' and the 'economic' were both enmeshed and virtually identical.[3]

Agricultural relations of production were based on the *tımar* system. The vast majority of the land belonged to the sultan (*miri*). It was held by the peasants in secure tenure. The peasants were required to pay a tithe (*öşr*) to the *tımar*-holder, or *sipahi*, who used the revenue to sustain the local equivalent of troops. The *sipahi*'s ability to alter the use of the land, or to evict peasants, or to increase production, was strictly controlled by the higher-level representatives of the central authority (*sancak beyi*, *kadı*). Thus accumulation could be maintained at a level sufficient to sustain the *askeri* (or non-producer) class throughout the Empire, without permitting excess accumulation in local areas which could sustain the power of potential centrifugal forces.

Industrial crafts were governed by a guilds system, where production was in strict conformity with the norms of the state. The prices for food and raw materials were controlled, as was the right of the merchants to participate in specific markets. The major objective of the internal controls was to create an integrated economy with sufficient foodstuffs and other necessities for Istanbul and other cities, without however permitting unlimited accumulation by merchants or artisans. In addition, long-distance or international trade existed, but it was essentially in luxury items.

The system was not without its contradictions. The chronic shortage of silver led to the spread of moneylending, which created an underlying pressure on prices. But it would not be until the influx of Spanish silver in the sixteenth century and the population expansion that this factor began to undermine the self-contained system. The population expansion led to larger demands on the state institutions for grain.[4] At the same time, the European price inflation encouraged contraband trade, thus raising internal prices. This meant that state revenues became insufficient, and the traditional redistributive functions of the Ottoman state were threatened.

To counteract this revenue squeeze, the Porte pursued two fundamental policies: extension of tax-farming (*iltizam*) to the collection of the traditional tax on agriculture (*öşr*); and expansion of capitulatory rights to foreign merchants. Both policies led to a strengthening of centrifugal forces in the Empire.

Tax-farming of the *öşr*, replacing the *tımar* system, led to a slow transformation of the relations of production in the countryside, especially in Rumelia. Unlike in the *tımar* system, the tax-farmer had considerable autonomy in organizing the production system, which meant that he could take appropriate measures in response to the market and thus orient himself to the demands of a system based on accumulation. The other side of this autonomy was that he came to be free of the administrative and ideological duties of the *sipahi*. This removed constraints on the 'enserfment' of the agricultural producers, and on the increase of tax rates over the traditional norms. It also removed restraints on the practice of usury, which eventually led to an alienation of the land of a large portion of the peasantry.

Tax-farmers were drawn from various groups. The *mütesellim*, and representatives of the *sancak beyi* on the *has* (revenue grants of imperial family) or *zeamet* (revenue grants of high officials) lands under his direct control, took advantage of the long absences of the *sancak beyleri* during the sixteenth-century wars to usurp the tax income. Secondly, urban merchants, who had accumulated enough wealth in the inflationary period (or borrowed it from the bankers), were able to purchase a *mukataa* (right to farm taxes). Thirdly, local notables, *ayans* or their equivalents, also began to purchase *mukataa*, from the seventeenth century on. In addition, janissaries and members of higher levels of the bureaucracy often became tax-farmers themselves.[5]

As a result of a combination of forceful appropriation, usury, and abandonment of land by peasants, the size of the land units controlled by the tax-farmers grew, most notably in Rumelia. These large agricultural estates were called *çiftliks*. In western Anatolia, petty commodity production expanded. (Later, in Egypt, there would grow up similar large cotton estates.) Everywhere the economic and political power of the *ayans* grew, which was the counterpart of the central state's growing inability to control production and trade. This is often referred to as 'feudalization', and seen as part of the normal processes of the contraction of a world-empire. However, in this case, as the Ottoman Empire reached its zenith and began to contract, it was confronted by a dynamic, expanding capitalist world-economy. What started out as 'feudalization' would become in fact 'incorporation' into the world-economy and 'peripheralization'.

The *çiftliks*, first known in the sixteenth century,[6] entailed enserfment of labour and share-cropping relations, perpetuated essentially by the mechanism of usury. The landlords extended loans to the peasants at high interest rates. Unable to pay the excessive obligations, the producers were continuously overburdened with debts. The repayments assumed the form of produce to be delivered at harvest time at rates much below the market prices. In this manner, peasants eventually lost some of their land, and came to be employed as share-cropping tenants by the landlord. Although small peasant property was not completely destroyed, usury mediated the accumulation of capital in the hands of the new powerful landlords.[7]

The bigger landlords organized armed irregulars – *hadjuks*, *kırcalıs*, etc. – and launched raids in the countryside. The peasants, having already lost security of tenure through the introduction of tax-farming, subject to frequent intrusions by the armed forces of the *ayans*, suffering intensified labour services and augmentation of tax payments both in kind and in money, found their independence profoundly undermined. Field services which were virtually nominal in the sixteenth century – annually three days – became as much as two months in a year, not to mention the additional transportation and other labour services. Taxes paid to the landlord were as much as the sum of the tithe and poll tax paid to the state. The landlord normally appropriated half of the produce after the payment of state taxes.

Another salient feature of production in *çiftliks* was the novelty of the crop pattern. Cotton and maize appeared as the new commodities whose production progressively expanded. All export cotton was derived from *çiftlik* production. The *ayans* appropriated nearly half of total production and more than half of the high-quality cotton production destined for export.[8]

To a large extent, then, the transformation of social relations of production in agriculture was instigated by the demand of European markets. Tax-farming in the Ottoman Empire conditioned the specific mode of surplus appropriation of the *ayan* from the enserfed peasant in the *çiftlik*. This, in its turn, defined the boundaries of accumulation by the foreign merchants and their intermediaries, in their mission to expand commodity production. The *çiftlik* landlords were still nonetheless reluctant to transform totally production techniques, since increased labour productivity in a monetized economy might tend to allow the peasant to end this perpetual indebtedness, and thereby end the share-cropping relationship.

By the mid eighteenth century, increased European demand for Balkan production of cotton, grains, maize, cattle, and tobacco led the European states to press upon the weakened Ottoman state their demands for further commercial concessions. The capitulations were no longer the free largesse of the Ottoman state. They now became bilateral treaties which could not be unilaterally denounced by the Porte. The Treaty of Küçük Kaynarca in 1774 was critical in that it ended the Ottoman monopoly in the Black Sea trade and opened the Straits to the Russians (though this was not effective until the occupation of the Crimea in 1783).

The increasingly strong position of the foreign ambassadors and consuls allowed them to procure from the Porte privileges such as tax exemptions for non-Muslim Ottoman subjects. The latter became the agents of European traders, which further weakened the position of Muslim merchants in both overland and maritime trade. The role of these non-Muslim merchants was what permitted the particularly rapid incorporation of the Balkan zone.

In the middle of the eighteenth century, for the first time, imports to the Empire begin to exceed exports. This disrupted consumption patterns in the Empire, and tended to destroy the handicrafts system. In addition, it had a long-term effect on the Ottoman balance of payments, which placed the state in a world-debtor position.

The merchants played a key role in the ever closer integration of production processes into the world-economy. By a system of endebtment of landlords, the landlords were often forced to give rights to merchants to the surplus at below-market prices. The landlords, as we have seen, in turn increasingly held the direct producers in debt-bondage.

The combination of tax-farming and its resultant weakening of state controls on production, and the increasing concessions to foreign merchants and its resultant weakening of state controls on trade[9] created a set of centrifugal forces that undermined the basic authority of the Porte. Both the 'revolts' of individual *ayan* and the separatist movements in the Balkans and in the Middle East can be seen as results of the growing openness of the Ottoman Empire to the currents of the European world-economy.[10]

The initial response of the Ottoman state to this situation was a series of political measures seeking to recreate Ottoman centralism on an imperial scale. In the periphery of the Ottoman Empire, these measures proved to be largely ineffective. These lands had been annexed through military occupation and had been controlled militarily at the zenith of the Ottoman expansion. Their ability to secede from the Ottoman Empire was the result of the confluence of social forces created as a result of the growing organic links between these regions and the world-economy.[11] Furthermore, the processes of the world-economy led to a local articulation of economic processes along the lines imposed by the European system. These transformations occurred outside of the sphere of influence of the Ottoman state, for these lands had never been totally incorporated into the Ottoman system in the first place. As for the rise of individual *ayan*, political measures initiated by the state apparatus proved to be at least temporarily more effective.

In addition to extensive military reforms undertaken during the reigns of Selim III and Mahmud II (*c.* 1789–1839) the most important step in curbing the political autonomy of the local notables was the conclusion of the pledge of alliance (Sened-i İttifak) between the local lords and central bureaucracy (1808). Although at face value the document amounted to a recognition of the *ayan* in so far as it relied on their assistance, this was a temporary compromise on the part of the central bureaucracy owing to the latter's heavy involvement in prolonged wars at that moment.[12] As soon as the war with Russia was over in 1812, the central state actively fought against and curbed the tendencies of the *ayan* towards decentralization.[13] However, this wave of political recentralization proved to be only temporary. The incorporation of the Ottoman system within the world-economy continued notwithstanding.

Starting from the end of the reign of Mahmud II, the Ottoman state apparatus, concerned by the shortage in state finances, sought means by which to obtain part of the surplus flowing directly out of the Ottoman zone into the core countries of the capitalist world-economy, via this expanded participation in the world division of labour. The promulgation of the Gülhane Rescript in 1839, which was the beginning of the Tanzimat, represented in our view a legitimization of the now peripheral status of the Ottoman Empire in the world-economy, by providing a legal framework in which the state could attempt simply to secure its portion of the surplus in a system on which it had now itself become dependent.[14] Furthermore, through a series of commercial treaties signed between the Ottoman state and the European powers, European trade grew to the detriment of the local manufacture.[15] Another dimension of the Tanzimat era was its role in intensifying the inter- and intra-class contradictions within the Ottoman state. Increased exploitation of the peasantry, widespread peasant flights, measures taken by the big landlords to tie the peasantry to land, and the institutionalization of private property in land constituted some of the aspects of the inter-class struggle during this period.[16]

One of the most important consequences of the Tanzimat era was the changes in the mode of organization of the state apparatus that the 'reforms' brought about. Secularization and diversification of the governmental practices constituted the most important aspects of this change. In addition to already existing conflicts between the various levels of the Ottoman state structure, the rapid growth of the bureaucracy during Tanzimat generated new divisions and groupings among the different factions of the ruling bloc. In this configuration, the lower bureaucrats of the Porte and the *ulema*, both of whom were in relatively disadvantageous positions, staged protests through a movement called the Young Ottoman movement in the mid nineteenth century. In terms of its social roots, this movement remained circumscribed within the limits of the ruling bloc of the Ottoman Empire. The Young Ottomans aimed only at reshuffling the bureaucratic organization and in no sense did they seek to transform the existing parameters of the Ottoman state apparatus.[17]

During the second half of the nineteenth century the Ottoman state apparatus permitted the intrusion of European finance capital within the Ottoman Empire. Railway construction which was started in this epoch took place on the basis of 'state-to-state contracts'. These and other similar infrastructural investments served to further the commercial relations with Europe as well as constituting, in some cases, the first direct investment of foreign capital in the Empire.[18]

In spite of this direct intervention of the Ottoman 'state' on the 'economy', the state apparatus retained its 'dislocated' character, in that there was no mechanism of *representation* that would have translated the interests of the new economically dominant classes onto the political level. Furthermore, especially during Abdulhamid's reign, the palace tried to re-institutionalize a centralized administration, which only led to a further isolation of the state apparatus during the last decades of the nineteenth century. Throughout, financial difficulties of the Ottoman state apparatus persisted.

Finally, in 1856, borrowing from abroad was resorted to as a remedy. In twenty-five years, the debt incurred by the Ottoman state grew at an accelerating pace. In 1881, the Porte, having failed to pay the interest on a foreign debt of 200 million pounds sterling, was forced to permit its creditors to take charge of certain imperial revenues. The Public Debt Administration, a special institution set up to carry out this task, extended its control over the sources of imperial revenue as the amount and backlog of borrowing increased in the years that followed.[19] The PDA, on the one hand, kept the Ottoman bureaucracy from bankruptcy; on the other, it terminated the sporadic efforts of the palace to recreate Ottoman centralism. This institutionalization of the role of European finance capital within the Ottoman Empire effectively limited the bureaucracy's control over the appropriation and utilization of its revenues. The PDA in essence served to suspend the degenerated Ottoman bureaucracy within limits set by European finance capital. A similar process occurred in those areas of the Ottoman Empire which had become independent in the nineteenth century, such as the Balkan states and Egypt.

It is with the establishment of the Young Turk governments that we can discern the last stage in bringing this obsolete polity into line with the economic processes of peripheralization. Young Turk opposition that preceded the 1908 coup was different from the Young Ottoman movement in one fundamental way. Whereas the carriers of the Young Ottoman dissent had originated from among the ranks of the bureaucratic strata, the most important ideologues and practitioners of Young Turk opposition belonged to the circles that were located outside of the ruling bloc. As such they were able to formulate their dissent more coherently and translate this into a unified and organized struggle.[20] For peripheral structuration to be complete, the state apparatus as well as the economic processes had to go through a transformation along the lines that would be compatible with the demands of the world-economy. Transformation of the state apparatus during peripheralization involved its 'weakening' both 'internally' and 'externally' (that is, relative to other states in the world-economy). Whereas it is easy to discern the process of 'weakening' of the Ottoman state apparatus within the ambit of international relations, the problem is somewhat obscured when we trace the changes in its ability to control the internal processes during the period of its dissolution. However, a close reading of this history reveals that 'internally', the old 'strong' state apparatus of a world-empire had been progressively transformed into the 'weak' state apparatus of a peripheral zone of the world-economy. There was, in İnalcık's terms, a change in the 'concept' of state.[21] What some people argue was the creation of a more efficient state apparatus was in fact the creation of one that facilitated the operations of the world-economy.

For the transformation of the state apparatus in this direction to be complete, one last change needed to take place which would allow the political structure to fully respond to the needs of the economic forces located in the region. This was the work of the Young Turk regime of the early twentieth century. The concrete attempts of the Young Turk government at creating a 'national economy' and a 'national bourgeoisie' represented an attempt to ally with and profit from Germany's aspirations to use the Ottoman Empire as a 'semi-periphery' in Germany's struggle to achieve core status within the world-economy. From the establishment of the PDA to the end of World War I, the Ottoman state apparatus was, for the most part, in a state of chaos. But at the same time there occurred sustained economic growth within the Ottoman Empire.[22] This was however a 'growth' determined by the processes of the world-economy. What was going 'bankrupt' was not the Ottoman Empire as such but the old Ottoman state apparatus, giving way to a new structure, completing the peripheral structuration of the Ottoman Empire.

Up to now we have concentrated on the mechanisms of incorporation of the Ottoman Empire and its transformation into a peripheral structure. Specification of a more precise dating for these transformations is more difficult and controversial. Various studies have produced contradictory results as regards the periods of this history. Thus İnalcık's argument that the '1590's mark the main dividing line in Ottoman history'[23] finds its counter-position in Cook: 'There was no radical discontinuity in the history of the Ottoman state between the early fifteenth and the early nineteenth century.'[24] The few analyses produced from a world-system perspective also generate conflicting claims about the periodization. While Wallerstein argues that the Ottoman Empire was still outside of the world-economy in the sixteenth century, Faroqhi and İslamoğlu prefer to date the incorporation beginning in the sixteenth century.[25]

Although the 'classical age' of the Ottoman Empire involves a more or less smooth period of expansion from 1300 to 1600, the reversal of this pattern during the three centuries that followed involved fluctuations and contradictory processes. Looked at in the 'long term', the second period of the Ottoman Empire involved a more or less steady process of 'decline'. Though the actual emergence of a peripheral structure cannot be said to be complete before the end of the nineteenth century, the process of incorporation clearly occurred earlier.

Given the fragmented pattern of articulation with the world-economy that tore the Empire apart, it is difficult to give one specific date of 'incorporation' of the entity called the Ottoman Empire into the capitalist world-economy. Whether one wants to date the shift from *c.* 1600 or from *c.* 1750, it is our contention that what is conventionally called 'the Ottoman Empire' in the period after the point of incorporation is not the same object as the entity called the Ottoman Empire during the period of its historic upswing. During the second half of its history the Ottoman Empire involved different social relations, which have to be analysed under a different set of parameters. It was no longer an autonomous world-empire. It was now one more state operating within the framework of (and therefore the constraints of) the capitalist world-economy.

It is a truism that in early modern times there occurred a substantial reversal of the fortunes of 'East' and 'West'. The great empires of the East declined. Europe expanded to conquer the world. The Ottoman Empire was one such world-empire incorporated into the expanding capitalist world-economy. There are two ways to look at this phenomenon. We can seek the origins of the differential role of various zones of the world-economy in the different cultures these zones have historically produced. Some areas are presumed to have had values more consonant with modernity than others. Modernization then becomes the description of how the zones that lack the proper values and structure acquire them, how they 'modernize'. This is ideologically comforting for those who dominate the world-economy. They dominate because they are more 'efficient', more 'rational' in their institutional structures. They deserve to be emulated.

We approach this same phenomenon from a quite different perspective. It is not the difference of the 'advanced' and the 'backward', of the 'developed' and 'underdeveloped' that is the given. These differences are seen to be in fact the result of a world process of the internal development of an ever-expanding capitalist world-economy. This world-economy, when it expanded to include a zone like the Ottoman Empire, thereby reshaped, as we have seen, its productive systems and its state structure – and, we should add, the organizing principles (or ideology) of social life. When the Ottoman state or Ottoman agriculture 'reformed' itself, this was not a step towards being more modern, but a step towards further integration into the precisely peripheral role the zone had been assigned. The possibilities of transforming that peripheral role might be there at a later stage (as for other peripheral zones), but mobility within the world-economy of one zone has always been at the expense of counter-movement of other zones.

We cannot here trace the long-term trends of the capitalist world-economy as a whole and the systemic crisis towards which it is moving. We have merely been attempting to situate the history of the Ottoman Empire from the sixteenth to the nineteenth century as one best described as 'incorporation' into the capitalist world-economy, and its consequent 'peripheralization'.

Part II

State and agriculture

5 ❧ State and peasants in the Ottoman Empire: a study of peasant economy in north-central Anatolia during the sixteenth century

HURİ İSLAMOĞLU-İNAN

In this chapter I examine social and economic change in Ottoman rural society in north-central Anatolia during the sixteenth century. In doing this, I will argue that – contrary to accepted wisdom about the 'stationariness' or 'stagnation' of pre-industrial agrarian economies, especially the 'Asiatic' ones – peasant household economy in this region witnessed significant changes in the form of increased crop yields and productivity in response to a nearly 100 per cent growth in population and to increased commercial demand in the growing towns. Rural economic development did not take place in a vacuum; it cannot be understood in abstraction from historically evolved social-political relations of surplus extraction and of exchange. In the Ottoman Empire, these relations were structured by the political-juridical practices of the state that made possible the production, appropriation, and distribution of surpluses produced by peasants who had direct access to the means of production – the land. Not only were the power relations that focused on the state a primary stimulus to agricultural production or rural economic development; political-legal structures of the state largely shaped the manner and the extent to which population growth and commercial expansion in the sixteenth century affected changes in organization of peasant production (i.e., in productivity, in the levels of investment and technology) and in rural class relations. Put differently, my central argument is that population growth and commercial expansion in sixteenth-century north-central Anatolia did not have the outcomes – i.e., fragmentation and expropriation of peasant holdings, formation of large commercial estates, increased differentiation in the countryside – predicted in economic models of development.[1] They did not because such long-term changes in production and property relations and in land distribution cannot be expected to take place merely in response to changes in economic factors and in accordance with universal economic laws of supply and demand; structural changes in the rural economy and society require extra-economic coercion or state intervention on the part of classes whose interests such changes would serve, or a seizure of the state apparatus by those classes. In the sixteenth century, the Ottoman state sought to preserve the integrity of the peasant household economy that constituted its fiscal base. At the same time, perpetuation of that economy by means of political-juridical structures constituted the basis for the state's political authority. This should not, however, suggest that the Ottoman society was 'stationary', incapable of change: it did change but in a direction predicated by its own political-ideological (juridical) rationality. The object of this study is to delineate, through a detailed examination of surplus extraction and exchange relations and of changes in the peasant household economy, the specificity of rural social-economic transformation in sixteenth-century north-central Anatolia. This micro-history is only a preliminary step in understanding the specific transformation paths in other parts of the Ottoman Empire and in the periods following the sixteenth century when the impact of commercial expansion in the European capitalist economy was increasingly felt.

The study consists of two parts. First, I describe the basic social-economic structures of the Ottoman Empire and outline the conceptual framework for studying its internal dynamic. Second, I discuss the developments in the peasant household economy in sixteenth-century north-central Anatolia, in the context of the social-economic structures that characterized the Ottoman society in this region.

Conceptual framework: Ottoman society and social-economic change

In explaining the social-economic dynamic of Ottoman society, this study stresses the primacy of historically evolved power relations that focused on the state and that governed the spheres of production and exchange (distribution). Thus, in the production sphere, the state's political (administrative) controls not only ensured the continuity of agricultural production by free peasant producers with usufruct rights over the land but also made possible the extraction of surpluses from direct producers. These controls were, in turn, embodied in juridical-ideological practices whereby the state as dispenser of justice and perpetuator of the 'eternal order' sought to preserve the integrity of peasant holdings, prevent accumulation of land, and protect the 'free' status of the peasant. While most land belonged to the state, as I will later show, ownership of land was not a necessary condition of the state's absolute authority; establishment of an administrative-legal framework regulating agricultural production by independent peasants appears to have been a sufficient condition for the state's political domination.

In the sixteenth century, the *tımar* system provided the administrative framework for state intervention in the production and appropriation of peasants' surpluses. Under this system, the central state distributed revenue-grants or *tımar*s to its officials – bureaucrats and soldiers – who were empowered to collect taxes in areas assigned to them. The grantees, in exchange for the privilege of collecting taxes, had to support and deliver during time of war a specified number of mounted soldiers. In addition, they formed the administrative cadres representing the central authority even in the remotest village. But *tımar* holders were not the only representatives of the central state in the provinces; their activities were kept under the vigilant scrutiny of *kadıs* or judges – also state functionaries – who made sure that *tımar* holders did not step beyond their rights in their interaction with direct producers and performed their duties in accordance with the precepts of state legal codes. This characteristic of the Ottoman system, in turn, entailed a separation of juridical from administrative practices whereby holders of revenue-grants (or extractors of surplus) exercised no jurisdiction over the person or the land of peasants in their *tımars*. Such jurisdiction rested with the state which exercised it through the hierarchy of judges, who were responsible for administering and executing both the *şeriat* (Islamic law) and the administrative law (*kanun*) issued by the ruler.

Tımar holders or state officials were not, however, the sole extractors of peasants' surpluses in the form of taxes; the state also recognized the claim to surpluses of other groups, among them the Muslim religious establishment and the pre-Ottoman ruling elites. These groups were subordinated to the state's political authority to the extent that administrative-legal structures of the state intervened in the class relation between the producers and appropriators of surplus. This calls for an analytical distinction between the political-juridical sphere of state power and the state's role as extractor of surpluses (via the *tımar* system or other institutions). Confusion of these two aspects results in conceptions of the state as a class-like phenomenon with its entire political-juridical apparatus directed towards maximal appropriation of surpluses or revenues.[2] On the other hand, while the central state was a major recipient of tax revenues, state power cannot simply be reduced to the function of surplus extraction (i.e., to a class position); it had determinations outside the production or surplus-extraction process. First, the state's political power was premised on the reproduction of an undivided polity; the *tımar* system was the framework for a centralized, unfragmented political order. Second, state power rested on ideological-juridical structures that constituted the basis of its legitimation. Viewed in this perspective, state power in the Ottoman Empire formed an autonomous sphere that provided the 'conditions of existence' of the production and appropriation of agricultural surpluses. Thus, this study seeks to formulate the sphere of the political as defined by state power. This is central to an understanding of the Ottoman 'economic' dynamic which was subsumed to the logic of the political.

So far I have concentrated on the state's political intervention in the production process; but the state also intervened in the distribution or exchange of surpluses, imparting a political or non-market rationality to exchange relations. Thus, in the Ottoman Empire trade was subject to strict regulations.

In the case of internal trade, prices both in rural and urban markets were fixed by the state, and transactions were subject to *hisba* regulations enforced by state officials. Also the state sought to direct the flow of agricultural surpluses to designated areas, in order to ensure the provisioning of towns and of the capital city. Thus, trade regulations stipulated that both the food requirements of towns and raw materials for urban craftsmen were supplied from the produce of their hinterlands. To this end, the state legal codes specified that the peasant was to carry the grain tithe accruing to the *tımar* holder to a market place not further than a day's journey away. On the other hand, the flow of goods not produced in a given area as well as the provisioning of major cities was ensured through the granting of concessions to merchants whose activities were scrutinized by state officials. Of course, markets and trade were a major source of revenue for the state in the form of customs dues, market taxes, and from sales of concessions to merchants. More importantly, however, state controls over trade and markets largely aimed at limiting accumulation of commercial gains to those with a claim over agricultural surpluses. After all, markets primarily served the needs of revenue holders who sold either the entire amount of grain tithe collected in kind and forwarded the cash to the central treasury or converted part of their revenues into cash to meet the non-food requirements of their households and of the soldiers they raised. Peasants also sold part of their produce in markets, mainly for payment of money taxes, but, as I will later show, peasant surpluses did not constitute a major part of marketed surpluses.

State intervention in the internal nexus of exchange relations in barring accumulation of trade profits by revenue holders, sought to prevent the rise of local power nodules that could pose a threat to the state's political authority. In doing this, the state was ensuring the reproduction of the centralized polity. On the other hand, state controls over the production and appropriation of surpluses can be viewed as another facet of controls over distribution; measures aimed at the preservation of the integrity of peasant holdings and restrictions on the extent of surpluses appropriated by revenue holders significantly limited the amount of surpluses which these functionaries marketed.

The political determination of distribution (exchange) relations, in turn, describes the specific structure of commercial development in the Ottoman Empire. First, the state's political controls coupled with high costs of overland transport characteristic of pre-industrial societies resulted in a pattern of regional economies with limited trade relations outside a given region. Secondly, commercial development or the extent of commercial activity was largely determined by the marketing of surpluses extracted as taxes. Thus, it can be argued that, given the political rationality of the Ottoman system, the integration of peasant household economy into the larger society *via* the market was not to a large degree a function of the peasants' direct market involvement but occurred through the mediation of taxation. Thirdly, the extent of commercial activity largely varied with changes in the volume of the peasants' output, given that the product tax was assessed as a fixed percentage of total output. I will later try to show, in the context of developments in north-central Anatolia, how this pattern of commercial development shaped the degree and extent of changes in peasant organization of production and in rural class relations in the sixteenth century when population and commercial demand for agricultural goods were expanding. Central to that analysis is, however, the conceptualization of rural economic dynamic. What follows is an outline of such a conceptualization.

Agricultural production in pre-industrial societies is generally assumed to be essentially stagnant. In its neo-Malthusian or neo-Ricardian formulations,[3] this approach is introduced in terms of a homeostatic or eco-system with a built-in mechanism of self-correction whereby an inelastic supply of food, produced with fixed techniques, determines the level of population and therefore the demand for foodstuffs. Central to this reasoning is the assumption that, given the absence of technological change, the only way to increase food production in pre-industrial society was through the opening of new lands to cultivation. But good lands were scarce; as population grew, inferior lands were increasingly brought under cultivation; productivity of both land and labour declined. As a result, demand for foodstuffs outran their supply; with terms of trade favourable to agriculture, agricultural prices and rents rose, while wages declined. At the same time, increased population pressure on land led to fragmentation of peasant holdings; this coupled with high rents signalled the expropriation of peasant lands by landowners who sought to reap the gains from rising rents and prices. Thus, the peasant cultivator was faced with a choice between starvation in the countryside and migration to towns where plague eventually caught up with him. The outcome of these developments was a complete reversal of previous trends: decline in population was accompanied by falling agricultural prices and rents while wages soared. Two aspects of this model needs to be emphasized. First, it tends to equate the stagnation of pre-industrial agrarian economies with assumed technological backwardness. Secondly, it seeks to explain the changes in the organization of production and rural class relations in terms of strictly economic categories of supply and demand, of relative scarcity of factors, particularly of land, and in abstraction of social-political-legal relations specific to any given society.

Recently, however, the neo-Malthusian model has been criticized for its 'economism', for assigning potency and causality to the economic factor of population in bringing about changes in rural social-economic structures. These critics, most notable among them Robert Brenner,[4] stress the role of historically evolved class (or political power) relations in determining the manner and degree to which demographic changes will affect structural transformations. While the approach adopted here also emphasizes the primacy of political power relations in determining the course of social-economic development, it is critical of Brenner's views on a number of grounds. Most importantly, Brenner, concentrating on power relations, overlooks the dynamics of pre-industrial agrarian economies.[5] Thus, Brenner accepts too readily the neo-Malthusian characterization of these economies as essentially stagnant; he differs from the neo-Malthusians with regard to explanations of that stagnation. That is, once he explains the Malthusian cycle as a product of established class structures, Brenner does not question the 'stagnation' thesis about pre-industrial economies but concentrates on the driving role of class relations. As a result, he is unable to relate the dynamics of the production process to that of political structures and therefore cannot account for the intervention of these structures in the economy. The latter phenomenon, as I have mentioned earlier, in the case of the Ottoman Empire is a primary condition of the extra-economic (or political) rationality that Brenner seeks to delineate for the pre-industrial European societies.

One important manifestation of the dynamic of pre-industrial agrarian economies was their response to demographic changes. In these economies where small-scale family farming constituted the main economic unit, the reproduction of the production process (as distinct from the reproduction of surplus extraction relations that were reproduced on the political level) took place on that scale according to an economic-demographic logic.[6] Now the fact that this logic determined neither the conditions of economic development nor the relative positions or strengths of different classes need not imply that it could be ignored. On the contrary, the processes through which this logic is subsumed to the dominant political rationality need to be demonstrated. This, however, necessitates a departure from neo-Malthusian (or stagnationist) conceptions of pre-industrial economy. In attempting to delineate the rural economic dynamic in Ottoman society and to show the processes whereby the power relations which characterized that society affected economic trends, this study will adopt Ester Boserup's model of rural development.[7]

First, the Boserupian model reverses the Malthusian causality between agricultural production and population; in so doing, it treats population as an external factor with determinations outside of the production process, whereby demographic changes affect changes in agricultural production (or food supply) and not vice versa. Secondly, this approach does not view the relative scarcity of good lands as a necessary constraint on agricultural production. Not assuming technological stagnation to be a characteristic of pre-industrial economies, it seeks to show that peasant producers, when faced with increasing numbers, mobilized techniques – such as intensive cultivation of land through shortening of fallow, fertilization through crop rotation – that were available to them. These techniques were not used prior to population growth because they generally entailed intensive use of labour and therefore sacrifices in the peasant's leisure time or the time he spent in the production of non-food requirements.

From the point of view of the argument presented here, the Boserupian model offers a number of possibilities. Most significantly, by arguing for the responsiveness of rural production to the external factor of population growth, it allows for the introduction into the analysis of other external determinants of agricultural production. Of these I will stress the role of state taxation demands and therefore of power relations (or relations of extraction of peasants' surpluses in the form of taxes in kind) as a principal determinant of agricultural production in Ottoman society.[8] As such, the approach adopted here stands in sharp contrast to the neo-Malthusian formulations that tend to abstract the developments in the agrarian economy from the context of political-social relations in which they take place, while assigning these developments the role of shaping such relations. Also, the Boserupian model, by stressing the externality of the population factor, makes possible the analysis of extra-economic determinants of demographic growth, such as conditions of political stability, forced sedentarization of nomadic tribes, migration. Thus, population growth becomes a function of social-political factors outside of the rural production process, once again refuting the 'insularity' that Malthusian formulations assign to the pre-industrial economy.

In the context of the above theoretical considerations, I now turn to the study of social-economic structures in sixteenth-century north-central Anatolia.

Ottoman rural society in north-central Anatolia, 1520–75

The study of Ottoman rural society in north-central Anatolia during the sixteenth century is based on the data of Ottoman fiscal surveys for ten administrative districts (*nahiyes*).[9] These districts which formed part of the province (*vilayet*) of Rum are Cincife, Venk, Kafirni, and Yıldız in the *kaza* (seat of a *kadı* or judge) of Tokat; Çorumlu, Karahisar-ı Demirli and Katar in the sub-province (*liva*) of Çorumlu; and Niksar, Karakuş and Felis in the *kaza* of Sonisa (see map 5.1, p. 132). The sample comprises some five hundred rural settlements (see Table 5.21 p. 159) and three towns: Tokat, Çorum, and Niksar. The time span covered is largely determined by the availability of fiscal surveys; the years between 1520 and 1575 have been investigated. For areas in Tokat and Çorumlu, surveys dating from the fifteenth century are also available, thus providing a basis for comparison of developments in that century with those in the sixteenth century.

Surplus-extraction relations

In north-central Anatolia, the *tımar* system that constituted the dominant form of surplus-extraction in the sixteenth-century Ottoman Empire, was only partially applied. In this region as well as in the rest of central and eastern Anatolia that formed the former domains of Turco-Mongol dynasties, the *malikane-divani* system of surplus-extraction prevailed.[10] Under this system, ownership rights (*rakaba*) to the land rested with pre-Ottoman ruling groups designated as *malikane* holders; revenues from the land were divided between the legal owners – who held the land as their freehold property (*mülk*) or as *vakıf* (pious endowment) – and state appointees or *divani* holders who were entitled to revenues as part of their *tımar*. The concession of land ownership rights to pre-Ottoman ruling groups, however, represented a significant departure from the general pattern of the Ottoman land-tax system characterized by state ownership of land. The *malikane-divani* system was, in fact, a compromise between the pre-Ottoman land systems and the Ottoman fisc, dictated by the conditions of the Ottoman conquest of former Turco-Mongol lands and by the character of the ruling elites in these areas.

Central and eastern Anatolia first came under Ottoman influence during the reign of Bayezid I (1389–1402) through a series of tributary arrangements between the Ottoman sultan and the Turkish dynasties which had ruled in the area since the collapse of the Selçuk state in the thirteenth century.[11] But before Ottoman rule could be consolidated, the victory of Timur (Mongol ruler) over the Ottomans at the Battle of Ankara (1402) reinstated the Turkish dynasties in their former position of autonomy. Following a period of incessant struggle, the Ottomans were able to establish their control in this region around the mid fifteenth century, only by conceding to the powerful local elites the ownership rights to the land. These elites consisted of Turkish military rulers (*umera*) and the members of religious establishments. The latter group included the *ulema* (religious scholars) at mosque-*medrese* complexes (institutions of higher learning) and the *şeyh* families who were the custodians of *zaviyes* (dervish hospices).[12] This religious elite controlled large stretches of land as *vakıf* or pious endowments for religious institutions and constituted a very influential group in central and eastern Anatolia from Selçuk times. At the same time the interests of the *umera*, *ulema* and the *şeyh* families were intertwined since it was not uncommon for military rulers to convert their properties into *vakıf*.[13] The closely knit character of the historically entrenched local elites, in turn, must have been a significant barrier to the full application of the Ottoman land-tax system in this region.

In fact, the Ottoman central state was engaged in a continuous struggle with the local elites during the second half of the fifteenth and early sixteenth centuries to establish its political domination and to control larger shares of surpluses in the form of tax revenues in former Turco-Mongol lands. The data presented in Tables 5.1 and 5.2 on the distribution of revenues in north-central Anatolia for the period between 1520 and 1574 are suggestive of the nature of this struggle.[14] First, the data indicate that in the sixteenth century the central state managed effectively to limit the extent of revenues that accrued to legal owners and controlled or at least had a say over the dispensation of nearly three-quarters of the total tithe revenues from the districts under study. At the same time, there is a decline from the fifteenth century in revenues that accrued to local groups, especially to the *umera*. This is particularly the case for *divani* revenues: these revenues were originally allotted to Turkish military rulers who the central state appointed as *tımar* holders and entrusted with administrative functions during the initial stages of the conquest. It appears that, once the *umera* were drawn into the administrative-legal framework of the Ottoman state and were reduced to mere state officials, they could be replaced in the sixteenth century with other officials, more compliant to the demands of central authority.[15] Also the period between 1520 and 1574 witnessed an increase in the proportion of revenues (both *divani* and *malikane*) the government allotted to *tımar* holders and, to a lesser extent, in revenues allotted to the domains (*has*) of the sultan and provincial governors. These trends, in turn, point to an increased appropriation of the administration of these areas by the central state.

Second, the data on revenue distribution point to a rise in the share of *vakıfs* in total revenues, especially of family *vakıfs*. Under the *malikane-divani* system freehold properties of pre-Ottoman military groups could be sold and divided among heirs, resulting in discontinuities in ownership and in extreme fragmentation of these properties. In order to prevent fragmentation and, more importantly, to escape confiscation by the central state, these groups increasingly converted their properties into family *vakıfs*. But, since these lands were already parcellized at the time of conversion, no single family controlled any significant amount of revenues from family *vakıfs*. This, however, further underlines the trend towards the dissipation of the financial power base of local military elites, a process already underway with the penetration of the *tımar* system. The same cannot be said of *vakıf* holdings of mosque-*medrese* complexes and *zaviyes*. These underwent neither fragmentation nor changed hands over time. Moveover, both the *malikane* and *divani* revenues that accrued to *vakıfs* of mosque-*medrese* complexes show an increase during the sixteenth century. This increase was only partially due to the conversion of freehold properties of local elite families; more significantly, the central state in the sixteenth century was allotting a significant part of revenues that directly accrued to it, to mosque-*medrese* complexes.[16] It can thus be surmised that the central state sought the alliance of local *ulema* (religious scholars) who as teachers, judges, reciters of sermons at mosques controlled the ideological-juridical structures. These structures had formed the basis for legitimacy of the power of local Turkish dynasties. As such, alliance with the *ulema* was a means of co-opting that legitimacy and therefore further undermining the domination of local dynasties. On the other hand, it is not unlikely that the central state appointed the *kadıs* (or judges) in this area from the ranks of the local *ulema*, who then would be in a position of implementing the juridical precepts that constituted the basis for legitimacy of state power. This, in turn, could explain the prominence of *ulema* as claimants to surpluses in the sixteenth century.

But what were the implications for the organization of agricultural production, for rural class relations of appropriation of administration by the Ottoman central state through the introduction of the *tımar* system, on the one hand, and of cooptation of local ideological-juridical structures, on the other? In general terms, increased application of the *tımar* system and appropriation of the local ideological-juridical apparatuses allowed the central state to intervene in the class relation between the owners of land and the direct producers. Concrete manifestations of this intervention, in turn, define the character of rural structures under the *malikane-divani* system. First, under this system, legal owners of land were entitled to a rent, but neither the conditions nor the amount of this rent were determined by them. The amount of rent was specified in state legal codes as a single tithe (one-tenth of a peasant's total output) on grains and other produce and as one-half of the dues from beehives and mills. Legal owners were not free to cultivate their lands nor could they intervene in the production process undertaken by 'free' peasants with usufruct rights to small plots and whose rights and obligations were specified in state codes. All matters relating to the person and the land of the peasant were outside the purview of legal owners (or *malikane* holders); these were the responsibility of *tımar* holders who formed the administrative cadres and whose powers could be revoked by the central state. *Tımar* holders received the *divani* share of revenues which consisted of another single tithe on grains and other produce and the other half of dues on beehives and mills. In addition, however, *tımar* holders were responsible for the collection of all *resm-i çift*[17] or land cum personal taxes, sheep tax, penal fines. Moreover, peasant holdings could not be sold or purchased without the permission of *tımar* holders, who were responsible for the drawing of title deeds and who saw to the dispensation of holdings that fell vacant. Secondly, neither legal owners of land nor *tımar* holders exercised any jurisdiction over peasants; as was the case with state-owned lands, legal matters relating to peasants and their land were settled at the tribunal of the *kadı* or judges appointed by the central state. Finally, there were legal sanctions against accumulation of land in the hands of legal owners; though *malikane* holders could sell or purchase lands, such transactions were subject to validation by the central state.

In brief, direct intervention of the administrative (political) and juridical practices of the central state in the 'internal nexus' of surplus extraction or class relation between the legal owners and peasant producers deprived the former of any local power base and reduced them to the status of a 'rentier' class. As such, the *malikane* holders, though they held the ownership title to land, were dependent on the administrative-juridical apparatus of the state for appropriation of rural surpluses. This was tantamount to the establishment of the political domination of the central state and resulted in the gradual undermining of the claims of the pre-Ottoman ruling elite both to revenues and administration. In the sixteenth century, *tımar* holders who, in all likelihood, did not belong to this group, and the local *ulema* – co-opted by the state – emerged as the two major claimants to revenues in north-central Anatolia. On the other hand, the state's intervention in surplus-extraction relations aimed at preserving the integrity of peasant holdings and barring any controls by surplus extractors over the peasant-production process. In doing this, the central state was not merely seeking to secure its own fiscal base, but – perhaps more importantly – fulfilling its ideological role as the protector of the peasantry and the preserver of 'eternal order'. Embodied in juridical structures, this ideology[18] served to legitimize, in the eyes of peasants, the state controls over the production and appropriation of surpluses and constituted the basis of the state's political domination. In the next section I will discuss how this specific structure of surplus-extraction relations in north-central Anatolia affected changes in peasant organization of production and rural class relations in the sixteenth century, characterized by population growth and commercial expansion.

Dynamics of peasant household economy

Located in north-central Anatolian plateau, the districts under study were characterized by mountainous terrains intersected by various tributaries of the Yeşilırmak and the Kızılırmak and by trade and army routes linking eastern Anatolia with the west and the central plateau with the Black Sea coast (see Map 5.2, p. 133). Proximity to rivers and availability of irrigation largely account for the density of settlements in this area during the sixteenth century. On these fertile lands, cereals – with wheat and barley as the chief crops – constituted almost a monoculture. They were, however, complemented by a certain amount of stock raising, fruit growing, viticulture, horticulture, as well as cotton and rice cultivation in some of the districts under study. In the sixteenth century peasant economy in north-central Anatolia was predominantly engaged in the production for subsistence and for regional markets. These markets were generally towns located on trade and army routes, serving as commercial centres and also as cultural-religious centres housing major *medreses* (institutions of higher learning) and mosques. There were as many as twelve towns of varying sizes in this region during the period under study, and this high level of urban concentration may explain the paucity of rural markets. On the other hand, cotton goods and rice exported from north-central Anatolia to the Crimea and possibly to Istanbul were not produced by peasants. Cotton goods for export were primarily manufactured by urban craftsmen, while rice cultivation, requiring considerable investment in irrigation, was not generally undertaken on small peasant holdings. Rice was produced on large state farms by share-croppers with a different legal status from that of ordinary peasants. Thus, changes in peasant household economy in north-central Anatolia during the sixteenth century was largely a function of such regional developments as population growth and increased commercial demand in the growing towns, on the one hand, and of increased state demand for taxes on the other. What follows is an attempt to specify the impact of each of these factors on rural output, organization of peasant production, and on rural class relations.

Population growth and peasant household economy

The data of fiscal surveys for areas under study reveal a population growth at an average rate of well over 100 per cent during the period between 1520 and 1575 (see Tables 5.3 and 5.5 pp. 137–8 for population trends in individual districts). Whenever surveys from the second half of the fifteenth century can be located, they indicate that the upward trend began in this early period and, gaining momentum, continued into the sixteenth century. At the same time, population growth was characterized by an increase in urban population relative to rural population (cf. Tables 5.6 and 5.8 with Tables 5.3 and 5.5, pp. 137–40). But what were the causes of these phenomenal increases in numbers in north-central Anatolia?

When posed in terms of annual growth rates which, in fact, closely approximate to the way a population actually grows continuously over time, the implied rate of increase for each of the ten districts during the fifty-five year interval between 1520 and 1575 is about 2 per cent a year – a rate significant for any population (see Table 5.5, p. 138). This raises serious doubts about the population growth in these areas having been based primarily on natural fluctuations. When fertility is high, as has been generally assumed in the case of pre-industrial societies,[19] the mechanism bringing about population increase is a reduction in mortality, usually associated with improvements in environmental conditions rather than in medicine.[20] Since mortality initially is at a high level, a drastic reduction would have to occur to produce a natural increase rate of 2 per cent a year. On the other hand, while such a sharp decline in mortality seems implausible, given the trends in mortality variations in these societies, the absence of 'exceptional' mortality owing to famine, disease or war may account for part of the increase in population. But there is practically no way of determining how much of the increase could be attributed to natural fluctuations.[21] The fiscal surveys contain no information on deaths and births which constitute the key variables in computing natural fluctuations. Nor do they provide any clues as to the age of marriage – the key to fecundity in old demographic structures.[22]

Internal migration, on the other hand, emerges as one of the main explanations for the high rates of growth. While population movements within the Ottoman Empire were controlled and migration into towns was restricted, these took place to the extent of requiring state measures to stem the flow.[23] At the same time, movement between villages seems to have been a common phenomenon; such migration was legalized by the entry of the migrant into the tax lists after an undisputed residence of ten to fifteen years in his new village.[24] To this endemic mobility was added large displacements of population resulting from wars, social unrest, or economic crisis in the countryside. Significant increases in the numbers of *mücerreds* (bachelors) and *cabas*, or unmarried landless peasants who were expected to have an independent source of livelihood, strongly suggest increased migration into north-central Anatolia in the later sixteenth century (see Tables 5.4 and 5.7 pp. 137, 140).[25] Yet, as neither the surveys nor other sources record migration in any systematic manner, it is not possible to attempt a numerical evaluation of the extent of migratory fluctuations at any given period. The researcher must then be content with drawing some general impressions from varied and fragmentary data which are nevertheless valid.

The data for areas in north-central Anatolia suggest a strong correlation between the changes in the conditions of political-social stability and the fluctuations in the size of population during the period under study. Thus, alternating periods of political turmoil and peace were to witness massive movements of population into or out of the area. Moreover, not all migratory movements were voluntary. The state employed mass deportations both as a means of settling newly conquered lands and in order to establish law and order through the uprooting of rebellious populations, especially of troublesome tribes.

In north-central Anatolia, Ottoman rule was established by the mid fifteenth century, following turbulent years of struggle between local Turkish dynasties and the Ottomans for control over central and eastern Anatolia.[26] For the period between 1455 and 1485, the data of the surveys suggest a slow or zero population growth in rural areas around Tokat. In 1471, Tokat was sacked by the Turkish dynasty of Akkoyunlu, resulting in the city's depopulation. Although Mehmet II's victory over the Akkoyunlu in 1473 helped to consolidate Ottoman rule in the Tokat–Niksar region, it by no means marked the end of political turbulence. In the early sixteenth century, areas in north-central Anatolia became a focal point in the acute rivalry between the Shii Safavid dynasty in Iran and the Ottomans. Safavids, through skilful religio-political propaganda, won the support of the Shii Turkish tribes, the so-called Kızılbaş, in Anatolia and instigated their revolt against the Ottoman government. During the reign of Selim I (1512–20), when the Ottomans finally succeeded in suppressing the rebellion, they did so by killing large numbers of Kızılbaş, or forcing them to migrate to Iran.[27] At the same time, the Ottoman government sought to break the power of the tribes through a systematic policy of deportation. Tribal populations in this area, as well as in other parts of Anatolia, were uprooted and deported to newly conquered areas, most notably to the Balkans.[28] It is thus not surprising that during the years between 1485 and 1520 the rates of population growth in the districts around Tokat should fall below the already sluggish rates of increase observed in the earlier period. Only after 1520 did the areas in north-central Anatolia experience relative political stability under Pax Ottomanica. This coincided with the period of rapid demographic growth which continued at least until 1575 when the last of the sixteenth-century surveys was made.

Stable political conditions in north-central Anatolia were not, however, matched by similar developments in eastern Anatolia where Ottomans and

Safavids were locked in a life-and-death struggle during much of the period between 1520 and 1575. Thus it would seem that at least part of the population increase in this period may have taken place as a result of migration of people from the war-torn frontier areas into the Tokat–Çorum–Niksar region where law and order prevailed.[29] This westward movement of urban and agricultural populations may have, in turn, more than counterbalanced the relative depopulation of the region early in the sixteenth century in the aftermath of the Kızılbaş revolts.

Another factor which may have influenced the growth in rural population as indicated by the data of the surveys is the settlement of nomads. Fiscal surveys used in this study, however, do not systematically list pastoral nomads, who constituted an important component of the population in Anatolia.[30] Thus, from these surveys alone it was not possible to determine whether the increase in settled population in north-central Anatolia was accompanied by a decline in the number of nomads, but the overall figures for Anatolian population in the later sixteenth century indicate that the rate of increase in nomadic population was about half that of other sectors of the population – a fact which may be attributed to sedentarization.[31]

Sedentarization of nomads, on the other hand, was a primary concern of the central state, which sought to 'peasantize' the nomads and therefore bring them under its political domination. There were also revenue considerations; pastoral nomads were exempt from most of the taxes which the peasants were liable to pay. This seems to have been the case even when they engaged in the cultivation of the soil in their winter pastures or *mezraa*s (uninhabited arable lands). Thus, in the later sixteenth century, the documents increasingly point to a tendency on the part of central government to register the nomads as ordinary *reaya* (tax-payers) and the lands they worked as peasant holdings.[32] Finally, the state had a definite interest in protecting peasant production, which formed the basis of its political authority as well as being an important source of revenue. Therefore, disputes between nomads and villagers was probably an additional reason for assimilating the nomads and changing their status to that of ordinary peasants.[33]

The success of such administrative measures to realize the settlement of nomads is, however, open to question because nomads were probably resourceful enough to evade additional obligations to the state. Thus, in order to understand the sedentarization process, we need to consider the changes in the rural economy, such as increased frequency of cropping on *mezraa* lands in response to population growth. These developments I will discuss later in the context of the dynamics of agricultural economy. Here, it should be noted, however, that the central government during the period following the Kızılbaş uprisings deliberately refrained from any systematic efforts to settle the nomads. Instead, it limited its activities to the legitimization of settlement processes which had already occurred. Thus, when nomads were more or less settled in their *mezraas*, the latter were entered in the surveys as villages and their inhabitants as ordinary peasants.[34] But the state encouraged this process of gradual settlement through granting of preferential tithe rates to nomads who cultivated the land.

Thus, political factors – establishment of Pax Ottomanica and the state's encouragement of settlement of nomads – were the main causes of population growth in sixteenth-century north-central Anatolia. As such, population growth can be said to have taken place independently of the internal dynamic of peasant household economy or of levels of food production in that economy. Given this externality, I will discuss how population growth affected changes in peasant economy and, more importantly, how its impact was mediated by the political-legal structures of the state that directly intervened in the production and appropriation of rural surpluses.

Population growth in north-central Anatolia was accompanied by increases in the output of two major crops: wheat and barley. As the indices for population and production of these crops set out in Table 5.9, p. 141, show, production of both wheat and barley lagged behind population growth. But on the basis of these figures, can we assume that the rural economy in the later sixteenth century witnessed a subsistence crisis resulting from an unfavourable balance between population and resources – especially land – which, in turn, could explain the slow increases in grain output relative to those in population? Also, did the population pressure on land lead to fragmentation of peasant holdings, peasant dispossession, and to rural–urban migration?

M.A. Cook's estimates of man/land ratios for different parts of Anatolia show a deterioration in these ratios in the districts under study in the later part of the sixteenth century.[35] Based on the data of fiscal surveys, Cook shows that, while both the size of population and the extent of arable increased, population growth was more rapid than the extension of cultivation. At the same time, his findings suggest that fragmentation of peasant holdings was also under way and the unity of the traditional peasant holding, the *çift*, was not, in fact, maintained. Thus, Cook makes a case of increased population pressure on land and, citing the evidence of proliferation of entries in the later surveys relating to small-scale mountain clearings or *balta yeri*, argues that 'peasants were reaching the limits of cultivation as defined by their physical environment'.[36]

But, following Cook's argument, can we conclude that scarcity of land was the major limiting factor on peasant production in the later sixteenth century? After all, expansion of the arable was not the only means through which the peasants could increase crop yields when confronted with rising demand for their products; they could intensify land utilization through shortening of fallow or use of crop rotation with sown grass or fodder plants or through the introduction of soil fertilization and of irrigation. Direct evidence of the fiscal surveys relating to such practices in north-central Anatolia is less than satisfactory. Nevertheless, certain information included in the surveys suggests that intensification was under way in the later sixteenth century.

First, there is the evidence of the conversion of settlements listed as *mezraas* in the earlier surveys, into villages in the later surveys.[37] *Mezraas* were uninhabited cultivated lands generally attached to villages; they were cultivated either by villagers or nomads. With increased demand for grains, both peasants and nomads might be expected to intensify cultivation on these lands and to inhabit them on a permanent basis. Now at least part of the fragmentation – as evidenced in the increased numbers of smaller holdings in the later sixteenth century – may have been the result of subdivision of these *mezraa* lands and not necessarily of fragmentation of existing holdings.[38] I will return to this point in relation to changes in land distribution. Here, it is important to note that population growth does not necessarily entail fragmentation or extension of cultivation into marginal lands. It can result in increased frequency of cropping on lands which were at the disposal of peasants or nomads but were not intensively cultivated, either because there were not enough people to cultivate them or need for produce was not pressing enough. References in the earlier surveys to uncultivated arable in many villages which appear to have recently gone out of cultivation also substantiate this point.[39] That these references are absent from the later surveys suggests that these lands may have been under long fallow and their cultivation intensified in the later sixteenth century.

Secondly, the appearance in the later surveys of large numbers of *balta yeri* entries[40] that represent assartments from land under forest or scrub should not necessarily imply that peasants were bringing under cultivation less fertile lands. These lands, which were cleared by use of axes and fire, were frequently fertile enough not to require ploughing and therefore the use of draught animals. Moreover, weeding, a major activity on other lands, was not necessary on the assarts. Thus, by cultivating these lands, peasants did not only work less but also did not have to set aside land or crops for feeding the draught animals. Finally, it should also be mentioned that assarts provided high yields for two or three years, after which time they could be used as grasslands for animals, as land exposed to fire tends to become more grassy. Increases in the numbers of sheep raised in the areas under study in the later sixteenth century might indicate that at least some of the assarts were used as grazing areas.[41] Now what this discussion suggests is that there were factors other than scarcity of land that might have initiated the clearing of forest lands.

Third, surveys of the later sixteenth century include entries of leguminous crops – lentils, broad beans, chickpeas – which are absent in the earlier surveys (see Table 5.10, p. 142–3). At the same time, the survey data show that increases in barley yields were greater than those in wheat yields (see Table 5.14, p. 146–8). Since both these crops could be used as animal fodder, their increased production may suggest a move in the direction of intensification of land use by limiting grazing areas for draught animals. At the same time, introduction of leguminous crops is no insignificant indicator of peasant attempts at soil fertilization. These crops had a fertilizing property in their ability to bind nitrogen from the atmosphere and, when cultivated in rotation with such crops as wheat and barley, they might be expected to improve the seed productivity of these crops. In the absence of data on seed/yield ratios or on quantity harvested per unit land, we cannot establish the effect of the introduction of legumes in the rotation.[42] But the relatively high rates of increase in wheat and barley yields in the later sixteenth century suggest that this may have been a factor in influencing the rising trend (see Table 5.14, pp. 146–8). Another factor affecting soil productivity may have been the increased use of fertilizers in the form of manure resulting from the growth in animal husbandry in the later sixteenth century (see Table 5.15, p. 149).

Lastly, with regard to irrigation and the possible changes in the extent of irrigated lands, the evidence is also very limited as the surveys contain no reference to irrigation facilities or techniques. But the growth in such activities as truck gardening, fruit growing, and viticulture as well as rice cultivation on peasant plots, all of which required irrigation, indicates that peasants might also have stepped up their use of irrigation. In areas close to river-beds or streams, labour-intensive methods of irrigation may have been adopted; thus lifting the water from these sources and spreading it over the fields by means of human as well as animal labour may well have been undertaken. At the same time, the increased rice cultivation on state lands also suggests increased capital investment in irrigation works as well as diversion of more labour power to this activity. Finally, the surveys list significant numbers of water mills in the countryside, sometimes as many as five or six in a given village. This shows that harnessing of water power was a common practice. Moreover, the increase in the numbers of millstones in operation in the later sixteenth century also points in the direction of increased utilization of water power by peasants in response to increase in grain production[43] (see Table 5.16, p. 151).

The above discussion suggests that scarcity of land might not have been a primary constraint on peasant production in sixteenth-century north-central Anatolia. It appears that, though no major technological innovations took place at this time, peasants were aware of certain techniques of intensive land utilization which they mobilized in response to changes in demand patterns. Moreover, there is little reason to assume that the lands which were brought under cultivation in the later sixteenth century were necessarily of poor quality. The case of forest assarts substantiates this point. On the other hand, intensification of land use required more intensive use of labour. Not only did the peasants have to work harder: individual households might have resorted to hiring labour. Significant increases in the numbers of landless peasants or *caba* in the later sixteenth century points to the availability of such a labour force (Table 5.4, p. 137).[44]

Finally, population growth in sixteenth-century north-central Anatolia does not appear to have led to blatant discrepancies in land distribution or to set into motion a trend towards the destruction of peasant holdings. In fact, according to M.A. Cook, in the later sixteenth century the actual distribution of land was somewhat more egalitarian than the pattern of fragmentation suggests.[45] Thus, for instance, survey data show that in this period in districts around Tokat many tenures entered against the name of a single person were in fact shared; there is also evidence that tenures which came up for disposal tended to go to the landless; and, finally, most of the assarts listed in the later surveys were in the hands of otherwise landless peasants. Furthermore, there is no evidence to indicate that rural usury and peasant dispossession increased during the period of population growth. Also, there is nothing to suggest that the peasant dispossession that did take place was associated with the formation of large estates.[46]

What needs to be explained, however, is why the peasant household economy in north-central Anatolia was spared the fate that is frequently assumed to be that of pre-industrial societies during periods of demographic expansion. Viewing the rural economic developments in the context of surplus-extraction relations that characterized the Ottoman society, I will argue that the political-legal practices of the state were largely instrumental in the preservation of the integrity of peasant holdings. To this end, the state imposed legal sanctions against the division and the sale of peasant holdings. Thus, as I have shown earlier, fragmentation of holdings might not have been as dramatic as a casual reading of the survey data might suggest; proliferation of smallholdings may reflect more a sub-division of *mezraa* lands or open fields and less the sub-division of existing holdings. At the same time, state officials or *tımar* holders controlled certain amounts of land which they rented out to peasants. This practice, in turn, imparted to peasant production some degree of flexibility whereby the producer could vary the size of his holding according to the size of his household; and, more important, given that migration was a primary determinant of population growth in north-central Anatolia, these lands could be leased to newcomers, thus ensuring their cultivation. The decline in the extent of these lands during the later sixteenth century suggests that *tımar* holders were renting out their domain lands to peasants under favourable conditions.[47] On the other hand, willingness of *tımar* holders to do so, at a time when commercial demand for agricultural goods had risen – instead of turning their domains into large estates – points not only to the effectiveness of state measures limiting cultivation by revenue holders and sanctioning their use of corvée labour, but it also bespeaks the specific structure of commercial development in Ottoman society. Finally, if fragmentation and emerging scarcity of land were not significant barriers to increased agricultural production, can we then assume that population growth in sixteenth-century north-central Anatolia led to a subsistence crisis in the countryside, forcing peasants to migrate to towns?

Probably not. First, as I will show later, while wheat and barley production per capita declined, peasants increased the production of other food crops, among them fruits, vegetables, legumes, and sheep. Thus, it can be argued that peasants might have been forced to change their diets or eat less wheat; but this should not suggest that they were actually suffering from serious food shortages. Secondly, migration to towns which appears to have been significant, was probably more a response to increased employment opportunities in towns than an outcome of the inability of peasant economy to feed increased numbers. Peasants, especially the young ones, might have preferred to enter into the service of provincial administrators as irregular soldiers or join the *medreses* as students, rather than endure the drudgery of work that intensification of production entailed in their villages. In the later sixteenth century both the entourages of provincial administrators and the student body of *medreses* expanded. These developments, however, took place as a result of changes in power relations between the central administration, on the one hand, the *ulema* and provincial administrators, on the other. As such, they had determinations outside the peasant economy and cannot be explained in terms of changes in that economy under the impact of population growth.

Commercial development and peasant household economy

So far I have concentrated on the responses of peasant household economy to population growth. The later sixteenth century also witnessed significant increases in commercial demand for agricultural goods in rapidly growing towns in north-central Anatolia. What follows is an attempt to delineate the effect of increased commercial demand on the peasant household economy.

In order to gauge the effect of market demand on peasant production of cereals, I have attempted to estimate the changes in marketed surpluses per taxpayer in the areas under study during the sixteenth century.[48] The exercise, however, proved to be less than fruitful given our profound ignorance of equivalents of local measurement units in kilograms or in any standard measure that would allow for comparisons to be made over time and locality.[49] Hence, it was not possible to calculate the amount of grains peasants required for sustenance and then to establish what part of the produce might have been set aside for marketing, after deductions were made for tithe payments, milling losses, and seed requirements. Instead, I have estimated wheat and barley yields per taxpayer after making allowances for such deductions. The figures presented in Table 5.17, p. 153, show a general decline in wheat and barley yields per taxpayer during the sixteenth century. But does this also suggest a decline in grain surpluses marketed by peasants themselves at a time when aggregate grain output was increasing? If one is to assume that there were no significant changes in peasant consumption of wheat and barley, the answer to this question has to be affirmative. On the other hand, if one considers that peasants had to sell part of their produce for the payment of money taxes (land cum personal taxes, dues on mills and beehives, bride tax, penal dues) and also for purchasing finished goods in town markets, did a shift occur from home consumption (both by men and animals) of wheat and barley to that of leguminous plants or to lesser grains such as millet? Could the expanding urban demand further stimulate such a shift? To answer these questions we need to first look at the extent of government demands for wheat and barley and their effect on peasant production in this period.

These demands took the form of grain tithe collected in kind and of extraordinary levies at times of emergency or war. The tithe represented as much as one-fifth of the peasant's total output in the areas under investigation where a double tithe was extracted. Extraordinary taxes were also levied in kind (*nüzül*), requiring two-thirds or four-fifths to be paid in wheat and one-third or one-fifth in barley. Sometimes, though, they took the form of forced government purchases (*sürsat*).[50] It is not, however, possible to determine the magnitude of these impositions for the period under study, since they were not recorded in the fiscal surveys, and separate records of these are not available prior to 1590.[51] Yet, state demands for such tax deliveries from areas in north-central Anatolia must have increased considerably in the later sixteenth century when the imperial army repeatedly traversed these areas *en route* to Iranian campaigns. Thus, it can be argued that taxation demands siphoned off a significant part of peasants' grain surpluses, and the increases in total grain yields (see Table 5.14, p. 146–8) were to a large extent stimulated by increased state demands to meet the requirements of an army on the march.[52] This may, in turn, explain the higher rates of increase in barley yields, a staple food for army horses. At the same time, as I will later discuss, agricultural revenues collected in kind by holders of revenue grants represented the larger part of grain surpluses sold in regional markets.

Peasants, however, were not totally cut off from the market. Substantial increases in truck-gardening, fruit growing, and viticulture, especially in areas around towns, suggest that in the later sixteenth century peasants might have compensated for the relative decline in marketed grain surpluses by increasing the production of these crops that found ready markets in the growing towns (see Tables 5.18, 5.19, 5.20, pp. 154–8). In the case of these crops, it should also be noted that, at least in some regions of the Ottoman Empire, taxes recorded in the surveys referred to that part of the produce which was marketed; fruits, vegetables, grapes grown for peasant families' own consumption were probably tax exempt and therefore were not included in the survey estimates.[53] Thus, figures given in this study for 'total' production of these crops might, in fact, reflect total marketed amounts and not the amounts that were actually produced. If this were the case in north-central Anatolia, then increases in the production of fruits, vegetables, and grapes in the later sixteenth century can be taken as a direct indicator of increased market demand.[54] On the other hand, increases in cotton cultivation in the majority of districts under study was probably largely in response to the increased demand of domestic producers of cloth and fibres who had to produce more to clothe growing numbers. Given that cotton constituted a very small percentage of total production in most districts, and its share in that production did not significantly rise during the sixteenth century except in the districts of Felis, Karahisar-ı Demirli and Katar (see Table 5.10, pp. 142–3), cotton production to meet the requirements of urban craftsmen could not have been all that significant. Evidence for increased rural weaving activities in Karahisar-ı Demirli where cotton production also increased in this period substantiates this point.[55]

Production of rice, a strictly commercial crop, also increased in the later sixteenth century (see Tables 5.18, 5.19, 5.20, pp. 154–8). Certain *kanunnames* (legal codes) even specify at which stage of growth the crop was to be marketed.[56] I have earlier mentioned that organization of rice cultivation largely remained outside the domain of peasant household economy. In the Niksar region where rice cultivation was significant, the larger part of the yields accrued to the *has* (domain) of the ruler. In practice, this meant that the sultan's appointed agent or *emin* was responsible for providing the specified amount of seed and later for the disposal of yields. Although the surveys provide no information as to what actually happened to the ruler's share of the rice crop, it is probably not incorrect to assume that a significant part was sold to merchants on local markets, who carried it to other parts of the Empire.[57] At the same time, some rice must have been purchased by the *imaret*s (mosque complexes) and other urban institutions of which there were a large number in the towns of Rum, which included such major administrative and religious centres as Amasya and Tokat. Furthermore, share-croppers, or *çeltikçi*s, must also have marketed their share of the crop. In addition, it can also be assumed that the rice cultivated by ordinary peasants was destined for the market – since peasants cannot very well be expected to use this valuable crop for home consumption. Thus, the increase in rice yields in the later sixteenth century is a definite indicator of increased commercial demand for this crop.

On the other hand, to what extent there was a shift to rice cultivation in response to market demand and at the expense of other crops is not clear. The Ottoman central government was well aware of such a tendency and tried to protect other peasant produce from the onslaught of rice. In doing this, it attempted not only to ensure the production of subsistence goods but also to preserve the integrity of the small peasant producer. But, judging from the extent of government regulations limiting rice cultivation and the measures against those who cultivated more than the specified amount of seed, it may be concluded that the state was engaged in a continual struggle with the local officials as well as other notables who wanted to extend rice cultivation on their holdings, thereby accumulating large fortunes. To maximize their profits, these personages also made illegal impositions of corvée labour.[58] Hence, given the considerable temptation to increase rice yields, the production of this crop may also have taken place on a 'contraband' basis, and therefore the actual yields may have been greater than those recorded in the surveys. By the same token, the tendency toward the 'enserfment' of the peasantry on rice fields may also have been more significant than in other spheres of cultivation. At the present state of our knowledge of the specific conditions in rice-growing areas, however, such statements remain no more than mere speculations.

Finally, considerable increases during the later sixteenth century in the number of sheep raised by peasants in all districts under study, especially those in the hinterland of towns, also suggest a trend towards increased production for urban markets (see Table 5.15, p. 149). Given the paucity of our information on peasant diets and marketing practices, it is not, however, possible to estimate how much animal meat, tallow, hides or dairy products was actually consumed by peasants, and how many animals or what proportion of their yields were marketed. Low-meat diets were characteristic of certain *imaret* kitchens in sixteenth-century central Anatolia[59] and it is likely that ordinary peasants were even less able to afford this kind of nourishment. Similarly, little is known about the consumption of dairy goods and tallow. Such foods as cream, yoghurt and cheese appeared on the tables of the wealthy, though cheese was also consumed by modest-income groups in seventeenth-century İstanbul.[60] Tallow was probably used as cooking fat both by peasants and town-folk. Information is equally scarce on peasant usage of hides, though it can be assumed that out of this material were made *çarık*, or partially treated pieces of hide, which the peasants wrapped around their feet in lieu of shoes. At the same time, there must have been a market for hides in towns, where tanning was a major occupation. But with regard to these products, as well as to meat, it is probably not too incorrect to assume that the peasants preferred to offer them for exchange, given favourable market conditions, and minimize their home consumption. This would be particularly true at a time when the marketable grain yields were considerably reduced and the rural population was hard pressed for cash incomes to meet such non-food requirements as the payment of money taxes and the purchase of finished goods in town markets. Lastly, wool production was an important by-product of sheep-raising. Part of the wool produced by peasants might have supplied the urban weaver, while at least some was used by rural craftsmen.

Despite increased urban market demand for the products of sheep-farming, there is, however, little reason to suppose that a significant shift to pastoral activity occurred in the peasant economy resulting in conversion of fields to grazing lands. Grain cultivation safeguarded through state measures remained the dominant form of agricultural activity during the sixteenth century. But the importance of sheep-raising as a supplementary activity seems to have increased. From the perspective of the peasant household economy, this meant either certain lands were set aside for grazing or, if animals were grazed on fields, longer fallow periods were required. In the latter case, animal droppings on fields must have contributed to increased soil fertility. With regard to strictly grazing lands,[61] these are not recorded in the surveys in any systematic manner and therefore it is not possible to establish whether these were preserved or reclaimed in the later sixteenth century when peasants sought to increase grain yields. On the other hand, sheep farming was a much less labour-intensive activity than crop cultivation; the prospect of more work if grazing lands were converted into fields – at a time when peasants were already working harder – might have stopped them from reclaiming these lands. This consideration coupled with favourable market conditions could then explain in part the rise in sheep-farming in this period. Of course, arguments presented here on sheep-farming remain tentative without detailed studies of the economy of pastoral nomads who predominantly engaged in this activity. The issue is further complicated in the case of areas in north-central Anatolia where pastoral nomads were undergoing sedentarization and their activities cannot easily be differentiated from those of ordinary peasants.

In brief, the above discussion suggests that the market involvement of peasants was limited during the sixteenth century when commercial demand for agricultural goods was expanding. Appropriation of a substantial part of peasants' surpluses in the form of taxes in kind on two major crops – wheat and barley – significantly curtailed the production of these crops for the market. On the other hand, in order to meet their cash requirements – especially for payment of money taxes – peasants did engage in commercial production of fruits, vegetables and sheep, and this production did increase in the later sixteenth century, no doubt partly in response to increased urban demand for these goods. But such 'commercialization' was limited; grain production for taxes and for subsistence continued to dominate the rural economy in this period. Finally, cultivation of strictly commercial crops such as rice generally took place outside the peasant household economy and on state farms.

In contrast, to the limited market involvement of direct producers, however, increased commercial demand signalled an intensification in the market participation of revenue holders or groups with a claim over peasant surpluses; in sixteenth-century north Anatolia these groups were the *tımar* holders and the *ulema*. For one, given that the grain tithe collected in kind was estimated as a fixed proportion of total yields, increases in the aggregate supply of grains were translated into increased marketed surpluses by these groups. A rough estimate indicates that nearly two-thirds of the total grain tithe from areas under study – after allowances are made for consumption needs of individual groups – found its way to local town markets in the second half of the sixteenth century.[62] This amounted to nearly 13 per cent of total wheat and barley yields from these areas. It can thus be argued that food requirement of local towns was to a large degree met from the surpluses marketed by revenue holders who absorbed the price effects resulting from increased commercial demand for foodstuffs. On the other hand, more than half of the total income that accrued to revenue holders from sales of tithes and from money dues was, in all likelihood, spent locally.[63] Both the *ulema* and the *tımar* holders were major consumers of urban finished goods; their increased incomes coupled with the expansion in their entourages in the later sixteenth century might be expected to provide the primary stimulus for the expansion of urban craft production. Hence, regional urban development that characterized this period appears to have been largely an outcome of increased market involvement of revenue holders, who were the principal beneficiaries of increased commercial demand for agricultural goods.

Lastly, what needs to be considered are the changes in peasant organization of production and rural social relations in the period of commercial expansion. First, did commercial development in the sixteenth century result in significant changes in the economic division of labour between urban and rural areas, or in an increased specialization of agricultural production and dependence of the peasant household economy on towns for manufactured goods? One indicator of such changes would be the changes in the extent of rural craft production which in sixteenth-century north-central Anatolia largely consisted of weaving and spinning of wool and of cotton produced by the peasants themselves. The only evidence that the fiscal surveys provide of these activities is taxes levied on dye-houses.[64] Of the three dye-houses recorded in the rural areas under study (see Table 5.16, pp. 151–2), only one, and that in the tribal district of Karahisar-ı Demirli, shows a substantial increase in its revenues in the period between 1520 and 1575; the one in Kafirni near the city of Tokat shows a sharp decline in revenues, while income from the third dye-house in Yıldız (again near Tokat) remained constant during the same period. These trends, in turn, suggest that at least in Kafirni and Yıldız, peasants might have diverted some of their time and labour from craft production to intensive production of grains and of non-grain crops.[65] The latter activity, coupled with rising demand for cloths as their numbers increased, might have led to increased peasant purchases of cloths and yarns in towns. But this tendency towards increased market involvement of peasants was restricted by the 'limited commercialization' of agricultural production and the absorption of peasants' surpluses through taxes. This, in turn, imposed limits on the amount of cash the peasant had at his disposal (especially after the payment of money taxes) and therefore on the peasant's ability to purchase urban craft goods. On the other hand, in Karahisar-ı Demirli considerable increases in dye-house revenues point to an intensification of weaving and spinning activities in this region, where both cotton and wool (as evidenced in the rise in sheep-farming) production also rose during the sixteenth century. But it is not clear whether it was the peasants or nomads who increased their weaving and spinning activities; if it was the nomads, were they responding to increased peasant demand for cloths or yarns? At present, we know very little about the interaction between the peasants and the economy of pastoral nomads; but peasants of this region – as more of their labour and time was absorbed by intensive methods of agricultural production – might have increased their purchase of finished goods from nomads. Moreover, since they could enter into barter exchange relations with the nomads, peasants probably preferred nomad-produced goods to those of urban craftsmen, who demanded cash. In sum, given the 'limited commercialization' of peasant production largely dictated by the mode of surplus extraction that characterized the Ottoman society, increased commercial demand in towns in the later sixteenth century did not lead to increased specialization of production between urban and rural areas. Though peasants might have purchased more finished goods both in urban markets and from nomads in the later sixteenth century than in the earlier period, rural craft production continued to absorb both the time and labour of peasants in the later period.

Secondly, increased commercial demand did not have the effect of disrupting the organization of agricultural production around small peasant holdings. As I have discussed earlier in relation to the impact of population growth on rural economic and social structures, there is no evidence that peasant dispossessions increased in the later sixteenth century nor is there any indication of widespread formation of large commercial estates. Appropriation of peasants' surpluses in the form of taxes in kind on grains, coupled with legal sanctions against the sale and subdivision of peasant plots, ensured the cultivation of staple goods essential for peasant subsistence and for the provisioning of the army and towns. Also the political-legal structures of the state significantly limited capital accumulation in the countryside and therefore differentiation among peasant households. More importantly, these structures also imposed constraints on the amount of surpluses that was extracted by different groups of revenue holders and on their claims on land and on the labour of peasants. The concern of the central state for maintaining the integrity of peasant household economy is particularly pronounced in the restrictions on commercial production of rice; these restrictions primarily aimed at preventing expropriation of peasant lands and recruitment of peasants as share-croppers or corvée labour on rice fields by revenue holders who sought to expand the cultivation of this highly lucrative crop. Finally, revenue holders did benefit from increased commercial demand in the later sixteenth century; they did so through the marketing of peasants' surpluses they appropriated in the form of taxes. The effectiveness of the political-juridical framework of the state largely precluded the possibility for revenue holders to seize peasant plots and to engage in commercial production in the capacity of landlords or capitalists. Thus, the later sixteenth century witnessed a decline in the extent of domain (*hassa*) lands of *tımar* holders, who were increasingly renting or selling these lands to peasant producers at a time when market demand for agricultural products was expanding.

Hence, the analysis of the impact of urban commercial expansion on peasant household economy in sixteenth-century north-central Anatolia sheds some light on the 'commercialization' dynamic in Ottoman society shaped by the specific structures of surplus extraction and exchange in that society. First, central to this 'dynamic' was the response of peasant economy to commercial expansion through the mediation of taxation, on the one hand, and the 'limited commercialization' of peasant production on the other. As such, agricultural surpluses collected in the form of taxes constituted the larger part of marketed surpluses, and commercial expansion did not result in a transformation of peasant organization of production and or rural class relations. Secondly, 'commercialization' unleashed a tendency towards the development of regional economies. Within the framework of state regulations over internal trade, increased agricultural production contributed to the growth of regional towns, whereby their food and raw materials requirements were met by the produce of their hinterlands. At the same time, urban craft production was stimulated by the increased demand of revenue holders – who were the primary beneficiaries of the rise in urban demand for agricultural goods. Finally, this pattern of regional economic development, by allowing capital accumulation to take place in the hands of revenue holders, was to constitute the basis for the rise of local power nodules in the period following the sixteenth century.

Conclusion

The model of social-economic transformation revealed through the detailed study of a single Ottoman region in the sixteenth century has two characteristic features. One, rural economic development – i.e., increases in productivity, changes in technology – was to a larger extent stimulated by taxation demands and not, in any significant way, by market-demand patterns. By leaving the organization and control of the actual production process in the hands of direct producers with hereditary cultivation rights over the land, the Ottoman system afforded the peasantry the minimal space to increase yields in response to changes in demand patterns. That is, the system offered possibilities of economic development; but this development was largely dictated by extra-economic structures that described surplus-extraction relations and *not* by economic decisions of individual producers responding to favourable market-demand patterns. Thus, this study rejects views of development that ascribe the stagnation of pre-industrial economies to the intervention into the 'economic' sphere of non-economic factors (i.e., state or political-legal practices). Instead, I have argued that Ottoman economy owed its dynamism largely to state intervention in the economy in the form of taxation demands. As such, this study stresses the 'non-economic' or political rationality of economic development in Ottoman society.

Two, commercial expansion in the form of increased demand for agricultural goods did not result in any significant commercialization of agricultural production as to alter the social-economic structures in the countryside. Instead, different groups of revenue holders benefited from favourable market conditions in the growing towns through the sale of agricultural surpluses they extracted from the peasants in form of product taxes. On the other hand, extraction of surpluses from the direct producers with direct access to the land required extra-economic means of coercion. In the Ottoman Empire, revenue holders were dependent on the political-legal structures of the state for enforcing their claim to a share of the peasant's output. Not only did the state provide the repressive (coercive) apparatus that made surplus extraction possible; the juridical-ideological structures of the state legitimized this practice in the eyes of the peasant producer. The state, however, intervened to support the claim of revenue holders to surpluses only if those surpluses were produced by independent peasants with usufruct rights over the land. The state had a stake in the preservation of peasant household economy because peasants constituted its fiscal base. But, perhaps more importantly, the maintenance of a peasantry over which the state alone did exercise jurisdiction constituted the basis for the state's absolute political authority, the basis for the undivided polity.

In describing the structure of surplus extraction relations in north-central Anatolia, I have tried to show how the incorporation of pre-Ottoman ruling groups into the political-legal framework of the state ensured their dependence on the state for extraction of surpluses and therefore their subjection to the state's political authority. This structure of dependency of revenue holders on the political (coercive) and ideological (legitimating) apparatuses of the state largely accounts for why population growth and urban commercial expansion in the sixteenth century did not result in the destruction of the peasant household economy, i.e., fragmentation of peasant holdings, peasant dispossessions, formation of large estates, and increased social coercion of labour. Consequently, the *tımar* holders and the *ulema* at mosque-*medrese* complexes – who were the two major groups with a claim over peasants' surpluses – did not benefit from increased commercial demand for agricultural goods through forcefully converting peasant holdings into units of commercial production. Instead they enriched themselves through marketing of the product tax at favourable market prices. Moreover, since the product tax was assessed as a fixed proportion of total output, increases in aggregate yields in this period were translated into larger shares of surpluses that the revenue holders could market.

The later sixteenth century also witnessed the decline of the *tımar* system as changes in war technology shifted the balance from provincial cavalry to foot soldiers. From the point of view of provincial administrators or *tımar* holders this signalled the breakdown of the administrative framework that enforced their claim to surpluses. Thus, faced with the prospect of losing their privileged status, these soldiers took to plundering the countryside and resorted to illegal extortions of peasants' surpluses. This reaction which broke out in local disturbances throughout Anatolia – and came to be known as the Celali uprisings – represented not so much a resistance to the state's political-juridical structures which prevented commercialization of agriculture and therefore capital accumulation in the hands of provincial administrators; it was a resistance by this group to the prospect of being excluded from the political-juridical framework of the state which enabled them to appropriate agricultural surpluses.

Finally, once the *tımar* system was effectively replaced by tax-farming as the dominant form of taxation in the seventeenth century, agricultural production undertaken by independent peasant producers on small plots appears to have been reconstituted. Tax-farmers then enforced their claims over specified shares in the context of the political-legal practices of the state. Tax-farmers belonged to the ranks of local notables – *ulema* and merchants – and the economic trends of the later sixteenth century no doubt contributed to their ascendancy in the subsequent period. These developments remain outside the scope of this study and information relating to seventeenth- and eighteenth-century developments in north-central Anatolia is scarce. Yet recent research on European territories and for Anatolia in the nineteenth century[66] strongly suggest that, in response to increased European demand for agricultural goods, tax-farmers did not undertake radically to transform the rural social-economic structures and to bring about a commercialization of agricultural production. Instead they responded to increased commercial demand by claiming a larger share of the surpluses either through squeezing the peasants for more taxes or by not delivering to the state what was its due. While this signalled increased economic power of tax-farmers – who sold these surpluses on lucrative markets – and a decline in the actual amounts received by the state, these developments do not appear to have eliminated the political-juridical dependence of tax-farmers on the state in most Ottoman territories.

Thus, the pattern of social-economic development described here has certain generalizable features. Shaped by the historically evolved structures of Ottoman society, it is a pattern premised on regional economic development encouraging the rise of local power nodules which remained dependent on the state for enforcing their claim over surpluses produced by 'free' peasants. Such a model of rural development, of course, requires further elaboration in the light of micro-historical studies of different Ottoman regions at different time periods. But, I believe, it may provide a more appropriate framework for research on patterns of rural development in the Ottoman Empire, especially for the post-sixteenth century period, than the much-acclaimed thesis of the 'formation of large estates' and 'enserfment of peasantry' under the impact of commercial expansion.

Appendix I: Documentation for individual districts and towns

In order to avoid repetition and to save space in notes and tables, the dates of compilation of individual surveys used in this study are given in the following list. The list also contains the inclusive page numbers for each district and town under study in different surveys.

Abbreviations

KK Tapu ve Kadastro Müdürlügü Arşivi (Ankara), *Kuyudu Kadime Defterleri*
MM Başvekalet Arşivi (Istanbul), *Maliyeden Müdevver Defterleri*
TT Başvekalet Arşivi (Istanbul), *Tapu Tahrir Defterleri*

No. of survey	Date of compilation AH/AD	Name of district or town	Page numbers
TT, no. 2	859/1455	Cincife	165–76
		Venk	133–64
		Yıldız	165–87
		Tokat (city)	3–64
TT, no. 19	890/1485	Cincife	27–33
		Venk	35–48
		Yıldız	559–69
		Tokat (city)	3–26
TT, no. 79	926/1520	Cincife	28–34
		Venk	35–49
		Yıldız	117–28
		Kafirni	61–92
		Tokat (city)	1–27
TT, no. 287	961/1554	Cincife	85–95
		Venk	96–115
		Yıldız	183–207
		Kafirni	140–83
		Tokat (city)	1–18

No. of survey	Date of compilation AH/AD	Name of district or town	Page numbers
KK, no. 14	982/1574	Cincife	165b–71b
		Venk	171a–83b
		Yıldız	225b–46b
		Kafirni	203a–17b
		Tokat (city)	1–27b
MM, no. 354	860/1456	Çorumlu	132–57
		Çorum (town)	122–31
		Karahisar-ı Demirli	204–31
TT, no. 444	early reign of Süleyman I around 1520–30	Çorumlu	7–67
		Çorum (town)	1–6
		Karahisar-ı Demirli	307–33
		Katar	203–27
TT, no. 387	929/1523	Çorum (town)	389–401
KK, no. 38	984/1576	Çorumlu	20b–68a
		Çorum (town)	7b–19b
		Karahisar-ı Demirli	228b–52a
		Katar	253b–67b
TT, no. 54	935/1528	Niksar	101–44
		Niksar (town)	96–101
		Karakuş	82–94
		Felis	66–81
KK, no. 12	982/1574	Karakuş	69b–84b
		Felis	54b–66a
KK, no. 10	982/1574	Niksar	29a–215b
		Niksar (town)	7b–28a

Appendix II: Maps

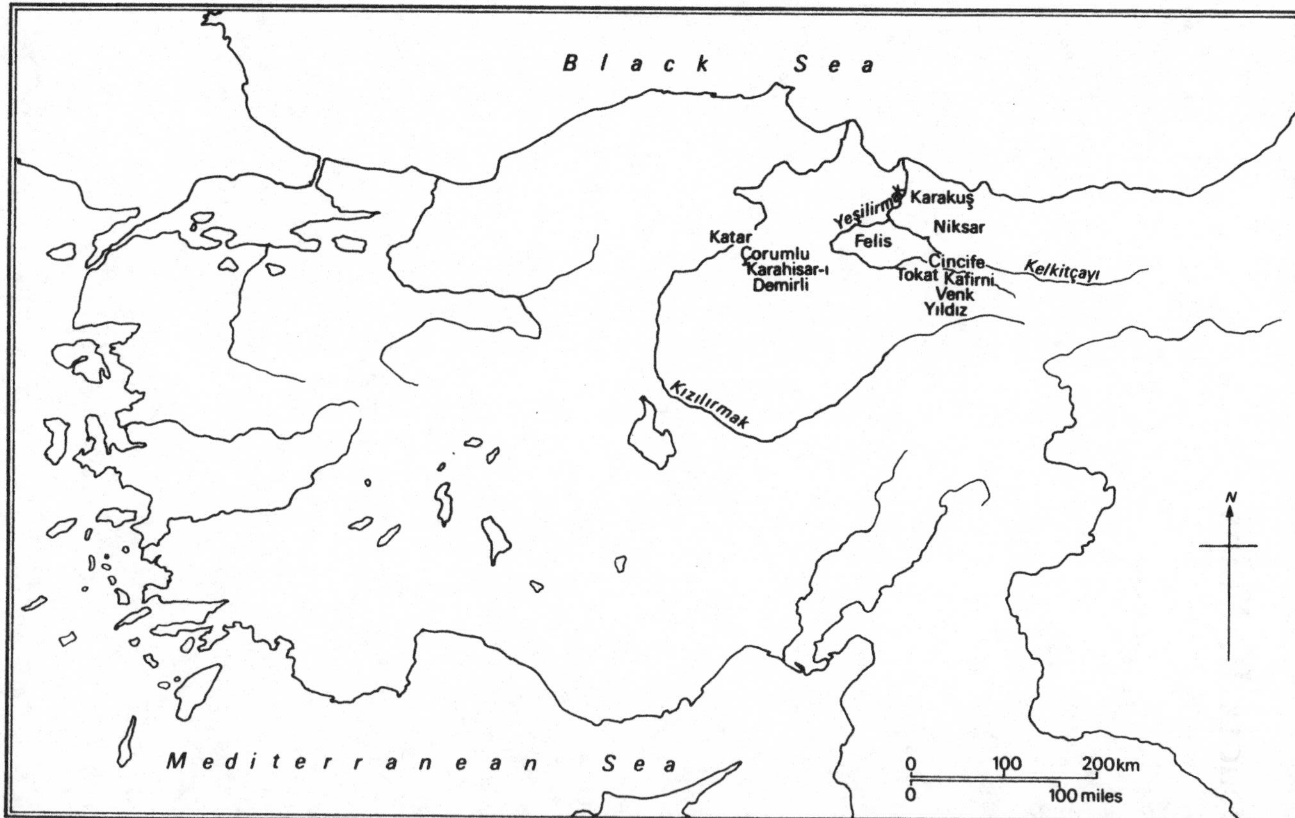

Map 5.1 Location of selected districts in Rum

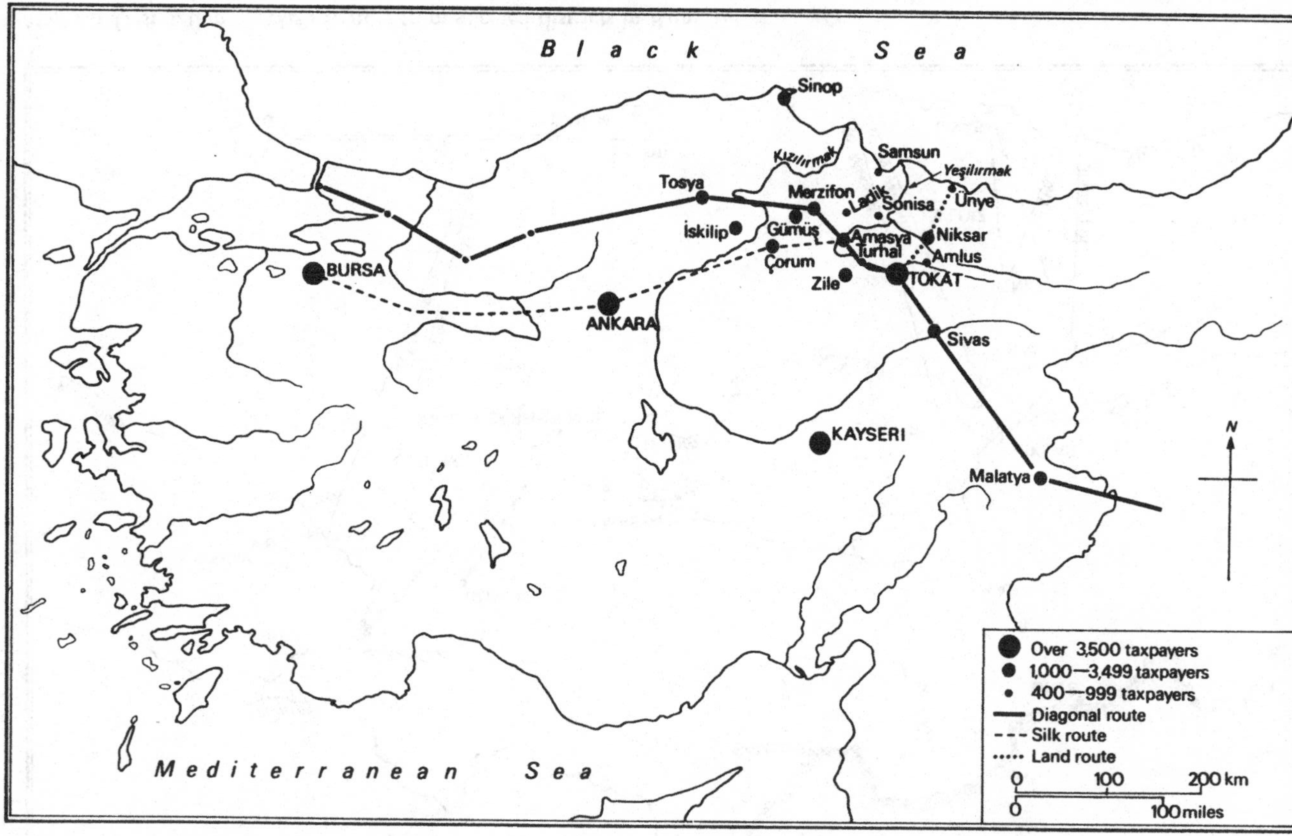

Map 5.2 Towns and trade routes in Rum

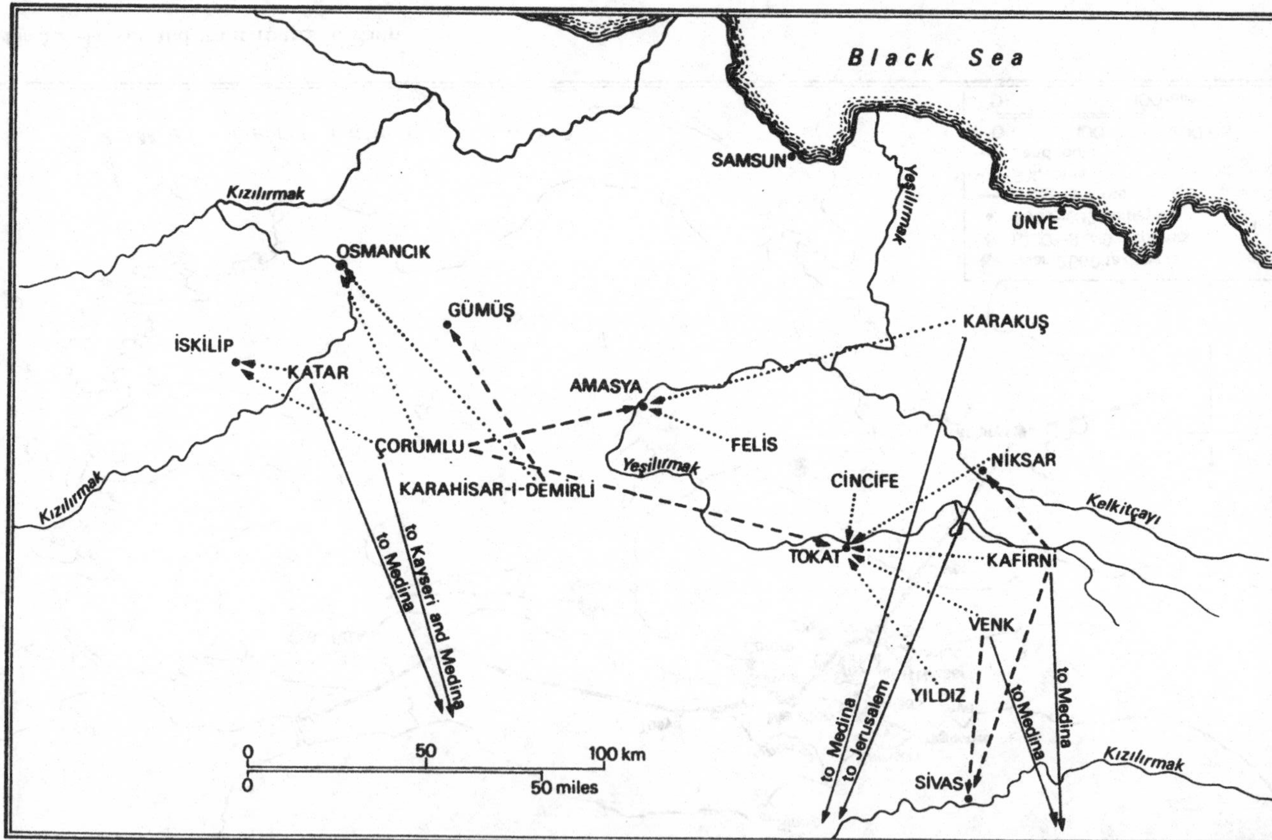

Map 5.3 Destination of *vakıf* revenues from selected districts in Rum

Appendix III: Tables

Table 5.1 *Distribution of* divani *shares among different revenue holders in ten districts of Rum for two selected periods in the sixteenth century*

Sample size: 487 settlements in 1520–30
491 settlements in 1574–6

Holders of *divani* revenues	Number of shares: 1520–30	Indv. categories as a % of total *divani* shares 1520–30	Number of shares: 1574–6	Indv. categories as a % of total *divani* shares 1574–6
Public *vakıf*	7	1.4	8	1.6
Family or Personal *vakıf*	—		—	
Zaviye	17	3.4	17	3.4
Mülk	5	1.0	4	0.8
Tımar	225	46.2	250	50.9
Zeamet	—		—	
Has-ı humayun or *hudavendigar* (property of sultan)	20	4.1	57	11.6
Has-ı mirmiran (property of governor of *vilayet*)			1	0.2
Has-ı mirliva (property of governor of *sancak* or *liva*)	10	2.0	17	3.4
Unspecified	203	41.6	137	27.9

Note —: None were recorded

Table 5.2 *Distribution of* malikane *shares among different revenue holders in ten districts of Rum for two selected periods in the sixteenth century*

Sample size:* 487 settlements in 1520–30
491 settlements in 1574–6

Holders of *malikane* revenues	Number of shares: 1520–30							No. of shares in terms of full shares 1520–30	Indv. categories as a % of total *malikane* shares	Number of shares: 1574–6							No. of shares in terms of full shares 1574–6	Indv. categories as a % of total *malikane* shares
	Full	3/4	2/3	1/2	1/3	1/4	Less than 1/4			Full	3/4	2/3	1/2	1/3	1/4	Less than 1/4		
Public *vakıf*	66	2	1	5	3	8	—	72	16.9	73	1	4	12	3	9	—	85.6	19.47
Family or personal *vakıf*	43	7	2	20	4	18	3	61.3	14.4	47	7	2	25	4	22	4	73.3	16.68
Zaviye (dervish hospice)	58	—	1	16	1	2	—	67.5	15.8	61	—	—	14	1	3	—	69.0	15.7
Mülk (freehold property)	81	8	6	50	13	20	14	127	29.8	79	5	5	47	8	18	14	118.6	26.9
Tımar	15	2	—	9	—	1	1	21.4	5.0	18	2	—	11	1	3	2	26.3	5.9
Zeamet	—	—	—	—	—	—	—	—	—	—	—	—	—	—	—	—	—	—
Has-ı humayun	—	—	—	—	—	—	—	—	—	4	—	—	—	—	1	—	4.25	0.96
Unspecified	72	1	1	4	2	1	—	76.26	17.9	61	—	—	2	1	—	—	62.3	14.2

* For 50 settlements in 1520–30 and 51 settlements in 1574–6 surveys do not distinguish between the *malikane* and *divani* shares nor do they specify the revenue holder. It has been assumed that revenues from these settlements accrued directly to the central government.

Note —: None were recorded.

Table 5.3 *Rural population in Rum: total number of taxpayers*

Name of administrative district	1455	1485	1520–30	1554	1574–6
Cincife	362	434	485	780	1,111
Venk	451	594	775	1,284	1,895
Yıldız	430	519	574	904	1,324
Kafirni	—	—	1,094	2,138	3,286
Çorumlu	—	—	1,974	—	3,522
Karahisar-ı Demirli	—	—	1,659	—	3,394
Katar	—	—	1,251	—	2,521
Niksar	—	—	2,181	—	6,100
Karakuş	—	—	638	—	1,838
Felis	—	—	688	—	1,362

Note —: Nothing recorded.

Table 5.4 *Proportion of unmarried males to total number of taxpayers in rural areas for selected periods during the sixteenth century (in percentages)*

Name of administrative district	1520–30		1554		1574–6	
	Caba	Mücerred	Caba	Mücerred	Caba	Mücerred
Cincife	31.1	22.3	47.4	31.2	20.5	42
Venk	24.2	25	40.6	38.5	24.4	48.4
Yıldız	23.2	20.7	39.4	32.3	27.2	41.5
Kafirni	29.3	29	41.9	35.7	29.1	46.7
Çorumlu	23.5	29	—	—	37.5	41.7
Karahisar-ı Demirli	28.2	31	—	—	28	48.3
Katar	35.6	27.9	—	—	36	42.7
Niksar	25.8	19.7	—	—	30.5	50.2
Karakuş	32.9	23.2	—	—	33.9	39.8
Felis	32.3	25.8	—	—	32.4	53.7

Note —: None, or unspecified in the records.

Table 5.5 *Percentage of rural population change: overall and annual rates of growth**

Name of administrative district	1455–85	1485–1520	1520–54	1520s–75	1554–75
Cincife	20(0.6)	11 (0.3)	61 (1.4)	129 (1.5)	42.4(1.7)
Venk	32(0.9)	30.5(0.8)	65.7(1.5)	144.5(1.6)	47.6(1.9)
Yıldız	21(0.6)	10.6(0.3)	57.5(1.3)	130.6(1.5)	46.4(1.8)
Kafirni	—	—	95 (2.0)	172.5(2.0)	53.7(2.0)
Çorumlu	—	—	—	78.4(2.1)	—
Karahisar-ı Demirli	—	—	—	104.6(2.2)	—
Katar	—	—	—	101.5(1.4)	—
Niksar	—	—	—	179.6(2.1)	—
Karakuş	—	—	—	188 (2.3)	—
Felis	—	—	—	98 (1.5)	—

* The figures in parenthesis represent average annual rates of growth.

Note —: None.

Table 5.6 *Town populations in selected areas of Rum*

Name of town	1455–60		1485		1520–30		1554		1574	
	Total no. of taxpayers	Bachelors	Total no. of taxpayers	Bachelors	Total no. of taxpayers	Bachelors	Total no. of taxpayers	Bachelors	Total no. of taxpayers	Bachelors
Tokat	3,116	—	1,892	87	1,888	365	1,506	—	3,868	1,258
Çorum	438[a]	10	—	—	1,339[b]	432	—	—	2,984	1,750
Niksar	—	—	—	—	327	88	—	—	1,127	488

[a]This count is based on Başvekalet Arşivi, *Maliyeden Müdevver*, no. 354. Owing to the great instability of administrative boundaries, it was not possible to use this survey to compare estimates of rural population over time.

[b]This count is based on the 'synoptic' survey (*icmal*), Başvekalet Arşivi, *Tapu Tahrir*, no. 387 (1522–3). The *mufassal* survey, Başvekalet Arşivi, *Tapu Tahrir*, no. 444 also compiled between 1520–30, and on which are based the estimates for rural population given in this study, does not include a complete list of taxpayers in the town of Çorum.

Note —: None.

Table 5.7 *Proportion of bachelors* (mücerred) *to total number of taxpayers in towns (in percentages)*

Name of town	1520–30	1554	1574–6
Tokat	19.3	—	32.5
Çorum	32.3	—	58.6
Niksar	27.0	—	43.3

Note —: None.

Table 5.8 *Percentage of urban population change: overall and annual rates of growth*

Name of town	Mid fifteenth century to 1485	1485–1520	Mid fifteenth century to 1520–30	1520–54	1520–30 to *c*. 1575	1554–76
Tokat	−39.2(−1.7)	−.2(0.0)	−39.4(−0.7)	−20.2(−0.7)	104.8(1.4)	156.80(4.8)
Çorum	—	—	205.7(1.6)	—	122.8(3.8)	—
Niksar	—	—	—	—	244.6(2.5)	—

Note: figures in parenthesis represent average annual rates of growth.
—: None.

Table 5.9 *Grain production and population indexes for areas in Rum*

Name of administrative district	Approximate date of survey	Wheat production	Barley production	Population
Cincife	1455	138	119	74
	1485	120	87	89
	1520	100	100	100
	1554	120	127	161
	1574	152	145	229
Venk	1455	119	118	58
	1485	138	96	76
	1520	100	100	100
	1554	118	138	165
	1574	147	182	244
Kafirni	1520	100	100	100
	1554	117	136	195
	1574	182	160	300
Yıldız	1455	213	273	80
	1485	135	105	90
	1520	100	100	100
	1554	119	165	157
	1574	136	141	230
Çorumlu	1520–30	100	100	100
	1576	146	175	178
Karahisar-ı Demirli	1520–30	100	100	100
	1576	106	137	205
Katar	1520–30	100	100	100
	1576	110	131	201
Niksar	1528	100	100	100
	1574	175	153	279
Karakuş	1528	100	100	100
	1574	198	185	288
Felis	1528	100	100	100
	1574	124	134	198

Note: Base = 100. The surveys dating from 1520–30, Başvekalet Arşivi. *Tapu Tahrir*, nos. 79, 444, and 54 are taken as base. Indexes for agricultural production are derived from Tables 5.11–5.14; population indexes are derived from Tables 5.3 and 5.5.

Table 5.10 *Individual crops as a percentage of total production*

Name of administrative district	Approximate date of survey	Wheat	Barley	Leguminous crops and minor cereals	Fruits & vegetables	Cotton	Flax & hemp	Rice
Cincife	1455	45	20.8	—	30.7	—	3.3	—
	1485	42.5	19.6	—	33.6	—	4.2	—
	1520	45.7	29.5	—	19.8	—	4.8	—
	1554	47.2	32.2	0.5	19.3	—	0.7	—
	1574	39.9	25.6	1.2	30.1	—	3.2	—
Venk	1455	65.5	30.7	—	2.6	0.3	0.9	—
	1485	65	25.4	—	9	0.4	0.2	—
	1520	59.7	33.5	—	6.3	0.2	0.2	—
	1554	52.9	35	0.9	9.3	0.2	1.6	—
	1574	52.5	27.1	1.6	15	0.4	3.2	—
Kafirni	1520	60.6	37.2	—	1.8	—	0.25	—
	1554	53.9	37.7	2.3	4.6	—	1.3	—
	1574	60.4	33.4	1	4.2	—	1	—
Yıldız	1455	63.5	36.4	—	—	—	0.1	—
	1485	70.3	29.3	—	—	—	0.4	—
	1520	64.2	34.4	—	0.07	—	1.4	—
	1554	54.9	40.9	3.3	0.6	—	0.5	—
	1574	61.9	34.5	1.8	0.3	—	1.5	—
Çorumlu	1520–30	65.9	31.6	—	2.5	0.08	—	—
	1576	59.9	34	0.9	5	—	0.2	—
Karahisar-ı Demirli	1520–30	66.8	28.5	—	1.2	3.3	—	—
	1576	56	33.7	0.4	5	4.5	0.5	—
Katar	1520–30	65	30.4	—	1.6	2.9	—	—
	1576	57.4	33.6	0.3	3	5.6	—	—

Niksar	1528	49	34.2	0.09	9.3	2.9	1.2	3.2
	1574	48.6	30.8	0.2	14	3.4	1.4	3.7
Karakuş	1528	52.6	36.9	—	7.1	3	0.4	—
	1574	53.5	36.1	1.4	4.8	3.9	0.2	—
Felis	1528	61.1	34.2	—	4.2	0.4	—	—
	1574	56	32.8	0.09	6.2	3.8	0.9	—

Note —: None.

Table 5.11 *Estimates of grain tithe and rates of change 1485–1520*

Name of administrative district	Money valuation per measurement unit: 1485	Money valuation per measurement unit: 1520	Rate of change in money valuation (%)	Total tax in *akçe* 1485	Total tax in *akçe* adjusted to new valuation	Total tax in *akçe* 1520	Rate of change in real tax revenue (%)
Cincife							
Wheat	1 *mud* = 50 *akçe*	1 *mud* = 100 *akçe*	100	7,600	15,200	12,600	−17
Barley	1 *mud* = 40 *akçe*	1 *mud* = 80 *akçe*	100	3,520	7,040	8,133	+15.5
Venk							
Wheat	1 *mud* = 50 *akçe*	1 *mud* = 100 *akçe*	100	18,400	36,800	26,580	−27
Barley	1 *mud* = 40 *akçe*	1 *mud* = 80 *akçe*	100	7,200	14,400	15,038	+4.4
Yıldız							
Wheat	1 *mud* = 50 *akçe*	1 *mud* = 100 *akçe*	100	13,900	27,800	20,625	−26
Barley	1 *mud* = 40 *akçe*	1 *mud* = 80 *akçe*	100	5,840	11,680	11,060	−5.3

Table 5.12 *Estimates of grain tithe and rates of change 1455–85, 1455–1520*

Name of administrative district	Money valuation per measurement unit: 1455	Money valuation per measurement unit: 1485 & 1520	Rate of change in money valuation (%)	Total tax in *akçe* 1455	Total tax in *akçe* adjusted to new valuation	Total tax in *akçe* 1485 & 1520	Rate of change in real tax revenue (%)
Cincife							
Wheat	1 *mud* = 60 *akçe*	1 *mud* = 50 *akçe* (1485)	−16.6	10,440	8,700	7,600 (1485)	−12.6
		1 *mud* = 100 *akçe* (1520)	66	10,440	17,400	12,600 (1520)	−27.6
Barley	1 *mud* = 40 *akçe*	1 *mud* = 40 *akçe* (1485)	0	4,840	4,840	3,520 (1485)	−27
		1 *mud* = 80 *akçe* (1520)	100	4,840	9,680	8,133 (1520)	−16
Venk							
Wheat	1 *mud* = 60 *akçe*	1 *mud* = 50 *akçe* (1485)	−16.6	18,940	15,784	18,400 (1485)	+16.5
		1 *mud* = 100 *akçe* (1520)	66	18,940	31,566	26,580 (1520)	−15.8
Barley	1 *mud* = 40 *akçe*	1 *mud* = 40 *akçe* (1485)	0	8,880	8,880	7,200 (1485)	−19
		1 *mud* = 80 *akçe* (1520)	100	8,880	17,760	15,038 (1520)	−15.3
Yıldız							
Wheat	1 *mud* = 60 *akçe*	1 *mud* = 50 *akçe* (1485)	−16.6	26,320	21,934	13,900 (1485)	−36.6
		1 *mud* = 100 *akçe* (1520)	66	26,320	43,866	20,625 (1520)	−53

Barley	1 *mud* = 40 *akçe*	1 *mud* = 40 *akçe* (1485)	0	15,120	15,120	5,840 (1485)	−61.3
		1 *mud* = 80 *akçe* (1520)	100	15,120	30,240	11,060 (1520)	−63

Table 5.13 *Estimates of grain tithe and rates of change 1554–75*

Name of administrative district	Money valuation per measurement unit: 1554	Money valuation per measurement unit: 1574	Rate of change in money valuation (%)	Total tax in *akçe* 1554	Total tax in *akçe* adjusted to new valuation	Total tax in *akçe* 1574	Rate of change in real tax revenue (%)
Cincife							
Wheat	1 *kile* = 5 *akçe*	1 *kile* = 6 *akçe*	+20	15,141	18,169	23,064	+27
Barley	1 *kile* = 4 *akçe*	1 *kile* = 5 *akçe*	+25	10,345	12,931	14,780	+14.3
Venk							
Wheat	1 *kile* = 5 *akçe*	1 *kile* = 6 *akçe*	+20	31,403	37,683	46,966	+24.6
Barley	1 *kile* = 4 *akçe*	1 *kile* = 5 *akçe*	+25	20,792	25,990	34,233	+31.7
Kafirni							
Wheat	1 *kile* = 5 *akçe*	1 *kile* = 6 *akçe*	+20	65,127	78,152	121,332	+55.2
Barley	1 *kile* = 4 *akçe*	1 *kile* = 5 *akçe*	+25	45,553	56,941	67,015	+17.7
Yıldız							
Wheat	1 *kile* = 5 *akçe*	1 *kile* = 6 *akçe*	+20	24,573	29,487	33,790	+14.6
Barley	1 *kile* = 4 *akçe*	1 *kile* = 5 *akçe*	+25	18,227	22,783	18,787	−17.5

Table 5.14 *Estimates of grain tithe and rates of change 1520, 1554, 1574*

Name of administrative district	Money valuation per measurement unit: 1520–1530	Money valuation per measurement unit: 1554 & 1574–76	Rate of change in money valuation (%)	Total tax in *akçe* 1520	Total tax in *akçe* adjusted to new valuation	Total tax in *akçe* 1554 & 1574	Rate of change in real tax revenue (%)
Cincife							
Wheat	1 *kile* = 5 *akçe* (1520)	1 *kile* = 5 *akçe* (1554)	0	12,600	12,600	15,141	+20
		1 *kile* = 6 *akçe* (1574)	+20	12,600	15,120	23,064	+52.5
Barley	1 *kile* = 4 *akçe* (1520)	1 *kile* = 4 *akçe* (1554)	0	8,133	8,133	10,345	+27
		1 *kile* = 5 *akçe* (1574)	+25	8,133	10,166	14,780	+45
Venk							
Wheat	1 *kile* = 5 *akçe* (1520)	1 *kile* = 5 *akçe* (1554)	0	26,580	26,580	31,403	+18
		1 *kile* = 6 *akçe* (1574)	+20	26,580	31,896	46,966	+47.2
Barley	1 *kile* = 4 *akçe* (1520)	1 *kile* = 4 *akçe* (1554)	0	15,038	15,038	20,792	+38
		1 *kile* = 5 *akçe* (1574)	+25	15,038	18,797	34,233	+82
Kafirni							
Wheat	1 *kile* = 5 *akçe* (1520)	1 *kile* = 5 *akçe* (1554)	0	55,580	55,580	65,127 (1554)	+17
		1 *kile* = 6 *akçe* (1574)	+20	55,580	66,696	121,332 (1574)	+82

Barley	1 *kile* = 4 *akçe* (1520)	1 *kile* = 4 *akçe* (1554)	0	33,492	33,492	45,553 (1554)	+36
		1 *kile* = 5 *akçe* (1574)	+25	33,492	41,865	67,015 (1574)	+60
Yıldız							
Wheat	1 *kile* = 5 *akçe* (1520)	1 *kile* = 5 *akçe* (1554)	0	20,625	20,625	24,573	+19
		1 *kile* = 6 *akçe* (1574)	+20	20,625	24,750	33,790	+36.5
Barley	1 *kile* = 4 *akçe* (1520)	1 *kile* = 4 *akçe* (1554)	0	11,060	11,060	18,227	+65
		1 *kile* = 5 *akçe* (1574)	+25	11,060	13,272	18,787	+41.5
Çorumlu							
Wheat	—	—	—	—	—	—	—
	1 *kile* = 5 *akçe* (*c.* 1520)	1 *kile* = 6 *akçe* (1576)	+20	70,994	85,192	124,917	+46.6
Barley	—	—	—	—	—	—	—
	1 *kile* = 4 *akçe* (*c.* 1520)	1 *kile* = 5 *akçe* (1576)	+25	32,837	41,046	(1554) 71,982	+75.3
Karahisar-ı Demirli							
Wheat	—	—	—	—	—	—	—
	1 *kile* = 5 *akçe* (*c.* 1520)	1 *kile* = 6 *akçe* (1576)	+20	78,627	94,352	99,737	+5.7
Barley	—	—	—	—	—	—	—
	1 *kile* = 4 *akçe* (*c.*1520)	1 *kile* = 5 *akçe* (1576)	+25	32,758	40,947	56,229	+37.3

Table 5.14 (*cont.*)

Name of administrative district	Money valuation per measurement unit: 1520–1530	Money valuation per measurement unit: 1554 & 1574–76	Rate of change in money valuation (%)	Total tax in *akçe* 1520	Total tax in *akçe* adjusted to new valuation	Total tax in *akçe* 1554 & 1574	Rate of change in real tax revenue (%)
Katar							
Wheat	1 *kile* = 5 *akçe* (*c.* 1520)	1 *kile* = 6 *akçe* (1576)	+20	47,333	56,799	62,333	+10.4
Barley	1 *kile* = 4 *akçe* (*c.* 1520)	1 *kile* = 5 *akçe* (1576)	+25	22,152	27,690	36,478	+31.7
Niksar							
Wheat	1 *kile* = 5 *akçe* (1528)	1 *kile* = 6 *akçe* (1574)	+20	69,961	83,953	147,225	+75.3
Barley	1 *kile* = 4 *akçe* (1528)	1 *kile* = 5 *akçe* (1574)	+25	48,771	60,963	93,513	+53.4
Karakuş							
Wheat	1 *kile* = 6 *akçe* (1528)	1 *kile* = 6 *akçe* (1574)	0	16,372	16,372	32,461	+98.2
Barley	1 *kile* = 5 *akçe* (1528)	1 *kile* = 5 *akçe* (1528)	0	11,629	11,629	21,511	+84.9
Felis							
Wheat	1 *kile* = 6 *akçe* (1528)	1 *kile* = 6 *akçe* (1574)	0	24,672	24,672	30,669	+24.3
Barley	1 *kile* = 5 *akçe* (1528)	1 *kile* = 5 *akçe* (1574)	0	13,391	13,391	17,953	+34

Table 5.15 *Taxes levied on animals in Rum*

Name of administrative district	Approximate date of survey	Sheep-tax (in *akçe*)	Number of sheep	Sheep per taxpayer	Dues from beehives (*divani*) (in *akçe*)	Total dues from beehives	Number of beehives
Cincife	1455	400	800	2.2	—	—	—
	1485	1,130	2,260	5.2	280	560	280
	1520	580	1,160	2.4	373	746	373
	1554	1,202	2,404	3	57	114	57
	1574	5,480	10,960	9.8	212	424	212
Venk	1455	120	240	0.5	—	—	—
	1485	865	1,730	2.9	804	1,608	804
	1520	345	690	0.9	865	1,730	865
	1554	1,791	3,582	2.8	1,336	2,672	1,336
	1574	2,968	5,936	3.1	1,536	3,072	1,536
Kafirni	1520	1,633	3,266	2.9	1,446	2,892	1,446
	1554	5,550	11,100	5.2	2,815	5,630	2,815
	1574	10,068	20,136	6.1	2,398	4,796	2,398
Yıldız	1455	340	680	1.6	—	—	—
	1485	1,519	3,038	5.8	284	568	284
	1520	860	1,720	2.9	277	554	277
	1554	1,707	3,414	3.7	222	444	222
	1574	1,526	3,052	2.3	208	416	213
Çorumlu	1520–30	2,859	5,718	2.9	3,002	8,671	4,335
	1576	5,014	10,028	2.8	2,183	4,786	2,393
Karahisar-ı Demirli	1520–30	3,467	6,934	4.2	2,416	5,263	2,631
	1576	3,555	7,110	2	2,006	4,252	2,126

Table 5.15 (*cont.*)

Name of administrative district	Approximate date of survey	Sheep-tax (in *akçe*)	Number of sheep	Sheep per taxpayer	Dues from beehives (*divani*) (in *akçe*)	Total dues from beehives	Number of beehives
Katar	1520–30	4,124	8,248	6.6	710	1,326	663
	1576	7,298	14,596	5.8	640	1,280	640
Niksar	1528	7,452	14,904	6.8	2,955	5,910	2,955
	1574	15,500	31,000	5	2,888	5,776	2,888
Karakuş	1528	1,373	2,746	4.3	203	470	235
	1574	2,848	5,696	3	213	469	234
Felis	1528	610	1,220	1.8	122	595	297
	1574	1,725	3,450	2.5	212	482	241

Note —: None.

Table 5.16 *Commercial and manufacturing taxes in rural areas*

Administrative district	Approximate date	Market dues (*bac pazar*)	Taxes on mills (*asiyab*) and number of millstones[a]	Taxes on dye-houses (*boyahane*)	Toll-tax (*resm-i rah*)	Others
Cincife	1520	—[b]	330 (8 *hacer*)	—	—	—
	1554	—	360 (10 *kıta*)	—	—	—
	1574	—	558 (13 *kıta*)	—	—	4090 Wine-tax (*resm-i şire*)
Venk	1520	—	691 (9 *hacer*)	—	—	—
	1554	—	859 (14 *kıta*)	—	—	—
	1574	—	932 (18 *kıta*)	—	—	—
Kafirni	1520	—	1,772 (28 *hacer*)	2000	—	—
	1554	—	1,843 (29 *kıta*)	2200	1500[c]	—
	1574	—	2,269 (38 *kıta*)	1254	—	—
Yıldız	1520	—	455 (11 *hacer*)	400	1500	430 butter (*revgan*)
	1554	—	427 (10 *kıta*)	400	1500	—
	1574	—	540 (15 *kıta*)	400	—	—
Çorumlu	1520–30	—	3,454 (60 *hacer*)	—	—	—
	1556	—	3,575 (65 *bab*)	—	—	—
Kararisar-ı Demirli	1520–30	—	1,843 (37 *hacer*)	300	—	—
	1576	425[d]	3,124 (59 *bab*)	1000	—	—
Katar	1520–30	—	215 (5 *bab*)	—	—	—
	1576	—	266 (6 *bab*)	—	—	—
Niksar	1528	—	1,776 (53?)[e]	—	—	970 Wine-tax şire (*resm-i şire*)
	1574	—	2,532 (72?)	—	—	—

Table 5.16 (*cont.*)

Administrative district	Approximate date	Market dues (*bac pazar*)	Taxes on mills (*asiyab*) and number of millstones[a]	Taxes on dye-houses (*boyahane*)	Toll-tax (*resm-i rah*)	Others
Karakuş	1528	—	1,647 (37?)	—	—	—
	1574	—	1,763 (42?)	—	—	—
Felis	1528	—	2,445 (21?)[f]	—	—	—
	1574	—	1,371 (26?)	—	—	—

[a] The figures in parenthesis refer to the number of millstones in operation. The terminology of the surveys for millstones vary from one period to the next. The terms used are: *hacer* or stone, *kıta* merely indicating a unit, and *bab* which literally means 'gate'.
[b] —: None.
[c] This figure includes *tamga* or stamp tax. Başvekalet Arşivi, *Tapu Tahrir*, no. 287, p. 160.
[d] *Bac pazar* is included in the total for tithe revenues, sheep tax, mill tax, and personal taxes. The above figure is arrived at by deducting the total amount (12,575 *akçe*) for these taxes from the grand total of 13,000, *Kuyudu, Kadime*, no. 38, p. 228b.
[e] The terminology used for millstones in the surveys for the districts of Niksar, Karakuş, and Felis is varied and it is not always clear whether or not a *kıta* is the equivalent of *hacer* or *bab*.
[f] This figure includes 1,090 *akçes* representing *mukataa* revenues from *asiyab-ı dibek* or millstones. These were not assessed the same way regular taxes on mills were assessed.

Table 5.17 *Wheat and barley production per taxpayer: Rum for selected periods during the sixteenth century*

Name of administrative district	Approximate date of survey	Wheat production per taxpayer (in *akçe*)	Wheat production per taxpayer (in *kile*)	Barley production per taxpayer (in *akçe*)	Barley production per taxpayer (in *kile*)
Cincife	1520	161	26.8	107.3	21.5
	1554	120	20	83.2	16.6
	1574	105.9	17.6	67.7	13.5
Venk	1520	213	35.5	125	25
	1554	149.3	24.8	103.6	20.7
	1574	113	18.8	78.5	15.7
Kafirni	1520	320.6	53.4	204.7	40.9
	1554	186.8	31	135.2	27
	1574	184.8	30.8	103.9	20.8
Yıldız	1520	219.6	36.6	123	24.6
	1554	165	27.5	129.8	25.9
	1574	129.6	21.6	72.9	14.6
Çorumlu	1520–30	194.9	32.5	100.5	20.1
	1576	169.6	28.2	95.4	19
Karahisar-ı Demirli	1520–30	224	37.3	100	20
	1576	116	19.3	71	14.2
Katar	1520–30	231	38.5	113.2	22.6
	1576	125.8	20.9	73.9	14.8
Niksar	1528	196.5	32.7	142.2	28.4
	1574	114.4	19	73.2	14.7
Karakuş	1528	92.9	15.5	64.6	12.9
	1574	66.7	11.2	46.5	9.3
Felis	1528	102.8	17.2	57.8	11.5
	1574	68.8	11.4	40.4	8

Table 5.18 *Indexes for the production of non-cereal crops*

Name of administrative district	Approximate date of survey	Leguminous plants and minor cereals	Fruits & vegetables	Vines	Cotton	Rice	Flax & hemp
Cincife	1455	—	178	244	15	—	34
	1485	—	96	244	—	—	50
	1520	—	100	100	100	—	100
	1554	100	371	55	—	—	24
	1574	327	631	166	—	—	149
Venk	1455	—	28	89	168	—	450
	1485	—	30	519	222	—	88
	1520	—	100	100	100	—	100
	1554	100	219	92	112	—	945
	1574	222	405	258	348	—	2,315
Kafirni	1520	—	100	100	—	—	100
	1554	100	325	—	—	—	651
	1574	52	397	358	—	—	739
Yıldız	1455	—	—	—	—	—	24
	1485	—	—	—	—	—	38
	1520	—	100	—	—	—	100
	1554	100	1,076	—	—	—	49
	1574	53	566	—	—	—	148
Çorumlu	1520–30	—	100	100	100	—	—
	1576	—	423	36	25	—	—
Karahisar-ı Demirli	1520–30	—	100	100	100	—	—
	1576	—	454	1,457	165	—	—
Katar	1520–30	—	100	100	100	—	—
	1576	—	323	167	235	—	—

Niksar	1528	100	100	100	100	100/100[a]	100
	1574	291	311	180	185	142/185	179
Karakuş	1528	—	100	—	100	—	100
	1574	—	109	—	351	—	110
Felis	1528	100	100	—	100	100/	—
	1574	540	174	—	1,156	124/—	—

[a]The first figure refers to the value of total rice yields under share-cropping arrangements; the second to the tithe on rice cultivated in peasant plots.

Note: Base = 100. Surveys dating from 1520–30, Başvekalet Arşivi, *Tapu Tahrir*, nos. 79, 444, and 54 are taken as base. For districts around Tokat, in the event that no taxes were recorded for a given crop in the 1520 survey, 1554 survey (Başvekalet Arşivi, *Tapu Tahrir*, no. 287) is taken as base. Indices presented here are derived from Tables 5.19 and 5.20.

—: None.

Table 5.19 *Percentages of change in real revenues from non-cereal crops*

Name of administrative district	Dates over which changes are recorded	Leguminous plants and minor cereals	Fruits & vegetables	Vines	Cotton	Rice	Flax & hemp
Cincife	1455–85	—	−47.3	−2	—		+4.4
	1485–1520	—	+4	−59	—	—	−33
	1520–54	—	+271	−44.8	—	—	−76
	1554–74	+227.3	+70	+202	—	—	+521
	1520–74	—	+531	+66	—	—	+49
Venk	1455–85	—	+1.7	+470	+20	—	−81
	1485–1520	—	+235	−161.5	−55	—	+13
	1520–54	—	+119	−8	+12	—	+845
	1554–74	+122.4	+85	+180	+211.4	—	+146
	1520–74	—	+305	+158	+248	—	+221
Kafirni	1520–54	—	+225	—	—	—	+551
	1554–74	−48	+22	—	—	—	+13.6
	1520–74	—	+297	+258	—	—	+639
Yıldız	1455–85	—	—	—	—	—	+54.5
	1485–1520	—	—	—	—	—	+160.6
	1520–54	—	+976	—	—	—	−50.5
	1554–74	+46.5	−48	—	—	—	+200.7
	1520–74	—	+466	—	—	—	+48.7
Çorumlu	(1520–30)–1576	—	+323	−64	−74	—	—
Karahisar-ı Demirli	(1520–30)–1576	—	+354	+1,357	+65	—	—
Katar	(1520–30)–1576	—	+223	+67	+135	—	—
Niksar	1528–76	+191.5	+211.5	80.1	+85.3	+42.5/+85[a]	+79.6
Karakuş	1528–76	—	+8.9	—	+251	—	+10
Felis	1528–76	+440	+74.4	—	+1,056	+24	—

[a] The first figure refers to the rate of change in the value of total rice yields under share-cropping arrangements; the second to that of tithe on rice cultivated in peasant plots.

Note —: None.

Table 5.20 *Revenues from non-cereal crops (in akçe)*

Name of administrative district	Approximate date of survey	Leguminous plants and minor cereals	Fruits and vegetables	Vines	Cotton	Flax & hemp	Rice	
							Share-cropping	Tithe
Cincife	1455	—	990	6,150	30	780[a]	—	—
	1485	—	480	5,540	—	750	—	—
	1520	100	998	4,525	359[b]	1,000	—	—
	1554	168	3,704	2,495	—	240	—	—
	1574	671	7,689	9,200	—	1,820	—	—
Venk	1455	—	320	430	90	225	—	—
	1485	—	300[c]	2,260	100	45	—	—
	1520	—	2,009[d]	870	90	102	—	—
	1554	519	4,401[e]	801	101	964	—	—
	1574	1,408	9,935[f]	2,741	383	2,894	—	—
Kafirni	1520	—	1,553	200	—	240	—	—
	1554	3,073	5,046	—	—	1,563	—	—
	1574	1,953	7,518	875	—	2,166	—	—
Yıldız	1455	—	—	—	—	60	—	—
	1485	—	—	—	—	85	—	—
	1520	—	25	—	—	443	—	—
	1554	1,473	269	—	—	219	—	—
	1574	960	170[g]	—	—	803	—	—
Çorumlu	1520–30	—	2,510[h]	138	80	—	—	—
	1576	1,711	12,966[i]	60	25	411	—	—
Karahisar-ı Demirli	1520–30	—	984[j]	114	3,253	—	—	—
	1576	611	5,451[k]	2,026	6,539	766	—	—
Katar	1520–30	—	580	570	2,132	—	—	—
	1576	290	2,286[l]	1,162	6,113	—	—	—

Table 5.20 (*cont.*)

Name of administrative district	Approximate date of survey	Leguminous plants and minor cereals	Fruits and vegetables	Vines	Cotton	Flax & hemp	Rice: Share-cropping	Rice: Tithe
Niksar	1528	134	4,231[m]	10,045[n]	4,160	1,777	135,179	4,492
	1574	475	16,073[o]	22,072	9,402	3,892	235,112	10,152
Karakuş	1528	—	2,189	?[p]	1,033	106	—	—
	1574	823	2,365	470	3,625	117	—	—
Felis	1528	10	1,706	?[q]	160	—	4,840	—
	1574	54	2,975	823[r]	1,850	682	6,000	—

Note: The figures included in this table represent the money equivalent of taxes recorded in various surveys. No adjustments are made to changes in official values therefore the changes in total revenues derived from a given crop from one period to the next do not reflect real changes. Percentages of change in real revenues are given in Table 5.19.

—: None.

[a] This figure includes 600 *akçes* levied on flax and walnuts. In 1485 survey in all but one instance taxes on flax are combined with those on walnuts, on gardens (*bostan*), or on cotton.
[b] This sum includes 300 *akçes* levied on cotton and flax combined
[c] 300 *akçes* are taxes on vines, and fruits combined
[d] 1,082 *akçes* are taxes on vines, fruits, and walnuts combined.
[e] This sum almost exclusively represents taxes on fruits (*meyve*)
[f] 1,800 *akçes* are taxes on vines and fruits combined
[g] Except for 50 *akçes* levied on walnuts this total refers to taxes on gardens (*bostan*). In 1554 survey, except for 60 *akçes* on onions, the total also refers to taxes on gardens.
[h] 613 *akçes* are taxes on vines and fruits combined.
[i] 6,915 *akçes* are vines and fruits combined.
[j] 950 *akçes* are vines and fruits combined.
[k] 976 *akçes* are vines and fruits combined.

[l] 1,208 *akçes* are vines and fruits combined.
[m] 1,161 *akçes* are vines and fruits combined.
[n] 970 *akçes* are taxes on 'grape-juice' (*şire*) and vines.
[o] 4,057 *akçes* are fruits, vines, and garden produce combined.
[p] 1,190 *akçes* are fruits, vines, and garden produce combined.
[q] 640 *akçes* are fruits, vines, garden produce combined.
[r] 1,182 *akçes* are fruits, vines, garden produce combined.

Table 5.21 *Number and types of settlements included in the samples for individual districts in two periods in the sixteenth century: 1520–30 and 1574–6*

Name of administrative district	Total number of settlements identifiable in 1520–30 and 1574–6	Number of villages exluded		Number of *mezraas* included		Number of *mezraas* excluded		Number of *mezraas* that developed into villages	Proportion of *mezraas* to total no. of settlements (%)	
		1520–30	1574–6	1520–30	1574–6	1520–30	1574–6		1520–30	1574–6
Cincife	10	—	1	3	3	—	—	—	30	30
Venk	32	1	—	4	3	—	2	1	12.5	9
Kafirni	78	2	3	9	9	3	—	—	12	12
Yıldız	20	—	1	2	2	—	3	—	10	10
Çorumlu	80	3	9	18	18	1	1	—	20	20
Karahisar-ı Demirli	76	2	6	44	35	13	51	9	58.5	46.5
Katar	40	1	2	5	2	4	6	3	12.5	5
Niksar	105	—	11	30	28	—	4	2	28.5	26.6
Karakuş	22	6	10	—	—	—	3	—	—	—
Felis	28	2	5	4	4	3	5	—	13	13

Note —: None.

6 ❧ The cotton famine and its effects on the Ottoman Empire

ORHAN KURMUŞ

The Cotton Famine

As far as its effects on the Lancashire cotton industry are concerned the cotton famine is considered an almost closed chapter in history. What little is published touches upon the subject only indirectly,[1] a consensus having been reached quite some time ago.

A recapitulation of the main findings of previous studies leads to the conclusion that the term 'cotton famine' is, in fact, a misnomer. For, although the supply of cotton from the southern ports of the USA had ceased because of the Civil War, there were enough stocks of raw material in England, in ports and in mills, to keep the Lancashire cotton industry going for at least seventeen weeks in 1861. Even when the crisis became most acute in Lancashire in 1862, no shortage of cotton existed.[2] The lowest level of stocks was reached in 1863 when there were about 120 million lb of raw cotton at ports and about 18 million lb at mills. These unusually large stocks had been the product of the good harvest in the USA in 1860 which had been hastily shipped to Liverpool in anticipation of war. From the point of view of raw-material stocks the 'cotton famine' was not so much of a catastrophe as were the shortages that occurred in 1846, 1850 and 1857.

Although the American Civil War was not really responsible for the economic and social distress widespread in Lancashire in the early 1860s it was, nevertheless, instrumental in reviving anxiety about the future of an uninterrupted supply of raw cotton. The establishment of the Manchester Cotton Supply Association (MCSA) in 1857 was an early indication of this concern. The main idea behind the formation of the MCSA was that heavy dependence on American supplies was potentially dangerous for the Lancashire cotton industry.

By the early nineteenth century, the USA had largely replaced Brazil and the West Indies as the chief supplier of cotton to the British market. During 1806–10 the average share of US cotton in total British cotton imports was 53.1 per cent

Table 6.1 *British cotton imports from Turkey (lb)*

Years	1725	1755	1775	1785	1787	1789
Quantity	667,279	738,412	2,175,132	2,190,027	3,227,964	4,406,892

Source: British Museum, Add.MSS 38376 *Liverpool Papers*, vol. 187, fos. 55–126.

in terms of quantity. Two decades later it rose to 74.5 per cent, continued to increase during the 1830s and 1840s, finally reaching 81.1 per cent in 1846–50.[3]

It seems that the Lancashire cotton manufacturers paid little attention to this dangerously high ratio of supplies from the USA mainly because they were more interested in developing new markets for their products than in trying to find alternative sources for the supply of their raw material.[4] It was this latter objective that the MCSA had in view when it was formed.

A study of the MCSA's efforts to extend the cultivation of cotton in various countries promises to be a fruitful area of research. Such a study may help to illuminate the hitherto unknown aspects of England's foreign relations. It may also show how these relatively backward countries responded to the demands of the MCSA, and with what results. The following sections constitute an account of what happened in the Ottoman Empire in general, and in western Anatolia in particular, during and after the cotton famine.

Attempts to regenerate Turkey as a supplier of cotton

Among many other countries, the MCSA considered Turkey as a potential source of cotton imports. This consideration was not unfounded because Turkish cotton had been imported into England as far back as 1586 and, as A.C. Wood puts it, 'it was to the cotton wool imported from Cyprus and from Smyrna . . . that the Lancashire cotton industry owed its foundation'.[5] Another observer of the period asserts that until 1780 almost all cotton imported into England came from İzmir.[6] However exaggerated this claim may be, there is some evidence to show that British cotton imports from Turkey were quite large throughout the eighteenth century (see Table 6.1).

In addition to cotton wool Turkey had also supplied England with considerable quantities of cotton yarn. In 1697 England bought 483,136 lb of cotton yarn from Turkey; in 1725, 146,340 lb, and in 1735 about 106,760 lb.

İzmir was the chief exporter of Turkish cotton. During 1785–7 about 95 per cent of Turkish cotton exports originated from İzmir. Also, in 1783–93 İzmir exported about 252,000 bales of cotton wool and about 16,500 bales of cotton yarn to France. That is why the chairman of the MCSA described İzmir as the New Orleans of the eighteenth century.[7]

The beginning of the nineteenth century witnessed a fall in the quantity of cotton imported into England from İzmir. Two factors operating simultaneously were responsible for this fall. First, Turkish cotton was eclipsed by American cotton which was better in quality and cheaper in price. Second, the Levant Company, which had been the main importer of Turkish produce, was prohibited from buying Turkish cotton unless it was exchanged in payment for British goods exported to Turkey.[8] Thus in 1817, the value of raw-cotton imports from Turkey was as low as £799.[9] Cotton prices in Turkey fell considerably and it ceased to be profitable to grow cotton except for local needs.[10]

The earliest indication of the revival of interest in Turkish cotton can be seen in the leading articles of a newspaper published by an Englishman in İstanbul. For two months the newspaper tried to propagate the idea that Turkey had all the requirements for the successful cultivation of cotton and that there was a ready market for cotton in Europe, especially in England, which could absorb practically unlimited quantities.[11]

After the formation of the Asia Minor Cotton Company in 1856,[12] a more systematic approach was adopted by the MCSA in 1857. The Association, through the Foreign Office, sent a questionnaire to all British diplomatic agents in Turkey and asked them to report on the present and potential state of cotton growing in their districts. One of the most promising replies came from İzmir.[13] The British Consul stated in his report that the diminished cultivation of cotton was capable of great extension if the producers were supplied with American seed and practical help. He also pointed out that the present state of camel transportation was pathetic and the newly started İzmir–Aydın railway would be of great importance to the extension of cotton culture. Irrigation was not usually employed because it was generally unnecessary. Even with the very inferior native seed, and a very rude plough which did not open the ground more than three inches, average yield per acre never fell below 500 lb of clean cotton. The processes of cleaning, pressing, and packing were carried out with extremely primitive technology. There was not a single gin in the region. One man, using a hand roller, was capable of turning out a mere 7 lb of clean cotton a day which, in turn, was pressed into bags by foot pressure.

The MCSA found the situation in western Anatolia very promising and decided to start a campaign aimed at the encouragement of cotton production.[14] The first step was to ensure that the producers substituted good-quality American seed for native seed, because in its then state İzmir cotton could only be classed with the inferior Indian cotton. Sixty bags of good seed were shipped from Liverpool and on arrival at İzmir were immediately forwarded to the interior.[15] Although a very large part of the 1858 crop was destroyed by locusts, it was reported that there was an extension of land under cotton, and total production was estimated to be about 330,000 lb. In 1859, the output increased to 7.5 million lb and more American seed was sent to İzmir.[16]

Encouraged by its initial success the Association sent an agent to İzmir to organize and coordinate a more effective movement. In his reports the agent recommended three important measures. He drew attention, first of all, to the fact that under the existing tax system it was unrealistic to expect a considerable increase in the output of cotton. The tithe on cotton should be abolished altogether.[17] or a method should be initiated under which cotton growers would be exempt from taxation in alternating years,[18] or the Turkish government should be persuaded to abolish the tithe on cotton in exchange for higher duties on cotton manufactures imported from England.[19] Secondly, if cotton growing in Turkey was expected to develop on a scale commensurate with the urgency of the wants of England, 'demand . . . must be backed by money invested in creating the required supply'.[20] So, the MCSA had to send competent instructors to teach the practical aspects of cotton culture, American seed had to be furnished in abundance without delay, and publications of the MCSA extensively distributed. Thirdly, the beneficial effects of the İzmir–Aydın railway on the revival of cotton cultivation were emphasized. The early completion of the line would reduce transport rates considerably, and merchants would be able to establish an efficient network of trade and communication. Also the improved machinery necessary for the cultivation and cleaning of cotton would be conveyed to the interior more easily. Therefore, the report went on, the railway should be encouraged and supported by all possible means. A vigorous support, a strong pull, was all that was needed to finish the line. This strong pull was to take the form of more Lancashire names and capital in the company.[21]

In İstanbul an equally interesting development was taking place. The British-owned newspaper *Ceride-i Havadis* rigorously continued its campaign which was as diversified in its form as its content. Starting with the imminent danger of a civil war in the USA,[22] it went on to explain how profitable it was to grow cotton,[23] then gave free advice to the Turkish government on the methods and forms of support to be given to cotton producers,[24] and finally taught the producers the modern methods of cotton growing and ways of fighting cotton diseases.[25]

The İzmir–Aydın railway company was also doing its share to promote cotton culture. A delegation, comprising of some İzmir merchants and officials of the company, set off for İstanbul and explained to the government how beneficial it would be if the government, alongside its encouragement of cotton production, gave special assistance to the railway.[26] The company also played an active role in the formation of an association at İzmir aimed at the dissemination of information about cotton.[27] The directors of the company published a report on the two-sided relationship between cotton and the railway, stating that the support given to cotton was futile unless the same encouragement was extended to the railway.[28] The secretary of the company 'did all in his power to make the issue known in Manchester and elsewhere by the circulation of reports, and by correspondence with several Chambers of Commerce'.[29]

Gradually, these efforts bore fruit and in late 1862 an Imperial Command granted the following privileges to cotton growers:[30]

(i) Any piece of crown wasteland could be taken gratis for the purpose of cotton cultivation.
(ii) Such land would be exempt from taxation for five years.
(iii) All kinds of cotton would pay the same export duty, which was fixed on the basis of lowest-quality cotton.
(iv) Tools and machinery to be used in cotton growing and cleaning would be exempt from import duty.
(v) The government would distribute free cotton seed, and provide free instruction and literature.

In April 1863 the government distributed nearly 295 tons of seed in Anatolia.[31] In May, in İzmir, 311,715 lb of seed were given away to prospective producers.[32] (In 1862 it had been only 47,040 lb.)[33] The first part of the MCSA campaign, the substitution of American seed for native seed, was apparently successful. However, reports by the agents of the Association produced serious doubts about the credibility of the intentions of the Turkish government to encourage cotton growing. It was alleged that the abolition of tithes and other exemptions had not in fact taken place but existed only on paper.[34] The Association, after investigating the allegations and having found that their intelligence was correct, acted immediately and passed resolutions to the effect that the Turkish government should stick to its promises and carry out the announced measures.[35] The reaction of the Turkish government was very harsh. If the Association, it was said, did not want to damage its reputation, it should stop making 'extravagant and preposterous demands'.[36] Having apparently failed to fulfil its promises, the Turkish government later resorted to the use of ineffectual incentives in the form of silver and gold medals to producers who met certain production requirements.[37]

In England, Lancashire cotton brokers formed three companies all of which had 'the purpose of encouraging the growth of cotton in Asia Minor'. The Asia Minor Company, the largest of the three with a capital of £500,000, sent three of its directors to İzmir to investigate the possibility of increasing western Anatolia's cotton output.[38] The other two companies, the Ottoman Cotton Company and the Asia Minor Company, arranged practical courses on modern methods of cotton growing and especially on the extra care that had to be given to the fragile American cotton.[39]

Results

Total cotton output in 1861 was estimated to be about 9.7 million lb, and the British Consul in İzmir predicted that more land would be brought under cultivation in the following year.[40] Subsequent reports showed that the total area under cotton had increased four times in 1862 compared with 1861.[41] Near Aydın, while in 1862 there were 4,500 acres under cotton, in 1863 some 13,000 more acres were brought under cultivation. A farmer, near Nazilli, boasted of growing cotton on 4,400 acres. The environs of Torbalı, where the railway was passing, had set aside 3,800 acres in 1862, which increased to 8,700 acres in 1863. At Bayındır, 1,050 acres had originally been devoted to cotton in 1862, another 1,850 acres were added in the following year.[42] Even in Denizli, where the railway was to be extended in the future, land under cotton increased by 1,600 acres in 1863.[43]

Towards the end of 1863 it became clear that the total output of cotton within the İzmir Consular District was not less than 45,000 bales, an equivalent of 31.5 million lb of clean cotton.[44] The high price of cotton persisted in 1864 and it was expected that Turkey would produce and supply England with larger quantities.

In June 1864 the Foreign Office decided to conduct a large-scale survey of cotton culture in Turkey. A questionnaire was prepared and sent to all British consular representatives in the Ottoman Empire.[45] In their reports the British consuls answered twenty-five questions on various aspects of cotton growing in their districts. It is reasonable to assume that these reports cannot possibly reflect the true conditions prevailing in these areas in so far as statistical facts are concerned, simply because reliable statistical information was not available to the consuls. Hence, all quantitative 'facts' in these reports cannot but be regarded as 'guesstimates' by the consuls. However, they are quite useful in establishing orders of magnitude and used here only in this context.

A review of the consuls' replies to the Foreign Office circular reveals that there had been a considerable increase in the area of land under cotton in 1864. The reports show that, while in 1863 cotton was planted in about 480,000 acres in seventeen districts, in 1864 the total area under cotton reached 1,145,000 acres, an increase of almost 140 per cent. Similarly, the quantity of American and Egyptian seed planted increased from 996,200 lb in 1863 to 4,421,000 lb in 1864.

The largest expansion took place in the Adana–Maraş–Aleppo district, from 310,000 to 745,000 acres. It was reported that producers of sesame seed and rice stopped growing these crops and devoted all their land to cotton. This expansion, however, was not in the direction desired by the MCSA because there was no substitution of American or Egyptian seed for native seed.[46]

In Macedonia, on the other hand, not only was there an extension of cotton culture (from 50,000 acres to 140,000 acres in 1864) but also the use of American seed increased from 800,000 lb to 4,000,000 lb. It seems that Macedonia's progress owed much to Akif Paşa, governor of Salonica, who took stringent measures for the importation and the distribution of American seed as well as the protection of the crop.[47]

The consuls' reports are unanimous in agreeing that the increased production of cotton was financed chiefly by local merchants and brokers. The methods of finance differed from one region to another but three main forms could be discerned:

(i) A fixed share of the output, from 50 to 75 per cent, was taken by the merchant in return for his defrayment of the entire costs of production. (This method was very widespread in Mosul, Jaffa, Adana, Maraş, and Bursa.)

(ii) Money was lent to producers at rates of interest from 33 to 50 per cent a year. Land, agricultural implements, and oxen were usually shown as collateral and seized by the lender in case of default. (Practised in parts of Palestine and İzmir.)

(iii) Advance buying of the entire crop at a price determined in the sowing season. (Although considered illegal under Ottoman law, this method of finance was widely used in European Turkey.)

In western Anatolia the expansion of cotton production (from 29,000 to 53,750 acres) was not as spectacular as it was in Macedonia or in southern Turkey but it displayed a determined effort towards increasing the use of American seed. As should be expected, the overwhelming majority of plots newly brought under cotton were in the immediate neighbourhood of the İzmir–Aydın railway.[48] Furthermore, producers were reported to have discovered that the lands best suited to the growth of cotton had until then been used for grain. When they started sowing cotton instead of grain, fears were expressed about the possibility of a deficient grain harvest.[49] During 1865 cotton production suffered a temporary setback because of the hard state of the ground in the spring. It was reported that the quantity of seed sown in 1865 was at least 25 per cent less than in 1864.[50]

The low level of technology in cotton cleaning and pressing had always been a great hindrance in the past. Exporters' requirements were that cotton should be free of seeds and any exogenous material, and that the bales should be pressed and packed properly.[51] 'Some of the more intelligent and wealthy merchants gave their full attention' to this fact and, starting from 1862, set up small factories for cleaning and preparing the raw product for exportation.[52]

One of them even claimed to have invented a revolutionary mechanism with the use of which twenty gins could be attended by a single person, enabling the factory to increase its output by 28 per cent, a saving of £50 a day.[53] By the late

Table 6.2 *Cotton exports from İzmir*

Years	Quantity of cotton exports (bales)	Value of cotton exports (£)	Value of total exports (£)
1863	33,720	1,674,536	4,832,979
1864	35,615	1,267,920	4,046,338
1865	37,918	2,076,086	3,842,285
1866	34,262	521,600	3,606,240

Source: Quantity data from C.D. Scherzer, *La province de Smyrne* (Vienne, A. Hölder, 1873); last two columns from PRO, FO 78/3070; PRO, FO 83/395; 'Statistical tables relating to foreign countries, pt ix', *Accounts and Papers* (1864), vol. 60, p. 325.

1860s there were thirty-four factories, all in railway towns, employing more than seven hundred gins.[54]

Table 6.2 gives the quantity and value of cotton exports from İzmir. There is a general lack of data showing the share of exports to England in total cotton exports from İzmir. The only available figure indicates that in 1864 England imported £866,952 worth of cotton from İzmir, which was approximately 68 per cent of the total value of İzmir cotton exports.[55]

The Turkish cotton boom ended in 1865 with the conclusion of peace in the United States. The price of cleaned cotton decreased from about 19s per lb in 1864 to 12s 3d in 1865, and it was as low as 9s 3d in 1867.

It is quite difficult to pass a judgement on whether the efforts of the MCSA were successful in reviving cotton culture in Turkey. This will involve a comparison of the results obtained in various countries where similar measures were introduced. The Association itself was not completely satisfied with Turkey's performance. It was observed that 'the Ottoman Empire has not made much progress as a cotton growing country as there seemed reason to anticipate'.[56] The blame was put on the Turkish government because it had failed to fulfil its promises. In Turkey another culprit was found: peasants. It was claimed that they, despite the warnings of instructors sent by the government, tilled the land exactly the way they tilled it for wheat or barley and did not plant the seeds until June, whereas they should have planted them in early April.[57]

Another line of explanation ran in terms of the psychological attitude of farmers. A contemporary writer asserted that 'The majority of peasants regarded these measures as another means of government deception. "We cannot afford to accept these favours", they said, "because in the end the government will come up with something which will make us regret what we have done".'[58] The British consul in Jaffa reported in the same vein. According to him, producers in his district were very distrustful of the government's promotion activities because they thought that these activities were designed to increase the tithes on agricultural production.[59]

The extent to which the aspirations of the MCSA were fulfilled is not of chief interest here. What is more important is the issue of what the re-introduction of cotton precipitated as far as the economic development of western Anatolia is concerned. First of all, it meant a large-scale transition to a cash-crop economy. It was true that the İzmir region had already been more commercialized than many areas, with the possible exception of İstanbul. The efforts to revive cotton culture and the consequent expansion in the volume of trade led to the organization of commerce on such a scale that the İzmir region by far surpassed the rest of the Empire with its highly sophisticated and technical handling of commercial affairs.

The transportation and warehousing of cotton was a hazardous affair as the bales were very prone to catch fire. The merchants had long been yearning to see an insurance company in İzmir. In 1863, the London Sun Insurance Company opened an agency in the city, the first of its kind in Turkey. Although the rates were considered very high, almost all warehouses were insured against fire.[60] Two banks, the Imperial Ottoman Bank and the Ottoman Financial Association, were established in 1864.[61] The former immediately opened branches in the interior and specialized in long-term loans, especially to small farmers. The Ottoman Financial Association, on the other hand, limited its activities to İzmir and its immediate vicinity, specializing in financing merchants who required short-term loans in their business routine.[62] The operation of the banks was widely acclaimed, especially by foreign merchants who had been threatened with being shut out from the interior trade as a result of the activities of wealthy natives who started purchasing the produce from growers beforehand and selling it to the merchants at great profit.[63] The banks enabled foreign merchants to borrow at relatively low rates of interest and compete against native speculators. They also helped small producers by partially freeing them from the usurers.

The increased volume of trade necessitated a new type of local administration in western Anatolia. New and more sophisticated services had to be offered to the inhabitants; more stringent measures had to be taken to secure the regularity of trade; and relations between merchants were to be based on a more controlled and sounder basis. In as far back as 1860 the government was petitioned by a number of İzmir merchants 'who were most anxiously desirous that the Porte should grant permission for a municipality in Smyrna'.[64] In fact, there was already a municipal organization in the city. What the petitioners wanted was one exactly the same as the municipality of İstanbul.[65] Behind this move was the desire for representation in municipal and other councils, and thus to gain a fair amount of control in the administration of the city, especially in the regulation of trade. From 1864 onwards, when the municipality was reorganized on the same footing as in İstanbul, the British merchants continually asked the government for more powers in the running of the province.[66]

The opening of underwater telegraph communication with Europe, and overland with the rest of the Empire; the enlargement of the existing and the opening of new commercial courts; the establishment of the English daily *Smyrna Mail*, 'advocating the commercial interests of the city', the building of a new and modern quay at the harbour must also be mentioned as examples of different kinds of development which were taking place.

All these were indications that İzmir was undergoing a tremendous transformation compared with the rest of the Empire. It would be misleading to attribute all these developments to the efforts of Lancashire cotton manufacturers and merchants. After all, western Anatolia was not the only region where such measures were introduced, but no other region exhibited the progress recorded by İzmir.

The main impact of the İzmir–Aydın railway was that many towns, which had previously been unable to send their produce to İzmir because of high camel rates, came into contact with the main market. As 'production for the market' became the principal target, cash crops were substituted for traditional ones. Existing land-use patterns started to change under pressure from the market. Distribution of land between different uses changed considerably and existing boundaries of cultivation expanded. To sum up, a forceful movement started towards an expanded and integrated regional market.

Without the joint efforts of the Turkish government and Lancashire cotton manufacturers to revive cotton culture, these developments could have taken place but at a slower pace. Cotton played the role of an active catalyst accelerating the ongoing process. In other words, the American Civil War and its effects in the world markets represented a strong push in the direction of commercial expansion and accelerated development in western Anatolia.

Whether the Turkish cotton boom was the beginning of or only a stage in the integration of the Ottoman economy with the capitalist world is a subject for further debate. What is beyond doubt is that it was instrumental in linking the fortunes of large masses of peasant producers in Anatolia to the vagaries of market conditions in capitalist countries.

7 The Middle Danube *cul-de-sac*

BRUCE McGOWAN

We are accustomed to thinking of the Danube as a great natural waterway, which is what it has become in the twentieth century after numerous improvements at its mouth and at various places along the mainstream and on its tributaries. But before these improvements were made the whole middle course of the Danube west of the Iron Gate (Đerdap, near Orsova in today's Rumania) was more a barrier than a boatway. Merchants from the Ottoman side ('Greeks' as they were called by their contemporaries) crossed the river to carry on a sporadic north–south trade in the seventeenth century, then a trade which became a steady stream in the eighteenth century, owing especially to the Central European appetite for Macedonian cotton.

However, this trade crossed the great river from south to north and did not depend much upon transport along its course. For the banks of the Danube were marshy and undrained and offered treacherous footing to bargemen and barge horses until great investments of labour were made, above all during the early decades of the nineteenth century. At the Iron Gate rowers were able to pass only when the water was right for them. But the passage was problematic at the best of times and impossible for boats over a certain size. At the southwestern end of the Danubian basin the narrow Kupa, a tributary of the Sava and of the Danube, also forced commerce into a trickle.

During the later Ottoman centuries, and until access to the Hungarian plain was forced open by railroads, the Middle Danube can be seen as a kind of backwater, or *cul-de-sac*. Until then the potential for trading the surpluses of the region via the Black Sea and via the Adriatic was quite disappointing. The Ottoman authorities knew this well since they drew the grain supply for their capital city from the shores below the Iron Gate, whereas above the Iron Gate the Danube was used only for purposes which transcended trade – for military movements and for communications. The great agricultural potential of the Hungarian plain was only partially tapped even after the coming of railroads, since by that time the grain of Odessa had won the day. Therefore, although the transformation accomplished by steam in the nineteenth century put an end to

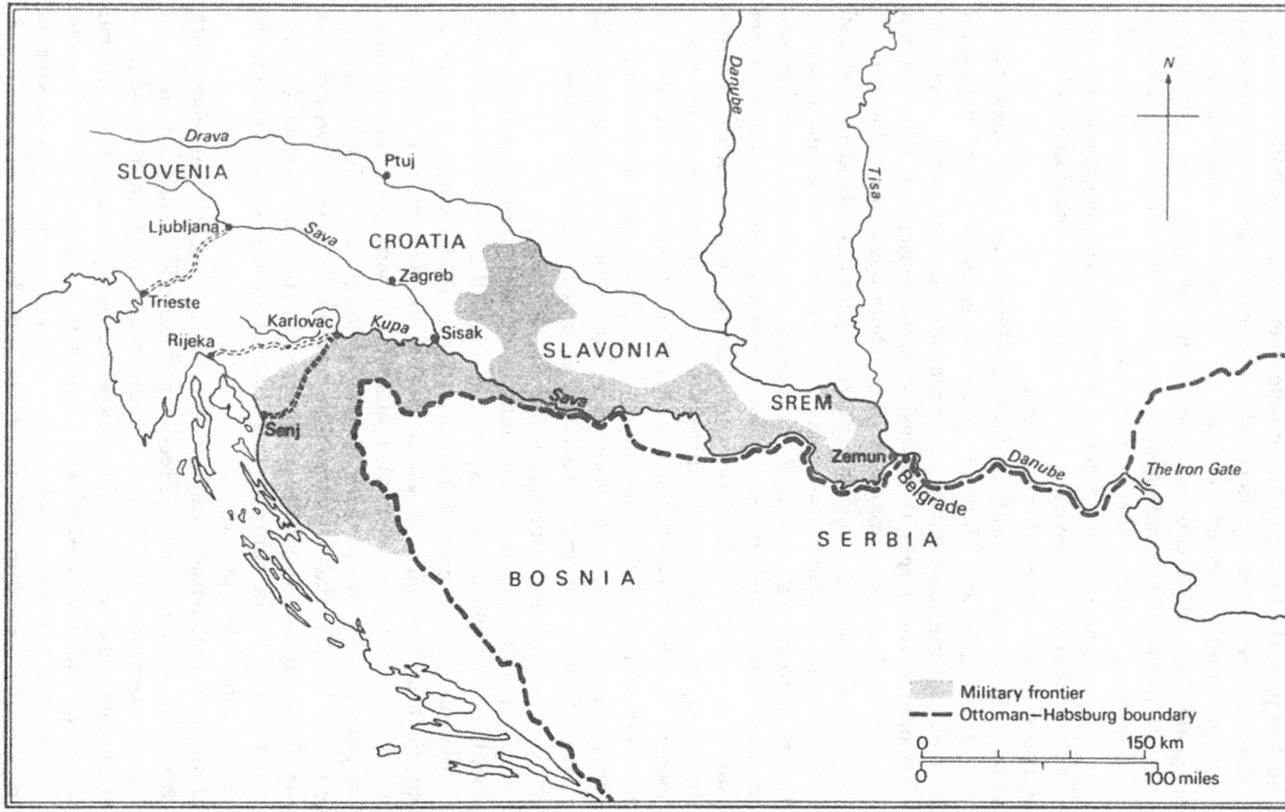

Map 7.1 The Middle Danube in the eighteenth century
Source: Igor Karaman, *Privreda i Drŭstvo hrvàtske u 19. stoljecá* (Zagreb, 1972), p. 42.

the landlocked past, the timing of that development was not wholly fortunate.

Until the steam revolution, patterns of land use throughout the Danubian basin were profoundly affected not only by the natural environment, by technology, and by social structures, as would always be the case, but also by relatively poor prospects for trading surpluses via water routes. The affected areas include those north of the Danube which were reconquered by the Habsburg house in the war which ended at Karlowitz (1699), and also the southern side of the Danube–Sava line, which remained in Ottoman hands until the foundation of the modern Serbian state.

Slovenia, at the far west of the affected belt, evolved in a manner distinct from that of neighbouring Croatia. During the sixteenth, seventeenth and eighteenth centuries the long-term economic trends in the Slovenian provinces include the appearance of numerous forges, the diversification of agriculture in a direction away from monoculture, and a parcellization of holdings associated with both. From the beginning of the sixteenth century, superior landholders used and abused their judicial powers to make allodium from the forests and meadows formerly used as commons.[1] Taking Roman law as the precedent, services and taxes on peasant small-holders and cottars were increased, bringing them further under the control of the privileged stratum. At many locations forges were established, which also brought increasing pressure on the use of the forests. Forge owners also led a campaign, parallel to that of the landholders, in bringing cottars and smallholders into dependent relationships. The products of these forges – agricultural tools, wire, nails, etc. – formed a major part of Austrian exports to the Ottoman provinces[2] accompanied by the perennially desirable Austrian coinage, especialy *thalers*.

But, despite relationships between landholders and peasants which could have provided labour for allodial exports, no marked trend of this kind took place. Viticulture, in support of local and regional consumption patterns, absorbed much of the available labour dues. And, even though there were imperial patents (1767, 1768) which aimed at dividing up all common meadows, pastures, and forests, many common pastures still survived undivided into the 1820s.[3] This is a fact which runs counter to the example provided by Rumania of that day, and which can be taken as evidence that an easy outlet for agricultural products (in contrast to industrial products) was lacking in Slovenia throughout this period.

Agrarian trends in Croatia during the sixteenth, seventeenth, and eighteenth centuries were in the same general direction as those in Slovenia but went much further, to the extent that Civil Croatia (governed separately from the Military Frontier District) can be said to have experienced a version of the 'second serfdom', or 'refeudalization' which was common to so much of Eastern Europe in this period. The key features of this development were the limitations on resettlement which were imposed on the peasantry between 1514 and 1538, followed by the progressive introduction of the *tlaka*, an annual debt of service, incumbent first upon the village as a collectivity, then upon the peasant as an individual.[4]

In Croatia, as in Slovenia, noble privileges were used to turn each stage to the advantage of the landholding stratum. During the inflation of the late sixteenth century, cash tithes were replaced by tithes in kind. The landholding class used its privileges to extend its own access to town markets and to fairs in order to sell the tithed products and correspondingly to restrict the access of peasants and townsmen alike.[5] Landholders also enjoyed the right of first purchase of all peasant products, inevitably at confiscatory prices.[6]

In the seventeenth century, the sale of tithes was deemed insufficient as a means of exploiting the market privileges of the landowning class. Hence tithes in kind began to give way to the onerous *tlaka*, which by the end of that century overshadowed tithes in importance. By clearing land and by usurping land formerly used either by peasant households or as village commons, superior landholders gradually assembled large allodial plots of their own, a common feature of the second serfdom. The ratio of allodium to rusticum was in Croatia between 1:3 and 1:5, a ratio typical of East European *Gutsherrschaft* agriculture.[7] The eighteenth century saw a progressive intensification of the *tlaka* labour due as the basis for allodial agriculture.[8]

Yet trade directed towards distant markets was not the aim of Croatian allodial agriculture. Over half the value of allodial surpluses was in wine and most wine was sold in the domestic markets.[9] Until the dissolution of the traditional bonds of peasant dependence in 1848–9 and the subsequent penetration of the railroads, Croatian agriculture was largely landlocked and regional in character.

Srem and Slavonia, to the north of the Military Frontier District, which in turn abutted Ottoman territory across the Sava, were provinces reconquered by the Habsburgs in the great war which freed Hungary from Ottoman rule (1683–99). Because the estates into which these new provinces were divided were huge, the population sparse, and the land abundant, it was not until half a century had gone by, during which period the two provinces were under military rule, that the despised labour due (*tlaka*) was introduced as a peasant burden. In 1755 the Commission under Graf Serbolini noted that allodial holdings in the Slavonian Virovitica district were scarcely organized, and that money rents prevailed.[10] But the *urbar* (land tax register) of 1756, reflecting the views of the landholding stratum, introduced annual labour service as the norm for Slavonia. The peasants of Srem, being even closer to the competing regimes of the Military Frontier District and to the Ottoman territories across the Sava, were allowed to buy exemption from the *tlaka*, though they continued to work on allodial properties for pay.[11]

It was these newer provinces which were best placed to trade grain outside the

Habsburg domains. The Ottoman garrisons at Belgrade, Smedrevo and Šabac were frequently, perhaps regularly, supplied by grain from across the Sava down to the time of the first Serbian uprising in 1804.[12] In return Serbia sent pigs which were fattened north of the Sava before being herded west and north to feed Vienna and the garrisons of Bohemia and Moravia.[13] This symbiosis reflects the scantiness of population in Serbia relative to the size of its garrisons in the decades following the Treaty of Belgrade (1739) which returned northern Serbia to Ottoman rule. It also infers grain surpluses available north of the Sava for the purpose of fattening pigs.

Maps and figures supplied by Benda show that the trade in grain from Srem and Slavonia did not exceed local importance. In common with southern Hungary, these provinces shipped grain surpluses to Vienna only when harvests were very poor. Otherwise the river road was too long and too dangerous. Vienna was supplied in normal years by the northwest Hungarian counties around Györ, Sopron, Moson, and Pozsony.[14] Italy, likewise, received grain from the Croatian and Hungarian Banats only when poor harvests there raised prices to extraordinary levels. Therefore, although allodial agriculture, supported by the *tlaka*, was a prominent feature of the Slavonian economy in the late eighteenth and early nineteenth centuries, demand conditions were seldom such as to tempt the landholder to great efforts. The grain exports of Hungary/Croatia were only marginally larger in the 1840s than they had been in the 1770s.[15] One author says of conditions on the latifundia of Srem and Slavonia that even in 1848 their owners 'lived solely from feudal incomes, [were] not occupied with economic affairs, and [paid] no attention to the progress of agriculture . . .'[16]

A first step towards breaking through the western barrier to the sea was taken in 1717 when Charles VI, in the aftermath of Venetian defeats, proclaimed Trieste and Rijeka as free ports, and the Adriatic a free navigation zone. In the following year the Treaty of Passarowitz freed the Sava also for navigation.[17] But decrees and treaties left the physical barriers unchanged. A first attempt to change the physical facts was begun in 1723 when a newly enfranchised imperial trading company began work on a road from Karlovac to Rijeka (the Carolinian) with the help of peasant labour. The company's mandate, in keeping with the mercantilist outlook of that time, was to seek an outlet for the surpluses of the Danube–Sava basin.

But the Kupa River, which fed the Carolinian, was not a generous river. Cargoes which reached Sisak, at the juncture between the Sava and the Kupa, had to be reshipped up the Kupa to Karlovac on boats of only a tenth the size of those which could ply the Sava. From Karlovac onward goods had to be reloaded onto pack horses for the trip to Rijeka.[18] This made the route so expensive as to be of limited use in normal times, at least for the shipment of bulky goods such as grain.

When in the disturbed war years of 1768–74 a first opportunity arose to exploit higher grain prices, a need was felt to improve the road by adapting it for wagon traffic (1771). When in 1776 Rijeka was rejoined to the Hungarian crown, the Hungarian–Croatian nobility began to take a more active role in trade, with the result that Joseph II opened a second road, passing from the Karlovac junction to Senj on the coast, completed in 1779. The desolate, heavily wooded middle section of the Carolinian road remained a problem for wagoners, so that in 1811 a new road to Rijeka was opened from Karlovac, the same route which is today followed by the Zagreb–Rijeka highway. The opening of this new road doubtless owed a great deal to the second episode of higher grain prices (1805–9) occasioned by the disturbances of the Napoleonic period. But except for periods of extraordinary prices the expenses incurred by shipping bulky goods overland were prohibitive.

A way out of the dilemma was at one time sought through a project to canalize the Kupa River and to bring boats along it as far as the vicinity of Rijeka.[19] But this project failed, after enormous expenditure (1807) and has never since been resumed. The relative expensiveness of the Karlovac–Rijeka route is reflected in the fact that the inner provinces of Hungary persisted, until the coming of the railroads, in shipping what they could via Ptuj to Trieste, a route which also had long overland stretches and which was also expensive.[20]

At the eastern end of the middle Danube zone the Iron Gate section of the Danube formed an almost absolute barrier to bulk trade until the middle of the nineteenth century. Much river trading had taken place in Hungary during the first decades of the nineteenth century. Hungarian grain needed an outlet and much faith was placed in steamboats as a means of reaching markets. But here are the words of Count Stephen Szechenyi, a man who backed and encouraged the Hungarian effort to improve river navigation, speaking in 1834:

> From Moldova to Skele Gladova [two miles below Orsova], a distance of about 14 miles, the Danube is not navigable; both passengers and goods have to be forwarded by rowing boats . . .
>
> What articles have we got to export? Wood, grain, wine, etc.? These are cheaper on the lower Danube than here. But someone may say that we have got iron, glass, cloth and such like. To them I reply that we do not produce large quantities of these articles, but the wide-awake Englishman is already to be seen at the mouth of the Danube disposing of such wares.
>
> Neither the Wallachians nor we have ever done any trade worth mentioning from Semlin [Zemun] downwards; the whole trade is exclusively in the hands of the Turks . . . The Iron Gates were to them not an obstacle, but a strong defense of their national existence.

And in 1835: 'We see that the Danube between Pressburg and the Black Sea is of no commercial importance to Hungary in view of the fact that trading ships draw at least 5 feet (of water).'[21]

Improvements of the Iron Gates at Đerdap were, in fact, accomplished in the period 1848–9 by the Austrian Danube Steam Navigation Company in return for a franchise allowing the Company an exclusive right to trade on the Austrian and Hungarian Danube until 1880.[22] The mid-century improvement let pass boats of 150 tons. Towards the end of the century (1890–6) improvements were made which would allow boats of up to 650 tons to pass through a 2½ km canal around the worst part of the straits.[23]

However, by the 1830s the cheaper grain of the Russians was bypassing the mouth of the Danube. Its presence was important even in the Adriatic ports.[24] Therefore when railroad lines were opened to Trieste and Rijeka soon after mid century it was not grain which was the major bulk export, but timber. The coming of the railroads in the mid-Danubian basin had opened an era of timber cutting and land clearing throughout the Danube–Sava basin.[25]

Until the coming of the railroads in the latter half of the nineteenth century, the eastern and western ends of the mid-Danubian basin were plugged as though by pincers. The Ottomans deliberately closed the Black Sea straits as a matter of policy. Here was a second inland backwater which was closed by nature.

The effects of this enclosure upon the landholders of Slovenia, Croatia, Slavonia and Srem are fairly apparent. They satisfied themselves with a slack allodial agriculture based to a large extent on wine, much of it sold in west Croatian markets, and until 1848 were content to draw upon the unpaid and inefficient labour of their peasantry while making little effort to be more efficient.[26]

The effect of the enclosure on the Ottoman side of the Sava–Danube line is a little more problematic. The bottling up of grain surpluses probably encouraged trade in pigs and other livestock, which persisted throughout the nineteenth century. Yet the lack of incentive for a grain trade on the rivers must have had a dampening effect on Serbian agriculture also, just as it had to the north.

About the presence of great numbers of '*chiftliks*' and '*chiftlik* holders' in eighteenth-century Serbia there is no doubt. By 1748, only a decade after the return of the Ottoman garrisons in northern Serbia, the Belgrade *divan* was forced to recognize the growing *chiftlik* problem and its pernicious connection with the problem of collecting taxes. In 1759, 1775, and 1792 the *sipahi*s of Serbia obtained decrees from the Porte forbidding the formation of *chiftlik* villages by Janissary *ağas* and their ruffians.[27] But what was the nature of these Serbian *chiftlik*s of the eighteenth century?

Our knowledge of the economic and transport conditions prevailing on the middle Danube in that period supports the doubt, lacking other evidence, that these were *chiftlik*s of the late Macedonian type, established to carry on commercial agriculture, in spite of Vuk Karadžic's statement that tenants on *ağa chiftlik*s performed services for the *chiftlik* holder.[28] It is hard to see where Janissary *chiftlik* holders could have sold surpluses profitably and regularly since the Janissaries themselves controlled the garrison markets. Far more probably, most Janissary *chiftlik*s had little connection with commercial agriculture organized for the market, and were in fact merely devices for skimming revenues which rightly belonged to the central government.

There is now reason to believe that revenue skimming was in fact the common mode and *raison d'être* of the so-called *chiftlik*s of the Balkans in the seventeenth and eighteenth centuries. A recent study by the writer shows, on the basis of evidence taken from Ottoman provincial registers, that the typical '*chiftlik*' of those centuries was small indeed, and that commercial agriculture resembling the later Macedonian type was in the eighteenth century narrowly restricted within a few southerly zones.[29]

One obvious premise, i.e., that peasant disabilities of the 'second-serfdom' type coexisted, in all the areas just discussed, with a slack or even slight allodial agriculture, may disturb those who would place such disabilities in lockstep with the development of commercial, especially export-oriented agriculture. There is no contradiction here. Disabilities such as the *tlaka*, on the Habsburg side of the border, or usurpation of tenures and restrictions on movement, on the Ottoman side, reflect above all the political power of one class over another. The advantages possessed by a landholding or land-usurping class *can* be made to serve commercial agriculture if such opportunities exist. But these advantages may also be seized, maintained and strengthened in the absence of compelling market opportunities, providing only that the power of one rural class over another goes largely unchecked, as happened in most of Eastern Europe in the early modern period and progressively in much of Ottoman Europe only slightly later.

8 Commodity production for world-markets and relations of production in Ottoman agriculture, 1840–1913

ŞEVKET PAMUK

During the three quarters of a century preceding World War I, Ottoman foreign trade, most of which was with industrialized Europe, expanded at unprecedented rates. In the second half of the nineteenth century, especially after 1880, substantial amounts of European capital were invested in railroads and in other forms of infrastructure in the Ottoman Empire, further contributing to the expansion of that trade. These changes in the sphere of circulation had far-reaching effects on the sphere of production. Some branches of handicrafts-based manufacturing activity began to decline under the competition of industrial imports. Patterns of production in the Ottoman economy began to shift towards agricultural commodity production for world-markets.

This study deals with some aspects of the latter process. Most importantly, it will examine the relations of production in Ottoman agriculture, particularly the patterns of landownership and tenancy, and their evolution during a period of rapid expansion in commodity production. It will be limited to the 'core' areas of the Empire, Northern Greece, Thrace and Anatolia.[1] In the first section below, we examine the extent and long-term rhythms of the expansion of agricultural commodity exports from the Ottoman Empire during the nineteenth century and assess the relative importance of domestic urban and European markets in the commercialization of Ottoman agriculture. The second and third sections discuss some critical features of Ottoman agriculture and present an aggregate picture for landownership and tenancy patterns in the Asiatic provinces during the mid century. Section 4 analyses the impact of the penetration of capitalism and the expansion of commodity production on patterns of landownership and tenancy and, more generally, on mechanisms of surplus appropriation from the direct producer on a region-by-region basis for the latter part of the nineteenth and early twentieth centuries.

Foreign trade and the expansion of commodity production

Long-term trends

While the volume of Ottoman trade with Europe was not stagnant during the eighteenth century, a substantial jump is observed in the rate of expansion of the trade volumes in the aftermath of the Industrial Revolution, particularly after the Napoleonic Wars. Simple calculations indicate that the total European trade (imports plus exports) of the areas that constituted the Ottoman Empire during the second quarter of the nineteenth century (including Wallachia and Moldavia but excluding Libya, Egypt and Morea) expanded by approximately one half during the half century between 1730 and 1780 at average annual rates below one per cent. The value of this trade was around 3 million British pounds during the decade of the 1780s. In the next half century between 1780 and 1830, the European trade of the same areas grew by about 80–90 per cent at annual rates below one and a half per cent. In contrast, during the following quarter of a century until the eve of the Crimean War, the value, in current prices, of the European trade of these areas tripled despite the rapid decline in the prices of European manufactures. The expansion during the second quarter of the nineteenth century corresponds to average annual rates of approximately 5 per cent, so that by 1853 Ottoman trade with Europe excluding Russia had exceeded 16 million British pounds sterling.[2]

Clearly, the timing of the quantitative jump in the trade volume came in the aftermath of the Industrial Revolution and the emergence in Europe of economies in need of raw materials, foodstuffs and markets for their manufactures. In the case of the Ottoman Empire, the expansion of trade was further facilitated by the signing of separate Free Trade Treaties with each European power, the important consequences of which were to extend beyond the nineteenth century. The expansion of Ottoman trade and agricultural commodity exports continued until World War I. Despite the loss of population and territory throughout the century, total exports of the Empire from Ł4.7 million in 1840 to Ł28.4 million in 1913 while the imports increased from Ł5.2 million in 1840 to Ł39.4 million in 1913. In constant 1880 prices, these correspond to a nine-fold increase in exports and a ten-fold increase in imports. The rates of expansion of the exports from northern Greece and Anatolia show similar trends, approximately eight-fold increase in current and eleven-fold increase in constant prices.[3] Since the share of agricultural commodities in total Ottoman exports remained very high throughout the period under study – close to 90 per cent in 1913 – the above figures accurately reflect the expansion of agricultural commodity exports.[4]

We do not have equally reliable information regarding changes in the levels of agricultural production during the same period. Ottoman statistics for agricultural production do not become available until after the turn of the century. In the absence of direct measures, tithe-assessment and tithe-collection figures can perhaps be taken as crude measures of the long-term trends in agricultural production, but we should caution that even these tithe figures are incomplete. Although available figures start in 1863, for many years of the following half century assessment and collection statistics for many of the administrative units are simply unavailable. Nonetheless, a crude estimate regarding long-term changes in the volume of agricultural production can still be attempted. Our calculations suggest that the volume of annual gross agricultural production in the areas of the Empire under study here more than doubled between the early 1860s and World War I.[5] While this doubling represents a substantial increase in the levels of production, it also implies that the rate of growth of exports far exceeded the rate of growth of agricultural output. As a result, the share of exports in total agricultural production and in the national product rose rapidly until World War I.

There are no estimates for the 'national product' of the Ottoman Empire for the early part of this period, but an estimate for 1913 indicates that 14.1 per cent of the gross national product was being exported in that year. More importantly, the share of agricultural exports (excluding minerals) in net agricultural production rose from 18.4 per cent in 1889 and 17.8 per cent in 1899 to 22.3 per cent in 1910 and 26.5 per cent in 1913.[6] These ratios indicate fairly high degrees of commercialization of agriculture and of external orientation of the Ottoman economy, particularly for the later dates. However, they also hide substantial differences in the rates of marketization and exportation of different crops.

However, reviewing the century-long expansion of commodity production in Ottoman agriculture by comparing aggregates at two end points, 1840 and 1913, as we have done above, might be misleading. First, by focusing on the end points we run the danger of missing the long-term fluctuations in economic activity in the industrialized centre countries and their consequences on Ottoman exports and agriculture.[7] Second, aggregate, economy-wide exportation rates do not reveal very much about the regionally uneven nature of the penetration of capitalism, especially in the case of the Ottoman Empire, where regional differentiation was quite pronounced even prior to the nineteenth century. Therefore, in examining the expansion of commodity production in agriculture, it would be more fruitful to pursue a line of inquiry that emphasizes both the regional differences and the long-term fluctuations in that process.

Commodity production for domestic markets

In contrast to that of the export markets, the role of the domestic market in the expansion of commodity production in agriculture was rather limited during the nineteenth century. It is difficult to determine the share of domestic markets, local or otherwise in total agricultural production, but several observations can be made. We know that, while there was some interregional trade by sea within the Empire, the volume of overland domestic trade in foodstuffs remained low until the construction of railroads. Internal trade networks were weakened even further with the construction of railroads by foreign capital, since these railroads linked the agronomically attractive areas to major ports of export and import.[8]

In the absence of substantial volumes of interregional trade, the rate of growth of the urban population and of urban markets can perhaps be taken as a rough measure for the rate of growth of agricultural commodity production for domestic markets. The population of towns with over 20,000 inhabitants in Anatolia, northern Greece and Thrace rose from 1.4 million, or 17 per cent of the total population, in the 1830s–1840s to 3.3 million, or 22 per cent of the total population of these areas, in 1912.[9] These figures point to relatively large urban markets for the eighteenth and early nineteenth centuries but rather slow rates of urban growth during the nineteenth century. Moreover, no less than 45 per cent of the total increase was due to the growth of İstanbul, which remained dependent upon imports of foodstuffs, especially of cereals from Wallachia, Moldavia, and more recently from Russia, which lie outside the areas considered in this study.[10] Therefore, while the share of domestic urban markets in agricultural commodity production was quite high at the beginning of the nineteenth century, the rate of growth of the urban markets was nowhere near the rates of expansion of agricultural exports outlined earlier. In fact, on the basis of simple calculations, we estimate that as much as three-quarters of the expansion in agricultural commodity production that took place between 1840 and 1913 in the areas included in this study were induced by world-market demand.[11]

Changing composition of agricultural output

Commercialization of agriculture is usually accompanied by a shift in the composition of agricultural output from cereals and other subsistence crops towards industrial raw materials and other cash crops. However, since cereals were an important part of the expansion of commodity production in the Ottoman case, such a shift was not as pronounced as the commercialization and export orientation of agriculture. Official Ottoman statistics indicate that in 1907, 88 per cent of all cultivated land in northern Greece and Thrace was set aside for wheat, barley and other cereals. These crops accounted for 76 per cent of the total value of agricultural production excluding animal products. Similarly, in 1910, cereals covered 84 per cent of all cultivated land and accounted for 77 per cent of the value of agricultural output excluding animal products in the Anatolian provinces of the Empire.[12]

As for the composition of agricultural exports, Ottoman statistics indicate that during the period 1878–1913, no single crop dominated the exports, and only rarely did the share of any single commodity exceed 12 per cent of the value of total exports. Despite the doubling of the value of total exports from 1878 to 1913, the aggregate share of the more important commodities did not change substantially. The share of the eight most important commodities, tobacco, wheat, barley, raisins, figs, raw silk, raw wool, and opium in the total value of exports was 51 per cent during 1878–80; the same share stood at 44 per cent in 1913.[13] Similarly, the foreign-trade statistics of European countries indicate that in the earlier period, 1840 to 1878, none of these commodities had substantially larger shares in the total value of Ottoman exports.[14]

Land, labour and the state during the nineteenth century

In this section we focus on all relations of production in Ottoman agriculture except landownership and tenancy. By relations of production we refer to a subset of all relations between economic agents that take place during the production process. More specifically, we define relations of production as the specific economic forms and mechanisms of surplus appropriation from the direct producers in a surplus-generating economy.[15] These forms and mechanisms are not limited to property relations concerning land and other means of production; they include market processes. For example, while land rent in its different pre-capitalist forms or state taxation of the direct producer constitute extra-market mechanisms of appropriating the surplus product, the unequal relations between the usurer and/or merchant and the peasant producer or wage labour in a capitalist farm are mechanisms of surplus appropriation that involve market processes.[16] We should also emphasize that it would be unrealistic to expect that at a given time in a given socio-economic formation there will exist only one mechanism of surplus appropriation. While their relative importance may change over time, different extra-market and market mechanisms will coexist.

After the disintegration of the *tımar* system, the Ottoman Empire had entered a period of decentralization. As the military and political power of the central government declined, the *ayans* and *derebeys* (valley lords) became increasingly more powerful in the provinces. They emerged as provincial administrators and tax collectors, usurers, merchants, and *de facto* owners of land tracts of *miri* (state) lands. They expanded their share of the agricultural surplus by withholding tax revenues from the government and by increasing the rates of exploitation of the direct producers. However, it is unclear to what extent they relied on their power as tax collectors, usurers, and merchants and to what extent they transformed the existing forms of agricultural organization by establishing large, semi-feudal estates (*çiftliks*) for commodity production. Undoubtedly, both processes were under way. But, while we are not in a position to assess the relative importance of *çiftliks* in the Balkan provinces of the Empire, in view of the relatively low levels of commodity production we find it unlikely that they had become the dominant form in Anatolia by the late eighteenth and early nineteenth centuries. Even in the İzmir region, where commercialization of agriculture had proceeded to a greater extent than elsewhere in Anatolia, the power of the most important *ayans* derived, above all, from tax collection in agriculture and long-distance trade.[17]

One of the most important developments in the early part of the nineteenth century was the rapid change in this balance of power between the central government and the locally powerful elements. Sened-i İttifak, signed in 1808, represented the zenith of the power of local *ayans* and *derebeys*, but it also signalled the beginning of a centralization drive by the Ottoman state. In the following decades, particularly between 1831 and 1837, the central government moved swiftly to destroy the economic basis of provincial opposition. In 1831 the *tımar* system was formally abolished. All forms of *de facto* ownership of *miri* lands were eliminated and large estates were expropriated. Lands which reverted to the central government were then leased to *mültezim* for tax-collection purposes. It is difficult to say to what extent these measures fulfilled the objectives of the central government, but there is evidence that, even in eastern Anatolia and northern Syria, lands in the hands of Kurdish tribal lords were confiscated, and that some were distributed to the small peasantry.[18] Later, the Land Code of 1858, enacted under pressure from European powers, recognized private ownership of land, and in 1867 ownership of land by foreign citizens was recognized. However, by this time the balance of power between İstanbul and the provinces had shifted decisively in favour of the former.[19]

Another important characteristic of nineteenth-century Ottoman agriculture was the relative proportions of labour and land, the relative scarcity of the former and the relative abundance of the latter. Following rapid increases during the sixteenth century, the population of the Anatolian countryside, but not necessarily of northern Greece, showed a net decline between 1600 and 1800.[20] A complex set of factors – the dissolution of the *tımar* system, frequent wars, heavy exploitation of the peasantry, and the general economic and fiscal crisis – contributed to this outcome.

The population of Anatolia began to grow in the nineteenth century. An important source of this trend was the immigration of large numbers of Muslims from the Caucasus and from the European provinces as these areas seceded from the Empire.[21] Throughout the nineteenth century, the Ottoman central bureaucracy was very much aware that the expansion of agricultural production which constituted the primary source of fiscal revenue depended critically upon relieving the labour shortage and providing inexpensive means of transportation. Immigrants were settled along the Anatolian railway in Eskişehir, Ankara and Konya and in agronomically favourable areas of western Anatolia and Antalya.[22] In addition, attempts were made to settle the nomadic tribes in regions where labour shortage was particularly acute, such as the Çukurova plain.[23] Despite these policies, relative scarcity of labour, regional variations notwithstanding, continued to be an important characteristic of Ottoman agriculture until World War I.[24]

The obverse side of the coin is the relative availability of land.[25] Throughout the nineteenth century, extensive techniques of agriculture were employed in most parts of northern Greece and Anatolia. Cultivated lands were left fallow every two or three years.[26] Uncultivated marginal lands were always available for 'purchase' from the state at nominal prices or in return for regular payments of tithe for ten years, particularly in areas where the absence of inexpensive forms of transportation made commodity production for long-distance markets difficult.

Under the circumstances, in areas where land had become a commodity, land prices reflected differential rents but basically excluded absolute rent. In general, land prices followed the short-term and long-term fluctuations in world-market conditions for agricultural commodities. Along with the expansion of world-market demand and of exports, land prices rose from 1840 until the early 1870s. They declined during the Great Depression of 1873–96, only to rise again during the subsequent upswing which continued until the outbreak of the War.[27] The availability of marginal lands meant that, despite the relative scarcity of labour and the primitive nature of agricultural implements, substantial amounts of new land could be brought under cultivation during periods of high world-market demand and favourable terms of trade. If the large increases in area under cultivation and agricultural production indicated by the official Ottoman statistics are to be believed, an explanation of these increases must include the above considerations, recent immigration and the role of the railroads.[28]

These relative proportions of land and labour tended to improve the bargaining position of the small peasant producer. Peasant households which owned a pair of oxen and the most basic implements, or those which could borrow them, cultivated their own land. When marginal land was not available, peasants share-cropped for small or large landlords. Those households which did not own a pair of oxen, frequently the most critical of the means of production, or those which were forced to sell their oxen because of poor harvests and permanent usury, offered their labour services to large landlords as share-cropping tenants. Although the landlords had the right to cancel a tenancy arrangement, evictions were infrequent.

Around the turn of the twentieth century, large landowners in the highly commercialized agricultural regions of İzmir–Aydın, Adana, and Salonica began to employ imported implements and labour-saving machinery in order to reduce their dependence on relatively scarce labour.[29] However, in a social formation where marginal land was available and labour scarce, wages were bound to remain relatively high. Large farms using year-round wage labourers could not take over at the expense of simple commodity production by peasant households. If necessary, peasant households could exert much greater effort and accept much lower levels of consumption.[30] Consequently, once commodity production either by small owner-producers or by share-cropping tenants was re-established by the central government during the early part of the century, it survived until World War I.

Another factor in the survival of simple commodity production by peasant households was the central government. Throughout the century, the Ottoman state attempted to prevent the emergence of a powerful landlord class that might expand its share of the agricultural surplus at the expense of the state and even challenge the rule of the central bureaucracy.

At the same time, however, the state heavily taxed the small peasantry. Among a variety of taxes falling upon rural classes, *aşar* (tithe) as a predetermined percentage of gross agricultural product constituted the main source of fiscal revenue for the Ottoman state.[31] After the disintegration of the *tımar* system, tithe revenues were auctioned off to *mültezim* (tax-farmers) who not only reduced the state's share of the surplus but increased the rates of exploitation of the direct producers.[32] Despite the strengthening of the state apparatus during the nineteenth century, the tax-farming system could not be abandoned until World War I, despite several state attempts in that direction.[33] Locally powerful tax-collectors continued to keep a large part of the tax revenues.

After the Tanzimat Decree of 1839, the tithe was fixed at 10 per cent of the gross agricultural output, paid mostly in kind in the earlier period but increasingly in money terms later in the century. Moreover, during the years of lower agricultural prices, the tax-collectors frequently demanded and received payment in cash. The 10 per cent rate was likely to increase to as much as 15 per cent whenever the fiscal crisis of the state intensified.[34] The collection of tithe along with other forms of rural taxation such as *agnam* (animal tax) meant that as much as a quarter or more of agricultural production was taxed.[35] In addition, the taxes were highly regressive, falling mostly on the unprotected small peasantry, while the large landowners were usually underassessed.[36]

Given the low levels of productivity, dependence of the harvest on weather conditions, and heavy state taxation, both the smaller owner-producers and the tenants were permanently indebted to usurers at interest rates ranging anywhere from 20 to 120 per cent.[37] Whatever was left after the tax-collector and, in the case of the tenant, the landowner had had their shares, was appropriated by the usurer.[38] The small producers frequently had to struggle to survive from one year to the next. For these peasants, capital improvements in land and implements were unheard of. At the same time, the traditional manufactures in the cities were being destroyed under the competition of imported industrial commodities. Urban areas, therefore, offered no prospects of employment, and the availability of marginal lands prevented mass emigration from rural areas.[39]

During years of exceptionally poor harvests, the state ensured that tax-collectors arrived at the harvest place before the usurers by postponing all payments to moneylenders until the following year. Moreover, in its attempts to protect its fiscal base, the small peasant, against powerful landlords and increasing concentration of landownership, the state issued decrees during periods of crisis to enforce the existing law against the appropriation of any owner's land because of inability to pay back debts.[40] Under these circumstances, complaints by moneylenders that the defaulting peasants were not being arrested, though infrequent, were not unheard of.[41]

Different groups dominated moneylending activities in different regions. In areas where semi-feudal relations of production and/or powerful landlords prevailed, the latter usually doubled as usurers. For the large landowners usury not only provided a means of appropriating a larger share of the surplus, but, given the relative scarcity of labour, permanent indebtedness of peasants secured tenants for their land. On the other hand, in central Anatolia where small peasant ownership was dominant and in regions where production for the market had expanded to a greater degree, merchants, tax-collectors, and other moneylenders residing in urban centres controlled usury.[42]

Land ownership and tenancy patterns in the Asiatic provinces

There is a very important and useful survey of land-ownership and tenancy patterns in the Asiatic provinces of the Ottoman Empire in the late 1860s which will serve as the starting point for our subsequent analysis. The report was prepared by the British consul in Trabzon as part of a larger, comparative study of European land-tenure systems in connection with British government policies towards Ireland.[43] The date of the study, 1869, is particularly important, coming three decades after the confiscation of large landholdings, a decade after the Land Code of 1858, and towards the end of the first wave of rapid expansion of agricultural exports, which lasted until the early 1870s. In order to prepare the survey, Consul Palgrave states that he travelled extensively in Anatolia, Syria, and Iraq, both 'observing and talking with the more knowledgeable people'. Clearly, the accuracy of such a survey needs to be questioned, and the approximate nature of Palgrave's figures suggests caution. Hence, in what follows we will treat Palgrave's study as a rather crude reflection of the actual patterns of ownership and tenancy.

As stated by Palgrave, the Asiatic provinces of the Ottoman Empire had a total surface area of 1,219,000 square kilometres. Fully one-half of this land was considered unsuitable for cultivation, and two-thirds of the remainder was occupied by forests and pastures, leaving as cultivable land a total of 21,662,000 hectares.[44] Twenty-five per cent of all cultivable land belonged to *vakıfs* (endowments) which were left relatively untouched during the 1830s. The Land Code of 1858 had reduced *miri* lands to 5 per cent of all cultivable land by 1869. The rest, or 70 per cent of all cultivable land, was *mülk*, or private property.

As Table 8.1 summarizes, 75 to 82.5 per cent of all cultivable land was in small holdings ranging from 2 to 20 hectares, with the average somewhere between 6 and 8 hectares. In the study, large holdings were defined as those greater than 20 hectares, with an average of 120 hectares. Large holdings comprised 17.5 to 25 per cent of all cultivable land.

One-seventh of all *mülk* land, or 10 per cent of all cultivable land, was under large holdings, being cultivated either by labour hired on an annual basis or, in most instances, by share-croppers (*ortakcı or maraba*) whose tenancy agreements were subject to renewal by the landlord every year. The remaining six-sevenths of *mülk* lands, or 60 per cent of all cultivable land, was under small holdings. One-third of these small holdings were cultivated directly by small peasant owners with an average of 6 hectares per farm. The other two-thirds of the privately-owned small holdings were cultivated by small tenants either under fixed rent or, more usually, under share-cropping arrangements, at an average of 8 hectares per farm.

Of the *vakıf* and *miri* lands which together constituted 30 per cent of all cultivable land, one-half was under small holdings of less than 20 hectares. One-half of these were being cultivated by lifetime tenants whose position was 'practically equivalent to ownership of land'. The other half of the small *vakıf* and *mülk* holdings were being cultivated by share-cropper tenants. As for the large *vakıf* and *mülk* holdings, half of them were being cultivated by share-cropper tenants at an average of 8 hectares per tenant. The remaining quarter of all *vakıf* and *mülk* lands were originally in the form of large holdings, but because of various restrictions placed on them by the Evkaf İdaresi (Board of Endowments) had been divided up into small holdings and were being cultivated by direct producer tenants.[45]

It should be noted that according to Palgrave no less than 40 per cent of all cultivable land was being rented out by small landowners to small tenants. He does not offer any explanation for the unusually high frequency of this phenomenon, but several reasons might be suggested. His category 'small' inevitably hides a good deal of differentiation among households owning, according to his definition, fewer than 20 hectares. The primitive nature of agricultural implements and techniques in nineteenth-century Ottoman agriculture set at a relatively low level the amount of land that could be cultivated by an average household using a team of oxen.[46] Holdings of 'small' owners beyond that size had to be rented out. Similar differentiation with respect to ownership of implements and livestock might have led small tenants to cultivate additional plots without relying on hired labour.[47] Moreover, in the 'life-cycle' of a household, there will be periods of relative labour surplus – when the offspring are of working age but before they leave – and periods of labour deficiency.[48] The frequency with which the Ottoman Empire was involved in wars during the nineteenth century and the high rate of casualties inevitably compounded the scarcity of labour in rural areas, particularly of young adult

Table 8.1 *Landownership, land distribution, forms of tenancy and relations of production in the Asiatic provinces of the Ottoman Empire* c. *1869*

Size of holding	Form of operation	Form of ownership: *Mülk* Private property (0.70)	Form of ownership: *Vakıf* Endowment (0.25) and *Miri* State (0.05)	Form of surplus appropriation from the direct producer (in addition to state taxation, usury and merchant capital whenever applicable)
Small	Small peasant ownership Owners as direct producers	A (0.20) Avg. 6 hectares per holding owners/producers: 23.7%	D (0.075) Avg. 8 hectares per holding tenants for life, *de facto* small peasant ownership Direct producers: 7.1%	A None B rent payments to small owners C rent payments to large owners, wage labour
2 to 20 hectares (0.75 to 0.825)	Small owners to small tenants Mostly share-cropping; some fixed rent	B (0.40) Avg. 8 hectares per tenant Direct producers: 37.95	E (0.075) Avg. 8 hectares per tenant Direct producers: 7.1%	D None
Large Greater than 20 hectares; average 120 ha (0.175 to 0.25)	Large owners to small tenants Mostly share-cropping; some fixed rent, some year round wage labourers; in addition 200,000 seasonal wage workers	C (0.10) Avg. 8 hectares per tenant Owners: 0.6% Direct producers: 9.4%	F(0.075) Avg. 8 hectares per tenant Large holdings broken up owing to restrictions by Evkaf Idaresi *De facto* small holdings Direct producers: 7.1% G (0.075) Avg. 8 hectares per tenant Direct producers: 7.1%	E, F, G } Rent payments to *vakıf* trustees or to state

Note: Figures in parentheses represent shares in total cultivable land.
Percentages represent shares in total number of households in agriculture.

Source: Parliamentary Papers, Accounts and Papers (1870), 'Report on land tenure in (the Asiatic provinces of) Turkey', by Consul Palgrave.

males.[49] Such demographic factors may account for a good deal of the small-to-small tenancy arrangements.[50] Finally, absentee ownership by urban dwellers may have been a major factor in the relatively high frequency of these small-to-small tenancy arrangements.[51] Despite these potential explanations, we are inclined to treat this particular figure of 40 per cent with more caution than others in the Table 8.1.

After the confiscation of many of the large estates during the 1830s, share-cropping became the dominant form of tenancy in the large *mülk* lands.[52] Arrangements varied from region to region, depending upon the relative power of the landlord and the tenant, the quality of the land, and custom. In most cases the product was equally divided after government taxes and dues were paid and an allowance was made to the side which supplied the seeds, implements, and livestock.[53] The length of the tenancy arrangement also depended upon the relative strength of the two sides. Particularly in areas where finding tenants was not a major problem, landlords preferred to keep the arrangement subject to renewal every year in order to extract the maximum effort and the maximum surplus from the tenants. For reasons discussed earlier, share-cropping remained the dominant form of labour organization in the large holdings until World War I.

Around mid century a small and decreasing number of large holdings were being operated by labourers hired on an annual basis.[54] In addition, according to Palgrave's estimates, around 200,000 seasonal wage labourers were employed throughout the Asiatic provinces of the Empire in the production of cash crops, which required peak seasonal labour.[55] With increasing export orientation and increases in the production of cash crops such as cotton, it appears that the numbers of seasonal wage labourers began to expand, especially after the late 1890s in the regions of Salonica, İzmir–Aydın, and in particular, Adana.

If we momentarily abstract from the distinctions between *mülk*, *vakıf* and *miri* lands, we can regroup the data presented in Table 8.1 and arrive in Table 8.2 at a more summary picture regarding the distribution of direct producers among different forms of landownership and tenancy. This summary picture shows more clearly the dominance, by Palgrave's estimation, of small holdings and small producers in the Asiatic provinces of the Empire around the mid nineteenth century. The early nineteenth century was a period of the strengthening of the central government, confiscation of large estates, distribution of land to small producers, a decline in the power of local notables, and a general centralization of the Ottoman social formation.[56] Palgrave's report was prepared three decades after most of these changes had taken place. The long-term impact of the increasing commercialization and export orientation of agriculture on patterns of landownership and tenancy, whatever that would be, was yet to materialize. Under these circumstances, the dominance of small holdings and small peasant producers in Anatolia and in other Asiatic provinces should not be surprising.[57]

Table 8.2 *Summary distribution of landownership and tenancy patterns in the Asiatic provinces of the Ottoman Empire* c. *1869*

Type of direct producer	Reference to forms in Table 8.1	Share in all direct-producer households (%)	Share of total cultivable land (%)
Small peasant owner-producers	A,D	31.0	27.5
Share-croppers, other tenants renting from small owners (small–small)	B,E,F	52.4	55.0
Share-croppers, year-round wage labourers, other tenants in large holdings (small–large)	C,G	16.6	17.5

Source: See Table 8.1

On the other hand, however, one major theme of Palgrave's report was what he considered to be the unfavourable consequences of the confiscation of large estates and the abolition of the earlier land-tenure system. Therefore, there may well be a bias in the report towards overestimating the extent of small holdings. Even if an allowance is made for this potential bias, the conclusion remains that the great majority of cultivable lands were under 'small' holdings around the mid nineteenth century.

One important shortcoming of the Palgrave survey is its aggregate nature, which, given the substantial regional variations in landownership and tenancy patterns and the regionally uneven nature of the penetration of capitalism into Anatolia, limits the insights it offers into the dynamics of change in Ottoman agriculture during the nineteenth century. For example, substantial regional variations should be expected in the size of 'small' and 'large' holdings, depending upon agronomical factors and the availability of irrigation.

Moreover, there is not always a one-to-one correspondence between apparent forms of tenancy and the mechanisms of surplus appropriation from the direct producer. The same tenancy relationship, for example, share-cropping, between a large landowner and a small tenant may represent either semi-feudal relations of production or petty-commodity production, depending upon the relative positions and power of the owner and the tenant and the nature of the relationship in the more general context of the socio-economic formation.[58] Only a region-by-region analysis of the historical evolution of relations of production and of the relative importance of commodity production will help draw the distinction between these two cases.

Regional patterns of landownership and tenancy

As some of the relevant indicators summarized in Table 8.3 indicate, agriculture in the core areas of the Ottoman Empire, namely northern Greece, Thrace, and Anatolia, showed substantial regional variations with respect to relative proportions of land and labour, agronomical factors, composition of output, and relative importance of local urban markets by the end of the nineteenth century. Equally important were regional differences in proximity to major ports, availability of inexpensive forms of transportation, and the timing of the construction of railroads by foreign capital, as well as the degree and timing of world-market-induced commercialization. In this section we will examine the patterns of landownership and tenancy in northern Greece, Thrace and Anatolia during the nineteenth century, utilizing a framework that emphasizes the considerable differences in these variables.[59]

Our analysis will be carried out in terms of three types of regions. Region Type I includes northern Greece and Thrace, western Anatolia, the eastern Black Sea Coast, and the Adana region, the latter two being special cases within the broader picture. These areas were pulled into commodity production for world-markets at a relative early stage in the nineteenth century, if not earlier, and by 1913 they represented the most commercialized, most export-oriented regions of the Empire. Region Type II consists of central Anatolia, which was isolated from long-distance markets until the construction of the Anatolian railway by German capital in the early 1890s. In the following two decades, cereal production in central Anatolia for İstanbul and European markets expanded rapidly under small and middle peasant ownership. Region Type III includes eastern Anatolia, with its central and southern tiers, both of which remained mostly isolated from the impact of world-markets and the penetration of world-capitalism. Small peasant ownership was relatively stronger in the central tier, while feudal and semi-feudal relations of production dominated in southeastern Anatolia and northern Syria.

Eastern Anatolia

Eastern Anatolia was less affected by the world-market-induced commercialization of agriculture than was any other region during the nineteenth century. Because of the absence of railroads until the early 1910s, agricultural produce of the region could not be directed towards long-distance markets on a regular basis. In years of good harvest, limited amounts of cereals were shipped by camel caravans through Aleppo to the export port of İskenderun. The markets of Mousul, Baghdad, and distant India emerged as occasional outlets for the cereals

Table 8.3 *Indicators of regional differentiation in Ottoman agriculture around 1900*

	Labour and land							Distribution of farm size			
								Percentage of farms			
	Total population (millions)	Cultivated area (thousand sq km)	Rural population density (per sq km)	Composition of agriculture output (% share of cash crops)	Importance of urban markets (% share of urban population)	Density of railroads (km per 1000 sq km) in 1875	in 1900	under 10 *dönüms*	10 to 50 *dönüms*	over 50 *dönüms*	Average farm size *dönüms*
	1A	1B	1C	2	3	4A	4B	5A	5B	5C	5D
Regions											
Northern Greece	1.63	4.6	310*	10.9	15*	n.d.	n.d.	30	52	18	19
Thrace	1.15	4.4	233*	11.9	11	n.d.	n.d.	55	28	17	24
N. Greece and Thrace	2.78	9.0	268*	11.4	13	5.3	13.7	40	42	18	21
W. Anatolia/Marmara	5.20	14.9	220*	18.6	37*	2.2	13.7	31	46	23	35
E. Black Sea	1.34	3.7	342	3.2	6	—	—	43	42	15	18
Adana	0.50	4.7	91	35.1	15	—	1.7	17	36	47	77
Central Anatolia	4.70	19.6	215	6.6	11	—	2.5	23	52	25	35
Eastern Anatolia:											
Central Tier	1.15	5.2	194	10.1	12	—	—	41	41	18	21
Southern Tier	0.81	6.5	101	9.7	20	—	—	23	37	40	58

* Figure approximate

Notes and sources:

1A Total population in 1907–9: from T. Güran, 'Osmanlı tarım ekonomisine giriş, 1840–1940' (Introduction to Ottoman agricultural economy, 1840–1940) (University of İstanbul, 1978), unpublished Ph.D. dissertation, p. 5, based on the Ottoman Agricultural Census of 1907–9.

1B Land under cultivation in 1907–9: Güran (1978), p. 5, based on the Ottoman Agricultural Census of 1907–9.

1C	Rural population/land under cultivation. Rural population has been estimated by subtracting the urban population figures derived from C. Issawi, *The economic history of Turkey* (Chicago, University of Chicago Press, 1980), pp. 34–5 from column 1A.
2	The share of industrial crops and vineyards in total area under cultivation. From Güran (1978), p. 20, based on the Ottoman Agricultural Census of 1907–9.
3	Population of towns over 20,000 in 1912/Total population in 1907–9.
4A	Length of railroads per 1000 sq km in 1875; (–) indicates the absence of railroads.
4B	Length of railroads per 1000 sq km in 1900; both based on V. Eldem, *Osmanlı imparatorluğunun iktisadi şartları hakkında bir tetkik* (A study of Ottoman economic conditions) (İstanbul, Türkiye İş Bankası Kültür Yayınları, 1970), pp. 164–5.
5A	(Farms under 10 *dönüm*)/(Total number of farms); 1 *dönüm* = 0.0913 hectares
5B	Percentage of farms between 10 and 50 *dönüms*.
5C	Percentage of farms over 50 *dönüms*.
5D	Average farm size in *dönüms*. Source for 5A–5D: Güran (1978), p. 28, based on the Ottoman Agricultural Census of 1907–9.

Definitions of regions (Names of *sancaks* and other administrative units)

Northern Greece:	Salonica, Monastır
Thrace:	Edirne
Western Anatolia and Marmara:	İzmit, Biga, Hüdavendigar, Aydın (İzmir)
Eastern Black Sea Coast:	Trabzon
Central Anatolia:	Kastamonu, Ankara, Konya, Sivas
Eastern Anatolia, Central Tier:	Erzurum, Mamuretülaziz
Eastern Anatolia, Southern Tier:	Diyarbakır, Bitlis, Van

of the region only after the turn of the century.[60] However, in general, barriers posed by transportation costs isolated eastern Anatolia from the rest of the Empire and the European markets throughout the century. Consequently, while bad harvest years led to near famine conditions, unusually good harvest years were almost equally disastrous for the small peasantry. Prices collapsed and the peasants could not pay back their debts to the usurers. A limited amount of mohair constituted the major export commodity of the region during this period.[61]

Southeastern Anatolia including Aleppo was the most urbanized region of Anatolia during the seventeenth and perhaps even in the eighteenth century. Although the overall population density was low and virtually no urban growth occurred during the nineteenth century, more than a fifth of the population continued to live in the medium-sized towns of the region (see Table 8.3). Hence, there was a considerable amount of commodity production for local urban markets. The province of Mamuretülaziz can be singled out in this respect. In that province, small- and medium-sized landowning Turkish and Armenian peasants specialized in the production of fruits, vegetables, and other commercial crops for the urban markets of the region.[62]

With respect to patterns of landownership and tenancy, the central and southern tiers of the region followed different paths. In the southeastern Anatolian provinces of Diyarbakır, Bitlis, and Van, the Ottoman state had recognized in the sixteenth century the autonomy of the Kurdish tribal lords in exchange for military obligations and orderly payments of tribute. The political, administrative and legal autonomy of the tribal lords and the lord–peasant bonds remained strong until the nineteenth century. The centralization attempt by the state during the 1830s resulted in the expropriation of some of the large holdings.[63] However, these measures could hardly affect the political, social and economic power of the tribal lords in the region. During the rest of the century, they benefited from a number of opportunities to regain their holdings.[64]

First, the Land Code of 1858 recognized the existing *de facto* distribution of landownership, thereby making the tribal lords legal owners of large tracts of land.[65] After 1858, these landlords began to buy amounts of *miri* land back from the state at low prices.[66] However, many of these tracts remained uncultivated because of the difficulties of finding tenants, and transportation barriers against production for long-distance markets.[67] Second, the Kurdish tribal lords relied on their economic and non-economic power to secure tenants as they reduced small peasant owners to share-cropper status through usury and other means. While in other regions of the Empire the state occasionally interfered in this process in support of the small owner-producer, the centuries-long autonomy of the Kurdish tribes and lords remained unbroken during the nineteenth century.[68] Undoubtedly, a good deal of small peasant ownership did survive, given the relative proportions of land and labour in the area and the difficulties of expanding commodity production in large estates for long-distance markets. Nonetheless, the official Ottoman statistics summarized in Table 8.3 confirm that, by the first decade of the twentieth century, southeastern Anatolia was second only to the Adana region in terms of inequalities in the distribution of farm size.

In the central tier of eastern Anatolia, which included the provinces of Erzurum and Mamuretülaziz, feudal and semi-feudal relations of production were not equally powerful. The ethnic composition of the population was distinctly different, consisting mostly of Turks and Armenians.[69] In addition, the density of population in agriculture was higher than that of the southern tier. These factors combined with others to lead to a pattern of ownership dominated by small and middle holdings (see Table 8.3). The absence of inexpensive forms of transportation limited the possibility of production for long-distance markets and the area under cultivation. Cereal shipments were undertaken only when famine prices prevailed elsewhere. While subsistence agriculture and animal husbandry dominated in Erzurum, in Mamuretülaziz, where agronomical factors were favourable, commodity production for regional markets and the cultivation of cash crops developed to a relatively high degree. In this context, state taxation and usury were the main mechanisms of surplus appropriation from the direct producer. Finally, in the period up to 1913, with the exception of Mamuretülaziz, there was virtually no improvement in the agricultural techniques and implements that had been in use in the eastern Anatolian region for many centuries.[70]

Western Anatolia, Thrace and northern Greece

Because of favourable agronomical conditions and proximity to major ports, agriculture along the coastal areas of western Anatolia, Thrace and northern Greece had been relatively more commercialized than other regions of the Empire even before the second quarter of the nineteenth century. Salonica and İzmir were important ports of export in the eighteenth century.[71] When the Free Trade Treaties of 1838–41 took away the power of the Ottoman state to impose temporary, year-to-year restrictions on the exportation of foodstuffs and raw materials, these regions and their immediate hinterlands were the first to show rapid increases in exports. The first wave of expansion of exports continued until the early 1870s, when the mid-century upswing of the world-economy came to an end. The years of the Crimean and American Civil Wars were particularly important in this stretch as they generated considerable demand for primary commodities. The second wave of export expansion for these regions did not come until the end of the century, when the world-economy entered another long-term upswing.[72] Along with increasing commercialization and export orientation of agriculture, raisins, tobacco, figs, cotton, raw silk and olive oil became the most important export commodities in these areas.[73]

It should also be emphasized that in these regions, costs of transportation to the nearest ports, while by no means insignificant, did not constitute the kind of absolute barrier they were in eastern Anatolia. The construction of railroads by European capital in the hinterland of İzmir during the early 1860s and in Thrace and northern Greece in the early 1870s substantially reduced transportation costs, but most of the early expansion of exports in these areas had occurred before the completion of railroad construction.[74]

Prior to the second quarter of the nineteenth century, feudal obligations and feudal relations of production were not strong in western Anatolia and Thrace despite the substantial political and economic power of the *ayans* as local administrators, tax collectors, merchants, and *de facto* owners of large tracts of land. During the centralization drive of the state, the power of *ayans* was reduced, and some of their large *de facto* holdings were expropriated and distributed to the small peasantry. Hence, the expansion of commodity production for export and the penetration of foreign capital in infrastructure, trade, and banking proceeded under a pattern in which small peasant owner-producers and small peasant tenants in small holdings coexisted with some large holdings. A British consular report from the İzmir area in 1863 states that 'by far the largest proportion of cultivated land is owned by peasants' in farms of 3 to 20 acres (1.2 to 8 hectares).[75] According to another estimate, in the province of Edirne which covered Thrace, two-thirds of all farms were under 20 hectares, and an additional 30 per cent were between 20 and 40 hectares.[76]

In contrast, large holdings and the *çiftlik* system prevailed in the Salonica and Monastır provinces of northern Greece throughout the nineteenth century.[77] In 1859, it was estimated that three-fourths of all land in the province of Monastır was in the hands of large landlords.[78] For the province of Salonica, one estimate states that 40 per cent of all farms were larger than 200 hectares in 1863.[79] In comparison to the western Anatolian provinces of the Empire, the lord-peasant bonds were quite strong in northern Greece. Despite the official abolition of corvée in the European provinces of the Empire in 1881,[80] and once more with the Tanzimat Decree of 1839,[81] it did not disappear in this area until after mid century.[82]

Given the relative scarcity of labour, availability of marginal lands, dominance of small peasant ownership and the limited nature of capital accumulation in these regions of the Empire, transformation of large holdings into capitalist farms employing wage labourers on a year-round basis was unlikely.[83] Instead, the large landowners preferred to rent their land out to share-cropper families who represented a relatively inexpensive source of labour power, particularly for the cultivation of crops which required labour year-round.

Tenant families came from the ranks of the poor peasantry which did not have the means to cultivate marginal lands on their own.[84] Even under a tenancy arrangement, they could not, by themselves, meet the relatively large outlays associated with the cultivation of cash crops. Moreover, it was difficult for them to endure a bad harvest year if they accepted a fixed rent arrangement. Under these circumstances, share-cropping remained the most frequently adopted tenancy arrangement in western Anatolia, Thrace, and northern Greece. Fixed rent tenancy was adopted mostly on *vakıf* lands where there was little supervision by the absentee landowners and where the tenants were relatively better off.[85]

Two different forms of share-cropping in large holdings need to be distinguished here. Share-cropping in large estates of southeastern Anatolia represented feudal or semi-feudal relations of production where the lord-peasant bonds were quite strong and the tenant's obligations to the landlord went beyond the purely economic obligation of rent payments. On the other hand, in the Type I regions (see Table 8.1) of western Anatolia and on the Black Sea coast, where lord-peasant ties were weaker and where commodity production had expanded to a much greater extent, share-cropping represented a more limited, economic arrangement for rent payments. A careful contemporary observer draws the following picture for the İzmir area in 1890:

> The mode of exploitation used by the agriculturalists changes depending upon the size of the holding. In the *çiftliks* which range from 2,000 to 80,000 *dönüms*, that is from 200 to 8,000 hectares, share-cropping is almost exclusively adopted except in the *kaza* (county) of Scala-Nuova [Kuşadası] where fixed rent is principally used. The share-cropper and his family provide the labour and the owner furnishes the work animals and the seed. When the time comes, they share equally without taking into account the seeds. The *çiftliks* from 500 to 2,000 *dönüms*, that is from 50 to 200 hectares, are cultivated directly by their owners with share-cropping in part. The holdings between 10 and 50 *dönüms*, 1 to 50 hectares, are worked directly by their owners with the help of day workers, if necessary, during harvest time.[86]

During periods of long-term expansion of the world-economy, demand for the agricultural exports rose rapidly and the terms of trade moved in favour of the Ottoman Empire.[87] During these periods[88] large landowners must have attempted to expand their holdings and reduce small peasant holders into share-cropper tenants. However, the limits to this process arising from the special characteristics of the Ottoman social formation need to be stressed. First, the small peasant owners were ready to exert high levels of effort and be content with very low levels of consumption, which made it easier for them to retain their holdings despite the heavy burden of state taxation and the appropriation of the rest of the surplus by usurers and merchants.

Moreover, the central government attempted to support the small peasantry against large landowners by prohibiting the expropriation of the lands of defaulting owners.[89] How effectively or how frequently this law was enforced was a matter that depended upon the economic and political conjuncture and the local power of landowners.[90] However, as farm size distribution statistics summarized in Table 8.3 show, small and middle owners and tenants in small holdings, heavily taxed and frequently if not permanently indebted, continued to coexist with those with large holdings and to account for a substantial part of the commodity production for export until World War I.

British attempts to establish large-scale capitalist farms should also be examined here. After the construction of the İzmir–Aydın railroad by British capital and the modification of the Ottoman Land Code in 1866 to allow for landownership by foreigners, British citizens began to purchase substantial amounts of land and operate large, export-oriented capitalist farms in the hinterland of İzmir. According to one estimate, in the İzmir area, British capitalist farmers had purchased up to one-third of all cultivable land by 1868 and most of the cultivable land by 1878.[91] These capitalists imported substantial amounts of agricultural implements and machinery for their farms.

This attempt to transform the existing mode of production by the infusion of large amounts of capital was important in its own right. Equally important, in our view, are the reasons for the unqualified failure of the British attempts at capitalist farms as well as of other colonization projects in the Ottoman Empire. In western Anatolia where marginal land was readily available and labour relatively scarce, the British farmers could not easily secure wage labourers for their large holdings. In the formal colonies, governments resorted to a head tax or other means in order to break up the existing mode of production and establish wage labour, whenever necessary. However, the Ottoman Empire maintained its formal political independence throughout the nineteenth century, allowing thus for a considerable degree of independence from the Great Powers in certain issues. In this case, the Ottoman government resisted pressures from Britain and did not attempt to separate small producers from their land, especially since the small peasantry constituted the very fiscal base of the Ottoman state.[92]

Eastern Black Sea coast

The patterns of change in other coastal areas of Anatolia differed from those of western Anatolia. The western half of the Black Sea coast was not suitable for extensive cultivation. In the eastern half, Trabzon had been a major port on the transit route to Iran.[93] Agricultural commodity exports from Trabzon and to some extent Samsun expanded during the upswing of 1840–73. The secondary ports, Ordu, Giresun, and Rize, emerged in the next long-term expansion from 1896 to 1913. Tobacco in the plains around Samsun and hazelnuts further to the east were the major export crops. However, the commercialization and export orientation of the region never reached levels achieved in western Anatolia.[94]

The expropriation of large holdings during the 1830s affected the patterns of landownership and tenancy for the rest of the century.[95] In 1863, it was reported that 100 per cent of all farms in the Trabzon area were under 4 hectares.[96] Although agricultural population density was higher in this region than anywhere else in the core areas of the Empire (see Table 8.3), marginal land was still available. The relatively limited commercialization of agriculture, the labour-intensive nature of the export crops, and other reasons discussed earlier with respect to western Anatolia prevented the re-emergence of large holdings.

Adana

The southern Anatolian coast provides a different story. The plain of Antalya, which was to become a highly fertile and important agricultural area during the twentieth century, was sparsely populated and was not opened up to cultivation until the late 1890s when large numbers of immigrants leaving Crete after the war of 1897 were settled there.[97] In the decade preceding World War I, Italian capital began to be interested in the area both in terms of its agricultural potential and as an outlet for the Italian textiles industry, which was attempting to enter markets already dominated by major European powers.

Economic conditions in the plain of Adana to the east had improved considerably during the period of its occupation by İbrahim Paşa, son of Mehmet Ali of Egypt. Irrigation projects were initiated and agriculture flourished.[98] However, with the departure of İbrahim Paşa in 1840, security conditions in the area deteriorated, the irrigation systems were not maintained, and agricultural production declined rapidly. Improvements in the irrigation and drainage systems were not attempted until the time of the American Civil War. One estimate puts the population of the entire plain including the cities and the nomads at 100,000 in 1862.[99] (Compare with the 1907–9 population given in Table 8.3.) The last of the *derebeys* was eliminated from the area by the Ottoman army in 1864. Because of these circumstances, the world-wide cotton crisis which accompanied the American Civil War had a relatively limited impact in the plain of Adana.

With the draining of the delta, large amounts of land were opened to cultivation in the early 1870s.[100] Proximity to a port of export and the high quality of irrigated land rapidly transformed the area into one of the most export-oriented regions of Anatolia, specializing in cotton production. The subsequent evolution of landownership and tenancy patterns owed much to the recent absence of cultivation, to settlements, and to the relative scarcity of labour in the area. As the locally powerful groups were able to extend ownership to large tracts of fertile land, securing labourers posed a serious problem from the outset. The large land owners and the state, which wanted to expand its fiscal base in the region, encouraged seasonal migration into the area during the peak cotton-harvest season. More important, serious attempts were made to settle the nomadic Türkmens of the region in the agricultural lowlands.[101]

The severe drought of 1885 and the destruction of the cotton crop gave the central government the opportunity to introduce higher-quality seeds from Egypt. The commercialization of agriculture accelerated during the upswing of 1896–1913. With the arrival of the Anatolian railway to Mersin and the purchase of the Mersin–Tarsus extension by German capital from the original British owners, the area rapidly entered the German sphere of influence.[102] The Anatolian railway company provided credit to landowners to adopt higher-quality seeds, import implements and machinery from Germany, and undertake irrigation investments in their large-scale farms.[103] By 1913 the plain of Adana had been transformed into the most commercialized agricultural region of the Empire, dominated by large farms cultivating cotton for export. Every harvest season, these farms employed anywhere from 50,000 to 100,000 migrant wage labourers arriving from as far as Harput, Bitlis and Mousul.[104] (See Table 8.3 for the distribution of farm size.)

Central Anatolia

The rapid expansion of commodity production in central Anatolia started with the construction of the Anatolian railroad by German capital in the early 1890s linking Eskişehir, Konya, and Ankara to İstanbul. In the earlier period, high costs of caravan transportation to Mediterranean and Black Sea ports had virtually isolated central Anatolia from both the rest of the Empire and the European markets. Only mohair and opium were shipped long distances on a regular basis.[105] The Anatolian railroad converted large areas of uncultivated dry farming land to wheat and barley production for both export and the İstanbul market, which was dependent upon imported grains from Rumania, Bulgaria, Russia, and upon flour from France.[106] In 1889, Anatolian grain made up only 2 per cent of all grain received in İstanbul.[107] Within a decade of its construction, as many as 400,000 tons of cereals were being shipped annually on the railroad.[108] Novichev puts the ratio of marketization in the province of Konya at 26.4 per cent of the total production for wheat and 25.5 per cent for barley in the year 1912, when total cereal shipments on the railroad did not exceed 300,000 metric tons.[109] Anywhere from one-tenth to one-fourth of the railed grain was sent to İstanbul. In addition, a significant amount was consumed by the military units within the Empire. The construction of the Anatolian railroad did not simply reduce the imports of cereals from abroad. As much as three-quarters of the transported cereals, mostly barley, were destined for the European market.[110]

With respect to landownership and tenancy patterns, the differences between central Anatolia and eastern Anatolia, particularly its southern tier, need to be emphasized at the outset. Although the *ayans* were quite powerful in central Anatolia during the eighteenth century, their influence was reduced, large holdings were broken up, and lord-peasant bonds were weakened during the 1830s. As a result, centuries after the dissolution of the *tımar* system, the Ottoman state was able to reassert its power in the region. Because of the absence of inexpensive forms of transportation and relative scarcity of labour, large amounts of land not substantially lower in quality than those already under cultivation remained untilled until the 1890s and even after construction of the railroad. Small holdings and small peasant ownership dominated. State taxation and usury were the main mechanisms of appropriating the surplus from the direct producer.[111]

When the Anatolian railway provided the transportation link, a shortage of labour emerged as the major obstacle in the way of expansion of cereal production in the region. To solve this problem, large numbers of immigrants from the seceding areas of the Empire, particularly from the Balkans, were settled along the railway.[112] The distribution of state lands to the immigrant families reinforced the existing small-middle ownership pattern.[113] The establishment of commodity-producing households in large numbers and the availability of large amounts of land made the separation of direct producers from land and the emergence of wage labour extremely difficult.[114]

Two developments of the 1880s need to be underlined here: world wheat prices continued to decline rapidly, and the long-standing historical position of Germany as a net exporter changed to one of a net importer of wheat.[115] Not coincidentally, the construction of the Anatolian railroad by German capital started towards the end of the same decade. However, given the primitive nature of agricultural techniques and the permanent indebtedness of the small peasantry, sustained increases in the volume of rail shipments and transformation of the area into a bread basket for Germany could hardly be expected. Hence, after the turn of the century, the Anatolian railway company was actively involved in the agriculture of the region, extending credit to middle farmers for seeds, land-improvement schemes, and irrigation projects.[116] Had it not been for the outbreak of the World War, this particular form of intervention by foreign capital would have accelerated the ongoing differentiation of agricultural producers to consolidate a class of middle peasants in central Anatolia.

Conclusion

Several important studies on nineteenth-century Ottoman agriculture in northern Greece and Anatolia have been undertaken in recent years.[117] They have paved the way for a broader perspective on the penetration of world-capitalism and its spatially uneven impact. In this chapter we undertook a region-by-region, comparative analysis of the dynamics of change in nineteenth-century Ottoman agriculture. The conceptual problem is a familiar one: how did the relations of production change in a socio-economic formation as it came into contact with world-capitalism, as commodity production for export increased and as foreign investment in infrastructure and in trade expanded?

Our analysis has focused on the forms of surplus appropriation from the direct producers, on the policies of the Ottoman state which heavily taxed the small peasant producers and, at the same time, attempted to support them against the emergence of a powerful class of large landowners and on the long-term rhythms of the penetration of world capitalism. With respect to the latter, it had already been emphasized that foreign investment and the world-market-induced expansion of commodity production did not follow an unbroken line over the course of the century. The rate of growth of the external trade of the Ottoman Empire accelerated during periods of expansion of the world-economy. Similarly, foreign capital came in waves, the logic and the timing of which was closely tied to the long-term economic cycles in the capital-exporting countries and their rivalry. The complex interaction of these factors led to major regional differences in patterns of landownership and tenancy.

We can now group direct producers in early twentieth-century Ottoman agriculture into four basic categories:

(1) servile tenants in southeastern Anatolia whose dependence on the landlords was not limited to economic factors;
(2) a limited number of wage labourers, mostly seasonal, who were concentrated in the most commercialized, most export-oriented regions;
(3) some fixed-rent and mostly share-cropping tenants in large-, middle- and small-sized holdings, whose relations with the landowners did not go beyond the economic; and
(4) owner-producers in small- and middle-sized holdings.

We have emphasized that, regional variations notwithstanding, the last two categories constituted the overwhelming majority of direct producers in Ottoman agriculture. In other words, small peasant ownership and petty-commodity production remained central characteristics of Ottoman agriculture during the nineteenth century as capitalism was beginning to penetrate and dominate the rural areas. We would suggest, finally, that dynamics of contemporary agrarian change in these areas of the world cannot be fully understood without due attention to this historical legacy – regional variation and petty-commodity production.

9 ❧ Primitive accumulation in Egypt, 1798–1882*

ALAN R. RICHARDS

This paper provides an interpretation of eighteenth- and nineteenth-century Egyptian history. I use two sets of categories. First, I use the notion of 'the modern world-system', a conception of the reproduction process of any local society which locates it within a larger, international process of reproduction through the international division of labour. In this view, there have been two varieties of world-systems: empires and the modern, capitalist system. In both, the 'basic linkage between the parts of the system is economic'; however, unlike empires, the modern world-system 'is larger than any juridically defined political unit'.[1] Second, I employ the categories of technical and social relations of production. The former is essentially the same as technology (how people interact with nature to reproduce themselves), while the latter comprises the division of labour and class relations, i.e., the locus of decision-making power over natural resources, produced means of production, and, therefore, over human labour (how people interact with each other to reproduce themselves). I shall argue that, before the period of Muhammad ᶜAli, Egypt was part of the 'Ottoman world-system'. As a result of the conjuncture of the growth of the European capitalist world-system with the internal social relations of Egypt, a systemic crisis was created. But because of these internal social relations, a resolution of the crisis was impossible unless the 'rules of the game' were altered. The solution to the crisis pursued by Muhammad ᶜAli (and Ali Bey before him) was the 'solution' of establishing an 'Egyptian world-system' or empire. But, in fact, in the process of pursuing such a solution, Muhammad ᶜAli initiated the integration of Egypt into the capitalist world-system. As a direct consequence the social and technical relations of production in agriculture were transformed.

Indeed, one might argue that such a transformation of the relations of

*Since the first publication of this article in 1977, the author has modified his position on a number of issues discussed here. For these modifications see Alan R. Richards, *Egypt's agricultural development, 1800–1980: technical and social change* (Boulder, Colorado, Westview Press, 1982).

production *was* the process of integration. If one grants that capitalism is, and has been since its inception, an international social system (that is, a set of rules governing the division of labour, the production of goods, and their distribution), then it is clear that when a 'society' moves from one world-system with its set of rules (say, the Ottoman Empire) into the capitalist world-system with a different set of rules, the rules governing this society are altered. In the language of systems theory, the capitalist world-system, like any complex system, has a 'control hierarchy', in which higher-order rules control the lower. The rules of distribution and production in Egypt would thus be modified by the more inclusive fundamental rules governing the system as a whole.[2] To put it more simply, the study of Egypt's integration into the capitalist world-system is the study of the development of capitalism in that country. Here I adopt the Marxian view that capital is a social relation between the direct producers and those who can extract part of the net product (surplus) by virtue of their ownership of non-human productive resources. Capitalism requires the separation of the direct producer from the means of production; it implies that large numbers of people lose decision-making power over the natural resources needed for the production of material life. The process by which this separation is first achieved is 'original accumulation'. Such an 'original' or 'primitive accumulation' is a necessary condition for the rise of capitalist relations of production.

Since the principal natural resource in Egypt was (is) land, original accumulation in Egypt is very largely the story of how large numbers of peasants lost decision-making power over their land. This does not imply simply that the individual peasant family had possessed complete decision-making power over the land and then lost it to someone else. Rather, the process involved the dissolution of old, quasi-communal forms of land tenure (although the extent to which tenure was communal differed between the two principal regions of the country) and their replacement by private property in land. Such a change concentrated decision-making power over land. Given the importance of the control over land to the reproduction process of Egyptian society, the land-tenure system constitutes the primary social relation whose transformation I wish to trace.

Although the separation of the peasant from the land is a necessary condition for fully capitalist social relations, it is not sufficient.

> A presupposition of wage labor . . . is free labor and the exchange of this free labor for money. Another presupposition is the separation of free labor from the objective conditions of its realization – from the means of labor and the material for labor.[3]

The first aspect of capitalist social relations was only partially fulfilled in Egypt. First, of course, the existence of the corvée meant that the Egyptian peasant was not free in Marx's double sense (free to sell his labour power on the market and free from the possession of any other commodity to sell). The system of exploitation which came to be employed on large estates (*ᶜezbah*s) included the pre- or non-capitalist feature that a section of the work force was remunerated not in cash, but rather with small parcels of land on which to produce their own subsistence *directly*. This feature of rural social relations, coupled with the direct coercive power which estate holders exercised on their lands and the system of debt peonage for small peasants, resident ᶜ*ezbah* workers, and migrant labourers alike is the key to understanding the often-made statement that Egypt's integration into the capitalist world-system created a social system of 'agrarian capitalism'.[4] Nevertheless, an analysis of the degree of supervision of the work force and of the amount of labour time which the agricultural worker spent working for the owners of the land reveals important differences between Mamluk and 'post-cotton' Egypt. In particular, I shall argue that the scope of the decision-making power which the fellah exercised in agricultural production was narrower under the ᶜ*ezbah* system than under the Mamluk system. The peasants also came to work more hours per year than had been the case in the eighteenth century. Both the decline in the decision-making power of the direct producer and the initial increase in labour time are, of course, general features of the development of capitalism. Not only was Egypt capitalist because it had private property rights in land and labour and was selling a commodity on the international capitalist market; the structure of social relations at the point of production itself also had important capitalist features.

I think that it can be shown that the transformation of the social relations of production, the rise of private property in land and the attendant peasant land loss, was directly connected to the integration of Egypt to the world-economy. The key export crop in Egypt was cotton. As we shall see, large-scale production of cotton required considerable changes in the irrigation system. The way in which this technical change was carried out, with corvée labour and heavy land taxes, directly affected the peasants, causing many of them to lose their land. Further, as the agricultural economy became more and more oriented toward the production of cotton for export, foreigners, especially Europeans, became increasingly interested in the country. They lent large sums to the government and were a constant source of pressure on the government to establish private property in land. To become part of the capitalist world-market, Egypt needed capitalist institutions with which those foreigners wishing to do business in Egypt were familiar.

The nature of this original accumulation had important consequences for the future. New groups rose to positions of power in the countryside, and some old groups strengthened their position. These dislocations created the environment within which the ᶜUrabi revolt of 1882 occurred; they were a necessary, although not sufficient, condition for the outbreak of the revolt. Since the revolt precipitated the British intervention and later occupation, which, in at least one prominent historical interpretation,[5] precipitated the division of all of eastern Africa among the European powers in the late nineteenth century, the importance of these dislocations is obvious.

The social relations of production of the pre-capitalist order

Since an understanding of the nature and consequences of the transformation of the relations of production in nineteenth-century Egypt requires an overview of the pre-capitalist order, I will start by sketching the social relations of production (including trade patterns) in Mamluk or Ottoman Egypt (1516–1798) and then describe the basin system of irrigated agriculture, or the physical relations of production in the nineteenth century before the British intervention and occupation in 1882. This will involve a discussion of the changes in the irrigation system, the emergence of private property in land, the origin of the principal social classes, and the emergent forms of land and labour exploitation. The main theme is 'primitive accumulation' and its relationship to the changes in agricultural technology. At the same time, I wish to demonstrate how the ʿUrabi revolt of 1882 had its social roots in this transformation of production relations.

Egypt had two principal functions in the Ottoman imperial system. First, it supplied foodstuffs, both in the form of tribute and as commodities, to İstanbul and the Holy Places of Arabia. Other areas of the Empire, such as Rumelia, Anatolia, and Syria, received foodstuffs as well. Secondly, Egypt was the focal point of an extensive transit trade between Africa, Arabia, and the rest of Asia on the one hand and the Mediterranean countries on the other. Revenues obtained from customs duties formed part of the tribute sent to the Porte. Within one hundred years of the conquest, however, both the Ottoman imperial system as a whole and the Egyptian component of it were in decline, and by the mid eighteenth century Egyptian society was in full-scale crisis. The dynamic and origins of this crisis may be sketched as follows. The decline of central authority in İstanbul and the decline in government revenues led to the creation of a system of tax-farming (*iltizam*), which increased the tax burdens on the peasantry. The decline in the transit trade in coffee after 1725 put downward pressure on government revenues; this joined with a strong demand for revenue to finance internal and external wars of the ruling class of large tax-farmers to intensify pressures on the peasants. The heavier tax burden, the increase in Bedouin activity, and random ecological shocks (flood variations and epidemics) depopulated the countryside. However, this crisis did little to alter the social relations of production in agriculture itself. Certain features of those relations, primarily the organization of access to land and the lack of direct contact between the ruling class and the peasantry, inhibited the transformation of these social relations. That would only come with the resolution of the crisis by the integration of Egypt into the European capitalist world-system in the nineteenth century. The rest of this section is devoted to elaborating and documenting these assertions.

Scholars have long emphasized Egypt's function as the granary of the Ottoman Empire, supplying wheat, rice, lentils, beans, etc., to Rumelia,

Anatolia, Syria, and the Hejaz.[6] She also exported raw materials for manufacturing to the rest of the Empire, primarily flax (to Syria and the Greek Islands) and indigo (to Syria). Her own manufactured cloth was exported to the Maghreb, Arabia, Rumelia, Anatolia, Syria, and Darfur.[7] Also, the researches of André Raymond have shown that Egypt was the centre of a large and flourishing entrepôt trade between the Orient and Africa on the one hand and the Mediterranean on the other.[8] Coffee had replaced spices as the mainstay of this trade by 1700. Grown in the Yemen and re-exported via Egypt to the rest of the Ottoman Empire and to Europe, the coffee trade dominated Egyptian trade to such an extent that Raymond had gone so far as to call it 'the principal economic activity of Europe'.[9] The transit trade comprised about 25 per cent of all Egyptian imports and perhaps 40 per cent of all exports. For our purposes here, it is important to note Raymond's estimate that the taxes on the trade comprised approximately 50 per cent of the total government revenues, the other 50 per cent coming from agricultural taxation.

The coffee trade underwent a relative decline after its zenith in the years between 1690 and 1725. The Europeans were not able to dislodge the Muslims from the coffee trade by force as they had done earlier with pepper and spices. The Ottomans held Aden until 1830 and the superior naval technology of the Europeans, so telling in the Indian Ocean, was less significant in the closed and placid Red Sea.[10] Instead, the Europeans were able to set up their own coffee plantations in the Caribbean.[11] From a world-systems perspective, the rise of plantation colonies not only contributed to the resolution of the 'general crisis of the seventeenth century',[12] but also weakened the economic position of the 'external arena' (e.g., Egypt), preparing it, so to speak, for membership in the periphery of the system. West Indian coffee first arrived in Marseilles around 1730, and by 1786–9 some 21 per cent of French coffee was sold in the Levant. Its price was roughly 25 per cent lower than that of Yemeni coffee. There appears to be an interaction among declining trade volume, increased per unit levies on trade, and higher, less competitive coffee prices. Formally, the problem was that while the demand for Yemeni coffee was relatively elastic, ruling-class demand for tax revenues was inelastic for reasons discussed below. Therefore, any fall in the volume of revenue would lead to an increase in its 'price', or per unit taxation. When these per unit levies were translated into higher prices, sales, and therefore revenues, also fell, and the process repeated itself. By 1764 the competition of West Indian coffee was sufficiently severe that its importation into Egypt was prohibited.[13]

The competition of European trade led not only to a decline in total trade volume and in government revenue, but also to a problem in the balance of trade. As alluded to above, Egyptian trade was composed of two sectors: trade with Africa, Arabia, and the Orient on the one hand, and trade with the Mediterranean, both Christian and Muslim, on the other. The strong Egyptian deficit on the first account was covered by a strong surplus on the latter. In 1700–

30 European trade, with a balance favourable to Egypt, contributed to equilibrium in Egyptian trade. But, by the end of the century, Europe was selling more to Egypt than she was buying. Raymond ascribes this to two forces: (1) the decline in the coffee and the other transit trades (the mainstay of Egyptian–European commerce), and (2) the rapid decline in Egyptian cloth exports to France after 1730.[14] The resulting imbalance contributed to the depreciation of the Egyptian currency. The roughly contemporary decline in the inflow of Sudani gold aggravated the depreciation.[15] Presumably, this depreciation of the currency raised the price of imports of European goods, largely luxury products and arms.[16] We shall see that there are reasons for supposing that the demand for luxury goods and arms by the ruling class was inelastic, and perhaps shifting out in the eighteenth century. The depreciation therefore contributed to increased demands for revenue.

Be that as it may, it would be unwise to over-emphasize the role of Europe for Egyptian trade. Overall, trade with Europe accounted for about one-seventh of Egypt's total trade.[17] The trade with İstanbul alone surpassed that with Europe. Egypt was, at this time, part of the Ottoman, not the European capitalist, world-system. Aside from the transit trade, Egypt exported some textiles to Europe (nine-tenths of these to France), and some rice and wheat to Marseilles and Livorno. Towards the end of the century, it appears that large quantities of wheat were exported to France. Girard reported that in the last three years of the eighteenth century, some 800,000 *ardeb*s of wheat were sent to Marseilles.[18] However, this trade suffered from several severe handicaps. Both demand and supply were highly unstable. Only in times of famine (*disette*) was there a demand for Egyptian grain in Europe.[19] Similarly, the vagaries of the Nile flood caused sharp fluctuations in the amount of grain which was available for export. Egyptian government policy contributed to the frailty of this trade. The export of rice and wheat to Christendom, for example, was illegal.[20] Although a clandestine trade existed and was at times openly encouraged by the Beys, European traders were exposed to *avania*s and extraordinary levies at virtually all times.[21]

To summarize the preceding discussion, we note that Egyptian trade played a vital role in the Ottoman world-system and in the local economy. Egypt supplied large quantities of foodstuffs to other parts of the Ottoman Empire, as well as some textiles and raw materials for manufacturing. The transit trade in coffee was a critical component of the whole. Its decline, along with the decline in other exports, reduced government revenues, created balance-of-trade deficits, and contributed to the depreciation of the currency. The role of European competition and the increasing demands for revenue from the ruling class seem to be the principal forces behind this stagnation and decline in trade. Increased insecurity of trade routes inside Egypt and in the eastern Mediterranean also contributed to the decline. But to understand the government's demand for revenue, we must understand the structure of the social relations of production in agriculture, and to these we now turn.

The fiscal crisis of the Ottoman state required decentralizing provincial administration.[22] In Egypt such decentralization took the form of grants of *iltizam* or tax-farming. Under this system, Mamluks (elite warrior-slaves) were responsible for supervising tax-collection. They then paid a fixed sum to the *emins* (salaried representatives of the Ottoman Treasury) and pocketed what was left, and the surplus of *fa'id*. In return for this privilege of tax-collection, the holder paid an initial fee. As Hansen has stressed,[23] this switch to *iltizam* was a form of borrowing by the government, in which the latter forswore future revenues (the *fa'id*) in exchange for the payment now. By 1671 officials sent from the Porte had little authority.[24] As the *emins*ᶜ importance dwindled, the Mamluks became the dominant power in the land.[25]

For our purposes here, three aspects of rural social relations are of interest: (1) the allocation of decision-making power over land and the systems used for exploiting it; (2) the structure of social relations *within* the ruling class; and (3) the system of village solidarity *vis-à-vis* demands of the ruling class. Let us examine these in turn. The *tasarruf* or use of the land was divided between the *multezim* (tax farmer) and the peasants.[26] The latter's land (*ʾard al-fellah*) was reserved for their use, and they paid a variety of taxes on it to the *multezim*. The land reserved for the exclusive enjoyment of the *multezim*, the *ʾard al-wasiyyah*, was estimated at roughly 10 per cent of the *ʾard al-fellah* at the end of the eighteenth century.[27] There were three ways of exploiting this land. First, the *multezim* might rent out the land to the village shaykh or headman who would direct the agricultural operations of the other peasants. Secondly, he might exploit the lands directly using paid labour. Thirdly, he might use corvée labour.[28] Supervision of the agricultural activities on these lands was carried out by a variety of personnel from the Mamluk's 'household'. Each powerful *multezim* had a sort of military lieutenant (*qa'imaqam*), himself a Mamluk, who generally lived on the *ʾard al-wasiyyah* and who was in charge of supervising cultivation and taxation.[29] But he did not do this directly. Rather, he was assisted here by a variety of local officials, and the actual supervision of cultivation and other agricultural operations was the responsibility of the village shaykh and another villager, the *khawli*.[30] In addition, there were a host of other officials, perhaps the most prominent being the *sarraf* or treasurer, usually a Copt, who kept the accounts. All of these individuals received tax exemptions and payments in kind.[31] Peasant labour was paid in cash (for cultivation), in kind (for harvest), or not at all (if corvée labour).[32] Much of the labour came from among the local villagers holding usufructory rights to the *ʾard al-fellah*, but there were some landless peasants. Many of these appear to have been peasants whose lands had not been watered by the annual Nile flood; they were, therefore, landless only temporarily.[33]

The system of tax-farming led to increasing burdens on the peasant. In the first place, changes in military technology and changes in trade led to pressure on government revenues. In part, the Egyptian Mamluks tried to solve these problems by sending less tribute to İstanbul.[34] But this alone could not solve the problem because the second aspect of rural social relations, those within the ruling class, raised the Mamluks' demand for revenue and rendered such demand inelastic. Each Mamluk 'house', composed of the head of the house and his military slaves, was in severe competition with the others. Although they did form coalitions, these appear to have been unstable and no single faction was able to establish a centralized, powerful regime of their own. Doing so was especially difficult since (1) the inclusion of the offspring of Mamluks as members of the house perpetuated conflicts of revenge, and (2) the Mamluks were formidably armed (by the seventeenth century) with carbines and pistols.[35]

This structure of conflict and mutual distrust meant that each Mamluk house had a large and inelastic demand for resources in order to obtain the arms needed for defence and aggression and the luxury goods needed as symbols of power to retain the loyalty of followers. Recall that the price of these goods was pushed up by the depreciation of the currency and that revenues from trade were declining. The only solution was to tax the peasants more. Average taxation in terms of gold per *feddan* (slightly more than an acre) increased by roughly 35 per cent from the sixteenth to the end of the eighteenth century.[36] These were the official taxes, usually in kind for lands planted in wheat or beans, in cash for land planted in either millet or maize.[37] Most of the in-kind payments were transported along the Nile to Cairo, where they were stored in giant warehouses between Bulaq and Misr al-Qadimmah.[38] There it was sold, or shipped directly as tribute to İstanbul or the Holy Cities of Arabia. Some of the goods were consumed in Cairo, and the rest was exported.[39] Other extraordinary levies were common. The corvée for the *ʾard al-wasiyyah* has already been mentioned; in the sixteenth century, peasants had been paid for the corvée labour on irrigation works, but by the eighteenth century they were not.[40] Other levies were imposed; the costs of feeding Mamluks whenever they arrived in the village, the costs of tax-collection itself, and the cost of transporting the taxed goods to market were all borne by the peasants.[41] Shaw describes the collection of taxes at harvest time as 'large scale raiding operations, with resultant depopulation, famine and devastation'.[42] By the time of the French invasion, after over a century of war, Bedouin raids, and oppressive taxation, the population had declined to about two and a half million. Comparisons with earlier times are difficult; however, Ömer Lütfi Barkan estimates between four and five million in the sixteenth century.[43] This is lower than the estimate for Roman times of 'seven and a half million exclusive of Alexandria – one of the very few ancient population figures we have that is likely to be accurate'.[44]

Why didn't the Mamluks realize that they were 'killing the goose that laid the golden egg'? Hansen has argued that from the *multezim*'s point of view there was an 'optimal rate of taxation'. This was the rate which would provide the maximum *long-run* revenue, which in turn implied taxing peasants just below the level at which they would abandon their lands and flee to the cities, to the desert and swamps, or to Syria.[45] But the structure of social relations *within* the ruling class largely precluded this. In game-theoretic terms, ruling-class conflict took the form of the 'prisoners' dilemma', a non-zero sum game whose solution is suboptimal for both players. Two Mamluks might agree that they would both be better off if they stopped fighting each other, thereby reducing their demand for arms and luxury goods, which in turn would lead them to tax their peasants less heavily and so induce them to remain on the land. But if one Mamluk reduced his taxes and his acquisition of arms, but the other did not and then attacked, the result for the first Mamluk was complete catastrophe. In the not-so-long run, most Mamluks would be dead. In the absence of any central ruler strong enough to impose his will on the entire country, each Mamluk house had to press for enough revenue to protect itself against attack. They were therefore driven to squeeze the peasants until, in the words of the seventeenth-century peasant poet, 'my testicles are like palm fibre'.[46]

Nevertheless, the peasants were not entirely defenceless. The village unit afforded them some protection and, more importantly for our analysis, protected the structure of social relations within the village and between the village and the ruling class. It was this third feature of rural social relations which ensured that the dynamic of crisis outlined above would not, in itself, lead to a transformation of social relations. This protective organization had two parts. The first was the organization of peasant land. In this, as in other respects, Lower (northern) Egypt differed from Middle and Upper Egypt. In the latter region, 'lands were held communally and assigned to individual cultivators annually as soon as the extent of the Nile flood became apparent'.[47] Because variations in the Nile flood caused considerable differences in the land available for cultivation in a given year, it was difficult to establish separate boundaries. Land was therefore distributed by the village shaykh in accordance with the ability of a family to cultivate the land.[48]

In Lower Egypt, where boundaries could be established more easily, individual families cultivated a fixed area of the *ʾard al-fellah*, in contrast to the communal system of the Saʿid (Upper Egypt). These areas, called *athar*, were handed down from father to son. The son had to pay the *multezim* an investiture tax, and then the land, or rather its use, was his. The usufruct could be sold, but this seems to have mostly involved pawning the land, rather than outright sale.[49] The *multezim* could, however, remove a peasant from his land for failure to pay his taxes. Such a peasant then either stayed in the village as an agricultural labourer, or fled.[50] The actual legal protection afforded the *individual* peasant, then, was not so great as might at first appear. However, the peasants *as a group*, the village, did not lose land abandoned for failure to pay taxes to *ʾard al-wasiyyah* of the *multezim*. Rather, the shaykh would give the land to another peasant.[51]

The second organizational feature protecting the peasants was that neither the Mamluks nor the Bedouin shaykhs (who held power in Upper Egypt until 1760) had much to do with the peasants directly. The *multezims* or their representatives dealt with the village shaykhs, not the individual peasants.[52] The shaykh was in charge of distributing land in Upper Egypt, as we have seen; in Lower Egypt, he was responsible to some extent for organizing work on the *ᵓard al-fellah*. If a *multezim* rented his *ᶜard al-wasiyyah*, he rented it to the shaykh who then dealt with the problem of getting the villagers to work it. If the *multezim* worked his land with a corvée, then the shaykh supervised it. No one, however, tried to tell the peasants which crops to raise.

> The fellahs enjoy furthermore total discretion as to the kind of produce they wish to raise: they can sow wheat, rice, *doura*, as they prefer.[53]

The shaykhs were responsible for both the maintenance of order and the collection of taxes, in the sense that they were held responsible if the tax-collection came up short. The peasant did come into contact with the Mamluks at harvest and tax-gathering time, but the contact was minimal, limited to a beating or two.

There may have been some direct contact between peasants and *multezims* through the circulation process of the economy. If a peasant did temporarily alienate his land, then he would have pawned it to those who had cash. These were, perhaps, the *multezims*.[54] The *multezims* always supplied working capital on their *ᵓard al-wasiyyah*, but here, too, they went through the shaykhs. I have not been able to find any evidence on how extensive such financial contact may have been; most social historians (e.g., Shaw, Baer, and Rivlin), as well as the primary source of Lancret's testimony, emphasize the lack of direct contact between Mamluks and peasants. The village *as a whole* was responsible for taxation and for the corvée; allocation of the individual fulfilment of these two duties, given the collective quota, was the role of the village shaykh.[55]

This isolation, and especially the organization of peasant land, lent stability to the social relations of production in the countryside.[56] The increased tax burden, resulting from Mamluk myopia, their increased need for revenue, and the decline in trade revenues induced peasants to abandon their lands and to flee, but it did not lead to any change in what was produced, how it was produced, or how the labour was organized and supervised. The crisis of Mamluk society led to quantitative regression, but not to qualitative transformation.

The physical relations of production of Mamluk Egypt: the basin system of irrigation

This 'corporate' social structure rested upon a particular system of irrigated agriculture. Since Egypt's integration into the world-economy as a cotton producer involved the transformation of both the social relations described above and also the agricultural technology, it will be helpful to outline briefly the main features of the irrigation system and the related patterns of land use. This is what I mean by 'physical relations of production' in the historical context of nineteenth-century Egypt.

The basic system of irrigation had been used in Egypt since the time of the Pharaohs.[57] The topography of the Nile Valley resembles the back of a leaf: the land slopes down gradually from the high land lying along the banks of the river and canals toward the desert. The high land along the banks of the river was flooded perhaps once every fifteen to twenty years when the annual Nile flood was unusually high.[58] The remainder of the land, comprising some 75 per cent of the cultivated area in the Delta (Lower Egypt) and nearly 90 per cent in the valley,[59] was divided into basins by a system of dikes, some running perpendicular to the Nile, others parallel to it. Canals dug through the high land along the banks allowed the rising flood waters to flow into these basins. The water, rich with the sediment carried off from the Ethiopian highlands, was allowed to stand on the fields and soak in after being trapped there by the dikes.[60] After standing for some forty days, the water was either allowed to drain back into the Nile,[61] or flowed on into the next, lower basin.[62]

The irrigation system had a number of important effects upon land use patterns and the maintenance of soil fertility. First, little, if any, fertilizer was required for the basins, since they were supplied with nutrients by the flood every year. Girard asserts that fertilizer was not used on land which was 'irrigated naturally', i.e., on basin lands.[63] They were used on the higher land, which makes sense since these lands were not flooded annually. Secondly, crops sown after the flood required relatively little land preparation: in Upper Egypt, the seeds were simply sown broadcast as the waters receded.[64] In the Delta, the land was ploughed perhaps two times with a scratch plough and then was watered twice during the growing season of wheat (one of the principal basin crops). In Upper Egypt, no additional waterings were given. Land planted in clover (*birsim*) was not ploughed in either region.[65] The French savants who accompanied Napoleon noted that Egyptian basin agriculture required much less labour per unit of land and per unit output than contemporary French peasant agriculture.[66] Thirdly, the basin lands were 'washed' every year and the higher lands were flooded from time to time, thus preventing the build-up of salts in the soil. Although this was helpful for the ecology of the soil, the excessive floods were very destructive of human life by destroying crops and inaugurating the usual cycle of famine and plague. The model of the regression of Mamluk society given above would be incomplete without the inclusion of the aggravating impact of such events. Fourthly, these lands lay fallow for a considerable time before the arrival of the flood in late July–early August. During this period the soil heated up, cracked, and was aerated. Fifthly, crops whose growing season included the dry, pre-flood months had to be grown near the river in order to obtain the necessary water. Since these lands were high, as

Table 9.1 *Labour inputs for crops under the basin system of irrigation, 1801*

Crop	Man days/*feddan* (1 *feddan* ≈ 1 acre)
Durah (millet)*	85
Maize*	65 (irrigation and harvest only)
Wheat *al-bayady* (dry season)	15
Barley *al-bayady*	7½
Birsim (clover)	13–15
Beans *al-bayady*	20
Wheat *al-shitwi** (winter crop)	86
Barley *al-shitwi**	70
Flax*	72 (irrigation only)
Cotton*	500 plus harvest
Onion*	80

* indicates that the crop required labour for irrigation.

Source: M.P.S. Girard, 'Mémoire sur l'agriculture, l'industrie, et le commerce de l'Égypte', *Description de l'Égypte, état moderne*, II, pt. 1, 565–81.

previously noted, and since the Nile was low during this season, the water had to be raised a considerable distance to the fields. This required a great deal of labour. Some rough figures for the labour needed for the different crops are given in Table 9.1.

The cropping patterns were in large part dictated by the timing of the flood and the structure of the irrigation system. The basin lands were cropped once per year and followed a two-year rotation of wheat and barley alternating with *birsim* and beans.[67] In addition to these staple crops, cash crops such as sugar, indigo, and rice were grown. These latter required a great deal of labour; indigo, for example, was cultivated for four years and required nine men per *feddan* for eight months of the year.[68] It was grown by 'well-to-do proprietors' and/or peasant cooperatives.[69] Cotton was grown under the basin system, but it was not a particularly profitable crop.[70] It was grown as a perennial crop in Upper Egypt, although an annual variety was cultivated in the Delta.[71] Since its growing season was from February to October, the area planted with it was constrained both by the need to be on high ground to protect it from the flood (although it was possible to build supplementary dikes to serve this purpose), and, more importantly, by its heavy water requirements during the summer when the Nile was at its nadir. Its watering required about 480 man days per *feddan* (two men per *feddan* for eight months of the year).[72] If cotton was to be grown on a large scale, the irrigation system, the physical relations of production would have to be transformed. In the process, the social relations of production were also altered. The process by which Egypt became a major cotton exporter can be viewed as a dual transformation of the relations of production. Let us now turn to this transformation.

Muhammad ʿAli and the beginnings of cotton cultivation

Muhammad ʿAli's massacre of the Mamluks resolved the 'prisoners' dilemma' within Egypt by destroying organized military opposition within the ruling class. In this he had simply succeeded where others, such as Ali Bey Bulut Kapan, had failed.[73] But this did not imply any lessening of the tax burden on the peasants, for Muhammad ʿAli embarked on a program of 'primitive accumulation'. Indeed, such a program was a necessary component of the resolution of the prisoners' dilemma. At the core of this process was the need for a large standing army, both to acquire 'colonies' in the Sudan, western Arabia, and Syria, and to defend his position in Egypt against possible Egyptian rivals and the Porte. Of course, this was very costly, especially since a modern army would have to be created from scratch. The problem was how to acquire the resources necessary for such a plan. Since his principal goal, independence, necessarily implied conflict with the Ottoman sultan, and since, as we have seen, the overwhelming majority of Egypt's trade had been with the Empire, Muhammad ʿAli needed (and proceeded) to reorient Egyptian trade toward the West. As Rivlin has pointed out, the irony is that the pursuit of independence from the Ottoman Empire led Egypt towards dependence on the West.[74] By 1823, some 76 per cent of Egyptian exports were going to Europe.[75] The consequences of this reorientation were far-reaching, as we shall see.

To facilitate revenue collection and to protect his centralized power, Muhammad ʿAli abolished the *iltizam* system and replaced it with the *ihtikar*, or monopoly system. This system had three essential features. First, taxes were collected directly, by government employees receiving a salary. Secondly, peasants delivered crops at prices fixed by Muhammad ʿAli at levels below the market price.[76] Thirdly, he monopolized both internal and external trade. At first, this system was limited to the traditional crops of the country; it was inaugurated in Upper Egypt in 1812 when the entire grain crop was seized.[77] But increasingly he turned towards cotton as an export crop. This not only helped to integrate Egypt into the European world-system, but also contributed to peasant land loss. However, the *ihtikar* system was incompatible with the increasing contact with Europe. The usual difficulties of running a centralized bureaucracy in a pre-industrial society joined with European pressures to force Muhammad ʿAli to abolish the system and to share the power. In doing so, he laid the foundations for the rise of social groups which would dominate the century, the pashas and the shaykhs. At the same time, his policies had helped to weaken, but not to destroy, the protective social relations of the village, thereby beginning their transformation into capitalist forms.

Thus Muhammad ʿAli's reign is important for three reasons. First, he initiated the integration of Egypt into the European world-system as a supplier of agricultural goods. As a part of this process, he introduced the cultivation of long-staple cotton into the country and began the transformation of the Delta from basin to perennial irrigation. Secondly, his policies redistributed the control over inputs into agricultural production; his policies laid the foundations of the country's class structure. Thirdly, the peasants were brought into direct contact with the government for the first time, disrupting and partially transforming village social relations at the point of production. The suffering and dislocation of peasant life caused by this contact make Egypt a classic case of the thesis that the first dealings which peasants have with the central government in the modern era is military, oppressive, and violent. This dislocation was an essential part of the redistribution of land. In Egypt original accumulation was primitive indeed. For the rest of this section, I will be concerned with these changes which Muhammad ᶜAli wrought in the technical and social relations of production.

Since Muhammad ᶜAli needed revenue, and since it had to come from Europe, he needed something to sell there. This meant an agricultural good of some sort. We have seen that, in the late eighteenth century, France and Italy were importing wheat from Egypt. One might suppose that the logical response to this problem, given the information costs of finding new markets, would simply be to expand these exports. But here Egypt suffered from several disadvantages. France placed a sliding-scale tariff duty on grain imports in 1819. The Restoration government raised the rates in 1821 to such an extent that imports of grain were permitted in only one month from 1821 to 1830.[78] Tariffs remained essentially unchanged until the Second Empire in the 1850s.[79] For the period of Muhammad ᶜAli's reign, wheat exports to France could not provide the kinds of revenues which he required. The same, of course, applied to Great Britain with its Corn Laws from 1815 to 1846.[80] In the rest of the Mediterranean, Egypt faced new and formidable competition from Black Sea grain. Italy became 'dependent on Russian hard wheat for her pasta'.[81] Egyptian threshing techniques (crushing the grains with a *nurag*, a heavy wooden sled with iron disks drawn by oxen) contributed to its weak competitive position in the wheat export market.[82] On the other hand, there was a strong demand in Europe for long-staple cotton, and its price was between two and four times as high as Egyptian short-staple cotton.[83] Foreign experts were brought in and given charge over several villages in 1821 and 1822. The resulting cotton was of high quality and fetched a high price in European markets. This provided Muhammad ᶜAli with the incentive to extend its cultivation.

As we have seen, however, such an extension would have been quite difficult under the basin system of irrigation. Consequently, Muhammad ᶜAli embarked upon a large-scale program of public works to supply the necessary summer water. New canals were constructed and old ones were deepened. Altogether some 240 miles had been dug by 1822.[84] *Saqiyah*s (water wheels) and *shaduf*s (counter-weight-lifting devices) were also constructed. The labour for these projects was provided by the corvée, which is discussed below. By the early 1830s, 600,000 *feddan*s could be placed under summer cultivation, in comparison with 250,000 in 1798.[85]

At first, Muhammad ʿAli tried to induce the peasants to raise the crop by offering high prices and supplying working capital. Initially he offered 175 per *qantar* ($\approx$99 lbs) and 'made generous advances . . . of seed, oxen, and water-raising devices'.[86] Prices offered to the cultivators had declined to 100–150 piastres per *qantar* in 1826 and, although the evidence is fragmentary, they do not seem to have risen much until 1834. Yet it appears that Muhammad ʿAli's prices were more or less in line with international prices, falling in the late 1820s and then rising again in the early 1830s.[87]

However, there is evidence of peasant resistance to cotton growing. In some areas they would surreptitiously remove the cotton seeds which they had planted 'in the hope of convincing the [local] Bey that the soil was not suitable for cotton cultivation'.[88] In 1834 army officers and soldiers were sent to supervise the work in the fields.[89] Rivlin asserts that there was 'a noticeable lethargy among the fellaheen toward cotton cultivation'.[90] There are perhaps two reasons for this. Until 1836, the peasants were not paid in cash, but rather in tax credits.[91] And there were labour-power problems: cotton was a labour-using crop and the amount of labour power which was available in a given village was declining owing to conscription, corvée, and flight. Consequently, peasants might well have preferred to assure their subsistence crops before undertaking the cultivation of cotton.

Muhammad ʿAli laid down strict rules on how cotton should be grown, rules derived largely from the advice of his foreign experts and later codified in the *Laʾihat Ziraʿah al-fellah* (Regulations of Peasant Agriculture).[92] These extremely precise instructions were enforced by a hierarchical command structure with Muhammad ʿAli at the apex and the *qaʾimaqam* and village shaykh at the base. The law obliged the latter to go to the fields *every day* to inspect the peasants' labour. Severe beatings were prescribed for the slothful or disobedient.[93] Formerly beaten at harvest time (a practice which continued), the peasants were now also beaten throughout the eight-month cotton-growing season. The same command hierarchy enforced government decisions on the crop mix for each locality and collected taxes. In short, the government told the peasants what to plant, when to plant, and how to plant. This direct governmental interference in the physical production process contrasts sharply with the Mamluk system, although the mediating role of the shaykh provided some continuity with earlier practices.

The peasants under Muhammad ʿAli: the beginning of primitive accumulation

The interference by the government in the lives of the peasants in this period was extensive. In this section, I wish to examine the effects of Muhammad ʿAli's policies on the peasantry and their response to the situation. The origins of 'primitive accumulation' in the sense of peasant land loss are to be found in this conflict, so it would be wise to look at it in some detail. There were the agricultural regulations discussed above. A far greater burden, however, was impressment, either in the corvée, or worse, in the military. The corvée, of course, had existed for centuries as a means of maintaining the dikes and canals of the basin system. However, villagers worked to maintain the irrigation works of their *own* village. The effects of their labour were, therefore, clearly visible and obviously benefited them and their families, thereby legitimizing the system. But under Muhammad ʿAli, peasants were now dragooned to work far from their homes. They received little, if any payment – perhaps one piastre per day for giant public works like the Mahmudiyya Canal in the Delta, nothing for other projects.[94] ʿAmr estimates that 400,000 peasants worked for four months per year on these works.[95] Often they had to supply their own food, water, and tools. Since they were working away from their village, they received few benefits from their work. Even if they were working in their own areas, they may have received few benefits, for, as we shall see later, towards the end of Muhammad ʿAli's reign the lands benefiting from summer water were often appropriated by government officials. If they did have land which could be planted in summer crops, they lost this opportunity (such as it was) by being forced to work on the corvée. After the formation of large estates, the large landowners arranged to have corvée labourers work on their estates and to get their own peasants exempted from the corvée.[96] Under these conditions it is hardly surprising that the peasants were reluctant to be drafted into the corvée. The government, however, compensated for peasant reluctance with the usual brutality. For instance, when the Mahmudiyya Canal was built, soldiers acting as overseers rounded up the peasants and brought them to work with cords around their necks. There were many casualties. Estimates range from 12,000 to 100,000 dead over a three-year period.[97]

The oppression of the corvée was certainly secondary to that of military conscription, however. Muhammad ʿAli had decided to fight his wars with native Egyptian troops, because imported Mamluks would have become a threat to his power and because he realized that their brand of unruly warfare had been shattered by Napoleon's disciplined squads. To fill his military registers, he impressed peasants into the army for life. They were therefore deprived of any chance of family or clan life, were badly paid, miserably fed, and led by Turkish officers who despised them.[98] Although these conditions prompted army mutinies in 1827 and 1832, the peasants in the villages presumably knew little about army conditions and cared less – they simply regarded the idea of conscription as anathema, for it would totally disrupt their lives forever.

The peasants responded to these measures in three ways: by rebelling, by fleeing from the land, and by mutilating themselves. Revolts were fairly numerous. In 1812, when the grain crop was seized for the first time, the Upper Egyptians of the area rebelled and were massacred by Muhammad ʿAli's Albanian cavalry. In 1816 groups of peasants refused to grow the crops which they had been ordered to raise and had to be coerced before they would do so. In

May, 1823, the people of Minufiyya province rebelled against conscription and high taxes. The greatest revolt of the era broke out in April, 1824, in Upper Egypt, extending from Isna to Aswan. The rebels were led by a North African shaykh, Ahmad ibn-Idris, 'who declared that he had been sent by God and His Prophet to end the vexations which the Egyptian people suffered and to punish Muhammad ᶜAli for introducing innovations which ran contrary to the dogma of Islam'.[99] Part of his activities was dividing the contents of government warehouses (*shunas*) among the people.[100] At first the revolt spread, with uprisings as far north as Girga. Many of the fellahin troops sent to quell the revolt joined the rebels, until finally the Turkish mercenaries and Muhammad ᶜAli's bedouin allies crushed the rebellion with the usual carnage.[101] Revolts also occurred in Sharqiyya province in the Delta.[102] Sporadic revolts continued in the 1830s, the most significant one taking place in 1838, again in Upper Egypt, and again prompted by the draft. Since these revolts were never joined by any non-peasant group in society, and since the government had an adequate and passably loyal military force in the bedouins and the cavalry, all of these revolts were crushed fairly easily.

Self-mutilation was a somewhat safer means of thwarting the government and was widespread. Blinding one eye, especially the right one, cutting off the right index finger, and pulling the front teeth seem to have been the most common forms.[103] This worked so well that, in Girga, a province of ninety-six villages, there were only seven suitable recruits. The practice of blinding seems to have fallen off somewhat when Muhammad ᶜAli formed a one-eyed regiment, but there is no evidence to suggest that his order to throw those who deliberately maimed themselves into the galleys as slaves had any effect.

Finally, the peasants simply fled. About two thousand families went to Syria with their flocks where they were granted refuge by Muhammad ᶜAli's enemy, ᶜAbd-allah of Akkah. They also fled to distant villages, to swamps, to bedouin tribes, and to the larger towns and cities, especially Alexandria. One major round-up netted between six and seven thousand refugees in that city. By 1831 25 per cent of the cultivable land in Upper Egypt was lying fallow because of the labour shortage,[104] despite frequent government attempts to catch the refugees and forcibly return them to the land.

The rise of the pasha and shaykh classes under Muhammad ᶜAli

Muhammad ᶜAli's attempts to transform the agricultural technology in Egypt brought the peasants into direct contact with the central government for the first time. This contact and the peasant response to it deprived large numbers of peasants of decision-making power over the land. But his policies not only stimulated peasant land loss; they also created a new class of large landholders and strengthened a middle group, the village shaykhs. We must now turn from the victims to the beneficiaries of primitive accumulation.

The combination of the world economic crisis of 1836–7, the decline in government revenue due to peasant flight from the land, and foreign (largely British) pressure forced Muhammad ʿAli to decentralize decision-making power over the land and to abandon his monopoly system. This decentralization took the form of land grants of *ʿuhdah*, *ibʿadiyyah*, and *chiflik*. These grants formed the basis for the creation of large estates. *ʿUhdah* grants resembled the old *iltizam* in that the fellahin paid their taxes to the *mutaʿahhid* (*ʿuhdah* holder) instead of to the government. However, the *mutaʿahhid* could not impose a tax burden on the peasants higher than the official government tax rate. But like *multezims*, part of the land grant was reserved for his own use, for which he could use the unpaid labour of fellahin and upon which he paid no taxes. Muhammad ʿAli still issued orders on land use, however. The *mutaʿahhid* supervised cultivation to ensure that these orders were carried out and provided working capital. He also 'exercised judicial and executive powers previously discharged by government servants'.[105] The second category, *ibʿadiyyah*, were grants of uncultivated lands. The recipient of such a grant paid no taxes on the land if he brought it under cultivation. In 1842 'Muhammad ʿAli was compelled . . . to grant almost complete rights of ownership [to *ibʿadiyyah*], including the right of sale and transfer',[106] this being the first sort of land to gain such status. Finally, *chiflik*, 'the most important factor in the formation of large estates in the last century',[107] were grants to Muhammad ʿAli himself and to the royal family. There were other miscellaneous grants of land and the three main categories sometimes overlapped. The origin of *chifliks* is of interest here: 'the greater part of them consisted of villages abandoned because of the heavy tax burden and transferred to the royal family'. It appears that they were 'almost exclusively in Lower Egypt and mainly in Gharbiya and Sharqiyya'.[108] *ʿUhdah* were also often obtained by a grantee's paying off the accumulated tax arrears of a village.[109] Rivlin summarizes the tenure changes as follows:

> In a twenty-three year period (1821–1844) the best Delta land most suited to cotton cultivation had passed into the hands of large landholders. The peasants . . . held land which did not benefit from the program of irrigation works . . . Furthermore, the status of peasant-held land remained unchanged; it was state land burdened with the *kharaj* (land tax) and to which the peasants had rights to usufruct only.[110]

Although the statistics of the period are very rough, it is possible to get a general idea of the changes in landholding wrought by Muhammad ʿAli. Rivlin's figures are given in Table 9.2.[111] ʿAmr asserts that in the early years of Muhammad ʿAli's reign (*c.* 1813–48) the total cultivable land of some two million *feddans* was divided as follows:[112]

(1)	*Ibʿadiyyah* and *çiftliks*	200,000 *feddans*
(2)	*Awsiyyah* (lands of old, presumably non-Mamluk *iltizam* holders)	100,000 *feddans*
(3)	*ʾarad al-mashayikh* (shaykhs' lands)	154,000 *feddans*
(4)	*ʾarad al-rizqah* lands given to foreign experts and advisors)	6,000 *feddans*

Table 9.2 *Land tenure under Muhammad ʿAli*

	Peasant Land (in *feddans*) 1820	1844	Land held by estate-holders 1844
Lower Egypt	1,003,866	674,914	1,464,559
Upper and Middle Egypt	952,774	1,339,000	112,000
Total	1,956,640	2,013,914	1,576,559

Source: Rivlin, *Agricultural policy*, p. 73.

(5) *ʾarad al-athri* (peasant land) (no numbers)
(6) *ʾarad al-ʿaraban* (bedouin land) (no numbers)

Grant holders of all types, including shaykhs, held roughly 28 per cent of the cultivated area in about 1820, but nearly 44 per cent of it by 1844. This latter figure is certainly an underestimate, since Rivlin's figures do not include shaykhs' lands. If we exclude the shaykhs' lands from the calculations, giving us a rough measure of the increase in cultivable land held as *ʿuhdah, chiflik* and *ibʿadiyyah*, we have a change from about 10 per cent to 44 per cent from 1818 to 1844. Even adding in *wasiyyah* land still brings the amount of cultivated land held by non-peasant grant holders in 1818 to 15 per cent of the total. One might recall that the Napoleonic scholars estimated that the total land area which the Mamluks held for their own use under the *iltizam* system (*ʾard al-wasiyyah*) was about one-tenth the area of peasant land.[113] These numbers are, of course, extremely rough. Nevertheless, they do provide an indicator of the very large increase in estate lands which scholars agree occurred during this period. The grantee holders did not wield much independent power in the late 1830s and 1840s, for the state was still sufficiently powerful to thwart any possible attempts to challenge the ruler. But these land grants went far toward creating a ruling class of landlords.[114]

This new Turco-Egyptian landlord class was supplemented by some native Egyptians, at least in the bureaucracy, although the highest officials remained Turks. Muhammad ʿAli needed manpower to fill the posts which the expansion of the civil and military bureaucracy created.[115] Since Muhammad ʿAli was suspicious of his Turkish subordinates, he needed a group of officials who would carry out his orders more effectively, or at least, that he thought he could rely upon. The native Egyptians could fulfil both needs because they were newcomers to power, raised up by Muhammad ʿAli and therefore more dependent on him than were the Turks. The appointment of Egyptian officials had an additional advantage for Muhammad ʿAli. Since they were less secure in their tenure than the Turks, he could afford to pay them less, thereby lowering government expenditure. The new Egyptian bureaucrats made up for this loss by extorting the difference between their pay and that of the Turks from the peasants. They were uniquely qualified to do this because many of the appointees were village shaykhs or their sons or relatives.[116]

This brings us to the 'middle' group whose power increased during Muhammad ᶜAli's reign, the village shaykhs. Like the Egyptian bureaucrats with whom they were closely associated (indeed, they were often the same person), their power began its growth only in this period, during the second half of Muhammad ᶜAli's reign. Initially, his policies only weakened them. The abolition of *iltizam* 'stopped up the source of most of the payments from which the village shaykhs had benefited'.[117] Muhammad ᶜAli intentionally limited their power somewhat in the second half of his reign. They acquired a good deal of the land which was abandoned by peasants fleeing conscription, although there are no figures that I know of which would show just how much.[118] No doubt they also managed to turn their powers of tax-collection to their own advantage, as did everyone in the administration. Corruption was endemic and widespread among Muhammed ᶜAli's bureaucrats. Rivlin cites a British consular report which estimated that the central government received no more than 60 per cent of the taxes which were collected.[119] No doubt the army officers and bureaucrats in Cairo took the lion's share, but the shaykhs could endure the bastinado as well as anyone and their physical endurance quite probably enriched them. Finally, their position as directors and supervisors of agricultural labour was extended considerably. As we shall see, these shaykhs, as a 'middle' group in the countryside, played an important role in the events of the next generation.

In summary, although Muhammad ᶜAli did not introduce capitalist production relations on a full scale, defined here as private property in land and the creation of a landless class and a 'free' labour market, he did contribute toward their later rise. First, for the first time peasants were brought into direct contact with the central government, a contact which caused major dislocations in peasant life. Muhammad ᶜAli weakened the protective organization of the village and its internal solidarity by his land grants, but by retaining collective tax obligations, including the labour tax of the corvée, he did not entirely destroy it. Secondly, such dislocations contributed to the foundation of a new class of large landowners and to the strengthening of a middle group, the shaykhs. In short, the outlines of the class structure of nineteenth-century Egypt began to emerge during his reign and as a result of his policies. Thirdly, he made important changes in the agricultural technology by beginning perennial irrigation and by introducing the cultivation of long-staple cotton. Finally, he acquainted Europeans with the possibility of Egypt as a source of supply of an important raw material for their factories. The Muhammad ᶜAli years were a time of beginnings.

The transformation of the social relations of production, 1848–82: tenurial institutions

The transformation of both the social and the technical relations of production continued and intensified from the death of Muhammad ᶜAli in 1848 to the British intervention of 1882. Government attempts to extend the cultivation of the cash crop, cotton, required the digging of summer canals and the extension of the transportation network. These projects required labour and capital. The former was supplied by the corvée, the latter by borrowing abroad and by increased taxation. As the size of the foreign debt mounted, taxes were increased further in an effort to meet the payments. The combination of these measures, aimed at the transformation of the physical relations of production, with the rise of private property rights in land, altered the social structure: peasants lost land to pashas, shaykhs, and moneylenders, either through flight, forfeit for non-payment of taxes, or foreclosure for failure to pay private debts. This dual transformation of physical and social production relations generated resistance and upheaval, culminating in the ᶜUrabi revolt in 1881–2. For the remainder of this paper, I will try to trace the acceleration of this transformation of the relations of production to see how it affected the principal social groups.

The transformation of tenurial institutions took place in several stages. It was a complex affair, and I shall only sketch it here. There are two issues to be discussed: one, the change in the definitions of the various legal categories of land, and two, the growth of private-property rights for these various categories. What happened to the *ᶜuhdah* holders is by no means clear. However, it appears that ᶜAbbas (*r.* 1848–54) confiscated a large number of them.[120] This did not, apparently, help the peasants much. It seems to have meant a return to more direct taxation. Further, ᶜAbbas seems to have granted full ownership rights to some *ᶜuhdah* holders.[121] Some new *ᶜuhdahs* were created under Ismaʾil (*r.* 1863–79). He then abolished them between 1866 and 1868 by granting ownership rights to their holders in return for payment of tax arrears.[122] I shall have more to say about the relationship between taxes and the rise of private property in land later. *Ibᶜadiyya* and *chiflik* seem to have continued as before, although both were expanded by Ismaᶜil. He made extensive grants of both kinds between 1863 and 1870. The former kind was especially prevalent in the northern Delta provinces of Buhaira and Gharbiya.[123]

These categories were more or less subsumed by two other categories which were created by Saᶜid (*r.* 1854–63) in his Land Law of 1854. The measures taken by Saᶜid and Ismaᶜil greatly increased the security of both sorts of tenure, although they favoured one over the other. The first sort was known as *ᶜashariyya*, since in 1854 a tax of 10 per cent was imposed on them (*ᶜashr* = 'ten' in Arabic). The second category was *kharajiyya* or *athariyya*, which included all peasant holdings. *ᶜAshariyya* included *chiflik*, some *ibᶜadiyya* land, and some other sorts of land, including, later, the *ᶜuhdahs* granted by Ismaᶜil.[124] Such lands form a subset

Table 9.3 *Land tenure, 1863–80*

Year	ᶜ*Ashariyya* Area (*feddans*)	Per cent	*Kharijiyya* Area (*feddans*)	Per cent
1863	646,177	14.5	3,759,125	85.5
1875	1,194,288	26.0	3,509,168	74.0
1880	1,294,343	27.4	3,425,555	72.6

Source: G. Baer, *A history of landownership in modern Egypt*, p. 20.

of all land held in large grants: *ib*ᶜ*addiyya* grants under ᶜAbbas fell outside the category, as did ᶜ*uhdahs* granted before ᶜAbbas. Nevertheless, the growth of this type of land can be taken as a lower-bound estimate of the growth of large landholding at the expense of the peasants. I shall examine reasons for supposing that the actual land loss of the peasants exceeded this lower bound later on. Baer's figures are given in Table 9.3.

From this it can be seen that the peasant holders of *kharajiyya* land lost some 300,000 *feddans* to the large ᶜ*ashariyya* holders from 1863 to 1880. All ᶜ*ashariyya* land was declared to be full private property in the Land Law of 1858. This law also provided for foreign ownership of land, although some restrictions remained here until about 1873.[125]

The second category of land, *kharajiyya* or *athariyya*, presents a somewhat more complicated case. In 1846 the peasants were allowed to mortgage the usufruct; at the same time, the seizure of the usufruct for failure to pay taxes was formally recognized. In 1854 they were allowed to inherit the usufruct, and Saᶜid's Land Law of 1858 further secured this inheritance.[126] However, the peasants still held and inherited only the usufruct since the government could confiscate the land without indemnity. An exception to this right of confiscation was that anyone who erected buildings, constructed a *saqiyya*, or planted trees on *kharajiyya* land became the full owner.[127] Also, *kharajiyya* could not be endowed as *waqf* without the express permission of the ruler.

Under Ismaᶜil the government's need for cash gave impetus to the creation of private property from *kharajiyya* land. In 1871 the Muqabala Law 'freed from one-half his tax liability anyone who paid six years' taxes in advance and stated that the difference would never be claimed'.[128] They would also become full owners of the land. At first people held back, but as the government made payments compulsory in 1874, those who could muster the capital came through. By 1881, private ownership of land was the general rule.

The transformation of the physical relations of production, 1848–76: public works and the cotton boom

The impetus behind these changes was the government's increasing need for revenue, revenue which was used, in part, for considerable public works. As a

Table 9.4 *Public-works spending of Isma^cil*

Work	Cost ('000 £E)	Remarks
Suez Canal	12,000	After deduction of £E4 million for shares sold
Canals	12,600	£E 1,500 per mile
Bridges	2,150	430 bridges
Sugar mills	6,100	64 mills with machinery
Alexandria harbour	2,542	
Port of Suez	1,400	
Alexandria waterworks	200	
Railways	13,361	910 miles
Telegraphs	853	5,200 miles
Lighthouses	188	15 in Mediterranean and Red Sea
Total	51,394	

Source: H.H. Abbas, *The role of banking in the economic development of Egypt*, unpubl. Ph.D. dissertation, University of Wisconsin-Madison, 1954.

result, the infrastructure of Egypt was considerably improved. The length of railroad track tripled. Between 1851 and 1856 the Alexandria–Cairo railroad was built. In 1856–7 the Cairo–Suez line was finished, and side lines to Samanud and Zagazig in the Delta were constructed. By 1877, Egypt had 1,519 kilometres of standard-gauge railroad. This made marketing for export much easier and extended the area where export crops could be grown profitably. Other public works were the improvement of the harbour facilities at Alexandria, and a large program of irrigation works. Isma^cil had 8,400 miles of canals dug, the largest being the Ibrahimiyya Canal in Middle Egypt, thus bringing perennial irrigation to a portion of that area for the first time.[129] Isma^cil's spending on the country's infrastructure can be summarized as shown in Table 9.4. The problem was, of course, that this spending could only be financed through increased taxation and foreign borrowing, particularly when one adds the spending on luxuries for the court and military adventures in the Sudan. By 1876, Isma^cil was in debt some nine and a half million pounds.[130]

The change in tenurial relations, the extension of irrigation and the improvement in transportation facilities laid the groundwork for the spread of cotton cultivation in Egypt. Two factors stimulated the growth of this crop. First, although there is some doubt here, there were government attempts to increase the amount of taxes collected in cash. We do not know how successful this was; we do know that ^c*ashariyya* landholders were explicitly allowed to pay either in cash or in kind by the law of 1854. Owen doubts that there was enough money in circulation at the time to allow all peasants to pay in cash. Nevertheless, the attempts to increase cash payment of taxes probably did induce some peasants to try to raise a marketable crop.[131] In the 1850s this may have been wheat; in 1856 the US consul was reporting that wheat was more profitable than cotton. The repeal of the Corn Laws in England, the liberalization of French tariff policy under Napoleon III, and the Crimean War all helped to stimulate production in Egypt. Whereas average annual wheat exports were 485,021 *ardebs* (1 *ardeb* ≈ 5.5 bushels) in the period 1840–3, and 527,065 *ardebs* in 1848–50 for the 1850s (1852–8), average annual exports climbed to 1,143,770 *ardebs*, reaching a maximum of 1,674,852 *ardebs* in 1855 and a minimum of 752,572 in 1857.[132] Wallace presents some peasant testimony that, at least in some areas, the fellahin abandoned the cultivation of cotton upon the death of Muhammad ʿAli in 1848.[133] However, by 1860, Egypt was already the sixth most important supplier of the British cotton market, with Britain taking 65 per cent of the crop.[134] When the US Civil War broke out and the Union Navy blockaded or occupied southern ports, British textile manufacturers turned to Egypt as a source of raw material, a move which doubled the value of Egyptian exports.[135] Area figures are not available for the period, but the growth of cotton cultivation can be traced in the export figures, since very little cotton was retained for home manufacture. Although the cotton boom collapsed, with social consequences discussed below, cotton exports remained well above their pre-1860 level (see Table 9.5).

The position of the social classes, 1848–80: the pashas

Thus, in general, the period 1848 to 1880 saw the extension of capitalist institutions (private property in land) and the development of Egypt as an exporter of an important primary product, cotton. The question we now ask is how the different groups in the countryside were affected by these changes. Who gained ownership of what sort of land? How was this reflected in the methods of cultivation? How was agricultural labour organized? How did the landless class emerge? What social forces lay behind the ʿUrabi revolt of 1882?

First, the class of Turco-Egyptians consolidated their position as large landowners during this period. As we have seen, they had been given extensive grants of land under Muhammad ʿAli and other viceroys and had had private property rights extended over these lands during the period under consideration. We have seen how their holdings expanded at the expense of peasant lands and how they acquired tracts of uncultivated land. They also enjoyed lower tax rates than the peasants. Table 9.6 shows figures given by Baer.

The rates on *ʿashariyya* lands rose during the period, but the differential remained: in 1877 *kharajiyya* land taxes in the Delta were from 120 to 170 piastres per *feddan*, and went as high as 200 per *feddan*. The national average on this sort of land was 116.2 per *feddan*. *ʿAshariyya* landholders, on the other hand, paid an average of 30.3 piastres per *feddan*.[136] When under the Muqabala Law of 1871 *kharajiyya* lands became private property if six years' taxes were paid in advance, the Turco-Egyptians, along with the shaykhs and foreigners, must have been the

Table 9.5 *Volume and price of Egyptian cotton exports*

Year	Volume (*qantars*)	Price (*rials/qantars* = 1/5 £E)
1858	502,645	12.75
1860	501,415	12
1861	596,200	12
1862	721,052	13
1863	1,181,888	23
1864	1,718,791	36.25
1865	2,001,169	45
1866	1,288,762	21.25
1867	1,260,946	35.25
1868	1,253,455	22.25
1869	1,289,714	19
1870	1,351,797	22.5
1871	1,966,215	19.5
1872	2,108,500	15.75
1873	2,013,433	21
1874	2,575,648	19
1875	2,206,443	19.5
1876	3,007,719	15.5
1877	2,439,157	13.12
1878	2,583,610	13
1879	1,680,595	16.38
1880	3,000,000	14.52
1881	2,510,000	13.83
1882	2,811,000	14.24
1883	2,140,000	14.71
1884	2,565,000	13.52
1885	3,540,000	12.37
1886	2,788,000	11.71
1887	2,864,000	12.37
1888	2,964,000	12.3
1889	2,780,000	13.27
1890	3,203,000	13.4
1891	4,054,000	11.52
1892	4,662,000	9.06
1893	5,117,000	9.3
1894	5,073,000	8.49
1895	4,840,000	8.46
1896	5,220,000	10.03
1897	5,756,000	8.68
1898	6,399,000	7.18
1899	5,604,000	7.90
1900	6,512,000	10.84
1901	5,391,000	10.87
1902	5,526,000	9.81
1903	5,860,000	13.65
1904	6,147,000	14.41
1905	6,376,000	12.18

Table 9.5 (*cont.*)

Year	Volume (*qantars*)	Price (*rials/qantars* = 1/5 £E)
1906	6,033,000	15.11
1907	6,977,000	16.87
1908	6,913,000	14.42
1909	6,813,000	13.44
1910	5,046,000	21.49
1911	7,477,000	17.6
1912	7,367,000	17.25
1913	7,375,000	18.28
1914	7,369,000	19.02

Table 9.6 *Tax rates by land categories* (piastres/feddan)

	ʿAshariyya 1854	*ʿAshariyya* 1864	*Kharajiyya* 1856
Lower Egypt	26	35	90–100 Lower and Upper Egypt
	18	25	
	10	18	
Upper Egypt	20	31	
	14	21	
	8	14	

Source: Baer, *A history of landownership in modern Egypt*, p. 18.

main beneficiaries.[137] The way in which land became private property favoured the Turco-Egyptian 'pashas'.

Furthermore, they had the best land – the most fertile tracts lying along the summer canals, lands which were the most suitable for cotton cultivation. This had been true since Muhammad ʿAli's original grants.[138] 'The Englishman, Thomas Clegg, who made a tour of the Mediterranean cotton areas in the mid 1850s reported that something like three-eighths of the total Egyptian crop came from the estates of ʿAbbas and the family of Ibrahim alone.'[139] They were able to use their power to get water, to appropriate animals, and to get fellahin to work their land on corvée. They could afford to erect *saqiyas* more easily.[140] The lower tax rates on their lands and their greater wealth presumably gave them a longer time-horizon than the smaller cultivators.

All of these advantages were reflected in their superior techniques of cultivation. They planted their lands in cotton 'only once every four or five years, thus preserving the quality of the soil'[141] in the 1850s. They paid greater attention to seed selection and spaced their rows of cotton three feet apart.[142] The result of these techniques was higher yields:

> By the end of the 1850s a marked difference was being observed in the crops produced by the two groups – that from the large estates being known as . . . 'princes'' cotton and generally enjoying a premium of 1½ to 2 dollars a cantar on account of its greater cleanliness and length of staple . . . *Balli* (peasant) cotton rarely produced more than two cantars a feddan, whereas those with money to invest in the oxen and *saqiyas* necessary to provide adequate watering could provide one to one and a half cantars more.[143]

In short, there were few advantages in agricultural production which the pashas did not have: higher-quality land; more of it; more money; longer 'time-horizons'; lower tax rates; and the ability to dragoon the one input which they did not own outright, labour power. It seems highly probable that these individuals benefited greatly from the expansion of cotton production in the 1860s.

It is unclear precisely how the pashas exploited their estates. However, if we look at the period 1848–80 as a whole, we can draw a few tentative conclusions. Central to the discussion here is the probable emergence of the ᶜ*ezbah* system at roughly the time of Muhammad ᶜAli's moves toward decentralization of agricultural administration.[144] As the word implies,[145] ᶜ*ezbahs* were hamlets, established by the landlord at some distance from the local village. The essence of the system was the granting of parcels of land to peasants to grow their subsistence crops (maize and beans) and fodder for the animals (*birsim*) in exchange for labour services in the landlord's cotton fields. These subsistence plots were rotated in accordance with the general rotation of the fields among crops and fallow. Agricultural operations as a whole were supervised by the owner or his agent, especially the cultivation and harvest of cotton, questions of irrigation and drainage, and crop rotation. Supervision of the labour for food and fodder crops was unnecessary, since the peasants had every incentive to produce as much as possible. Admittedly, this sketch summarizes what we know about the system from information starting in the 1880s and 1890s.[146] But it seems likely that some such system was practised on the large estates earlier. First, we have the assertions of Lozach and Hug, and Ayrout noted above on the date of origin of the system. Secondly, Bayle St John, travelling in Egypt in the 1850s, reported that on estates, 'almost everywhere the fellah is allowed to possess a small allotment, which he cultivates when he is able'.[147] He also noted that the estate holder could use the labour of those who worked on it, and often paid no wages to the fellahin.[148] Thirdly, the evidence presented in the preceding paragraph on techniques of cotton cultivation on the estates indicates that it was probably a closely supervised crop in 1850s. The peasants had *much* less incentive for working hard in the cotton fields, work for which they received little, if any, direct remuneration, than they had for carefully tending the maize, bean, and clover patches. Yet the cotton grown on the estates produced higher yields of cotton than did small farms, and different techniques were used. Cotton labourers must, therefore, have been supervised.

Despite their considerable power, several factors mitigated the pashas' power and the security of their wealth. According to Muslim inheritance law, land must be divided equally among all heirs. This produced a tendency toward fragmentation, and numbers of the families of high officials lost their estates in this way.[149] However, the result seems to have been that those who continued in power or continued to have money simply acquired other lands, with the result that some large landowners held lands in different and dispersed areas, rather than in contiguous plots forming vast estates. If the land units became small enough, it seems likely that share-cropping (*métayage*) was the principal mode of land and labour exploitation. Share-cropping was the principal mode of exploitation for medium properties in the 1880s and later,[150] and Gali asserted in 1889 that the system was less widespread then than it had been in the past.[151] This is what one would expect on *a priori* grounds, since (1) the supervision costs of the ᶜ*ezbah* system would rise sharply with fragmentation, and (2) the poverty of the fellahin would make it difficult for them to pay cash rents or to give guarantees. Share-cropping would then be the logical alternative. Gali notes that the risks of Nile flood variations also contributed to the choice of share-cropping.[152] For the period of 1850–80, the available evidence is simply too scanty to permit any conclusions about how much estate land was cultivated under a *métayage* system and how much under the ᶜ*ezbah* system. Such an assessment is made particularly difficult by the fact that, within the ᶜ*ezbah* system, the subsistence plots were sometimes cultivated on a share basis.[153] One can note, however, that the inheritance laws, and therefore one of the pressures toward choosing a *métayage* system, could be and were evaded by turning land into *waqf*.[154]

In addition to fragmentation, the power of the central government made the tenure of property insecure for the Turco-Egyptians. Because officials got their land through politics and the favour of the viceroy, they could lose them in the same way. Saᶜid destroyed some of the fortunes of the grantees who had been favoured by ᶜAbbas. When evidence that an official had fallen from favour appeared,

> the peasants plunder him with impunity. Old claims are raked up against him; new ones are forged; his crops are destroyed; his cattle are stolen; he becomes . . . 'a thing to be eaten'.[155]

It was really only with the British occupation and administration that *all* land could be considered entirely free from confiscation. Nevertheless, Egypt in the nineteenth century was far from being an Oriental despotism à la Wittfogel. Large landowners were fairly well protected by the 1858 law and there were other mechanisms for circumventing the ruler's power, such as turning land into *waqf*. The viceroy also needed the cooperation of his fellow Turco-Egyptians, so he couldn't antagonize them too much. There is no question that he exercised a great deal of arbitrary power, but not so much that he prevented the Turco-Egyptians from being the wealthiest and most powerful group in Egypt.

The position of the social classes, 1848–80: the village shaykhs

They were not the only powerful group, however. Since the Turco-Egyptians turned office-holding into landholding, it is reasonable to suppose that the native Egyptian officials did the same. During Saᶜid's rule, and especially during that of Ismaᶜil, the government appointed increasing numbers of Egyptians to the post of *mudir* or provincial governor. Under Ismaᶜil, for example, a fellah, Hamid Abu-Satit, became *mudir* of Girga and then Qena provinces. During his time in office, he acquired seven thousand *feddans*. ᶜUrabi Pasha, leader of the revolt in 1882, held eight and a half *feddans* from his father, a village shaykh, but managed to expand his holdings to 570 *feddans* by the end of his army career.[156] It seems, however, that most of such officials who owned land had acquired it before they became officials, usually by virtue of being village shaykhs.[157]

Indeed, the village shaykhs showed the most notable rise in wealth and power of any group during this time. They became important landowners, were often quite wealthy, and were frequently the most important persons in the countryside. Their wealth and power derived directly from their political position as intermediaries between the government and the peasants. By exploiting this key role, by taking advantage of economic trends, and by joining the civil service, some of them rose to positions of wealth and power comparable to the Turks, as in the examples given above. Of course, the shaykhs had always held a special position in the Egyptian social structure and had always linked the peasants to the government. What happened between 1850 and 1880 was that the functions of the shaykh expanded as the state performed new tasks and undertook new projects. The rise of private property in land allowed them to convert their power into land, always at the expense of the peasants.

Their rise began during Muhammed ᶜAli's reign, as shown above, when they were responsible for taxation. ᶜAbbas granted them an additional function which enhanced their power. He established manpower quotas from each village for the army and the corvée, and he made the shaykhs responsible for filling them.[158] This put them in an ideal position to extract bribes from the peasants in exchange for exemptions from the draft or corvée. This was not as important during the reign of ᶜAbbas as it would have been under Muhammed ᶜAli, since there were no foreign wars to fight and no major public works projects were undertaken. Still, the corvée and the draft continued, and the shaykhs continued to get land which the peasants abandoned when they fled from these two scourges. The shaykhs also used their power to supervise the transfer of land when a fellah died without heirs to defraud peasants and to aggrandize their own fortunes.[159]

Saᶜid attempted to weaken the shaykhs' power, although with limited success, by reducing their authority in land distribution and in taxation. In 1855 land transfers were taken out of their hands and put into the hands of the *mudir*. The Land Law of 1858 which secured inheritance of usufructory rights on peasant land undermined the shaykhs' power to redistribute land. The abolition of collective taxation (except for the corvée) reduced their power in tax affairs. Finally, Saᶜid extended conscription to include the shaykhs' sons, who had previously been exempt.[160]

Such a weakening was only temporary and was limited because the shaykhs remained the government's representatives and agents in the villages.

> They had a large and sometimes decisive say in fixing tax assessments; they determined virtually alone the classification of land for purposes of taxation; and they decided which land should be classed as 'unproductive' and therefore tax exempt. It was on the strength of what the *umdah* told him that the *mudir* decided which land should be expropriated for public use.[161]

The shaykh remained 'the Pasha in miniature'.[162]

If Saᶜid left the shaykhs with considerable power, Ismaᶜil raised them to their apogee. They continued to be responsible for the corvée and continued to reclassify land under various tax brackets. The weakening of the central government toward the end of his reign only strengthened them by removing any checks on their arbitrary exercise of power, so that by the time of the British intervention, 'the general impression of contemporary observers was that the village shaykhs were practically uncontrolled, virtually masters of the country'.[163] We shall see, however, that they had competitors for this position in the countryside.

As a result of their power, the shaykhs accumulated considerable wealth and lands, although not so much as the Turco-Egyptians. Baer estimates that the higher Turkish officials held estates of between 1,500 and 2,500 *feddans* apiece, whereas large shaykh estates were between 800 and 1,000 *feddans*.[164] Some owned as much as 3,000 *feddans* and more, but these seem to have been exceptional.[165] Their lands came chiefly from former peasant holdings, for they seem to have been the main beneficiaries of peasant flight from the land.[166] It is likely that the richer shaykhs exploited their lands using the ᶜ*ezbah* system, whereas the more modest ones used share-cropping. Wallace in 1876 speaks of landless peasants 'associating themselves with richer neighbours', and Villiers Stuart in 1883 reported conversations with shaykhs resident on their ᶜ*ezbahs*.[167] Their long experience as supervisors of agricultural operations must have served them well in either case.

The position of the social classes, 1848–80: the peasants and land loss

Finally, there were the fellahin. The ways that they lost their land, alluded to at various times above, can be summarized here: (1) outright seizure – the land grants of Muhammed ᶜAli; (2) flight from the land to escape corvée, conscription, or taxes; (3) failure to pay taxes; and (4) foreclosures for non-payment of private debts. The steady rise in the land tax rates and their heavy incidence on the fellahin have been noted above. Although ᶜAbbas reduced the size of the army, conscription continued with the result that whole villages sometimes left and fled to the hills, as in the area near Luxor recorded by Bayle St John.[168] When ᶜAbbas abolished the *ᶜuhdahs*, he demanded tax payment from the peasants; a 'large-scale exodus' ensued.[169] Saᶜid's tax increases also led to mass flights. He then limited the peasant's right of return to the land and sold the *raqaba* or title of the land to officials and to foreigners.[170] Under Ismaᶜil, not only the increase, but also the timing of these increases contributed to peasant land loss: as the cotton boom collapsed, taxes were increased. In 1868, the British consul at Alexandria reported that the peasants were paying 70 per cent more in taxes than in 1865.[171] Wide-scale flight from the land ensued.[172]

Taxation contributed to peasant land loss in another way, through debt and foreclosure. Its rise seems to have begun during the cotton boom. We have seen how cotton prices rose in the 1860s and how output responded. It should be noted, first, that most cotton grown before 1860 was grown on the large estates. Estimates vary; the best available study, that of Owen, asserts that 'only a fraction' of the total cotton crop was grown on peasant-held land in this period.[173] But after the precipitous price climb (see Table 9.5), they did increasingly plant the crop. In part, this was no doubt a response to the ordinary sort of price incentives. There is much evidence, however, that the heavy tax rates played a role as well, leading in some cases to overcropping:

> The fellahin being hard pressed for money, took to raising as much of it [cotton] as possible, regardless of the fact that the overcropping might in a few years impoverish the soil . . . [A]s the over-cropping did not suffice to provide all the money which the peasants required for the payment of their taxes and other purposes, and as the influx of Europeans and European institutions furnished new means of easily borrowing money on land and other securities, the peasants gradually sank into a state of indebtedness from which a very large section of them can never hope to extricate themselves.[174]

Wallace points to a phenomenon of some interest, the rise of moneylending; there is other evidence that these loans increased.[175] If the peasants were growing cotton, this fact is not surprising. Although peasants' techniques (the *balli* method) differed sharply from those of the landlords, using less labour, land, and seed than the methods of the pashas, increased cotton production would have increased their need for working capital, inducing them to borrow. However, most observers at the time (e.g., Wallace, Villiers Stuart, and Lady Duff Gordon) emphasized the increased burden of taxes as the cause of most peasant debt. These moneylenders lent at rates which varied from 1 to 5 per cent per month.[176] These loans, incurred during the boom, proved burdensome later: (1) the price of cotton fell sharply (see Table 9.5); (2) their cattle were wiped out by a plague in 1863; and (3) tax rates rose after the boom collapsed, as noted above. Bankruptcies and land sales followed.[177] This form of land loss continued and accelerated during the 1870s, especially after the establishment of Mixed Courts in 1875.

The fruits of accumulation: the ʿUrabi revolt

Social transformations on the scale described above usually do not occur without resistance and upheaval, and Egypt was no exception. All of the social developments described above contributed to the ʿUrabi revolt of 1882. Although the causes of the actual military uprisings are certainly most complex, involving a great deal of intrigue, false starts, misunderstandings and the like by Egyptian political figures and the foreign ministries in London and Paris, a number of important facts about the social composition of the rebels, their targets, and sources of support up to the intervention of the British seem critical. I am not trying to offer a detailed explanation for all of the manoeuvres which occurred; I merely wish to place the revolt within the context of the transformation of the relations of production outlined so far.[178] As mentioned above, ʿUrabi Pasha belonged by birth and career to the class of shaykhs and native government officials. Men such as this were also his principal co-plotters; it was a revolt of the junior officers, a product of the recruitment of native Egyptians.[179] These men were angry about their failure to advance further because the Turco-Egyptians blocked their way, monopolizing the highest ranks. Furthermore, there were 'cutbacks in every branch of administration under Anglo-French control from 1876–1882'.[180] All that was needed to trigger a revolt was a collapse of legitimacy, which had in fact happened when Ismaʿil was forced to place tax-collection under the aegis of the *Caisse de la Dette Publique*, the corporation which had been formed by foreign creditors to reclaim their loans to the Khedive in 1876, and to abdicate in 1879.

At least initially, the shaykhs sided with ʿUrabi. We have seen how their power grew throughout this period, and, although their wealth was still less than that of the Turco-Egyptians, they had become increasingly insubordinate to the pashas and the higher (i.e., Turkish) authorities.[181]

> The backbone of the Arabist party, in so far as that party represented a national movement and not a military movement, was to be found amongst this class. The greater part of the yeomanry of the country were sympathetic with Arabi; he was their kith and kin; they looked to him to deliver them from the usurer and the pasha.[182]

The shaykhs had a specific grievance: the *Caisse de la Dette Publique* was proposing to abolish the Muqabala Law as part of its program of fiscal reform. Since the notables had benefited from this law, they protested its repeal.[183] They also called for the reform of tax responsibility and for the abolition of the tax on animals.[184] The initial split was between the native Egyptian bureaucrats and their allies (often their blood relatives), the shaykhs on one side and the Khedival house, the Turco-Egyptian landlords, and foreigners, whether Greek moneylenders or French financiers, on the other.

The question of where the peasants would fit in must not have had an obvious answer at the time. They had lost their land to pashas, shaykhs, and moneylenders; both pashas and shaykhs oppressed them with tax-collection and corvées. If anything, one might expect the peasants to prefer the pashas. There is some evidence that they regarded the shaykhs as rather more oppressive than the pashas, possibly because the peasants had so little personal contact with the latter.[185]

However, although the shaykhs made loans to the peasants, most peasant land loss from debt was to foreigners, especially Greeks, Syrians, and Lebanese Christians, not to shaykhs.[186] The moneylenders exploited their new legal position under the Mixed Courts and the peasants' need for cash for taxes with the usual ruthless tactics. For instance, peasants lost land worth £ E 50 per *feddan* for £ E 10 debt.[187] The overall result was a tidal wave of peasant debt:

> Between 1876 and 1882 legal mortgages alone rose according to Lord Dufferin, from five-hundred thousand to seven million pounds (approximately), of which five million pounds were village mortgages. To this an estimated three or four million pounds worth of debts to moneylenders should be added. By 1882 the Mixed Courts had handled foreclosures to the value of £ E 24,000.[188]

The situation of the peasants was becoming desperate.

In this situation the government's inability or unwillingness to protect them was critical. The government acquiesced, or was compelled to acquiesce, in the financial rule of the very foreigners who managed and profited by the Mixed Courts' mortgage proceedings. In addition, the fact that the local moneylenders were Christians delegitimized them in the eyes of Muslim peasants. ʿUrabi's promise to cancel peasant debt and to 'banish the usurers' tipped the balance: Villiers Stuart, a member of parliament and of a fact-finding mission for that body after the occupation, repeatedly reported land loss to Greek and Levantine moneylenders through the mechanism of the Mixed Courts as the reason for peasant discontent.[189] Their support for ʿUrabi was largely the result of his promise to 'banish the usurers',[190] although his promises of tax reduction must also have been popular.[191] Wallace reported that students from al-Azhar (many of whom were the sons of shaykhs) appeared in the villages, agitating against the foreign infidels, including, apparently, the moneylenders.[192] The peasants did not actually join ʿUrabi's forces, but they did become increasingly insurbordinate from 1876 on. In 1879, armed bands were formed against tax-collectors in the area between Suhag and Girga. Revolts occurred against the corvée in the rice-growing areas in 1880. 'In 1882, the British consuls reported a general state of rebelliousness among the peasants.'[193]

There were, then, all the makings of a full-scale revolution: a discontented class of rising, well-to-do but politically subordinate men both in the countryside and in the cities, closely linked with each other; a weakened and discredited central government; a peasantry in the throes of change from one set of social relations of production to another, and who had a specific, acute grievance which was due to new and unheard of innovations (mortgage foreclosure). Finally, these peasant grievances were appealed to by the leaders of the discontented 'middle' group.

But, of course, the revolt failed, going the way of so many indigenous uprisings against foreign penetration and the dislocations which such foreign, capitalist penetration fostered. The British intervened when riots in Alexandria gave them their excuse to crush the revolt. The Turco-Egyptians retained their hold on the land, although they had to cede much political power to the British. The failure of the revolt seems to have been the result of this intervention, although the incompetence of the leadership undoubtedly helped.

Some insight into the reasons for the failure of the revolt can be gained by comparing the Egyptian case with that of other countries which experienced peasant revolts as a result of the transformation of production relations from pre-capitalist to capitalist. Eric Wolf[194] demonstrates that the middle peasants, defined as those peasants who have at least enough land on which to support a family and hence do not have to enter the market for either labour or land (although they may buy and sell other inputs and outputs), played a crucial role in all of the major peasant revolutions of this century: Mexican, Russian, Chinese, Vietnamese, Algerian, and Cuban. Their importance derives from two facts: (1) they have a limited amount of leverage against more powerful groups because of their (potential) economic self-sufficiency, and (2) they are vulnerable to economic changes which will weaken them, separate them from their land and reduce them to dependent relations.

> His is a balancing act in which his balance is continuously threatened by population growth, by the encroachment of rival landlords; by the loss of rights to grazing, forest, and water; by falling prices and unfavorable conditions of the market; by interest payments and foreclosures.[195]

The Egyptian case presents some important differences from those cases which Wolf studied. We have seen that the shaykhs were supporters of ʿUrabi in the early stages of his political struggle with the Khedive and the pashas. Clearly, these men are better viewed as 'rich peasants' or 'kulaks' than as 'middle peasants' as Wolf defines them. They were beneficiaries, not victims, of the dissolution of the old, pre-capitalist village community. They were, to a lesser degree, part of the power system which was being used to transform the countryside, rather than outside of it as were the middle peasants, in the case studied by Wolf. Unlike the middle peasants, the political status of the shaykhs rose as market relations spread.

It should be remembered, as well, that the ʿUrabi revolt was a *military* revolt, by military men. The shaykhs' support was mostly verbal. There is a resemblance here to the behaviour of rich peasants during the Chinese revolution: 'Only when an external force, such as the Chinese Red Army proves capable of destroying these other, superior power domains, will the rich peasant lend his support to an uprising'.[196] It would appear that the existence of this 'external force' was, in fact, crucial; it seems that the mere appearance of the

British forces dissolved the support of the provincial notables for ʿUrabi.[197] Most of all, the shaykhs wanted to be on the winning side.

It is also necessary to emphasize that the issue of legitimacy, couched in more-or-less traditional Islamic terms, played a very important role in the rebellion. Foreclosures were contrary to traditional Muslim law, the *Shariʿah*. The accession to power of European Christians over the finances, an important government function, would naturally have been anathema to the *ʿulema*. These men were the 'city cousins' of the village shaykhs. As in Algeria, there were linkages between an urban elite and peasants. As in Algeria, some form of Islam provided the two groups with a common sense of 'us' as opposed to 'them'. But, unlike Algeria, the links were between an urban elite and *rich*, not middle, peasants. In the face of superior force, the *ʿulema* would back the winners, supplying a theological reason for their actions.[198] These social factors, plus the obvious differences in terrain (there are no inhabited 'peripheral areas' in Egypt like the Kayble mountains of Algeria), may help to account for the failure of the ʿUrabi revolt.

Conclusion and summary

I have argued in this paper that the phenomenon of primitive accumulation in Egypt was inseparable from that country's integration into the capitalist world-system. Capitalism came to Egypt with cotton; the coming of capitalism and cotton resulted in a large number of peasants losing all decision-making power over their land. In short, they were dispossessed. We have seen that peasants lost land because they fled, finding their land owned by someone else if they managed to return, or because they failed to pay their taxes or debts. In what way can the loss of land for these reasons be attributed to the rise of cotton cultivation and to the spread of capitalism into Egypt? Recall that there were three reasons for flight from the land: the corvée, taxation, and conscription. The corvée was the way that labour was mobilized to change the irrigation system in order to permit the cultivation of cotton. Growing cotton demanded summer irrigation; summer irrigation demanded summer canals; the construction of these canals was accomplished with forced labour. Peasants who fled from this forced labour would find their land in someone else's hands, should they be lucky enough to survive and return. There is, therefore, a direct connection between the rise of cotton cultivation and peasant land loss.

But the extension of cotton cultivation required not merely labour to dig summer canals; railroads, improved harbours, infrastructure of all sorts were also needed. These required not merely labour, but also capital. This could be raised either directly by taxation, or by borrowing, which, in turn, ultimately rested upon taxation to pay off creditors. The increased tax burden, was intimately connected with the spread of cotton cultivation for export. Again, there is a direct link between cotton cultivation and peasant land loss.

At first glance, flight from the land to avoid military conscription might seem unrelated to the spread of capitalism. In a sense, this is no doubt an accurate assessment. Muhammad ᶜAli conscripted peasants in order to field an army capable of defending his claims to autonomy from the Ottoman Empire. In trying to set up his own empire, his own world-system, he was, of course, acting in the best tradition of his predecessors, such as Ali Bey. Yet the *outcome* of the policy was the extension of capitalist social relations. The situation is similar to the choice of cotton versus wheat. Muhammad ᶜAli promoted cotton because he wanted revenue for his 'empire'; the effect was to initiate Egypt's integration into the capitalist world-system. There is a second parallel with the cotton/wheat choice. Just as developments in the core of the world-system (Western Europe) and in the semiperiphery (Russia) shaped the choice of beginning cotton cultivation rather than merely increasing wheat exports (via tariffs and wheat exports, respectively), so did they affect the choice of *conscription* as the means of raising an army. Russian expansion into the Caucasus inhibited the flow of Mamluks (a flow which the Porte could block in any case), and Muhammad ᶜAli had the example of the military power of Napoleon's invading army. In part, then, he chose conscription because his goals and the prevailing political constraints gave him little choice, and in part because of the 'demonstration effect' of the performance of the army of the revolutionary French bourgeoisie in Egypt.

This 'demonstration effect' can be seen at work in another aspect of the spread of capitalism into Egypt. Part of the reason for the heavy tax burden on the peasants, at least under Ismaᶜil was the latter's extravagant expenditures in Cairo and Alexandria. This, too, was an imitation of the West. Ismaᶜil was trying to create 'all the paraphernalia and creature comforts of Western civilization . . . in a matter of years'.[199] Such emulation should be seen as an integral part of the extension of the capitalist mode of production into Egypt. As Marx put it: 'Production not only supplies a material for the need, but it also supplies a need for the material . . . The need which consumption feels for an object is created by the perception of it.'[200] Part of Egypt's integration into the capitalist world-system was a tendency toward the 'hegemony' of European capitalist norms over local ones in the eyes of the local ruling class.[201]

A peasant might not flee from higher taxes, however; he might borrow instead. Borrowing was in part directly related to taxation, in that many peasants simply got loans to pay the tax-collector. In part the link was indirect, in that peasants borrowed the working capital to produce cotton and then would use the receipts from the sales of cotton to pay the taxes. In both cases, the rise of the moneylender accompanied the rise of cotton cultivation and paralleled the peasant's loss of land. The hold of these moneylenders was well established by the 1870s, with important consequences for later events.

This particular mechanism of primitive accumulation also blocked the complete transition to capitalist social relations. Small peasants, resident *ᶜezbah* workers, and *tarahil* (migrant labour) labourers were all in debt, giving rise to relations of personal dependence. The time which a resident *ᶜezbah* worker spent working for the estate owner (e.g., in cotton labour) was more clearly differentiated from the time which he spent reproducing his own and his family's life (e.g., labour on the patches of maize which had been allocated to him). Because of debt-peonage, his cotton-field labour was often openly unpaid labour. Such patterns persisted after the British occupation. *Tarahil* workers were often indebted to their labour contractor and were under pressure to work a certain number of days without pay for him.[202] It is interesting to note in passing that this class of money-wage labourers (and thus the class that at first sight displays the most nearly-capitalist social relations) was also the class which perhaps more than any other preserved the old, pre-capitalist 'mediated' social relations. An estate owner did not hire *tarahil* labourers directly, but rather hired them *via* a contractor, much as a Mamluk did not hire peasants or obtain them on corvée directly for work on the *ʾard al-wasiyyah*, but went through the village shaykh instead.

It would seem, then, that the notion of 'primitive' or 'original' accumulation applies to nineteenth-century Egypt, provided that we recognize that 'primitive accumulation' is a necessary, but not sufficient, condition for the development of fully-fledged capitalist social relations. The relations which did emerge have been aptly described as a form of 'backward colonial capitalism'.[203] The non-capitalist features of rural social relations, mentioned at various times above, may be summarized here. First, until the abolition of the corvée under the British, agricultural labour in Egypt was not 'free' in Marx's double sense, but only in its 'freedom' from anything but labour power to sell. Secondly, small landowning peasants, resident *ᶜezbah* workers, and migrant labourers alike were often entangled in the web of debt-peonage.[204] Thirdly, *tamaliyya* (permanent agricultural labourers) workers were paid not in cash but with grants of land for growing their subsistence crops. Central to the Marxian conception of capitalist social relations is that these social relations take the form of *commodity* relations; capitalism is, in the first instance, a form of commodity-producing society. Not only is the worker free to sell his labour power, not only is this the only commodity which he has to sell, but selling his labour power is the *only* way in which he can reproduce his daily life. Not only are his labour power and his product commodities, but so also are the goods that comprise his 'consumption basket', the goods which reproduce his labour power. Marx held that a consequence of turning all goods needed for the reproduction of society into commodities was that exploitative social relations were 'concealed'. The worker did not know when he was working for himself (reproducing his labour power) and when he was working for the owner (producing a surplus appropriated by the dominant class). He simply received a money wage, the same for each hour (abstracting, of course, from overtime). Since under normal capitalist conditions commodities exchange at their prices of production in the long run and not at their labour values (the two being unequal except in special cases), the extraction of surplus labour time by the owners of the means of production is further concealed.[205] But the *tamaliyya* worker did not obtain his food on the market; rather, he produced it himself with his own labour. When working in the maize and bean patches, he knew that he was working to reproduce himself and his family. In contrast, his work in the cotton fields was more clearly work 'for the boss'. This would have been especially true if the money wage received for such work was absorbed as debt-payment to the landlord. Under such conditions, the resident *ᶜezbah* worker was, indeed, similar to a worker on the *ʾard al-wasiyyah* of the *multezim* Mamluk times. Like so many workers on the capitalist periphery, the work relations of the labourers on the *ᶜezbah* were openly coercive and 'unmediated'.

For all that, there remained important differences between the *ᶜezbah* worker and the eighteenth-century peasant. First, there is little question that the nineteenth century saw the creation of a substantial landless class. Unlike the eighteenth-century peasant, the resident *ᶜezbah* worker held no rights of *any* kind to his subsistence plot. He could not inherit, lease, or dispose of the plot in any way. The size of the plot itself was changed by the landlord in accordance with changes in the market prices of food crops.[206] By contrast, peasants of Mamluk times who paid their taxes were insured of their usufructory rights to the *ʾard al-fellah*. Unfortunately, we have few reliable numbers on the increase in the landless class. There were wage workers under the Mamluk regime. However, some (perhaps most) of these were peasants whose lands had not been reached by the Nile flood,[207] indicating that they, at least, did not form a permanent class. Nor is there any indication that the landless formed a substantial percentage of the peasant population at that time. On the other hand, by World War I, perhaps one-third to one-half of the agricultural population was landless.[208]

A second difference between eighteenth- and nineteenth-century agrarian social relations was the degree to which the direct producers were supervised. Landlords at the end of the nineteenth century entered directly into the process of production (usually by means of overseers); consequently, the work force was more closely supervised than it had been under the Mamluk regime. The landlord supervised all the cotton labour, decided the crop mix and crop rotation, regulated questions of water, etc. This was a far cry from the administration of the *ʾard al-fellah*. Of course, labour on the *ʾard al-wasiyyah* was supervised and was often unpaid. However, since the area of such lands was roughly 10 per cent of the area of peasant lands, and since primarily the same crops were grown on the two sorts of land, we might conclude that Mamluk peasants divided their time in roughly the same proportions. By contrast, the *ᶜezbah* worker spent twenty-five days per month working under supervision for the landlord. It seems safe to conclude that the *ᶜezbah* worker was more closely supervised and had less decision-making power over his day-to-day labour than did the Mamluk peasant. Share-croppers on the *métayage* system were also closely supervised.[209] Such a decline in the decision-making power of the direct producer is, of course, a feature of the development of the division of labour under capitalism.[210] In this important sense, the ᶜ*ezbah* worker was a capitalist worker. Whereas in Mamluk times the ruling class had been content to skim off the surplus product of the worker, under the ᶜ*ezbah* system, as in the Manchester mills spinning and weaving Egyptian cotton into cloth, the owners entered directly into the process of production itself.[211]

Finally, it seems likely that the total amount of peasants' labour time increased owing to the changes in the irrigation system. This is consistent with the notion of capitalism as the 'means of appropriating the (potential) leisure time of others',[212] and with Ibrahim ᶜAmr's assertion that the amount of labour required of Egyptian peasants under capitalist agriculture exceeded that required in Mamluk times.[213] Egyptian basin agriculture was famous for providing high yields per unit land area with relatively little labour compared with Europe.

> As things are at present these people get their harvest with less labor than anyone else in the world . . . they have no need to work with plough or hoe . . . they merely wait for the river of its own accord to flood their fields.[214]

> The land [given over to wheat production] produces fourteen times the amount sown . . . In France, wheat lands produce 5–8 to 1 . . . the cultivator, without working as hard as in our country, obtains each year such a prosperous outcome.[215]

This happy state of affairs was due to the particular, and perhaps unique, features of the agricultural technology. As Hamdan has pointed out, basic cultivation was a special combination of hydraulic, irrigated agriculture and dry farming.[216] In a sense, it combined the most favourable features of two different agricultural systems, the high yields per unit area of hydraulic with the relatively low input of human labour per unit output of dry farming.[217] On the one hand, the crops were irrigated, receiving nutrients from the silt and solutions in suspension in the flood waters. But, apart from dike construction, much of the work of irrigation and fertilization was done by the river, not by the peasants. This stands in contrast to paddy-rice cultivation in Asia, in which a gently moving quantity of water must constantly furnish the plants with moisture and nutrients, and the soil must be ploughed repeatedly until it is 'puddled,' etc.[218] This requires a great deal of labour. The peculiarities of the climate in Egypt and the timing of the Nile flood, as well as the scarcity of water for large portions of the year, dictated the growing of small grain cereals, wheat, barley, and millet. These are classic 'dry-farming' crops and require little labour relatively to, say, rice. Since there was little ploughing, no fertilizer application, and relatively little irrigation work, basin agriculture required relatively little labour per unit

Table 9.7 *Labour requirements of various crops, 1943–4*

Crop	Adult male workers per *Feddan*	Boys per *Feddan*
Wheat	19	9
Barley	15	3
Beans	16	1
Onions	32	59
Birsim	22	2
Millet	52	10
Maize	26	12
Rice	32	43
Cotton	47	69

Source: Mahmoud Anis, 'The national income of Egypt', *L'Egypte contemporaine* (Nov./Dec. 1950), 755.

of output. The generally low labour requirements of the system are underscored when we remember that there was a long fallow period for *all* basin fields, not just fallow in rotation with other crops.

This is significant, because as we have seen, most cultivated land was in basins: 75 per cent in the Delta and nearly 90 per cent in the Saᶜid. Crops grown on the perennially irrigated high lands required a lot of labour (see Table 9.1), but these crops were sharply limited in area.

The transition to perennial irrigation (and then from the three-year to the two-year crop rotation within the perennial system from 1890–1914) meant an increase in labour relative to the basin system. In the first place, of course, the transition itself required considerable labour. Secondly, the increased number of crops which could be grown per year meant more labour. It is true that the labour required for flood and summer crops was lower under the perennial system than under the basin (see Table 9.6; cf. Table 9.1). But it seems likely that this was more than compensated for by (1) the increase in the number of crops per year; (2) the rise in the labour required for the 'basin' crops, wheat and barley (but not, apparently, beans); and (3) most important of all, perhaps, the widespread adoption of cotton. It was not merely that more crops per year were grown; one crop that came to be widely grown was a relatively labour-using crop. Furthermore, there is little reason to suppose that the amount of labour needed to maintain the irrigation system declined because of the switch: basin dikes no longer needed to be built, but irrigation canals had to be cleaned and maintained. It seems fair to conclude that the changes in the irrigation system resulted in more work and less leisure for the peasants. (See Table 9.7.)

In summary, Egypt's integration into the world-system in the nineteenth century transformed the social and technical relations of production. The conjuncture of the coming of cotton production, bringing irrigation works, corvée, and heavy taxation in its train, with the rise of private property rights in land dissolved the protective organization of the peasant village, radically redistributed access to land and to other non-human resources, and proletarianized large sections of the peasantry. As a consequence, peasants worked harder and under closer supervision than previously. The social relations which did emerge were not fully capitalist, however, since payment in grants of land and debt-peonage systems were widespread. Such relations are, perhaps, to be expected in peripheral areas in the capitalist world-system. This last mechanism tended to reduce small peasant landowners to the same level of living as the resident *ᶜezbah* workers. The heightening of inequalities which the process of Egypt's integration into the capitalist world-system engendered had ominous consequences for future agricultural development. In the period of the British occupation and administration, the small peasant landowners further intensified their agricultural production largely in an attempt to forestall complete land loss to moneylenders. Coupled with a British failure to invest in adequate drainage, this intensification led to declining cotton yields and to soil deterioration, damage which was not repaired until the late 1930s.

Part III

Industry and labour

10 Price history and the Bursa silk industry: a study in Ottoman industrial decline, 1550–1650

MURAT ÇİZAKÇA *

Industrial decline, unlike industrialization, is a relatively little-known aspect of economic history, and because most countries have experienced it at some time, it is a phenomenon deserving of more scholarly attention. In this article I argue that price history, when used in conjunction with simple economic reasoning, is a useful mode of analysis of industrial decline.

The Ottoman Empire, which covered most of Eastern Europe and the Near East in the sixteenth century, did not escape the worldwide inflation that is generally known as the 'price revolution'.[1] But the spread of the price revolution to the Near East and its impact upon Ottoman industrial performance are questions that require further specific research.

In this article I concentrate on the city of Bursa, the most important centre of silk trade and industry in the Near East during the period 1550–1650.[2] Bursa was a major entrepôt through which not only Persian but also locally produced raw silk was sent to Europe, mainly via Italy. Competition for the raw material existed between the cloth producers of Bursa and the weaving centres of Europe. This competition forms the basis of my analysis, and I will argue that major changes in price trends reflect, among other things, the intensity of European competition for raw silk. Another type of competition existed in the sale of cloth. Bursa, again, was a major centre where European cloths – mainly woollens and light silks – were sold and competed directly with the locally produced cloths. Obviously, the price trend of Bursa cloths reflects this sales competition as well.

*This article is based on the author's doctoral dissertation, 'Sixteenth–seventeenth-century inflation and the Bursa silk industry: a pattern for Ottoman industrial decline?' (University of Pennsylvania, 1978). The following scholars helped the author in various stages in the preparation of this article: T. Naff, H. İnalcık, J. Brown, G. Danişman, C. Issawi, A. de Maddalena, J. Lee, S. Faroqhi, F. Birtek, and G. Libecap. Special thanks are due to Ö.L. Barkan, M. Wolfe, H. Sahillioğlu, M. Genç, H. Van der Wee, and C. Poni. While the author is grateful to all of them, he lays claim to any and all remaining errors. An earlier version of this article was presented at the Seventh International Economic History Congress, Edinburgh, 1978.

Although this study concentrates on a single industry in a single town it provokes thought in more general directions. If European competition in the purchase of raw materials and in the sale of final products could affect Ottoman markets so clearly through the price mechanism, then we can expect similar patterns to emerge in other major Ottoman cities and industries. Indeed, recent research appears to support this argument. Braude's work on the Salonica woollen industry showed that the price scissors mentioned above for Bursa existed in much the same way in that city. European competition, on the demand side, pushed wool prices to enormous heights while on the supply side it depressed woollen-cloth prices by rapidly increasing exports of woollens to the Ottoman Empire.[3] This unfavourable price structure yielded a result similar to the situation observed for the silk industry in Bursa. The preliminary results of my own ongoing research indicate that the stamp-tax farm of Salonica suffered deficits in 1560, 1566, 1572, 1575, 1581, and 1583.[4]

The sixteenth century was a period of rapid population growth for the Ottoman Empire. Because agriculture could not absorb the excess rural population, migration to the cities rapidly ensued.[5] Yet neither could the declining urban industries absorb the excess population, and so massive unemployment resulted. The works of the late Professor Akdağ confirm this point, and demonstrate how unemployed peasants took refuge in urban pious organizations and became 'students' at *medreses*.[6] 'Student' riots soon followed, which formed the explosive material of the much more violent Celali uprisings in the next decades.

Except for one work by the late Professor Barkan, there are no published studies available for Ottoman textile prices.[7] Consequently, the bulk of the price data for this study had to be collected from primary sources, among which the most important were the Bursa court registers dealing with inheritance. Conflict among a silk merchant's heirs was taken to court, where the *kadı* (judge) would divide the property after having first determined its extent. To measure the value of raw silk he usually relied upon prevailing market prices. It is these prices, registered by the judges, that constitute my data. They have been collected for the period 1550–1650.

Utilizing data from such sources evidently presents certain difficulties. First, the prices were determined in courts and not directly in the market. The registered prices were frequently arrived at by groups of experts, *ehl-i vukuf*, who may have made wrong evaluations or, in some cases, reached a 'convenient' price with the heirs. Secondly, the documents sometimes omit necessary information, such as the quantity or quality of the product, which results in wide variations in the prices of the same product. Finally, because of errors in the documents, such as multiplication mistakes, one does not always know if the price or the total value was written wrongly.

To assure reliability in my tables and graphs, I eliminated all suspect data; almost half of the data I had obtained was sacrificed. Notwithstanding these

Table 10.1 *Composite index of prices of main types of raw silk*

Years	Composite index of a *lodra*[a] of silk (in *akçes*)[b]	Years	Composite index of a *lodra* of silk (in *akçes*)
1548	59	1595	197.06
1557	83.78	1597	224.79
1559	80.83	1603	351.05
1566	94.4	1607	233.05
1569	68.44	1608	224.79
1570	41.89	1614	189.98
1571	74.93	1617	174.64
1572	81.42	1622	338.07
1573	67.85	1627	306.8
1575	71.98	1629	294.41
1576	83.19	1630	99.71
1577	80.24	1634	240.72
1578	99.71	1635	373.47
1579	84.37	1636	315.65
1580	84.37	1637	394.12
1581	136.29	1639	250.75
1582	151.63	1646	199.42
1583	144.55	1647	216.53
1584	250.16	1648	129.80
1585	158.71	1650	100.89
1587	178.18	1651	143.96
1588	182.90	1652	93.81
1589	192.93	1653	175.23
1594	207.09		

[a]*Lodra* was a weight unit, the exact metric equivalent of which is subject to dispute.
[b]*Akçe* was the basic Ottoman coin which included varying amounts of pure silver over time.

Source: Murat Çizakça, 'Inflation and the Bursa silk industry', p. 106.

drawbacks, the data drawn from the inheritance registers are the most voluminous, continuous, and realistic prices available. My main concern is with general trends rather than absolute magnitudes, and so these data are sufficient.

Since there were several hundred types of raw silk, only the most frequently observed types were selected and grouped into five major categories: *harir-i ham* (raw silk), *harir-i şehri* (Bursa silk), *harir-i gilâni* (Persian silk), *harir-i heft renk* (seven-coloured silk), and *boyanmış ipek* (dyed silk). In order to obtain a simple and clear price trend the weight average of these prices was calculated for each year.[8] The outcome of this procedure can be seen in Table 10.1 and Figure 10.1. It should be added here that no attempt will be made to express nominal prices in pure silver so as to isolate the price trend from monetary effects, because accurate information on this is lacking.[9]

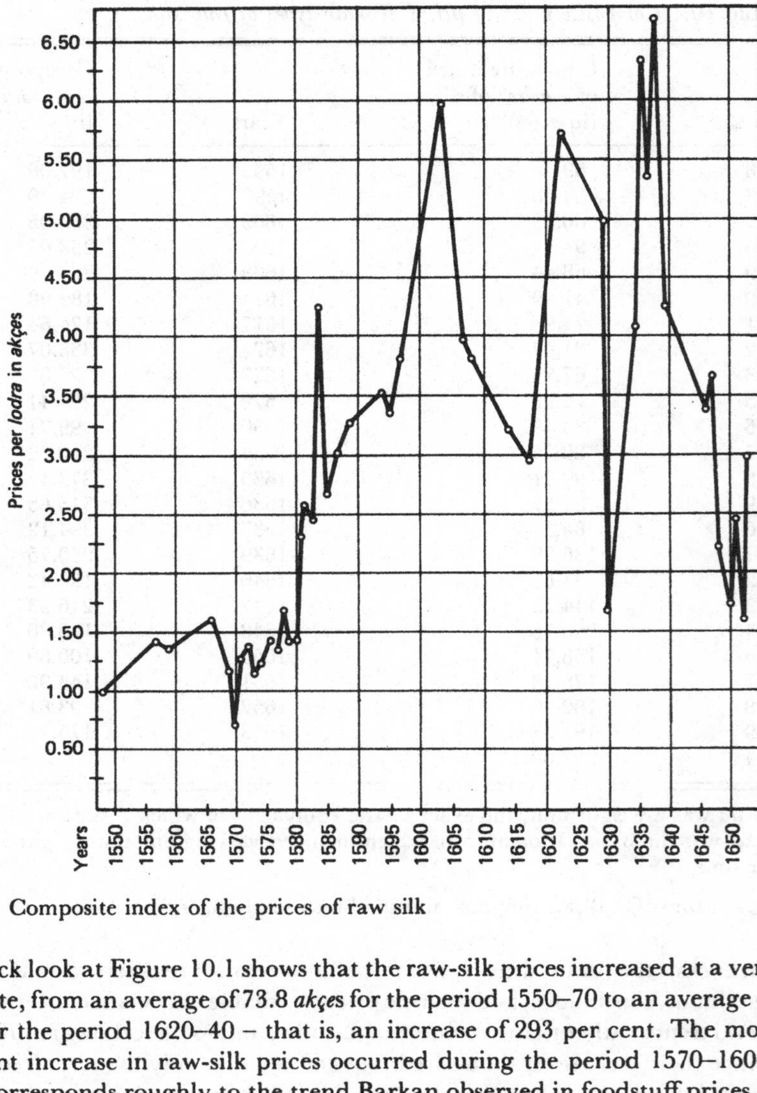

Fig. 10.1 Composite index of the prices of raw silk

A quick look at Figure 10.1 shows that the raw-silk prices increased at a very rapid rate, from an average of 73.8 *akçe*s for the period 1550–70 to an average of 290.4 for the period 1620–40 – that is, an increase of 293 per cent. The most consistent increase in raw-silk prices occurred during the period 1570–1604, which corresponds roughly to the trend Barkan observed in foodstuff prices.[10]

Silk-cloth prices

The court registers of Bursa, and in particular the inheritance registers, which were used for compiling the prices of raw silk were likewise relied upon for cloth prices, and the methodology applied in both instances was much the same. Understandably, the variety of cloth types was far greater than that observed in

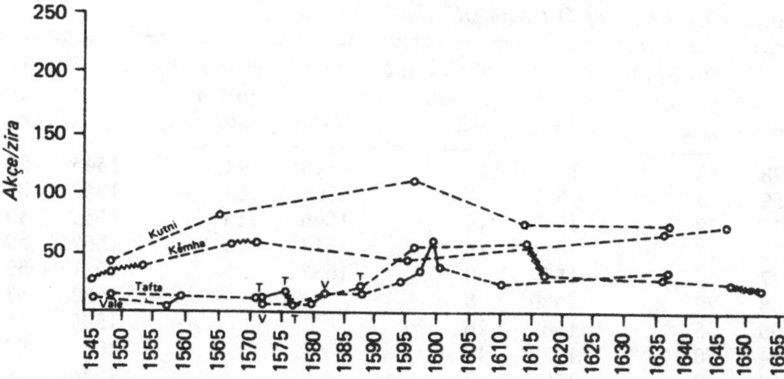

Fig. 10.2 Silk-cloth prices (per *zira*)

raw silk, for the same raw silk could be woven and painted as well as mixed in different ways with other inputs. My first task was to reduce the manifold cloth types into three major groups: silk, woollen, and cotton. Silk was further divided into five subgroups: *kemha, atlas, kutni, tafta*, and *vale* (cf. Table 10.2).[11] Of these, the price trend of *atlas* is not included in my calculations because, according to Dalsar, Venetian exports of *atlas* to the Ottoman markets, particularly in the 1600s, increased greatly. Thus *atlas* prices may actually reflect the prices of Italian rather than Ottoman cloth.[12] In Figure 10.2 one clearly sees that the prices of a *zira* of various silk cloths also increased, but the rate of increase of these prices was much less than that of raw-silk prices.[13]

Interpretation of observations

A number of factors may account for the different rates of increase observed in the prices of raw silk and silk cloth. For raw-silk prices, on the supply side we may argue that, since part of Bursa's raw silk came from Iran, Ottoman–Persian wars might have pushed up the prices by cutting the supply routes. Indeed, during the period under consideration, the first war with Iran occurred between the years 1578 and 1590, which coincide with a period of rapid increase in raw-silk prices. It would be misleading, however, to draw conclusions from this observation alone, for the period 1550–1650 witnessed three more wars with Iran (1603–12, 1615–18, and 1624–39). Figure 10.1 shows that, whereas one can observe a clear relationship between the Persian wars and silk prices during the period 1578–90, the relationship becomes rather inconsistent for the later years. In all this, we are hampered by our ignorance of the exact share of Persian silk in the total silk supply available in Bursa.[14] Nevertheless, political relations with Iran remain a factor to be considered when analysing raw-silk prices.

On the demand side, it is possible that a silk-cloth industry was developing elsewhere in the Empire, competing with the weavers in Bursa for the raw

Table 10.2 *Prices of Ottoman silk cloths* (in *akçes*)

Years	Prices of a *zira* of *tafta*	Years	Prices of a *zira* of *vale*	Years	Prices of a *zira* of *kutni*	Years	Prices of a *zira* of *kemha*
1548	15	1545	14	1548	44	1545	29
1559	15	1557	7	1565	81	1548	35
1572	12	1559	14	1596	113	1553	40
1576	17	1571	13	1614	75	1567	59
1577	7.5	1572	9	1637	75	1571	59
1588	22	1580	8			1583	53
1596	55	1582	16			1595	45
1614	60	1588	18			1636	67
1617	32	1594	27			1646	74
1636	30	1597	35				
1647	25	1599	60				
1652	20	1600	40				
		1610	25				
		1637	35				

Source: Murat Çizakça, 'Inflation and the Bursa silk industry', pp. 242–5.

material and thus pushing up the prices. Preliminary results of a separate inquiry into the tax-farm yields of Ottoman industries indicated that İstanbul might have functioned in this way. During the years 1594–1602 tax-farm yields of the İstanbul dye-houses increased from 31,666 *akçes* to 216,666 *akçes*.[15] Recent research, however, indicates that this tremendous increase in the activities of İstanbul dye-houses was probably caused by a remarkable increase in cotton rather than silk-cloth production. Faroqhi and İslamoğlu showed that towards the end of the sixteenth century cotton production in Adana increased by 142 per cent, as a 'function of increasing demand for cotton in İstanbul'.[16] Certainly, the feverish activity of İstanbul dye-houses may have been partly geared to the dyeing of silk cloth, but so far we have no sure evidence to support this argument.

Thanks to the works of European scholars we are much better informed on the next alternative, namely, European competition. European demand for raw silk was growing, and the competition could indeed have caused the observed price trends; and in our current state of knowledge that remains the most likely explanation. It is unfortunate that continuous statistics on European trade with the Levant do not exist for the sixteenth century. But we know that the Italians, particularly the Venetians, had imported large quantities of Ottoman silk since the Middle Ages, and had supplied northern Europe with this product. Furthermore, the French and Italian silk industries used Levant silk as a supplement to their own locally produced silk.[17] More specifically, the use of Levant silk as a supplement to European silk gained momentum as a result of a technical development in Italy. The spread of the hydraulic mill from Bologna to the rest of Italy, notably to Venice, resulted in a great expansion of the production of *orsoglio alla bolognese*.[18] Because Ottoman silk was needed to supplement the *orsoglio*, we can envisage a positive relationship between the increased production of *orsoglio* and the imports of Ottoman silk. Carlo Poni, an authority on the mechanization of the Italian silk industry, has explained the situation as follows:

This mechanization concerned only the production of a special thread, called the *orsoglio 'alla Bolognese'* or *organzino*, which was used as a warp. This thread could not directly compete with the Bursa cloth. But with this strong, fine and good thread – the best during the sixteenth and the eighteenth century – the Italian and later the European weavers could produce new types of cloth, which fashion proposed and imposed in the European market. The Turk[ish] silk, like the southern Italian one, was used in order to make the weft. The demand for this raw silk increased with the production of the warp in northern Italy, and the enlargement of the market of luxury goods . . . All this can explain the decline (stagnation) of the prices of Turk[ish] cloth and the increase of the prices of raw silk.[19]

Clearly, increased exports of Ottoman silk to Europe were a major factor behind the increasing raw-silk prices in Bursa. We lack statistics for Italy's Ottoman trade, but do have some supporting evidence on the role of demand elsewhere in Europe. Ralph Davis, in his study of English imports from the Middle East, has shown that between 1621 and 1721 English imports of raw silk from the Middle East increased by 275 per cent.[20] That a country like England, not particularly famous for its silk industry, should have increased its raw silk importation so drastically may look strange. But we know that, with the successful mechanization of the Italian silk industry, large quantities of cheap and good-quality Italian thrown silk were smuggled into England.[21] It is very likely that the English, like the Italians, used Levantine silk to supplement the *orsoglio*.

Another region of Europe, the Low Countries, was also very active in the Levantine markets at the end of the sixteenth and early seventeenth centuries.[22] Van der Wee has shown that Italian *organzino* was used as an input in the textile industries of Flanders, and so it is very likely that the Dutch also used the Ottoman raw silk to supplement the *organzino*.[23] Indeed, in the 1550s four million guldens' worth of silk and silk products from Italy *and* the Levant was imported into the Low Countries. This was the largest item of import, followed by English cloth.[24]

Furthermore, it should be added that throughout most of the seventeenth century the bulk of the English and Dutch demand for raw silk was concentrated on the Levant; direct importation of silk in large quantities around the Cape of Good Hope had to wait until the 1670s and 1680s.[25] In short, I contend that this concentrated European demand was a major factor behind the rapidly increasing silk prices in Bursa.

At this point we should examine the several reasons why European but not Ottoman weavers were able to purchase increasing quantities of Ottoman raw silk despite its rapidly increasing price. First, as mentioned above, technological developments and their speedy diffusion in Europe led to a great reduction in the average cost of silk twisting.[26] There is evidence that the hydraulic mill, the chief invention, did not spread to Bursa until the nineteenth century.[27] Secondly, the massive expansion of the rural industries in Western Europe led to considerable savings in wages.[28] Although the putting-out system existed in the Ottoman Empire, we cannot determine the extent to which it affected Ottoman wages. More importantly, its rapidly increasing price notwithstanding, Ottoman raw silk was not expensive for the English and the Dutch. They benefited from successive depreciations of the Ottoman currency and the resulting exchange rates which favoured the relatively stable English pound and Dutch florin.[29] It would be interesting to compare the prices of raw silk in Europe and in Bursa; however, my attempts at obtaining raw silk prices in Europe were frustrated by lack of data for the period in question.[30]

Let us now turn our attention to the relatively small increase in silk-cloth prices in Bursa. Europeans reduced their demand for Ottoman silk cloth, and the Ottomans themselves may have begun to prefer European cloth to domestic products.[31] It is also possible that the increase in prices was retarded by a considerable increase in the supply of cloth, which might have come about in several ways. First, the imports from European countries may have increased for reasons exogenous to the Ottoman economy, such as the reduction of costs, hence prices, and quality improvements in European textile industries. Secondly, the domestic supply of cloth may have increased as a result of internal developments, such as the expansion of traditional urban or rural industries. In short, on the supply side we have to determine if it was European competition or increases in domestic production that accounts for the observed price trend.

Unable to examine the demand-side alternatives, we can at least consider the supply side. First, there is the argument that cloth importation from abroad saturated Ottoman markets, depressing cloth prices in general. That increasing quantities of Dutch, English, and French woollens were indeed exported to Turkey is well known.[32] But when we begin to weigh the effects of the increased export of European woollen cloths on the prices of Ottoman silk fabrics, we encounter certain problems. Comparison of the prices (in *akçes*) of European woollens with Ottoman silk cloth reveals that Ottoman silk cloth was the cheaper.[33] In view of the deteriorating exchange rate between the Ottoman *akçe* and European currencies, this is what we would expect. But then how did the Europeans succeed in exporting increased quantities of these expensive woollens to the Ottoman Empire?

To answer this question we must first look briefly into developments taking place outside the textile industries. As is generally true during periods of rapid inflation, the late-sixteenth-century Ottoman economy experienced a redistribution of income that favoured a small percentage of the population while impoverishing the masses.[34] The demand of those who benefited from this situation (important army officers, large *çiftlik* [plantation] owners, provincial commanders who had the right to collect taxes in kind, and merchants) would gradually become more inelastic, and their consumption of expensive luxury products such as European woollens would not necessarily decline – indeed, it might increase.

Deterioration of the income distribution in the Ottoman Empire may also explain the idiosyncratic demand structure observed in that part of the world. When expensive and traditional broadcloth exports from England to the war-torn Continent declined, the Ottoman Empire absorbed them in ever-increasing quantities; conversely, when cheaper new draperies found eager markets in the western Mediterranean, they did not enter the Levant.[35]

It can be argued that it was the Ottoman demand and the increased exports of broadcloth to the Levant which facilitated the transition in England from the production of broadcloth to the new draperies. In other words, had it not been for its outlet in the Ottoman markets, Suffolk would have been depressed even more. As for the new draperies, the Ottoman peasantry was probably too impoverished by then to consume even these cheaper products. It is also possible that the increased domestic cotton production mentioned earlier captured the bulk of the Ottoman market for light and cheap fabrics. On the other hand, if domestic cotton-cloth production was indeed so successful, then it can be considered another factor in the depression of silk-cloth prices in Bursa.[36]

The substitutability of woollens for silk cloths is not really so puzzling as might at first appear. Some of the Bursa silk cloths, particularly *kemha*, were heavy, thick fabrics suitable for winter wear. Among the different silk-cloth types observed in Figure 10.2, *kemha* prices are the most nearly stagnant, which suggests that they were the ones most affected by increased imports of European woollens. In short, notwithstanding the cheapness of domestic silk cloth, the increased exports of high-quality European woollens to the Ottoman markets seem to have depressed the prices of certain types of Ottoman silk cloth. The reader is cautioned here from assuming that only the heaviest types of Ottoman silk cloths were affected in this way. Although the heavy, thick broadcloths rather than the light, new draperies formed the bulk of the English woollen exports, this was not so with the Dutch and Flemish exports. Indeed, Brulez showed clearly that large quantities of Hondschoote sayettes were exported to Italy, particularly to Venice and Ancona, whence they were in all probability re-exported to the Ottoman markets.[37] We thus have a situtation in which European woollens competed with the Ottoman silk cloth from both ends – English broadcloths affected the heavy silk cloth and the Flemish and later Dutch sayettes affected the lighter silk cloth.

The increase in English exports of woollens from the 1590s onwards eventually reduced the prices of those woollens relative to Ottoman silk cloth. The prices given in Table 10.3, which were obtained from the Bursa court registers, reflect the downward trend in English prices. Clearly, the English

Table 10.3 *Prices of English woollen cloth* (Çuka-i London) *in Bursa*

Years	Price of a *zira* of cloth (in *akçes*)
1624	240
1637	280
1639	210
1649	219
1651	69
1653	117

Source: Murat Çizakça, 'Inflation and the Bursa silk industry', p. 248.

luxury woollens which originally had been bought only by the highest income groups were becoming available to the lower income groups as well. But how could English merchants reduce their prices so drastically in Ottoman markets, despite the debasements of the *akçe*? One might also wonder about the basic cost to the English industry, namely, the price of raw wool in England. It has been shown that the average price of wool in England for the period 1590–1609 was 81 per cent higher than for the period 1541–60.[38] On the other hand, Beveridge indicated that woollen-cloth prices in England remained stagnant for the most part, and Table 10.3 shows that they actually declined in Ottoman markets.[39]

What we observe in the English woollen industry is a price structure that was in general similar to that observed in the Bursa silk industry – in both, the rate of increase of raw-material prices was higher than the rate of increase of cloth prices. As will be demonstrated below, this price structure resulted in a sharp decline and then a persistent stagnation in the production of silk cloth in Bursa. But in England, after a relatively short crisis, the woollen industry recovered, diversified, and re-entered the world markets with new products.

The English woollen industry owed its resilience to various well-known factors. First, although during this period the woollen industry experienced no technological breakthrough comparable to the tremendous achievements in the cotton industry in the eighteenth and nineteenth centuries, it nevertheless underwent gradual improvement in all its phases, particularly in the shuttle mechanism, which rapidly increased production of cloth. Second, development of the putting-out system and the industry's spread to the countryside reduced labour costs by employing part-time rural workers in their own cottages. Third, the size of the English woollen industry allowed economies of scale. According to Braude, by the 1600s, 'Total English output may have been greater than that of all Italy and the Ottoman Empire combined.' Consequently, 'the industry marshalled tremendous capital sources which could more easily sustain bad years'.[40] Fourth, although English wool prices rose in the sixteenth century, elsewhere prices were rising even faster. Between 1550 and 1600 English wool prices rose a little over 80 per cent, but 'during this same period the Balkan price rose 244 per cent, that is, about three times as much'.[41] Fifth, the structure of the English chartered companies allowed them to dump cloth in the Ottoman markets. This last advantage was probably the most significant one, and deserves further examination.

The Levant Company bought Ottoman raw materials, mainly silk, in the competitive markets of the Levant.[42] The silk was in turn sold at monopolistic prices in England. Because English policy prohibited bullion exports, the Levant Company offered broadcloth in exchange for Turkish silk. Having paid extremely low prices for the broadcloth in England's oligopsonistic market, the Levant Company sold it at low prices in Ottoman markets.[43] This dumping and resulting losses in West–East trade were more than compensated by huge profits when the raw silk was sold in England.[44] This, in conjunction with the other reasons outlined above, explains why England could export to the Levant increasing quantities of high-quality woollens at ever-decreasing prices, despite the successive debasements of the Ottoman currency.

The effects on the Italian and Ottoman woollen industries of the massive English and Dutch entry into Ottoman markets have been studied elsewhere.[45] As far as the Ottoman silk industry is concerned, I believe that this entry acted as a depressing force on cloth prices. Exports of Italian silk cloth to the Levant also sharpened competition in the sale of cloth in Bursa. The mechanization of the silk industry in Italy doubtless lowered costs, hence prices, while maintaining or even improving the quality of the product. Indeed, the silk industry in Venice was one of the few industries to survive the seventeenth-century crisis.[46] That Ottoman markets were significant in its survival is supported by Dalsar's observation that, particularly after the 1600s, *atlas* exportation to the Levant increased greatly.[47] To conclude, European competition appears to have been a crucial factor behind the sluggish cloth prices in Bursa after 1600. Further research on the volume and content of trade, however, and especially trade between Italy and the Ottoman Empire, is urgently needed.

Finally, the development of the Ottoman silk industry, either in Bursa or elsewhere, must also be considered as a possible factor in the trend of cloth prices. We have noted that cloth production in İstanbul was increasing, but we lack specific knowledge of its industry's development. (Actually, the problem of internal trade remains a vast area for research in Ottoman economic history.)[48] The further alternative, the expansion of cloth production in Bursa itself, will be addressed in the remainder of this article.

Conclusion

The present analysis of silk prices in Bursa reveals a 293 per cent increase in raw-silk prices between 1550–70 and 1620–40. I have demonstrated elsewhere that other basic cost factors, such as dye-stuffs, also tended to increase.[49] Whereas costs were increasing rapidly, analysis shows that prices of the final product were rising at a much slower rate. Faced with such a price structure, decline in profitability would seem inevitable unless the Bursa silk industry experienced a major improvement in productivity. Unfortunately, virtually no sketches of Ottoman machinery are available, which is perhaps because of the Moslem distaste for paintings. Thus Ottoman technological history remains a vast mystery.[50]

During my inquiries in Bursa I discovered foot-operated treadle-reels, *mancınık*, and spool-winders as well as hand-operated looms and silk twisting machines, all of which were in good working order. Leila Erder notes that these primitive machines still dominated the scene at the beginning of the nineteenth century. It seems that more advanced techniques, such as hydraulic mills and steampower reeling, were introduced mainly by Europeans, almost suddenly and under very special circumstances during the 1830s.[51] By implication, Ottoman textile technology in the period 1550–1650 was relatively unsophisticated, and incapable of overcoming the decline that inhered in the price structure. Let us now test this argument.

The production trend of the Bursa silk industry (both raw silk and cloth) can be obtained indirectly by studying the tax-farm records, *mukataa defterleri*. The government farmed the right to tax silk, brought to Bursa from Iran and from Ottoman provinces. We can estimate the volume of silk supply in Bursa by following the trend of the auction prices of the scale tax farm, *Mizan-ı Harir Mukataası*. This method is valid because, generally, these prices emerged from tough competition between the tax-farmers,[52] and because the tax rate that farmers collected on the amount of weighed silk apparently remained constant.[53] Similar considerations apply to the *Damga-ı Akmişe Mukataası*, the tax-farm of stamp duties on cloth. In this tax-farm all cloth produced in Bursa was stamped by the state and a stamp tax, *damga resmi*, was collected.[54] Assuming that the tax rate remained constant, it follows that there was a positive relationship between the amount of taxes collected and the volume of cloth production in Bursa.

Figure 10.3 shows the auction prices of the raw-silk tax farm, *Mizan-ı Harir Mukataası*, and of the stamp tax-farm, *Damga-ı Akmişe Mukataası*. Respectively, these prices depict approximate trends for Bursa's raw-silk supply and volume of cloth production. To illumine the relationship between these trends a third factor, raw-silk prices, has been depicted. The horizontal axis indicates the major political events of the period, that is, Venetian and Persian wars and Celali uprisings.

With respect to the consequences of stagnant cloth prices, we saw above that costs in the Bursa silk industry were increasing. A producer faced with rising input costs usually tries to transfer them to his consumers in the form of higher prices. Of course, the ability to do so without suffering drastic reductions in sales

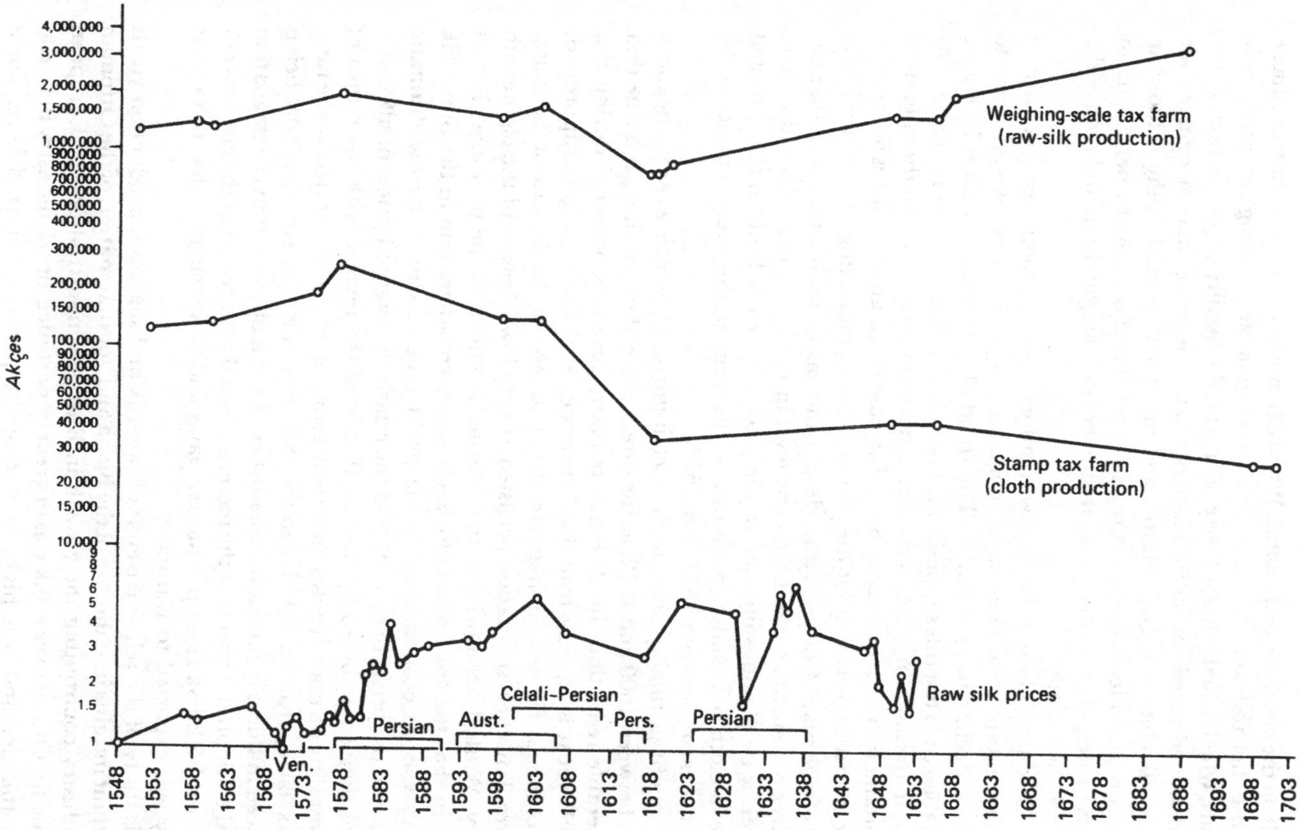

Fig. 10.3 Composite index of raw-silk prices of tax-farms

depends on the elasticity of demand. When demand is elastic, the cloth producer is forced either to leave the industry or to economize by using less costly raw materials, which usually has adverse effects on the quality of production. From the evidence adduced earlier in this paper, one can argue that the demand for Ottoman silk cloth was quite elastic, and that the Ottoman clothiers took the latter recourse. Indeed, the court registers are full of documents pertaining to attempts by desperate clothiers to circumvent guild regulations and reduce the quality of their cloth.[55]

The Ottoman cloth producer was subject to the combined pressure of increasing input costs and elastic demand. Together these would seem to conduce a decline in production. The trend of the stamp tax farm in Figure 10.3 enables us to test this supposition. The period 1550–77 shows a considerable increase in the auction prices of the stamp tax farm, implying that the volume of cloth production was increasing. Some increase in the auction prices of the raw-silk tax farm also is evident for the period, likewise indicating an increase in the supply of raw silk.[56] Consequently, despite increasing production of cloth, raw-silk prices remained at about the same level in 1577 as in 1557. After this time, however, a tremendous increase in the price of raw silk leads to the expected decline in cloth production, as shown by the trend of the auction prices of the stamp tax farm between 1577 and 1618.

One might justifiably point to the Celali uprisings, which were particularly violent between 1600 and 1612, as the direct cause of this decline. It is true that considerable reductions in all Bursa tax-farm revenues occurred during this period;[57] yet it is equally true that, once the revolts were largely suppressed, many of the tax farms exhibited a tendency to recover. In the case of the stamp tax farm, however, stagnation persisted at very low levels until the eighteenth century. While I acknowledge the destructive effects of the uprisings, I must maintain that the chief reason for such long-term stagnation in the Bursa silk industry was an economic one – the profit squeeze caused by the dramatic increases in the prices of raw silk and the relatively stagnant prices of silk cloth. My position is reinforced by the fact that after the revolts, with the return of relative safety on major routes, there was a surge in the auction prices of the raw-silk tax farm, from which I deduce that raw silk was entering and being produced in Bursa in increasing quantities. But it is obvious from the stagnation in local cloth production that the increased supply of raw silk in the city was not consumed by Bursa cloth producers. Davis and Ülker suggest that this excess supply was exported to Europe.[58]

This study of the relative trends of raw-silk and silk-cloth production yields important insights into the fate of the Bursa and, for that matter, of the Ottoman silk industry confronting the growth in Europe's industrial power. European demand for Ottoman raw silk was of great importance for the industry in Bursa. When this demand was high, as during the period considered here, Bursa increasingly specialized in the production of raw silk, and cloth production suffered. When this demand slackened, however, as in the eighteenth and early nineteenth centuries, then Bursa's cloth production recovered. The relative trends were reversed once more during the nineteenth century when European, particularly French, demand for Ottoman raw silk reached enormous proportions as a result of the application of steampower to weaving. Transformation of the industry was then completed and Bursa specialized almost entirely in producing the raw material with which it supplied the hungry industries of Europe.[59]

11 Notes on the production of cotton and cotton cloth in sixteenth- and seventeenth-century Anatolia

SURAIYA FAROQHI

At present it is still too early to attempt a monograph on this important branch of production in Ottoman Anatolia during the sixteenth and seventeenth centuries. Through the work of İnalcık, Dalsar, and Ergenç, the manufacture and sale of silk and angora fabrics for this period is more or less clearly understood.[1] However, almost nothing is known about the cultivation of cotton, the production of cotton fabrics, and the trade therein. Given the prime importance of textiles in any pre-industrial economy, an attempt to understand the problems of urban–rural differentiation, of marketing systems and of the connection between internal and external trade must, however, take account of cotton production. This sector had been of considerable importance even before the Ottomans gained control of southern Anatolia. Cotton was a staple carried by Venetian ships in the later Middle Ages, and Pegolotti highly recommended the quality of cotton grown in what is now the Çukurova.[2] Given these circumstances, a provisional report on Ottoman source materials located so far may well be of some use. In the long run, it will hopefully be possible to undertake a more exhaustive study.

Among archival documents, there are various types that should be consulted. To establish the areas where the raw material was cultivated, we have the tax registers (*tahrir*).[3] Occasional information on marketing dues serves to indicate places where the cotton crop was offered for sale. For the production of the cloth itself, our most significant data come from records of tax-farmers (*emin, mültezim*) who farmed sales taxes or dyers' workshops (*boyahane*).[4] Scattered documents can be gleaned from the registers known as *mühimme defterleri*, or registers of important affairs, and also from the *şikayet defterleri*, or registers of complaints.[5] The former series, encompassing a huge number of directives to provincial administrators of various ranks, has been extensively used by scholars, and certain selections have even been published.[6] On the other hand, the 'registers of complaints' merit more notice than they have attracted so far. Essentially they constitute replies to petitions made either by subjects or by provincial members of the Ottoman administration, which not infrequently relate to financial and economic matters. In addition, registers kept by the *kadı*'s courts in various towns provide a great deal of useful information, owing to the fact that it was one of their main functions to document legal transactions between individuals.[7]

Distribution of cotton planting seems to have been quite similar to what can be observed from modern maps.[8] Among the most productive areas were the plain between Adana and Tarsus, known today as the Çukurova, and the area between the two Menderes rivers, in those days divided between the provinces (*sancak*) of Aydın, Saruhan and Kütahya.[9] But cotton was also of some significance in the area of Alanya, Erzincan and Malatya.[10] In many other places, the plant occurred in minute quantities of little economic significance, for instance in the area of Amasya-Merzifon, around Tokat and elsewhere.

In most cases we have no indication of the absolute quantities produced. Cotton was usually measured in *kantar*, or else in *men* (*batman*), which latter unit was sometimes considered to be equal to one twentieth of a *kantar*.[11] Since however there existed a wide variety of *kantars* in local use, many of them unknown to us, quantities thus expressed are of very limited value to the modern researcher. However, the area around Malatya can be considered an exception. Here the tax registers define the *batman* as 2,400 *dirhem*,[12] so that if the standard Anatolian *dirhem* was intended, the *batman* should have amounted to 7.4 kg. Therefore it is likely that this *batman*, which was also used in Divriği, corresponded to the unit current in Tokat, Erzurum and Van, which continued to be employed until the nineteenth century as the so-called caravan *batman*.[13]

Now if we add up the amount of cotton demanded from the peasants living in the administrative unit immediately surrounding the city of Malatya (the so-called *nahiye* of Kasaba), we arrive at the amount of 1,121 *batman-men*. Since in Malatya the tax regulations specified that one fifth of total produce be collected as taxes,[14] the official estimate of the total harvest amounted to 41,847 kg or 42 metric tons. This appears to be a low figure when compared to the production of this area in more modern times, which was recorded to be about a thousand tons in 1952.[15] However, the *nahiye* of Kasaba was probably much smaller than the Malatya area used as a base for twentieth-century statistics. Moreover, we must take account of the vast increase in the demand for cotton during the nineteenth and twentieth centuries.

A very rough estimate of Anatolian cotton production in the 1570s can be arrived at in the following manner. According to a computation by Mustafa Soysal,[16] the province (*sancak*) of Adana in those years contained 6,506 ha devoted to cotton, which should have produced about 200 kg each. This results in a hypothetical harvest of 1,301,200 kg, or about 1,300 metric tons. On the other hand, adding up the cotton taxes collected in the province of Tarsus, we arrive at a total of 27,345 *men*.[17] Since Anatolian *men* generally corresponded to something between about 5 and 8 kg, the cotton tax should have amounted to somewhere between 137,000 and 219,000 kg. As moreover in the province of Tarsus dues made up one tenth of total produce, this resulted in a stipulated harvest ranging between 1,370 and 2,190 metric tons. If on the other hand we assume a *men* to equal one twentieth of a *kantar* and count a *kantar* as 56 kg just as Soysal has done, the *men* should have corresponded to only 2.8 kg, and we arrive at an estimated total harvest of about 770 metric tons.

Under these circumstances, the total estimate for the two provinces should range between about 2,100 and 3,500 metric tons. To pass from this estimate to a second one encompassing all of Anatolia is unfortunately rather difficult, since in the other major producing area, namely the province of Aydın, cotton dues were recorded only in money and not in quantities. If however we assume that production in the Çukurova made up about one half of the production of total Anatolia, we arrive at an estimate somewhere between 4,200 and 7,000 metric tons. However, these figures give us no more than a general order of magnitude and will need revision when the areas in question have been studied in more detail.[18]

For the production of cotton cloth, called *bez* or *boğası*, we can discern several centres, among them the *sancak*s of Aydın, İçel and Hamid. As elsewhere some reference has been made to the *sancak*s of Aydın and İçel,[19] we will here concentrate on Hamid. Our basic source in this respect is an account concerning the activities of a group of tax-farmers.[20] During the years between 930 and 938/1523 and 1532 they farmed the stamp tax on cotton fabrics (*damga-ı boğası*) for the administrative districts of Afşar, Yalvaç, Eğridir, Agras (modern name: Atabey), Keçiborlu, Gönen, Uluborlu, Burdur, Isparta, and Barla in the province of Hamid and the districts of Antalya, Köprüpazarı and Teke-Karahisar (near the ruins of ancient Perge)[21] in the province of Teke (Table 11.1).

When making use of this very instructive series of figures, certain precautions must however be taken. Since the accounts were compiled for fiscal purposes, the main aim was to establish whether the tax-farmers had fully discharged their obligations. If they had not, it was imperative to establish how much money they still owed the central administration. If, on the other hand, one and the same farmer took the dues collection of several administrative units upon himself, there was no reason to separate the revenues generated by these districts. Such a practice may leave us with aggregates that are often much less interesting than the original figures would have been.

Even more discouraging is the fact that even totally alien taxes may be aggregated in this fashion. In our case we occasionally have to deal with amounts of money that constitute the sum of the stamp tax on cotton cloth and of a market tax on grain known as *bac-ı keyl*.[22] To make things yet more difficult, the scribe occasionally forgot to record the full amount as owed by the tax-farmers and noted down only the amount actually delivered to the Treasury, as well as deductible expenses. In such cases we can only compare the figures recorded with the totals ascribed to that particular administrative district for other years in the series. If there is approximate correspondence, it is permissible to conclude

Table 11.1 *Stamp taxes on* boğası, *1523–32*

	930/1523–4	931/1524–5	932/1525–6	933/1526–7	935/1528–9	937/1530–1	938/1531–2
Yalvaç, Afşar	5070	5577	6084	5577	5577[a]	4056[a-b]	4056[a-b]
Eğridir, Agras	9019				3549[a-c]	3042[a-d]	4056[a-c]
Keçiborlu	807	800			1521[a]	1414[a]	2028[a]
Gönen, Uluborlu	20,280					6584[d]	6884[d]
Uluborlu		8112	8112	9633	8112	6284	
Gönen, Agras					10,380		
Agras						4656	4056
Eğridir, Barla, Agras		21,701	24,336[e]	22,308[e]	1421[f]	1814[f]	2828[f]
Gönen, Isparta							
Isparta	2531				3042	2928	3242
Burdur	1314				1014	1300	1014
Total, Hamid	39,021	36,190	38,532	37,518			
Antalya, Köprüpazar, Teke-Karahisar		12,958	9126[g]	46,644[h]			
Antalya, Teke-Karahisar	15,210		2885[i]				
Teke-Karahisar						12,588	
Total, Teke	15,210	12,958	12,011				

[a] includes *bac-ı keyl*
[b] Yalvaç alone
[c] Eğridir alone
[d] Gönen alone
[e] includes Burdur and Keçiborlu
[f] Barla alone
[g] without Antalya
[h] for 3 years, without Teke-Karahisar
[i] Antalya alone

that few arrears remained, and the taxes recorded can be taken as an approximation of the taxes really collected. When it is probable that arrears were considerable, we have no option but to discard the figures. For that reason 934/1527–28 and 936/1529–30 yield almost no usable data.

If, as is probable, the amount of stamp tax collected corresponded more or less to the amount of cloth offered for sale, the totals for the different administrative districts should indicate where the most active markets for cotton cloth were located.[23] Considering the difficulty of transport, we can assume that most of the cotton cloth stamped in a given market had been produced in the immediate vicinity. Of course there may have been distorting factors, such as the greater or lesser zeal of the tax-collectors in different places, or differences in the reliability of their accounting. But for the time being, we have no option but to ignore these difficulties.[24]

Since most administrative districts are documented more than once, and the figures usually show only slight variation from year to year, the geographical distribution of cotton weaving is probably best ascertained by taking averages for each administrative district. This method has been followed for the province of Hamid. In Teke, where data are rather sparse, it seems more practical to operate with individual figures.

In Hamid, the stamp tax from the administrative district of Uluborlu amounted on an average to 8051 *akçe*. As Uluborlu was the only substantial town in this area and the administrative district contained very few villages, we are probably correct in assuming that the cotton cloth in question was mainly produced by urban weavers. Moreover, a tax register compiled about forty years later does in fact acknowledge the activity of weavers in this place.[25] They possessed a special market which was their collective property and which would have produced 200 *akçe* a year if rented out.

Second in importance was the administrative district of Gönen, whose central place certainly was never more than semi-urban.[26] As an average, stamp dues in this area amounted to about 6,734 *akçe*. We can assume that a large part of the cloth in question was woven by families that still maintained some ties with the land, and the same should have been true of all the other administrative districts in Hamid as well. As a further centre in the marketing of cotton cloth, the little town and administrative district of Agras (modern Atabey) deserve mention, with an average stamp tax of 4,356 *akçe*.[27]

As far as the province of Teke was concerned, total revenue from the stamp tax generally amounted to less than one half of what was being collected in Hamid. It is most interesting that only a small part of these dues came from the town of Antalya proper. In 932/1525–6, the entire administrative district of Antalya produced only 2,885 *akçe*, while Teke-Karahisar and Köprüpazarı were assessed at 9,126 *akçe*. If the figure for 937/1530–1 is anything of a guide, a big market in cotton cloth was probably located in Teke-Karahisar, which was expected to yield 12,588 *akçe*. As a comparison, in 933/1526 the farm for Antalya and Köprüpazarı had been assessed at 46,644 *akçe* for a three-year period, or 15,538 *akçe* a year. Under these circumstances, it is probably fair to say that the outlying areas of the province accounted for at least three quarters of the total stamp tax, and possibly for more.

Now even Antalya during those years was a town of very modest proportions.[28] It is also very likely that Teke-Karahisar was no more than a village, and rather an isolated one at that.[29] Thus, in Teke even more obviously than in Hamid, the production of cotton cloth was a rural activity. Since the data on Aydın and İçel convey the same impression,[30] there is some justification for assuming the existence of fairly widespread commercialized weaving, at least in certain parts of the sixteenth-century Anatolian countryside.

Also, there is considerable evidence for the fact that trade in rurally produced cotton fabrics was not just intended to supply the immediately surrounding areas, but İstanbul as well. Two documents, one dealing with Gülnar and the other with the province of Hamid, specify the length and width of the fabric to be delivered. In the case of Gülnar this was to be large enough that a *kaftan* could be lined with a single piece.[31] Now procuring a special order from İstanbul undoubtedly involved considerable time and expense, which certainly would not have been incurred unless the extent of the trade justified it. Moreover, in the case of Hamid, the central administration was directly involved. For the document in question, of which we possess two different versions, was issued upon the complaint of a court official, the chief tailor (*terzibaşı*). However, decrees from İstanbul do not seem to have been very effective in setting standards, for in one of the texts we find the remark that earlier edicts of the same content had been disregarded. Therefore an attempt was made to shift enforcement of the sultan's orders on to the shoulders of those who handled the cloth once it had been woven.

Among these, the documents name bleachers and dyers (*kassar*, *boyacı*) and of course the officials in charge of the stamp tax. Thereby, the latter again appears to have been intended not just as a means of producing revenue, but also as a way of ensuring standard qualities. Finally, the merchants are mentioned. Also, the documents in question obviously assume that at least some of the craftsmen handling cotton cloth were organized in guilds, since reference is made to 'their' guild officials, namely *şeyh* and *yiğitbaşı*. How far the guild organization had penetrated into small semi-rural settlements is at this point still an open question. Unfortunately, the *kadı* registers concerning most of the towns in question have not survived for the sixteenth century.

In the case of the Gülnar weavers, the decree of 1564–5 makes no mention of a guild organization. Yet the people in question seem to have lived and worked within a reasonable distance from one another, probably in the little town of Gülnar itself. For not only did they maintain enough communication with one another to agree to send a messenger to the Porte, the *kadı* was also instructed to call them all together and admonish them. Moreover, the latter official was ordered to make sure that the producers of *boğası* made no more than a 10 per cent profit, a standard rule known from many handlists dealing with the regulation of markets.[32] This rule too would scarcely have been enforcable by one or two officials – i.e., the *kadı* and the market overseer known as *muhtesib*[33] – unless there was some kind of formal or informal organization among the producers to support them.

Other aspects of the organization of production present further difficulties. Among other things, we do not know how spinners and weavers were provided with the necessary raw materials. In Aydın no very elaborate organization may have been in existence, and we are free to assume that peasants worked up raw materials produced on their own lands, or at least by their fellow villagers. While we have no data on agricultural production in the province of Teke, a similar situation may well have prevailed there. But the area of Gülnar, so productive in cotton fabrics, does not seem to have grown the raw material in significant quantities.[34] And in Hamid, cotton was of negligible importance as an agricultural crop. In the administrative district of Uluborlu almost no cotton tithes were mentioned,[35] even though the register was very specific about many other crops grown in this area.

That there must have been a fairly lively trade in cotton yarn is indicated by the fact that in many towns a special tax was levied on this commodity. If a city was located in the centre of a cotton-producing area, revenue from this source might amount to the respectable sum of 16,000 *akçe*.[36] Many towns, such as for instance Sivas,[37] and probably Ayntab (Gaziantep)[38] had special areas set aside for the trade in yarn of all kinds. That this must have been a reasonably lucrative business is indicated by the fact that wealthy state officials competed with one another to rent shops to the yarn merchants.

Towards the middle of the seventeenth century, Bolu, a little provincial town in the northern part of central Anatolia, also possessed its own group of Armenian merchants, who dealt both in yarn and in *boğası*.[39] While they had set up their stalls in front of the covered market, they also spent considerable time travelling from village to village. Were they only supplying yarn for household consumption? Or were certain settlements in this forested and inaccessible area eking out a meagre living by weaving cloth for the market? If so, what was the role of the merchants? It is possible that they only provided the yarn, but one cannot help wondering whether they did not take a hand in selling the finished product as well.

At the same time, it is very likely that there was a market for woven cloth even outside of the cities. From the middle of the sixteenth century, there survives the answer to a complaint from two merchants with Iranian connections (*acem tüccarı*), a certain Badros and his confrère. They were dealing in fine muslin (*tülbend*) and regularly visited the towns of Şeyhli, Kaymas, Kandıra, and other small places in the administrative district of Üsküdar.[40] This seems to have excited the anger of local merchants, who attempted to stop the trade of the two outsiders. The latter asked for official protection, which was duly granted. One wonders where the muslin in which they traded may have come from. It may have been from Iran itself, or else picked up somewhere along the way, in Erzincan or in Tokat. Only further inquiry into the trade in fabrics all over Anatolia will furnish a reply.

We obtain further information concerning the mechanics of the cotton trade from an early seventeenth-century document proposing to regulate the distribution of cotton and linen fabrics in İstanbul.[41] The setting is familiar: In the past all fabrics of this type which were brought into the capital had been sold in one place, the business building known as the *bodrum han*. But recently traders had adopted the habit of buying and selling wherever they wished. As a result, the Treasury suffered a loss in taxes, not only directly as traders avoided the customs duties which were probably being levied in the *han*, but also indirectly. For apparently there was considerable competition between linen drapers regularly organized in guilds, who paid taxes, and travelling salesmen who could avoid most charges. Moreover, the guildsmen complained that they were being made to pay high prices on the wholesale level, and in consequence were unable to sell their wares. Remedies as proposed by the central administration are also familiar: the sale of cotton and linen fabrics was to take place in one location only, and the linen drapers were to purchase their wares through the mediation of their guild officials.[42]

In this context, it would be highly desirable to connect the traders delivering their goods to the İstanbul linen drapers with the yarn and cloth merchants of whom we have already caught a glimpse as they tramped the highways and byways of Anatolia. But that is just what we are not yet able to do. It is likely that local cloth markets formed the missing link. Quite possibly the seller of raw cotton and yarn, the local buyer of finished *boğası* and the wholesaler in the İstanbul market were in certain cases one and the same person. But at present all this is no more than a hypothesis.

As to the prices paid for the finished cotton cloth, we find a few indications in sales documents, and more could probably be located in various towns of Anatolia. A casual search in the Ankara registers reveals that *boğası* was sold by the piece (*kıta*). Around 1591–3, a piece of *boğası* sold for 80–140 *akçe*, while for unspecified linen or cotton cloth (*bez*) we also find records of sales by the bale (*top*) or ell (*arşın*).[43] While data on the cotton trade in late-sixteenth-century Ankara are few and far between, other towns may provide further data in the future. However, it is probably too much to hope for continuous series in any one place.[44] If employed with caution, data from estate inventories may also be used.[45] At least in certain places, there were various standards of size and quality in existence, although the documents are not always very specific in describing them. Prices of course differed accordingly. It seems to be even more difficult to locate prices of raw cotton.

As has been established in studies of the Levant trade,[46] cotton was also one of the raw materials exported by European merchants, although throughout the seventeenth century its significance, at least in English commerce, could never even remotely compare with that of the trade in raw silk. Yet it is apparent that export of cotton goes back at least to the last years of the sixteenth century. An imperial decree from the year 1004/1595–6 refers to the fact that such purchases had even been legal for a while, at least as far as the ports of İzmir, Foça, and Çeşme, were concerned.[47] For some of the merchants involved in the trade had procured themselves an order from the sultan legalizing their activities, a permission which was ultimately revoked. In the area of Adana and Ayas, the former Lajazzo living on as a minor local port, European traders appear to have purchased cotton in spite of all orders to the contrary.[48] It appears that the reason behind Ottoman prohibitions was concern for the supply of İstanbul, which could not be allowed to go short in either foodstuffs or raw materials. Even though the cultivation of cotton was increased considerably at least in the area around Adana,[49] supply could not keep pace with increased demand, and the purchasers by European traders imposed additional strain.

Again the documents pose many more questions than they answer. Nothing is said about the nationality of the traders. Considering the fact that the foreign merchants most frequently visiting İzmir in the late sixteenth and early seventeenth centuries appear to have been Englishmen, Frenchmen, and Venetians, it is very likely that members of one or the other of these communities had also been exporting cotton from the province of Aydın.[50] Moreover, we would like to know something about the quantities involved, and at what time the latter became large enough to disorganize internal trade. Nor do the documents tell us anything about the sellers and about the intermediaries who probably arranged many business deals. Questions of this type can only be answered by patient research among archival materials.

Yet a few conclusions can be drawn even now. First of all, the weaving of simple cotton cloth was in many areas predominantly a rural activity. Secondly, it was carried on in close connection with the market. Raw materials in quite a few cases must have been provided commercially, and linkage to distant buyers ensured. In passing, a further document from the *mühimme* registers reveals that here lay an opportunity for profitable investment. We hear of a *kadı* in the province of Hamid who had committed all kinds of abuses and invested his ill-gotten gains in the *boğası* trade.[51] It is very possible that there was even some kind of putting-out system in operation. At the same time, guild organization, with its possibilities of purchasing raw materials in common, may well have spread to certain settlements that remained very small in terms of population. About the details of organization in this branch of production we remain ignorant. Nor do we know how the weavers were affected by the upheavals of the later sixteenth century and the subsequent period, or by the export of raw materials as practised by European traders. But in spite of all these uncertainties, we retain the impression that the Anatolian countryside of the sixteenth century was affected by commercialization to a considerable degree.

12 ❧ The silk-reeling industry of Mount Lebanon, 1840–1914: a study of the possibilities and limitations of factory production in the periphery

ROGER OWEN

Between 1840 and 1914 nearly two hundred silk-reeling factories were established in the Ottoman province of Mount Lebanon and its neighbouring districts. In the first decade of the twentieth century they employed some 14,000, mostly seasonal, workers, the majority of them women, and produced around 500,000 kg of raw-silk thread a year, roughly a fifth of the total output of the Levant[1] (see Table 12.1). There was then an enormous reduction in activity during the difficult conditions experienced in Mount Lebanon in the First World War. But silk production was revived again in the 1920s, only to receive a second major blow as a result of the collapse of the international price during the early part of the Great Depression. Output sank to about a quarter of its previous peak but managed to sustain this level for the rest of the 1930s and through the early years of the Second World War before the industry disappeared for good almost as soon as Lebanon achieved its political independence in 1943.

The ups and downs of Lebanese silk production provide a powerful illustration of many of the problems and possibilities facing factories established on the European periphery. It owed its start to the French weavers' search for alternative sources of silk thread once their own domestic reeling industry had been nearly decimated as a result of silk-worm disease in the 1850s; and its vast expansion in the following decades to a combination of growing French demand and of continued French financial interest in Lebanese commerce and manufacturing. But, like numerous other examples of non-European nineteenth-century industrialization, its techniques and methods of organization remained more or less unchanged up to the First World War with the result that it became vulnerable to competition from the raw-silk producers of Europe and of China and Japan. It will be argued later that the reasons for this technical and organizational stagnation can be explained partly by the way in which it was integrated into the pre-existing system of economic and social relations in Mount Lebanon itself. Like any other manufacturing process which was heavily dependent on a locally produced raw material, the development of a silk

Table 12.1 *World production of raw-silk thread, 1871–5 to 1910–14 (annual averages in kg, 000)*

	1871/5	1881/5	1891/5	1901/5	1910/14
France	658	631	745	591	396
Italy	2,880	2,760	4,428	4,326	3,828
Spain	138	86	86	80	81
Austria–Hungary	none	153	257	315	314
(Total Europe)	3,678	3,630	5,518	5,312	4,619
Levant (including Syria/Lebanon)	676	700	1,107	2,304	2,419
Shanghai*	2,996	2,448	4,030	4,227	5,495
Canton*	945	894	1,373	2,128	2,259
Japan	691	1,360	3,006	4,865	10,156
India	562	406	261	256	166
(Total Asia less Levant)	5,194	5,108	8,670	11,476	18,076
World total	9,546	9,438	15,295	19,092	25,114

* Figures for exports not total production

Sources: L'Union des Marchands de Soie de Lyon, *Statistiques de la Production de la soie*, in Matsui, *History of the silk industry*, p. 57.

industry can only be properly understood by an examination of the complex inter-relationship between external factors deriving from the world-market and the organization of Lebanon's own agricultural sector – in which mulberry leaves are grown, silk worms produced and raised and cocoons delivered to the factories. To make such an examination still more complicated, it was not only silk thread which was traded internationally but eggs and cocoons as well.

The first modern Lebanese silk factory was erected around 1840 by a French entrepreneur called Portalis in the little village of Btater in the mountain district of the Shuf.[2] It was based on the relatively simple technology embodied in the Chambon method perfected in Europe in the 1820s and 1830s. This involved the construction of basins (tanks) of hot water in which the silk cocoons were dipped to unloose the gum which bound them together, and the import of power-operated reeling machines on which the thread from the cocoon was unwound.[3] Portalis also brought over European female spinners to teach the local women the art of spinning to 'two ends', a method by which each operative was put in charge of a process which involved teasing out the thread from two cocoons at once and directing it over two sets of reels to make two separate lengths of yarn.[4] It has been asserted that the productivity of factory workers spinning to two ends may not have been any greater than that of those who continued the traditional practice of reeling by hand.[5] Where the importance of this innovation did lie was in the fact that its employment in a factory allowed the controlled production of the type of thread of consistent quality which the new European weaving machines required.

Table 12.2 *Cocoon and silk-thread production in Syria/Mount Lebanon, 1861–1913 (annual averages)*

	Cocoons kg, 000	Silk thread kg, 000
1861–4	1,390	
1865–9	2,180	
1870–4	1,900	160 (1873–4 only)
1875–9	1,930	146
1880–4	2,980	223
1885–9	3,280	277
1890–4	4,680	443
1895–9	5,020	441
1900–4	5,210	479
1905–9	5,410	486
1910–13	5,640	489

Sources: (*Cocoons*) Figures from L'Union des Marchands de Soie de Lyon, *Statistiques de la production de la soie en France et à l'étranger* in Saba, 'Development and decline', pp. 60–1. This differs slightly from the figures in Ducousso, *L'industrie de la soie*, p. 101. (*Thread*) *Statistiques de la production de la soie* in Chevallier, 'Lyon et la Syrie', p. 286. These differ slightly from the ones given in Ducousso, *L'industrie de la soie*, pp. 100–1, and Z. Kanzadian and L. de Bertalot, *Atlas de géographie économique de Syrie et du Liban* (Paris, 1926), p. 62.

Other entrepreneurs quickly followed Portalis' example, stimulated by the huge rise in the price of raw silk in the 1850s and 1860s and by the growing demand from France. By the early 1850s there were 9 or 10 foreign-owned factories and another 5 or so constructed by local bankers and merchants.[6] This number rose to 67 for Mount Lebanon and its surrounding districts in 1867, of which 10 were French.[7] Expansion then continued, in spite of the fall in the international price of silk in the 1870s which led to the closure of so many plants in other parts of the Middle East such as Anatolia and Persia. There were an estimated 105 factories in Mount Lebanon and Syria in 1885 (5 of them French), 150 in Mount Lebanon in the early 1890s and over 190 in Mount Lebanon and Syria in the first decade of the twentieth century (6 of them French).[8] It should be noted, however, that some of those in the latter period were very small, consisting of only a very few basins, and that the vast majority of them relied on manual methods rather than machines to turn their reels.[9]

With this increase in the numbers of factories, output of silk thread grew rapidly, from about 150,000 kg in the early 1870s to just under 450,000 kg a year in the early 1890s, almost all of which was exported to France[10] (see Table 12.2).

Table 12.3 *Two estimates of the average price of Syrian silk thread during the period 1892–1913 (francs/kg)*

	(1)		(1)	(2)		(2)
1892	45	1901	40.375	47	1910	51
1893	54.5	1902	43.875	51	1911	50
1894	38.75	1903	48.875	55	1912	49
1895	39	1904	40.5	49	1913	52
1896	35.75	1905	42.5	51		
1897	36.875	1906	49.125	53		
1898	36.875	1907	59	73		
1899	51	1908	51	50		
1900	41.875	1909	52.5	55		

Sources: (1) Ducousso, *L'industrie de la soie*, p. 144 (based on three-monthly averages for the type 'Uso Lyon')
(2) Kanzadian and de Bertalot, *Atlas*, p. 62.

This in turn required a considerable expansion in the planting of mulberry trees, in the production of cocoons and, as will be seen later, in the import of silk-worm eggs. According to the estimates presented by the Lebanese historian, Ismail Haqqi, by the beginning of the twentieth century some 31,500 hectares, or about 40 per cent of Mount Lebanon's cultivated land, was devoted to the mulberry while perhaps 165,000 people out of a total population of 400,000 were involved in some part of the process of providing the silk factories with raw materials.[11]

Several features of this process of rapid expansion deserve attention. First, following the example set by Portalis and the first French entrepreneurs, the vast majority of the factories were established in the mountainous districts just north and south of the Beirut–Damascus road, inhabited mainly by Maronite and Greek Orthodox Christians[12] (see Map 12.1). Such a rugged location had many disadvantages from the point of view of ease of transport, at least until a sizeable road-building program was put under way in the 1880s, but it did mean that the factories were close to the villages which cultivated the mulberry trees and where silk production had been concentrated for many centuries, as well as to an area where there was a supply of cheap labour.[13] Both factors were of great importance. The cost of collecting and transporting cocoons was particularly high and, throughout the world, the majority of factory owners, including the Japanese, preferred to locate their plants close to the source of supply.[14] Again, while some of the first entrepreneurs may well have believed that they could recruit skilled labour from among the traditional silk-reelers put out of business by European competition, the majority attached more importance to finding women willing to do the bulk of the work. But here there was a problem. Many mountain families were unwilling to release their daughters for work in the

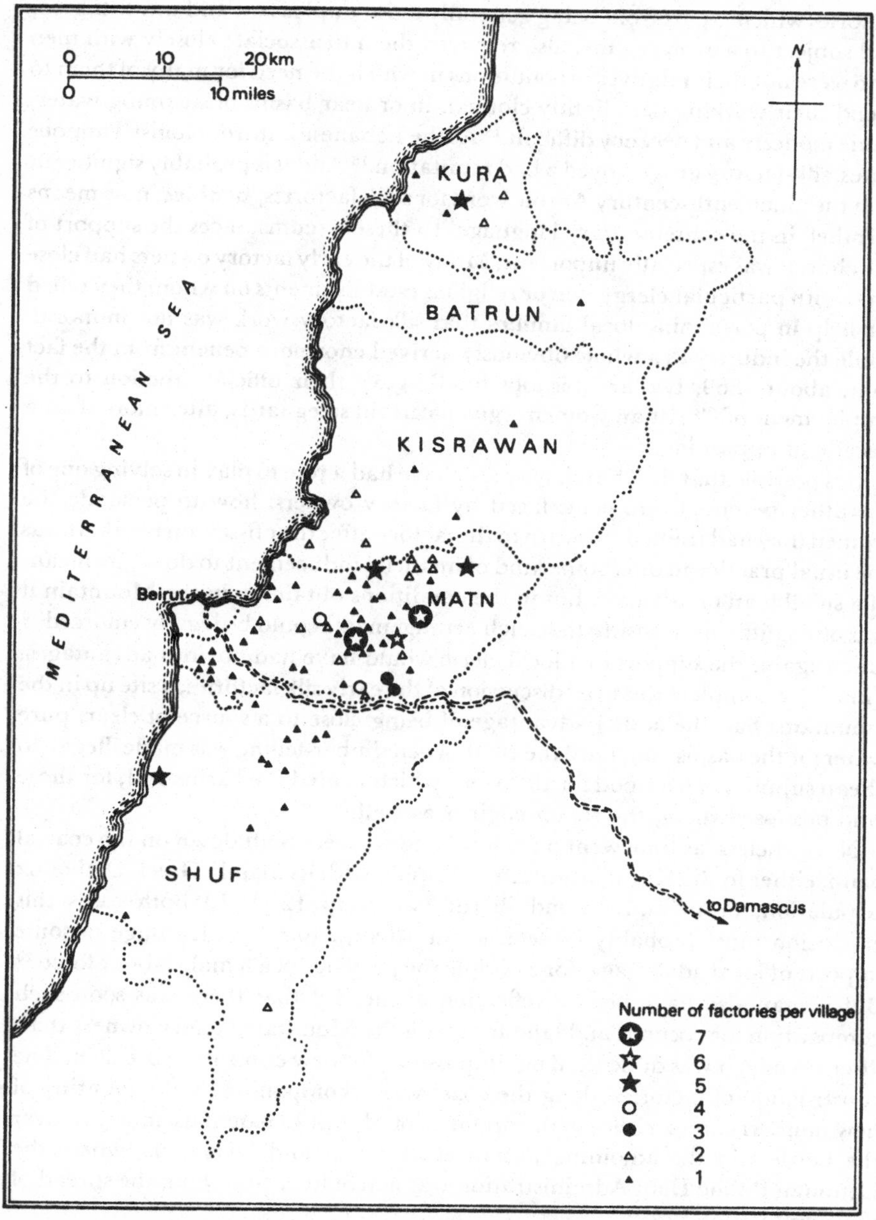

Map 12.1 Silk factories in operation in Mt Lebanon *c.* 1913

factories which, apart from being generally dark, unpleasant and unventilated, and subject to a grim regime, also required them to associate closely with men who were not their relatives in conditions in which the need for many of them to spend their working day, lightly clothed, in or near basins of steaming water, made modesty and decency difficult.[15] As the Lebanese anthropologist Tannous notes, silk-factory girls enjoyed a bad reputation.[16] And it is probably significant that the nineteenth-century Arabic word for such factories, *karakana*, now means 'brothel' in the contemporary language. In these circumstances the support of the church was especially important. Many of the early factory owners had close links with particular clergymen or religious establishments on whom they relied for help in persuading local families that silk-factory work was not immoral, while the industry as a whole obviously derived enormous benefit from the fact that, about 1869, two archbishops finally gave their official sanction to the employment of Christian women – given certain safeguards, after more than a decade of opposition.[17]

It is possible that the church may also have had a role to play in solving one of the other perennial problems faced by factory owners: how to persuade the women they had trained to return to the factory after the off-season break. It was the usual practice to offer some kind of financial inducement to do so, by means of a small loan or advance; but in the conditions obtaining in the Mountain it was often difficult to ensure that such arrangements could be legally enforced.[18] Once again, the support of a local cleric would have had obvious advantages. Finally, to complete this brief discussion of the early silk factories, a site up in the mountains had the added advantage of being close to a source of clear, pure water for the basins and, until the 1880s when timber-felling was made illegal, to cheap supplies of firewood for the ovens which heated the basins and, for those who possessed them, the steam engines as well.[19]

Nevertheless, as time went on, a few factories were built down on the coastal plain, either in the Kura, just south of Tripoli, with its mainly Greek Orthodox population, or in and around Beirut (see Map 12.1). In both cases this expansion must probably be seen as an attempt to take advantage of some important local advantage, for example the presence of a female labour force.[20] But it may also have been a reflection of the fact that there was soon such competition for cocoons and labour among the Mountain factory owners that, after a while, it was difficult, if not impossible, for new entrants to break in. The construction of factories along the coast was accompanied by the planting of new mulberry trees, either in the province of Mount Lebanon itself, or just over the borders in the adjoining provinces of Beirut and Damascus, where the Ottoman Public Debt Administration was active in encouraging the spread of their cultivation.[21]

A second feature of factory expansion was that the vast majority of new plants were constructed within the boundaries of the province or *mutasarrifiya* of Mount Lebanon, which enjoyed a special form of quasi-autonomous authority established by international agreement under the Règlement Organique of 1861.[22] This gave the local inhabitants considerable advantages over their neighbours in the rest of the Ottoman Empire in terms of lower taxes, better security and freedom from conscription, while silk producers enjoyed the particular benefit of freedom from the Ottoman silk tithe and the fact that contracts and commercial agreements were subject to the European-dominated Commercial Tribunal in Beirut.[23] Set against this, however, the silk industry as a whole suffered certain disadvantages in the longer run, two of which were of particular importance. The first relates to the supply of silk-worm eggs. During the 1870s there was a considerable effort by local merchants to develop a consistent, disease-free, type of egg suitable for Lebanese conditions.[24] But, when these efforts came to nothing just after 1880, Lebanese silk-worm cultivators had no alternative but to rely on foreign imports, which were not only more expensive than native ones but also tended to be more prone to disease and sudden fluctuations in quality.[25] Mount Lebanon would thus have derived considerable benefit if the Ottoman Public Debt Administration had been allowed to extend its supervision of Ottoman egg production to the province in the early 1890s. But these attempts were thwarted by a group of Lebanese and foreign merchants (including a number who were involved in selling imported eggs) on the grounds it would involve the creation of a monopoly which was contrary to the principles of Free Trade supposedly enshrined in the Règlement of 1861.[26] Two decades later, when a second attempt to revive local production made considerable inroads into the market for imported eggs silk-worm cultivators would also have benefited from some body to control quality and regulate marketing procedures, as, for example, in Japan.[27] But, given the powerful position of foreign merchants and the passive role of the local administration, such a development was virtually impossible. Second, and even more important, the creation of Mount Lebanon as an administrative entity with a special economic and political status tended to accelerate those trends which were already pushing it in the direction of a closer relationship with Europe at the expense of its links with the surrounding Ottoman provinces. As far as silk was concerned this was to be of special consequence after the First World War when there was some effort to redirect exports away from Lyon and back towards the silk-weaving establishments of Damascus, Homs and Hama in the Syrian interior. But, by then, the opportunities for exploiting this potential market were much reduced.[28]

Finally, to return to the subject of the factories themselves, almost all of them were established not by foreigners but by local Lebanese and Syrian entrepreneurs, the majority of them Christian but perhaps fifteen or so Druze or Muslim.[29] Such a development may seem odd at first sight, given the many advantages which the first French owners enjoyed by way of cheap credit and their close links with Lyon mills[30] However, as the major historian of the industry, Gaston Ducousso, argues convincingly, it can be explained quite easily in terms of certain structural features which gave local entrepreneurs a significant edge over their foreign competitors. For one thing, technology was simple and the amount of capital required to start even a medium-sized factory very low.[31] For another, Lebanese owners were much better placed to obtain a regular supply of cheap cocoons from a scattered peasant population in conditions in which, as already noted, legal contracts were particularly difficult to enforce.[32] As cocoons formed the major part of the costs of production (perhaps as much as 75–80 per cent) this was obviously a factor of major importance.[33] Ducousso might also have added that local entrepreneurs were often better able to maintain a regular labour force from season to season by using ties of kinship and local power relations just as much as straightforward economic inducement.[34] The point is an important one and helps to explain not only the central role played by Lebanese entrepreneurs but also the fact that the industry was well placed to cut costs at times of falling prices by the simple expedient of reducing factory wages or paying the producers less for their cocoons. Lastly, if conditions became really difficult, local producers were often better able to tide themselves over a bad season or two by temporarily closing down their operations.

Having said all this, it is important not to push the point about the purely local or native character of the Lebanese and Syrian entrepreneurs too far. Many of them were French protégés (or protected persons) with all the political and economic advantages this entailed. More importantly, they were at work in an industry which was largely dependent on French expertise, French capital and French commercial organisation. It was the first French entrepreneurs who provided their local successors with a model by way of factory lay-out and industrial procedure, a model which the latter were in all cases content simply to follow.[35] It was also the French bankers and silk weavers who provided much of both the fixed and the working capital necessary to erect and to operate a silk-reeling establishment. According to Ducousso, writing of conditions in the early twentieth century, such a plant required something like 200 to 250 francs a basin for its construction (and thus about 8,000 to 10,000 francs for an average factory) and another 3,500 to 5,000 francs a basin each year as working capital, mainly for the purchase of cocoons.[36] In 1909, according to one calculation which he quotes, a little over half the 12 to 15 million francs required for cocoon purchase came from France, either directly to well-established factory owners or via loans from Beirut banks – at rates of interest which were clearly determined in France itself.[37] Finally, to use Ducousso's data yet again, certain key French firms, notably those of Eynard and Mourgue d'Algue, played a central role in the export of silk thread as well as in the supply of credit, the import of silk-worm eggs and the provision of insurance.[38]

It would now be useful to examine the structural features of the Lebanese silk industry in more systematic fashion. Perhaps the best place to begin is by noting that the question of its organization and linkages seem to have become a subject

Table 12.4 *Cocoon production in Syria/Lebanon, 1920 to 1941–2 (kg, 000)*

1920	800	1930	3,575	1940–1	600
1921	1,100	1931	2,760	1941–2	600
1922	1,900	1932	1,762		
1923	2,225	1933	1,400		
1924	2,855	1934	NK		
1925	2,944	1935	600		
1926	2,955	1936	NK		
1927	3,185	1937	800		
1928	3,370	1938	900		
1929	3,480	1939	800		

Sources: Saba, 'Development and decline', p. 63; Comité Exécutif du Premier Congrès Libanais de la Sériculture, *Annual Reports*.

for debate and discussion just before the First World War when there was a feeling in some quarters that it was running into serious difficulty. The acting British vice consul in Beirut, James Elroy Flecker, expressed these sentiments most forcefully when he noted, in his commercial report for 1911, that the industry was 'probably doomed'.[39] The same current of unease can be found running through Ducousso's book, *L'industrie de la soie en Syrie et au Liban* (1913), which seems to have been written, in part, to draw attention to the ways in which Lebanon was falling behind its international competitors and to suggest some ways in which the situation might be improved. The particular reasons underlying this dark view of the future are a bit difficult to understand but would seem to have had something to do with two separate sets of circumstances. One was the increasing import into Beirut of Japanese and Chinese thread which cost only half that of the local product.[40] The other was the temporary closure of some Mountain factories on the grounds that they could no longer find enough female labour, and the re-allocation of some of the agricultural land on the coastal plain from mulberries to alternative crops.[41] In the former case, the shortage of labour was linked to an acceleration in emigration, particularly among Christians, which in the decade just before the First World War was estimated to be running at some 15,000 a year – out of a total adult working population of not more than 200,000[42]. At the very least this must have made for some upward pressure on wages. Nevertheless, there is no sign that the total output of thread was declining just before the First World War (see Table 12.2) and, in view of the industry's recovery in the 1920s (Table 12.4) it would seem that critics like Ducousso may well have underestimated its strength, its resilience and its own special advantages.

Ducousso's observations on the state of the industry concentrate on two particular aspects: one, of the organization of the factories themselves, the other, the process by which they were supplied with cocoons. I will deal with them in this order. As far as the factories were concerned, Ducousso makes the important point that, with the exception of the four plants owned by the French firm of Veuve-Guerin at Krey, they had made little or no effort to update either their technology or their organization. At a time when both the French and the Italians were making strenuous efforts to switch to the more productive method of spinning to four or six ends (in which each spinner dealt with four or six threads at a time), only Veuve-Guerin was making the same transition in the Mountain, with the result that, on average, Lebanese yields were very much lower per basin than in Europe.[43] Again, only Veuve-Guerin had introduced what was becoming standard equipment in Europe (and also to some extent in Japan): new plant for stifling the crysalis inside a cocoon by dry heat rather than steam.[44]

Ducousso obviously recognized that there were many problems connected with training local workers to spin to four or six ends, a process which was both more skilful and much more onerous.[45] And he also underlines this point, if only by inference, when he asserts that Veuve-Guerin's switch had been accompanied by the establishment of an orphanage in the same village, the stated purpose of which was to provide the girls with a practical education in silk-reeling – thus, of course, ensuring the factory of a docile set of skilled operatives.[46] But the main thrust of his argument certainly follows straight from the conventional wisdom regarding any system of capitalist industrial enterprise: that capital has to be constantly accumulated, technique continually developed, individual units regularly increased in size, if there is to be any chance of survival against better-organized competitors. But, although in Mount Lebanon this may have been the logic at work for the few French factories, it is clear that, for the rest, there were powerful tendencies pulling in exactly the opposite direction. For them the major dynamic seems to have been one pushing in the direction of the multiplication of small, undercapitalized, technologically stagnant units – and it is interesting to ask why.

There has been too little research so far to provide a very well-documented answer. Nevertheless, there is good reason to argue that the reasons underlying the development of the Lebanese system can be found in an examination of a combination of mutually reinforcing internal and external factors. As far as the internal ones are concerned, silk production was an activity in which, in its Lebanese context, there was little advantage to be gained by increasing the size of the factory beyond a certain, small limit, and many benefits to be gained from the use of local village relationships to transfer part of the costs of labour and raw materials, and as much as possible of the risks, back to the peasant families themselves. From a technical point of view, where no steam power was used to turn the reels, there do not seem to have been any economies to be gained from having a factory of more than about forty or so basins.[47] From the point of view of cheap inputs, the fact that there were no large towns and no extensive system of agriculture meant that entrepreneurs had no alternative but to look for their cocoons and their labour in tiny peasant communities, where the power of personal relationships was going to be an extremely important asset. This last point can be reinforced, I think, by pointing out that of the 88 villages and small towns in Mount Lebanon which contained a silk factory just before the First World War, 32 contained more than one (and 13 more than 2), a fact which I take to mean that the advantages enjoyed by an owner in terms of personal relationships was more than enough to outweigh the disadvantages of having to compete for labour and cocoons within a very small area.[48]

To turn now to the external factors, these would seem to have hinged on two particular features. First, the fact that Lebanese silk thread appears to have occupied a privileged position among the silk weavers of Lyon on account of its resistance, elasticity and ability to take any dye meant that French bankers and merchants – as well as their local Beiruti associates – were under no special pressure to encourage the rationalization of its production or the reduction in its price *vis-à-vis* its Asian competitors.[49] Secondly, these same bankers and merchants must have been quick to see the benefit to themselves of a situation in which competition between a large number of small factory units for the eggs they imported (for sale to the cocoon producers) or for commercial credit allowed them to obtain a larger share of the profits (Ducousso estimates this at $33\frac{1}{3}$ per cent) than they could have done from an industry dominated by a few large firms. Just as the owners themselves increased their own profits by their ability to push down the cost of wages and cocoons, so too the Beiruti merchants were able to augment theirs by forcing the factories to pay heavily for their working expenses. In these circumstances it would have been difficult for most owners to accumulate the capital they needed to modernize their plants, even if there had been any other incentive for them to do so.

The second part of Ducousso's criticism of the organization of the Lebanese silk industry concerns the way in which the production of cocoons was dominated by poor peasant families, working small plots of land, who lacked both the skill and the economic stimulus to practise it properly.[50] The yields of the eggs put out to hatch into worms was one of the lowest in the silk-producing countries of the world, something which he ascribes, largely, to the fact that the huts in which they were placed were small and dirty, that the peasant experienced great difficulty in keeping them at the correct temperature and that the worms were not fed or looked after with sufficient care.[51] There was a further disadvantage in that the cocoons when produced were bought in small lots by brokers and then sold to the factories in such a way that proper sorting for quality and type was difficult. All this was clearly a reflection of the fact that production was carried out in small units by peasants who were often share-cropping tenants of larger landowners and whose isolation made them relatively easy to be exploited by the cocoon brokers, who often doubled up as usurers and egg merchants and were thus able to keep many of their clients perpetually in debt.[52] Once again, the implication of Ducousso's argument is that silk-worm raising should have taken place in larger, better-organized units, as it did in

Europe and many parts of Asia.[53] But in a Lebanese context this would have involved a full-scale reorganization of rural economic and social relations, which was clearly impossible.

Reading Ducousso as well as the writings of local Lebanese who also wished to make their industry more competitive, it is not difficult to feel the latter's sense of frustration.[54] As a rule they were perfectly well aware of developments in the rest of the world, particularly in Japan where there was a period of particularly rapid progress in the two decades before the First World War.[55] What was especially important was that this was a process which involved interconnected improvements on all fronts, from an increase in the yields of mulberry trees, through the establishment of well-regulated cocoon markets to the rapid introduction of steam-powered reeling machines. Capital was used more effectively than in Syria/Lebanon, for example as a result of the fact that the mulberry trees produced several harvests of leaves, thus allowing a more continuous feeding of silk worms and a more regular flow of cocoons to the factories. Meanwhile, there was a rapid improvement in local technology with the introduction of purely Japanese inventions like the apparatus for drying cocoons or Japanese-made reeling machines. Finally, there was a continuous reduction in dependence on foreign working capital so that, for example, by 1913–14 nearly two-thirds of Japanese silk exports were financed by Japanese financiers.[56] The result was not only a huge increase in output but the capture of a large share of the American market which, by the First World War, was as large as that of all the European countries combined.

Nevertheless, it does not take more than a moment's thought to realize that the Japanese path was intimately associated with the larger developments in the country's socio-economic system and not one which could be copied elsewhere. In the event, a better comparison for Mount Lebanon is with countries like China, which also failed to reorganize their methods of cocoon production or to pass much beyond the stage of simple industrial processes like the Chambon method of reeling.[57] As in China, the Lebanese system developed within the context created by the interaction of world-economic forces and the domestic socio-economic structure. As in China this allowed development of a certain kind, encouraging the proliferation of simply organized factories while systematically discouraging those forces which might have promoted technical progress.[58] As in China, the possibilities open to industrialists were severely circumscribed by the fact that cocoon production took place in an agricultural sector which made its improvement and rationalization particularly difficult.

As a postscript it might be useful to provide a brief sketch of the further history of silk production in Mount Lebanon up to its final collapse. In spite of Flecker's gloomy prognostication, it was quite a long time dying. Although famine, blockade and the uprooting of hundreds of thousands of mulberry trees during the First World War reduced output to only a tenth of its pre-war level, there was then a period of rapid revival in the 1920s: by 1927–8, 113 factories were again at work, producing some 330,000 kg of thread, roughly three-quarters of the early-twentieth-century average.[59] This upsurge owed something to the activities of the French Mandatory authorities which took steps to encourage the replanting of mulberry trees, to establish a few model silk-rearing houses for training purposes and to make it easier to import new European machinery. Nevertheless, only a handful of factories were reorganized and re-equipped (local estimates vary from six or seven to fifteen) and the bulk of the industry was carried on as before, with workers' productivity remaining at only just over half that of contemporary Italy or France.[60] Once again its resilience is to be found not in its capacity to change and to develop nor in its technical progress but in its links with the French commercial interests which provided credit and its ability to keep down costs by exploiting the vulnerable position of the Lebanese peasant population.

The huge fall in prices in the early 1930s produced another period of worry and concern, marked this time by the establishment of the first Congrès Libanais de la Sériculture in Beirut with a preparatory committee consisting of a number of leading Lebanese factory owners and silk and egg merchants and a permanent Executive Committee which made what, by local standards, were energetic efforts to improve techniques, particularly those related to the production of cocoons.[61] Its activities included the use of a small government subsidy to distribute free eggs to producers between 1932 and 1934, to disinfect some of the larger 'magnanaries' or silk-worm-rearing houses and to construct new ones.[62] But the French-dominated Mandatory government would do little to help and if the industry managed to survive both the fall in prices and the virtual cutting off of all French credit in 1934 it was only because of its ability to cut costs as well as a successful attempt to exploit the local market for thread by expanding its production of the lower-quality type known as Scandaroun.[63] In this way some fifty or sixty factories remained at work for most of the 1930s and early 1940s, with an output of something like a quarter of the 1920s' peak.[64] The industry then disappeared almost completely in the quite new economic conditions after 1945. When I myself visited Lebanon in 1967–8 there was only one factory left.

13 ❧ The silk industry of Bursa, 1880–1914*

DONALD QUATAERT

The Ottoman Empire, along with other non-Western areas, confronted the problem of economic survival in the nineteenth-century era of European industrialization. European capital and manufactures intruded everywhere, destroying the old while creating new marketing patterns, formed economic and financial satellites and, in the process, disrupted existing equilibriums. While the Ottoman state participated in the vast expansion of world-trade, increasing its commerce sixteen-fold between 1850 and 1914, the trade relationship generally was unfavourable. The decay in Ottoman industry continued and, at the end of the century, agricultural commodities from a growing market sector comprised at least three-quarters of exports. Ottoman subjects supplied raw materials to the industrial nations and purchased from them processed foodstuffs (e.g., flour and sugar) and manufactured goods (notably textiles).

Within the Empire, the Western presence grew larger as foreign capital built railroads, harbour-works, tramways and factories and as European merchants travelled in once-remote regions. By 1914, private foreign investment had reached approximately 66 million pounds sterling. Ottoman finances concomitantly fell under increasing European control. Once-novel foreign loans became a common Ottoman method of meeting fiscal needs in the third quarter of the century and, by 1914, the outstanding debt totalled some 150 million *liras*. As World War I approached, the Ottoman Empire assumed the character of a European economic appendage, bound to Western consumer needs and investment capital for its economic existence.

The adjustments involved in this basic transformation of the Ottoman economy and their effects on the different business sectors of the Empire are

*I gratefully acknowledge that the research here reported was assisted by grants awarded by the Foreign Area Fellowship Program (1970–1) and the Joint Committee on the Near and Middle East of the American Council of Learned Societies and the Social Science Research Council (1975). My thanks to the staffs of the Başbakanlık Arşivi (İstanbul) and the Zentrales Staatsarchiv (Potsdam) for their cooperation and assistance. This article originally was accepted for publication in 1978 and appears in a slightly different version in *Collection Turcica, I. Contribution à l'histoire économique et sociale de l'empire ottoman* (Paris, Éditions Peetens, 1984), pp. 481–503.

relatively unknown. The broad outlines of economic change are beginning to emerge in the literature but little research has been done on specific commodities, types of agriculture, product changes in response to foreign demand, and the role of foreign capital in the different sectors. Furthermore, the composition of the entrepreneurial class involved in the transformation has been noted but not traced in detail. Another gap in our knowledge concerns labour conditions.

The present study seeks to examine the altered economic structure and its effects on a single sector, the Bursa silk industry. It discusses changes in silk output, describes the foreign and indigenous elements involved in those changes, and examines working conditions. The case of the Bursa silk industry, with its extraordinary export orientation, an unusually high growth rate, and almost complete collapse in the 1914–23 period, is probably not typical. Yet, an extreme case often offers more insight than 'typical' experience – and the parameters of typical cases are as yet unknown. Besides, the investigation of one industry will, one hopes, furnish a basis for similar studies which should improve our understanding of structural economic changes in the late period of the Ottoman Empire.

The city of Bursa, with a late nineteenth-century population of approximately 90,000, is situated within easy reach of sea transport, some 42 kilometres from the Sea of Marmara. The relationship between this ancient city (Prusa) and silk reached back into the Byzantine epoch and continued, with varying fortunes, throughout Ottoman times. The prosperity of Bursa for centuries rested upon its silk-cloth manufacture, the object of sales to Ottoman and European consumers. By the mid-nineteenth century, however, French and Italian competitors, as well as taste changes, stripped Bursa of its foreign outlets: Ottomans but few others purchased the finished silk goods manufactured in the city.[1]

In response, the industry turned to producing the basic raw materials utilized in silk weaving – silk-worm eggs, cocoons, and raw silk – for shipment to European weaving facilities.

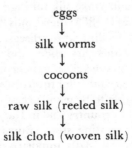

eggs
↓
silk worms
↓
cocoons
↓
raw silk (reeled silk)
↓
silk cloth (woven silk)

Fig. 13.1 Stages in silk production

Technological improvements introduced into the reeling but not the weaving segment of the industry dramatized this shift from finished to primary commodity production. Whereas steam-powered weaving establishments were lacking until 1908, steam-powered reeling mills at Bursa dated from the 1830s and became widespread in subsequent decades.[2]

In their new capacity as primary producers, Bursa silk raisers experienced prosperity during the early 1850s, based largely on the misfortunes of France. Pebrine, a disease which caused sterile silk worms or weak offspring, appeared in the French silk-raising districts and devastated their production. French cocoon production plummeted from twenty-six to eight million kg between 1853 and 1856.[3] The reduced supply relative to demand pushed egg, cocoon and raw-silk prices to unprecedented heights; French silk-raisers turned to foreign, uninfected sources, including Bursa. With the active encouragement of French merchants, large landholders in the Bursa area planted new tracts of mulberry orchards while local egg-raisers increased the volume of eggs sent into incubation. Production of the valuable white cocoon mounted and reached perhaps four million kg in the mid 1850s, while raw-silk production totalled *c.* 600,000 kg.[4]

The prosperity of Bursa, however, already was challenged by the opening of the Chinese trade during the 1840s and 1850s and the slightly later (1857) initiation of silk exports from Japan. Concomitantly, pebrine radiated outward from France and reached Turkey in 1857. Within a decade, raw-silk production fell by two thirds, to 192,440 kg.[5] Difficulties increased in 1869 when the newly opened Suez Canal facilitated a flood of Oriental silk into European markets. After the collapse brought on by pebrine and the competition of the Far East, Bursa production and exports continued their downward slide. In the early 1880s, total Turkish silk production barely averaged 150,000 kg per year; silk exports in 1885 were valued at less than half the already depressed 1872 levels. Overall, as measured by weight, cocoon production in Bursa province reportedly fell some 80 per cent between the boom of the 1850s and 1881.[6]

During these decades of decline, the Ottoman government unsuccessfully intervened to save the industry by offering incentives such as tithe exemptions to those willing to continue or undertake silk raising.[7] A solution to the pebrine problem appeared to be at hand in 1865 when Louis Pasteur devised a simple yet effective technique for controlling the disease. His method involved micrographic examination of the chrysalides and moths and a painstaking selection of disease-free breeding stock. Using these procedures, silk-raisers were slowly able to obtain healthy specimens for future breeding. While some French silk-growers, unwilling or unable to bear the necessary costs, resisted Pasteur's technique, most breeders in that country and in Italy adopted the practice and began producing a healthy breeding stock. Bursa residents recognized the opportunity and, in the 1860s and 1870s, imported these eggs at a cost of three million francs per year[8] – a raw-materials exporter temporarily importing in an effort to resume its former role. Despite initial successes, some Bursa raisers, tempted by the high profits, engaged in fraudulent practices which resulted in diseased eggs and inferior raw silk. Also, committees formed to inspect imported eggs permitted the entry of diseased specimens; in addition, committee members prevented competitors from obtaining healthy eggs. Although some silk-raisers and merchants went to France, studied the Pasteur method, and implemented it at Bursa, their efforts could not overcome corruption, indifference, and lack of capital.[9] Silk-raising at Bursa appeared doomed.

Beginning the late 1880s, market conditions, foreign capital, and entrepreneurs favourably combined to produce a fascinating reversal of silk-production trends. Rapid growth continued unchecked until the eve of World War I. Fresh cocoon production nearly tripled: volume rose from an annual average of 2.5 million kg in the 1880s to over seven million kg during the first decade of the twentieth century while the sparse data indicate that the value of cocoons more than doubled in a decade (Table 13.1). The amount of locally produced silk worm eggs annually sent into incubation increased from an average 31,000 ounces in the late 1880s to an average 192,000 ounces between 1902 and 1905. Reciprocally, the incubation of imported eggs fell from an annual average of 59,000 ounces to less than 1,000 ounces (Table 13.2). Unable to satisfy local demand for silk worm eggs in the 1880s, Bursa, after 1900, annually exported over 400,000 ounces, primarily to Russia and Persia.[10] And finally, annual raw-silk-production levels probably approached 700,000 kg just prior to World War I (Table 13.3). All statistical indicators note a new phase of prosperity for the industry beginning in the late 1880s.

Market conditions played a role in the turnaround. From the 1860s existed an apparently insatiable global demand for raw silk which producers were hard-pressed to meet. The United States, as the volume of its raw-silk imports rose four-fold between the 1870s and World War I, became the largest consumer of silk: with the impetus of American demand, the Japanese government and private silk-raisers almost quadrupled raw-silk production between 1868 and 1893, then tripled it again before 1914.[11] On a global scale, the continuing rise in demand for raw silk doubled world raw-silk production between 1880 and 1900; by 1912, it nearly had doubled again, to some twenty-seven million kg. Within the context of American–Japanese domination, Bursa played a minor role, producing perhaps 3 per cent of global raw-silk output.[12] Vital to Bursa were the needs of France, the second largest consumer of raw silk after the United States. The pebrine onslaught permanently reduced French raw-silk production levels. Between the 1850s and 1914, local sources provided French industries with only one-seventh of their total needs: at the turn of the century, for example, France produced less than 600,000 kg of raw silk while the French silk-cloth industry required *c.* four million kg.[13] Bursa enjoyed a virtually guaranteed market and sold at least 80 per cent of its total production to France to help fill the gap.[14]

Market demand, however, does not account fully for the growth of the Bursa

Table 13.1 *Fresh cocoon production in Bursa province and the district (*sancak*) of İzmit, 1884–1914 (annual average in millions of kg)*

1884	2.4
1888–90	3.1
1891–5	4.1
1896–1900	5.2
1901–5	6.3
1907–9	7.6
1913	6.8
1914	3.1

Note: Value of production (in millions of *kuruş*): 1894–53.2; 1895–45.5; 1896–58.6; 1904–104.5. *Hüdavendigâr vilâyet salnamesi* (Yearbook for the province of Hüdavendigar), 1302 (1884), p. 361, indicates that the value of cocoon products in the district of Bursa, the centre of the industry, was 14 million *kuruş*.

Sources:
1884: *Revue commerciale du Levant, bulletin mensuel de la chambre de commerce française de Constantinople*, 31 May 1908, pp. 797–802.
1885, 1909, 1913–14: Vedat Eldem, *Osmanlı imparatorluğunun iktisadi şartları hakkında bir tetkik* (A study of the economic conditions in the Ottoman Empire) (Ankara, TİSA Matbaacılık Sanayii, 1970), p. 128.
1888–1908: *Hüdavendigâr vilâyet salnamesi*, 1325 (1907), pp. 267–8.
1886, 1887, 1906, 1910–12: not available.

silk industry. In this regard, the history of silk production in Persia is relevant. Persia, another long-time silk supplier, also had suffered from the onslaught of pebrine. Despite the favourable market conditions outlined above, the Persian silk industry failed to recover; its production in 1909 was only half the 1850 levels.[15] Thus, the response to market conditions in the Bursa industry differed sharply from that of Persia. What factors in the local Ottoman environment might help explain the difference?

In 1881, six years after extensive borrowing had engendered the financial

Table 13.2 *Silk-worm egg incubation and export in Bursa province and the district of İznit, 1888–1905 (annual averages in 1,000 ounces of 25 grams/oz)*

	Imported eggs incubated	Indigenous eggs incubated	Eggs exported
1888–90	70	31	0
1891–5	9	106	59
1896–1900	3	144	289
1901–5	1	192	423

Source: Hüdavendigâr vilâyet salnamesi, 1325 (1907), pp. 267–8.

collapse of the Ottoman government, the Ottoman Public Debt Administration was formed by European bond-holders of the huge Ottoman debt. To repay its loans, the İstanbul regime 'absolutely and irrevocably' ceded to the European consortium a variety of important revenues: whole sectors of the Ottoman economy were alienated from the government and functioned under direct European financial control. By 1914, revenues ceded to the organization exceeded four million *liras* and comprised 15 per cent of all Ottoman tax revenues. In addition, the Debt Administration, as agent for the İstanbul regime, collected other revenues to service new loans and railroad construction. The consortium functioned as the singlemost visible symbol of European economic control in the Ottoman Empire.

Among the revenues ceded to the Debt Administration were the silk tithes of Bursa province and other regions.[16] These tithes provided a minor if rising proportion (perhaps, ultimately, 6 per cent) of the total ceded revenues. Bursa province and the district (*sancak*) of İzmit accounted for some nine-tenths of the silk tithes collected and were the objects of most Debt Administration efforts to promote silk production.[17] For several years the organization tightened silk-tithe collection procedures but adopted no direct measures to increase revenues by developing the industry. The sultan, for his part, ordered that means be found to raise silk-tithe proceeds and asked silk merchants for recommendations.[18]

The passive posture of the Debt Administration came to an end in late 1886 or early 1887 with the intervention of Hermann Scholer, German vice-consul in Bursa since 1881 and a silk merchant residing in the city. Scholer's rather dubious reputation, spotted with allegations of fraud and questionable business practices, did not close the ears of the Debt Administration to his proposal that the industry be revived through adoption of the Pasteur technique. Although Scholer apparently had himself in mind for directorship of such a program, the Debt Administration instead asked Pasteur for recommendations.[19] Pasteur referred the organization to the head of the Sericulture Station at Montpellier, who in turn recommended Kevork Torkomyan. Torkomyan, an Ottoman

Armenian, had been sent abroad by his government to study agronomy, had graduated from the Montpellier Agricultural School in 1883, and subsequently had been employed on the imperial estates. He made the condition of his acceptance of the offer the establishment of a silk station at Bursa, for the dual purpose of educating egg-raisers and disseminating proper silk-worm-breeding practices.

In January, 1888, through the intervention of high Debt Administration officials, the sultan approved Torkomyan's appointment and two weeks later consented to the foundation of the silk station.[20] These measures inaugurated the revival of Bursa silk production. Other programs followed in rapid succession. In 1891, the Debt Administration began sponsoring silk-raising competitions at Bursa as a means of upgrading production standards. Similar competitions, in which winners received valuable microscopes and cash awards, later were held annually in the nearby silk towns of Bilecik and İzmit.[21] To protect the local raisers, the Debt Administration, in 1891, instigated the imposition of import duties on silk-worm eggs entering Turkey.[22] The government also became more actively involved and granted a three-year tithe exemption for all newly established mulberry orchards in the province of Bursa; three years later, it exempted Bursa silk-worm raisers from the profit tax (*temettü vergisi*).[23] In addition, the government established a model silk-worm nursery at its School for Practical Agriculture in Bursa, perhaps with Debt Administration financial assistance.[24] Finally, and of vital importance to the future of silk production, the Debt Administration and the government co-sponsored the establishment of mulberry plantations from which saplings, some sixty million between 1890 and 1910, were distributed without charge to cultivators near Bursa and in various other parts of the Empire.[25]

Occasionally, the İstanbul regime moved beyond Debt Administration initiatives. In 1899, for example, when the foreign consortium failed to deliver the promised number of mulberry bushes, the government provided funds to purchase one-half million plants from Bursa nurseries and sent them to waiting cultivators.[26] More generally, however, the government, unwilling to commit its limited fiscal resources to a sector from which it derived little immediate benefit, followed the lead of the Debt Administration. To cite one example: in 1895, the Finance Ministry (Maliye Nezareti), over the objections of government agricultural specialists, withdrew from a previously favoured scheme to co-finance the formation of silk-raising institutes at other silk centres and indicated that the Debt Administration could fund the project alone.[27] Foreign groups provided most of the techniques, capital, and supportive milieu necessary to defeat pebrine and revitalize the industry.

A major force in the victory over disease and decline was the Silk-raising Institute (Séricicole Institut/Harir Darruta'limi), founded on the advice of Scholer and Torkomyan and financed by the Debt Administration. Over the course of Torkomyan's three-decade-long career at the institute, some 2,032 persons received training in Pasteur practices,[28] a cadre which deserves much of the credit for the revival of the silk industry. The Institute opened its doors in 1888/1304 with an initial class of twelve students and, in early 1894, moved to larger, permanent quarters.[29] Torkomyan was aided in his teaching duties by Scholer and, after 1895, by Yervant Beyazyan, another Ottoman Armenian sent to France for agricultural education.[30] The Institute offered two programs of instruction in Pasteur practices. The first, for full-time students, involved a two-year curriculum and culminated in an examination before Torkomyan and government agronomists. The second program provided instruction and certificates to those who enrolled in part-time studies and subsequently were tested in Pasteur methods. The attrition rate among candidates suggests standards were high. Some two-thirds of the full-time students taking the examinations passed and received the necessary approval.[31]

In the Bursa area, silk-worm eggs were raised not only in nurseries specifically erected for that purpose but also in homes and cottages as well. In the former case, the eggs were sold to silk-worm raisers who tended them until the caterpillars had spun their cocoons. Silk-worm raisers purchasing eggs often lacked the necessary capital for immediate payment and engaged in share-cropping. In some towns and villages around Bursa, one-sixth to one-half of the total cocoon production was turned over to the egg supplier in payment for the eggs. In another case, where a Bursa firm had set up a branch in central Anatolia, one-tenth of the cocoon production was paid to the supplier of eggs. Share-cropping and domestic industry were practised throughout the era of Debt Administration control.[32]

When the larvae hatched, it was usual for the women in the family to gather the mulberry branches and assume responsibility for raising the silk-worms.[33] At the time, the predominance of women in silk-worm raising was explained by the following tale, printed in a government publication. A bachelor was using 620 grams of eggs to produce a certain amount of cocoons – and the amount was decreasing. After he married, his wife volunteered to take over the work. Secretly, she used only 128 grams of eggs. The husband discovered this and lamented his imminent doom since she, using about one-fifth the eggs he had used, surely would produce only one-fifth the cocoons. She retorted with the promise to sell her trousseau to recoup the husband's losses if she didn't obtain at least the same volume of cocoons. In the end, of course, her production from 128 grams of eggs exceeded her husband's yield from 620 grams.[34] This story, which neatly justifies women's leading role in terms of greater skills, obscures the actual reason. Silk-raising families engaged primarily in growing food crops for their livelihood. The income from silk-raising was supplemental in nature, a secondary activity requiring most attention in the off-peak agricultural seasons. Not their higher skill levels, but the quality of women as extra-income producers seems the more satisfactory explanation for female control of silk-raising in Turkey.[35]

The productivity of Bursa egg and cocoon raisers compared favourably with that of other areas, both elsewhere in Anatolia and abroad. In the late 1890s, silk-producing countries globally averaged 39 kg of fresh cocoons per ounce (of 25 grams) of egg while, for example, Diyarbakır producers obtained 20 to 28 kg per ounce. Areas around Bursa often averaged 45 kg per ounce of seed and yields of better than 100 kg were recorded in several of the silk-raising competitions.[36]

When the cocoon had been formed, the silk-raiser's work was completed (unless she reeled the silk at home). Debt Administration inspectors, aided by government officials, then registered the amount of the crop for tithing purposes. The fresh cocoon raiser could sell freely but always under the supervision of these authorities.[37] By overseeing the production and sale of eggs and cocoons, the Debt Administration sought to protect the quality of its revenue source and assure full payment of taxes. Other controls were imposed over the industry.

In October, 1893, the Ottoman government passed into law an important proposal sponsored by the Debt Administration. This piece of legislation specified that only individuals possessing a certificate or diploma from the Bursa Silk-raising Institute or its foreign equivalent could engage in the sale or production of silk-worm eggs and cocoons.[38] In effect, the regulation restricted egg and cocoon raising to Insititute beneficiaries. Lists of the diploma and certificate recipients were published periodically, announcing the competence of those who had acquired the exclusive legal right to engage in silk-raising. These lists provide a means of determining the identity of innovators who took advantage of the opportunity provided by the foreign capital and spearheaded the technical changes in the egg and cocoon phases of silk production.

Between 1888 and 1905, 1,234 persons from the Ottoman Empire attended the Institute and obtained certificates or diplomas; of these, 72.9 per cent were from the Bursa area.[39] Among the Bursa silk-raisers, 73.3 per cent were of either Greek or Armenian origin and some three quarters of this sub-group had Armenian names. The proportion was approximately inverse to the population composition of the Bursa region – *c.* 17 per cent Greek and Armenian and *c.* 83 per cent Muslim.[40] The Bursa area was not atypical in this respect: 85 per cent of those from other Ottoman regions who attended the Institute also possessed Greek and Armenian surnames with the Armenians accounting for two-thirds of the group.[41] Thus, the Ottoman minorities, notably the Armenians, controlled the silk-worm egg and cocoon production phases of the industry.

The experiences elsewhere in the Empire demonstrate that the eggs and cocoons produced around Bursa were utilized in a unique manner. After 1891, the Bursa area not only exported eggs abroad but also shipped them to other provinces, assisting in the foundation or expansion of silk-raising.[42] The egg production of many other areas, by contrast, either satisfied only local demand or was exported for raising. Further, the bulk of cocoon production at Bursa was not exported but reeled into raw silk prior to shipment out of the country. Again by way of contrast, Aleppo sent 90 per cent of its cocoons abroad and retained 10 per cent for local needs.[43] Elsewhere in Syria and Lebanon, an extensive cottage industry manually reeled the raw silk and wove finished silk fabrics.[44] Bursa again was unique in that a considerable proportion of its raw silk derived not from manually operated reeling devices in peasant homes and workshops but rather from a network of reeling mills, many of them steam-powered. The raw silk, the role played by steam power, and working conditions in the mills – form the foci of the following discussion.

Bursa raw-silk production, while roughly paralleling trends in egg and cocoon raising, did not fall as sharply during the crisis of the late 1850s and 1860s. Local mill operators sought to maintain production by importing eggs and cocoons, an effort inspired by the unabated foreign demand for raw silk. For reasons discussed earlier, these measures only partially succeeded and raw-silk output declined further in the 1870s.

When the Debt Administration revived local egg and cocoon production, the reeling industry responded quickly. Table 13.3 indicates that raw-silk production more than tripled between the late 1880s and 1908. But, while output rose substantially, a decreasing proportion of the raw silk was consumed locally. One observer noted that Bursa artisans were weaving 51,000 kg of finished silk cloth in the early 1890s, some 20 per cent of total raw-silk production. Within a decade, as raw-silk output rose from 200,000 to 600,000 kg, the amount woven in the area fell absolutely, to as little as 12,000 kg. Between 1900 and 1908, local craftsmen annually wove only 2 to 7 per cent of Bursa raw-silk output into fabric.[45]

The role which steam power played in silk-reeling was documented by an Ottoman government survey of 'industrial establishments' as they had existed in 1913. The survey defined such establishments as those with a capital value in excess of 1,000 lira which utilized more than 750 man days per year, and possessed motors developing at least five horsepower. The silk-reeling mills meeting these standards were steam powered and all were located in the city of Bursa.[46] Owners of the steam-reeling mills were heirs of a tradition in Bursa which dated back to perhaps the 1830s and was well-established in the 1850s.[47] The history of this tradition in the use of steam power for silk-reeling is obscure, in part because nineteenth-century Ottoman and European observers failed to distinguish between steam-powered mills and non-steam factory establishments.[48] The main outlines, however, are clear – after 1840, both factory establishments and steam-powered mills proliferated and replaced the previously dominant practice of manual silk-reeling in the home. In the first decade of the twentieth century, 165 mills of both types utilized 9,200 basins (containers of heated water into which the cocoons were submerged to facilitate reeling on to wheels). Altogether, these mills employed 19,000 persons in the province of Bursa and adjacent district of İzmit.[49] A half decade later, in 1913, the government classified 41 Bursa mills as 'industrial establishments'; these steam-

Table 13.3 *Raw-silk production in the Bursa area, 1876–1908 (annual average in 1,000 kg)*

1876–80	85
1881–5	140
1886–90	186
1891–5	264
1896–1900	401
1901–5	517
1906–8	610

Note: Percentage of production consumed by local industry: 1900–5; 1901–7; 1905–3; 1906–4; 1907–2; 1908–6.

Sources: Production – derived from 'Silk', *Encyclopedia Britannica*, 11th edn, XXVII (1911), 104. For similar figures, see *USCR*, 1901, LXV, 244, p. 311, and Zentrales Staatsarchiv, Potsdam, Auswärtiges Amt (ZStA,AA), Nr 53738, Bl. 174r and Nr 53736, Bl. 106. A. Gündüz Ökçün, *Osmanlı sanayii: 1913, 1915 yılları sanayi istatistiki* (Ottoman industry: industrial statistics for the years 1913, 1915) (Ankara, Sevinç Matbaası, 1970), p. 160, indicates Bursa-area production exceeded 702,000 kg *c.* 1912.
Consumption – *The Statesman's Yearbook* (New York, St, Martin's Press), for 1903, 1907, 1908, 1909, 1910, pp. 1171, 1535, 1573, 1277, and 1274 respectively. ZStA,AA, Nr 53739, Bl. 125, using different figures, indicates that in 1903 and 1904, 3 and 5 per cent respectively were consumed locally.

powered mills contained 2,313 basins and employed 4,600 workers, 20 per cent all 'industrial establishment' employees. Other, manually powered reeling establishments in the city used 127 basins and fewer than 300 workers. On the eve of World War I, steam silk-reeling mills predominated in the city and the owners of these mills controlled the most advanced sector of the Ottoman silk industry.[50]

Proprietors of the steam-reeling mills and beneficiaries of the Silk-raising Institute shared two characteristics. Both groups were at the forefront of their respective sectors: the graduates introduced the Pasteur technique and the mill owners applied steam power for the reeling of silk. Also, both groups generally were outside the mainstream of Ottoman society. Beneficiaries of the Institute, we have seen, primarily came from the Ottoman minority populations. Most owners of the steam-reeling mills were either members of the same minority groups or foreigners.

Greeks and Armenians owned at least 23 and perhaps as many as 26 of the 41 mills while 6 mills were the property of foreigners, primarily of French extraction. The Ottoman government, owner of two mills, rented one to a family of foreign origin residing in Bursa. No more than 10 owners had Turkish names; these accounted for about one-quarter of the mills. Examining the ownership lists from the perspective of agglomeration demonstrates that 7 families – all but one of foreign or minority extraction – owned or operated 19 mills, 46 per cent of the total.[51]

Another source, utilizing French consular records at Bursa, indicates foreign and minority dominance was not confined to these larger 'industrial establishments' but extended over the entire silk-reeling industry of the Bursa area. An itemized list noted the location, size, owner and manager of 131 reeling mills (apparently both steam and non-steam powered), utilizing 7,685 basins in the city and province of Bursa. Twenty-six per cent of the 38 mills in the city were owned by Turks, the remainder by foreigners and the Ottoman minorities. In the rest of the province, the ownership distribution was identical: some 24 of the 93 reeling mills (26 per cent) were in the hands of Turkish owners.[52]

The impression of Ottoman minority and foreign predominance reflected in the lists of steam- and non-steam-reeling mill owners and Institute beneficiaries contrasts strongly with Muslim control of the silk trade in the earlier Ottoman period.[53] Although the nature and speed of this transformation from Muslim to non-Muslim ascendancy has yet to be traced in detail, certain elements in the shift can be noted here. The geographic position of Bursa, in western Anatolia close to the coast and İstanbul, exposed it to earlier and probably more intensive European economic infiltration. Security of life and trade at Bursa was greater than elsewhere in Anatolia, a function of its location and historic importance to the Ottoman regime. Attracted to this accessible, secure production centre with an existing cadre of skilled workers, European merchants and entrepreneurs gradually assumed an important role in the economic life of the city. A turning point occurred in the 1840s when scores of experienced silk producers and steam-reeling-mill operators, mainly from France, emigrated to Bursa. Henceforth, foreigners played a direct and important role in the silk industry of the city. This European penetration upset the traditional indigenous balance in the industry. Muslims may have found it distasteful to participate in an increasingly European, Christian economic environment. Alternatively, their entry or continuation in silk-raising may have been discouraged or blocked by Europeans who favoured the Christian elements of the Bursa populace. In this milieu of emerging European economic supremacy, the Ottoman Christians clearly benefited most, although the precise relationship between the foreigners and the entrepreneurship of the minorities is still uncertain. The derivation of such entrepreneurial groups from the socio-cultural periphery of many countries has been noted,[54] and it is not unusual to find that the Christian Armenians and Greeks, living on the margin of a primarily Muslim Ottoman society, more eagerly pursued opportunities in the silk industry.

Perhaps more striking since it violates common assumptions concerning Ottoman entrepreneurship is the significant proportion of the steam- and non-steam-reeling mills owned by Turks (one quarter of the total). In some cases, Turkish owners actively managed their factories and supervised the day-to-day operations. Others were members of the high bureaucracy who traded their status in the government for a share in the profits of factories financed and managed by others. Alternatively, persons with wealth accrued through office or landholding may have sought a higher rate of return and played the role of investor, leaving management in the hands of employees more familiar with the industry.[55] Whatever the terms, the participation of Muslim Turks suggests that the conventional notion of the group by nature disinclined to enter into commercial and industrial enterprises is an overstatement and in need of further study.

The work force in the mills emerged slowly and painfully, in a manner reminiscent of early European industrialization. During the 1840s and 1850s, several mills in the area were burned or destroyed by local residents. While European observers attributed the incidents to religious fanaticism and the like, the labourers who were involved may have been Ottoman-style Luddites.[56] Workers' unwillingness to endure the discipline of regular work hours in the newly established factories made it difficult to maintain a stable work force. In response, the mill owners, resorting to a tried-and-true European practice, required employees to obtain and carry work cards. Only with such a card, noting the employee's reliability, experience, and conditions of recent employment, could the individual obtain a new position.[57]

Approximately 95 per cent of all workers in the Bursa mills were women and girls, many in their pre-teens. Although some Turkish and Jewish women were employed, the vast majority were Armenian and Greek. The shared religion of employees and employers did little to ease working conditions. Wages in the mills, by Ottoman standards, were quite low. In 1913, the average Ottoman 'industrial establishment' worker drew twelve to fifteen *kuruş* per day but reeling-mill employees at Bursa received a daily pay ranging from two to four *kuruş*.[58] Many of the girls and women lived in dormitory-like quarters near the factories, were awakened by a watchman and marched off to start a sixteen-hour work day. Beginning at 9 a.m. with a factory-provided breakfast which they regarded as 'poisonous', the women laboured until 1 a.m. A break, perhaps as brief as twenty minutes, afforded the opportunity to eat *in situ*, with resumption of work signalled by a whistle blast. There are reports of sexual abuse as well as

Table 13.4 *Silk tithes collected by the Debt Administration in Bursa province and the district of İzmit, 1882–1905 (annual averages in 1,000 lira)*

1882	15
1888–90	37
1891–5	50
1896–1900	62
1901–5	81

Sources: For 1882, see Cuinet, *La Turquie d'Asie*, vol. 4, p. 60; for 1888–1905, see *Hüdavendigâr vilâyet salnamesi*, 1325 (1907), p. 268.

beatings and other forms of maltreatment, but the extent of brutal practices is uncertain. The Young Turk Revolution of 1908 brought in its wake an upsurge of labour unrest in many Ottoman cities. The 4,600 steam-mill employees at Bursa complained of their plight in class-conscious terms and demanded a redress of grievances, particularly an end to night work.[59] The women went on strike in August 1910, but with few apparent results:[60] the employment conditions sketched above prevailed until the collapse of the industry during World War I and the Turkish War of Independence.

In the two and a half decades prior to World War I, the Bursa silk industry emerged as a prosperous and growing sector of the Ottoman economy. As egg production multiplied many times over, fresh cocoon and raw-silk output rose three- to four-fold. When the silk tithe is used as a measure, the total value of silk products seems to have increased at least five-fold during the same period (Table 13.4). All this had little to do with the Ottoman regime or the majority of its subject population. The silk tithes of the Bursa area accrued to the Debt Administration for application against a European-owned public debt, the payments for which were scheduled to extend well into the twentieth century. Foreigners had provided the market, the techniques and much of the capital, while the Armenian and Greek minorities dominated the industry in all its phases. The development of Bursa silk production was a venture encouraged by foreign interests, largely but not solely effected by the Ottoman minorities, and of primary benefit to European creditors of the beleaguered Ottoman treasury.

Epilogue

In 1911, with the war against Italy for Tripolitania, the Ottoman state began a decade of nearly continuous warfare. The decision of the İstanbul government to join the Triple Alliance spelled the destruction of the Ottoman Empire and

Table 13.5 *Fresh cocoon production in Turkey, selected years, 1913–38 (in millions of kg)*

1913	7.8	1924	0.8
1914	3.5	1929	2.0
1915	2.9	1930	1.7
1916	2.2	1931	1.0 estimated
1917	1.5	1933	1.9
1918	1.3	1934	1.2
1919	0.8	1935	2.0
1920	1.0	1936	2.1
1921	1.4	1938	2.3

Sources:
1913–1920: Great Britain, *General report on the trade and economic conditions of Turkey, dated January, 1921* (London, HM Stationery Office, 1921), pp. 14–16.
1921: Bursa province only. Great Britain, Department of Overseas Trade, *Report on the economic and financial conditions in Turkey, February, 1922* (London, HM Stationery Office, 1922), p. 35.
1924: *Ibid., Report on the economic and commercial conditions in Turkey, April, 1925* (London, HM Stationery Office, 1925), p. 12.
1929–31: *Ibid., Report on economic conditions in Turkey, May 31st, 1932* (London, HM Stationery Office, 1932), p. 15.
1933, 1936, 1938: Great Britain, Naval Intelligence Division, *Turkey*, II, Geographical Handbook Series, March, 1943 (London, HM Stationery Office, 1943), p. 207.
1934–5: Great Britain, Department of Overseas Trade, *Report on economic and commercial conditions in Turkey, 1936* (London, HM Stationery Office, 1937), p. 10.

was followed, in 1923, by the creation of the Turkish Republic. During this period of foreign, civil and national-liberation wars, the Bursa silk industry virtually disappeared. Cocoon production fell from 7.8 to 0.8 million kg between 1913 and 1924 (Table 13.5) while, in approximately the same period, the overall value of silk production in Turkey declined from about one million *liras* (gold) to 175,000 *liras* (gold). As few as seven reeling mills in the entire country survived the prolonged conflicts.[61]

The collapse of the silk industry may be attributed to a number of factors. The declaration of war in 1914 isolated Bursa from its leading trade partners and overnight eliminated its export markets. Bursa was occupied by the Greek army of the Athens government from July 1920 to September 1922; the city and its environs were the site of bitter battles between the Greek and Turkish armies. Further, the influx of refugees from the lost Balkan areas introduced new populations unacquainted with silk-raising. Perhaps two-thirds of all mulberry bushes in the region were cut down for firewood (despite government prohibitions), or destroyed in the fighting.

With the foundation of the Turkish Republic, the Debt Administration lost its control over the silk industry and ceased to function as an opportunity provider. Moreover, European animosity towards or mistrust of the new state, as well as stringent restrictions on outside capital, made foreign investors reluctant to aid in development programs. The disappearance of the Debt Administration as an active force in silk-raising paralleled that of the Armenian and Greek populations. The decline in the silk industry in fact is discernible in 1912–13 when new laws providing for Christian conscription into the Young Turk armies and the growing Turkish nationalism of that regime stimulated an outward migration of the minorities. Between 1912 and 1923, wartime casualties, emigrations, deportations, the 'Armenian question' which is the subject of contemporary disputes among historians, and population exchanges after the war left republican Turkey with a fraction of the former Ottoman minority populations. Armenian, as well as Greek, entrepreneurs were largely absent in the Republic.

For a time, world demand continued to mount. France, the pre-eminent market for Bursa silk, consumed nearly twenty times the amount of silk which French sources could supply in 1924. World silk output in 1919 approximated that of 1913; by 1924, it had increased 43 per cent. Between 1925 and 1929, however, silk prices fell by a third. The global depression followed with a further collapse in prices and stagnation in the world silk trade.[62]

Republican Turkey's inheritance in silk was, therefore, meagre. Almost totally lacking were the foreign organization, foreign capital, experienced silk-raisers and, finally, the market. Kemal Atatürk's administration, confronted with the formidable tasks of creating a nation and rebuilding a war-ravaged economy and society, devoted the bulk of investment capital (drawn largely from internal savings) to the development of industries furnishing basic consumer goods. With no vested interests speaking on its behalf, the promotion of silk production remained subordinate to the creation of an economic infrastructure. In *c.* 1938, silk production in republican Turkey peaked, at a level one-third that achieved by Bursa before World War I.[63]

14 ❧ A provisional report concerning the impact of European capital on Ottoman port workers, 1880–1909*

DONALD QUATAERT

While the incorporation of the Ottoman Empire into the European-dominated world-economy correctly is seen as a monumental event, its impact on the various, specific elements of Ottoman social and economic life is just beginning to receive attention. European commercial and capital penetration profoundly affected Ottoman workers, eroding the livelihoods of some, transforming those of others while creating totally new occupations for still others. The process of incorporation was a gradual one, occurring over several centuries and continuing until the formal dismantling of the Ottoman state after World War I. Moreover, it occurred unevenly, drastically affecting one region at an early date while others remained comparatively untouched until the twentieth century. Examples from the sixteenth–seventeenth centuries demonstrate the early and nearly complete eradication of certain occupational groups, such as wool-cloth makers in Selanik.[1] Early twentieth-century Ankara provides an example of guildsmen in a geographically more remote, less-incorporated sector, surviving but having lost their joint productive–distributive functions. Marketing operations in Ankara often were assumed by non-Muslim merchants who took over the high-rent main streets of the bazaars where shopkeepers sold goods made in Europe or by wage/piece workers labouring in the sidestreets.[2] At Bursa, the silk industry thrived after a fashion, but no longer as the producer of the famed and finely crafted silk cloths. Instead, dozens of silk-reeling mills operated with modern, steam-powered equipment, usually under the control of persons with minority or foreign surnames. Inside the mills, some 4–5,000 semi-skilled wage labourers (usually female) spun silk for shipment to Europe.

*An earlier version of this paper was presented to the IIe Congrès International d'Histoire Économique et Sociale de la Turquie, Strasbourg, 1–5 July 1980, and appears in the proceedings volume of the conference. An expanded and revised version of this study of the İstanbul port workers and their struggles with the Quai Company, based on additional research in Paris and İstanbul, forms a chapter in my *Social disintegration and popular resistance in the Ottoman Empire, 1880–1908* (New York, New York University Press, 1983), pp. 95–120.

The list of those whose means of making a living were altered by European economic penetration could be extended, but the point seems clear enough for our present purposes – for many Ottoman workers, the European incursion was of major and personal significance. The instruments of that penetration – the transportation and communications systems – facilitated Ottoman incorporation into the world market by closely linking surviving handicraft bastions, such as at Ankara, to Europe. While such innovations transformed the livelihoods of the guildsmen, modern transportation also created thousands of new positions, notably on the railroads and in the telegraph service. Railroads took away much of the long-haul caravan trade on parallel routes, but they also gave hauleteers new employ on the multitude of feeder networks that sprang up to supply the Anatolian and Baghdad trunk lines. European investment in the Ottoman transport sector, that is, affected Ottoman workers in complex and various ways. In this sense, Europeanization/modernization of Ottoman transport facilities was a microcosm of the incorporation process that engendered a host of profound but, as already stated, poorly understood changes. The present paper represents this author's preliminary findings on the encounter of some Ottoman transport workers with foreign capital. Here, the transport sector serves as a case study of the Ottoman incorporation into the world-economy and illustrates some of the manifold kinds of interactions possible between Ottoman social and economic forces and those of foreign capital penetration. Within the framework of this case study, the example of port workers in İstanbul shows how European capital took over an already existing transport facility, radically transformed its physical plant, and correspondingly affected the lives of those customarily employed at or near the docks.

The port workers

In November 1890, a group of investors, primarily French, obtained from the Ottoman government the right to construct and exploit a set of port facilities at İstanbul. The concession included the erection of quais on both sides of the Golden Horn – on the Galata side from Tophane to the old bridge and on the Stambul side from Sirkeci to Azapkapı. Also granted were a variety of rights, for example, to establish a steam-ferry service within the monopoly zone of the quais, to construct a tramway on the quais and to build a number of warehouses and depots. By 1895, the Galata portion of the project essentially had been completed. The company, officially named the Quai, Dock and Entrepôt Corporation of İstanbul, reduced the scope of its operations on the Stambul side to the Sirkeci–Karaköy bridge section, completing its construction by 1899.[3]

The need for such a port, with its ample dockside space for large vessels, stemmed from the technological revolution in sea transport – the replacement of sail by steam. In 1873, for example, the shipping handled by the port of İstanbul equalled 4.5 million tons, 51 per cent steam and 49 per cent sailing vessels. By the

1880s, the sailing share already had dropped to 8 per cent of the total as increasing numbers of steamships crowded into the port. Total tonnage had risen to 10 million tons in 1900 but sailing vessels accounted for only 581,000 tons, or 5 per cent of the total. The dominance of steam over sail at İstanbul and elsewhere in the late nineteenth century stemmed from its greater speed and reliability. Such ships also were considerably larger; sailing ships calling at İstanbul in the late nineteenth century averaged 120–170 tons while steamships averaged 1,000–1,500 tons and were increasing steadily in size and carrying capacity.[4] Fuller İstanbul (and Ottoman) participation in world-trade required ports with the ability to handle the large ships. The new port works at İstanbul both met the need and accelerated the trend towards steamships.

As the port facilities were completed, the larger ships more frequently on-and-off loaded directly at the dockside. The government-company agreements, moreover, assured the firm's monopoly over activities within the concession zone. Both the nature of the facilities and the concession documents jeopardized the livelihoods of Ottoman port workers. The workers involved here were porters (*hamals*) and boatmen (*kayıkcı*, *sandalcı* and *mavunacı*). Both groups largely were recruited in Anatolia. The *hamals* in our case study were organized into the *emtia dahiliye gümrüğü hamalları*, a sub-group of the İstanbul *hamal* guild. Until the Ottoman Bank incident and the massacres of the 1890s, most İstanbul *hamals* generally had been of Anatolian Armenian origin from around Lake Van.[5] Thereafter, most were recruited from among the Anatolian Muslim populations, both Turkish and Kurdish.[6] Many came from quite considerable distances; in one case, an İstanbul *hamal* (Muslim) was encountered on the road east of Maraş, heading still eastward to his home.[7] One newspaper relates the drowning of a twelve-year-old *hamal*,[8] which suggests that some porters were very young. The boatmen similarly were of Anatolian background and, as did the porters, worked in İstanbul for temporary but often extended periods. Their ethnic origins are a bit uncertain at present – one report[9] states they were Lazes and Kurds from the Black Sea ports while another source[10] says they were Turkish, Greek and Armenian. The boatmen (and mostly probably the porters as well) lived as bachelors in groups of about six, paying an old man to cook, clean and arbitrate disputes among them.[11] Although, as we shall see, both the porters and boatmen were attached strongly to the customary rights of their respective guilds, the conditions of their existence mitigated against the development of modern class consciousness. Their identity, however long their urban residence, remained that of villagers usually; the place of their employ was only an ephemeral phenomenon, a temporary state to be endured but not of decisive importance. They married women from the home village, sent money back to support their wives and children, visited them infrequently but finally returned to take up permanent residence.[12]

When working in İstanbul, their guilds traditionally had established patterns of behaviour with government officials. The erection of the harbour works, however, substituted the French company for the Ottoman government in the lives of the workers and placed them in a new and direct relationship with a foreign firm. With the final completion of the facilities in 1899, the implications of the concession arrangements for the workers began to emerge more clearly. In that year, the state and the company formally agreed to a definitive set of fees to be charged for the various on–off loading, storage and carrying services. Thereafter, in essence, the company dictated the level of charges the porters and boatmen could expect for their services. That is, porters' and boatmen's fees were no longer set by guild–government agreement as before but through a state-company negotiation in which the guildsmen were represented only indirectly. Nonetheless, many of these measures went unimplemented for several years as the government retained a community of interest with the guilds. Until 1907, the state–guild relationship continued to function rather well, at company expense. The guilds, surely with at least tacit government approval, successfully frustrated the concessionaire's efforts to streamline operations by bringing the workers fully under its control. Government support of the workers during a part of this 1899–1907 period may be attributed in part to the sultan's concern that a clause in the concession document would become a wedge for the establishment of extra-territorial claims by European powers in the Ottoman Empire. He feared that the port company's rights to land reclaimed from the sea in the harbour area would lead to extra-territorial port zones, such as those then plaguing Chinese rulers. To thwart such an eventuality, the sultan around the turn of the century unsuccessfully sought to purchase the company outright.[13] For this purpose, the port workers could have provided a useful means of pressurizing the company. Even when Abdul Hamid abandoned his attempt, the government seems to have retained an alliance with the workers, possibly as a means of checking further encroachments by the foreigners.

In 1907, however, the Ottoman state abandoned the port workers to the company. As a part of the deal to obtain a customs-duty increase from 8 to 11 per cent, the government consented to a number of changes (called reforms) in the administration of customs. The more serious inroads were made into the occupation of the porters, while the boatmen were the less affected. The agreement to establish more regular customs procedures, i.e., more in conformity with European practices, included actual company control of porters and their punishment by dismissal for incapacity or abuse.[14] The traditional *hamal* right to collect fees directly from the merchants whose goods they were carrying was denied and the porters now were to receive payment from the Quai Company in accordance with its own tariff schedule. The porters effectively lost their monopoly to the company, which now possessed the ability to set the fees and regulate, to some degree, *hamal* affairs. The company reaction to the *carte blanche* was instantaneous and unambiguous. Alleging that porters were illegally collecting fees from merchants, the company refused work to forty-two *hamals* and forcibly removed them from the quai. The government dismantled the guild committee (*esnaf heyeti*) and the remaining porters (reportedly fifteen) in this sub-group were given employ by the company. The firm thereby began to implement fully the regulations set out in the earlier agreements. It thus successfully interposed itself between the porters' guild and their customers, interfering in those relationships while, in the process, assuming an overseeing role that had belonged to the Ottoman state. Further, as stipulated in the 1907 agreement, merchants were permitted to haul their own goods up to the customs house,[15] a measure taking jobs from some porters. The boatmen's position also suffered further erosion. Initially, to provide some compensation for business lost upon construction of the quais, the company had permitted the boatmen's (*mavunacı*) guild to handle ship–quai–ship transport in such cases where sea transport was necessary.[16] The company, however, had retained the right to determine unilaterally the numbers of such boats needed. Also, it seems that the company, to avoid unrest among this group of workers, previously may have been allowing the boatmen to offload some ships directly tied up to the quai. This practice ceased with the 1907 arrangement which allowed the company to reduce the volume of goods handled by the boatmen. And finally, as in the case of the porters, the boatmen now collected their fees from the company.[17] The extent to which negotiations for the customs revisions were directed to such minutiae as the number of porters and boats employed in the port underscores the intimate relationship between the European merchant, investor and diplomat in the Middle East.

While the company juridically was justified in reasserting itself over the workers, the latter were hardly mollified by such legalistic references to treaties or government appeals to the need for increased revenues. A year after corporation and state combined against them, the Young Turk Revolution seemed to afford the porters and boatmen an opportunity to win back their lost positions. Within less than a week of the constitutional restoration, the forty-two displaced *hamal*s forcibly reclaimed their jobs at the quai. The boatmen (*mavunacı/kayıkcı*), in a probably simultaneous set of events, again denied the right of the company to set fees and began collecting them personally from the merchants. The company unsuccessfully tried to use force. Then, on 30 July 1908, it officially complained to the central regime, stating that the fees were going to the local government (the municipality?) and threatening suit.

For more than six months an extensive series of confrontations and negotiations ensued involving the various groups of port workers, the company, Young Turk officers and members of the Committee of Union and Progress (CUP) and most government ministries. The period was particularly tumultuous, one of special uncertainty as the meaning of the constitutional restoration came to be defined more clearly. Through September, wave upon wave of strikes broke in almost every part of the communication, transportation and industrial sectors. Thereafter, until early 1909, Ottoman port cities were agitated further by the boycott against Austria–Hungary. In the course of these events, over twenty documents passed among the contending parties on the question of worker and company rights. This correspondence contains few direct references to the strikes and none at all to the boycott. Rather, the focus is upon the claims of the aggrieved parties and their demands to the government for redress. The company, throughout the exchange, insisted upon the illegality of the porters and boatmen's actions and demanded that the state immediately halt such activities. The workers, led by the forty-two returned *hamal*s, protested vigorously and rather effectively in defence of their views and their jobs. On 13 August 1908, many thousands of dock workers at İstanbul struck, returning to work two days later, following arbitration by CUP members Dr Ali Riza Tevfik Bey and Major Selim Serry (*sic*) Bey. The two, according to newspaper accounts, listened first to the workers and then spoke with company agents.[18] The efforts, so highly praised in the French press of İstanbul, also seem to have included police and army protection for 'foreign strike breakers'.[19] Less than a week after such arbitration, ten striking porters on the Stambul quai, reportedly ringleaders, were arrested by the government.[20] The head of the gendarmerie warned the boatmen against striking and work resumed.[21] While the Stambul side of the concession zone was in turmoil, porters on the Galata/Tophane side similarly pressed for guild rights and took over that quai.[22] On 10 September 1908, yet another strike (of presently undetermined dimensions) hit the Quai Company.[23] During the following week, a 'great crowd' of porters stormed the Galata/Tophane quai and again seized it from the company. The goal this time seems to have been shacks set up at the end of the quai for coal loaders employed by the company. Back on the Stambul side of the quai, the boatmen (*kayıkcı*) similarly prevented the company from seizing barracks (*baraka*) of porters who had been dismissed earlier. On this occasion, the company specifically berated the government for not sending troops to expel the workers.[24]

In a move probably designed to defuse the workers' anger, the company, in early October, ceased using its own small boats to shuttle passengers and goods from ship to quai and permitted the boatmen's guild to (re)assume this function.[25] All the while, however, it continued to insist on its legal right not to utilize the guild's services.

At this juncture, after half-hearted government efforts to dislodge the protesting porters and boatmen, the Austro-Hungarian annexation of the Ottoman provinces of Bosnia and Herzegovina brought the port workers into an alliance with the Young Turks. Both groups had been shaped by the ongoing process of European penetration but the details of their coalition remain sketchy. My own research shows that port workers in many areas, including İstanbul, cooperated closely with local CUP groups and played a vital role in engineering and sustaining the boycott of Austro-Hungarian goods that lasted from October 1908 until February 1909. Four examples from among the many available will be offered here to support the claim of active porter/boatmen participation. At the İstanbul harbour, in late October, men from the lighters refused to allow Austrian ships to off-load[26] while, in mid November, we find the porters and lightermen of the İstanbul port allied with the CUP and refusing to on- or off-load any Austrian ships.[27] A similar report was issued on 20 December, while a week later the boatmen were said to be working hand in glove with the boycott committee.[28]

The involvement of the port workers in this boycott illustrates clearly elite Young Turk mobilization of lower strata energies against the same, in this case, Austrian target. The motives of the two groups, however, were quite different. The Young Turk appeals were made on the basis of nationalism, on the need to avenge the humiliation that the annexation had brought to the Ottoman state. The port workers, for their part, probably reinterpreted this call in more readily understood terms, viewing the annexation as a Christian affront to Islam. That is, the Young Turk leaders and their port worker followers adopted the same course of action – boycott – on behalf of the nation on the one hand and the faith on the other.[29]

The broader significance of the port workers' participation in the boycott is unclear. Ironically, it seems to have helped them little in their struggle with the Quai Company. On the one hand, government measures of repression in August–September had been unconvincing. On the other, the workers' enthusiasm for the boycott may have aroused the Ottoman government to act against them for two quite different reasons. First, as the boycott dragged on, non-Austrian merchant interests were infringed upon, unwittingly or otherwise, and numerous diplomatic protests were filed with the Ottoman regime against the 'hideous' and 'vulgar' actions of the port workers. Thus, the Ottoman bureaucrats in office who received the protests were pressured to move against the workers now doubly guilty of disturbing the international order by struggling with the company and by their boycott actions. Secondly, on the eve of the first Ottoman elections of the post-revolutionary period, the alliance of the workers with the CUP may have troubled some of the unionists' political rivals holding government office, providing such officials with yet another inducement for reprisals.[30]

Dating from mid November, in the midst of the boycott, the policy of the various government ministries – from the Interior, Justice, Commerce and Public Works to the Grand Vizierate – generally was unfavourable to the workers. The Ministry of Commerce and Public Works again investigated the legal bases of the guilds' claims and, on 15 November, informed the grand vizier that both the concession documents and the sultan's *irade* (decree) made clear that the contractual rights of the company were being violated. Two weeks later Kâmil Paşa reviewed the correspondence and ordered the definitive expulsion of the *hamals* from the port area, threatening police action in the event of non-compliance. These guildsmen responded with an appeal to the grand vizier in the name of the constitution (*kanun-u esas*) and asked for his intercession with the company. Their petition stated that the dismissal of the forty-two porters was against the customary practices and usages of all guilds. If the company were not prevented from firing them, the petition warned, the general (*umum*) porters' guild and their own local guild (here called the *emtia dahiliye iskele başı*) of *hamals* would leave work.[31]

The porters, in subsequent correspondence, continued to insist on their traditional rights, stating they were altogether independent of the company and not subject to its dictates. The quarrel reached a resolution of sorts on 8 February 1909, when the grand vizier, in response to the *hamals*' petition, devised a compromise in consultation with the Quai Company director. M. Granet agreed to re-hire thirty of the released *hamals* and employ them, on a daily-wage basis, at various places of his choosing. The remaining twelve would be employed elsewhere, among the porters in the customs house. No porter, it was stated, would have the right of complaint or appeal. Further, prosecution of the 'ringleaders' who were arrested in late August would continue and, the grand vizier specifically stated, the porters' takeover of company functions had been illegal. Whether or not this decision to insist on the impropriety of the porters' actions while arranging for their employment was a holding action, a reward for their boycott activities, or a demonstration of government reluctance to move against its own subjects on behalf of a foreign corporation presently cannot be determined. We do not now have any additional data on the porter–Quai Company controversy.

The conclusion of the struggle with the boatmen is even more obscure. While the grand vizier, in December 1908, was considering the porters' petition, he complained to the Marine Ministry that government officials on the docks were not offering the company sufficient protection against the boatmen. Near mid December, the company resumed use of its own boats and asked the government for assistance. Kâmil Paşa noted that the boatmen's guild was interfering with the legal rights of the company and rendering the government vulnerable to lawsuit. He therefore ordered the gendarmerie to take the necessary actions against the boatmen.[32] Uncowed, the boatmen initiated their own suit against the company. In the course of the litigation, the Quai Company alleged that the court (which one is not indicated) had granted excessive numbers of delays that worked to the advantage of the guild. The suit continued into February 1909 but there are no recorded results among the archival documents consulted.

Conclusion

The 1890 decision to revamp the port facilities at İstanbul had important consequences for Ottoman economic and political life. As seen, many workers' occupations became dysfunctional with the introduction of the new technology. Also, the creation of a foreign corporation in control of the port removed the pre-existing groups of workers from the jurisdiction of the state to that of the firm and drove a wedge into guild–government interactions. The state certainly lost some legitimacy in the eyes of at least those whose jobs were eradicated or jeopardized and who were kept from their posts by state military action at the behest of the company. It is clear, in sum, that the Quai Company contributed to destabilization in the late Ottoman Empire.

And yet, the consequences of foreign-capital penetration in this case were not felt as quickly or completely as might be expected. In fact, the workers offered a quite tenacious resistance to the economic effects of foreign investment.[33] The guild and government for their part held together for a surprisingly long period of time, suffering their first truly serious breach with the customs agreement in 1907. The need of the company to demand this reassertion of its rights years after signature of the original concession indicates they were not being honoured. The 1908 revolution seemed to offer the workers a chance to recoup the losses of the previous year. In response to their takeovers and resistance to company force, the government often moved slowly and reluctantly. The footdragging of the judiciary in the case of the boatmen and the unwillingness of some dockside officials to drive off the porters and boatmen suggests a continued sharing of views between the workers and at least certain levels of state functionaries.

Part IV

Trade and markets

15 ❧ The Venetian presence in the Ottoman Empire, 1600–30

SURAİYA FAROQHİ

Introduction

It is the aim of the present study to describe the commercial and political relations between Venice and the Ottoman Empire during the first quarter of the seventeenth century. This period is of considerable interest in the economic history of the Mediterranean since, during the years immediately before 1600, Venice for the last time in its history had possessed a major stake in the Levant trade.[1] Unlike the crisis of the early sixteenth century, after the Portuguese had first managed to insert themselves into the trade of the Indian Ocean,[2] the crisis of the early 1600s, immediately following a brief period of prosperity, proved irreversible from the Venetian point of view. Therefore it is of interest to find out what happened to the Venetian network of diplomatic representatives, consuls and ordinary merchants during a period of considerable economic and political difficulty. Moreover the interplay of this network with the Ottoman authorities, both central and provincial, was of crucial importance for the history of Venetian trade.

Thus the present study concentrates upon the interaction between political and commercial aspects of the Ottoman–Venetian relationships. *Bailos* (Venetian representatives), consuls and merchants have been studied in some detail, and thus the manner in which Venetian official representatives interacted with the home authorities in Venice, and with the locally resident merchant community, is reasonably well known.[3] Equally, we now possess a considerable number of studies dealing with merchant organizations, both of the 'traditional' type represented in Venice, and of the 'regulated companies', by means of which, to name but one example, English merchants were to make such a prominent place for themselves in the Levant trade.[4] While much less is known about Ottoman mercantile organization, a number of studies does exist and, at least on a general level, we can describe the manner in which Ottoman merchants of the sixteenth or seventeenth century did business.[5] On the other hand, very little is known about the interaction between Ottoman and Venetian merchants or about the attitude which the Ottoman state took toward the commercial relations which its subjects entertained with Venice.

Matters are complicated by the fact that Ottoman state power was apparently organized at a number of different levels. Persons and institutions at various levels of the political hierarchy could interact with their Venetian counterparts in ways that were not necessarily approved of by the central authorities in İstanbul. At the lowest level, Ottoman merchants, frequently but not necessarily of non-Muslim background, might cooperate with Venetian traders in the illegal exportation of grain, a practice that the Ottoman central authorities tried to repress with varying degrees of success.[6] With respect to an intermediary level, represented by local and provincial authorities, European observers of the seventeenth and eighteenth centuries often commented upon the special facilities which foreign merchants enjoyed in İzmir or Aleppo.[7] This was most probably owing to the fact that provincial governors and *kadıs*, not to mention tax-farmers and janissaries doing duty as watchmen, depended on commercial dues for much of their income, and were in consequence inclined to do nothing that might frighten the merchants away. On the other hand, provincial governors and fortress commanders on the Morean or Albanian coast might closely cooperate with corsairs from North Africa, without necessarily heeding the orders from İstanbul that forbade these practices.[8] Ottoman policies toward its tributary state, the tiny but commercially active Republic of Dubrovnik, might also be interpreted as part of the tendency to organize political relations on distinct and semi-autonomous levels. For Dubrovnik was permitted to do what Ottoman merchants could not do, namely trade with known enemies of the Ottoman state while at the same time functioning in many respects as part of the Ottoman body politic.[9]

Many historians have tended to view at least most of these phenomena as symptoms of Ottoman decline, which is supposed to have occurred from the late sixteenth century onward. However, it is also possible, once one rids oneself of the fascination which the growth or contraction of Ottoman political power exercised upon contemporaries, to interpret this phenomenon in quite a different way.[10] It is well known that members of the Ottoman bureaucracy had very definite views with respect to the position which their own state, as a Muslim polity organized according to the principles of Near Eastern and particularly Iranian statecraft, should occupy toward the world at large.[11]

On the other hand, practical circumstances often favoured policies which were not easy to fit into the model of the ideal Muslim and Near Eastern state, which was expected to expand continuously through Holy War or *gaza*. The establishment of long-term peaceful relations through the *ahidname* (capitulations) was a case in point; the abrogation of the rule that a non-Muslim, residing on Islamic territory for more than a year, became a protected subject of the relevant Muslim state (*zimmi*) was another.[12]

For political reasons, the Ottoman authorities might espouse these policies, but to induce provincial administrators to accept them might be a difficult task on the 'ideological' level, irrespective of the amount of coercive power that the central administration might be able to mobilize. For Ottoman local administrators who, for instance, opened their ports to North African corsairs, could easily feel that they were representing the traditions of the authentic Ottoman *gazi* state, and, what is more, the North African corsairs must have agreed with them on this matter.[13] Moreover, since the Ottoman central authorities in principle accepted the ideology of the *gazi* Muslim state, motivation to act against refractory fortress commanders who aided the North African corsairs preying upon infidel shipping must in many cases not have been very high. Thus the difficulty of enforcing the *ahidnames* (capitulations, privileges) can be easily understood without necessarily involving the model of 'Ottoman decline'.

Another aspect of the 'organization of political and commercial relations on distinct and semi-autonomous levels' was the fact that tasks considered distasteful from the point of view of the Ottoman state ideology might be relegated to the initiative of lower-level authorities. The role of Dubrovnik, an intermediary in trade and diplomacy as mentioned above, might be cited as an example. Another case in point was the fact that foreign merchants often had day-to-day dealings only with temporary officials (*emins*) and even more frequently with tax-farmers (*mültezim*). For *emin* and *mültezim* did not constitute part of the regular Ottoman bureaucracy, and in many cases were non-Muslims. Moreover, the tax-farmer, as opposed to a regularly appointed official, was generally allowed a large measure of independence, provided he regularly paid the Treasury the amounts of money stated in his contract. Within the same context, one might mention the fact that İzmir throughout most of the seventeenth century did not constitute a provincial (*sancak*) capital, but retained a relatively low status in the administrative hierarchy as a district (*kaza*) centre.[14] Thus European merchants in this very active port town dealt only with quite low-level authorities, and were permitted to behave in a relaxed fashion which would have been quite unthinkable in most of the other Ottoman port towns.[15]

In this context, a few words must be said concerning the manner in which the Ottoman central bureaucracy viewed the problems raised by the existence of foreign trade. On the positive side, there were the benefits accruing to the Treasury from customs revenues. This matter is frequently touched upon in rescripts which the Ottoman administration issued upon requests from the Venetian *bailos*. This emphasis on customs revenues may have been partly due to the fact that Venetian petitions themselves frequently dwelt upon this theme, for a rescript made out on behalf of the sultan customarily contained a detailed summary of the document in response to which it had been issued. But references to customs revenues also occur quite independently, and must have been of some importance in the thinking of Ottoman officials. In addition to this purely utilitarian point of view, Ottoman rescripts also contain a more 'ideological' motivation, namely that it was becoming to the state to protect merchants, and to provide its own subjects and those of friendly rulers with the means of earning their daily bread.

On the negative side, there was the difficulty of enforcing export prohibitions. The exportation of war material was prohibited by the *şeriat*, although legal authorities of the Caliphal period did not necessarily agree on exactly what was to be regarded as war material.[16] However, the Ottoman authorities rarely if ever invoked the *şeriat* as a basis for these prohibitions, which were apparently motivated by purely practical considerations. In fact many European states of the medieval and early modern period enforced similar prohibitions, quite apart from the fact that the popes at times tried to ban all trade with Muslim countries. Among the considerations primarily important to the Ottoman central administration were the needs of the armies, the navy, the palace, the enormous capital city of İstanbul and, to a lesser degree, the needs of local craftsmen.

Thus, while certain prohibitions, such as those relating to horses, arms, or gunpowder, were universally enforced throughout the Empire, others, such as the prohibition to export grain, were at times partially abrogated by export licences. Yet other prohibitions might be of purely local or regional significance. To mention but one example, the exportation of raisins from the Aegean coast of Anatolia was forbidden, for this area was meant to supply İstanbul. On the other hand, raisins grown in Thessaly or Morea were available for exportation, since they had not been earmarked for the consumption of any particular sector of the Ottoman internal market.[17]

At the same time, the Ottoman Empire did not place any restrictions upon imports. This was motivated by the fact that the administration concerned itself only to a very limited extent with the protection of local producers, although protective measures occasionally resulted as a by-product of other considerations.[18] Or rather, where imports were concerned, the Ottoman administration tended to subordinate the protection of producers to the protection of consumers. For the motive behind an open-door policy toward imports was that such a policy should result in an abundant supply of goods on the market, leading to a low level of prices. Therefore, even though Ottoman authors such as Naima[19] might complain about the abundance of luxury imports, in practice nothing was done to stem the flow.

In the present study, an attempt has been made to describe Ottoman–Venetian relations such as they appeared from the Ottoman point of view. Even though the description is largely concerned with concrete facts, the central theme is the manner in which Ottoman officials perceived the state which they administered. An attempt has been made to interpret Ottoman–Venetian relations during the early seventeenth century, without referring to the unrealistic model of an Ottoman state which kept on declining for several centuries in succession. Rather, it has been assumed that the commercial and political relations of the Ottoman Empire were organized at different levels, and that it lay within the logic of the Ottoman political system to maintain a certain degree of autonomy as far as the different levels were concerned. In extreme cases, the logic of the Ottoman political system might even permit local administrators to do what a rescript emanating from the central bureaucracy expressly prohibited. In the case of a strongly centralized state, such as the Ottoman Empire undoubtedly was in certain respects, such an assumption may at first appear surprising. However, it was discovered long ago that the supposedly absolutist regimes of the pre-industrial period in Europe might equally include certain sectors in which state involvement was minimal.[20] Under these circumstances, the alternative explanations sketched out in the present study seem to deserve a certain amount of consideration.

Historical background

It has often been remarked that Venice broke off its alliance with Spain and the pope, and concluded a separate peace with the Ottoman Empire in 1573, in order to safeguard its commercial position in the eastern Mediterranean.[21] Obviously the loss of Cyprus was considered a minor evil, even though the island's cotton and sugar had markedly contributed toward making the voyages of the medieval Venetian merchant galleys a commercial success. At least in the short run, this policy bore its fruits. In the last years of the sixteenth century, trade with the Levant for a brief span seemed to have regained its former prosperity. Even on the island of Cyprus, Venetian merchants were fairly active. They also constituted one of the more important groups of foreign traders engaged in the sale of woollen cloth and in the purchase of silk and spices in Aleppo.

However, at the beginning of the seventeenth century and particularly since the 1630s, Venetian trade in the Mediterranean was very visibly on the decline. The reasons for this crisis have been investigated by many different scholars and now seem to be well established. Its shipping had long been one of the weak points in Venice's economy: now it was affected both by piracy and by commercial competition on the part of the English and Dutch.[22] In the sixteenth century, the woollen industry had compensated for losses in other branches of trade.[23] But the contraction of the Ottoman market, and competition from English broadcloth, both led to a decline of the Venetian woollen industry. Moreover the Dutch, who established their first entrepôts in Indonesian waters during those years, managed to cut off the flow of spices through the Red Sea in a much more radical fashion than the Portuguese had ever succeeded in doing. Therefore, both from the sellers' and from the buyers' points of view, Venetian merchants in the Mediterranean found themselves on the losing side.

In addition, the policies adopted by Venetian merchants and patricians, which at first glance might be considered successful adjustments to a changing situation, contributed toward weakening the city's position in international trade. Wealthy inhabitants invested in landholding on the Terraferma, and high grain prices justified this inclination toward rural life from a commercial point of view.[24] Venice increasingly turned into a regional port serving northern Italy, and its control over the northern part of the Adriatic was by now more an illusion than a reality. Even the concentration of Venetian manufacturing upon luxury and semi-luxury products was bound to weaken the city's position in the markets of the eastern Mediterranean. For with serious fiscal difficulties and price increases besetting the Ottoman economy in the last quarter of the sixteenth century, the capacity for customers to absorb highly priced Venetian imports was bound to diminish. Thus, even though Venice in the first half of the seventeenth century managed to avoid a complete collapse of its economy, its role in Mediterranean trade was permanently affected.

In addition to its economic difficulties, Venice in the early seventeenth century was confronted with serious political problems. In the face of papal power at the height of the Catholic reformation, Paolo Sarpi asserted the claims of the Venetian state to regulate the secular aspects of ecclesiastic life.[25] At the same time, Venice lived in a state of undeclared war with the Spanish viceroy of Naples. Closer to home, in 1618 a plot was uncovered to seize power in Venice itself, which had been hatched by mercenaries employed in the Venetian army. It was widely assumed that the preparations for this attempted *coup d'état* had at least been connived at by the Spanish ambassador accredited with the Serenissima.

On Venice's eastern frontier, the piracies of the Uskoks, freebooters employed by the Austrian Habsburgs in their border warfare with the Ottoman Empire, by the beginning of the seventeenth century constituted a serious liability to Venice both politically and economically. Apart from the fact that Venetian shipping was being attacked, the constant threat to the lives and property of Ottoman merchants positively invited an intervention on the part of the sultan in the northern Adriatic. For, regarded from the Ottoman point of view, Venice could at the very least be held responsible for not adequately policing the seas in its immediate vicinity.[26]

During the sixteenth century, Venetian politicians had often been willing enough to close their eyes to the problem. However, in the early seventeenth century the situation was no longer the same, once Spanish predominance in Italy made it vitally important for the Venetians to maintain peaceful relations with the Ottoman Empire. For a considerable time the problem of the Uskok and their piracies was argued over by Venetian and Habsburg authorities. Finally, apart from waging war against the Austrian archduke who had made himself most notorious as a protector of the Uskoks, the Venetians secured the services of a high Austrian official not unamenable to judicious bribery. Under the aegis of this administrator, who for a while represented the Austrian authorities in the pirate centre of Senj (Segna), a beginning was made toward resettling the Uskoks in the interior. However, it was not until 1618 that the process was completed, and the piratical activities of the Uskoks finally came to an end.

Ottoman sources on Ottoman–Venetian relations

To date, these political and economic problems have been studied mainly on the basis of Venetian and, to a lesser extent, of other European archival materials. In this context, Ottoman sources have generally been neglected. During the last twenty years Turkish scholars such as Tayyip Gökbilgin and Şerafettin Turan have however taken a certain interest in the Ottoman materials to be found in Venetian archives, and in the activities of Ottoman merchants who inhabited the Fondaco dei Turchi.[27] On the other hand, very little work has been done with the material available in İstanbul or with the documents preserved in the *kadı* registers of Bursa.[28] Nor can the present study do more than illustrate the potential of the Ottoman archives even for the seventeenth century, which is on the whole less well covered by official documents than the 'classical' period that preceded it.

Among Ottoman archival series, the *mühimme defterleri* (registers of important affairs) are relatively well known and have frequently been used.[29] Beginning in the last years of Kanuni Süleyman's reign (1520–66), they cover the Cyprus war and the subsequent peace negotiations with Venice. This series permits us to catch a glimpse of Venetian trade, resumed almost immediately after the cessation of hostilities in 1573. For the following years, we possess occasional references to Venetian shippers trading in Ottoman territory, particularly if they were caught while trying to export goods whose exportation was forbidden. But, on the whole, it cannot be claimed that Ottoman–Venetian relations in times of peace are adequately covered by the documents contained in the volumes of *mühimme* records.

However, much richer documentation is available in the so-called *ecnebi* registers (registers of matters connected with foreigners), which cover both the affairs of individual foreigners residing in the Ottoman Empire and what might properly be considered inter-state relations.[30] These registers survive from the early seventeenth century onward. Documents dealing with Venice and with Dubrovnik are often collected in the same registers, possibly because Ottoman scribes liked to spell Dubrovnik (Ragusa) as Dobra-Venedik. Owing to the intensity and long history of Ottoman–Venetian relations, a relatively large number of registers concerning Venetian affairs can be found in the Prime Ministry Archives in İstanbul.

In these registers, we usually find copies of the capitulations (*ahidname*) in the form in which they had been approved by the reigning sultan.[31] However, since the Venetian *ahidnames* of the late sixteenth and early seventeenth centuries varied very little from one sultan to the next, the main interest of the *ecnebi* registers lies in the fact that they reflect day-to-day application of the *ahidname*. Steensgaard has correctly remarked that only a minority of all local disputes was ever referred to İstanbul.[32] Even so, the *ecnebi defterleri* show that the number of disputes and complaints involving foreign merchants and decided in the Ottoman capital was not inconsiderable. Moreover, cases once decided apparently possessed some value as precedents. Therefore the responsible diplomats had these documents confirmed every time a new sultan ascended the throne, even if the cases these rescripts referred to had long ceased to be of much practical importance. In the specific case to be dealt with here, Sultan Osman II (1618–22) reigned only for a short period, and was after a brief interlude succeeded by his brother Murat IV (1623–40). Thus a large number of documents had to be submitted for confirmation within a relatively short time span, and this fact probably accounts for the richness of the two registers which have been studied in the present article.

In addition registers of miscellaneous rescripts, of which a few examples survive for the mid sixteenth century, and which become increasingly frequent as time passes, also contain individual documents relating to the Venetians in the Ottoman Empire. Particularly *kadıs* and district governors (*sancakbeyi*) of ports much frequented by foreign merchants often received special instructions from the Ottoman central administration with respect to these visitors. In most cases, it is hard to judge why certain rescripts should have been entered into the *mühimme defterleri* and not into the *ecnebi* registers or collections of miscellaneous rescripts.[33] Very probably, certain rescripts were in fact copied into more than one register; in addition, two or more rescripts of very similar character might appear in the same collection of documents.

However, it appears that the *ecnebi* registers contained only rescripts which had been solicited by the diplomatic representative of the state to which the register referred, that is, in this particular instance by the Venetian *bailo*. Documents responding to queries from provincial or local administrators, even if they had a direct bearing upon Venetian affairs, were rarely included in the *ecnebi* registers. Therefore one can expect to find in these collections mainly documents favourable to the interests of the Venetians, for it was Ottoman chancery custom to avoid issuing a rescript, if the petition presented by the *bailo* or other foreign representative had been rejected. On the other hand, rescripts limiting the scope of Venetian activity are more likely to be found in the *mühimme defterleri* or in the collections of miscellaneous rescripts mentioned above.

Major issues in Ottoman–Venetian relations

On the basis of about three hundred rescripts analysed for the purposes of the present study, a variety of topics can be treated in a more or less detailed fashion.[34] On the political side, there was the eternal problem of the frontier. As Halil İnalcık has stressed, Sultan Mehmet the Conqueror (1451–81) had conceived a policy of systematically reducing the Venetian colonies on the borders of the Ottoman Empire, and during his reign Venice lost control over the Morea.[35] Under later sultans this policy was pursued at a slower pace, though never given up: as late as the mid seventeenth century, Ottoman forces were to conquer the Venetian colony of Crete. Even in the early eighteenth century, when both Venice and the Ottoman Empire had lost their former position in world politics, the Ottomans were still strong enough to prevent the Venetians from regaining a foothold in the Peloponnese.[36] Thus, daily skirmishes between Venetian governors on the Dalmatian coast, on one side, and Ottoman provincial administrators or corsair captains on the other must be seen in the context of long-term policies. In fact, the period covered by the present study might be described as the relatively peaceful interlude which separated the Ottoman conquest of Cyprus from the long war for the domination of Crete.

On the other hand, Ottoman–Venetian relations in Dalmatia cannot be adequately described without taking into account the role of the Spanish viceroys of Naples. In one of the *ecnebi* registers studied here, we find an interesting document relevant to abortive peace feelers on the part of Spain, which ostensibly originated with the court of Naples. Corsairs and pirates professing allegiance to the Spanish crown, and subjects of Naples attempting to purchase grain on the Dalmatian coast constitute the more routine matters treated in the rescripts at our disposal.

Many of the rescripts dealing with the conditions under which the Catholic religion might be exercised in towns and cities like Bandırma, İzmir, or Aleppo must also be interpreted in the context of European religious controversies. Inside Italy, Venice was opposed to the pope and to Spain, and recognized Henri IV as king of France when the latter was still a Huguenot.[37] On the other hand, the Catholic reformation of the later sixteenth and early seventeenth centuries was an important force in Venetian public life.[38] Moreover, to pose as the defender of the Catholic priests resident in Jerusalem was a matter of prestige in European politics. The frequency of references to the 'Kemame kilisesi' (Church of the Holy Sepulchre in Jerusalem) in the rescripts solicited by the Venetian *bailo* must be evaluated in this context.

Of more immediate interest to the historian dealing with Ottoman–Venetian relationships is the geographical distribution of individual Venetians and their consuls throughout the Ottoman Empire. Consuls are relatively easy to trace, since the appointment of these functionaries had to be confirmed by the Ottoman authorities before the former could take up their official duties. Usually, the Ottoman document of appointment also contained a summary of the *ahidname* which constituted the guidelines for the consul's activity.[39] As far as individual merchants were concerned, those whose business affairs progressed smoothly entered the Empire and departed again without leaving a trace in the Ottoman rescripts. But those who were somehow involved with local authorities, particularly where inheritances were at issue, have frequently found their way into the registers, and their activities can be reconstructed to a certain extent.

In addition, there is the vast number of Ottoman rescripts which directly concern the organization of trade. Some of them deal with the conflicts between Venetian merchants and local Ottoman authorities; disagreements were often engendered by legally or illegally levied taxes. Enforcement of export prohibitions constituted another frequently disputed matter. Occasionally competition from English shippers, which contributed materially to the decline of Venice as a commercial power in the fifty years following the end of the Cyprus war, is also reflected in the Ottoman rescripts. Unfortunately, the rescripts analysed here contain practically no quantitative information. However, the wide range of topics covered, and the occasional vividness of detail more than make up for this shortcoming.

International politics in the Adriatic

Since less than a hundred kilometres of sea separated the Ottoman possessions in Albania from Spanish-controlled Naples, it is not surprising to find a number of references to *harbî İspanya keferesi* ('Spanish infidels from the abode of war') among the rescripts granted to the Venetians. Ottoman governors of Klissa, Kırka, Hersek (Herzegowina), Delvina, and Alonya (Vlorës) were instructed to cooperate with Venetian naval commanders against possible attack on the part of the Spaniards, presumably the viceroys of Naples.[40] This cooperation was to take the shape of an exchange of information concerning the movements of the common enemy. However, in view of the fact that relations between Ottoman and Venetian lower-level authorities in Dalmatia tended to be much less friendly than those between the two governments themselves, it is difficult to say how much of this cooperation in fact materialized.

The persistence of distrust, in spite of what were, for the time being, cordial political relations, is reflected in a rescript dealing with a minor political event. Some Spanish corsairs based upon a port in the Kingdom of Naples, had landed on the Venetian island of Istandin (Tinos).[41] There they were driven off by the local Venetian authorities, and, among the booty the corsairs left behind, were some goods which very obviously belonged to Muslim owners. Acting in accordance with the relevant provisions of the capitulations, the Venetian authorities in Istandin decided to send the goods to the neighbouring Ottoman island of Andra. For this purpose, they requested a rescript that would allow the messengers entry into Ottoman territory. In the Ottoman reply, addressed to the *kadı* of Andra, the latter was instructed to receive the messengers and to make out a properly sealed receipt for the goods they were to deliver. But, above all, the *kadı* was enjoined to make sure that the men from Tinos stayed in Andra only for the minimum amount of time needed to discharge their commission and were sent back to Venetian territory as soon as possible. Unfortunately, the document does not say whether there was anything specific that the messengers from Tinos were to be kept from finding out, or whether the order was simply intended as a general measure of precaution.

Since Spain and the Ottoman Empire were officially at war, direct trade relations were obviously not permitted by the Ottoman authorities. However, in the daily course of frontier relations, this prohibition was occasionally ignored.[42] Thus the sultan reminded the *kadı* of Draç (Durrës, Durazzo) and other Ottoman administrators active on the Albanian coast that merchants from the Spanish domains, probably Neapolitans, were in the habit of trading in the area. Some of the visitors seem to have openly declared their nationality, others claimed to be from the port of Dubrovnik (Ragusa) which recognized Ottoman suzerainty. Yet others may have declared themselves Venetians, and the relevant rescript seems to have been issued at the instigation of the latter, although the text does not contain any references to an initiative on the part of the *bailo* in İstanbul. For, among the instructions issued to local Ottoman administrators, it was emphasized that *bona fide* Venetians, whose government maintained friendly relations with the Ottoman Empire, were not to be molested under the pretext that they were Spanish subjects.

However, Ottoman–Venetian cooperation during these crucial years went beyond the ordinary courtesies of border relations. In 1618, the Catholic inhabitants of the Valtelline had revolted against the authority of the Protestant Graubünden (Ligues grises). The Spanish governor of Milan had seized the opportunity to establish garrisons in a strategic area, which linked the Spanish possessions in northern Italy with the Low Countries by way of Franche-Comté.[43] This move in turn directly affected Venetian interests, since a Valtelline controlled by Spain threatened communications with France at the time when a Franco-Venetian alliance opposed the aspirations of the Spanish viceroys in Italy. Under these circumstances, Venice applied for aid to the Ottoman sultan, requesting permission to recruit mercenaries on Ottoman territory.[44] It is probable that at the court of İstanbul the significance of the conflict was well understood. For in a rescript dated Dec. 1624/Jan. 1625 and addressed to the provincial governor (*beylerbeyi*) of Bosnia as well as to the lower-level governors of İskenderiye (Shkodra), Delvina and Morea, the Ottoman chancery explained that the Spaniards had conquered the locality of 'Valtuniye in Frengistan'. This place being located in immediate proximity to the Venetian domains, it was considered likely that the Spaniards would use 'Valtuniye' as a springboard for an attack upon Venetian territory. Under these circumstances the Venetians, as allies of the Ottoman Empire, should be permitted to recruit mercenaries who would, of their own free will, serve Venice in its struggle against Spain. It is possible that the Ottoman authorities were thinking of the Morlacci, mountaineers living in the districts bordering on Venetian territories in Dalmatia, who in later years sometimes revolted in support of Venetian war aims. Or else the Porte may have been thinking of Albanians, who in the sixteenth century had occasionally fought on the battlefields of distant Scotland.[45] At the same time, it is noteworthy that a sultan granted his subjects official permission to participate in what was, after all, a conflict not directly affecting Ottoman interests. Obviously it was not feared that the departure of a few hundred or even of a few thousand men would significantly affect the tax revenues or the security of the districts they had inhabited. This state of affairs might be interpreted as a warning not to exaggerate the short-term political consequences of demographic difficulties in the early-seventeenth-century Ottoman Empire.[46]

Even more explicit concerning the informal Venetian–Ottoman alliance of those years is a document dated May 1626 and addressed to the authorities of Dubrovnik.[47] This rescript concerns a Spanish peace offer, a matter which had been in the air since the Count-Duke Olivarez had become prime minister to Philip IV in 1622. For Olivarez was known to favour more or less peaceful relations with the sultan, in order to free Spanish armies for the war against the Protestant princes of Europe.[48] Seen from a 'Realpolitik' point of view, this choice made sense. Ottoman–Spanish borders, both in North Africa and in the Adriatic Sea, were stabilized to a point that it would have taken a major military effort to upset them.[49] Moreover, the outcome of such an effort, in the light of the experiences gathered during the 1570s, was unforeseeable to say the least. On the other hand, the Netherlands, the German territories and the French borderlands constituted a much more accessible prize, while Philip II's policy of pursuing a war on both fronts against the Ottomans and against the Protestant powers of Europe had resulted in a dangerous over-extension of the financial resources of the Spanish crown. Previously, Anthony Sherley (English adventurer, 1565–1633?) had hoped that the initiative for peace would come from the sultan.[50] But in 1625–6, the time was obviously ripe for a proposal from the Spanish side.

Ostensibly, the initiative came from the Spanish viceroy of Naples, and not directly from Madrid. The preliminary negotiations seem to have been encouraging to the Spaniards, for a second embassy was sent out in 1626. However, while the embassy was on its way, the Ottoman court's evaluation of the situation radically changed. In its letter to the Dubrovnik councils, the Ottoman chancery explained that the Spanish crown was the ancient enemy of the sultan, and that any peace overtures on the part of Spain were simply meant to permit a concentration of forces against Ottoman allies in Europe. The text does not state who these allies were. But presumably Venice was being referred to, because France, the traditional ally of the Ottomans, got involved in a war with the Spanish Habsburgs only in 1628.[51] It must be assumed that the Venetian *bailo* had worked behind the scenes to effect this change in policy and to avert a peace which directly threatened the interests of Venice. As Anthony Sherley had already remarked, Venice could maintain its position as the 'hinge of Europe' no longer, once the Ottoman Empire and Spain were at peace.[52]

The fact that the letter rejecting the Spanish peace offers was addressed to the governing council of Dubrovnik highlights the position of this small trading republic as a privileged gateway into or out of the Ottoman Empire, according to the circumstances. On the authorities in Dubrovnik devolved the responsibility of sending back the Spanish emissaries, and even of transmitting the order to return, if the envoys had already set out for the Ottoman border. It is well known that Dubrovnik merchants in the sixteenth and seventeenth centuries not infrequently gathered political information, both on behalf of the sultan and on behalf of his adversaries. Thus the role of the Dubrovnik councils as an intermediary between the Ottoman Empire and the Christian powers of the western Mediterranean formed part of an established diplomatic pattern.[53]

Piracy and border conflicts

In spite of the Ottoman–Venetian alliance, border conflicts on the Dalmatian coast were not infrequent. Within this context, the rescripts which the Ottoman central authorities addressed to the provincial governor of Bosnia, and to local authorities in places like Novi or Klissa, were usually reminders of the fact that the Ottoman Empire maintained treaty relations with Venice, and admonitions to keep the peace. Thus the local governor (*sancakbeyi*) of İskenderiye (Shkodra), along with all *kadıs* and fortress commanders in the province, was ordered to maintain good relations with Venetian subjects, and to consult with Venetian authorities whenever the need presented itself.[54] More specifically, the *bey* of Herzegowina was informed of the fact that a fortress commander stationed near the Venetian castle town of Kotor (Cattaro) was demanding taxes (*haraç*) from the inhabitants of certain Venetian villages. The sultan indicated his displeasure at this state of affairs, as contrary to the privileges he had granted, and enjoined the governor to remedy the situation.[55] Moreover the Ottoman central authorities ordered the governor of Bosnia to see to it that double taxation of villages close to the Ottoman–Venetian border was brought to an end. In this case, oppression of the villagers had apparently been connived at by local authorities both Venetian and Ottoman.[56]

Other border conflicts arose out of the fact that Venice's few remaining possessions in Dalmatia were completely surrounded by Ottoman territory. Access to these fortified ports from the land side therefore had to be regulated in some detail. As an example of how such conflicts were resolved one might cite the case of a janissary named Bekir, who, apparently upon his own initiative, had set up a customs house taxing European merchants approaching the Venetian port of Split (Spalato).[57] According to the Venetian complaint, these taxes constituted illegal innovations (*bidat*). In consequence, Ottoman local officials were ordered to investigate, and to suppress the customs station if the complaint was based on fact. In another instance, the Venetian *bailo* complained of the activities of an unnamed military commander, who supposedly had set himself up in an unauthorized fortress commanding access to Spalato.[58] The robberies committed by this personage, so the Venetian petition explained, hurt not only the interests of passing merchants, but those of the Ottoman fisc as well. For traders could be expected to avoid this route in the future, thus depriving the sultan's treasury of much needed customs revenues.

However, in spite of such difficulties, the port of Spalato attracted a considerable amount of traffic and constituted a serious competitor to Dubrovnik. Therefore the governing circles of the latter town came to an agreement with the Ottoman tax official responsible for the collection of tolls from merchants crossing the border between the Ottoman Empire and Dubrovnik.[59] Since both the tax-collector (*emin*) and the Ragusans had an obvious interest in diverting traffic from Spalato to Dubrovnik, the Ottoman tax-collecting official took measures to force traders bound for Spalato to visit Dubrovnik instead. In spite of the latter town's subordination to the Ottoman Empire, which normally resulted in the sultan's support for Dubrovnik in its conflicts with commercial competitors, in this case the Ottomans gave priority to the alliance with Venice. Accordingly, when the Venetians complained of the tax-collector's behaviour, the Ottoman authorities ordered the punishment of the *emin*, although nothing is known about either the nature of the punishment or its effectiveness.

Much more serious, however, than occasional conflicts between Venetian merchants and local Ottoman administrators were the problems arising out of the activities of pirates and corsairs in the Adriatic. Scholars such as Tenenti and Lane have remarked how, at the turn of the sixteenth century, Venetian shipping was attacked both by Northerners, who were at least partly motivated by commercial competition, and by the corsairs of North Africa.[60] In addition, the state of undeclared war between Venice and the Spanish viceroys of Italy made the Venetians vulnerable to attacks by corsairs based upon ports in the Kingdom of Naples. Moreover, the Uskok problem had been eliminated only in 1618, after considerable damage had been done to Venetian shipping. For a while, it appeared as if the overall economic position of Venice would remain permanently affected by this onslaught upon its carrying trade.

However, as the seventeenth century wore on, the importance of shipping within the Venetian economy declined, and, in consequence, the city became less vulnerable to pirate attack. Certain scholars have therefore tended to regard the impact of piracy more as a conjunctural accident[61] than as a long-term reason for Venetian economic decline. However, if one considers the fortunes of Venice as closely connected with long-distance maritime trade, then the piratical activities particularly of English shippers should be considered as a factor which strongly contributed toward the weakening of the Venetian position.

Not all the many aspects of Adriatic piracy are reflected in the rescripts which the Ottoman sultans accorded the Venetians. Surprisingly enough, the Uskoks are mentioned only in passing, and that in connection not with the Venetians but with the Ragusans.[62] Nor has the presence of corsairs and pirates from the Northern seas and from the island of Malta made any impact on Ottoman–Venetian relations during the early years of the seventeenth century. On the other hand, the activities of corsairs and pirates from the Ottoman domains are amply documented. This is true both of the North Africans, subject to the Ottoman sultan but negotiating direct treaties with foreign powers, and of the Albanian or Morean captains regularly active in the waters of the Adriatic.

Ottoman rescripts particularly dwell upon the fact that the activities of North African and 'Adriatic' corsairs were connected. For, since the North Africans operated far away from their bases, they obviously needed a place in which to revictual. In many cases they also disposed of the booty on Rumelian territory, for this saved the risk and expense of carrying goods and slaves all the way to North Africa. Acting upon Venetian complaints, the sultans sent out rescripts admonishing those fortress commanders who most frequently cooperated with the corsairs of the Magrib: the commander (*ağa*) of Novi (Herzegnovi), the district governor (*sancakbeyi*) of Avlonya (Vlorës) and the commanders (*dizdar*) of the ports of Preveze, Modon, Anavarin (Navarino), and Limasol.[63] The rescript issued by the Ottoman chancery threatened not only the accused commanders but also their superiors, the provincial governors with deposition and unspecified dire punishment if the peace was not respected.

On the other hand, there is little reference in these formal texts to the reasons why local commanders acted in the fashion described. Among the more important motivating forces doubtlessly figured the notion, based upon the *şeriat* that Holy War could be interrupted only by brief truces and not by lasting peace.[64] Furthermore, there was the image of Venice as one of the major enemies of the Empire which, if a somewhat outmoded idea by the early years of the seventeenth century, must still have been vivid in the minds of Ottoman frontier warriors (*gazi*).

However, certain rescripts emanating from the Ottoman central government propounded the exact opposite, and asserted something that the recipients must have found very hard to accept, namely that the Venetians were ancient and faithful friends of the Ottoman Empire, and could therefore expect preferential treatment with respect to other Christian allies.[65] One of the very few further explanations which the Ottoman administration gave to make its policy palatable to its subordinates was the observation that existing treaty relations with Venice made it impossible to regard booty taken from Venetian citizens as legitimate.[66] Therefore glory as a *gazi* could no longer be gained from the struggle against the Venetians, but efforts must henceforth be aimed at other states.

Among the concrete measures by which the Ottoman government attempted to control politically inexpedient piracy, one might name the attempt to limit shipbuilding in the Ottoman Adriatic ports. As a routine measure, local administrators were ordered to burn the boats of coast-dwellers who had made themselves a reputation as pirates. But matters went beyond these punitive measures, for instance the inhabitants of the locality of Iskradin, not far from the Venetian fortress of Şibenik (Sebenico), were in the year 1621–2 forbidden to build boats large enough to hold twenty-five or thirty men, even for trading purposes.[67] As an excuse, the relevant rescript proclaimed that in the past the men of Iskradin had never used boats of this size. However, it is very possible that the Venetians in requesting this order from the sultan were not simply concerned with the problem of piracy, but also with undesirable competition in local carrying trade.

Among the more narrowly military measures against pirates, the Ottoman administration envisaged a certain amount of common action with the Venetians. Rescripts addressed to the authorities in Tunis, Rhodes and Morea, from the year 1624–5, refer to an attack upon the Venetian possessions of Korfu and Kefalonia by a conjunction of North African and Morean corsairs.[68] In this context it is mentioned that the plunderers had been put to flight by the appearance of the *derya beyleri*. This term normally refers to district governors officiating in the seaboard provinces of the Ottoman Empire, so presumably the *derya beyleri* who drove away the attackers were commanders in the Ottoman fleet. In another rescript the *kadıs*, district governors, and fortress commanders of the İnebahtı (Lepanto, Naupaktos) and Aya Mavra (Leukas) areas were advised of the fact that Venetian galleys, patrolling the Adriatic against pirates, might visit Ottoman ports under the addressees' jurisdiction.[69] It was stressed that, as long as the Venetian naval units committed no unfriendly act, they were to be treated as allies. However, it is well known that on the issue of piracy, Ottoman–Venetian communications not infrequently broke down, even to the point of resulting in a cannonade between the Ottoman fortress of Avlonya (Vlorës) and a Venetian naval unit in 1638.[70]

Ecclesiastical affairs

A comparatively large number of rescripts solicited from the sultan by the Venetian *bailo* deal with the affairs of Catholic churches and priests. Certain rescripts were requested to secure the position of churches used by Venetian residents. Thus, by the reign of Ahmed I, İzmir was being frequented by a large enough number of Venetians for a Frankish church to have come into existence in which the Venetians worshipped along with other European residents.[71] Older was the European Catholic church of Aleppo, for it was claimed that it had been assigned to the French and Venetians when they first returned to trade in the city, that is about fifteen years after the Ottoman conquest in 1516.[72]

More significant are the instances in which the *bailo* interceded on behalf of small groups of Roman Catholics who were scattered over the territories of the Ottoman Empire. Thus certain monks in the province of Bosnia were having difficulties with unnamed local residents. It seems that the latter reproached the monks for not furnishing their contingent of boys to the levies of future janissaries undertaken on behalf of the Ottoman central administration, and for not sending a gift to the sultan on his accession. The Bosnian monks were granted a rescript of protection,[73] and in a comparable fashion, the Venetian consul at Aleppo took an interest in the affairs of the Maronite community residing in this city. Disputes between the Maronite patriarch and his flock, complaints concerning the intervention of Greek Orthodox and Syrian patriachs in the affairs of the Maronites, and even a conflict involving an exchange of real estate between the local Maronite and Armenian churches are consequently all documented in the registers dealing with Venetian affairs.[74]

Much more sustained, however, was the interest of the Venetian *bailo* in the sanctuaries of Jerusalem and surroundings, that is, particularly the Church of the Holy Sepulchre (Kemame) and the Church of the Nativity in Bethlehem. A rescript dated 1031/1621–2 even claims that the friars guarding the Holy Sepulchre were Venetian subjects (Venedik *reayası*).[75] As a result, the Ottoman administration did not consider it unusual that the Venetian *bailo* intervened on behalf of the friars, and particularly on behalf of the Latin Guardian of the Holy Places, who controlled access to the sanctuaries of the Holy Sepulchre and the Dormition.[76]

But in addition to the *bailo*, the 'Frankish' monks of Jerusalem also possessed an effective protector in the administrator of a pious foundation established on behalf of the soul of Sultan Kanuni Süleyman.[77] For, since the dues paid by European pilgrims formed part of the foundation endowment, the administrator had every interest in keeping the sanctuaries in good condition, so that they might be visited by a large number of pilgrims. In fact, judging from the strongly worded rescript that the foundation administrator procured for the Latin monks of Jerusalem, one might even speculate that his protection was more effective than that afforded by the *bailo*.

Even so, the *bailo*'s intercession resulted in a sizeable number of Ottoman rescripts protecting the interests of Catholic monks and laymen temporarily or permanently residing in the Ottoman Empire. This observation can be adduced as evidence for the opinion that the French capitulation of 1604, which includes an article protecting the interests of Catholic priests and churches in Palestine, was not intended to grant the French king an exclusive right of intervention in this matter.[78] Quite to the contrary, it is very likely that the Ottoman administration took a pragmatic view of the whole situation. In the early seventeenth century, the French commercial presence in the Ottoman Empire did not amount to very much, while the Venetians both did a good deal of business and maintained a close political relationship with the sultan. Under these circumstances the effectiveness of an ambassador's intervention was based upon that official's status at the Ottoman court, and much less upon the letter of the capitulations.

Between politics and commerce: the *ahidname* and its application

In principle, relations between Venice and the Ottoman Empire were regulated by the *ahidname*, which European diplomatic terminology generally called capitulations. However, in view of the difference between 'capitulations' of the sixteenth or seventeenth century, and their nineteenth- or twentieth-century homonyms, it appears preferable to call the earlier documents 'grants of privileges'. This more neutral term also stresses the proximity of the *ahidname*s granted foreign rulers by sixteenth- or seventeenth-century sultans, to the guarantees accorded cities or states that became part of the Ottoman realm by 'voluntary' surrender. Charters of this latter type had for instance been issued to the former Genoese colonies of Galata and Chios, and Ottoman chanceries equally referred to these documents as *ahidname*s.[79]

It is worth remarking that the *ahidname* was primarily a political document, dealing with the relationship between two states. Commercial matters were touched upon, but appear as somewhat marginal issues. One may suppose that the Ottoman administration regarded commercial relations as problems of a more local nature, to be decided *ad hoc* as need arose.[80] Moreover, in spite of a long sequence of territorial and economic losses, the Venetian state of the late sixteenth and early seventeenth centuries must have still appeared formidable enough to ensure the 'primacy of politics'.

Among the provisions of the *ahidname*, the clause that gave rise to most dispute was one that at first glance would appear to be a mere side-issue, namely what was to happen to the estates of Venetians who died on Ottoman territory. Where subjects of the sultan were concerned, the fisc claimed the estate of people dying without legal heirs. Thus, in every major settlement, there was an official who confiscated such inheritances on behalf of the sultan. Exemptions from this ruling were however granted to various categories of people apart from foreign merchants, such as for instance participants in the pilgrimage caravan to Mecca.[81]

Owing to difficulties of travel and communication, legal heirs might often find it impossible to present themselves at the time the inheritance was being divided. Later on, they were likely to run into difficulties when they attempted to claim their share from an official determined to hold on to what he had got. Therefore disputes of Ottoman subjects with the officials in charge of confiscating heirless property were extremely common, and the Venetian complaints on this issue simply form part of a large pattern. It is in this context that one must interpret the numerous rescripts enjoining local *kadı*s and district governors to see to it that the estates of deceased Venetians were handed over to the *bailo*. Some of these cases were indeed rather picturesque: thus, upon the death of the Venetian consul in Gelibolu (Gallipoli), the *bailo* in İstanbul had quite a bit of trouble extricating the consul's residence from the hands of the official in charge of heirless property.[82]

Another issue frequently taken up by Ottoman rescripts was the status of long-term Venetian residents. Here a fairly serious legal problem awaited resolution. For, while Ottoman legists granted that the ruler could promulgate laws, it was always assumed that these laws should not conflict with the Muslim religious law or *şeriat*.[83] In actual fact, even though the Ottoman bureaucracy took the rules of the *şeriat* very seriously, solutions not easily incorporated into the Islamic legal system were adopted on a number of issues. One of these was the abrogation of the rule that a non-Muslim from a country which had entered into official relations with a certain Muslim ruler became a subject of the Islamic polity after a year's residence.[84] This 'naturalization' would have involved the payment of all locally levied taxes, such as the poll tax (*cizye*), dues in money and in kind, demanded particularly in times of war (*nüzul*, *avarız*), and many others of a similar nature. In spite of continuous complaints about irregular contributions demanded from foreign merchants, long-term Venetian residents were usually very anxious to assert the fact that they were not subjects of the Ottoman Empire – behaviour which indicates that their position was more advantageous than they would readily have admitted.[85]

Under these circumstances, a rescript defined the procedure by which a resident Venetian might become a Christian subject of the Ottoman Empire. This was either by marriage to a local Christian woman or by making a declaration of intent.[86] In the absence of these two features, even very long residence did not make a Venetian into an Ottoman subject. Nor was the ownership of real property crucial, although in the eyes of many people the acquisition of such property seems to have created a presumption of intent to become an Ottoman subject. Thus the sultan's administration permitted Venetians as well as other foreign merchants to live in the Ottoman territories for many years, while at the same time retaining all the advantages commonly accorded to visiting traders.

Another important aspect of the privileges granted to the Venetians needed occasional clarification, namely the authority of *bailo*s and consuls within the Venetian community. At first glance, the legal situation seems unambiguous: according to the *ahidname*, disputes among Venetians were to be settled by the *bailo*.[87] Moreover, local authorities were not to hear these cases once they had been decided by the *bailo*, even if one of the parties requested such a hearing,[88] and disputes involving the *bailo* himself could only be resolved in İstanbul.[89] That local authorities could not re-try a case decided by the *bailo* was in conformity with Ottoman judicial practice, for a case decided by a *kadı* could also be reviewed nowhere but in İstanbul. On the other hand, this partial assimilation of the *bailo* to the status of an Ottoman judicial official must have been difficult for certain local authorities to accept. References to the honourable social position of the *bailo*, and to the eminent status of the Venetians as long-time friends of the Ottoman Empire, which abound in rescripts sent out by the Ottoman central administration, thus failed to make a great impression upon provincial and local administrators.

Another aspect of the *bailo*'s position demanded official clarification in the course of a complicated dispute which seems to have taken place sometime in the early seventeenth century, probably during the brief reign of Sultan Osman II (1618–22). Certain traders, about whom nothing is said in the available documents but who must have been Ottoman subjects, had purchased woollen cloth and other fabrics in Venice, insured their goods, and then loaded them onto a state galley bound for the Venetian port of Split (Spalato).[90] This convoy was attacked by a Spanish flotilla, and the goods were lost. Thereupon the merchants lodged a complaint in İstanbul. In their opinion, because of the insurance contract concluded in Venice, the Venetian government had stood surety for the safe delivery of the goods. As a result, the merchants demanded compensation from the Venetian *bailo* in İstanbul, whom they regarded as the legal representative (*vekil*) of the government in Venice.

The *bailo* denied both points: neither had the Venetian government accepted responsibility for the safe delivery of the goods, nor had he himself been sent to İstanbul to represent the Venetian government in what he must have regarded as a civil matter. Apparently the case went through a number of phases, but finally the Ottoman government accepted the *bailo*'s position. After the administration had decided against the *bailo*'s responsibility in cases involving Venetian insurance policies, merchants with complaints involving such matters were probably forced to take their cases to Venice, although the grand vizier's intervention might also be solicited. In a sense, the sultan's decision was in conformity with the *ahidname*, which stated that the *bailo* could not be held responsible for other people's debts.[91]

From the *bailo*'s point of view, the decision of the Ottoman administration meant that his status as a diplomatic representative was reinforced. The position taken by the Ottoman government is in harmony with the hypothesis that the latter viewed Ottoman–Venetian relations as primarily a matter between states, and regarded the commercial aspect as something of a side-issue. On the other hand, the Ottoman merchants involved in the affair seem to have taken the opposite position, and at one point they apparently came quite close to having their interpretation officially accepted. Whether the Ottoman government's decision in favour of the *bailo* affected the use of Venetian ships and insurance facilities by Ottoman merchants is unfortunately not documented in the source material at hand.

Consuls

At the beginning of the seventeenth century, Venice still possessed an appreciable network of consuls throughout the Ottoman Empire. Among them, the consul of Aleppo was the most prominent. In Ottoman documents of the time, he was often called a *baylos*, that is, put on the same footing as the official Venetian representative in İstanbul. In addition, the consuls of Tripolis (Syria), or Alexandria (Egypt), and of İskenderun (the port of Aleppo), were placed in charge of fairly large groups of Venetian merchants.[92] However, the rescripts studied here do not refer to the affairs of these last-named officials, and concentrate instead upon the consuls of Rumelia and Anatolia.

On the Albanian coast, the consulate of Avlonya (Vlorës) must have been anything but a sinecure. Venetian boats frequently approached the coast to trade in salt, and, for many of these shippers, Avlonya must have constituted the most accessible consulate.[93] More important was the fact that corsairs from North Africa not infrequently sought shelter under the guns of Avlonya. Complaints about Venetians who had been sold as slaves in contravention of the privileges granted by the Ottoman sultan quite often reached the consul, who was then expected to intervene. Thus the Ottoman central administration was informed of the activities of a Jewish merchant of Avlonya, who acted as a middleman for the North African corsairs.[94] Probably the information which the Venetian consul in Avlonya passed on to İstanbul often placed him in a rather delicate position as far as local power politics were concerned. Most likely it is due to this particular situation that a rescript was issued in the year 1624–5, which was meant to protect the Venetian consul from all molestation.[95]

As a last remnant of its seaborne empire, Venice in the early seventeenth century still maintained consuls on several Mediterranean islands. Thus there was a Venetian representative on Naxos, an island which had only been fully incorporated into the Ottoman Empire during the second half of the sixteenth century.[96] In addition, there were consuls on the island of Mürtadabad (probably Kea), on Chios and on another island which has not as yet been identified.[97]

However, the most important island consulate was certainly on Cyprus, from where Venetian shippers continued to export cotton well into the seventeenth century. Originally, the Ottoman administration had forbidden the exportation of Cyprus cotton, but apparently the prohibition was not enforced for very long.[98] One of the rescripts in the *ecnebi* registers even contains a few figures that permit us to gauge the importance of the Venetian Cyprus trade.[99] A certain Ludovico, son of Pietro, a Venetian who had lived on the island for eighteen years, had represented the Dutch as consul on Cyprus while entering into a partnership with the resident Venetian consul. After Ludovico's death, the provincial governor of Cyprus and other local authorities tried to lay their hands upon the inheritance. During the ensuing dispute, it was asserted that Venetian and Dutch merchants had entrusted Ludovico with more than 100,000 *kuruş*es worth of goods and ready money. Moreover, Ludovico had become a rich man in his own right, who was owed money by an impressive number of Cypriots, both Muslim and Christian. In addition, he had even acquired real estate from debtors who had been unable to repay him. Thus it appears that, during the first quarter of the seventeenth century, the Cyprus trade was far from dead, and that a few Venetian merchants even managed to grow rich on it.

On the Dardanelles, the consulate of Gelibolu (Gallipoli) did not serve any immediate commercial purpose. Rather, it was meant to help merchants passing through the Dardanelles when they got into difficulties with the Ottoman authorities. For ships leaving the Ottoman Empire were inspected when passing the fortresses of Kilidbahır and Seddbahır to make sure that they did not export goods of which there was a scarcity in İstanbul.[100] In addition, shippers passing though the Dardanelles paid a number of dues, a fact which also often resulted in situations in which the aid of a consul was needed. Thus it is probable that the consul of Gelibolu transmitted the complaints of certain Cretan shippers, who reported that the dues they were expected to pay upon passing the Dardanelles had been increased from about 1,000 *akçe* to 5,000–6,000 *akçe*. In another instance, a palace official tried to collect dues over and above the customary amounts from Venetian and French boats entering or leaving the Sea of Marmara. In this case as well, the consul of Gelibolu probably informed the *bailo* and thereby set the complaint mechanism going.[101]

On the Marmara coast, the Venetians maintained consulates in Bandırma and in Silivri. In spite of its modest size, a certain amount of business was done in the port of Bandırma, since we hear of two Venetians renting a storehouse in this place and purchasing leather and raw wool.[102] No information survives concerning commercial activity in Silivri. But, since we know of Venetian merchants visiting the area and trading on the shores of the Sea of Marmara, one must assume that the consulate had been instituted to take care of their needs.[103]

Inland, the only consulate of importance was Ankara. In the early seventeenth century, Venetians and Poles were particularly prominent among the merchants visiting this city, which was famous for its mohair and mohair yarn. Certain Venetians resided at Ankara for long periods of time; some of them are on record as renting private houses over several years, thus avoiding the crowding and discomfort of public hostelries.[104] However, the best quality mohair yarn could not legally be taken out of the Ankara area, for the tax collected from locally woven mohair cloth constituted a revenue item of some importance to the Ottoman Treasury.[105]

Venetian merchants in the Ottoman provinces

In the meantime, other Venetian traders visited the fairs of the Balkans and the Morea. Thus a rescript dated 1031/1621–2 recommends a merchant trading on the island of Ağrıboz (Euboa) and in the Morea to local governors.[106] In this document, the Ottoman administration particularly stressed the need to make sure that janissaries in charge of policing the fairs did not overcharge the merchants whom they were supposed to protect. In fact, visits of Venetian merchants to the celebrated Thessalian fair of Maşkolur had been documented in Ottoman sources for the second half of the sixteenth century.[107] In the early seventeenth century, however, Maşkolur was no longer mentioned as a place frequented by Venetian traders, although the Thessalian fairs were at the time a major centre of Ottoman internal trade.[108]

Venetian traders in Thessaly and the Morea during the second half of the sixteenth century seem to have been mainly concerned with the exportation of raisins and currants, although the Venetian island of Ƶante was itself a major producer of dried fruits. The role of Venetian traders in this context is stressed by a rescript issued in 1573–4, when, after the end of the Cyprus war, merchants from Venice again began to visit the Ottoman Empire.[109] The return of the Venetians particularly affected the profits of the tax-farmer who had contracted for the dues payable from Morean raisins and currants; for in a previous petition to the Ottoman central administration, the latter had complained that, owing to the non-arrival of Venetian exporters, the market price of currants had dropped to almost nothing.[110] In the documents of the early seventeenth century studied here, no direct reference is made to the exportation of Morean currants on the part of Venetian merchants. Probably the latter were by this time feeling the effects of competition from English traders, whom we find established in Balyabadra (Paleopatras) at the end of the sixteenth century. However, conflicts between Venetian shippers and the tax official (*emin*) of Holomiç (Higoumonitza) indicate that age-old Venetian relations with the Morea had not totally disappeared.[111]

Interestingly enough, two rescripts refer to Venetian merchants who had obtained permission to purchase white sturgeon (*morina balığı*) and caviar in the Black Sea port of Kilia.[112] In one instance, the text appears to refer to a strictly individual case. In the other, one must assume that Venetian merchants had established a somewhat more long-lasting relationship; for the rescript in question refers to the fact that two merchants, named Constantine and Giulio, were in the habit of travelling this route every year. These documents should be taken to mean that occasionally the Ottoman authorities relaxed their policy of closing the Black Sea to European merchants, particularly when political relations with the traders' home country were good.[113] However, only in the document referring to a strictly individual case is the merchant who was accorded official protection unambiguously described as a Venetian. In the second instance, all we know is that the Venetian *bailo* intervened on behalf of the traders, which could be owing to the fact that Constantine and Giulio had close business relations with Venetian merchants, or else had taken up employment of some sort in the household of the *bailo*. Under these circumstances, Venetian trade in sturgeon and caviar in all probability did not reach a very impressive level.

In addition, Ottoman rescripts of the early seventeenth century mention Venetian salt traders on the Dalmatian coast. Documents referring to this trade frequently repeat the routine formula that, since many Ottoman localities in this area suffered from a lack of salt, traders supplying this vital commodity should be protected by *kadı*s and provincial governors.[114] However, in this sector the Venetians had to compete with the shippers of Dubrovnik (Ragusa) who were generally in a better position to obtain commercial privileges on Ottoman territory. Thus in certain localities, such as the salt-trading centre of Gabela, no shipper, Venetians included, was permitted to sell salt before the Ragusans had emptied their warehouses.[115] But even so, there existed a number of Venetians who possessed salt depots on the Dalmatian coast, and Ottoman local administrators who tried to lay hands on their goods. However, it is impossible to determine the amount of business which remained in the hands of Venetian merchants, whose government but a century or two earlier had monopolized the Adriatic salt trade.

In addition to the trade of Venetian citizens proper, the commercial activities of the inhabitants of certain Venetian colonies must be taken into consideration. The inhabitants of Zante (Ottoman: Zaklise) continued to enjoy the privilege of buying a certain quantity of grain whenever they delivered their tribute, and were in this respect assimilated to the Ragusans.[116] Thus it appears that, even though the Ottoman Empire no longer exported large quantities of grain to Venice, as had been the case in the mid sixteenth century, certain vestiges of this trade had survived the difficult years around 1600. On the other hand, Cretan shippers helped to supply İstanbul with lemon juice, honey, olive oil, and cheese, and could also be found trading in western Anatolia.[117]

This modest every-day trade of the Cretans, who at the same time undertook voyages to Egypt, seems to have possessed some importance in the eyes of Ottoman administrators in the capital. Thus, as a reason for protecting these traders from exactions on the part of local authorities in the Dardanelles area, a rescript explicitly refers to the fact that the shippers might cease to visit Istanbul. Local authorities were admonished to keep this consideration in mind and to refrain from demanding taxes which were not commensurate with the amount of profit that the Cretans might be able to make.

The new port of İzmir

Apart from Aleppo, the Venetian trading community mentioned most frequently in Ottoman records was that of İzmir. This is worth noting, because according to Venetian sources at the beginning of the seventeenth century most Venetians apparently did business in Syria or Egypt, and not in Anatolia.[118] However, the frequency with which the Ottoman central authorities issued rescripts addressed to the *kadı* of İzmir indicates that the Venetian presence in this latter town was of greater significance than has been assumed to date. Unfortunately, little is known about the early urban development of İzmir or about its trade before the 1680s. However, the town increased from about 2,500 inhabitants in the second half of the sixteenth century to an approximate 90,000 toward the end of the seventeenth, attracting immigrants from as far away as Macedonia.[119] Thus it is possible that the 'construction site' atmosphere of the city generated a certain amount of conflict and tension, which in turn focused the attention of the Ottoman central administration upon both local and foreign merchants doing business in İzmir.

Seventeenth-century İzmir differed from all other contemporary Anatolian towns because it constituted the only major port city of the peninsula, whose *raison d'être* lay in international trade. Venetians brought mainly woollen cloth and occasionally glassware, which was becoming a fashionable item in wealthy Ottoman circles. In return they purchased raw cotton and cotton yarn and in addition small amounts of wax and leather. Sometimes woollen cloth and cotton were bartered, with money only used as a standard of exchange.[120] Sale on credit and more or less disguised interest payments were also not unknown.[121]

From the rather small number of commercial disputes recorded in the *ecnebi* registers, it appears that Venetians usually did business with Christian or Jewish merchants established in İzmir. However, some Venetian traders also ventured out into the countryside, buying cotton directly from the producers. These more adventurous merchants managed to secure an additional advantage, as a command from the sultan permitted them to pay their customs duties on the basis of the price actually paid in the countryside, and not on the basis of the substantially higher price which prevailed in İzmir proper.[122]

In the early seventeenth century the legal exportation of cotton from the Ottoman Empire in general, and from İzmir in particular, was a recent innovation. This trade had existed throughout the second half of the sixteenth century, but as a contraband venture, since the Ottoman administration then regarded cotton and cotton yarn as a kind of war material. It is not clear why this policy was reversed in the 1620s: an increase in local production, a reduced need for sailcloth in the absence of naval wars, and a growing need for cash revenues must all have played a part. Under the circumstances, certain Venetians wished to have their right to export cotton confirmed by special decree. For local administrations in İzmir either insisted that the exportation of cotton was still prohibited, or else they were unwilling to concede this right to the Venetians, even though they admitted that it had been granted to the French and English.[123] Thus the favourable relationship of Venice with the Ottoman Empire was of only limited use to Venetian merchants, since they were being eclipsed by the dynamism of their European competitors.

European, or more particularly English, competition was also reflected in the disputes concerning the non-payment of the dues known as *cotimo* and *bailaggio*, which constituted one of the chief sources of income for Venetian consuls in the Ottoman Empire.[124] By the beginning of the seventeenth century, it had become common enough for Venetian merchants to transport their goods on English ships. However, in such cases merchants were none too eager to pay the *cotimo* and *bailaggio* to the Venetian consuls. As a result, the latter were not infrequently deprived of the money they needed to operate effectively.

In this matter, the Ottoman authorities seem to have upheld the position of the consuls, enjoining the English shippers, and even non-Muslim Ottoman subjects upon occasion, to pay their dues to the Venetian consul. While it is probable that rescripts of this type were not obtained without some lobbying behind the scenes, the position expressed in them conformed to the known attitude of the Ottoman administration. It was usually deemed expedient to strengthen the authority of the acknowledged head of each particular community residing on Ottoman territory, so that the latter could be made responsible for the behaviour of the group as a whole. Thus the case of the Venetian consuls conforms to a well-established pattern.

Aleppo: customs and the regulation of trade

Even though the trade of early-seventeenth-century İzmir was expanding fast, Ottoman as well as Venetian authorities were mainly concerned with the Venetian presence in Aleppo and its port İskenderun. This state of affairs explains why the Venetians demanded, and the Ottoman chanceries made out, an impressively large number of documents addressed to the governors and *kadıs* of Aleppo, which referred to one aspect or another of Venetian trade.

From the Ottoman rescripts dealing with the Venetian colony in Aleppo, one gains the impression that the latter's rights and duties had been defined mainly by Sultan Kanuni Süleyman (1520–66). His name is usually mentioned at the head of a long line of sultans who had confirmed rescripts regulating the status of the Venetian community in Aleppo. This fact is worth noting because Süleyman's predecessor Selim I (1512–20), soon after conquering Syria from the Mamluks, had issued two *ahidname*s to the Venetians, while under his grandson Selim II (1566–74), the peace concluded after the Cyprus war redefined the Venetian position in the Ottoman Empire. Süleyman I really appears to have issued a sizeable number of rescripts dealing with the Venetian presence in Aleppo. But it is probable that the prestige which his reign enjoyed, half a century after his death, also contributed to the frequency with which his name was invoked.[125]

Rescripts relating to Venetian affairs in Aleppo will here be treated under three headings. First of all, a number of documents define the position of the Venetian trader *vis-à-vis* the Ottoman authorities, both central and provincial. A second set of documents deals with the rights and obligations of Venetian merchants with respect to ordinary Ottoman subjects, be they merchants, guildsmen, or even simple neighbours. In addition, a number of documents clarify the position of the Venetian consul, or *baylo*s of Aleppo according to Ottoman official parlance. While the *ahidname* is frequently invoked in these rescripts, analysis shows that the documents are mainly concerned with problems arising from day-to-day business dealings, about which the *ahidname* has comparatively little to say.

According to a rescript confirmed by Sultan Ahmet I (1603–17), Venetian merchants trading in Aleppo could not be forced to make purchases, either of silk or of any other goods.[126] This injunction was probably intended to protect traders against provincial governors, who might be tempted to resuscitate the trade monopolies of certain Mamluk sultans.[127] With even more emphasis, the rescripts declared that Venetian traders could not be obliged to sell to provincial governors under the pretext that the goods they offered for sale were needed by the Ottoman state.[128] It appears that this justification was sometimes proffered by provincial governors when they more or less confiscated certain goods, for the merchants in question usually had a great deal of trouble before they received even partial payment.

Conventional wisdom current among Ottoman officials in the central administration was very much opposed to expedients of this type. Thus in the last quarter of the sixteenth century, an official letter sent by the authorities in İstanbul to the *Şerif* of Mecca had explained to the latter that, if Indian merchants no longer visited Jiddah in large numbers, this was due to the fact that the *Şerif*'s men had very often mistreated them. According to the officials who had drafted the rescript, the *Şerif* only needed to make sure that the Indian merchants were treated with justice, and they would not fail to return.[129] Thus Ottoman official ideology concerning the protection of merchants did not remain a dead letter, but, at least to a certain degree, could be expected to inform official policies.

Of equal significance was the permission given to Venetian importers of woollen or silk cloth to set their own prices.[130] This meant that the Aleppo *muhtesip*, an official concerned with the regulation of the market place, was not to concern himself with the prices of imported Venetian cloth. However, this ruling did not apply in İstanbul, where Venetian fabrics, along with Genoese velvets and a rather enigmatic 'Spanish' cloth, were sold at officially determined prices just as if they had been locally produced.[131] However, the exemption granted to the Venetian merchants fits in very well with Halil İnalcık's observation that long-distance and wholesale traders, even if they were subjects of the Ottoman Empire, were generally exempt from the rules enforced by the market inspector.[132] As a result, both Ottoman long-distance traders and their Venetian *confrères* established in Aleppo were left free to make as large a profit as the market would bear.

A number of rescripts regulated the importation of money from Venice into the Ottoman Empire. Venetian merchants paid for part of their purchases in Aleppo with the money earned through the sale of woollen cloth and a few other items of less importance. Whatever they needed over and above this amount was imported either in the shape of unminted silver, or else as Venetian coins (*kuruş*). This silver, once it had been brought to Aleppo, was inspected in the place where the consul resided, and a special rescript assured the importers that the inspection should not take place in the office of the local customs inspectors.[133] The excuse frequently proffered by the customs inspectors for their intervention, namely that they were simply trying to prevent the outflow of silver to Iran, was not considered acceptable in this context. At the same time, the Ottoman authorities confirmed an older rescript that fixed the rate of exchange at 34 *para* to the Venetian *kuruş* and forbade the local authorities to pay only 33 *pare* as they had been wont to do.[134]

A rescript dated 1620–1 – in this case we are dealing with a text recently promulgated and not with the simple confirmation of an older document – regulates the dues to be paid by the Venetian community for the money which it imported into the Ottoman Empire.[135] When recounting the antecedents for the rulings to be enforced, the Ottoman authorities admitted that the Venetians imported relatively small amounts of silver, which were mainly intended for day-to-day consumption. In the past, Venetian merchants had been permitted to import up to 30,000 *kuruş* without any charges; from what they imported over and above this limit, an unspecified amount of dues was to be paid to the sultan's privy purse. Recently, however, local tax officials had apparently demanded 2 per cent of all the money imported by the Venetians, and had even produced a rescript from the sultan to back up their claim. Apparently the case of the French, from whom a similar payment had regularly been demanded, had served as a precedent. However, ultimately the administration in İstanbul ceded to representations on the part of the Venetians, who seem to have claimed that the French, who imported only money and practically no goods, should not be treated in the same manner as themselves.[136] Thus the Ottoman administration went back to the previous regulation, namely an outright exemption for the first 30,000 *kuruş*, and for the remainder, unspecified payments to the sultan's privy purse. This regulation is remarkable in that it probably reflects a relative abundance of silver in circulation. For, if the opposite situation had prevailed, it is very likely that the Ottoman administration would have permitted the importation of silver without charge.

Certain Venetian merchants seem to have profited from the relatively high value of silver relative to gold in the coastlands of the eastern Mediterranean by purchasing gold from the local population.[137] Remarkably enough, these transactions were not forbidden, even though the Ottoman administration of the sixteenth and seventeenth centuries frequently demanded that Syrian taxes be paid in gold.[138] Therefore one would have expected the Ottoman central administration to try to monopolize local gold resources. Quite to the contrary, however, the sultan only demanded that the consul testify to the Venetian citizenship of the merchant in question, so as to prevent fraud. It is not clear what Venetian merchants did with the gold they had acquired in this fashion. However, since the Ottoman rescripts of the time also depict Venetian traders as exporting precious stones,[139] one feels tempted to associate the acquisition of gold and the purchase of jewels from possibly Indian merchants, who generally demanded payment in gold.

As can be expected, quite a few rescripts deal with the protection of Venetian merchants against demands for money over and above the regularly established customs duties. A clause prohibiting such levies had been explicitly inserted into the *ahidname*. But, since it was very difficult to enforce, various rescripts were requested by the Venetian *bailo* to clarify particular cases. Thus a document originally issued by Sultan Süleyman I, and subsequently confirmed by his successors, stressed the fact that Venetian merchants should pay a duty of 21 per cent on the spices they purchased in Aleppo (*öşr-i bahar*).[140] On the other hand, customs officials were forbidden to demand payments beyond this amount, as they had been accustomed to do under a variety of pretexts; thus the officials had demanded fees for their servants, for the handling of the bales, and for the issuance of receipts. In addition, the janissary guards employed by the Venetian consul also often collected a share from the value of the goods they were supposed to protect.[141] These abuses were prohibited by special rescript, while other texts dealt with an even more difficult matter, namely the fraudulent overestimation of the value of duty-paying goods by the Aleppo customs authorities. A further rescript determined that, if a Venetian merchant sold goods under the condition that customs duties were to be borne by the purchaser, the contract was to be deemed valid at law.[142]

At the same time, another document established the procedure to be followed by customs officials in the event of Venetian boats being shipwrecked. This rescript can be interpreted as an elaboration of two separate sections of the *ahidname*. For the latter formulated the principle that the victims of a shipwreck were to be protected and whatever was salvaged of their belongings restored to them. In addition, the *ahidname* also contained the provision that irregular taxation should be repressed as far as possible,[143] a desideratum which, on a more general level, characterized the ideal state as envisaged by the Ottoman central bureaucracy. Accordingly, the sultan decreed that goods belonging to Venetians, which had been salvaged from a shipwreck on the return voyage, were to pay no customs dues, if the owners could document that they had already acquitted themselves in Aleppo, İskenderun, or elsewhere.[144]

Certain rescripts also discuss the goods traded by Venetians, and more particularly the question which wares could or could not be exported. Imports did not give rise to any problems, and are therefore but rarely referred to. Apart from the obligatory woollen cloth, glassware also found a certain outlet on the market of Aleppo.[145] Much more varied was the list of goods exported: silk, some of it grown in the Tripolis region, cotton, wool, indigo, gall nut for tanning, spices, rhubarb, and precious stones.[146]

Of this list, only cotton presents a certain problem. A rescript dated 1618–19 permits the export of this commodity and claims to be a confirmation of earlier decrees, issued on behalf of Sultans Selim II (1566–74) and Murat III (1574–95). However, we know from numerous other sources that during the period in question the export of cotton was still prohibited. Possibly an exceptional permission of limited duration had been granted, such as the English had also requested for Tripolis in the year 1586–8.[147] Under Sultan Mehmet III (1595–1603) the list of specifically permitted goods was extended by the addition of raisins, pistachios and morocco leather, a commodity otherwise frequently reserved for the Ottoman internal market.

In the relevant rescript,[148] the granting of a sweeping permission to Venetian exporters is motivated by fiscal considerations. According to the text, certain unnamed persons had been causing trouble to the Venetian merchants of Aleppo, and these activities had resulted in a loss of customs revenue. Thus political considerations, which according to the Ottoman view were of primary importance in the Ottoman–Venetian relationship, were to a certain degree reinforced by the interests of the sultan's Treasury.

Aleppine and Venetian traders

Another complex of rulings incorporated in the registers under investigation attempted to clarify the position of Venetian merchants in Aleppo *vis-à-vis* ordinary inhabitants of the Ottoman Empire, mainly merchants or craftsmen, but also local administrators of pious foundations. Thus it was specified that Venetians resident in Aleppo, who rented storerooms or other accommodation, could not be evicted if they regularly paid their rent.[149] This ruling was of particular importance since most European merchants rented accommodation in a *han*, a building not dissimilar to the *fondacos* of Venice. Throughout the larger cities of the Ottoman Empire, these structures generally belonged to pious foundations which turned them over to the highest bidder, often for a period of three years. Whoever was awarded the contract then paid a fixed amount of money to the foundation chest, and could keep whatever profit he made beyond the stipulated sum. Under these circumstances, the contractor might feel tempted to evict tenants whenever he could find someone else willing to pay a higher rent. Such a course of action might have been made attractive by the fact that the current tenant had made certain improvements to the fabric of the building. It was with this situation in mind that a rescript issued by Sultan Mehmet III (1595–1603), and confirmed in 1618–19, determined that evictions of this sort were illegal, and that the old procedures should be respected.[150] No particular conclusions can be drawn from the fact that confirmation of this rescript was requested and granted in the early seventeenth century rather than at any other time, for confirmations of this type were often purely a matter of routine. On the other hand, the original date of issue during the very last years of the sixteenth century indicates the commercial prosperity of Aleppo during this particular period, which is already known to us from other sources.

Equally important was the ruling that court cases arising from commercial dealings between local merchants and Venetians were to be heard only if the original transaction had been recorded in the *kadı*'s register (*sicill*), and the latter official had issued a special document stating the facts of the case (*hüccet*).[151] This privilege was not unique, for, apart from the Venetians in Aleppo, the merchants of Dubrovnik from at least the fifteenth century onward were the beneficiaries of a similar ruling.[152] In this fashion, the dependence upon witness, which characterizes Islamic law, was lessened and problems arising from the principle held by Muslim legists, that on most issues a non-Muslim might not testify against a Muslim, could be minimized.[153] For if the *kadı* had issued a written document, the only witnesses needed would be those that could testify to the authenticity of the *hüccet*; and with respect to a document made out in the *kadı*'s court, Muslim witnesses would generally not be lacking.

Another rescript codifying the application of Muslim religious law with respect to the Venetians deals with the problem of stolen goods. In the introduction the rescript refers to the fact that Venetian ships carrying their wares to the Ottoman Empire were sometimes attacked by Christian pirates and the merchandise robbed. Later, the stolen goods were turned over to certain non-Muslim traders in Aleppo. The Ottoman government decreed that Venetians in such situations should be permitted to claim the return of goods bearing the Venetian mark, even if subsequent owners asserted that they had purchased these wares in good faith.[154] As an additional guarantee, the decree provided that disputes concerning the recovery of Venetian goods robbed by pirates could be settled only in İstanbul.[155] Though the document had originally been issued on behalf of Sultan Kanuni Süleyman (1520–66), it must have been very timely throughout the piracy-ridden years of the later sixteenth and early seventeenth centuries.

The Venetian consul in Aleppo

A separate set of regulations dealt with the status of the Venetian consul, or in Ottoman terminology the *baylos* of Aleppo. Certain rescripts reminded local authorities of the honourable (*vacibürreayet*) status of the consul as a Venetian noble, and stressed his right, laid down in the *ahidname*, to decide disputes among Venetians. Other documents deal with the privilege of the consul to appoint janissaries of his own choice as guardsmen (*yasakçı*), and with the remuneration these men were to receive.[156] This latter issue was often rather a thorny matter, in which Venetian representatives in other cities of the Ottoman Empire also requested help from the central administration. In addition, the right of the consul to travel to İskenderun and Tripolis (Syria), or else to visit Jerusalem was expressly placed on record.[157]

Curiously enough, a considerable number of rescripts were concerned with the food supply of the Venetian consulate in Aleppo. Apart from the fact that the consul could receive a certain amount of wine without paying taxes, this official, with the blessing of the Ottoman authorities, seems to have secured supplies for the Venetian community in general. Thus we hear that the consul ordered beef and sold it to resident Venetians at a price determined by himself, the market supervisor having no say in the matter.[158] Equally the consul might provide for bakers and tailors to serve the Venetian community; the men he hired for these jobs were to be excused certain services to the Ottoman state.[159] Thus it almost appears as if the Ottoman authorities saw the Venetians residing in Aleppo as forming part of the consul's household; and the fact that the entire colony was concentrated in two commercial buildings (*han*) probably did much to strengthen this view.

Privileges interpreted: the 'little *ahidnames* of Aleppo'

Most of the matters treated in the present study, and many others as well, were first decided in individual rescripts issued by various sultans, and confirmed by their successors when they acceded to the throne. However, for the sake of convenience the most important rulings, which generally had first been codified in the reign of Sultan Süleyman I (1520–66), were summarized in four documents,[160] addressed not to the governors and *kadıs* of Aleppo, but 'to whomever it may concern'.

These documents generally contain very little that might be regarded as an introduction or conclusion; under these circumstances, nothing can be said about their genesis. But minus the diplomatic formalities of oaths and invocations, these texts might almost be regarded as the 'privileges granted to the Venetian community in Aleppo'. At the same time, this set of documents provides clues to the actual application of the *ahidname*, to the manner in which the Ottoman authorities viewed the Venetian merchants trading in Aleppo, and, of course, to the matters which the *bailo* considered as particularly important for the continuation of Venetian trade in this city.

Moreover, it is obvious that N. Steensgaard has sensed the right thing when he supposes that there must have been other legal texts, apart from the *ahidname*, which determined the status of foreign merchants in the Ottoman Empire.[161] The principal legal base was Muslim religious law (*şeriat*), but almost equally important were the rescripts issued by various sultans, either in response to queries from provincial administrators, or else to complaints from the Venetians themselves. The 'little *ahidnames* of Aleppo' must be taken as a digest which conveniently summarized current Ottoman administrative practice.

Conclusion

In the present study, we have attempted to answer a concrete question, namely why certain articles forming part of the privileges granted to the Venetians, or as a matter of fact to other foreign traders, were notoriously difficult to enforce. Examining this problem, we have been able to make a number of observations concerning the functioning of the Ottoman state in the late sixteenth and early seventeenth centuries. For the purpose of argument, we have eliminated the traditional explanation that the Ottoman central government was often not in a position to impose its will upon the provincial administrators it employed. Not that this assumption is completely invalid; in fact, for the eighteenth century it appears a fairly realistic proposition. But the weakness of the Ottoman central government under the sultans of the late sixteenth and early seventeenth centuries should not be exaggerated. The present study has attempted to show that one can understand the behaviour of Ottoman provincial authorities without forever referring to the time-honoured explanation of 'Ottoman decline'.

It has been noted that the Ottoman central authorities frequently cited the *ahidname* even where it had no direct bearing on the case which they had been called upon to judge. This shows that, in spite of the problems arising from its application, the *ahidname* was by no means an empty piece of paper, but was in fact regarded by the Ottoman government as the document which regulated the Venetian presence in the territories governed by the sultan. At the same time, both the *ahidname* and the sultan's government were primarily concerned with inter-state relations. Thus commercial problems were left to local authorities, to regulate within the general framework of Ottoman procedure; the latter, of course, did not exclude the *ahidname*. It is in this sense that the existence of the 'little *ahidname*s of Aleppo', which in their tenor are very different from the general Venetian *ahidname*, should be interpreted.

Even though they rarely referred to the fact, Venetian merchants benefited from the positive attitude which the Ottoman administration generally took toward trade and traders. At least in Aleppo, the Venetians enjoyed privileges commonly accorded Ottoman wholesalers, that is, an exemption from the obligation to sell at officially fixed prices. Since, at the same time, foreign merchants were not required to pay most of the taxes demanded from Ottoman subjects, the Venetians' position relative to that of local traders was not bad, even if, on the negative side, one takes *avania*s and forced loans into account. Moreover, as the exportation of Syrian and Anatolian cotton was no loger prohibited from the early seventeenth century onward, a new and potentially lucrative branch of commerce was opened up. Certainly the English and Dutch profited more from these opportunities than did the Venetians. But, as far as the Ottoman central administration was concerned, during the later sixteenth and early seventeenth centuries merchants from Venice were given considerable encouragement.

On the other hand, provisions of the *ahidname* proved difficult to apply when they contradicted well-established Ottoman usage, particularly usage based upon Muslim religious law. In the same fashion, the notion of a long-lasting peace and quasi-alliance with the once formidable enemy Venice should have appeared unacceptable to people who viewed the Ottoman Empire as a state constantly expanding into new territories by means of Holy War. What is more, the proponents of the 'peace policies' at the Ottoman centre had assimilated the same traditions as their recalcitrant subordinates. Thus it is very probable that the behaviour of the fortress commanders of Avlonya or Limassol aroused a certain amount of sympathy in the authors of the very rescripts sent out to admonish them. The notoriously lenient behaviour of many Venetian naval commanders toward Catholic pirates posing as crusaders might constitute a parallel in this respect.[162]

Thus two separate but compatible explanations are being offered for the behaviour of Ottoman provincial authorities *vis-à-vis* Venetian and other foreign merchants. One of them is concerned with what might be called the ideological legitimation of the Ottoman state. The other is based upon the hypothesis that, in spite of its well-known centralization, the Ottoman state organized itself on various levels, which were allowed a degree of autonomy in their day-to-day functioning. Particularly relations with foreign merchants, as a necessary but not very prestigious administrative task, were to a certain extent left to the initiative of tax-farmers and temporary officials. Thus the Ottoman administration could minimize its own contact with foreign merchants, and, to a degree, afford to ignore the arrangements into which the latter might enter with local administrators.

Whatever privileges the Ottoman central authorities might have been willing to grant in their negotiations with European diplomatic representatives, application of the *ahidnames* took place only to the extent to which these privileges could be fitted into what the Ottoman bureaucracy regarded as 'proper procedure'. Ottoman officialdom may not have obeyed all the orders it received from above, but it followed intelligible principles in what it accepted and what it rejected. In this sense, one might even claim that the very limitations upon the applicability of the *ahidnames* document the cohesion, and not the decline, of a flexible and long-lasting state mechanism.

16 A study of the feasibility of using eighteenth-century Ottoman financial records as an indicator of economic activity

MEHMET GENÇ

I

Among the major questions facing Ottoman economic historians, particularly those working on recent centuries, we can include the following: what were the major effects on Ottoman economy of the series of rapid changes in eighteenth-century Western Europe that culminated in the Industrial Revolution? Was there, in fact, as has been assumed, a growth in the volume of Ottoman foreign trade, varying in rate according to region and sector beginning in the eighteenth century, and, if so, what were its dimensions and significance? In Western Europe, the expansion of foreign trade is generally accepted to a have been an important motor force in the series of complex and interrelated changes in all sectors of the economy that resulted in the Industrial Revolution. Did such an expansion have similar stimulating effects on the Ottoman economy? That is, was it accompanied by an increase in industrial production and in the volume of domestic trade, or, on the contrary, did it bring about a decline in these activities?

Obviously, to answer these and similar questions, we need, first, a series of homogeneous quantitative data that lends itself to aggregation. However, up to now there has been little attempt in Ottoman economic history at such quantification. This gap in research has been abetted by the lack of quantitative data and, one supposes, vice versa. Certainly, we cannot hope to find for the Ottoman Empire – or for any other pre-industrial society – series of homogeneous statistical information ready for immediate use according to the requirements of modern scientific research. Although the Ottoman archives contain an enormous wealth of historical information, this wealth does not always facilitate quantitative research. The most important, and often the only, documents which can be used for statistical purposes consist of figures recorded in transactions incurred to meet the financial needs of the state. Even though the accuracy of these figures, the majority of which are related to taxes, may be questioned; still, because they are more or less the products of a conventional procedure and not fabricated to prove a point, I have assumed that they would not be false or deliberately contrived, and therefore that it would be worthwhile to make a study of the feasibility of using them as quantitative material for research in Ottoman economic history. Hence, first, I will try to explore whether there is, in fact, a relationship between the figures collected and used by the Ottoman financial authorities for tax purposes and the real volume of economic activity. If not, can such a relationship be constructed? To what extent is this possible and what would be the degree of error involved. Finally, what economic phenomena might be revealed by a relationship constructed in this way?

II

Most taxes in the Ottoman Empire which might be related to real volumes of economic activity are those which in fiscal literature would be called indirect taxes. Ideally, if taxation was costless, if there was no corruption or smuggling and if tax rates were clear and consistent, tax-collection figures could be used as an exact measure of the value of the resources taxed. This is, however, an ideal situation that no fiscal administration, either in the past or in the present day, can claim to have realized. The exact opposite would be a situation where tax returns have no relationship whatsoever to the real volume of economic activity. This also, by the nature of things, is a hypothetical situation. Generally, historical 'reality' lies somewhere in between these two extremes, exactly where depending on the period in history, the level of economic development and the effectiveness of financial administration. Yet, to my astonishment, I found that the eighteenth-century Ottoman data conform very closely to the second ideal situation described above; tax figures are almost totally unrelated to the real volume of economic activity.

Indeed, throughout the eighteenth century, tax returns in many sectors of the economy that should have shown major changes varied less than 1 per cent over periods as long as forty or fifty years, and frequently did not vary at all. For instance, Svoronos has shown that between 1720 and 1770 the volume of trade passing through the port of Salonica increased by 400 per cent.[1] By contrast, in the same period customs revenues from this port increased only by something around 0.5 per cent. Various sources indicate that the port of İzmir developed considerably in the eighteenth century. Yet between 1750 and 1800 the revenues delivered to the Treasury from the *kantar* tax on goods entering and leaving İzmir remained constant at 4,400 *kuruş*es. Similarly, the customs revenues from Kavala, an important port in the northern Aegean, remained steady at 5,170 *kuruş*es for the forty-six years between 1748 and 1793. Hence, the constancy of these tax revenues from so many sectors could not simply mean that the volume of activity in these sectors had also remained steady for so long. Even if we assume that the tax-farmers (*mültezim*) had concealed any increases in revenues, how can we explain the cases in which revenues declined? To suppose that no decline ever took place, and that everything simply continued as if time did not exist is simply not possible. Of course, Ottoman society was traditional and change of all sorts was perhaps minimal, but even so, in any economy where the agricultural sector was dominant, there must have been short-term cyclical movements. As my research progressed, I saw that no matter how much the actual tax revenues collected from any economic activity may have increased in time, the amount of revenues handed over to the Treasury did not change. Since one of these two values stayed fixed and the other was varied, no definite or meaningful relationship between the two could be established. Finally, in the course of my inquiry as to why there was such a difference between the real value of tax revenues and the amount that entered the Treasury, and, even more importantly, why there was no relationship between these values, as well as the question of why there was no competition between tax-farmers, I confronted an important characteristic of the tax-farming system. From the end of the seventeenth century on, taxes – in particular a large portion of the indirect taxes which ought to be meaningful for establishing trends in economic history – were being farmed out not for a year or any specified length of time, but for a lifetime (*kayd-ı hayat*), a practice containing features which would help to explain the immobility of the figures mentioned above.

III

This new system, called *malikane* by the Ottomans, was a special version of the *iltizam* system, one with the longest possible term.[2] As with the *iltizam* system the taxes were still sold by auction, but with this difference: in the normal *iltizam* system, it was the amount of tax revenues owed to the Treasury every year that was fixed by auction. In this new system, the yearly amount was determined by the Treasury and there was no question of its being lowered or raised by auction. Now what was decided by auction was the amount that had to be paid by individual bidders to gain the right to life-term possession of the tax-farm.

This sum, called *muaccele* in the Ottoman fiscal sources, was a form of capitalization that corresponded to the present value of the financial benefits that the buyer would acquire by having lifetime rights to the tax-farm that was being auctioned. This figure was not arrived at through complex capitalization and discount calculations. The questions the potential purchasers were in a position to answer were fairly simple: what was the annual revenue yielded by the *mukataa* (or the tax-farm)? What portion of this revenue had to be paid to the Treasury? How much would the remaining net surplus be? The potential purchasers had the means to answer these questions fairly correctly, and the financial authorities were prepared to help them in every way. As will be made clear below, it was to the benefit not only of the purchasers but also of the Treasury that the purchasers be furnished with the most reliable information. The stability of the annual payments to the Treasury – which at first seemed so puzzling to me – actually served the important purpose of increasing the purchaser's ability to predict his future expenses.

The amount of the *muaccele*, paid in return for lifetime rights to the yearly net profit brought by the *mukataa*, was determined by the competition between the buyers, with the proviso that it would not sink below a limit set by the Treasury and usually amounting to a figure corresponding to two to eight times the annual net profit. All bids were recorded in a register open to the public which was kept by a department of the *defterdarlık* (Treasury). Bidding remained open for a long enough time for prospective buyers to acquire all relevant information. Sale was made to the highest bidder. The purchaser, who deposited the sale price, *muaccele*, in the Treasury, was given a *berat* (certificate) clearly outlining his rights and responsibilities as a *malikane* owner. Within the limits determined by law and described in the *berat*, he could manage the *mukataa* as he pleased. He could, if he desired, sell it to another. No government official other than the *kadı* (judge) had the right to control or to interfere with the activities of the *malikane* owner.

The system had certain attractions for the purchasers. In practice, under the *iltizam* system it was difficult for the same man to hold a *mukataa* for a long period of time. At any time someone else could come along with a higher bid and take the *iltizam* away from him. The new system thus offered greater security and stability than the old. The *malikane* owner knew that, without any further financial sacrifice, the *mukataa* was his, should he desire it, till the end of his life. His future revenues were not subject to any external risks, except for those inherent in the *mukataa* itself. Any measures which he took to develop the tax source and increase its productivity would lower the inherent risks and increase his profits. Through this mechanism, the new system worked in favour not only of the *malikane* owner but also of the entire economy and therefore of state finances. This was what legitimized the new system in the eyes of the Ottoman fiscal authorities.

At the end of the seventeenth century when the *malikane* system was estabished, however, there were other factors leading the state in the direction of this practice. Long years of warfare had brought the budget deficit to a point at which a balanced budget was inconceivable. While expenses were increasing rapidly, revenues were not merely failing to keep pace, but, partly because of the wars, and partly because of the widespread and long-term depression faced by the Empire in the seventeenth century, they were actually declining. In this situation, we can consider the above-mentioned change in the *iltizam* system *as a form of internal borrowing* by the state from the *mültezim* group, as if the state were capitalizing on the possible future profits of this group in advance and in the name of specified individuals. The only important risk the state faced was the possibility that the tax source might develop in the future in such a way as to bring in a higher amount of revenue than expected at the time of sale. In 1695, when the system was first applied, the Empire was in the midst of a twelve-year-long war and was more worried about financing immediate payments than about future losses of revenue. Moreover, it did not seem necessary to make provisions for an increase in revenues, given the psychological atmosphere created by the economic stagnation which had prevailed for so long. In any case, losses to the state owing to an increase in revenues were limited to the lifetime of the *malikane* owner, since when the owner died the *malikane* was once again going to be sold by auction. If in the meantime the yearly profit had increased, the new *muaccele* amount was going to increase proportionally. In this way the state could partially compensate for its losses through increases in the *muaccele* revenues at periods corresponding to the average lifetime of the *malikane* owners. In addition, it could save the tax source from the destructive effects of a yearly or frequent change in *mültezims*. The losses it might endure were a small price to pay for this.

IV

Given these conditions, what was most important for the fiscal authorities was the maximization of these periodic *muaccele* amounts. The starting minimum value of the *muaccele* was determined by the Treasury, depending on market conditions, at two to eight times the annual profit that would accrue to the purchaser. Maximization of the *muaccele* revenues thus determined was possible only by creating conditions conducive to competition among the potential buyers.

The body of potential buyers, the great majority of whom were soldiers, bureaucrats or men of religion belonging to the middle or upper levels of the *askeri* class, seems to have stayed constant in number at around one thousand throughout the eighteenth century. Ostensibly, the structure of the *askeri* class would appear to have presented an obstacle to the maintenance of free market conditions. In fact, this class was not a monolithic, undifferentiated whole, but consisted of a number of quasi-independent sub-groups made up of palace members, the Porte, the bureaucracy, the *ulema* (religious scholars) and, in the strict sense of the word, soldiers. It therefore had the potential to sustain conditions of competition. Furthermore, the central state, pressed by urgent needs to maximize the *muaccele* revenues, used its authority to ensure that competitive conditions were maintained and improved upon. Finally, whatever the particular conditions of the *mukataa* up for sale may have been, the fact that bidding revolved around relatively homogeneous 'fixed annual cash revenues' was a factor that definitely facilitated the continuation of a secure competitive environment.

It seems a reasonable assumption that there would be a fixed relationship between the annual profit accruing to the purchaser of a *malikane* and the sum, the *muaccele*, that he paid for this; and that for all *mukataas* sold by auction in the same market in the same period of time, this relationship would express itself in a

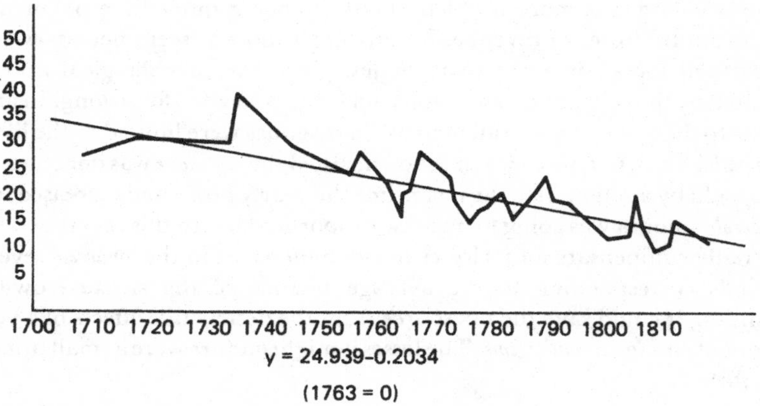

Fig. 16.1 Profit-rate trend – return on *muaccele* investments

series of proportions that would all fluctuate around the same mean. Hypothesizing that this proportion would change only as a function of time under the influence of certain factors, I made a study of 150–200 cases. From these, taken from the 120 year period between 1700 and 1820, a fairly clear trend emerged for the profit rate on the İstanbul market, where over 90 per cent of the *malikanes* were concentrated. This trend (shown in Figure 16.1) reveals the rate of return to investments in the İstanbul *malikane* market during the eighteenth century.[3]

The importance of this profit-rate trend, valid for all *malikanes* sold on the İstanbul market, is that, if we know the sale price of a particular *mukataa*, it allows us to determine the approximate amount of annual profit that the *mukataa* would bring to the purchaser at the year of purchase.

There are regular records in the Ottoman archives of the *muaccele* amounts paid at various times for *mukataas* sold as *malikanes*. Therefore, using the current profit rate trend as a key, and applying it to a time series of the *muacceles* of each *mukataa*, one can easily obtain a series revealing the annual profit accruing to the owners of each *mukataa*. If we take the owner's net profit and add to it the amount of tax that had to be delivered to the Treasury annually, which amount was also uniformly recorded in the Ottoman documents, we then obtain the gross annual income accruing to the *malikane* owner from his *mukataa*. This gross income and the figures used to obtain it are shown in detail in the Appendix (pp. 360–73) in tables relating to twenty-one *malikanes* I have chosen as typical. (The unit of account in these is an Ottoman *kuruş*, equal to 120 *akçes*.) We shall discuss below how and to what extent this gross income reflects, taking the tax rates into consideration, the volume of relevant real economic activity.

In these tables, column (a) shows the *muaccele* amount, column (b) shows the profit rate from Figure 16.1 corresponding to the year of this *muaccele*, and column (c) shows the product of (a) and (b), which is the probable profit of the *malikane* owner. Column (d) shows the amount owed annually to the Treasury. Column (e) shows the sum of (c) and (d), which corresponds to the gross income of the *malikane* owner. The last column is an index of the figures in column (e).

If we assume that the tax rates do not change or if, determining the degree of change, we can make adjustments accordingly, then we can be more or less certain that the figures in column (e) will reflect the changes in the volume of real economic activity related to the *mukataa*. I should add immediately that I do not mean that there will be an exact equivalence but rather that there will be a correlation or parallelism. Let me clarify this with an example.

Consider Table 16.1 containing data on the revenues on the export tax levied on cotton and cotton thread exported from the Empire. Between the years 1734 and 1791 this tax was levied at a constant rate of 1 *akçe* per *okka* of raw cotton and 2 *akçe* per *okka* of cotton thread. We have no way of knowing what the relative proportions of cotton and cotton thread exported were. If we assume that cotton and cotton thread were exported in equal proportions, then, for example, the 22,951 *kuruş*, gross revenue in 1750 from column (e) corresponds to an export volume of 2,008,590 *okkas*, and the 67,488 *kuruş*, gross revenue from 1787 corresponds to a volume of 6,073,920 *okkas*. Was this in fact the amount exported? The answer is, of course, no. I can say with a fair degree of confidence, however, that although I do not know the exact amounts exported, whatever the amount was in 1750, in 1787 it had increased by 200 per cent.[4] This is the first important result that can be obtained from knowledge of the gross tax revenues of the *malikane* owner. We cannot use these figures to determine the absolute volume of economic activity. In order to do that, we would need several other pieces of information that we do not have. It is appropriate to discuss these here because they affect not only our ability to determine the absolute level of activity but also the reliability of our estimations of the above-mentioned fluctuations.

The figures in the (e) columns of the appended tables are approximate estimations of what the *malikane* owners received, or rather what, according to my assumptions and calculations, they should have received. In order to calculate the *potential total gross* tax revenues, from which one could ideally derive the real volume of activity, the most important addition one would have to make to these figures is that of the cost of taxation.

Taxation costs undoubtedly varied according to the type of tax levied. Therefore, to find a figure which one could use in deriving the real volume of economic activity, one would have to make separate calculations for every *mukataa*. This would have been a difficult and risky operation, so I have not attempted it in my analysis. However, in the course of my research I derived the following impression: in the eighteenth century, taxation costs for most of the indirect taxes which might be used in attempts to estimate the volume of economic activity, such as customs duties, transit and market duties (*bac*), stamp duties (*damga*) and *ihtisab* (commercial transactions) duties, were confined to within 5 to 15 per cent of the total revenues. Of course one must assume that if the tax rates remained constant, when the general price-level rose, as it did in the second half of the eighteenth century, then the relative importance of the taxation costs within the tax yield would also have tended to increase.

The second factor to be considered is smuggling, the effects of which, by definition, cannot be empirically measured. The rate of smuggling changes as a function of the subjective weight of the tax burden, of the actual efficiency of the fiscal organization and of the nature of the deterrents applied. This is a complex and fluid phenomenon which can only be quantified through indirect and aggregate calculations that are simply not possible at this point in the study of Ottoman economic history. For the moment all we can say is that Ottoman tax rates, especially those in consideration here and those like them, were in general very low; moreover, some of them remained constant *de jure*, while a good many others remained so *de facto*. Therefore, as the price-level rose, the relative weight of the taxes declined. In the period from 1734 to 1792, for example, the customs rate on cotton exports remained 1 *akçe* per *okka*. In 1734 when the price of cotton was 22 *akçe* per *okka*[5] the tax rate amounted to close to 5 per cent. In the 1780s, when the price of cotton had risen to 122–140 *akçe*s per *okka*, the tax rate amounted to only 0.7–0.8 per cent. This situation, common to most of the taxes shown in the appended tables, should have reduced the tendency towards smuggling during the course of the eighteenth century by making it less profitable. It is worth noting that this downward trend would have the effect of compensating for probable increases in the cost of taxation.

Finally, a third and equally important factor is that *malikane* owners usually did not administer their *mukataa*s themselves; they farmed them out instead. Therefore some portion of the tax revenue must have been reserved as the income of the tax-farmer (*mültezim*). Hence, to arrive at the real value of the tax revenue we must add an amount corresponding to the *mültezim*'s income to the gross revenues of the *malikane* owner as shown in column (e). It is difficult to estimate what proportion of the revenue might have been set aside as income for the *mültezim*, but we can assume that the proportion remained relatively stable and did not fluctuate widely. If this proportion exceeded reasonable limits, then the *malikane* owner, rather than farming out the *mukataa*, was likely to collect the taxes himself or to appoint someone close to him for this purpose. Having invested a sizeable sum (perhaps borrowed) under competitive conditions, the *malikane* owner probably showed a limited tolerance to a decline in returns on his investment.

We can consider this general rule of thumb as valid also in the cases of taxation costs and smuggling; the *malikane* owner, seeking to maximize his revenues or at least to prevent any major decline in them, would try to minimize wide fluctuations in his share (column e) of the potential total tax revenues. It was in his power to do so to the extent that, as owner, he had been granted complete authority over the financial and economic management of the *malikane*.

What proportion of the potential total tax revenues would these three factors together comprise? An exact answer is out of the question. A very rough estimate might place 30 per cent as a low limit and 50 per cent as an upper limit. To use such doubtful and widely separated proportions in trying to arrive at the potential total tax revenues would leave us with such large margins of error as to render the whole operation meaningless. By studying the internal conditions of each *mukataa* one could perhaps minimize the margins of error. I must add, however, that the Ottoman sources do not seem to offer much promise in this respect.

V

Even if we do not know exactly the potential total tax revenues or the absolute level of the volume of economic activity, so long as the percentage of the potential revenues that the *malikane* owner received remained constant, then, I repeat, we can estimate with some certainty the changes over time in the volume of real economic activity. The accuracy of our approximations depends on the degree to which this percentage indeed remains constant, and, of course, on the validity of our other assumptions.

But how realistic is this theoretic scheme? For example, did the approximately 200 per cent increase in the export of cotton and cotton thread between 1750 and 1787 – which I estimated – actually take place? Unless the correlations I have proposed can be empirically verified, no matter how rational and consistent they may seem, they obviously will be of no operational value. It is clear that data suited for such verification are so limited as to be non-existent. Indeed, had such data been readily available, all these calculations and assumptions would have been redundant. Nevertheless, it is still possible to attempt a partial verification based on some existing fragmentary data. Robert Paris has provided us with data on exports of cotton and cotton thread to France, the biggest buyer from the Empire in the eighteenth century.[6] This data, given in Table 16.1a, at least makes possible a meaningful comparison. In order to facilitate the comparison of the figures in Tables 16.1 and 16.1a, these tables are followed by a graph of their indexes (Figure 16.2). The graph makes it clear that there was at least a partial parallelism between 1740 and 1760. In the period 1760–70 a widening gap appears between the two curves. If it were possible to show that the relative importance of France in Ottoman cotton and cotton-thread exports declined at a rate that corresponded to the growth of this gap, then our verification would be complete. Unfortunately we do not have the quantitative data that would allow us to demonstrate this.

We do, however, have some information, partly quantitative partly qualitative, that can be added. Ottoman cotton exports to England in 1750, valued at 598,605 pounds sterling, were 10 per cent of exports to France.[7] In 1775 this figure had risen by more than 250 per cent to 2,175,132 pounds sterling. It now was equivalent to approximately 20 per cent of the exports to France. Furthermore, although we do not have any reliable figures, there are numerous indications that there was a significant increase in the export of cotton and cotton thread overland to Central Europe in the second half of the eighteenth century. Another piece of information serves to corroborate the increase shown by these mainly qualitative sources. Until 1770 the export tax on cotton and cotton thread was taken only on goods shipped by sea. After this period, tax was also levied on shipments made overland. As a result, as can be seen in column (d) of Table 16.1, the annual payment to the Treasury increased from 5,600 *kuruş* to 13,758 *kuruş*. The only way it seems possible to explain this increase in tax revenues – a phenomenon rarely encountered in the *malikane* system – is by a significant increase in the volume of activity being taxed. Were it possible to quantify this additional information and add it to that included in the graph, the two curves might have been brought closer together. Unfortunately we are not in a position to do this.

Another example offers a better possibility for comparison. This example, from the customs farm at Salonica, is not only more complete but it also reveals a more obvious correlation. Table 16.2 contains data on the customs *mukataa* at Salonica; in Table 16.2a are the values in *kuruş* given by Svoronos for the total imports and exports from that port.[8] Figure 16.3 includes the indexes of these two series of figures. Svornos' data are averages over very long periods and the exact degree of their correlation with the data in our tables has not been estimated; even so, a high degree of correlation is quite obvious.

These examples allow us to believe that our figures, although they may contain as much as a 40 per cent margin of error in relation to the absolute level of the volume of real activity, give us a much closer approximation of reality when used to indicate relative changes over time in the volume of any particular activity.

VI

I have described as small the probability of error involved in estimating changes over time in the volume of activity of various sectors of the economy. This probability cannot easily be described by an exact mathematical proportion. It is a function of changes in the *malikane* owners' relative share (e) of the potential total gross tax revenues (p). So long as this proportion (e/p) does not change, the probability of error will remain low. But if e/p changes over time, then the probability of error will change at the same rate and in the same direction. In other words, if e/p increases, then our estimations will tend to show the increase in the level of activity of expanding *mukataa*s as greater than it really was and the decrease in contracting *mukataa*s as less than it really was. On the other hand, if e/p decreases, then our estimations will tend to show as less than it really was the increase in the level of activity of *mukataa*s that were expanding and as greater than it really was the level of decrease in *mukataa*s that were contracting. In both cases, the probability of error would be the same in absolute terms as the rate of change in e/p.

The nature of this probability of error is such that, in addition to allowing us to compare changes over time in the activity of any sector of the economy as reflected in the activity of a single *mukataa*, it also, more importantly, allows us to compare changes over time in the activities of any two separate *mukataas*. In the latter case our probable margin of error will be much less than it is in the former. If we look at the relative degree of change over time of two *mukataas*, one of which (a) represents expanding activity, and the other (b) represents contracting activity, whatever the degree of error may be in our original estimations, there will be virtually no error in our calculations of the degree of relative change between them. The following table, showing the hypothetical effects of an increase or a decrease in e/p, seeks to clarify these perhaps confusing statements.

I *Expanding* mukataa *(a)*

Year	e	Change in e (%)	p	Change in p (%)	e/p (%)	Change in e/p (%)
1 First case – increasing e/p						
1750	100		200		50	
1800	180	+80	300	+50	60	+20
2 Second case – decreasing e/p						
1750	100		200		50	
1800	120	+20	300	+50	40	−20

II *Contracting* mukataa *(b)*

1 First case – increasing e/p						
1750	100		200		50	
1800	90	−10	150	−25	60	+20
2 Second case – decreasing e/p						
1750	100		200		50	
1800	60	−40	150	−25	40	−20

In *mukataa* (a) the actual increase in activity is 50 per cent. However, based on an increasing (e), our estimations would have shown a rise of 80 per cent. Similarly in (b), where the actual decrease was 25 per cent, our estimations would have shown it as 10 per cent. The degree of error in our estimations can obviously be linked to changes in the e/p ratio. On the other hand, when we take the relative degree of change over time between two different *mukataas*, then the change in this e/p ratio no longer has any effect.

In *mukataa* (a) the actual expansion, from 200 to 300, is 50 per cent; while in

(b) the actual decrease, from 200 to 150, is 25 per cent. Thus the change in the revenue of these two *mukataas*, both of which started out at the same level, is such that one now registers twice the activity of the other. Our estimates in column (e) reflect exactly this same proportion of change. *Mukataa* (a) has risen by 80 per cent from 100 to 180 and *mukataa* (b) has declined by 10 per cent from 100 to 90. Our estimations of the degree of change in each *mukataa* were not correct. But even so, using these unreliable estimates, the results we got for the degree of relative change between them, namely that (a) had grown to twice the size of (b), are the same that we would have acquired if we had been able to use the correct figures.

It should be clear that the above argument is based on an important assumption. This assumption is that e/p will change in the same direction and at the same rate for every two *mukataas* being compared. Within what limits is this assumption reasonable?

There are a number of factors influencing the share (e) that the *malikane* owner (or owners) will receive of the total tax revenue (p). As we stated previously, (p) contains a number of factors that we cannot hope to quantify. If we leave aside smuggling and taxation costs, the compensatory effects of which will cancel each other out, then the determining factor will be the income of the *mültezims*.

The *malikane* owners, the great majority of whom lived in İstanbul, numbered about a thousand, and, as bureaucrats, soldiers and *ulema*, were almost identical with the central authority. Living in general at a great distance from the actual location of the *mukataa*, they were in effect a *rentier* class that had little to do with the actual collection of taxes. The *mültezims*, on the other hand, lived mostly in the provinces where the *mukataa* was located or in some nearby provincial centre. They were what were called in Ottoman sources *ayan ve eşraf*.[9]

The way the total tax revenue was divided between the *mültezims* and the *malikane* owners was no doubt decided separately for each *mukataa* as a result of bargaining between individuals. In a collective sense, the outcome of this bargaining was determined by the relative bargaining strength of the two groups, both of which represented different interests and different kinds of solidarity. The *malikane* owners were almost a part of the central authority: they had similar interests, a high degree of solidarity and inter-communication. They were a highly integrated social group that could act in unison. The *mültezim ayans* were people with influence in local social relations who could use their knowledge of the region to advantage in matters connected with tax-collecting, for instance, in employing suitable and inexpensive personnel. It is unlikely that the struggle between these two groups to determine the way in which the tax revenues were divided had results which varied widely for each *mukataa*. It is more reasonable to assume that the revenues of all *mukataas* were divided between the two groups in the same proportions, which varied according to the balance of the bargaining powers of the two groups. I think we can assume, just as we did for the profit rate, that, in the majority of cases, the proportion e/p tended to change in the same direction and at the same rate for all *mukataas*.

There is one more important point we should make here. In the hypothetical table on p. 355 above, I assigned, for purposes of clarity, unrealistically exaggerated values to the relative changes in e/p. The proportion of the total gross revenue of a *mukataa* accruing to a *malikane* owner might well have been, for example, 50 per cent. A change of 10 per cent in this proportion, that is a decrease to 40 per cent or a rise to 60 per cent, is more than could have been normal. The 20 per cent gap between these two extremes corresponds more or less to the amount of revenue obtained from *mukataas* included in the state budget in the second half of the eighteenth century. It is difficult to conceive that a sum of this magnitude, which was to be divided between a thousand *malikane* owners and an approximately even number of *mültezims*, could have been transferred collectively from one group to the other without causing serious social upheaval.[10] From this point of view we would be better off accepting that the change in e/p, to which for the sake of convenience we assigned a value of 10 per cent upwards or downwards in the hypothetical table, would be more likely to fluctuate around 5 per cent. This would mean a lower limit of 45 per cent and an upper limit of 55 per cent. In this case, our probable degree of error both in estimating the changes in a *mukataa* and in estimating the relative degree of change between two separate *mukataas* drops to 10–20 per cent.

Thus we can posit that the degree of change in e/p will not be extreme and that for the majority of *mukataas* this change will be in the same direction. Of course, any two individual *mukataas* may be exceptions to this general rule and to the extent that this probability exists individual comparisons may be erroneous.[11]

This leads us to the third stage at which the *malikane* data can be used. Rather than comparing individual *mukataas*, we can group *mukataas* according to the various sectors of the economy and then compare these groups. At this stage the probable errors that we are faced with in the case of individual comparisons will tend to cancel each other out, and the probability of error will approach zero. The more *mukataas* we include, the lower will be our potential for error. It was ultimately with this in mind that I set about analysing 200 *mukataas* from the major sectors of the Ottoman economy in the eighteenth century. Tables of the data appertaining to twenty-one *mukataas*, with accompanying graphs constructed from indexes of the figures in column (e) of the tables, are presented in the Appendix to this chapter (see pp. 350–3 above for an explanation of tables and graphs). The tables have been divided into two main groups. The nine *mukataas* represented in the first eleven tables (Tables 16.1 and 16.2 are the same as Tables 16.10 and 16.11) belong to the trade sector. A sub-group of this (Tables 16.3, 16.4 and 16.5) relates to the domestic-trade sector. It is comprised of the customs taxes of the cities of Trabzon, Tokat and Varna, cities which did not have important foreign-trade connections. A second sub-group comprises the customs taxes or similar taxes of six cities to which foreign trade was very important. The twelve tables from Tables 16.12 to 16.23 relate to the stamp (*damga*) tax and other taxes belonging to the industrial sector. All but two of the twelve tables related to industry deal with various branches of the textile industry. The overwhelming importance of the textile industry in the eighteenth-century Ottoman economy should not be cause for great surprise given the textile industry's predominance in other pre-industrial societies.

Until my analysis of the 200 samples is completed, I will not attempt a comprehensive discussion of the appended tables and graphs. Rather than making generalizations about a century of an immense Empire's existence, a century which saw deep-rooted changes and a variety of convergent and divergent developments, I will confine myself here to a few short observations.

The first thing to emerge from a study of these tables and graphs is the following: in almost all the branches of the economy represented by these twenty-one *mukataa*s (the exceptions being the Varna customs and the Adana iron mines), the trend is clearly toward increased activity. Until the 1760s we do not witness a significant differentiation with respect to sectors. Perhaps one can speak of a relatively faster rate of increase in the foreign trade sector, but some branches of the industrial sector were also developing rapidly. Among these were Trabzon linen production, Danubian wool and cotton textiles, and dyeing and printing in Serez (Tables 16.23, 16.16 and 16.20). One can speak of a 100 per cent increase in production in these industries between 1730–40 and 1760–70. In the same period, with the exception of the Varna and Tokat customs, all the *mukataa*s in the trade sector show an increase of at least 100 per cent. After 1760–70, we see that, with the exception of the Serez dyeing and printing industry, which continued to grow at the same rate, the growth rate in the industrial sector began to decline. It is true that there was development in the cotton-textiles industry in Kastamonu, Ankara and Şumnu, but this was only the continuation of a process of slow development originating in the first half of the eighteenth century. In the same period there was total stagnation in the customs of Trabzon, Tokat and Varna, as well as those of Kavala, İstanbul and the Danube, which were partly dependent on domestic trade. By contrast the revenues from the cotton and cotton-thread export tax and from the customs of Salonica and İzmir, where foreign trade predominated, grew at an increasing rate. In the industrial sector a peak was reached in the 1780s and was succeeded by stagnation or decline. In none of the twelve graphs of the industrial sector was the pre-1780 peak ever reached again. The customs of the domestic trade centres of Tokat, Varna and Trabzon grew only at a low rate until the 1810–20s when, with the exception of Tokat, they were opened to international trade. By contrast the growth rate of the revenues of the *mukataa*s in the foreign-trade sector, which had been steady in the first half of the eighteenth century, accelerated tremendously in the second half of the century.

A significant pattern emerges from a comparison of the graphs dealing with foreign trade and the graphs dealing with industry: all six of the foreign-trade graphs show a continued increase after the 1790s, while all twelve of the industry graphs, with the exception of Table 16.4, data for which could not be traced after 1795, and Table 16.10, which begins to decline only after 1805, show either decline or stagnation. In sum, we can conclude that native industry in the Ottoman Empire followed a path roughly parallel to developments in foreign trade until the third quarter of the eighteenth century. After that, however, it began to move increasingly in the opposite direction. It is worthy of note that Ottoman industry started to decline, not only with respect to foreign trade but also with respect to its own past levels of production, in just those years that are generally accepted as the beginning of the Industrial Revolution in Western Europe. It would seem, then, that there is need for a revision of the generally accepted notion that it was only towards the middle of the nineteenth century that the negative impacts of the Industrial Revolution were felt on Ottoman industry.

(translated by Anthony Greenwood)

Appendix

The following tables were constructed from information found in unpublished documents in the Prime Ministerial Archives in İstanbul. These documents are listed below by name of collection and number:

I Maliyeden Müdevver:

1080	9506	9543	9923
1691	9511	9562	9957
1884	9512	9580	9976
2449	9513	9598	9983
3422	9517	9602	10009
5463	9521	9610	10066
7575	9536	9619	10238
9359	9540	9666	18577
			19201

II Kâmil Kepeci:

187	199	2380
190	200	2381
191	203	3201
192	204	5101

III Cevdet, İktisat: 1869
Cevdet, Maliye: 15397, 29227

Table 16.1 *Cotton and cotton-thread export tax (mukataa-ı resmi-i miri-i penbe ve riştе-i penbe)*

Year	*Muaccele* (*kuruş*) a	Profit rate b	Annual profit to owner c (=a×b)	Annual payment to Treasury d	Gross yearly revenue e (=c+d)	Index
1734	3,000	30.9	927	5,500	6,427	28
1747	31,800	28.2	8,967	5,500	14,467	63
1750	63,000	27.7	17,451	5,500	22,951	100
1756	72,000	28.3	18,939	5,500	24,436	106.5
1763	96,000	24.8	23,808	5,600	29,408	128.1
1771	146,000	23.2	33,872	5,600	39,472	171.9
1775	253,000	22.3	56,419	13,758	70,177	305.8
1783	236,000	20.7	48,852	13,758	62,610	272.8
1787	270,000	19.9	53,730	13,758	67,488	294.1
1790	244,320	19.3	47,154	13,758	60,912	265.4
1791	280,500	19.1	53,575	14,358	67,933	295.9

Table 16.1a *Cotton and cotton thread exported to France*

Year	Average annual export (quintals)	Index
1700–2	21,262	32
1717–21	34,551	52
1736–40	45,672	68.8
1750–4	66,403	100
1786–9	106,784	160.8

Source: Paris, *L'histoire du commerce de Marseille*, p. 511.

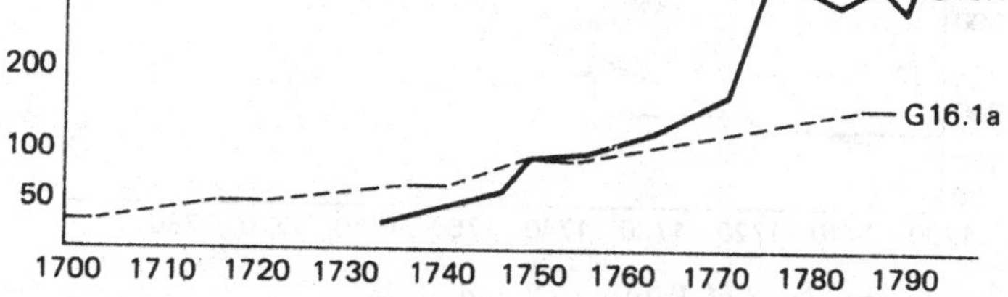

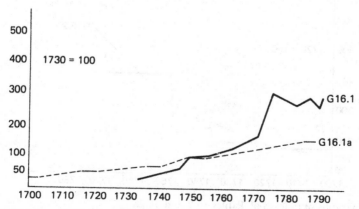

Fig. 16.2 Graphs of indexes of Tables 16.1 and 16.1a
Graph 16.1: Cotton and cotton-thread export tax
Graph 16.1a: Amount of cotton and cotton thread exported to France

Table 16.2 Mukataas *of the customs of Salonica (mukataa-ı gümrüğ-ü Selanik)*

Year	*Muaccele* (*kuruş*) a	Profit rate b	Annual profit to owner c (=a×b)	Annual payment to Treasury d	Gross yearly revenue e (=c+d)	Index
1707	3,500	36.1	1,260	16,500	17,760	71.5
1722	7,000	33.3	2,331	22,500	24,831	100
1739	66,000	29.8	19,668	22,600	42,268	170.2
1746	80,000	28.3	22,640	22,600	45,240	182.2
1774	300,000	22.7	68,100	49,000	117,100	471.6

Table 16.2a *Volume of trade at the port of Salonica*

Year	Total import and export (in *kuruş*)	Index
1700–18	900,000	81.8
1722–37	1,100,000	100
1738–43	1,600,000	145.5
1744–9	1,450,000	131.8
1750–70	3,500,000	318.2
1771–7	6,000,000	545.5
1778–87	7,500,000	681.8
1786–1800	9,500,000	863.6

Source: Svoronos, *Le commerce de Salonique*, p. 323.

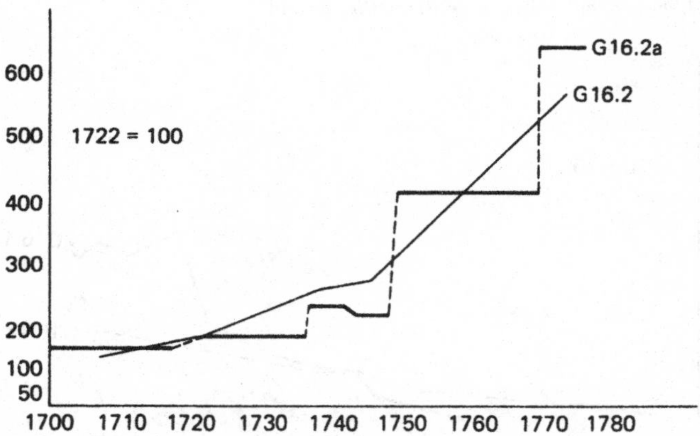

Fig. 16.3 Graphs of indexes of Tables 16.2 and 16.2a
Graph 16.2: Income of the *malikane* of the *mukataa* of the Salonica customs
Graph 16.2a: Volume of trade at the port of Salonica (in *kuruş*)
Source: Svoronos, *Le commerce de Salonique*, p. 323

Table 16.3 *Trabzon customs (mukataa-ı gümrüğ-ü iskele-i Trabzon ve tevabiha)*

Year	*Muaccele* (*kuruş*) a	Profit rate b	Annual profit to owner c (=a × b)	Annual payment to Treasury d	Gross yearly revenue e (=c+d)	Index
1722	15,500	33.3	4,995	7,775	12,770	85.2
1726	18,000	32.5	5,850	7,805	13,665	91.2
1732	22,500	31	6,975	8,000	14,975	100
1745	59,200	28.7	16,990	8,000	24,990	166.8
1766	64,000	24.3	15,552	8,000	23,552	157.3
1779					25,000	166.9
1790					30,000	200.3
1802					31,000	207
1807					17,500	116.8
1810					29,500	197

Table 16.4 *Entry customs at Tokat (mukataa-ı amediye-i Tokad)*

Year	*Muaccele* (*kuruş*) a	Profit rate b	Annual profit to owner c (=a × b)	Annual payment to Treasury d	Gross yearly revenue e (=c+d)	Index
1717	6,600	34.3	2,264	12,650	14,914	80.5
1722	8,000	33.3	2,664	12,861	15,525	83.7
1731	18,000	31.5	5,670	12,861	18,531	100
1788	60,000	19.7	11,820	12,851	24,681	133.2
1800					22,500	121.4
1813			5,318	13,420	18,738	101.1

Table 16.5 *Varna customs*

Year	*Muaccele* (*kuruş*) a	Profit rate b	Annual profit to owner c (=a × b)	Annual payment to Treasury d	Gross yearly revenue e (=c+d)	Index
1730	12,000	31.7	3,804	6,674	10,478	100
1740	12,800	29.7	3,802	6,674	10,476	100
1778	14,400	21.7	3,125	6,674	9,799	93.5
1784	21,730	20.5	4,454	7,345	11,799	112.6
1792	32,000	18.8	6,016	7,345	13,361	127.5
1811	40,000	14.9	5,960	8,345	14,305	136.5
1823	148,000	13	18,980	8,873	27,853	265.8

Table 16.6 *İstanbul* kantar *tax (mukataa-ı resm-i kantar-ı İstanbul ve tevahiba)*

Year	*Muaccele* (*kuruş*) a	Profit rate b	Annual profit to owner c (= a × b)	Annual payment to Treasury d	Gross yearly revenue e (= c + d)	Index
1741	23,500	29.5	6,932	7,000	13,932	40.4
1765	80,250	24.6	19,741	10,500	30,241	87.6
1774	126,000	22.5	28,350	10,500	38,850	112.6
1779	137,600	21.5	29,584	10,500	40,084	116.2
1784	125,120	20.5	25,650	10,500	36,050	104.5
1787	120,000	20	24,000	10,500	34,500	100
1789	124,260	19.5	24,790	10,500	35,290	102.3
1795			25,000	10,500	35,500	103
1807				13,500	62,500	181.1

Table 16.7 *Niğbolu, Rahova and Ziştovi customs*

Year	*Muaccele* (*kuruş*) a	Profit rate b	Annual profit to owner c (= a × b)	Annual payment to Treasury d	Gross yearly revenue e (= c + d)	Index
1736	3,050	30.5	930	7,462	8,392	58.1
1768	38,000	23.7	9,006	7,462	16,468	114.1
1774	28,000	22.5	6,300	7,462	13,762	95.3
1783	33,300	20.7	6,893	7,337	14,430	100
1791	34,100	18.9	6,445	7,537	13,982	96.9
1806	84,000	15.9	13,356	8,859	22,215	154

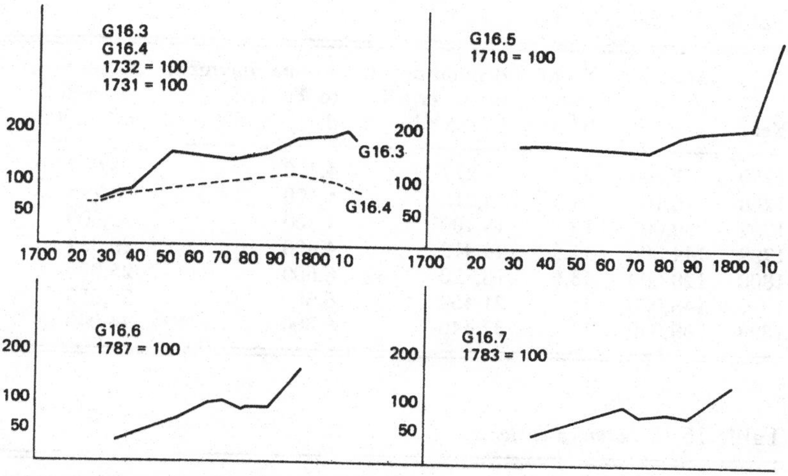

Fig. 16.4 Graphs of indexes of Tables 16.3 to 16.7
Graph 16.3: Trabzon customs
Graph 16.4: Entry customs at Tokat
Graph 16.5: Varna customs
Graph 16.6: İstanbul *kantar* tax
Graph 16.7: Niğbolu, Rahova and Ziştovi customs

Table 16.8 *Kavala customs*

Year	*Muaccele* (*kuruş*) a	Profit rate b	Annual profit to owner c (=a×b)	Annual payment to Treasury d	Gross yearly revenue e (=c+d)	Index
1734	7,030	28	1,970	5,170	7,140	54.9
1759	28,000	25.8	7,224	5,170	12,394	95.3
1766	32,120	24.4	7,837	5,170	13,007	100
1769	32,800	23.5	7,708	5,170	12,878	99
1770	34,200	23.2	7,935	5,170	13,105	100.7
1785	33,600	20.2	6,787	5,170	11,957	91.9
1793			16,800	5,170	21,970	169
1800			19,000	7,086	26,086	206.6
1808	182,860	15.6	28,526	9,100	37,626	289.4

Table 16.9 *İzmir* kantar *tax*

Year	*Muaccele* (*kuruş*) a	Profit rate b	Annual profit to owner c (=a×b)	Annual payment to Treasury d	Gross yearly revenue e (=c+d)	Index
1750	1,000	27.7	277	4,400	4,677	23.6
1768	16,100	23.7	3,815	4,400	8,215	41
1792	60,000	19	15,400	4,400	19,800	100
1799	144,000	17.3	24,912	4,400	29,312	148
1808	120,000	15.6	18,720	6,600	25,320	127.8
1812	143,000	15	21,450	6,600	28,050	141.4
1823	288,000	13	37,440	6,600	44,040	222.4

Table 16.10 *Salonica customs*

Year	*Muaccele* (*kuruş*) a	Profit rate b	Annual profit to owner c (=a×b)	Annual payment to Treasury d	Gross yearly revenue e (=c+d)	Index
1707	3,500	36.1	1,260	16,500	17,760	71.5
1722	7,000	53.3	2,331	22,500	24,831	100
1739	66,000	29.8	19,668	22,600	42,268	170.2
1746	80,000	28.3	22,640	22,600	45,240	182.2
1774	300,000	22.7	68,100	49,000	117,100	471.6

Table 16.11 *Cotton and cotton-thread export tax (mukataa-ı resm-i miri-i penbe ve riştе-i penbe)*

Year	*Muaccele* (*kuruş*) a	Profit rate b	Annual profit to owner c (=a×b)	Annual payment to Treasury d	Gross yearly revenue e (=c+d)	Index
1734	3,000	30.9	927	5,500	6,427	28
1747	31,800	28.2	8,967	5,500	14,467	63
1750	63,000	27.7	17,451	5,500	22,951	100
1756	72,000	26.3	18,936	5,500	24,436	105.5
1763	96,000	24.8	23,808	5,600	29,408	128.1
1771	146,000	23.2	33,872	5,600	39,472	171.9
1775	253,000	22.3	56,419	13,758	70,177	305.8
1783	236,000	20.7	48,852	13,758	62,610	272.8
1787	270,000	19.9	53,730	13,758	67,488	294.1
1790	244,320	19.3	47,154	13,758	60,912	265.4
1791	280,500	19.1	53,575	14,358	67,933	295.9

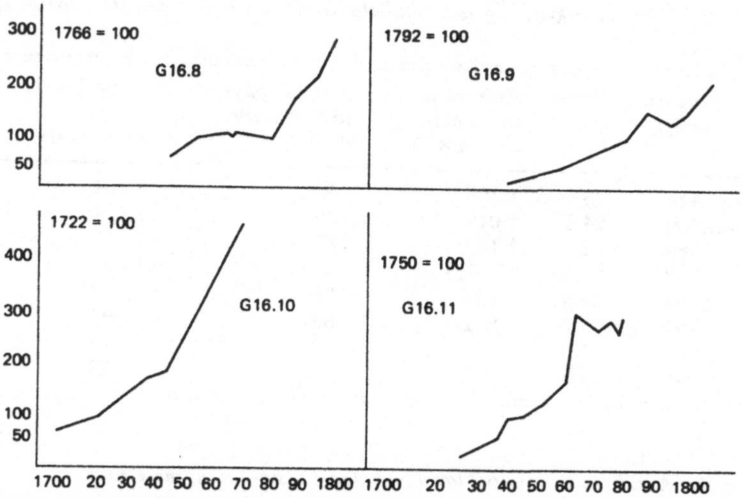

Fig. 16.5 Graphs of indexes of Tables 16.8 to 16.11
Graph 16.8: Kavala customs
Graph 16.9: İzmir *kantar* tax
Graph 16.10: Salonica customs
Graph 16.11: Cotton and cotton-thread export tax

Table 16.12 *Tax on Bursa silk-textiles press (mukataa-ı resm-i mengene-i kutni ve peşimi ve keremşud-i Bursa ve tevabiha)*

Year	*Muaccele* (*kuruş*) a	Profit rate b	Annual profit to owner c (=a×b)	Annual payment to Treasury d	Gross yearly revenue e (=c+d)	Index
1750	37,500	27.7	10,387.5	2,750	13,137.5	80.2
1757	57,750	26.2	15,130.5	2,750	17,880.5	109.2
1774	60,000	22.7	13,620	2,750	16,370	100
1776	60,000	22	13,200	2,750	15,950	94.7
1778	45,000	21.7	9,765	2,750	12,515	76.4
1782	58,000	20.8	12,064	2,750	14,814	90.5
1796				3,300	12,000	73.3
1807				4,740	10,338	63.1

Table 16.13 *Bursa silk-dyeing tax (mukataa-ı hassa-ı boyacı başılık-ı ipek-i elvan der Bursa)*

Year	*Muaccele* (*kuruş*) a	Profit rate b	Annual profit to owner c (=a×b)	Annual payment to Treasury d	Gross yearly revenue e (=c+d)	Index
1763	4,425	25	1,106	58	1,164	94.2
1766	4,300	24.4	1,049	85	1,134	91.4
1768	4,769	23.7	1,130	85	1,215	98
1769	4,908	23.5	1,153.5	85	1,238.5	100
1774	3,128	22.5	1,154	85	1,239	100
1788	4,125	19.7	812.5	85	897.5	72.3
1797	2,000	17.8	356	90	446	36
1807	2,970	14.8	441	138	579	46.7

Table 16.14 *Edirne* mengene *tax (mukataa-ı resm-i mengene-i Edirne)*

Year	*Muaccele* (*kuruş*) a	Profit rate b	Annual profit to owner c (=a×b)	Annual payment to Treasury d	Gross yearly revenue e (=c+d)	Index
1751	150	27.5	41	220	261	90.5
1793	250	18.6	46.5	242	288.5	100
1811	200	14.9	29.8	242	271.8	94.2

Table 16.15 *Edirne silk-textiles stamp tax (mukataa-ı resm-i damga-ı esnaf-ı sandalcı ve bürüncükcü der Edirne)*

Year	*Muaccele* (*kuruş*) a	Profit rate b	Annual profit to owner c (=a×b)	Annual payment to Treasury d	Gross yearly revenue e (=c+d)	Index
1774	9,500	22.3	2,138	224	2,362	184.2
1788	5,200	19.7	1,025	224	1,249	97.4
1793	5,200	18.8	978	224	1,282	100
1794	8,000	18.3	1,464	224	1,688	101.6
1800	8,000	17.1	1,368	224	1,592	124
1805	10,400	16.1	1,674	224	1,898	148
1836					64	5

Table 16.16 *Niğbolu, Ruscuk, Hezargrad, Tirnova, Yergöğü, Osman Pazarı and Şumnu woollen- and cotton-textiles stamp tax*

Year	*Muaccele* (*kuruş*) a	Profit rate b	Annual profit to owner c (=a×b)	Annual payment to Treasury d	Gross yearly revenue e (=c+d)	Index
1736	1,500	30.5	457.5	385	842.3	42
1738	2,000	30	600	385	985	49.1
1745	2,000	26.7	574	385	959	47.8
1746	2,400	28.5	640	385	1,025	51.1
1752	6,000	27	1,620	385	2,005	100
1757	8,600	26.2	2,253	385	2,638	131.5
1774	11,000	22.4	2,465	385	2,850	142.1
1775	9,800	22.2	2,175.5	385	2,560.6	127.7
1780	13,400	21.2	2,840.8	440	3,280.8	163.6
1787	14,000	19.9	2,796	440	3,236	161.4
1806	12,200	15.9	1,939.8	440	2,600	129.6
1807					216.5	10.8
1808					180	9
1809					175	8.5

Table 16.17 *Şumnu cotton-textiles stamp tax (mukataa-ı resm-i damga-ı astar der Şumnu)*

Year	*Muaccele* (*kuruş*) a	Profit rate b	Annual profit to owner c (=a×b)	Annual payment to Treasury d	Gross yearly revenue e (=c+d)	Index
1752	100	27.2	37.2	110	137.2	100
1782	710	20.8	147.7	110	257.2	187.8
1787	130	19.9	29.8	110	137.8	101.9
1805	200	16.1	32.2	110	142.2	103.6

Table 16.18 *Ankara cotton-textiles stamp tax (mukataa-ı resm-i damga-ı kirpas-ı Ankara)*

Year	*Muaccele* (*kuruş*) a	Profit rate b	Annual profit to owner c (=a×b)	Annual payment to Treasury d	Gross yearly revenue e (=c+d)	Index
1723	500	33.1	165.5	275	440.5	54.9
1734	650	30.9	200.8	382	582.8	72.6
1755	1,200	26.6	319.2	382	701.2	87.4
1772	2,020	22.9	462.6	382	850.6	106
1777	2,600	21.9	569.4	382	951.4	117.3
1780	2,000	21	420	382	802	100
1810	1,500	15.1	226.5	515.5	742	92.5

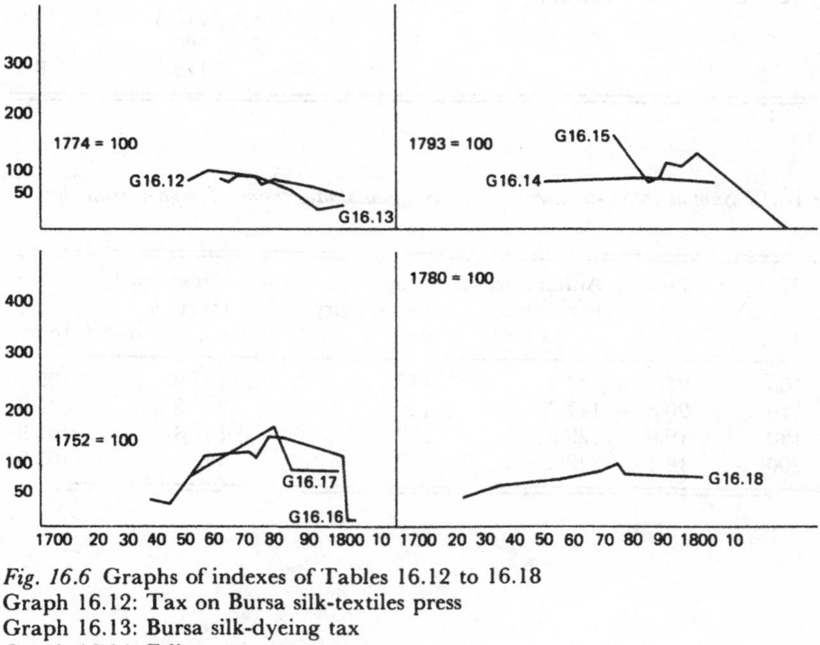

Fig. 16.6 Graphs of indexes of Tables 16.12 to 16.18
Graph 16.12: Tax on Bursa silk-textiles press
Graph 16.13: Bursa silk-dyeing tax
Graph 16.14: Edirne *mengene* tax
Graph 16.15: Edirne silk-textiles stamp tax
Graph 16.16: Niğbolu, Ruscuk, Hezargrad, Tırnova, Yergöğu, Osman Pazarı and Şumnu woollen- and cotton-textiles stamp tax
Graph 16.17: Şumnu cotton-textiles stamp tax
Graph 16.18: Ankara cotton-textiles stamp tax

Table 16.19 *Kastamonu cotton-textiles stamp tax (mukataa-ı resm-i damga-ı Kastamonu)*

Year	*Muaccele* (*kuruş*) a	Profit rate b	Annual profit to owner c (=a×b)	Annual payment to Treasury d	Gross yearly revenue e (=c+d)	Index
1740	10,200	29.7	3,030	1,050	4,080	75.3
1767	18,200	24	4,368	1,050	5,418	100
1787	30,000	19.9	5,970	1,050	7,020	129.5
1808	20,800	16.8	3,494	1,050	4,544	83.8
1816	33,000	13.9	4,587	1,050	5,637	104

Table 16.20 *Serez printing and dyeing tax (mukataa-ı damga-ı kârhane-i boyacı ve basmacı der nefs-i Siroz)*

Year	*Muaccele* (*kuruş*) a	Profit rate b	Annual profit to owner c (=a×b)	Annual payment to Treasury d	Gross yearly revenue e (=c+d)	Index
1741	600	29.5	177	68	245	14.5
1773	6,825	22.7	1,549	68	1,617	100
1776	11,400	22	2,508	68	2,576	159.3
1778	11,475	21.7	2,490	68	2,558	158.2
1760	11,475	21.2	2,427	68	2,495	154.3
1786	8,400	20	1,680	68	1,748	108.1
1795	12,400	18.1	2,244	68	2,312	143

Table 16.21 *Adana iron-mines tax (mahsul-u kürehan-ahen der cebel-i Gedin ma ahen-i Gedin)*

Year	*Muaccele* (*kuruş*) a	Profit rate b	Annual profit to owner c (=a×b)	Annual payment to Treasury d	Gross yearly revenue e (=c+d)	Index
1722	11,000	33.3	3,663	3,182	6,845	168.4
1766	3,600	24.5	882	3,182	4,064	100
1779	800	21.5	172	3,182	3,354	82.5
1791	850	19	161.5	3,182	3,343.5	82.2
1800	850	17.1	145	3,182	3,327	81.8

Table 16.22 *Niğbolu and Silistre leather-products stamp tax (mukataa-ı damga-ı sahtiyan ve meşin ve gön ve kavsele an taife-i debbağan der Niğbolu ve Silistre)*

Year	*Muaccele* (*kuruş*) a	Profit rate b	Annual profit to owner c (=a×b)	Annual payment to Treasury d	Gross yearly revenue e (=c+d)	Index
1779	1,100	21.5	236.5	550	766.5	100
1784	2,000	20.5	410	550	960	124.6
1788	4,250	19.7	837	550	1,337	184.3
1804	2,187.5	16.4	358.5	631.5	990	125.8

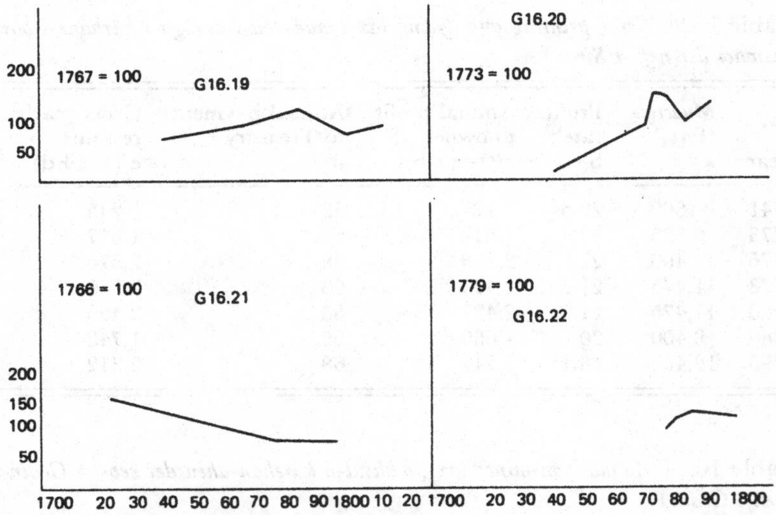

Fig. 16.7 Graphs of indexes of Tables 16.19 to 16.22
Graph 16.19: Kastamonu cotton-textiles stamp tax
Graph 16.20: Serez printing and dyeing tax
Graph 16.21: Adana iron-mines tax
Graph 16.22: Niğbolu and Silistre leather-products stamp tax

Table 16.23 *Trabzon linen stamp tax (mukataa-ı resm-i damga-ı bez-i keten-i Trabzon)*

Year	*Muaccele* (*kuruş*) a	Profit rate b	Annual profit to owner c (=a×b)	Annual payment to Treasury d	Gross yearly revenue e (=c+d)	Index
1734	3,000	30.5	915	1,833	2,748	37.9
1754	7,000	26.8	1,876	5,655	7,531	104
1780	7,300	21.2	1,590	5,655	7,245	100
1785	6,000	20.2	1,212	5,655	6,867	94.5
1810	15,750	15.1	2,378	4,763	7,141	98.5
1812	16,000	14.7	2,358	4,763	7,115	98.2

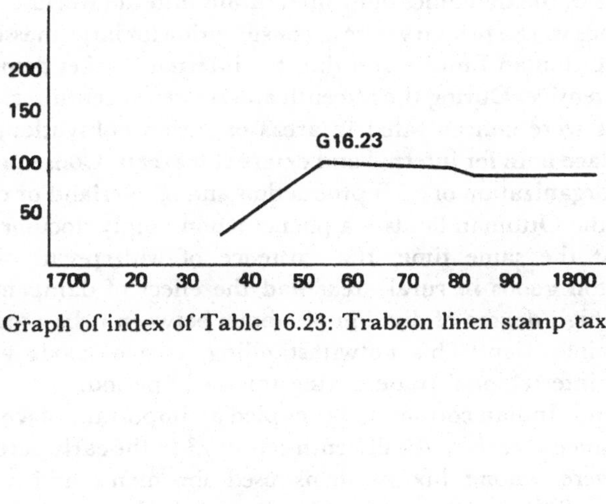

Fig. 16.8 Graph of index of Table 16.23: Trabzon linen stamp tax

17 When and how British cotton goods invaded the Levant markets

HALİL İNALCIK

Developments in both the production of cotton textiles and the trade in these goods are central to an understanding of the internal dynamics of the Ottoman economy as well as of the dynamics of its integration into the world-capitalist system. Cotton goods were a primary item of consumption for large masses of the population in the Ottoman Empire and thus the internal market demand for these goods was extensive. During the fifteenth and sixteenth centuries, cotton-weaving industries were concentrated in areas of cotton cultivation, where production took place both for internal and external markets. Consequently, a highly developed organization of craft production and of overland or caravan trade emerged in the Ottoman lands – a phenomenon amply documented in court records.[1] At the same time, the existence of widespread domestic production of cotton goods in rural areas had the effect of dampening the development to a high degree of division of labour between urban and rural areas and of specialization. This notwithstanding, cotton goods were an important item of interregional trade during this early period.

On the other hand, Indian cottons had occupied an important place among Ottoman imports since as early as the fifteenth century.[2] In the early period, fine Indian muslins were among luxury items used for men's and women's headwear. A price register dating from 1640[3] shows that in this period expensive Indian muslin varieties dominated the Ottoman market while cheaper cotton goods were all products of domestic industries. It thus appears that imports of these expensive cloths, more than those of spices and precious stones, were responsible for the substantial flow of silver stocks from the Ottoman Empire eastward to India.[4]

During the seventeenth century the increased import of Indian cotton prints as well as cheaper muslins had indeed a revolutionary impact on the world-economy.[5] The Ottomans viewed with growing concern the increased flow of silver specie eastward resulting from the expansion of the market for Indian cottons.[6] Given the availability of cheap raw cotton, cheap labour and necessary skills and techniques, the Ottoman weavers successfully imitated Indian textiles;[7] but, as customs registers indicate, this did not end or diminish their imports. In the case of European countries, it is generally accepted that attempts to replace the Indian textiles with local manufactures and therefore to control the eastward flow of species were among the factors that led to the Industrial Revolution.[8]

Given the popularity of Indian cotton goods, beginning in the second half of the eighteenth century the European cotton exports to the Ottoman Empire consisted primarily of imitations of the Indian products. As late as the mid nineteenth century the latter varieties constituted the bulk of European exports to the Levant. In this paper we shall discuss how British cottons replaced Indian ones in this important market. We shall see that this development unfolded in stages covering quite a long period, between 1770 and 1840. The first stage was characterized by the preponderance of English cotton-yarn exports over the local products; the second stage witnessed the triumph of English imitations of such Indian cottons as muslins and cotton prints over the original Indian products; in the final stage the English exports of coarse cotton cloths sought to penetrate the large rural market hitherto supplied by local manufacturers. We will argue that the principal determinant of this development in stages was the extent to which the English industry was able to offset the comparative advantages of low labour costs – which both the Indian and local Ottoman cotton industry enjoyed – through the introduction of new labour-saving technologies.

During the period preceding the Napoleonic wars (1793–1815), in the Levant market English cotton cloths faced competition not only from Indian but also from German, Austrian, and Swiss products. In this period, German cloths sold yearly in İzmir amounted to fifty-five to sixty thousand and in Bursa amounted to eighty thousand pieces.[9] To supply German cotton industries, substantial quantities of raw cotton and cotton yarn were exported to Germany from the Ottoman provinces, most significantly from such centres of production as the Serres–Salonica region and Thessaly.[10] Towards the end of the eighteenth century, Ottoman exports of cotton yarn alone amounted to as much as two and a half million kilograms yearly.[11]

Table 17.1 shows that German competition notwithstanding, as early as the 1770s England ranked first among the European exporters of cotton cloth to the Levant. France, while enjoying the lead in the export of woollens, trailed far behind England in cotton-cloth exports. Woollen cloths had always constituted the bulk of Ottoman textile imports from Europe until the invasion of cottons.

The seventeenth-century Ottoman traveller, Evliyâ Çelebi, noted[12] that in most Ottoman cities the members of the well-to-do classes wore clothes of imported woollens. Whereas, Çelebi observed, the clothes worn by lower classes, both urban and rural, were made of domestically produced cotton cloths. It was these rural and urban Ottoman masses that constituted the major market in cotton textiles, and it was the struggle to dominate this market that was to

Table 17.1 *Ottoman imports of cotton and woollen cloths from European countries in the 1770s (in French francs)*

Country exporting	Year	Muslins	Woollens
Great Britain	1777	691,000	656,000
Holland	1778	298,000	583,000
Venice	1782	97,000	—
Trieste (German and Austrian)	?	108,000	220,000
France	?	42,000	7,448,000

Sources: P. Masson, *Histoire du commerce français dans le Levant au XVIIIe siècle* (Paris, 1911), vol. II, pp. 495, 615; R. Paris, *L'histoire du commerce de Marseille, 1660–1789, V: Le Levant* (Paris, 1957), p. 552.

determine the course of the fundamental transformation of the Ottoman economy in the nineteenth century.

It should be kept in mind that throughout the eighteenth and the first decades of the nineteenth centuries European manufactures met with stiff competition from Indian muslins and cotton yarns in the Levant. This was primarily because the Ottoman genteel classes preferred the fine Indian cloths to their not so fine European imitations. It is sufficient to look at the Anglo-Ottoman customs regulations of 1806 which listed among English exports to the Ottoman Empire a variety of cotton goods manufactured in India.[13] These included: Indian cotton yarns (*rişte-i Hindî*) (immediately followed in the list, however, by English cotton yarns or *rişte-i penbe-i Ingiliz*), Indian tapes, various Indian muslins and turbans. Subsequent to the 1806 customs regulations, Aubin in 1812 listed[14] the following Indian cotton goods that England exported to the Levant: cossaes, calicoes, long cloths, terrendams, mulmuls, surbities, alliballies, f. mulls, s. mulls, cirbans, humhums, sursuckers, bassas, addatics, emmerities, guercks, doosooties, mamoodies, sallembores, jamdonies, alatches. Though the names of these cotton-cloth varieties are distorted almost beyond recognition as they were anglicized, it is still possible to trace their original Indian names, e.g. surbities for *şerbetî*, mamoodies for *mahmûdî*, sallembores for *salampur*, alatches for *alaca*, humhums for *hammamî*. On the other hand, English exports manufactured in England consisted primarily of imitations of the Indian varieties. Among these were calicoes (that competed with the Indian cossaes), striped cloths, and printed dyed calicoes, chintz cloth used for upholstery, *şerbetîs*, and Indian nankins. In 1826 muslins (*nezif* and *mermer* varieties) along with locally made ones, as well as Indian *savaşpur* or fine cotton cloth used for lining, were among the main cotton goods sold in the Ottoman market.[15] Already in this period the Ottoman Empire imported not only English printed cottons (*basma*) but also cottons of common use, cambrics (*patiska* or *batiste*) and coarse 'American' cotton cloth consumed by the masses.[16]

Effective competition with locally produced goods and their eventual displacement by imports largely depended on the exporting country's ability to produce goods at costs lower than those that characterized local industries. In the context of trade with Asian societies such as the Ottoman Empire and India, where cheap labour contributed to low costs of production, the exporting country in order to compete with local producers was faced with the problem of keeping labour costs below those in these countries. The spread of English cottons in the Levant market took place after the invention of new machines that enabled the English manufacturers not only to imitate the Indian products but also to sell them at lower prices. Thus, Hargreaves' spinning jenny (patented in 1770) and Arkwright's water frame (patented in 1769) led to unprecedented increases in the production of a variety of cotton yarns. But these machines were not equipped to make fine yarns used in the production of Indian muslins. Only after 1780 with the introduction of Samuel Crompton's mule (patented 1779) could finer and smoother yarn be produced. This last invention, in turn, made possible the spread of large quantities of English cotton goods in the Levant, and was indeed a turning point in England's export trade. Still, in order to compete effectively with the Indian products, English manufacturers had to await advances in bleaching and printing techniques.[17] In brief, capitalist development in England met this problem of lowering labour costs head-on through the introduction of new machines. Attempts to develop new technologies to expand production to larger markets were also undertaken in other capitalist countries, most significantly in France. As mentioned earlier, already in the eighteenth century Central European cotton cloths were competing with English products in the Levant. The Napoleonic wars and the subsequent trade embargo England imposed on the European countries, however, had crippling effects on cotton industries on the Continent.[18] As a result, England succeeded in eliminating its competitors in the Levant trade.

England attempted in the early nineteenth century to seize the muslin market in İstanbul from the Germans, as well as to undermine local production. According to C. Aubin,[19] a representative of a major English textile firm in İstanbul, during the Napoleonic wars prices of German muslins in İstanbul rose considerably. This was primarily an outcome of the increase in transportation costs as German cloths travelled to İstanbul via the land route when, under war conditions, access to the sea route via Fiume and Trieste was blocked. Confronted with the high prices of German cottons, Ottoman merchants in İstanbul sought to expand the production of fine cotton cloths. To this end, they planned to erect a large building housing four to five hundred looms. Aubin, while pointing to the possibility that this expansion of local industry might increase the demand for English cotton yarns of twist variety, strongly advocated that England should seize this lucrative market through exports of cheap- and high-quality muslins and crush the local enterprises. To initiate this process, Aubin sent to England samples of muslins sought after in the İstanbul market. Two years later in 1814 Isaac Morier enthusiastically observed that cheap English cotton cloths with their characteristic durability and bright colours found 'prodigious demand' in the Levant market from Cairo to İstanbul and that this trade was of utmost significance for England.[19a]

Of the English exports, cotton yarns were first to be introduced to the larger Levant market. In the 1790s, English cotton industries through use of new machines were able to lower the price of yarn significantly from 38 shillings per pound in 1792 to 5.5 shillings in 1812. Trade in yarns brought in very substantial profits, especially in the Levant where the mule and water-twist varieties (far superior to the local and to the Indian varieties) were introduced in this period. In the 1806 Anglo-Ottoman customs regulations, English cotton yarn figured as a major item among Ottoman imports. In the 1840s, the hand-looms in Diyarbakır (in south-eastern Anatolia) were using imported English cotton yarns that reached them via the eastern Black Sea port of Trabzon.[20] Similarly, cloth weavers in the cities of Aleppo, Damascus, İzmir, Bursa, and İstanbul were increasingly dependent on imports of English yarn.[21]

At the outset, the influx of English yarn imports dealt a severe blow to the spinning industries in Macedonia and Thessaly. But the large numbers of spinners in the cities and towns of Anatolia remained unaffected by this development. In Anatolia during the 1820s cheap cotton cloths were still made from locally produced yarns.

In 1831 David Urquhart attempted to estimate the production costs for cotton yarns and cloths in Ambelakia in Thessaly.[22] The import of cheap- and high-quality English yarns generally led to a fall in the prices of local yarn and to a decline in local wages. The latter development was primarily an outcome of the presence of large numbers of unemployed or, as Urquhart put it, 'people must go on working merely for bread, and reducing their price in a struggle for hopeless competition'. At the centre of this struggle were the women and children who provided the cheap labour in yarn spinning and whose efforts Urquhart characterized as 'most remarkable'. In this period the daily earnings of these Greek women and children, who mostly worked at home, fell as low as 20 *paras* or 6 pennies. Yet, they were unable to find purchasers for their product. Urquhart's estimates of production in the making of thread from 5 *okkas* (6.410 kg) of cotton are as follows:[23]

	piastres [*kuruş*]	paras*
Five okes [*okkas*] of uncleaned cotton, at seventeen paras	2	5
Labour of a woman for two days (seven farthings per day)	0	35
Carding by vibration of a cat-guard	0	10
Spinning, a woman's unremitting labour for a week	5	30
Loss of cotton, exceeding an oke of uncleaned cotton	0	20
Value of one oke of cotton-yarn	9	20

* 1 *kuruş* = 40 *paras*, 1 *kuruş* = 1.2 pennies, or 1 penny = 33.3 *paras*

'A woman's labour', Urquhart added, 'makes but 2d. per day, while field labour, according to the season of the year, ranges from 4d. to 6d.; and at this rate, the pound of coarse cotton-yarn cost in spinning 5d.'[24] In spite of these extremely low wages, however, producers of cotton yarn were unable to compete with imported yarn.

On the other hand, Urquhart continued,

> one oke of this thread weaves into forty pikes [three quarters of a yard or a Turkish *arşın* or *zira* equal to 59.5 cm], seven-eighths wide (thirty-two yards, twenty-one inches wide) worth twenty piastres, and is the work of one man for three days. This leaves the weaver about 10d. per day, and shows that we have not yet brought our *coarse cottons* into the same competition with theirs, as we have our yarn. Their own yarn being unequal, heavy in weaving and liable to break, the weavers prefer much the English yarn.[25]

The Ottoman cloth weavers preferred to make cloths from English yarn alone or use half English and half domestic yarn. The latter practice resulted in a more durable cloth, much sought after by the peasants. Also cloths made from English yarn alone were slightly more expensive. In brief, low production costs of local cloths resulting from the low wages of local weavers – compared with those of English workers – made it difficult for English cloths to compete with the local products. Thus, in 1830 the total value of English cotton cloth exports to the Ottoman Empire amounted to a mere 351 thousand pounds. Addressing himself to this question in 1831, Urquhart wrote:

> The coarse cloth which they [the very poorest class] require averages, as above stated, seventy pikes, at thirty paras per oke, or rather more than five shillings per pound – at least one fourth more than the value of such stuff in England, which makes £5,000,000. This embraces only the coarse and heavy stuffs, used by the peasantry . . . The Americans were the first to turn their attention to the coarse unbleached cotton stuffs. Plain goods now form one half of our assortments; but, as I have above remarked, although our handkerchiefs and imitation shawls are commonly to be seen throughout villages, and at the country fairs, we can scarcely be said to have entered on the branch to which our future commerce will be chiefly indebted.[26]

The same author also noted that local weavers, by keeping prices low and paying attention to the quality of their products, attempted to compete with the imports. Admitting that those attempts enjoyed a measure of success, Urquhart concluded:

> Still the consumption of eastern articles is immense, and the intricacy of their circulation throughout the country is quite surprising.[27]

He then proceeded to list some of the articles in this extensive internal trade such as cotton thread and cloth from Mosul and Mardin (in south-eastern Anatolia), dyed cotton cloth, red cotton thread, and imitations of Indian cloths from Diyarbakır (in south-eastern Anatolia), cotton cloths from İzmir, Urfa, Antep, Kilis, and Malatya.

A leading exponent of Adam Smith's principles of liberal economy,[28] Urquhart argued that if the Ottoman peasant left the production of cotton cloths to English manufacturers and concentrated on grain production, he would receive higher returns for his labour.[29] This outcome would follow almost automatically since free trade is a tradition in Turkey, guaranteed with the lifting of protectionist measures and the adoption of the *laissez-faire, laissez-passer* principle. Consistent with his liberal views, Urquhart also advocated the free flow of Ottoman goods into England and in particular the removal of high tariffs on wheat imports in the latter country.[30] Such measures would increase the profitability of peasants' production. At the same time, increased incomes of Ottoman peasants would create the purchasing power to buy English imports. This model of economic division of labour on a world scale, of inter-dependency, and of valuation of labour on the basis of an economic rationale was later in the nineteenth century to find widespread acceptance as the driving force behind England's economic penetration of different regions. What seems odd, however, is that the Ottoman reformist bureaucrats also embraced these views.[31] The Ottoman state during this period was far from following a systematic protectionist policy; periodic attempts to raise tariff duties were *ad hoc* measures aimed at increasing state revenues.[32] Yet, Ottoman bureaucrats – despite their liberal leanings – continued to be guided mainly by political and fiscal considerations. The opposite was the case in England where politics was subordinated to the dictates of a rational economic policy. This difference in the conception and behaviour is important, however, in explaining the dramatic developments in the relationships of the two countries during the rest of the century.

C. Aubin summarized the stages in the competition between the English and cheap Asian cotton goods in the following way: first the English cotton yarns of mule and water-twist varieties drove the Indian yarns from the Levant market; then around 1810 English imitations of Indian muslins, mainly because of their low prices, began to displace the Indian originals. The complete domination of the Levant market by English cotton goods and their replacing of Indian muslins and printed cottons, however, took place only after 1825. Thus, in 1833 David Urquhart could write '. . while we observe the avidity with which our goods are sought, the preference now transferred from Indian to Birmingham muslins, from Golconda to Glasgow chintzes, from Damascus to Sheffield steel, from Cashmere shawls to English broad cloth.'[33]

Table 17.2 shows that in the period between 1825 and 1830 Ottoman imports of English cotton yarns tripled, in 1835 they were six times the amount in 1825, and in 1860 as much as forty times that amount. Imports of cotton cloth increased five-fold between 1825 and 1830 and sixty-five-fold between 1825 and 1860. At the same time, during this period the share of exports to the Ottoman Empire of total English exports shows a continuous rise. When all Ottoman imports from England are taken into account, the Ottoman Empire ranked third among England's trade partners. In 1850 the total value of Ottoman imports from England was estimated at approximately 8.5 million pounds sterling, and approximately 3 million of this amount represented imports of

Table 17.2 *English exports of cotton goods, 1825–60*

	Exports to the Ottoman Empire		Total exports	
	Cloth (in 1,000 yd)	Yarn (in 1,000 lb)	Cloth (in 1,000 yd)	Yarn (in 1,000 lb)
1825	3,578	557	132,129	35,334
1830	15,940	1,528	219,335	64,645
1835	25,692	3,272	421,122	118,470
1845	46,793	5,830	673,268	135,144
1850	31,124	2,384	757,979	131,370
1855	132,605	8,446	1,230,827	165,493
1860	229,201	22,824	none recorded	none recorded

Sources: F.E. Bailey, *British policy and the Turkish reform movement* (Cambridge, Mass., 1942), pp. 247–70; for 1860 figures J.L. Farley, *The resources of Turkey* (London, 1862), p. 62; compare Orhan Kurmuş, *Emperyalizm' in Türkiye'ye Girişi* (Imperialist penetration of Turkey) (Istanbul, 1974), p. 149.

cotton cloth.[34] Later in the nineteenth century, England emerged as the biggest exporter of cotton cloth to the Ottoman Empire, leaving France, Austria, and Switzerland far behind. Thus, in 1878–80 Ottoman imports from England amounted to 45 per cent of the Empire's total cotton imports, while imports from France and Switzerland constituted 16 and 14 per cent respectively of that total.[35]

But how did the increased imports affect the Ottoman cotton cloth industry? Observing the adverse effects of this development on Ottoman weavers, Urquhart reported that out of 600 hand-looms in Üsküdar (a suburb of İstanbul) only 21 remained in 1821, in Tyrnavo (a town in Thessaly) only 200 out of 2,000 looms were in operation in 1830. Similarly, C. Hamlin in the 1840s wrote: 'Five thousand weavers in Scutari were without employ, and reduced to the most deplorable beggary. The fast colors and firm material of Diarbekr disappeared . . . and Bursa towels came from Lyons and Manchester . . . Thus all industries of Turkey have perished.'[36] An Ottoman document dating from 1868 described this pattern of decline in local industries as follows:

> While in the old days there were 2,750 hand-looms for cloth making in İstanbul and Üsküdar and as many as 3,500 Muslim and Christian subjects of the Ottoman state earned their livelihood at these looms, in the past thirty to forty years the numbers of these looms has dropped to 25 and the numbers of cloth weavers (*kumaşçı esnafı*), both masters and apprentices, dropped to 40 . . .[37]

This document too traced the beginning of the decline in Ottoman industry to the period between 1828 and 1838, thus confirming the accuracy of Urquhart's observations. Finally a French official document dated 1845 described the state of the local textile industry in Syria as follows:

À l'exportation générale, l'Angleterre occupe le premier rang; les toiles écrues, les coton filés, les impressions sont les principaux articles qui alimentent ses relations avec la Syrie . . . Leur bon marché (de ces étoffes) les avait fait préférer aux tissus indigènes similaires; delà ruine presque complète de l'industrie de Damas et d'Alep. Ces deux villes comptaient, il ya une vingtaine d'années, au delà de 25,000 métiers produisant des étoffes mi-soie, mi-coton; aujourdhui c'est à peine si le sixième a survécu.[38]

Other sources also confirm these accounts of the decline of Ottoman urban industries,[39] but what is significant for our purpose is that all these sources agree that the drastic effects of foreign imports on Ottoman manufactures became suddenly and strikingly visible in the period between 1825 and 1835.

It should be noted that in England this period was characterized by a sudden rise in the share of manufacturing together with mining and building industries in the total national income. According to the estimates by P. Deane and W.A. Cole,[40] between 1811 and 1821 this share jumped from 20.8 to 31.9 per cent, and showed an upward trend (though not as dramatic) in the subsequent decades. The growth rate of these industries during the period 1801–31 reached 4.7 per cent (the highest rate experienced until 1901), while the growth rate of agriculture, forestry, fishing stood at a mere 1.2 per cent.

Consistent with this overall pattern of development of the British economy, the cotton industry's peak period of growth was between *c.* 1816 and *c.* 1840. In this period, growth was primarily in response to increased demand in the home market. Later, foreign demand came to play a more important role in the production of cotton manufactures. At the same time, the period between 1816 and 1840 witnessed the largest capital investments in the cotton industry as machinery was introduced in the production bringing substantial returns of capital to the capitalists. It was during the 1820s that hand-looms began to be replaced by machines in the English cotton industry, and by 1850 only a negligible proportion of production was undertaken by looms. Thus, the revolution in the British cotton industry can be traced to the 1820s.[41] It can be argued that both the Industrial Revolution in England and the beginnings of decline in the Ottoman cotton industry occurred between 1820 and 1840.

As Urquhart indicated, as of 1833, English cotton cloths had not yet invaded the large Ottoman internal market but they competed with and subsequently triumphed over the fine Indian goods in such major urban markets as İstanbul, İzmir, Bursa, Damascus and Aleppo. The demand for cotton cloth of the large masses of population both in the countryside and in small towns continued to be met by local weavers. In rural areas the *manifaturacı*, or middleman who sold European machine-made goods, had not yet become indispensable.[42] Furthermore, for European goods to penetrate these local markets, European capitalism had to solve effectively the problems of poor transportation facilities and to persuade the Ottoman government to abolish internal toll taxes. The latter had the negative effect of raising the prices of imports, thereby preventing their ability to compete with local goods.[43]

British cotton-cloth exports to the Ottoman Empire show a drastic increase in the 1850s (see Table 17.2). A French report sent from Edirne in 1862[44] indicated that in this period, at least in some rural markets, European cotton goods were the major items of trade. Thus, forty million *kuruşes* worth of cotton cloths, mostly of English manufacture, and also calicoes or cheap printed cottons and madapolams (or imitations(?) of Indian *masulipatam*) were brought to Uzuncaova (situated between Filibe and Edirne), one of the largest rural markets in Rumelia. Twenty-five million *kuruşes* worth of these cloths were sold. Other European goods sold in this market were insignificant in value when compared to cotton cloths. (These were metals, colonial products, woollen cloths, and English cotton yarns, altogether worth seven million *kuruşes*.) On the other hand, the indigenous products sold in the same market included *aba* or felt cloth (worth one million *kuruşes*), sheep and goat skins (worth half-a-million *kuruşes*), iron (worth 200,000 *kuruşes*). Thus, it can be argued that the invasion of the rural interior by British cotton cloths actually occurred in the 1850s.

Lewis Farley's description of the state of the Ottoman economy in 1860 pointed to the complete de-industrialization. Farley, who visited the Ottoman Empire in order to assess its raw-material resources and its market potential for English manufactures, wrote:

> Turkey is no longer a manufacturing country. The numerous and varied manufactures which formerly sufficed, not only for the consumption of the empire, but which also stocked the markets of the Levant, as well as those of several countries in Europe, have in some instances, rapidly declined, and in others became altogether extinct.[45]

At the same time, he reported that the country was a very rich source of raw materials. Referring to the capacity of Ottoman territories to export raw cotton – an export item which became very important for England with the outbreak of the American civil war, he concluded:

> There can be no doubt, therefore, entertained as to the possibility of an immense increase of the quantity of cotton grown in Turkey . . . It is, in fact, this capability of supplying raw material at a low price and of excellent quality which gives to Turkish commerce that importance and consideration in which it is held by the European powers.[46]

Notes

Introduction: 'Oriental despotism' in world-system perspective

1 See Norman Daniel, *Islam and the West, the making of an image* (Edinburgh, University Press, 1960) for the European image of the Ottoman Empire in the nineteenth century.

2 For a description of this discourse see Perry Anderson, *Lineages of the absolutist state* (London, New Left Books, 1974), pp. 397–412; and, more importantly, Edward W. Said, *Orientalism* (New York, Random House, 1979).

3 For an excellent formulation of the Hegelian problematic of the 'self' and the 'other' see Said, *Orientalism*.

4 For discussion of ideal-type comparisons as applied to the history and the social structures of the Middle East and North Africa see Bryant S. Turner, *Marx and the end of Orientalism* (London, George Allen and Unwin, 1978).

5 Most representative of this literature are: Said, *Orientalism*; Turner, *Marx and the end of Orientalism*; Talal Asad (ed.), *Anthropology and the colonial encounter* (London, Ithaca Press, 1973); the articles in the *Review of Middle East Studies* (henceforth *ROMES*), 1(1975), 2(1976), 3(1978); Abdallah Laroui, 'For a methodology of Islamic studies', *Diogenes*, 83(1973), 12–39; Marshall Hodgson, *The venture of Islam* (3 vols., Chicago, The University of Chicago Press, 1974).

6 I. Wallerstein, *The capitalist world-system. Essays by Immanuel Wallerstein* (Cambridge, Cambridge University Press, 1980); *The modern world-system: capitalist agriculture and the origins of the European world-economy in the sixteenth century* (New York, Academic Press, 1974). For the application of this perspective to the Ottoman Empire, Wallerstein 'The Ottoman Empire and the capitalist world-economy: some questions for research', *Review*, II, 3(Winter 1979), 389–98. Also the articles by I. Wallerstein, H. Decdeli, and R. Kasaba and by İslamoğlu and Keyder in this volume.

7 For a discussion of the influence of the *Annales* School on recent Ottoman historiography see Halil İnalcık, 'Impact of the *Annales* School on Ottoman studies and new findings', *Review*, I, 3/4(Winter/Spring 1978), 69–96.

8 For a discussion of nineteenth-century origins of modern Orientalism see C.J. Adams, 'Islamic religion', Part I, *Middle East Studies Association Bulletin*, IV, 3 (October 15, 1970). For the founders of academic Orientalism such as Wellhausen, Nöldeke, Becker and Snouck Hurgronje see J.W. Fück, 'Islam as an historical problem in European historiography since 1800', in B. Lewis and P.M. Holt (eds.), *Historians of the Middle East* (London, Oxford University Press, 1962); V.G. Kiernan, *The lords of human kind: black man, yellow man and white man in an age of empire* (Boston, Little Brown,

1969); J. Waardenburg, *L'Islam dans le miroir de l'occident* (The Hague, Mouton, 1962); Talal Asad, 'Two European images of non-European rule' in Asad (ed.), *Anthropology and the colonial encounter*.

9 For a most striking example of the 'decline' thesis see G.E. von Grünebaum, *Classical Islam: A history 600–1258* (Chicago, Aldine Publishing Co., 1970). For a critique of this view see David Waines, 'Cultural Anthropology and Islam: the contribution of G.E. von Grünebaum', *Review of Middle East Studies*, 2(1976), 113–23.

10 For a discussion of Western political theory of Oriental despotism tracing it from Machiavelli's *Prince* see Anderson, *Lineages*, pp. 397–416, 462–72; for Baron de Montesquieu's discussion of despotism, see *The spirit of laws* (New York, Colonial Press, 1900), pp. 18, 25–8, 57–66, 122, 129. Also see Franco Venturi, 'Oriental despotism', *Journal for the History of Ideas*, 24 (1963), 133–62; R. Koebner, 'Despot and despotism: vicissitudes of a political term', *Journal of the Warburg and Courtauld Institutes*, 14(1951), 275–302.

11 The distinction between the civil society and the state and contrasting of the East and the West in the context of that distinction, found its most explicit formulation in G.W. Hegel, *The philosophy of history* (New York, Dover Publications, 1956). Also for a formulation of the comparison between East and West in the context of Gramsci's thought see P. Anderson, 'The antimonies of Antonio Gramsci', *New Left Review*, 100(November 1976–January 1977), 5–80.

12 For a comprehensive summary of Marx and Engels' scattered and fragmentary writings on the AMP and the tracing of the Hegelian ancestry of their formulations see Anderson, *Lineages*, pp. 464–96. The account given here is based on this summary.

13 The theoretical inadequacy of the AMP, especially in explaining the existence of highly developed state structures (such as those in the Ottoman Empire, Mughal India, China) in a classless society is discussed in Anderson, *Lineages*, pp. 481–95 and in Barry Hindess and Paul Hirst, *Pre-capitalist modes of production* (London, Routledge and Kegan Paul, 1975), pp. 178–201. Anderson also stresses the empirical shortcomings of the AMP and states that its description of Asian society does not correspond to the specific historical development of any society in Asia. Rejecting the geography-bound explanations of Asian history, Anderson, however, resorts to culturalist explanations of the kind favoured by Orientalists and Modernizationists. In doing so, he ascribes the failure of the Ottoman Empire to 'modernize' or to achieve capitalist development to its specific religious or cultural dispositions (pp. 397–400). Thus, his insistence on the necessity for depicting the specific social-economic structures and state systems in non-Western areas amounts to little more than an attempt at delineating the specific historical stagnation of the Ottoman Empire – an exercise that underlines the uniqueness of Western European development.

14 Two important works are those by Karl A. Wittfogel, *Oriental despotism* (New York, Vintage Books, 1981) and by Umberto Melotti, *Marx and the Third World* (London, Macmillian Press, 1977). These authors seek to provide a theoretical consistency to Marx and Engels' formulations. In doing so, Wittfogel, for instance, stresses the class character of the state embodied in a managerial bureaucracy in charge of hydraulic works. He then sees in this geographically determined political structure an 'essential' quality and seeks to explain the absence of Western-style democracies and the rise of 'totalitarian' regimes in modern-day Soviet Russia and in China in terms of their supposed agro-despotic heritage.

15 For an excellent critique of Wittfogel stressing this point as well as the theoretical inadequacies of his approach see Hindness and Hirst, *Pre-capitalist modes of production*, pp. 207–20.

16 Shlomo Avineri (ed.), *Karl Marx on colonialism and modernization* (New York, Doubleday, 1968); 'Modernization and Arab society', *Israel, The Arabs and the Middle East*, eds. Irving Howe and Carl Gershman (New York, Bantam Books, 1972). For an incisive critique of Avineri's thought and his Hegelian Marxism, see Bryant Turner, 'Avineri's view of Marx's theory of colonialism: Israel', *Science and Society*, 40(1976), 385–409; Turner, *Marx and the end of Orientalism*, pp. 25–38.
17 For such a conception of the Ottoman Empire see H.A.R. Gibb and H. Bowen, *Islamic society and the West; a study of the impact of Western civilisation on Muslim culture in the Near East*, vol. I, *Islamic society in the eighteenth century*, Parts 1 and 2 (London, Oxford University Press, 1950 and 1957). For a critique of this work, see R. Owen, 'The Middle East in the eighteenth century – on "Islamic" society in decline: a critique of Gibb and Bowen's *Islamic society and the West*', *ROMES*, 1(1975), 101–12.
18 This conception of the relationship between the rulers and their subjects finds its most lucid expression in H.A.R. Gibb, 'Religion and politics in Christianity and Islam', *Islam and international relations* (London, 1965); and G.E. von Grünebaum, *Islam, essays in the nature and growth of a cultural tradition*, 2nd ed. (London, Routledge and Kegan Paul, 1955); *Medieval Islam* (Chicago, The University of Chicago Press, 1946); and in the work of the Dutch Orientalist Snouck Hurgronje: G.H. Bousquet and J. Schacht (eds.), *Selected works of C. Snouck Hurgronje* (Leiden, Brill, 1957). For an excellent critique of 'Oriental despotism' based on the works of these authors see Talal Asad, 'Two European images of non-European rule'.
19 For a discussion of anti-humanism, absence of 'liberty' and 'progress' as well as of the irrationality of Islamic society see G.E. von Grünebaum, *Modern Islam* (Berkeley, The University of California Press, 1962).
20 For a critique of the institutional mode of analysis see İslamoğlu and Keyder, 'Agenda for Ottoman history'.
21 For the 'decline' thesis as applied to the Ottoman Empire see Gibb and Bowen, *Islamic society and the West*; Bernard Lewis, *The emergence of modern Turkey*, 2nd ed. (New York, Oxford University Press, 1968).
22 Asad, 'Two European images of non-European rule'. For an explicit statement of Dutch colonial role in Indonesia, see J. Waardenburg, *L'Islam dans le miroir de l'occident*; W.F. Wertheim, 'Counter-insurgency research at the turn of the century', *Sociologische Gids*, 19(September/December 1972). For a description of the intimate relationship between Orientalist research and French colonialism in Morocco, see Edmund Burke, III, 'The image of the Moroccan state in French ethnological literature: a new look at the origins of Lyautey's Berber policy', in E. Gellner and C. Micaud (eds.), *Arabs and Berbers: from tribe to nation* (London, Duckworth, 1973).
23 For the Middle East the textbook of the modernization paradigm is Daniel Lerner's *Passing of the traditional society* (New York, Free Press, 1958); for the nineteenth-century Ottoman Empire, W.R. Polk and R.L. Chambers (eds.), *The beginnings of modernisation in the Middle East* (Chicago, The University of Chicago Press, 1968) is a representative collection. For a critical review of modernization literature on the Middle East and North Africa see Turner, *Marx and the end of Orientalism* and also the articles in *ROMES*.
24 Turner, *Marx and the end of Orientalism*.
25 This approach is adopted in orthodox Marxist interpretations of Ottoman history.
26 Maxime Rodinson, *Islam and Capitalism* (Paris, Seuil, 1966).
27 See, for instance, Peter Gran, 'Late-eighteenth- to early-nineteenth-century Egypt: merchant capitalism or modern capitalism', in this volume.
28 Roger Owen, 'Islam and capitalism: a critique of Rodinson', *ROMES*, 2(1976), 85–93.

29 See n. 13.

30 For Wallerstein's critique of the modernization paradigm and his formulation of the world-system perspective as a methodology in social sciences see 'Modernisation: *requiescat in pace*'; 'The rise and future demise of the world capitalist system: concepts for comparative analysis'; 'A world-system perspective on the social sciences', in *The capitalist world-economy*.

31 For general theoretical formulations of this perspective see the articles by I. Wallerstein in *The capitalist world-economy* and *The modern world-system*.

32 For a discussion of internal trade also see Suraiya Faroqhi and Huri İslâmoğlu, 'Crop patterns and agricultural production trends in sixteenth-century Anatolia', *Review*, II, 3(Winter 1979), 401–36.

33 Çağlar Keyder's description of Ottoman rural crafts approximates to this conception: 'Proto-industrialization in the Ottoman Empire', *Insurgent Sociologist* (Winter 1980).

34 Suraiya Faroqhi, 'Sixteenth-century periodic markets in various Anatolian *sancaks*', *Journal of the Economic and Social History of the Orient*, XXII, 1(1979), 32–80.

35 For a discussion of the decline of the Muslim merchant class also see Peter Gran, *Islamic roots of capitalism: Egypt 1760–1840* (Austin, The University of Texas Press, 1979), pp. 3–34, 111–31.

36 For critical assessments of Wallerstein's work see Robert Brenner, 'The origins of capitalist development: a critique of neo-Smithian Marxism', *New Left Review*, 104(1977), 25–93; also see the special issue of the symposium on 'The modern world system by Immanuel Wallerstein', *Peasant Studies*, VI, 1(January 1977), 2–42. This issue includes articles by John Markoff, Robert A. Dodgshon, Jane Schneider, Domenico Sella, Edward J. Nell.

37 For a critical appraisal of the world-system perspective from the viewpoint of regional analysis see Carol A. Smith, 'Regional analysis in world-system perspective: a critique of three structural theories of uneven development', paper delivered at the conference of the Society for Economic Anthropology, Indiana University, Bloomington, Indiana, April 24–29, 1981. I am grateful to Ms Smith for letting me read this paper.

38 Anderson, *Lineages*, pp. 402–5.

39 Robert Brenner, 'Agrarian class structures and economic development in pre-industrial Europe', *Past and Present*, 70(1976), 30–5.

40 Barrington Moore Jr, *Social origins of dictatorship and democracy* (Boston, Beacon Press, 1967).

41 For recent formulations of this stance in the context of concrete regional analysis see Joel Kahn, *Minangkabau social formations* (Cambridge, Cambridge University Press, 1980); Katherine Verdery, *Transylvanian villagers: three centuries of political, economic and ethnic change* (Berkeley, University of California Press, 1983. Also, for a theoretical treatment of the subject, Eric Wolf, 'Crisis and differentiation in capitalism' in *Europe and the people without history* (Berkeley, University of California Press, 1984).

42 Bruce McGowan, 'The study of land and agriculture in the Ottoman provinces within the context of an expanding world economy in the 17th and 18th centuries', *International Journal of Turkish Studies*, II, 1(Spring-Summer 1981), 57–64.

43 Şerif Mardin, 'Power, civil society and culture in the Ottoman Empire', *Comparative Studies in Society and History*, 11 (1969), 258–81.

44 This conception largely borrows from Gramsci's writings. Antonio Gramsci, *Selections from the prison notebooks*, trans. and ed. Quintin Hoare and Geoffrey N. Smith (New York, International Publishers, 1980), pp. 206–69. Also Chantal Mouffe, 'Hegemony and ideology in Gramsci', *Gramsci and Marxist theory*, ed. C. Mouffe (London,

Routledge and Kegan Paul, 1979), pp. 168–209; Perry Anderson, 'The antimonies of Antonio Gramsci'; Christie Buci-Glucksmann, *Gramsci and the state*, trans. David Fernback (London, Lawrence and Wishart, 1980).

45 In this context, Talal Asad refers to a process of mutual accommodation between Islamic rulers and their subjects: Asad, 'Two European images of non-European rule', pp. 109–10.

46 For descriptions of this aspect of 'hegemonic' ideology see Halil İnalcık, 'Örf', *Encyclopedia of Islam*, 2nd edn.; 'Adaletnameler', *Belgeler*, II, 3–4(1965), 49–145; 'Suleiman the lawgiver and Ottoman law' *Archivum Ottomanicum*, 1(1969), 105–38.

47 For an excellent treatment of the role of the *ulema* in the production of 'culture' and the changes in that role during the late eighteenth and the nineteenth centuries in Egypt see Peter Gran, *Islamic roots of capitalism*, pp. 178–88. Also, Gran explores the relationship between the *ulema* and the mystical orders – the convergence and conflicting of their interests.

48 For the adoption of new modes of administrative organization, of new regulations during the Tanzimat period see Lewis, *Emergence of modern Turkey*; Roderic Davidson, *Reform in the Ottoman Empire, 1856–1876* (Princeton, Princeton University Press, 1963).

49 For changes in the modes of taxation and therefore in the role of the state see Roger Owen, *The Middle East in the world economy* (New York, Methuen, 1981), pp. 59, 292.

50 For instance, the nineteenth century in Egypt witnessed the decline of al-Azhar University in Cairo as bureaucrats educated in new state schools established by Muhammad Ali increasingly replaced the al-Azhar graduates in the reproduction of culture (P. Gran, *Islamic roots of capitalism*), pp. 178–88).

51 For a discussion of this absence see Şerif Mardin, 'Power, civil society and culture in the Ottoman Empire'. For a counter-argument and perceptive comments on popularist tradition in Islamic society deriving their legitimation from Islamic ideology see Asad, "Two European images of non-European rule', p. 110, n. 17. Asad also questions the arguments about 'Oriental' cynicism in relation to political life.

52 A group of Ottoman intellectuals known as the 'Young Ottomans' are representative of this mode of reaction: Şerif Mardin, *The Genesis of Young Ottoman Thought* (Princeton, Princeton University Press, 1962).

53 For the concept of 'traditionalization' see Abdallah Laroui, *The crisis of the Arab intellectual: Traditionalism or historicism* (Berkeley, The University of California Press, 1976).

54 For a discussion of the historicity of the distinction between secular and religious culture in the context of 'peripheralization' see Gran, *Islamic roots of capitalism*, pp. 178–88.

55 For a discussion of pan-Islamic ideology in the context of reaction to Western penetration see Edmund Burke III, *Prelude to protectorate in Morocco: Pre-colonial protest and resistance* (Chicago, The University of Chicago Press, 1976), p. 151.

56 Anderson, *Lineages*, pp. 397–400. Hans-Heinrich Nolte, 'The position of Eastern Europe in the international system in early modern times', *Review*, VI, 1(Summer, 1982), 25–84.

57 For recent contributions to the discussion of 'revolutions from above' see Ellen Kay Trimberger, *Revolutions from above: military bureaucrats and modernisation in Japan, Turkey, Egypt, and Peru* (New Brunswick, New Jersey, Transaction Books, 1978); Theda Skocpol and Ellen Kay Trimberger, 'Revolution and world historical development of capitalism', *Berkeley Journal of Sociology*, 22(1977–8), 101–14.

1 Late-eighteenth- early-nineteenth-century Egypt: merchant capitalism or modern capitalism?

1 The problem arose in my book *Islamic roots of capitalism: Egypt 1760–1840* (Austin, University of Texas Press, 1979), ch. 1, from the discovery of the various roles played by merchants in the larger world-market. I owe a debt to Maxime Rodinson's concept of a 'capitalist sector' in his *Islam and capitalism* (Austin, University of Texas Press, 1981). This concept marked a break with 'merchant capital' and anticipated the '*Grundrisse* phase' of current debates. Rodinson's term was the first recognition of the problem of the meaning of the Arabic *tâjir*. I regard Samir Amin as a direct heir of these insights. In *Arab Nation* (London, Zed Press, 1978), Amin reversed the classical Marxist position by posing both the European and the Arab merchant as being the basis of their respective capitalisms. This differs in two important ways from the critiques of merchant capital, by invoking first the importance of the world system as an ongoing process in developing what Rodinson would call a 'capitalist mentality', and insisting that the home, that is the unwaged domain, is part of the history of capitalism, through capitalist reproduction. The medieval 'capitalist mentality' was shaped by a world of guilds; it was the modern world system which disintegrated them and created a more capitalist Neo-Maturidite ideology from the sixteenth century. Furthermore, modern capitalist theory by conceding too much to Engels' theory of social productive labour, a theory which more than anything else undermined a true labour theory of value, has ignored the home as a fundamental institution of capitalism. Neither Rodinson nor Amin analyse the home except as pre-capitalist. This predisposes them to ignore the question of reproduction in their definitions of capitalism. Amin, of course, makes extensive use of the development-of-underdevelopment theme but he does so in the framework of the colonial era only. For Amin, Arab history is, from the sixteenth century, one of collapse (*Arab Nation*, p. 24); only at the end of the nineteenth century does Amin revert to a process theory of history with the idea of periphery capitalism.

2 A recent theoretical statement which reintroduces the role of distribution and summarizes the debates is André Gunder Frank, *World accumulation, 1492–1789* (New York, Monthly Review Press, 1978), ch. 7. Ultimately it is based on Marx's own self-clarifications and corrections in *Grundrisse* (London, New Left Books, 1973), 'The chapter on capital', esp. p. 408. For Egypt specifically, the publication of the fundamental work by André Raymond, *Artisans et commerçants au Caire au XVIIIe siècle* (2 vols., Damascus, Institute Français de Damas, 1973–4), shifts the discussion of Egyptian economy and polity out of the sterile Oriental despotism discourse into a history of trade and production, undercutting the utility of most of the theoretical books about Egypt ever written. More recently Terence Walz, *Trade between Egypt and Bilad As-Sudan, 1700–1820* (Cairo, IFAO, 1978), pp. 110 ff, gives an idea of the range of investments of one *wakāla* merchant.

3 Edward Said, *Orientalism* (New York, Random House, 1978); my review article for *Journal of the American Oriental Society*, 100(1980), 328–31.

4 'Political-economy of medical history: the rise of positivism in modern Arabic medicine and other fields', *Society, economy and medicine in Middle Eastern History*, ed. B. Musallam (Urbana, University of Illinois, forthcoming).

5 Gran, *Islamic roots of capitalism*, ch. 2. The struggle to control the lower classes by a government-sanctioned *ṣūfī* administrator is the background for Fred de Jong, *Turuq and Turuq-linked institutions in nineteenth century Egypt: a historical study in organizational dimensions of Islamic mysticism* (Leiden, Brill, 1978).

6 Gran, *Islamic roots of capitalism*.

7 Introduction to the literature of the agricultural crisis in the south of France in the late eighteenth century of a technical sort is in the Centre de la Méditerranée Moderne et Contemporaine, *L'ankylose de l'économie méditerranéenne au XVIIIe et au début du XIXe siècle: le rôle de l'agriculture* (Nice, Centre de la Méditerranée Moderne et Contemporaine, 1976); Michel Morineau, *Les faux semblants d'un démarrage économique: l'agriculture et la démographie en France au XVIIIe siècle* (Paris, Colin, 1970). And of a sociological sort in Barrington Moore, *Social origins of dictatorship and democracy* (Boston, Beacon, 1968).

8 Gran, *Islamic roots of capitalism*, chs. 3, 4, and *passim.*

9 Pierre-Philippe Rey, *Les alliances de classes* (Paris, Maspero, 1973).

10 Josef Muzikar 'Arab nationalism and Islam', *Archiv Orientalni*, V, 43(1975), 193–209, 302–23.

11 Olivier Le Brun and Chris Gerry, 'Petty producers and capitalism', *Review of African Political Economy*, 3(1975), 20–32.

12 Maurice Dobb, *Theories of value and distribution since Adam Smith* (Cambridge, Cambridge University Press, 1973), pp. 168 ff.

13 Gran, *Islamic roots of capitalism*, ch. 1.

14 An early rendition is F. Charles-Roux, *Les origines de l'expedition d'Egypte* (Paris, Plon-Nourrit, 1910); more recently Alain Silvera, 'Bonaparte and Talleyrand: the origins of the French expedition to Egypt in 1798', *The American Journal of Arabic Studies*, 3(1975), 1–14.

15 Paul Masson, *Histoire du commerce Français dans le Levant au XIIIe siècle* (Paris, Librairie Hachette, 1911), pp. 601ff, is a bit misleading, recording quite literally the pessimistic statements of merchants, intended of course to elicit sympathy.

16 Edouard Baratier, *Histoire de Marseille* (Toulouse, Edouard Privat, 1973), ch. 11.

17 Stanford Shaw, *Ottoman Egypt in the age of the French Revolution* (Cambridge, Harvard University Press, 1964), pp. 142–3; John Reudy, *Land policy in colonial Algeria: the origins of the rural public domain* (Berkeley, University of California Press, 1967), ch. 1.

18 Pierre Guiral, *Marseille et l'Algérie, 1830–41* (Aix-en-Provence, Publication des Annales de la Faculté des Lettres, 1956), pp. 26–30.

19 Talleyrand once quoted Napoleon to this effect: Talleyrand, *Memoirs of the Prince De Talleyrand* (London, Grolier Society, n.d.), vol. 1, p. 198. N. Bonaparte, *French expedition into Syria* (London, Cooper and Wilson, 1799), pp. 18–19, praises the commercial value of the nation, but so do many others!

2 Agenda for Ottoman history

1 See Aidan Foster-Carter, 'From Rostow to Gunder Frank: conflicting paradigms in the analysis of underdevelopment', *World Development*, IV, 3(1976), 167–80. Foster-Carter's new paradigm is limited to development theory. We are referring to a different body of literature in sociology, anthropology, and history, the representative works of which can be found in the following journals: *Critique of Anthropology, Economy and Society, Journal of Peasant Studies.*

2 L. Althusser and E. Balibar, *Reading capital* (London, New Left Books, 1972); André Gunder Frank, *Capitalism and underdevelopment in Latin America* (New York, Monthly Review Press, 1967); Immanuel Wallerstein, *The modern world-system* (New York, Academic Press 1974).

3 See H. İnalcık, *The Ottoman Empire: the classical age, 1300–1600* (New York, Praeger, 1973); H.A.R. Gibb and H. Bowen, *Islamic Society and the West*, I (London, Oxford University Press, 1962); B. Lewis, *The emergence of modern Turkey* (New York, Oxford University Press, 1968).

4 The current research conducted in Ottoman history can be classified into these two temporal blocks. Most recent doctoral dissertations take either the sixteenth or the nineteenth century as their period of study.

5 See Aziz Al-Azmeh, 'What is the Islamic city?', *Review of Middle East Studies*, 2(1976).

6 The division of the Ottoman society into two classes, the military and the *reaya*, originates in the work of N. Itzkowitz, 'Eighteenth-century Ottoman realities', *Studia Islamica*, XVI(1962), 73–94. Itzkowitz's work emerged as a critique of A.H. Lybyer, *The government of the Ottoman Empire in the time of Suleiman the Magnificent* (New York, Russell and Russell, 1966) which had divided the Ottoman society into Ruling and Muslim institutions. Also see Ö.L. Barkan, 'Edirne askeri kassamına ait tereke defterleri, 1545–1659', (Inheritance Registers of the Edirne Askeri Class, 1545–1659). *Belgeler*, III, 5–6(1966), 1–479.

7 For an elaboration of this circularity, see H. İnalcık, 'Capital formation in the Ottoman Empire', *Journal of Economic History*, XXXIX, 1(1969), 97–140. This traditional idea is formalized in the classic work of Nizam ül-Mülk, *Siyasetnâme*. The original is in Persian; the English translation by Hubert Darke bears the title, *The Book of Government; or Rules for Kings* (New Haven, Yale University Press, 1960).

8 See P. Wittek, *The rise of the Ottoman Empire* (London, The Royal Asiatic Society of Great Britain and Ireland, 1938) for an analysis which sees the *gaza* (holy war) tradition as the central factor in the formation of the Ottoman state.

9 For a comprehensive analysis of Islamic state ideology, see Marshall G. Hodgson, *The venture of Islam, conscience and history in a world civilization* (3 vols., Chicago, University of Chicago Press, 1974).

10 See İnalcık, *The Ottoman Empire*, p. 3.

11 The discussion that follows is largely based on the critical analysis of Gibb and Bowen by Roger Owen, 'The Middle East in the eighteenth century – an 'Islamic' society in decline: a critique of Gibb and Bowen's 'Islamic society and the West', *Review of Middle East Studies*, 1(1975), 101–12.

12 For a discussion of the historiography of 'Oriental despotism' see Perry Anderson, *Lineages of the absolutist state* (London, New Left Books, 1974). The contemporary analyses based on the idea of Oriental despotism originate in the work of Karl A. Wittfogel, *Oriental despotism* (New Haven, Yale University Press, 1957).

13 For the role of the notables, see A.H. Hourani, 'Ottoman Reform and the Politics of Notables', *Beginnings of Modernization in the Middle East: the nineteenth century*, eds. W.R. Polk and R.L. Chambers (Chicago University of Chicago Press, 1968), pp. 41–68; and Kemal H. Karpat, 'Structural change, historical stages of modernization, and the role of the social groups in Turkish politics', *Social change and politics in Turkey: a structural-historical analysis*, ed. K. Karpat (Leiden, Brill, 1973), pp. 11–92.

14 For a discussion of how the idea of secularism developed in the Ottoman context, see Niyazi Berkes, *The development of secularism in Turkey* (Montreal, McGill University Press, 1964).

15 'Modernization literature' is used to refer to the liberal paradigm in development literature current in the 1950s and 1960s, exemplified in the review, *Economic Development and Cultural Change*. For the Middle East, the standard modernization text has been Daniel Lerner, *The passing of traditional Society: modernizing the Middle East* (New York, Free Press, 1958). This paradigm finds its most complete statement in a conference held, appropriately enough, in Chicago. See Polk and Chambers (eds.), *Beginnings of modernization*.

16 See Şerif Mardin, *The genesis of young Ottoman thought: a study in the modernization of Turkish political ideas* (Princeton, Princeton University Press, 1962) for the extent of these ideological borrowings.

17 See Roderic H. Davison, *Reform in the Ottoman Empire, 1856–1876* (Princeton, Princeton University Press, 1963); F.E. Bailey, *British policy and the Turkish reform movement: a study in Anglo-Turkish relations, 1826–1853* (New York, H. Fertig, 1970); Stanford J. Shaw, *Between old and new* (Cambridge, Harvard University Press, 1971), and a number of doctoral dissertations supervised by S. Shaw.

18 By the Asiatic mode of production, we mean a situation in which the agricultural producer is a free peasant and his surplus is appropriated in the form of taxes by the state. Only state officials belong to the class of surplus appropriators. Thus the unit of reproduction is defined by the extent of the political authority. This situation reflects a distinct articulation of the political, ideological, and economic levels. Thus the Asiatic mode of production exists as a mode of production, provided that we accept the definition given in L. Althusser and E. Balibar, *Reading capital*.

In the late 1960s and the early 1970s, there was a debate in Turkey on the nature of the Ottoman Empire. The debate started with Sencer Divitçioğlu, *Asya Tipi Üretim Tarzı ve Osmanlı Toplumu* (Ottoman society and the Asiatic mode of production) (İstanbul, İstanbul Üniversitesi Yayınlarından, 1967), arguing that the Ottoman Empire was an example of the Asiatic mode of production. More orthodox participants in the debate rejected this view and coined terms as far-fetched as 'centralized feudalism'. This debate, however, was carried out within a narrow perspective without recourse to such essential concepts as 'social formation' or 'dominance'. Hence, even the most sophisticated contributions remained descriptive and ultimately empirical. This judgement can be extended to the entire literature (most of which appeared in *La Pensée*) generated by the concept of the Asiatic mode of production in the 1960s.

19 The argument in this section was originally formulated in Çağlar Keyder, 'The Dissolution of the Asiatic mode of production', *Economy and Society*, V, 2(1976), 178–96.

20 *Tımar* was not only for agricultural revenues. There were *tımars* applying to revenues from mines, etc. See Halil İnalcık, *Hicrî 815 Tarihli Suret-i Defter-i Sancak-ı Arvanid* (Copy of an official register for the province of Arvanid, year 815 Hicrî) (Ankara, Türk Tarih Kurumu, 1954). For a description of the institution see Ö.L. Barkan, 'Les formes de l'organisation du travail agricole dans l'Empire Ottoman aux XVe et XVIe siècles', *Revue de la Faculté des Sciences Économiques de l'Université d'Istanbul* I, 1(1939–40), 14–44. Halil İnalcık, *The Ottoman Empire*, and Gibb and Bowen, in *Islamic society and the West*, use a terminology proper to feudalism in describing the *tımar* institution. For an account of the Seljuk origins see C. Cahen, 'Ikta', *The Encyclopaedia of Islam*, 2nd edn. The *tımar* system did not apply to the collection of all revenue. On crown lands, the collection of taxes was entrusted either to tax-farmers or to salaried state officials.

21 *Öşr* was a traditional Islamic tax equal to one-tenth of the annual product. For a description of Ottoman taxes, see Halil İnalcık, 'Osmanlılarda Raiyyet Rüsumu' (Taxes paid by Ottoman subjects); *Belleten*, XXIII, 92(1959), 575–610, and Lütfi Güçer, *XVI–XVII Asırlarda Osmanlı İmparatorluğunda Hububat Meselesi ve Hububattan Alınan Vergiler* (The question of grains and taxes on grains in the Ottoman Empire during the sixteenth century) (İstanbul, İstanbul Üniversitesi Yayını, 1964). Gyula Kaldy-Nagy, 'The effects of the *tımar* system on agricultural production in Hungary', in L. Ligeti (ed.), *Studia Turcica* (Budapest, Akademiai Kiado, 1971), 241–8, describes the inception and effects of the *tımar* system in Hungary.

22 Legal and administrative authorities were not so clearly distinguished. Actually, the *sipahi* was also empowered to enforce and collect penal dues. See Halil İnalcık, 'Centralization and decentralization in Ottoman administration' in T. Naff and

R. Owen (eds.), *Studies in eighteenth century Islamic history: decline or change* (Carbondale, Southern Illinois University Press, 1977). The *sipahi-kadı* relationship is discussed in Halil İnalcık, 'Adaletnâmeler' (Legal statutes), *Belgeler*, II, 3–4(1965), 49–145.

23 For Ottoman guilds, see G. Baer, 'The administrative, economic, and social functions of Turkish guilds', *International Journal of Middle East Studies*, I (Jan., 1970), 28–50. For *hisba* see Halil İnalcık, 'Capital formation', p. 106.

24 Suraiya Faroqhi, 'Sixteenth century periodic markets in various Anatolian *sancaks*: İçel, Hamid, Karahisarı-ı Sahib, Kütahya, Aydın and Menteşe', *Journal of Economic and Social History of the Orient*, XII, 1(1979), 32–80, insists on this administrative determination. Also see Lüfti Güçer, *XVI–XVII, ıncı Asırlarda Osmanlı İmparatorluğunun Ticaret Politikası* (The commercial policy of the Ottoman Empire in the XVI–XVIIIth centuries) (manuscript, n.d.) for location and administration of markets. Markets were also found outside the settlement areas, where they were usually larger. In the sixteenth century, the number of village markets increased, thus showing a response to economic environment. After the sixteenth century, periodic fairs increased in numbers both in Anatolia and the Balkans, indicating a greater commercial involvement of the peasantry. For a list of eighteenth-century fairs in the Balkans, see N. Svoronos, *Le commerce de Salonique au XVIIIe siècle* (Paris, Presses Universitaries de France, 1956). For the markets in the Balkans, I. Asdrachas, 'Aux Balkans du XVe siècle: producteurs directs et marchés,' *Études balkaniques*, VI, 3(1970), 36–59.

25 The *derbent* organization was set up to protect the passes and the roads. Peasants were granted tax exemptions in return for their work maintaining roads, bridges, and passes. In time of the Celali uprisings and peasant flights, the maintenance of these routes was disrupted, threatening the security of merchants. For the *derbent* organization, see Cengiz Orhonlu, *Osmanlı İmparatorluğunda Derbent Teşkilatı* (Derbent organization in the Ottoman Empire) (İstanbul, İstanbul Üniversitesi Edebiyat Fakültesi, 1967).

26 See Mehmet Genç, 'A comparative study of the life term tax farming data and the volume of commercial and industrial activities in the Ottoman Empire during the second half of the 18th century', in *La révolution industrielle dans le Sud-est européen – XIXe siècle* (Sofia, Institut d'Études Balkaniques, 1976), pp. 242–79, for tax-farms on internal customs revenues (*mukataa*).

27 For the palace's concern over the provisioning of İstanbul, see Lütfi Güçer, 'XVIII. Yüzyıl Ortalarında İstanbul'un İaşesi İçin Lüzumlu Hububatın Temini Meselesi', (The provisioning of grains for İstanbul in the mid eighteenth century), *İktisat Fakültesi Mecmuası*, XI, 1–4(1949–50), 397–416. Also see R. Mantran, *Istanbul dans la seconde moitié du XVIIe siècle* (Paris, A. Maisonneuve, 1962), and M.M. Alexandrescu-Dersca, 'Contribution à l'étude de l'approvisionnement en blé de Constantinople au XVIIIe siècle', *Acta Orientalia et Studia* (Société des Sciences Historiques et Philologiques de la République Populaire Roumaine, Section d'Études, 1957), 13–37.

28 Contraband was carried out along the coastal areas, usually by Greek ships which were stationed on the Aegean islands. Its importance in the commercialization of agriculture and in the rise of the Greek bourgeoisie was great, especially during the eighteenth century. The story of contraband, sometimes involving 'feudalized' landlords, is yet to be told. Maurice Aymard, *Venise, Raguse, et le commerce du blé pendant la seconde moitié du XVIe siècle* (Paris, SEVPEN, 1966), for example, minimizes illegal trade. Traian Stoianovich, however, recognizes its importance. See 'Land tenure and related sectors of the Balkan economy, 1600–1800', *The Journal of Economic History*, XIII, 4(1953), 398–411; 'Le maïs dans les Balkans', *Annales, ESC*, XXI, 5(Sept.–Oct.

1966), 1026–40; 'Le maïs arrive dans les Balkans', *Annales, ESC*, XVII, 1(Jan.–June 1962), 84–93.

29 See Halil İnalcık. 'Capital formation'.

30 The Persian wars can be interpreted as attempts to secure trade over the silk route, and essential silk supplies (in the conquest of Tabriz, for example). The wars with the Karamani aimed at opening trade with Egypt. Balkan campaigns of the fifteenth century aimed at seizing the Belgrade road (the royal road of the Byzantine Empire) in order to circumvent Venice. See Radovan Samardzic, 'Belgrade, centre économique de la Turquie du Nord au XVIe siècle', La ville balkanique, XVe–XIXe siècles, *Studia Balkanica* (Sofia, 1970), 33–44.

31 For the trade of Bursa see Halil İnalcık, 'Bursa and the commerce of the Levant', *Journal of the Economic and Social History of the Orient*, III, 2(1960), 131–47. For the Black Sea trade see Halil İnalcık *The Ottoman Empire*, pp. 131–3.

32 For Ragusan trade, see J. Tadic, 'Le commerce en Dalmatie et à Raguse et la décadence économique de Venise au XVIIIe siècle', in *Aspetti e cause della decadenza economica veneziana nel secolo XVII*. Atti del Convegno, 27 giugno–2 luglio 1957. Venezia, Isola di San Giorgio Maggiore; *Civiltà Veneziana. Studi*, 9(Venezia, Istituto per la Collaborazione Culturale, 1961), 237–74. For Venice, see R. Woolf, 'Venice and the Terraferma: problems of the change from commercial to landed activities', in B.S. Pullan (ed.), *Crisis and change in the Venetian economy in the sixteenth and seventeenth centuries* (London, Methuen, 1968); F. Braudel, *The Mediterranean and the Mediterranean world in the age of Philip II* (2 vols., New York, Harper and Row, 1972) I; W. Heyd, *Histoire du commerce du Levant au moyen age* (Amsterdam, A.M. Hakkert, 1959); and Maurice Aymard, *Venise*.

33 The major article on the Mediterranean spice trade is Frederic C. Lane, 'The Mediterranean spice trade: further evidence of its revival in the 16th century', *American Historical Review*, XLV, 3(Apr. 1940), 571–90. See also R. Mantran, 'L'empire Ottoman et le commerce asiatique aux 16e et 17e siècles', in D.S. Richards (ed.), *Islam and the trade of Asia* (Philadelphia, University of Pennsylvania Press, 1970), pp. 169–79.

34 See Niels Steensgaard, *The Asian trade revolution of the seventeenth century: The East India companies and the decline of the caravan trade* (Chicago, University of Chicago Press, 1974).

35 For the silk trade, see Ralph Davis, 'English imports from the Middle East, 1580–1780', in M.A. Cook (ed.), *Studies in the economic history of the Middle East from the rise of Islam to the present day* (London, Oxford University Press, 1970), pp. 193–206. For English trade in the Levant, see T.S. Willan, 'Some aspects of English trade with the Levant in the sixteenth century', *English Historical Review*, CCLXXVI, 70(July 1955), 399–410; and A.C. Wood, *History of the Levant Company*, 2nd edn (New York, Barnes and Nobles, 1964).

36 For French trade, see P. Masson, *Histoire du commerce français dans le Levant au XVIIIe siècle* (Paris, Hachette, 1911). See also Robert Paris, *L'histoire du commerce de Marseille*, vol. V: *1660–1789. Le Levant* (Paris, Plon, 1957).

37 For Selanik, see N. Svoronos, *Commerce*; for the overland trade, see Traian Stoianovich, 'The conquering Balkan orthodox merchant,' *The Journal of Economic History*, XX, 2(June 1960), 234–313; and Virginia Paskaleva, 'Osmanlı Balkan Eyaletlerinin Avrupalı Devletlerle Ticaretleri Tarihine Katkı (1700–1850)' (A contribution to the history of commerce between the Balkan provinces of the Ottoman Empire and the European states) *İstanbul Üniversitesi İktisat Fakültesi Mecmuası*, XXVII, 1–2(1967–8), 265–92.

38 The peasant was 'free' in the sense that he was not a serf. He was, however, restricted in movement. He had to pay a tax if he wanted to leave his village permanently, and

his land could be confiscated if left uncultivated for three years in succession. See Ö.L. Barkan, 'Türkiye'de servaj var mı idi?' (Was there serfdom in Turkey?), *Belleten*, XX, 1–3(1956), 237–46; 'XV ve XVI Asırlarda Toprak İşçiliğinin Organizasyon Şekilleri', (Organization of Agricultural Labour in the fifteenth and sixteenth centuries) *İstanbul Üniversitesi İktisat Fakültesi Mecmuası*, I, 1(1939), 29–74; I, 2(1940), 198–245; I, 4(1940), 397–447.

39 Mehmet II, for instance, confiscated *vakıf* lands of the *ulema* faction and expanded *tımar* areas. His son, Beyazid II, however supported the *ulema* faction who were instrumental in his succession to the throne. In the nineteenth century, the *ulema* and the civil bureaucrats struggled to control the central administration.

40 Especially of guilds. Janissaries also became tax-farmers and engaged in contraband trade.

41 The most famous example was Mehmet Ali in Egypt. Tepedelenli Ali in the Balkans, Çapanoğlu, and Karaosmanoğlu in Anatolia were others. See K. Karpat, *Social change and politics in Turkey*.

42 Charles Tilly and Richard Tilly, 'Agenda for European economic history in the 1970's', *Journal of Economic History*, XXXI, 1(March 1971), 184–98.

43 Ö.L. Barkan, 'Tarihi Demografi Araştırmaları ve Osmanlı Tarihi', (Studies in Historical demography and Ottoman history), *Türkiyat Mecmuası*, X(1951–3), 1–27, and Ö.L. Barkan, 'XVI. Asrın ikinci yarısında Türkiye'de fiyat hareketleri', (Price movements in Turkey in the second half of the sixteenth century). *Belleten*, XXXIV, 136(1970), 557–607. M.A. Cook, *Population Pressure in Rural Anatolia, 1450–1600* (London, Oxford University Press, 1972), and Leila Erder and Suraiya Faroqhi, 'Population rise and fall in Anatolia, 1550–1620', *Middle Eastern Studies*, 15, 3(1979), 322–45, demonstrate the increase in Ottoman population, confirming Braudel's hypothesis of a general upsurge in population in the Mediterranean during the sixteenth century. The relative increase in urban population is shown by Ronald C. Jennings, 'Urban population in Anatolia in the sixteenth century: a study of Kayseri, Karaman, Amasya, Trabzon, and Erzurum', *International Journal of Middle East Studies*, VII, 1(1976), 21–57.

44 The same argument can be found in Emmanuel Le Roy Ladurie, *The peasants of Languedoc* (Urbana, University of Illinois Press, 1974), deriving from Braudel, *Mediterranean*.

45 *Avariz* which began as extraordinary taxes, were soon converted into regular taxes due to the endemic revenue crisis.

46 On *levends*, see Mustafa Cezar, *Osmanlı Tarihinde Levendler*, (*Levends* in the Ottoman Empire) (İstanbul, Güzel Sanatlar Akademisi Yayınları, 1965), and Halil İnalcık, 'Centralization', in Naff and Owen, pp. 27–8.

47 The Celali uprisings is the collective name given to unrest and brigandry in Anatolia from the 1590s to the mid seventeenth century. Population pressure and the price inflation were the probable causes of this movement which included smaller *sipahis*, *medrese* students, and irregular soldiers in the retinue of provincial administrators. The central authority, exceptionally, armed the peasantry to combat the bandits, which in turn created more rebels. From a devastated countryside, peasants fled to fortified towns or to unreachable mountainous areas; see Xavier de Planhol, *Les fondements géographiques de l'histoire de l'Islam* (Paris, Flammarion, 1968). The literature on the uprisings includes Mustafa Akdağ, *Celali İsyanları 1550–1603* (Celali uprisings, 1550–1603) (Ankara, Ankara Üniversitesi Basımevi, 1963), and William Griswold, *The great Anatolian rebellion 1000–1020/1591–1611* (Berlin, Klaus Schwarz Verlag, 1983). After the emergence of *ayans*, the bandits may have been absorbed into their retinues. See Neşet Çağatay, 'Osmanlı İmparatorluğu arazi ve reaya

kanunnamelerinde ilhak edilen memleketlerin âdet ve kanunları ve istilahların izleri', (Traditions and laws of annexed countries in Ottoman land and peasant jurisdiction), Report no. III, *Türk Tarih Kongresi* (Ankara, Türk Tarih Kurumu, 1948).

48 For the effects of the price inflation in the Ottoman Empire, see Ö.L. Barkan, 'Research on the Ottoman fiscal surveys', in Cook and Ö.L. Barkan, 'The price revolution of the sixteenth century: a turning point in the economic history of the Near East'. *International Journal of Middle East Studies*, VI, 1(1975), 3–28. See also Mustafa Akdağ, 'Osmanlı İmparatorluğunun kuruluş ve inkişaf devrinde Türkiye'nin iktisadi vaziyeti', (Economic situation in Turkey at the time of the foundation and rise of the Ottoman Empire), *Belleten*, XII, 51(1949–50), 498–564; and Halil Sahillioğlu, 'XVII. asrın ilk yarısında Istanbul'da Tedavüldeki Sikkelerin Rayiçi' (The exchange rate of *sikke* in circulation in Istanbul during the first half of the seventeenth century), *Belgeler Dergisi*, I, 2(1964), 223–8.

49 For a description of this assessment and an evaluation of the censuses as sources of data, see Ö.L. Barkan, 'Research on the Ottoman fiscal surveys', in Cook, *Studies in the economic history*.

50 They exacted not only salaries, but also 'gifts' from each new Sultan, a significant drain on the treasury. Every thirty-three years, when the lunar calendar fell exactly one year behind the solar calendar, the janissary had to be paid an extra three months' salary. These *sıvış* years coincided with the worst crises of the treasury and resulted in janissary rebellions. See Halil Sahillioğlu, '*Sıvış* year crises in the Ottoman Empire' in Cook, *Studies in the economic history*, pp. 230–52.

51 For the decline of the *tımar* system, see Mustafa Akdağ, 'Tımar rejiminin bozuluşu' (Dissolution of the *tımar* system), *Ankara Üniversitesi Dil ve Tarih Coğrafya Dergisi*, IV(1945), 419–31, and Bistra Cvetkova, 'L'évolution du régime féodal turc de la fin du XVI jusqu'au milieu du XVIII siècle', in Dimitre Kossav *et al.* (eds.), *Études historiques à l'occasion du XIe congrès international des sciences historiques, Stockholm, août 1960* (Sofia, 1960), pp. 171–206.

52 On this accumulation, see Mehmet Genç, 'Osmanlı Maliyesinde Malikane Sistemi', (*Malikane* system in Ottoman financial administration) in O. Okyar and Ünal Nalbantoğlu (eds.), *Türk İktisat Semineri* (Ankara, Hacettepe Üniversitesi, 1975).

53 For the *malikane* system see M. Genç, 'A comparative study', and İnalcık, 'Centralization', in Naff and Owen.

54 Usury in agriculture is, of course, not well-documented. See, however, Ronald C. Jennings, 'Urban population'; also see Suraiya Faroqhi, 'Agricultural activities in a Bektashi center: the Tekke of Kızıl Deli, 1750–1830', *Südost-Forschungen*, XXXV(1976), 69–96; and Halil İnalcık, 'Suleiman the Lawgiver and Ottoman law', *Archivum Ottomanicum*, I(1969), 105–38.

55 See Karl Marx, *Capital*, II, ch. 36.

56 See Karl Marx, *Capital*, III, ch. 4.

57 For a discussion of the origins of *ayans*, see H. İnalcık, 'Centralization', in Naff and Owen; also on *ayans*, see K. Karpat (ed.), *Structural change*.

58 Our primary concern here is to establish the connection between tax-farming and the rise of local potentates. We are not interested in how their local power bases originated, nor do we attempt to assess the significance of this group within the context of Ottoman history. It should be mentioned, however, that the development of *ayans* remains one of the least explored issues in Ottoman historiography, and ours is an attempt to place them within the context of 'feudalization'.

59 For commercialized agriculture in the Balkans, see Christo Gandev, 'L'apparition des rapports capitalistes dans l'économie rurale de la Bulgarie du nord-ouest au cours

du XVIIIe siècle' in *Études historiques à l'occasion du XIe congrès*, pp. 207–20. See also Traian Stoivanovich's three articles cited in note 28.

60 For the genesis of *çiftliks*, see H. İnalcık, 'Adaletnâmeler'; also on the *çiftliks* in the Balkans, see T. Stoivanovich, 'Land tenure and related sectors'.

61 For a discussion of the change in the status of the peasantry under the *çiftlik* system, see Suraiya Faroqhi, 'Rural society in Anatolia and the Balkans during the sixteenth century', *Turcica: Revue d'études Turques*, IX, 1(1977), 161–95.

62 See E.R.J. Owen, 'Cotton production and the development of the cotton economy in nineteenth century Egypt', in C. Issawi (ed.), *The economic history of the Middle East, 1800–1914* (Chicago, University of Chicago Press, 1966), pp. 417–29; and Helen Rivlin, *The agricultural policy of Muhammed Ali in Egypt* (Cambridge, Harvard University Press, 1961).

63 See A.J. Sussnitzki, 'Zur Gliederung wirtschaftlicher Arbeit nach Nationalitäten in der Türkei', in Issawi.

64 See Dominique Chevallier, 'Western development and Eastern crisis in the mid-nineteenth century: Syria confronted with the European economy', in Polk and Chambers, pp. 205–22.

65 See M.A. Ubicini, excerpts from *Letters on Turkey*, in Issawi, pp. 43–5, and Ömer C. Sarç, 'Tanzimat ve Sanayimiz' (The Tanzimat and our Industry) in Issawi, pp. 43–5.

66 For the text of the Anglo-Turkish Commercial Convention of 1838, see Issawi (ed.), *Economic history*, pp. 39–40, and for the railway project, see W. von Pressel, 'Les chemins de fer de Turquie,' in Issawi, pp. 92–3.

67 See Orhan Kurmuş, 'The role of British capital in the economic development of western Anatolia, 1850–1913', Unpublished Ph.D. thesis, University of London, 1974.

68 See Donald C. Blaisdell, *European financial control in the Ottoman Empire: a study of the establishment, activities, and significance of the administration of the Ottoman public debts* (New York, AMS Press, 1966).

69 For the revenue problem of the bureaucracy and how these articulated with peripheralization, see Keyder, 'Dissolution'.

3 State and economy in the Ottoman Empire

1 For the definition of redistribution as a mode of economic integration, see George Dalton (ed.), *Primitive, archaic, and modern economies: essays of Karl Polanyi* (New York, Anchor Books, 1964).

2 'World-economy' and 'world-empire' are concepts used by Immanuel Wallerstein in his essay, 'The rise and future demise of the world-capitalist system', *Comparative Studies in Society and History*, XVI, 4(September 1974). My use of the concept 'world-economy' differs from Wallerstein's on two counts. First, whereas Wallerstein appears to use the concept to refer to market as well as to pre-market 'world' systems, I use it exclusively to refer to market-determined economic systems. Second, and more importantly, whereas Wallerstein reduces the structure and the role of states within the world-economy to the marketing processes and to dominant class interests determined by the market situation, in what follows, I treat states as relatively autonomous structures keyed to the dynamics of international military rivalries, and geo-political as well as world-economic circumstances in which they find themselves. The best treatment of empires as political units is found in S.N. Eisenstadt, *The political systems of empires* (New York, The Free Press, 1969).

3 As I shall attempt to explain below a 'single system' does not necessarily mean a whole of identical parts.

4 Karl Polanyi, 'The economy as instituted process', in Dalton (ed.), *Primitive, archaic and modern economies*, pp. 139–74.

5 For a more detailed definition of peasant economy, see Daniel Thorner, 'Peasant economy as a category of economic history', *Peasants and peasant societies*, ed. Theodor Shanin (Harmondsworth, Penguin Books, 1971).

6 With regard to the status of the peasant household in the Ottoman Empire, see the following studies by Ömer Lütfi Barkan: 'Osmanlı İmparatorluğunda Çiftçi Sınıflarının Hukuki Statüsü', *Ülkü*, IX, 49, 50, 53, X, 56, 57, 59(1937–8); 'Türkiye'de Toprak Meselelerinin Tarihi Esasları', *Ülkü*, XI, 61, 63, 64(1938); 'Türkiye'de Servaj Var mıydı?', *Belleten*, XX, 78(1956). With regard to the status of land and the *tımar* system, see the following: Ömer Lütfi Barkan, *XV ve XVI Asırlarda Osmanlı İmparatorluğunda Zirai Ekonominin Hukuki ve Mali Esasları* (İstanbul, Edebiyat Fakültesi Yayınları, 1943); Halil İnalcık, 'Land problems in Turkish history', *The Muslim World*, 45(1955); and, also his 'Ottoman methods of conquest', *Studia Islamica*, 2(1954); Mustafa Akdağ, *Türkiye'nin İçtimai ve İktisadi Tarihi* (Ankara, Dil-Tarih ve Coğrafya Fakültesi Yayınları, vol. I: 1959, vol. II: 1971).

7 Marshall Sahlins, *Stone age economics* (Chicago, Aldine-Atherton, 1972), pp, 74–99.

8 On the nature of the Ottoman state, see the following works by Halil İnalcık, 'Osmanlı Padişahı', *Siyasal Bilgiler Fakültesi Dergisi*, XIII (December 1958); 'Osmanlı Hukukuna giriş: Örfi-Sultani Hukuk ve Fatih Kanunları', *Siyasal Bilgiler Fakültesi Dergisi*, XIV (June 1958); 'The nature of traditional society', *Political modernization in Japan and Turkey*, eds. Robert Ward and Dankwart Rustow (Princeton, Princeton University Press, 1964).

9 I mean by the 'circle of equity' the traditional Ottoman maxim that a ruler 'could have no power without soldiers, no soldiers without money, no money without the well-being of his subjects, and no well-being without justice'. Mentioned by İnalcık in his 'The nature of traditional society', and also emphasized in Normal Itzkowitz, *Ottoman Empire and Islamic tradition* (New York, Alfred A. Knopf, 1972), and Sencer Divitçioğlu, *Asya Üretim Tarzı ve Osmanlı Toplumu* (Istanbul, İktisat Fakültesi Yayınları, 1967).

10 See Gabriel Baer, 'The administrative, economic and social functions of the Turkish guilds', *International Journal of Middle East Studies*, I, 1 (January 1970).

11 See Halil İnalcık, 'Capital formation in the Ottoman Empire', *Journal of Economic History* (March 1960); also his *The Ottoman Empire: the classical age, 1300–1600* (London, Weidenfel and Nicolson, 1973), ch. 15.

12 See my *State and society in the politics of Turkey's development* (Ankara, University of Ankara Press, 1974).

13 For two recent attempts to retell the story, see Immanuel Wallerstein, *The modern world-system* (New York, Academic Press, 1974) and Perry Anderson, *Passages from antiquity to feudalism* and *Lineages of the Absolutist state* (London, New Left Books, 1974).

14 On the shifting of the trade routes, see A.H. Lybyer, 'The Ottoman Turks and the routes of Oriental trade', *The English Historical Review*, CXX (October 1925); Frederic C. Lane, 'The Mediterranean spice trade', *The American Historical Review*, XLV (April 1940). Lane argues that the Portuguese did not reduce the Levantine spice trade to permanent insignificance. On the impact of the price revolution, see Ömer Lütfi Barkan, 'The price revolution of the sixteenth century: a turning point in the economic history of the Near East', *International Journal of Middle East Studies*, VI, 1 (January 1975); also Barkan's, 'XVI Asrın İkinci Yarısında Türkiye'de Fiyat Hareketleri', *Belleten*, XXXIV, 4 (October 1970); Niyazi Berkes, *Türkiye İktisat Tarihi* (2 vols., İstanbul, Gerçek Yayınları, 1970), vol. 2.

15 This concept of specificity without self-completion is taken from Hamza Alavi, 'India and the colonial mode of production', *Socialist Register: 1975*, eds. Ralph Miliband and John Saville (London, The Merlin Press, 1975).
16 Immanuel Wallerstein, 'From feudalism to capitalism: transition or transitions', Paper delivered at the 89th meeting of The American Historical Association, Chicago, December 28–30, 1974 (mimeograph).
17 On the opening of Ottoman agriculture toward exports in the later sixteenth century, see Fernand Braudel, *The Mediterranean and the Mediterranean world in the age of Philip II* (2 vols., London, Collins, 1973), vol. I, pp. 593–4. Braudel cites as his source the works of Ö.L. Barkan and his students without, however, reference. For further information on this point, see note 36.
18 For this shifting nature of Ottoman trade in the seventeenth and eighteenth centuries, see Traian Stoianovich, 'Land tenure and related sectors of the Balkan economy, 1600–1800', *The Journal of Economic History*, XIII(Fall 1953); also his 'The conquering Balkan orthodox merchants', *The Journal of Economic History*, XX(June 1960); Halil İnalcık, 'İmtiyazat', *Encyclopedia of Islam*, 2nd edn; Yahya S. Tezel, 'Cumhuriyetin Devraldığı Tarım Yapısının Tarihi Oluşumu Hakkında Bazı Düşünceler', *Siyasal Bilgiler Fakültesi Dergisi*, XXVI, 4(1972).
19 İnalcık, 'İmtiyazat'.
20 These privileges constitute the troublesome story of the capitulations, which had their origin in the *aman* tradition, but evolved under financial and political difficulties into extra-territorial grants and immunities to which not only foreign merchants but also, in time, the so-called *dragoman* were given access. The *dragoman* were largely the members of the Christian communities who had attached themselves to foreign merchants as 'translators' (*dragoman*), clerks, accountants, etc., but in actual fact they were themselves merchants, benefiting from the imperial immunities, and serving as intermediaries between foreign merchants and the newly installed tax-farmers.
21 This does not mean that all small family holdings ceased to exist; just the contrary, they continued to be widespread. They survived, however, not as detached units but, most likely, as sources of cheap labour for the estates.
22 Much has been written on the destruction of the *tımar* system; see the following: Ömer Lütfi Barkan, 'The social consequences of economic crisis in later sixteenth-century Turkey', *Social aspects of economic development* (Istanbul, Economic and Social Conference Board, 1964); H.A.R. Gibb and Harold Bowen, *Islamic society and the West*, vol. I (London; Oxford University Press, 1950); İsmail Cem, *Türkiye'de Geri Kalmışlığın Tarihi* (İstanbul, Cem Yayınları, 1972); V.J. Parry, 'The Ottoman Empire: 1566–1617', *The counter-reformation and the price revolution*, The New Cambridge Modern History, vol. III (Cambridge University Press, 1968).
23 On the Celali rebellions, see the following works by Mustafa Akdağ: *Büyük Celali Karışıklıklarının Başlaması* (Erzurum, Atatürk Üniversitesi Yayınları, 1963); *Celali İsyanları, 1550–1603* (Ankara, Dil-Tarih ve Coğrafya Fakültesi Yayınları, 1963); *Türk Halkının Dirlik ve Düzenlik Kavgası: Celali İsyanları* (Ankara, Bilgi Yayınevi, 1975).
24 Yücel Özkaya, *Osmanlı İmparatorluğunda Ayanlık* (Ankara, 1977), p. 99.
25 See Stoianovich, 'Land tenure and related sectors'.
26 Perry Anderson, *Lineages of the absolutist state.*
27 The literature in Turkish surrounding the problem of feudalism vs. capitalism is both too numerous and too polemical to cite. On the more theoretically oriented discussions it is essential to consult at least the following: Rodney Hilton (ed.), *The transition from feudalism to capitalism* (New York, New Left Books, 1952); Andre Gunder Frank, *Capitalism and underdevelopment in Latin America* (New York, Monthly Review Press, 1967); Ernesto Laclau, 'Feudalism and capitalism in Latin America', *New Left*

Review, 67(May–June 1971); Immanuel Wallerstein, 'The rise and the demise of the world-capitalist system'; Hamza Alavi, 'India and the colonial mode of production'. See also for a very lucid comparison of England and France, and Eastern and Western Europe within the problematique of economic development (and transition from feudalism to capitalism), Robert Brenner, 'Agrarian class structure and economic development in pre-industrial Europe', *Past and Present*, 70(February 1976).

28 For a rather damning view of such traits of the Ottoman ethos, see Sabri F. Ülgener, *İktisadi İnhitat Tarihimizin Ahlak ve Zihniyet Meseleleri* (Istanbul, İktisat Fakültesi Yayınları, 1951); also Halil İnalcık, 'The Ottoman economic mind and aspects of the Ottoman economy', *Studies in the economic history of the Middle East from the rise of Islam to the present day*, ed. M.A. Cook (London, Oxford University Press, 1970), which is more concerned with the structure of economic organization and the dominant role of the state.

29 Stoianovich, 'Land tenure and related sectors', p. 402.

30 See Ira M. Lapidus (ed.), *Middle Eastern cities* (Berkeley, University of California Press, 1969), particularly the essay by Charles Issawi on 'Economic change and urbanization in the Middle East'.

31 Cited in Kemal Karpat, 'The transformation of the Ottoman state: 1789–1908', *International Journal of Middle East Studies*, III, 3(July 1972), 251.

32 The nationalist struggles in the Balkans and the great power politics which they involved are succinctly discussed in L.S. Stavrianos, *The Balkans: 1815–1914* (New York, Holt, Rinehart and Winston, 1963); see also his *The Balkans since 1453* (New York, Holt, Rinehart and Winston, 1958).

33 For an interesting case study of a *derebey*, see Dennis S. Skiotis, 'From bandit to pasha: first steps in the rise to power of Ali of Tepelen, 1750–1784', *International Journal of Middle East Studies*, II, 3(July, 1971). On the *ayan*, see Harold Bowen, 'Ayan', *Encyclopedia of Islam*, 2nd edn, and Bekir Sıtkı Baykal, 'Ayanlık Müessesesinin Düzeni Hakkında Belgeler', *Belgeler*, I (1964).

34 On the politics and economics of the 'Eastern Question', see M.S. Anderson, *The Eastern Question: 1774–1923* (New York, Macmillan and St Martin's Press, 1966); V.J. Puryear, *International economics and diplomacy in the Near East* (Stanford, Stanford University Press, 1935); George Lenczowski, *The Middle East in world affairs* (Ithaca, Cornell University Press, 1962); Frank E. Bailey, *British Policy and the Turkish reform movement* (Cambridge, Harvard University Press, 1942).

35 Nineteenth-century reform movements are effectively dealt with in the following works: Bailey, *British Policy*; Roderic Davison, *Reform in the Ottoman Empire, 1856–1876* (Princeton, Princeton University Press, 1963); Bernard Lewis, *The emergence of modern Turkey*, (2nd edn, New York, Oxford University Press, 1968); William R. Polk and Richard Chambers (eds.), *The beginnings of modernization in the Middle East* (Chicago, University of Chicago Press, 1968); Niyazi Berkes, *The development of secularism in Turkey* (Montreal, McGill University Press, 1964); Robert Ward and Dankwart Rustow (eds.), *Political modernization in Japan and Turkey* (Princeton, Princeton University Press, 1964); *Tanzimat*, (Ankara, Maarif Matbaası, 1940).

36 On the nature of the Tanzimat reforms two excellent articles by Halil İnalcık are 'Tanzimatın Uygulanması ve Sosyal Tepkiler', *Belleten*, XXVIII, 112(1964); 'Sened-i İttifak ve Gülhane Hatt-ı Hümayunu', *Belleten*, XXVIII, 112(1964).

37 An excellent study on the impact of reforms on the interaction of state and society in Palestine and Syria is Moshe Maoz, *Ottoman reforms in Syria and Palestine, 1840–1861* (London, The Clarendon Press, 1968).

38 On the land code of 1858, see Ömer Lütfi Barkan, 'Türk Toprak Hukuku Tarihinde Tanzimat ve 1274 (1858) Tarihli Arazi Kanunnamesi', *Tanzimat*, pp. 321–421.
39 A good study of the local assemblies during the Tanzimat period is İlber Ortaylı, *Tanzimattan Sonra Mahalli İdareler, 1840–1878* (Ankara, TODAİE Yayınları, 1974).
40 On the economic structure of the Ottoman Empire and the impact of free trade, see the various articles collected in Charles Issawi (ed.), *The economic history of the Middle East: 1800–1914* (Chicago, University of Chicago Press, 1966), particularly chs. 3–8 and 10–12; see also, Yusuf K. Tengirşek, 'Tanzimat Devrinde Osmanlı Devletinin Harici Ticaret Siyaseti', *Tanzimat*, pp. 289–320; other articles on economics and diplomacy in the same volume are of interest as well.
41 The text of the Anglo-Ottoman treaty of commerce is found in Issawi, *The Economic History*, ch. 3.
42 For a description of the decline and near disappearance of industrial crafts in the nineteenth century, see Ömer Celal Sarç, 'Tanzimat ve Sanayiimiz', *Tanzimat*, pp. 423–40; the same article is partly translated in Issawi, *The economic history.*
43 See Reşat Aktan, 'The burden of taxation on the peasants', in Issawi, *The economic history*, ch. 12.
44 For a stimulating article which contests for Western Europe the progressivist approach centred around the dynamic role of merchant capital, see John Merrington, 'Town and country in the development of capitalism', *New Left Review*, 93(September–October 1975).
45 On the dynamics of the balance-of-payments problem and its impact, see Çağlar Keyder, 'The dissolution of the Asiatic mode of production', *Economy and Society*, V, 2(May 1976).
46 On Ottoman debts, see İ. Hakkı Yeniay, *Yeni Osmanlı Borçları Tarihi* (Istanbul, İstanbul Üniversitesi Yayınları, 1964), and Refii Şükrü Suvla, 'Tanzimat Devrinde İstikrazlar', *Tanzimat*, pp. 263–83.
47 The Ottoman Debt Administration is examined in detail in Donald C. Blaisdell, *European financial control in the Ottoman Empire* (New York, Columbia University, 1929).
48 Two stimulating discussions of revolutions with an emphasis on the role of state elites are: Theda Skocpol, 'France, Russia, and China: a structural analysis of social revolutions', *Comparative Studies in Society and History*, XVIII, 2 (April 1976); and Ellen Kay Trimberger, 'A theory of elite revolutions', *Studies in Comparative International Development*, VII, 3(Fall 1972).
49 For a similar assessment of the Turkish revolution, see Şerif Mardin, 'Ideology and religion in the Turkish revolution', *International Journal of Middle East Studies*, II, 3(July 1971).
50 The sense in which I use the concept of ideology here is best expressed by Clifford Geertz in his brilliant essay 'Ideology as a cultural system', in his *The interpretation of cultures* (New York, Basic Books, 1973).
51 John H. Schaar, 'Legitimacy in the modern state', *Power and community*, eds. Philip Green and Sanford Levinson (New York, Vintage Books, 1970), p. 287.
52 In an interesting article, Alasdair MacIntyre compares the epistemological assumptions of the revolutionaries with that of the social scientists; see his 'Ideology, social science and revolution', *Comparative Politics*, V, 3(April 1973).
53 Intra-bureaucratic conflicts which occurred after the founding of the Republic are discussed in Frederick Frey, *The Turkish political elite* (Cambridge, MIT Press, 1965); see also, Walter Weiker, *Political tutelage and democracy in Turkey: the Free Party and its aftermath* (Leiden, Brill, 1973).

54 Cited in Osman Okyar, 'The concept of etatism', *Economic Journal*, LXXI, 297(March 1965).

55 For a more detailed analysis of this shift, see my *State and society in the politics of Turkey's development.*

4 The incorporation of the Ottoman Empire into the world-economy

1 This three-fold distinction may be found in elaborated form in I. Wallerstein, *The capitalist world-economy* (Cambridge, Cambridge University Press, 1979), chs. 1, 8, 9. See also for the most detailed account the article by Immanuel Wallerstein on 'spazio economico' in *Enciclopedia Einaudi* (Torino: Einaudi, XII (1981), 304–14).

2 The problem was laid out in I. Wallerstein, 'The Ottoman empire and the capitalist world-economy: some questions for research', *Review*, II, 3(Winter 1979), 389–98.

3 In non-capitalist systems, the 'economic' and the 'political' do not constitute distinct spheres of social activities. Rather economic activity is 'embedded' in the social organization. This view is informed essentially by the interpretation of K. Polanyi, *The great transformation* (Boston, Beacon Press, 1957) and 'The economy as instituted process', *Trade and market in early empires: economics in history and theory*, ed. K. Polanyi, C. Arensberg, A. Pearson (Chicago, Gateway Edition, 1971). See also M. Godelier, *Rationality and irrationality in economics* (New York, Monthly Review Press, 1972); T.K. Hopkins, 'Sociology and the substantive view of the economy', in Polanyi *et al.*, *Trade and market.* İlkay Sunar adopts this view in 'Antropologie politique et économique: L'Empire ottomane et sa transformation' *Annales, ESC*, XXXV, 3–4 (May–August 1980), 551–79.

4 See the debate summarized by M.A. Cook, *Population pressure in rural Anatolia, 1450–1600* (London, Oxford University Press, 1972).

5 See H. İnalcık, 'Centralization and decentralization in Ottoman administration', *Studies in eighteenth-century Islamic history*, ed. T. Naff and R. Owen (Carbondale, Southern Illinois University Press, 1977), pp. 27–52.

6 See S. Faroqhi and H. İslamoğlu, 'Crop patterns and agricultural production trends in sixteenth-century Anatolia', *Review*, II, 3(Winter 1979), 401–36.

7 T. Stoianovich, 'Land tenure and the related sectors of the Balkan economy, 1600–1800', *The Journal of Economic History*, XIII, 4(Fall 1953), 398–411; 'The conquering Balkan orthodox merchant', *The Journal of Economic History*, XX, 2(June 1960), 234–313.

8 T. Stoianovich, 'Land tenure', p. 404.

9 H. İslamoğlu and Ç. Keyder, 'Agenda for Ottoman history', Chapter 2 in this volume.

10 For the Balkans, see C. and B. Jelavich, *The establishment of the Balkan national states: 1804–1920* (Seattle, University of Washington Press, 1977); Stoianovich, 'Land tenure; and 'The conquering'; P.F. Sugar, *Southeastern Europe under Ottoman rule, 1354–1804* (Seattle, University of Washington Press, 1977); P.F. Sugar and I.J. Lederer (eds.), *Nationalism in Eastern Europe* (Seattle, University of Washington Press, 1969). For Syria, see Abdul-Kerim Rafeq, 'Changes in the relationship between the Ottoman central administration and the Syrian provinces from the sixteenth to the eighteenth centuries', *Studies in eighteenth century Islamic history*, ed. T. Naff and R. Owen, pp. 53–73. For Egypt, see A. Richards, 'Primitive accumulation in Egypt, 1798–1882', Chapter 9 in this volume.

11 J. Berque, 'The establishment of the colonial economy', *Beginnings of modernization in the Middle East: The nineteenth century*, ed. W.R. Polk and R.L. Chambers (Chicago, University of Chicago Press, 1968), pp. 223–43; A. Richards, 'Primitive accumula-

tion'. For Syria, see D. Chevallier, 'Western development and Eastern crisis in the mid-eighteenth century: Syria confronted with European economy', *Beginnings of modernization*, ed. Polk and Chambers, pp. 205–22. For the Balkans, see C. and B. Jelavich, *The establishment.*

12 İnalcık has a different interpretation of Sened-i İttifak. He argues that this document was an attempt at legitimizing and institutionalizing the feudal status of the big landlords. H. İnalcık, 'Sened-i İttifak ve Gülhane hatt-ı humayunu', *Belleten*, XXVIII, 112(1964), 607. Our argument derives from Ş. Mardin, *The genesis of Young Ottoman thought* (Princeton, Princeton University Press, 1962), p. 148 n.

13 İnalcık, 'Sened-i İttifak', p. 609; Mardin, *The genesis*, p. 148.

14 H. İnalcık, '"Tanzimat" ın uygulanması ve sosyal tepkileri' (The application and social consequences of Tanzimat), *Belleten*, XXVII, 112(1964), 623–90; Mardin, *The genesis*, pp. 157 ff.

15 C. Issawi (ed.), *The economic history of the Middle East 1800–1914* (Chicago, University of Chicago Press, 1966), pp. 39–40 for the text of the Anglo-Turkish commercial convention of 1838; see also F.E. Bailey, *British policy and the Turkish reform movement: a study in Anglo-Turkish relations, 1826–1853* (Cambridge, Mass., Harvard University Press, 1942), p. 126. For a discussion of consequences, see O. Köymen, 'The advent and consequences of free trade in the Ottoman Empire', *Études Balkaniques*, 2(1971); Y.A. Petrosyan, *Sovyet gözüyle Jön Türkler* (Young Turks from the Soviet point of view; Ankara, Bilgi Yayınları, 1974), p. 37; Ö.C. Sarç, 'Tanzimat ve sanayimiz' (Tanzimat and our industry), *The economic history of the Middle East*, ed. C. Issawi; S. Yerasimos, *Azgelişmişlik sürecinde Türkiye-II: Tanzimat' tan birinci dünya savaşına* (Turkey in the process of underdevelopment: from Tanzimat to the First World War; Istanbul, Gözlem Yayınları, 1975), pp. 657 ff.

16 Both the Ottoman officials and urban and semi-urban proprietors squeezed the peasantry to 'accept protection'. Peasants were doubly oppressed under these circumstances, and in most cases had to pay two rents: one 'legal rent' to the state and another 'protection money' to the landlords. See Stoianovich, 'The conquering', p. 255; K. Karpat, 'The land regime, social structure and modernization in the Ottoman empire', *Beginnings of modernization*, ed. Polk and Chambers; Richards, 'Primitive accumulation'.

17 The zenith of the Young Ottoman movement was the promulgation of the 1876 constitution. But not even the most liberal member of the commissions that drafted the constitution suggested any basic diminution in the sovereign rights of the sultan. It would be a mistake to consider the Young Ottomans as totally conservative. They put forth their dissent through numerous literary manifestos, newspaper articles, etc. In point of fact, the first daily newspaper in Turkish history was put out by some Young Ottomans. The change in the ideological climate of the country they ushered in and their seminal impact on the formation of a bourgeois ideology cannot be disputed. For an excellent account of the Young Ottoman movement see Mardin, *The genesis*; see also B. Lewis, *The emergence of modern Turkey* (London, Oxford University Press, 1976), pp. 143–5.

18 L. Rathman, *Alman emperyalizminin Türkiye' ye girişi* (The introduction of German imperialism into Turkey; Istanbul, Gözlem Yayınları, 1976); Issawi, *The economic history*, p. 61; A.D. Novichev, 'The development of commodity money and capitalistic relations in agriculture', *The economic history of the Middle East*, ed. C. Issawi, pp. 66–7; Yerasimos, *Azgelişmişlik*, pp. 919–64; Ş. Pamuk, *Osmanli ekonomisi ve dünya kapitalizmi: 1820–1913* (The Ottoman economy and world capitalism; Ankara, Yurt Yayınları, 1984), chapter 5.

19 F. Ahmad, *The Young Turks: the Committee of Union and Progress, 1908–1914* (London,

Oxford University Press, 1969), p. 70; Parvus Efendi, *Türkiye' nin mali tutsaklığı* (Turkey's financial enslavement; Istanbul, May yayınları, 1977); Petrosyan, *Sovyet gözüyle*, p. 153; Pamuk, 'Yabancı sermaye', pp. 1–10.

20 Ahmad, *The Young Turks*, pp. 16–17.

21 H. İnalcık, 'The nature of traditional society', *Political modernization in Japan and Turkey*, ed. R. Ward and D. Rustow (Princeton, Princeton University Press, 1964), p. 58.

22 V. Eldem, *Osmanlı imparatorluğunun iktisadi şartları hakkinda bir tetkik* (A study of the economic conditions of the Ottoman Empire; Ankara, Türkiye İş Bankası Kültür Yayınları, 1970); Pamuk, 'Yabancı sermaye'.

23 H. İnalcık, *The Ottoman empire: the classical age, 1300–1600* (New York, Praeger, 1973), p. 4.

24 M.A. Cook, 'Introduction', *A history of the Ottoman empire to 1730*, ed. M.A. Cook (Cambridge, Cambridge University Press, 1976), p. 9.

25 I. Wallerstein, *The modern world-system: Capitalist agriculture and the origins of the European world-economy in the sixteenth century* (New York, Academic Press, 1974), pp. 301 ff; Faroqhi and İslamoğlu, 'Crop patterns'.

5 State and peasants in the Ottoman Empire: a study of peasant economy in north-central Anatolia during the sixteenth century

1 These are primarily the demographic-determinist neo-Malthusian and trade-based models that explain social-economic change in pre-industrial societies in terms of changes in the 'objective' economic factors of population and trade. The neo-Malthusian model is widely applied to the study of developments in Western Europe between the fourteenth and eighteenth centuries, most notably by Emmanuel Le Roy Ladurie, M.M. Postan, and Pierre Goubert. The commercialization model, which traces its ancestry to the Pirenne thesis, is central to the works of Paul Sweezy and, more recently, of Immanuel Wallerstein, who applied it in explaining the rise of the world-capitalist system. For a critique of the 'economism' of these models see Robert Brenner, 'Agrarian class structures and economic development in pre-industrial Europe', *Past and Present*, 70(1976), 30–75; and 'The origins of capitalist development: a critique of neo-Smithian Marxism', *New Left Review*, 104(1977), 25–93. Brenner stresses the primacy of political-power relations or class relations in determining the course of social-economic transformation in different areas of Western Europe.

2 This confusion is implicit in the conceptualization of the Ottoman society by Huri İslamoğlu and Çağlar Keyder ('Agenda for Ottoman history', Chapter 2 in this volume). Also Brenner ('Agrarian class'), despite his emphasis on historically evolved structures of political power – especially that of state – as determinants of social-economic change in pre-industrial societies, is unable to define the sphere of political power. This is primarily because Brenner's conception of political power is circumscribed by class power; he therefore cannot account for state power with a class-free basis. As a result, Brenner reduces the state to a class-like phenomenon which has as its primary objective the maximizing of surpluses it extracts from direct producers in the form of taxes (as was the case in pre-industrial France). On the other hand, state power cannot be identified with class power; instead it enters the constitutive structure of class relations in pre-industrial societies (Perry Anderson, *Lineages of the absolutist state* (London, New Left Books, 1976), pp. 403–5). Moreover, because of this limited conception of state power, Brenner ignores the ideological-

juridical structures that constitute the basis for legitimation of state power and as such are central to the reproduction of class relations. Hence, Brenner's failure to incorporate the political and ideological-juridical structures – with determinations outside the production process – into his conception of class or power relations results in a reduction of these relations to mere positions in the production or surplus-extraction process. This, in turn, results in an 'economism' for which Brenner criticizes the neo-Malthusian and tradist views. I am indebted to İlkay Sunar for providing the outlines of the above critique of Brenner ('The role and the nature of Western impact in the economic transformation of the Ottoman empire', paper submitted to the Conference on Polity, Economy, and Society in Nineteenth Century Iran and Ottoman Empire, 17–21 June 1978, Babolsar, Iran).

3 For classic formulations of this approach see Emmanuel Le Roy Ladurie, *The peasants of Languedoc* (Urbana, Ill., The University of Illinois Press, 1977), and M.M. Postan, 'Medieval agrarian society in its prime: England', *Cambridge economic history of Europe*, vol. 1 (Cambridge, Cambridge University Press, 1966).

4 Brenner, 'Agrarian class', pp. 37–42.

5 For a critique of Brenner along these lines see Guy Bois, 'Symposium: agrarian class structures and economic development in pre-industrial Europe: against the neo-Malthusian orthodoxy', *Past and Present*, 79(May 1978), 60–9.

6 *Ibid.*

7 Ester Boserup, *The conditions of agricultural growth: the economics of agrarian change and population pressure* (Chicago: Aldine Publishing Co., 1965).

8 For a discussion of the role of coercion relations in stimulating agricultural production see Edward Nell, 'Economic relationships in the decline of feudalism: an explanation of economic interdependence and social change,' *History and Theory*, 6(1967), 313–50.

9 For a list of fiscal surveys used in this study and their dates of compilation see Appendix I, pp. 129–30. Also, for a detailed description of these surveys and the methods used in deriving the information on agricultural production, population, commercial and manufacturing activities included in the tables in Appendix III see Huri İslamoğlu, 'Dynamics of agricultural production, population growth, and urban development: A case study of areas in north-central Anatolia, 1520–1575', unpublished Ph.D. dissertation, University of Wisconsin-Madison, 1979.

10 A detailed description of this system is in Ömer Lütfi Barkan, 'Türk-İslam hukuku tatbikatının Osmanlı imparatorluğunda aldığı şekiller I: malikane-divani sistemi' (The application of Turkish-Islamic legal precepts in the Ottoman Empire and their forms of manifestation I: *malikane-divani* system), *Türk Hukuk ve İktisat Tarihi Mecmuası* 1(1939), 119–85. The system is also described in various *kanuns* (state legal codes). Ömer L. Barkan, *XV. ve XVI. asırlarda Osmanlı imparatorluğunda zirai ekonominin hukuki ve mali esasları* (Fiscal and legal basis of agricultural economy in the Ottoman Empire during the fifteenth and sixteenth centuries), vol. 1: *Kanunlar* (Legal codes) (Istanbul, Burhaneddin Matbaası, 1943), pp. 73–4, 77, 115–16, 182, 299–300.

11 For political and military histories of individual areas studied here, see *Islam Ansiklopedisi* (*IA*), s.v. 'Tokat', by Tayyib Gökbilgin; *Encyclopedia of Islam*, 2nd edn (EI^2), s.v. 'Çorum', by Franz Taeschner; *IA*, s.v. 'Niksar', by Besim Darkot. For a description of general conditions in the province of Rum also see Hüseyin Hüsameddin, *Amasya tarihi* (History of Amasya) (5 vols., Istanbul, Hikmet Matbaası, 1927–35).

12 For a detailed account of *şeyh* families in the Konya and Kırşehir regions of central Anatolia see Suraiya Faroqhi, '16–18 inci yüzyıllarda orta Anadolu'da şeyh aileleri' (*Şeyh* families in central Anatolia during the sixteenth-eighteenth centuries), *Türk*

iktisat tarihi semineri, ed. Osman Okyar and Ünal Nalbantoğlu (Ankara, Hacettepe Üniversitesi, 1975).

13 For a detailed description of such 'conversions' see İslamoğlu, 'Agricultural production', ch. 3.

14 The figures included in the tables do not represent amounts of revenue that accrued to individual groups of revenue holders. Instead all calculations are based on the number of shares each holder controlled. Thus, one full share represents total *malikane* or *divani* revenues from a single village, while various fractions of shares represent different proportions of these revenues from that village. This method is adopted because of the uncertainties involved with regard to the recording of *malikane* revenues in the fiscal surveys. For one, surveys do not list these revenues with any degree of consistency. On the other hand, when they are recorded – although in theory *malikane* and *divani* holders in a given village were entitled each to a single tithe from grains and other produce and one-half of dues from mills and beehives – in practice, the lump-sum money equivalents given as *malikane* revenues are frequently, though not always, less than the money totals for their *divani* counterparts. What considerations prompted the surveyors to allow for such discrepancies in their assessment of *malikane* revenues, we do not know. This practice, however, makes suspect any attempt to arrive at estimates of *malikane* revenues, particularly for those villages in which they are not recorded, based on the assumption that they would simply be equal to the amounts given for the respective *divani* taxes.

But the method used here also has its drawbacks. Villages varied both in size and in the extent of their resources and therefore the revenues derived from them varied. For instance, revenues accruing to a holder from a full share in one village were not equal in amount to revenues from a similar share in another village. Yet, while the procedure employed here does not provide an accurate description of the amount of revenues controlled by different holders, it still allows for an overall assessment of the distribution of revenues among different groups or institutions.

15 In the fifteenth century, *malikane* owners who were assigned administrative duties, were required to deliver a specified number of *eşkincis* or mounted soldiers to the imperial army. *EI*², s.v. 'Eshkinji', by Halil İnalcık.

16 The category of 'unspecified' shares that appear in the tables refer to those shares that directly accrued to the central treasury. Hence, it is assumed that revenues from these shares were collected by *emins* (state officials) who were responsible for the sale of the product tax on markets and who sent the cash returns to the treasury. In the later sixteenth century, the proportion of 'unspecified' shares in the total number of shares declined significantly – in the case of *divani* shares this proportion dropped from 41.6 per cent in 1520 to 27.9 per cent in 1574. These revenues were assigned to *vakıfs* of mosque-*medrese* complexes and to *tımars*.

17 For a discussion of *resm-i çift* taxes see Halil İnalcık, 'Osmanlılarda raiyyet rusumu' (Ottoman taxes), *Belleten*, 23(1959), 575–610.

18 For an excellent description of ideological-juridical practices in the Ottoman Empire see Halil İnalcık, 'Suleiman the Law-giver and Ottoman law', *Archivum Ottomanicum*, 1(1969), 105–38.

19 At the same time, E.A. Wrigley's studies have done much to establish that fluctuations in fertility actually occurred in pre-industrial societies and may be related to specific economic and social changes. For example, see his 'Family limitation in pre-industrial England', *Economic History Review*, 2nd ser., XIX, 1(1966), 82–109. David Herlihy also expounds this view in 'Population, plague and social change in rural Pistoia 1201–1430', *Economic History Review*, 2nd ser., XVIII, 2(1965), 225–44. Wrigley, however, admits in *Population and history* (New York,

McGraw-Hill, 1972), pp. 46–7, that the range of variation was relatively narrow.

20 Wrigley, *Population and history*, pp. 62–76.

21 I have attempted to gauge the extent of natural increase by tracing the descendants of taxpayers recorded in earlier surveys through the later surveys. But in the absence of family names, it has not been possible to establish familial ties in any satisfactory manner, even though the tendency of the surveyors to record families in more or less the same sequence in different surveys has been helpful. Only in cases where families in question were clearly defined, as is usually the case with *zaviyedars* (custodians of dervish hospices), this method has certain applicability. But since this exercise excludes the ordinary taxpayers who constituted the large majority of the population, I have decided not to pursue it.

22 On this problem and others related to natural fluctuations, see Roger Mols SJ, 'Population in Europe 1500–1700', *The Fontana economic history of Europe*, ed. Carlo M. Cipolla (6 vols., Sussex, Harvester Press, 1977), vol. 2, *The sixteenth and seventeenth centuries*, pp. 62–78.

23 The peasant was subject to the payment of a fine, or *çift-bozan akçesi*, if he decided to leave his village. The *sipahi*, if he had the approval of the judge, could force a peasant to return to his village of origin within fifteen years of his departure. H. İnalcık, *The Ottoman Empire: the classical age* (London, Weidenfeld and Nicolson, 1973), p. 111; Barkan, *Kanunlar*, p. 288. Sometimes the surveys recorded where a particular taxpayer might be located. This was generally the case if the taxpayer's actual place of residence was a town. In one of the edicts related to the preparation of the Karaman survey in 1584, it was clearly stated that no matter how long a time a peasant lived in Istanbul or Bursa, he was still entered in the tax lists of his village. *MM*, no. 16, p. 209; Barkan, *Kanunlar*, p. 24. Given the communal tax liability on the village level, such a measure meant that the entire village community had to suffer in the event any of its members emigrated. Hence, it was not uncommon for peasants to exert pressure on those who left the village to return.

24 Barkan, *Kanunlar*, pp. 65, 253, 283.

25 While the reliability of *mücerred* figures recorded in the surveys is open to question (see Leila Erder and Suraiya Faroqhi, 'Population rise and fall in Anatolia, 1550–1620', *Middle Eastern Studies*, XV, 3(1979), 322–45), increases in the proportion of bachelors to total adult males in the later sixteenth century call for an explanation. One interpretation, suggested by Michael Cook, is that this may point to a postponement of marriage age by males because of the economic distress caused by population pressure on land. *Population pressure in rural Anatolia, 1450–1600* (London, Oxford University Press, 1972), pp. 25–9. But rural population growth was also characterized by an increase in the proportion of *caba* or unmarried landless peasants who were expected to have an independent source of livelihood. It is likely that *cabas* worked as farm-hands on the land of others, particularly at harvest time, or performed odd jobs in villages. They might have constituted an itinerant labour force that moved from one area to another in search of employment – a passage from the *kanunname* of Yeni-il, a region in Rum, suggests that the Ottoman government was not always adverse to the movement of *cabas*, provided that they paid their personal taxes (Barkan, *Kanunlar*, pp. 75–6). Thus, the increased number of *cabas* in areas under study, may suggest the presence of peasants who may have moved into this region from other areas where adverse political and economic conditions prevailed. On the other hand, as I will later discuss, if one does not assume economic distress as a necessary outcome of population growth, at least part of the increase in the numbers of *mücerred* could also be an outcome of such migratory movements.

26 See above note 11.

27 On Kızılbaş uprisings, see Irene Beldiceanu-Steinherr, 'Le règne de Selim Ier: tournant dans la vie politique et religieuse de l'Empire Ottoman', *Turcica: Revue d'Etudes Turques*, 6(1975), 34–48; Walther Hinz, 'Das Steuerwesen Ostanatoliens im 15. und 16. Jahrhundert', *Zeitschrift der Deutschen Morgenlandischen Gesellschaft*, 25(1951), 17–201; Hanna Sohrweide, 'Der Sieg der Safavidan in Persien und seine Rückwirkungen auf die Schüten Anatoliens im 16. Jahrhunderts', *Der Islam*, 41(1965), 95–223. Ahmet Refik Altınay published in *Onaltıncı asırda rafizilik ve bektaşilik* (Heterodoxy and Bektashism in the sixteenth century) (İstanbul, A. Halit Kitaphanesi, 1932), some of the Ottoman government rescripts (*mühimme*) relating to the measures against the Kızılbaş.

28 On the deportation of Kızılbaş from areas in Rum to the Balkans and to Cyprus, see Ömer L. Barkan, 'Osmanlı imparatorluğunda bir iskan ve kolonizasyon metodu olarak sürgünler' (Deportation in the Ottoman Empire: a method of settlement and colonization), *İktisat Fakültesi Mecmuası* (*IFM*), XV, 1–4(Oct. 1953–July 1954), 213–16, 229.

29 Ronald Jennings in 'Urban population in Anatolia in the sixteenth century: a study of Kayseri, Karaman, Amasya, Trabzon, and Erzurum', *International Journal of Middle East Studies*, 7(1976), 31–2 emphasizes this westward movement in explaining the phenomenal rates of growth in the population of the city of Kayseri during the sixteenth century. He substantiates his point by singling out the growth in the numbers of Armenians whom the later surveys described as *şarkiyan*, thus pointing to eastern Anatolia as their place of origin. Of the districts studied here, similar entries can be found for Karakuş which witnessed a considerable increase in its Christian population in the later sixteenth century (*KK*, no. 12, p. 73a). At the same time, the term *cemaat-i şarkiyan* (community of the East) could also refer to nomadic groups which came from eastern Anatolia (*KK*, no. 12, pp. 63b, 59a). Furthermore, in the second half of the sixteenth century, there appears to have been a migration of tribal elements back to Anatolia from Iran (*IA*, s.v. 'Suleyman I', by Tayyib Gökbilgin). Lastly, the later surveys include a category of taxpayers listed as *hariçten ekerler*, participants in agriculture presumably from outside the traditional village context. See, for instance, *KK*, no. 14, p. 219a; *KK*, no. 38, pp. 247, 245a. This phenomenon may also suggest the presence of newcomers in this area.

30 For general descriptions of nomadic tribes in Ottoman Anatolia, see Faruk Sümer, *Oğuzlar (Türkmenler), tarihleri – boy teşkilatı – destanları* (Oğuzes – Turkmens: their history – tribal organization – epics), Ankara Üniversitesi Dil ve Tarih-Coğrafya Fakültesi Yayınları, no. 170 (Ankara, Ankara Üniversitesi Basımevi, 1972); 'Osmanlı devrinde Anadolu'da yaşayan bazı Üçoklu Oğuz boylarına mensub teşekküller' (Some groups belonging to Üçok tribes in Ottoman Anatolia'), *IFM*, XI, 1–4(1949–50), 437–508; and 'XVI. asırda Anadolu, Suriye ve Irak'ta yaşayan Türk aşiretlerine umumi bir bakış' (A general survey of Turkish tribes in Anatolia during the sixteenth century), *IFM*, XI, 1–4(1949.1950), 509–23; Ahmet Refik Altınay, *Anadolu'da Türk aşiretleri 966–1200* (Turkish tribes in Anatolia AH 966–1200/AD 1558–1792), Türkiyat Enstitüsü Yayınlarından (İstanbul, Devlet Matbaası, 1930). The surveys used in the present study occasionally list nomadic tribes. I have included these in the estimates for the total number of taxpayers whenever they could be traced in all surveys under study, but excluded them if they were entered in only one of the surveys. For instance, see *KK*, no. 12, pp. 63b, 65b, 58a, 55a, 66a, 59a–b, 78a; *KK*, no. 38, p. 38b. The entries are most frequent for the district of Katar, where nomads were usually listed under *resm-i çift* categories (*TT*, no. 444, pp. 337–48; *KK*, no. 38, pp. 253b–261b). I have, however, excluded from the counts for the town population of Tokat the tribes of İnallu and Emir Seyidlü which are listed in all surveys for this town, following the list of urban taxpayers.

31 For estimates of nomadic population in Rum see Ö.L. Barkan, 'Research on Ottoman fiscal surveys', *Studies in the economic history of the Middle East*, ed. Michael Cook (London, Oxford University Press, 1970), p. 170. For a comparison of growth rates of nomadic and settled populations, see Halil İnalcık, 'Impact of the Annales school on Ottoman studies and new findings', *Review*, I, 3–4 (Winter/Spring 1978), 75.

32 For a detailed investigation of this process in Karaman see Wolf-Dieter Hutteroth, *Landlichte siedlungen im südlichen innneranatolien in den letzten vierhundert jahren*, Gottinger Geographische Abhandlungen, no 46 (Gottingen, 1968), pp. 170–1, also *Mühimme Defterleri*, vol. 46, nos. 434, 435, 436.

33 For the relationships between nomads and settled populations, as well as for government regulations concerning nomads, see Lütfi Güçer, *XVI–XVII. asırlarda Osmanlı imparatorluğunda hububat meselesi ve hububattan alınan vergiler* (The question of grains and grain taxes in the Ottoman Empire during the sixteenth and seventeenth centuries), İstanbul Üniversitesi Yayınları, no. 1075 (İstanbul, Sermet Matbaası, 1964), pp. 11–19.

34 For similar developments in Karaman see Hutteroth, *Siedlungen*, p. 169.

35 Cook, *Population pressure*, pp. 11–29.

36 *Ibid.*, pp. 21–2.

37 For figures on *mezraas* that developed into villages in other areas, see Table 5.21, p. 159. At the same time, an increased number of tribal units which were listed under *resm-i çift* categories and paid agricultural taxes were entered in the later surveys. For instance, *KK*, no. 12, pp. 63b, 65b, 58a, 55a.

38 For evidence of fragmentation in Rum see Cook, *Population pressure*, p. 98.

39 *Ibid.*, p. 78.

40 For a description of these entries, *ibid.*, pp. 79–80.

41 For a general discussion of forest assarts see Boserup, *Agricultural growth*, pp. 24–7, 28–31.

42 With regard to the quantity of seed per unit area, the *kanun* occasionally specifies a minimum; see, for instance, *kanunname* of Mehmet II in F. Kraelitz, 'Kanunname Sultan Mehmeds des Eroberers', *Mitteilungen zur Osmanischen Geschichte* (1921); Barkan, *Kanunlar*, p. 46; and *Kanunname* of Rum in *KK*, no. 14, pp. 3a ff. Only in one case does the *kanun* refer to normal sowing (Barkan, *Kanunlar*, p. 47). To infer from references cited by İnalcık in 'Raiyyet', p. 581, note 26, that normal sowing increased in the period under study would be to compare the minimum to the norm. M.A. Cook's estimates for Rum show a normal sowing of ten *muds* per *çift*. But how much is a *mud?* See *Population pressure*, pp. 15, 68. With regard to soil productivity, Cook also estimated a yield of approximately three-fold, rather low by medieval European standards and even more so by modern Turkish standards. But, as Cook forcefully argues, this is not the kind of evidence that can tell us much about change in the sixteenth century (*ibid.*, p. 15).

43 Figures given for numbers of millstones in Table 5.16 for the early periods include those millstones described as *harabe* or as being in disuse. No such notations can be found for the later period. This may suggest an increase in the activity of mills in that period. For a discussion of water mills and use of water power in south-western Anatolia see Xavier de Planhol, *De la plaine pamphylienne aux lacs pisidiens, nomadism et vie paysanne* (Paris, Maison Neuve, 1958).

44 See above note 25.

45 Cook, *Population pressure*, pp. 22–5.

46 *Ibid.*, pp. 37–9.

47 *Ibid.*, pp. 74–5.

48 Similar attempts have been made for Ottoman territories in the Balkans. See, for

instance, I. Asdrachas, 'Aux Balkans du XV. siècle: producteurs directs et marchés', *Études Balkaniques*, 6(1970), 36–59; Bruce McGowen, 'Food supply and taxation on the Middle Danube, 1568–1579', *Archivum Ottomanicum*, 1(1969), 139–96.

49 On changes in grain measures over time in Hungarian territories, see Gyula Kaldy-Nagy, 'The administration of the *sancak* registrations in Hungary', *Acta Orientalia Academiae Scientiarum Hungaricae*, 21(1968), 198.

50 For a detailed discussion of these levies see Güçer, *Hububat meselesi*.

51 Exemptions from *avariz-i divaniye* and *takalif-i örfiye*, as these extraordinary levies were called, were granted to entire village populations in return for their work in maintaining roads, bridges, and passes (*derbents*). See, for instance, *KK*, no. 14, p. 183a; *KK*, no. 38, p. 233a; *KK*, no. 14, p. 222b. For similar exemptions granted to rice growers in Niksar see *TT*, no. 54, pp. 103, 106, 107.

52 İnalcık, 'Annales school', p. 89.

53 On the practice of differentiating between vegetables grown for home consumption and market-gardening see Kaldy-Nagy, 'Administration', pp. 203–4, for information on Hungary; in the provinces of Aydın and Menteşe in Western Anatolia, see *TT*, nos. 8, 148 and 337, and *KK*, nos. 129, 167, and 110. For instance, the inhabitants of the town of Ula in the province of Menteşe tried to prevent the central government from taxing their vegetable plots by claiming for them the status of house gardens (TT, no. 110, p. 89b). This may explain the relatively small sums recorded as *öşr-ü bostan* (tithe on gardens) in the areas under study.

54 The increased importance of viticulture is further demonstrated by the recording in the 1574 survey of a tax on *şire*, or unfermented grape-juice, in Cincife in the vicinity of Tokat. This tax, which amounted to as much as 4,090 *akçes*, may indicate a rise in the commercial production of *şire* – which was, in fact, the Ottoman euphemism for wine – in response to the demand in the town of Tokat. This is all the more likely since the peasants in this region – including a considerable number of Christians – probably did not pay taxes on the *şire* they made for home consumption. (Also see Tables 5.16 and 5.20, pp. 151–2 and 157–8.)

55 For increases in revenues from the dye-house in Karahisar-ı Demirli in the vicinity of Katar see Table 5.16, p. 151, and also the discussion on rural weaving activities below.

56 Information presented here on rice cultivation and its organization derives from invaluable discussions with Professor Halil İnalcık; see İnalcık, 'Rice cultivation and *çeltükci-reaya* system in the Ottoman Empire', *Turcia: Revue d'Etudes Turques*, XIV (1982). For government regulations on rice cultivation see Barkan, *Kanunlar*, pp. 17, 28, 31, 54, 113, 148, 200–5.

57 Professor İnalcık has informed me that rice was an important item in Black Sea trade and was exported from the north-central Anatolian rice-growing regions *via* such ports as Samsun, to the Crimea.

58 For such government regulations see Barkan, *Kanunlar*, pp. 113, 200–5.

59 For instance the *tekkes* (hospices) of Sadrettin Konevi in Konya and Seyid Gazi near Eskişehir, served very little meat. Suraiya Faroqhi, '*Vakıf* administration in sixteenth-century Konya' the *zaviye* of Sadrettin Konevi', *Journal of the Economic and Social History of the Orient*, 17(1974), 145–72.

60 Robert Mantran, *Istanbul dans la seconde moitié du XVIIe siècle, essai d'histoire institutionale, économique et sociale*, Bibliothèque Archéologique et Histoires de l'Institut Français d'Archéologie d'Istanbul, vol. 12 (Paris, Maison Neuve, 1962), pp. 201–2.

61 The number of *çayır, otlak, kışlak*, and *yaylak* entries recorded for each district under study in the later surveys are as follows: 8 in Yıldız (with a total tax of 255 *akçes*); none in Cincife; 3 in Venk (total tax of 120 *akçes*); 1 in Kafirni (total tax of 72 *akçes*); none in

Çorumlu; 2 in Karahisar-ı Demirli (total tax of 1,280 *akçes*). For a detailed description of these entries in the surveys, see Kemal Abdulfettah and Wolf-Dieter Hutteroth, *Historical geography of Palestine, Transjordan, and southern Syria in the late 16th century*, Erlanger Geographische Arbeiten, special volume 5 (Erlangen, 1977), p. 71.

62 For a detailed account of these estimations see İslamoğlu, 'Agricultural production'.

63 See Map 5.3, p. 134, for the destination of revenues from *vakıf* lands in the areas under study.

64 These taxes represent the amounts paid annually to the treasury by people to whom the revenues from these installations were farmed out. As such, they are not always accurate indicators of the amount of business carried out at dye-houses, because these franchises were often granted for three-year periods in return for advance payment of a fixed sum; actual receipts accruing to tax-farmers could be in excess of or below that sum. At the same time, while presence of a dye-house in a given region may point to textile production in that region, the opposite may not always be the case. Evidence for other parts of Anatolia suggest that villagers often did their own dyeing in their houses or cattlesheds. There is, of course, no way to assess the extent of such activities, thereby to determine the extent of rural production of fibres and cloths in areas where there were no dye-houses. Nevertheless, where there was a dye-house, it is probably not too inaccurate to suppose that tax-farmers exerted considerable pressure on rural craftsmen to have their dyeing done at the dye-house. Thus, for instance, one encounters complaints by villagers to the effect that the dye-house administrators sought to prevent them from doing their own dyeing (*Mühimme Defterleri*, vol. 74, p. 38).

65 For the role of production of non-agricultural goods in the economic development of peasant household economy see S. Hymer and S. Resnick, 'Model of an agrarian economy with non-agricultural activities', *American Economic Review*, 59(1969), 493–506; Jan DeVries in his critique of Boserup also emphasizes this aspect of the peasant economy ('Labour/leisure trade off', *Peasant Studies Newsletter*, I, 2(1972).

66 Bruce McGowen, 'The study of land and agriculture in the Ottoman provinces within the context of an expanding world economy in the 17th and 18th centuries', *International Journal of Turkish Studies*, II, 1(Spring–Summer 1981), 57–64. Also Şevket Pamuk, chapter 8 in this volume.

6 The cotton famine and its effects on the Ottoman Empire

1 For example, the lists of publications on the economic and social history of Great Britain and Ireland, annually published by the *Economic History Review*, contain one book on the subject published in 1978 and another one in 1979. These books, however, are not studies solely concerned with the cotton famine; see: B.H. Tolley, *Liverpool and the American cotton trade* (London, Longman, 1978); D.A. Farnie, *The English cotton industry and the world market, 1815–96* (London, Clarendon Press, 1979).

2 D.A. Farnie, 'The cotton famine in Great Britain', in B.M. Ratcliffe (ed.), *Great Britain and her world: essays in honour of W.O. Henderson* (Manchester, Manchester Univ. Press, 1975), pp. 157–8.

3 T. Ellison, *The cotton trade of Great Britain* (London, E. Wilson, 1886), p. 86.

4 Farnie, 'Cotton famine', pp. 159–60.

5 A.C. Wood, *A history of the Levant Company*, (2nd edn, New York, Barnes and Nobles, 1964), p. 74.

6 Ellison, *Cotton trade*, p. 81.

7 MCSA, *Cotton culture in new or partially developed sources of supply: report of proceedings* (Manchester, 1862), p. 30.

8 British Museum, Add. MSS 38350, *Liverpool Papers*, vol. 161, fos. 21–2.
9 Wood, *History*, p. 193.
10 British Museum, Add. MSS 38350, *Liverpool Papers*, vol. 161; two tables on fo. 12 and fos. 39–40, showing market prices and relative profitability of cotton cultivation in various countries, conclude that given the very low level of market price in Turkey it would be unrealistic to expect producers to grow cotton.
11 *Ceride-i Havadis*, 31 July–25 September 1840.
12 Not much is known about the activities of this company except that it was incorporated in London, see Public Record Office (PRO), BT 31/206 (629c).
13 PRO, Foreign Office (FO) 78/1307, Blunt to Clarendon, no. 59, 5 Dec. 1857.
14 PRO, FO 195/610, Blunt to Alison, no. 15, 29 April 1858.
15 PRO, FO 78/1391, Blunt to Malmesbury, no. 24, 20 April 1858.
16 PRO, FO 78/1533, Blunt to Russell, no. 34, 30 April 1860.
17 W. Sandford, *On cotton growing in Turkey and Syria* (London, J.E. Taylor, 1862), pp. 4–8.
18 *Cotton Supply Reporter*, 15 March 1862.
19 British Museum. Add. MSS 39111, *Layard Papers*, vol. 181, fos. 207–8.
20 Sandford, *Cotton growing*, p. 25.
21 *Ibid.*, pp. 10–24.
22 *Ceride-i Havadis*, 13 Feb. 1861.
23 *Ceride-i Havadis*, 10–12 March 1861.
24 *Ceride-i Havadis*, 14 March 1861.
25 *Ceride-i Havadis*, 9 Sept. 1861.
26 *Times*, 27 March 1861
27 *Times*, 29 March 1861
28 *Times*, 9 May 1861
29 *Times*, 28 Sept. 1861
30 *Türk Ziraat Tarihine Bir Bakış* (İstanbul, 1938), pp. 128–9.
31 *Ceride-i Havadis*, 12 April 1863.
32 PRO, FO 195/771, Blunt to Bulwer, no. 28, 1 Aug. 1863.
33 PRO, FO 78/1760, Blunt to Russell, no. 28, 23 May 1863.
34 British Museum, Add. MSS 39114, *Layard Papers*, vol. 184, fos. 33–6.
35 *Manchester Guardian*, 12 Aug. 1864.
36 *Cotton Supply Reporter*, 1 March 1865.
37 *Takvim-i Ticaret*, 10 Feb. 1866.
38 PRO, FO 78/1780, Company to Russell, 24 Feb. 1863.
39 *Times*, 31 March 1863; *Prospectus of the Asia Minor Co. Ltd* (Manchester, 1863); PRO, BT 31/778 (424c), The Ottoman Cotton Co. Ltd; PRO, BT 31/737 (230c), The Asia Minor Co. Ltd; PRO, BT 31/819 (629c), Asia Minor Cotton Co. Ltd.
40 PRO, FO 78/1687, Blunt to Russell, separate, 26 July 1862.
41 PRO, FO 78/1760, Blunt to Russell, no. 28, 23 May 1863.
42 PRO, FO 78/1760, Blunt to Russell, no. 31, 23 June 1863.
43 PRO, FO 78/1760, Biliotti to Blunt, 29 June 1863. According to G.B. Ravndall, *Turkey, a commercial and industrial handbook* (Washington, US Department of Commerce, Bureau of Foreign and Domestic Commerce, 1926), p. 97, between 1861 and 1865, land under cotton in western Anatolia increased ten times.
44 PRO, FO 78/1760, Blunt to Russell, no. 63, 21 Nov. 1863.
45 'Circular to Her Majesty's consuls in the Ottoman dominions regarding cotton cultivation together with a summary of their replies', *Accounts and Papers*, vol. 57 (1865), pp. 743–81.

46 *Ibid.*, p. 761. This region was known to possess the best soil for cotton growing but until the 1880s, when Adana and the port town of Mersin were connected with a railway, it did not show any remarkable growth in cotton exports.
47 *Ibid.*, p. 775.
48 PRO, FO 195/767, Mallouf to Vedova, 30 May 1864; PRO, FO 78/1831, Vedova to Russell, no. 27, 14 June 1864.
49 PRO, FO 78/1888, Cumberbatch to Russell, no. 34, 27 May 1865.
50 PRO, FO 78/1888, Cumberbatch to Russell, no. 48, 8 June 1865.
51 PRO, FO 78/1687, Blunt to Russell, separate, 26 July 1862.
52 PRO, FO 78/1760, Blunt to Russell, no. 28, 23 May 1863; PRO, FO 195/797, Memorandum by Consul Cumberbatch, 6 May 1865.
53 PRO, FO 195/797, Vedova to Cumberbatch, 16 July 1866.
54 C.D. Scherzer, *La province de Smyrne* (Vienne, A. Hölder, 1873), p. 104. For a detailed account of cotton-ginning enterprises in western Anatolia see O. Kurmuş, *Emperyalizmin Türkiye'ye Girisi*, 2nd edn (İstanbul, 1977), pp. 153–60.
55 PRO, FO 78/1788, Cumberbatch to Russell, no. 40, 8 June 1865.
56 W.O. Henderson, *The Lancashire cotton famine, 1861–1865* (Manchester, Manchester Univ. Press, 1934), pp. 46–7. Later investigations showed that the climatic conditions and the composition of soil in western Anatolia were not suitable for the growth of thin and long-fibred American cotton. Although native cotton, which had an average fibre length of 1.1 inches and a fibre diameter of 0.0008 inches, could be grown in abundance, it would not have been possible to use it efficiently in Lancashire mills which had been designed for the fine American cotton; see 'Report on agriculture in Asia Minor with special reference to cotton cultivation', *Accounts and Papers*, vol. 107 (1908), pp. 1–22.
57 *Türk Ziraat Tarihi*, pp. 136–7.
58 *Ibid.*, p. 131, quoting N. Kemal in *Hürriyet*, 20 July 1868. For the distrust of Turkish peasants of the Turkish government see, J.E. Pierce, *Life in a Turkish village* (New York, Holt Rinehart and Winston, 1964), p. 84. According to A. Bonne, the Middle Eastern peasant shows a profound distrust and disgust towards any kind of governmental activity: 'Every action of the Government is regarded by him as a trick to extort more taxation or to attain some other malicious end.' See his, 'Some aspects of the recent socio-economic changes in the Middle East', *Journal of the Royal Central Asian Society*, 27(1940), 286–300.
59 *Accounts and Papers*, vol. 57 (1865), p. 752.
60 PRO, FO 78/1760, Blunt to Russell, no. 67, 26 Dec. 1863.
61 PRO, FO 78/1888, Cumberbatch to Russell, no. 40, 8 June 1865.
62 PRO, FO 195/797, Mallouf to Vedova, 25 May 1864.
63 PRO, FO 83/337, Cumberbatch to Granville, no. 1, 4 Nov. 1870.
64 PRO, FO 195/646, Report on Smyrna for the quarter ended 31 March 1860.
65 PRO, FO 195/610, Blunt to Bulwer, no. 5, 17 Feb. 1860.
66 PRO, FO 195/910, Cumberbatch to Elliot, no. 44, 10 June 1868.

7 The Middle Danube *cul-de-sac*

1 P. Blažnik *et al.*, *Gospodarska in Družbena Zgodovina Slovencev* (Economic and social history of the Slovenes) (2 vols., Ljubljana, Slovenska Akademija Znanosti in Umjetnosti, 1970), vol. 1, pp. 153–4.
2 S. Gavrilović, *Prilog istoriji trgovine i migracije Balkan-Podunavlje XVIII i XIX stoljeća* (contribution to the history of trade and migration in the Balkan Peninsula . . .) (Belgrade, Srpska Akademija Nauka i Umjetnosti, 1969), p. 11.

3 Blažnik, *Gospodarska*, vol. 1, pp. 157, 168.
4 J. Adamček, *Agrarni odnosi u Hrvatskoj od sredine XV do Kraja XVII stoljeća* (Agrarian relations in Croatia from the middle of the fifteenth to the end of the seventeenth century) (Zagreb, Jugoslavenska Akademija Znanosti i Umjetnosti, 1980), pp. 773, 783, 789.
5 *Ibid.*, pp. 766, 794.
6 *Ibid.*, p. 762.
7 *Ibid.*, p. 781.
8 J. Adamček, 'Ekonomsko – društveni razvoj u Hrvatskoj i Slavoniji u 18. stoljeću' (Socio-economic development in northwest Croatia in the eighteenth century), in M. Gross (ed.), *Društveni razvoj u Hrvatskoj od 16. stoljeća do početka 20. stoljeća* (Social development in Croatia from the sixteenth to the twentieth century) (Zagreb, Jugoslavenska Akademija Znanosti i Umjetnosti, 1981), p. 65.
9 Adamček, *Agrarni odnosi*, p. 766.
10 S. Gavrilović, 'Uvodjenje urbara u Požeškoj županiji' (Introduction of the urbarial regime into the županate of Požega), *Godišnjak Filozofskog Fakulteta u Novom Sadu* (Annual of the Philosophical Faculty at Novi Sad), 3(1958), 61–9.
11 S. Gavrilović, 'Urbarijalno pitanje u sremskoj županiji sredinom XVIII stoljeća' (The agrarian question in the županate of Srem in the mid-eighteenth century) *Zbnornik za društvene nauke Matice Srpske* (Social science collection of the Matica Srpska), 27(1960), 20.
12 S. Gavrilović, *Vojvodina i Srbija u vreme prvog ustanka* (Vojvodina and Serbia at the time of the first rebellion) (Novi Sad, Institut za izučavanje istorije Vojvodine, 1947), p. 408; also V. Čubrilović *et al.* (eds.) *Istorija Beograda* (3 vols., Belgrade, Prosveta, 1974), vol. 1, pp. 678, 761.

13 Gavrilović, *Prilog*, p. 10.
14 G. Benda, 'Production et exportation des céréales en Hongrie (1770–1870)'. in B. Köpeczi and É. Balász (eds.), *Paysannerie française, paysannerie hongroise XVe–XXe siècle* (Budapest, Akademiai Kiadó, 1973), p. 192.
15 *Ibid.*, p. 194.
16 Vaso Bogdanov, quoted in I. Karaman, 'Osnovni podaci i neke napomene u slavonsko–srijemskom veleposjedu' (Basic data with some comments on the large estates of the Srem-Slavonia region), *Zbornik za društvene nauke Matice Srpske*, 20(1958), p. 41.
17 M. Kostić, 'O dunavskoj–savskoj trgovini, ladjama, ladjarima, i ladjarskim ćehovima u XVIII i XIX veka' (Regarding Danube–Sava trade boats, boat owners, and boatmen in the eighteenth and nineteenth centuries), *Istoriski Časopis*, 9–10(1959), 259.
18 Adamček, 'Ekonomsko-društveni razvoj, p. 72.
19 N. Petrović, *Plovidba i privreda srednjeg Podunavlja u doba merkantilisma* (Navigation and economy in the Middle Danube zone in the Mercantilist age), (Belgrade, Istorijski Institut, 1978), p. 432.
20 *Ibid.*, p. 232.
21 H. Hajnal, *The Danube* (The Hague, 1920), pp. 129–34.
22 *Ibid.*, p. 147.
23 'Djerdap', in *Enciklopedija Jugoslavije*.
24 I. Karaman, *Privreda i društvo hrvatske u 19. stoljeću* (Economy and society in nineteenth-century Croatia) (Zagreb, Školska Knjiga, 1972), p. 15.
25 Benda, 'Production', p. 193.

26 Karaman, *Privreda*, p. 17.
27 R. Tričković, 'Čitlučenje u beogradskom pašaluku u XVIII veku' (*Chiftliks* in the *pashalik* of Belgrade in the eighteenth century), *Zbornik Filozofskog Fakulteta* (Collection of the Philosophical Faculty) (Belgrade), 11/1(1970), 536, 540–1, 547.
28 B. Djurdjev *et al.* (eds.) *Historija Naroda Jugoslavije* (History of the Yugoslav peoples) (2 vols., Zagreb, Školska Knjiga, 1959), vol. 2, p. 1365.
29 B. McGowan, *Economic life in Ottoman Europe* (Cambridge, Cambridge University Press, 1981), pp. 45–79.

8 Commodity production for world-markets and relations of production in Ottoman agriculture, 1840–1913

1 By 'core' areas we do not claim to make an analytical distinction between different areas of the Empire. Rather, with the exception of the provinces of Syria and Iraq, we are referring to those areas that remained part of the Empire until the 1910s.
2 For a detailed examination of nineteenth-century Ottoman foreign trade, see ch. 2 of Ş. Pamuk, *Ottoman Empire and the world economy 1820–1913: trade, capital and production* (1986, forthcoming).
3 C. Issawi, *The economic history of Turkey, 1800–1914* (Chicago, University of Chicago Press, 1980), pp. 80–2 indicates that total exports from the five major ports of northern Greece and Anatolia increased from Ł 2,185,000 in the 'early 1840s' to Ł 13,200,000 in 1910–12. The rate of expansion of exports from these areas was actually higher owing to the emergence of secondary ports in the late nineteenth- and early twentieth-centuries. Moreover 1911–12 were war years and export volumes were considerably higher in 1913. For the relative importance of different Anatolian ports in 1890, see Maliye Tetkik Kurulu, *Osmanlı imparatorluğunda XIX yüzyılın sonunda üretim ve tüketim* (Production and consumption in the Ottoman Empire at the end of the nineteenth century) (Ankara, 1970) and V. Cuinet, *La Turquie d'Asie* (4 vols., Paris, E. Leroux, 1891–4).
4 See Appendix 1 of Pamuk, *Trade, capital, production* for the commodity composition of Ottoman exports.
5 It should be stressed that increases in tithe collections or assessments do not necessarily indicate increases in the volume of agricultural production. More precisely, the expansion of agricultural production probably remained well behind increases in the tithe revenues of the Ottoman treasury during this period. This was primarily due to the increasing effectiveness of the state in reducing the share accruing to the tax collectors and other middlemen. In interpreting year-to-year changes in tithe revenues it should also be noted that the rate of taxation out of the gross agricultural product did not remain constant; it was raised above 10 per cent to as much as 15 per cent during periods of crisis for the state treasury (see note 36 below). Our estimate for the increase in agricultural production attempts to take these factors into account in a rather crude way.

The following data provided the bases for our estimate:

(a) Tithe assessments for the entire Empire increased by 61 per cent between 1863 and 1874. (Source: S. Shaw, 'The nineteenth-century Ottoman tax reforms and revenue system', *Journal of Economic History*, 6(1975), 452). This was a period of roughly constant prices for Ottoman agricultural commodities.

(b) After the war of 1877–8, within the smaller boundaries of the Empire, tithe assessments for the Empire increased by 71 per cent and tithe collections rose by 69 per cent between 1887 and 1910. (Source: Shaw, 'Ottoman tax reforms', pp. 452–3.) The prices of the Ottoman agricultural mix were probably slightly lower in 1910 than they were in 1887, primarily owing to the significant decline in wheat prices.

(c) V. Eldem estimates, on the basis of region-by-region tithe-assessment figures, that gross agricultural production of the Empire, measured in constant 1913 prices, increased by 44 per cent between 1889 and 1911. (V. Eldem, *Osmanlı imparatorluğunun iktisadi şartları hakkında bir tetkik* (A study of Ottoman economic conditions) (İstanbul, Türkiye İş Bankası Kültür Yayınları, 1970), p. 308.)

(d) Tithe collections in the Anatolian provinces of the Empire increased by approximately 45 per cent between 1882 and 1902. (Source: D. Quataert, 'Ottoman reform and agriculture in Anatolia 1876–1908', (University of California, Los Angeles, 1973), Unpublished Ph.D. dissertation.)

6 Based on gross national product and net agricultural production estimates given in Eldem, *İktisadi şartlar*, pp. 302, 283.

7 See ch. 2 of Pamuk, *Trade, capital, production* for long-term fluctuations in Ottoman foreign trade and how they were associated with long-term fluctuations in the levels of economic activity in the industrialized centre countries during the nineteenth century.

8 The Anatolian railway was an exception to this pattern as a large part of the cereal shipments from central Anatolia was consumed in the İstanbul area. D. Quataert, 'Limited revolution: the impact of the Anatolian railway on Turkish transportation and the provisioning of İstanbul', *Business History Review*, 51 (1977), 139–60.

9 Issawi, *Turkey*, pp. 34–5.

10 Quataert, 'Limited revolution'.

11 Consider the following simple and admittedly crude calculation:

(a) Let us assume agricultural production of the areas considered in this study doubled between 1840 and 1912 (based upon tithe revenue figures; see above p. 180 and note 5).

$Q_{1840} = 100 \quad Q_{1912} = 200$

(b) We know that approximately 25 per cent of Q_{1912} was exported. (See above p. 180 and note 6.)

$X_{1912} = 50$

(c) Volume of agricultural commodity exports from the core areas of the Empire increased by tenfold between 1840 and 1912.

$X_{1840} = 5$

(d) Considering the dependence of İstanbul on imported foodstuffs, the share of domestic markets in the domestically consumed portion of the agricultural production is close to the share of urban population in total population:

$D_{1840} = 0.17 \quad (Q_{1840} - X_{1840}) = 16$
$D_{1912} = 0.22 \quad (Q_{1912} - X_{1912}) = 33$

(e) Then, the aggregate rate of marketization in agriculture was

$M_{1840} = (D_{1840} + X_{1840})/Q_{1840} = 0.21$
$M_{1912} = (D_{1912} + X_{1912})/Q_{1912} = 0.42$

(f) Therefore, approximately threequarters of the expansion in commodity production in agriculture that occurred between 1840 and 1912 was induced by world-market demand:

$(X_{1912} - X_{1840})/((D_{1912} + X_{1912}) - (D_{1840} + X_{1840})) = 45/62 = 0.73.$

12 Turkey, Orman ve Maadin ve Ziraat Nezareti İstatistik Dairesi (Statistics

Department of the Ministry of Forestry, Minerals, and Agriculture) and agricultural statistics for 1907 and 1909, cited in *1323 senesi Avrupay-i Osmani ziraat istatistiği* (Agricultural statistics for European Ottoman lands for the year AH 1323) (İstanbul, 1910/1326), and Turkey, Orman ve Maadin ve Ziraat Nezareti, *1325 Senesi Asya va Afrikay-i Osmani ziraat istatistiği* (Agricultural statistics for Asian and African Ottoman lands for the year AH 1325) (İstanbul, 1911/1927); T. Güran 'Osmanlı tarım ekonomisine giriş, 1840–1940' (Introduction to Ottoman agricultural economy, 1840–1940) (University of İstanbul, 1978), unpublished Ph.D. dissertation.

13 C. Aybar, *Osmanlı imparatorluğunun ticaret muvazenesi, 1878–1913* (Ottoman trade balance, 1878–1913) (Ankara, 1939) reprint of official Ottoman foreign trade statistics for 1878–1913. Based on the *Accounts and Papers*, Great Britain, Parliamentary Papers, Commercial Reports from consular offices in the Ottoman Empire, D. Quataert, 'The commercialization of agriculture in Ottoman Turkey, 1800–1914', *International Journal of Turkish Studies*, 1(1980), 40, states that nine agricultural commodities (cereals, grapes, tobacco, figs, raw cotton, valonia, opium, hazel nuts and olive oil) accounted for 70 per cent of total exports from the major ports in Anatolia around 1900. This figure is not inconsistent with the official Ottoman statistics since wheat, barley, and other cereals are aggregated as one commodity and since exports from the entire Empire should be expected to be more diversified than exports from major Anatolian ports.

14 Based on *Accounts and Papers* (1860–76), Annual Statement of the Trade of the United Kingdom.

15 'The specific economic form, in which unpaid surplus labor is pumped out of direct producers, determines the relationship of rules and ruled. It is always the direct relationship of the owners of the conditions of production to the direct producers . . . which reveals the innermost secret, the hidden basis of the entire social structure, and with it the political form of the relation of sovereignty and dependence, in short, the corresponding specific form of the state.' K. Marx, *Capital* (3 vols., New York, International Publishers, 1967), vol. 3, 791.

16 For a recent statement on this point, see K. Boratav, *Tarımsal yapılar ve kapitalizm* (Agrarian structures and capitalism) (Ankara, University of Ankara Press, 1980), pp. 12–15.

17 G. Veinstein, 'Ayan de la région d'İzmir et commerce du Levant, deuxième moitié de XVIIIe siècle', *Études Balkanique* XII, 3(1976), 71–83. In an important recent work B. McGowan reaches a similar conclusion for the Balkans during the seventeenth and eighteenth centuries. Paralleling the conclusions of Veinstein's work, McGowan's findings 'demote the importance of investigating *chiftlik* agriculture, and at the same time . . . reassert the importance of the fiscal struggle between Imperial center and the periphery.' B. McGowan, *Economic life in Ottoman Europe* (Cambridge, Cambridge University Press, 1981), p. 171.

18 B. Lewis, *The emergence of modern Turkey*, (2nd edn, London, Oxford University Press, 1968), pp. 90–2; *Accounts and Papers*, 'Report on land tenure in Turkey', 67(1870), p. 282; L. Steeg, 'Land Tenure' in E.G. Mears (ed.), *Modern Turkey* (New York, Macmillan Company, 1924), p. 238; Issawi, *Turkey*, p. 202. For the impact of the confiscation measures on eastern Anatolia, see selections in Issawi, *Turkey*, pp. 220–4 and *Accounts and Papers*, Commercial Reports from Diyarbakır for the year 1856; on the Black Sea region, see *Accounts and Papers*, Commercial Reports from Trabzon for the year 1867.

19 For legal aspects of the Ottoman land-tenure system in the nineteenth century, see Steeg, 'Land tenure'; also Ö.L. Barkan, 'Türk toprak hukuku tarihinde, Tanzimat

ve 1274 (1858) tarihli arazi kanunnamesi' (Tanzimat in the history of Turkish land laws and the legal code of 1274 (1858), *Tanzimat* (İstanbul, Maarif Matbaası 1940); Issawi, *Turkey*, p. 202, and Eldem, *İktisadi şartlar*, p. 70.

20 Issawi, *Turkey*, p. 1.

21 *Ibid.*, pp. 17–19. For the annual estimates of nineteenth-century immigration into the Ottoman Empire from different outlying areas, see Appendix 6, Table A6.1. For immigration into the core areas of the Empire, see A.C. Eren, '*Türkiye'de göç ve göçmen meseleleri* (Questions of migration and immigrants in Turkey) (İstanbul, Nur Gök Matbaası, 1966).

22 *Accounts and Papers*, Commercial Reports from Ankara, Konya and Antalya for the years 1893–1913.

23 *Accounts and Papers*, Commercial Reports from Adana for the years 1873–1913.

24 *Accounts and Papers*, Commercial Reports from consuls in Anatolia, Thrace and northern Greece, 1854–1913. Also see A. Ubicini, *Letters on Turkey* (London, J. Murray, 1856), pp. 325–8 and Köy ve Ziraat Kalkınma Kongresi (Congress of village and agricultural development), *Türk Ziraat tarihine bir bakış* (A survey of Turkish agricultural history) (İstanbul, Devlet Basımevi 1938), pp. 96–146, 204–10.

25 For a sampling of reports on the availability of large amounts of uncultivated land and 'excessive' land–labour ratios in different parts of the Empire, see *Accounts and Papers*, Commercial Reports for Monastır 1854, Bursa 1854–7, Diyarbakır 1856, 1862, 1863, Aleppo 1874, Edirne 1889, Ankara 1895. Also Güran, 'Osmanlı tarım', pp. 4–9, E.F. Nickoley, 'Agriculture', in Mears, p. 291; Ubicini, *Letters*; and Köy ve Ziraat Kalkınma Kongresi, *Türk ziraat tarihi*.

26 Nickoley, 'Agriculture', p. 291; Güran, 'Osmanlı tarım', p. 37.

27 Issawi, *Turkey*, pp. 206–7.

28 For the magnitudes of increases in area under cultivation and total agricultural production between 1909–10 and 1914–15, see *Turkey*, Orman ve Maadin ve Ziraat Nezareti (1910) and (1911) summarized in Güran, 'Osmanlı tarım', p. 5; Eldem, *İktisadi şartlar*, pp. 69–87, and Nickoley, 'Agriculture', pp. 284–5, 291–2.

29 *Accounts and Papers*, Commercial Reports from Izmir, Adana and Salonica, For the İzmir–Aydın area, also see Quataert, 'Ottoman reform', ch. 7, and O. Kurmuş, *Emperyalizmin Türkiye'ye girişi* (Imperial penetration of Turkey) (Istanbul, Bilim yayınları, 1974).

30 A.V. Chayanov, *The theory of peasant economy* (Homewood, Ill., published for the American Economic Ass. by R.D. Irwin, 1966), and H. Friedman, 'World market, state and family farm: social bases of household production in the era of wage labor', *Comparative Studies in Society and History*, XX, 4(1978), 554–64.

31 Tithe revenues that actually entered the Ottoman treasury rose from 4.25 million Ottoman *liras* in 1887–8 to 7.18 million in 1910–11. (1 British pound = 1.11 Ottoman *liras*.) Tithe revenues made up 27.1 per cent of all tax revenues in 1887–8 and 25.0 per cent of all tax revenues in 1910–11. Animal tax (*agnam*) collections added 11.5 and 7.6 per cent respectively. Shaw, 'Ottoman tax reforms," pp. 451–3. It is not clear what part of this substantial increase in tithe revenues was due to increases in agricultural production, what part due to more effective control of the tax-collections and tax-collectors by the state.

32 *İltizam*, year-to-year or short-term tax-farming system was increasingly replaced by the *malikane*, life-time tax-farming system during the eighteenth century. See M. Genç, 'Osmanlı maliyesinde malikane sistemi' (*Malikane* system and the Ottoman fisc), in Ü. Nalbantoğlu and O. Okyar (eds.), *Türkiye iktisat tarihi semineri* (Seminar on Turkish economic history) (Ankara, Hacettepe University Press, 1975).

33 Shaw, 'Ottoman tax reforms'; Quataert, 'Ottoman reform', ch. 1.
34 During the late 1860s when the budgetary deficits of the state could not be eliminated by large volumes of external borrowing, the tithe rate was raised to 15 per cent in 1868 and to 12.5 per cent during 1869–72. The rate was 12 per cent during 1873 and 1874 when the worst famine of the century hit central Anatolia. The rate was raised again to 11.75 per cent during the 1880s as the Great Depression of the world-economy and large debt payments to the Ottoman Public Debt Administration intensified the fiscal crisis of the state.
35 *Accounts and Papers*, 'Report on land tenure in Turkey', 67 (1870), p. 283. For a detailed list of the different forms of taxes paid by the rural classes see *Accounts and Papers*, Commercial Report from Trabzon for the year 1868. For road tax which could be paid either in cash or in labour services in road building, *Accounts and Papers*, Commercial Reports from Trabzon 1867, 1872, 1883, Salonica 1868; *Accounts and Papers* (1884), 'Special report on road building in Turkey'. Also, Shaw, 'Ottoman tax reforms', pp. 432–3, 457.
36 For the tax burden of the small peasantry, see R. Akkan 'The burden of taxation on the peasants', in C. Issawi (ed.), *The economic history of the Middle East, 1800–1914* (Chicago, University of Chicago Press, 1966); Köy ve Ziraat Kalkınma Kongresi, *Ziraat tarihi*, pp. 65–70, 206 and *passim*. For the arbitrary rule of tax-collectors, *Accounts and Papers*, Commercial Report from Aleppo for the year 1874.
37 Güran, 'Osmanlı tarım', pp. 133 ff. For a sampling of the rates of interest charged by usurers, see Issawi, *Turkey*, pp. 341–3. *Accounts and Papers*, Commercial Report from Aleppo for the year 1874.
38 For a detailed description of the living conditions of Anatolian peasants, see *Accounts and Papers*, 'Condition of the industrial classes in foreign countries', 68(1871), pp. 735–44.
39 Estimates indicate that urbanization in northern Greece and Anatolia as a whole remained limited during the nineteenth century. The size of both the total population in the core areas of the Empire approximately doubled between 1830 and 1912. The share of the urban population in the total is estimated to have increased from 17 to 22 per cent during the same period. Issawi, *Turkey*, pp. 34–5.
40 Barkan, 'Türk toprak hukuku'; Güran, 'Osmanlı tarım', p. 136; *Accounts and Papers*, Commercial Reports, *passim*.
41 For example, *Accounts and Papers*, Commercial Report from Trabzon, 1880.
42 *Accounts and Papers*, Commercial Reports from Diyarbakır 1856, Kavala 1858, Monastır 1859, Trabzon 1867, Ankara 1894.
43 *Accounts and Papers*, 'Report on land tenure in Turkey', 67(1870), pp. 276–92.
44 *Ibid.*, p. 286.
45 *Ibid.*, pp. 285–7. For a region-by-region distribution of farm size in northern Greece, Thrace and some parts of Anatolia in 1863, see the table prepared by Issawi, *Turkey*, p. 203.
46 Eight hectares for a household with one pair of oxen, according to Palgrave. See *Accounts and Papers*, 'Report on land tenure',
47 These middle peasants would, in effect, be bringing in their capital. In other words in this case the share-cropper was not only a labourer but was also his own capitalist. See Marx, *Capital*, III, 803.
48 Chayanov, *Peasant economy*, and Boratav, *Tarımsal yapılar*.
49 On this issue see, amongst others, Kurmuş, *Emperyalizm*, *passim*.
50 Boratav, *Tarımsal yapılar*.
51 *Accounts and Papers*, Commercial Reports, *passim*.
52 *Accounts and Papers*, 'Report on land tenure in Turkey', p. 284. This portion of the

report has been reprinted in Issawi, *Turkey*, pp. 223–4.

53 For regional variations in share-cropping arrangements, see *Accounts and Papers*, 'Report on land tenure', despatches from consuls in İstanbul, Edirne, Çanakkale, Trabzon, Monastır, Salonica, pp. 273–312. A summary is available in Issawi, *Turkey*, pp. 217–18. For an example of different forms of tenancy co-existing in a given area, see *Accounts and Papers*, Commercial Report from Trabzon for the year 1880. Also Güran, 'Osmanlı tarım', pp. 133–4.

54 *Accounts and Papers*, 'Report on land tenure', p. 289.

55 *Accounts and Papers*, Commercial Reports from İzmir, Adana and Salonica, 1896–1913.

56 Issawi, *Turkey*, p. 202, 220–3; *Accounts and Papers*, 'Report on land tenure', pp. 282–4.

57 The inclusion of Syria and Iraq in Palgrave's survey could not have biased his estimates in the direction of small holdings since we would expect that distribution of landownership was more unequal in these provinces of the Empire.

58 Boratav, *Tarımsal yapılar*, pp. 22–4.

59 For changing patterns of landownership and tenancy in other areas of the Ottoman Empire, in Syria and the Fertile Crescent, see I.M. Smilianskaya, 'From subsistence to market economy (Syria in the) 1850s', D. Warriner, 'Land tenure in the Fertile Crescent', and Warriner and G. Baer, 'The evolution of private landownership in Egypt and the Fertile Crescent', in Issawi, *Middle East*.

60 *Accounts and Papers*, Commercial Reports from Diyarbakır, Aleppo, Erzurum, Van, for the years 1900–13.

61 *Accounts and Papers*, Commercial Reports from Diyarbakır and Van, various years.

62 *Accounts and Papers*, Commercial Reports from Harput, various years.

63 *Accounts and Papers*, 'Report on land tenure'; Issawi, *Turkey*. pp. 220–1; *Accounts and Papers*, Commercial Report from Diyarbakır for the year 1856.

64 The analysis of the patterns of landownership is inevitably complicated by the presence of large numbers of nomads in the region. According to one estimate which appears rather high, the nomadic population in the provinces of Erzurum and Diyarbakır exceeded 600 thousand at the end of the 1860s. This, if true, would mean that the nomads comprised as much as one half of the total population of these two provinces at the time. See *Accounts and Papers*. 'Condition of the industrial classes in foreign countries', 68(1871), despatch from the consul in Diyarbakır.

65 Barkan, 'Türk toprak hukuku'; *Accounts and Papers*, Commercial Report from Diyarbakır for the year 1863.

66 *Accounts and Papers*, Commercial Report from Diyarbakır, 1863.

67 *Accounts and Papers*, Commercial Report from Diyarbakır, 1863, 1867, 1884, Van 1884.

68 For the observations of young Ziya Gökalp who grew up in the region, see S. Beysanoğlu, *Ziya Gökalp'ın ilk yazı hayatı* (Ziya Gökalp's early writings) (İstanbul, Şehir Matbaası, 1956), For a collection of cases of landownership disputes during the twentieth century which throws considerable light on the past, see N. Yalman, 'On land disputes in eastern Turkey', in G.L. Tikku (ed.), *Islam and its cultural divergence* (Urbana, Ill., University of Illinois Press, 1971).

69 *Accounts and Papers*, Commercial Reports from Erzurum, Harput; Issawi, *Turkey*, pp. 216–18, 224. While examining patterns of landownership and tenancy during the late 1920s and early 1930s, I. Husrev Tokin points to a similar ethnic distinction, without the Armenians, between the Kurdish settlements of the southern tier where lord-peasant bonds were very strong and the small and middle holdings in the Turkish villages in Erzurum. Husrev, *Türkiye' de köy iktisadiyatı* (Village economics in Turkey) (İstanbul, 1934), pp. 176–86. Also see A.J. Sussnitzki, 'Ethnic division of labor (in Turkey)', in Issawi, *Middle East*.

70 *Accounts and Papers*, Commercial Reports from Erzurum 1906, Van 1879, 1906, Aleppo 1902, Diyarbakır 1907; Issawi, *Turkey*, pp. 216–20; Quataert, 'Ottoman reform', ch. 7.
71 N. Svoronos, *Le commerce de Salonique au 18e siècle* (Paris, Presses Universitaires de France, 1956; P. Masson, *Histoire du commerce français dans le Levant au XVIIIe siècle* (Paris, Hachette, 1911); R. Paris, *Histoire du commerce de Marseille*, vol. V: *1660 à 1789. Le Levant* (Paris, Plon, 1957); Veinstein, 'Ayan'; N. Ülker, 'The rise of İzmir, 1688–1740' (University of Michigan, 1974), unpublished Ph.D. dissertation.
72 See ch. 2 of Pamuk, *Trade, capital, production.*
73 Nickoley, 'Agriculture', pp. 286–91; Quataert, 'Commercialization of agriculture', pp. 40–2; Issawi, *Turkey*, pp. 236–68.
74 Eldem, *İktisadi şartlar*, pp. 164–5; Issawi, *Turkey*, pp. 103–5, 108–11.
75 Issawi, *Turkey*, p. 203.
76 *Ibid.*
77 N.P. Mouzelis, *Modern Greece* (New York, Holmes and Meier, 1978), pp. 17–22.
78 *Accounts and Papers*, Commercial Report from Monastır for the year 1859.
79 Issawi, *Turkey*, p. 203.
80 *Ibid.*, p. 202.
81 İnalcık, 'The application of Tanzimat', *Archivum Ottomanicum*, 3(1973).
82 See, for example, evidence cited in *Accounts and Papers*, 'Report on land tenure in Turkey,' despatches by consuls in Monastır and Salonica.
83 Also, see Güran, 'Osmalı tarım', p. 86. For levels of agricultural wages, see Issawi, *Turkey*, pp. 204, 37–43.
84 *Accounts and Papers*, 'Report on land tenure', p. 284.
85 *Ibid.*, p. 284.
86 F. Rougon, *Smyrne* (Paris, Berger-Levrault, 1892), pp. 73–4.
87 See ch. 3 and Appendix 2 of Pamuk, *Trade, capital, production.*
88 For long-term fluctuations in land prices, see Issawi, *Turkey*, pp. 206–7.
89 See sources cited in note 42.
90 *Accounts and Papers*, Commercial Reports from Salonica, İzmir, Adana, Konya. Quataert, 'Ottoman reform', ch. 7, and Kurmuş, *Emperyalizm*, pp. 112–19.
91 Kurmuş, *Emperyalizm*, pp. 102–3.
92 The British were not alone in their hopes and attempts at colonization of Anatolia. For the little-known case of a fully-fledged German colony in the Amasya region, see *Accounts and Papers*, 'Condition of the industrial classes in foreign countries', 68(1871), p. 733.
93 C. Issawi, 'The Tabriz-Trabzon trade, 1830–1900: rise and decline of a route', *International Journal of Middle East Studies*, 1(1970) and Issawi, *Turkey*, pp. 124–6.
94 *Accounts and Papers*, Commercial Reports from Trabzon, Samsun.
95 *Accounts and Papers*, Commercial Report from Trabzon for the year 1867.
96 Issawi, *Turkey*, p 203.
97 *Accounts and Papers*, Commercial Report from Antalya for the years 1897–1899.
98 K. Ener, *Tarih boyunca Adana ovasına bir bakış* (A survey of the Adana valley throughout history) (İstanbul, 1961), pp. 200–17.
99 United States, Bureau of Foreign Commerce, *Commercial relations of the United States with foreign Countries*, Commercial Report from Adana for the year 1862.
100 *Accounts and Papers*, Commercial Reports from Adana for the years 1871, 1872, 1874.
101 *Accounts and Papers*, Commercial Reports from Adana for the year 1872; Ener, *Adana ovası*. For a study of the settlement policies of the state in this region, see A.G. Gould, 'Pashas and brigands: Ottoman provincial reform and its impact on the nomadic tribes of southern Anatolia, 1840–1885' (University of California, Los Angeles, 1973), unpublished Ph.D. dissertation.

102 A.D. Novichev, 'The development of agriculture in Anatolia', in Issawi, *Middle East*; Quataert, 'Ottoman reform', ch. 2; Pamuk, *Trade, capital, production*, ch. 4.
103 W.F. Bruck, *Die turkisch-Baum wollwirtschaft* (Jena, 1919); Novichev, 'Development of Agriculture'; Quataert, 'Ottoman reform', ch. 2.
104 Quataert, 'Ottoman reform', p. 168. Novichev, 'Development of agriculture', p. 69. For cotton cultivation in the plain of Adana, see Bruck, *Die-turkisch*, reprinted, in part, in Issawi, *Turkey*, pp. 242–5; *Accounts and Papers* (1908), 'Special report on cotton cultivation in Anatolia'.
105 *Accounts and Papers*, Commercial Report from Ankara for the year 1873.
106 Quataert, 'Limited revolution', and Novichev, 'Development of agriculture', pp. 66–8.
107 Quataert, 'Limited revolution', p. 151.
108 Quataert, 'Ottoman reform', Appendices.
109 Novichev, 'Development of agriculture', p. 66. However, in view of the limited reliability of the other figures cited by Novichev, these statistics should be treated with caution.
110 Quataert, 'Limited revolution', p. 149.
111 *Accounts and Papers*, Commercial Reports from Ankara, Konya.
112 *Accounts and Papers*, Commercial Report from Ankara, 1895; Issawi, *Turkey*, pp. 230–1; Eren, *Türkiye'de göç*.
113 Issawi, *Turkey*, pp. 230–1, *Accounts and Papers*, Commercial Reports from Ankara, Konya, various years.
114 H. Friedman makes a similar argument in explaining why commodity-producing households began replacing large capitalist farms employing wage labourers in wheat production during this period, especially in the North American plains. She also argues that the direction of technical progress did not favour capitalist farms during this period. See Friedman, 'World market, state, family farm', pp. 559–71.
115 *Ibid.*, pp. 574–8.
116 Quataert, 'Ottoman reform', ch. 2, Issawi, *Turkey*, pp. 229–31.
117 Quataert, 'Ottoman reform', Kurmuş, *Emperyalizm*; Güran 'Osmanlı tarım'; Issawi, *Turkey*.

9 Primitive accumulation in Egypt, 1798–1882

1 Immanuel Wallerstein, *The modern world-system: capitalist agriculture and the origins of the European world-economy in the sixteenth century* (New York, Academic Press, 1974), p. 15.
2 The analogies between Marxian political economy and systems theory are discussed thoroughly by Terence S. Turner, Dept. of Anthropology, University of Chicago, in an unpublished paper, 'The Ge and Bororo societies as dialectical systems: a general model'. I am indebted to Paul Christiansen for bringing this paper to my attention.
3 Karl Marx, *Grundrisse: introduction to the critique of political economy*, trans. M. Nicolaus (New York, Random House, 1978).
4 See, *inter alia*, the works of Samir Amin, Ibrahim ʿAmr, Mahmoud Hussain, and Anouar Abdel-Malek.
5 Ronald Robinson and John Gallagher with Alice Denny, *Africa and the Victorians: the climax of imperialism* (London, St Martin's Press, 1961).
6 See Stanford J. Shaw, *Ottoman Egypt in the age of the French Revolution* (Cambridge, Mass., Harvard Univ. Press, 1964), p. 6; André Raymond, *Artisans et commercants au Caire au dix-huitième siècle* (Damascus, Institut Français de Damas, 1973); P.S. Girard, 'Mémoire sur l'agriculture, l'industrie, et le commerce de l'Égypte', in *Description de l'Égypte: État Moderne*, vol. 2, 1 (Paris, 1813).

7 See Raymond, *Artisans*, pp. 191, 129–31; Shaw, *Ottoman Egypte*, p. 135.
8 See Raymond, *Artisans*, pp. 190 ff.
9 *Ibid.*
10 See Carlo Cipolla, *Guns, sails, and empires: technological innovation and the early phases of European expansion, 1400–1700* (New York, Minerva Press, 1965), pp. 102–3.
11 Specifically, coffee plantations were established in Surinam (1718), Martinique (1720), and French Guinea (1772). See D.B. Grigg, *The agricultural systems of the world: an evolutionary perspective* (New York, Cambridge University Press, 1974).
12 See E.J. Hobsbawm, 'The general crisis of the seventeenth century', in Trevor Aston (ed.), *Crisis in Europe, 1560–1660* (New York, Anchor, 1965), pp. 1–62.
13 See Raymond, *Artisans*, pp. 149, 156–7, 178–9.
14 See *ibid.*, pp. 180–4.
15 See *ibid.*, p. 196.
16 See Shaw, *Ottoman Egypt*, pp. 126–7.
17 See Raymond, *Artisans*, p. 194.
18 See Girard, 'Agriculture', p. 676.
19 See *ibid.*, p. 671.
20 See Raymond, *Artisans*, p. 180.
21 See, e.g., Paul Masson, *Histoire du commerce français dans le Levant au XVIIIe siècle* (Paris, Hachette, 1911).
22 On the crisis of the Ottoman state, see, *inter alia*, Halil İnalcık, 'The heyday and decline of the Ottoman Empire', in *Cambridge History of Islam* (2 vols., Cambridge, Cambridge University Press, 1970) vol. I, pp. 345 ff; Bernard Lewis, *The emergence of modern Turkey* (London, Oxford University Press, 1961).
23 See Bent Hansen, 'An economic model for Ottoman Egypt: the economics of collective tax responsibility', unpublished paper presented to the conference on the Economic History of the Near East at Princeton University, 16–20 June 1974, pp. 42–3.
24 See Stanford J. Shaw, 'Landholding and land tax revenues in Ottoman Egypt', in P.M. Holt (ed.), *Political and social change in modern Egypt* (London, Oxford University Press, 1968), pp. 91–103.
25 'By the end of the eighteenth century state lands were almost universally distributed throughout Egypt in the form of *iltizam* and fell into the hands of the wealthiest and most powerful men, most of whom were Mamluks. Of 6,000 *multezims*, it was estimated that 300 were Mamluks who held more than 2/3 of the cultivated land in Egypt', Helen A.B. Rivlin, *The agricultural policy of Muhammad ʿAli in Egypt* (Cambridge, Mass., Harvard University Press, 1961), p. 21.
26 The central government retained the legal title to the land even after the decline of its power.
27 See Michel-Ange Lancret, 'Mémoire sur le système d'imposition territoriale et sur l'administration des provinces de l'Égypte dans les dernières années du gouvernement des Mamlouks', in *Description de l'Égypte, état moderne* (Paris, 1809), vol. 1, p. 236.
28 See Comte Estève, 'Mémoire sur les finances de L'Égypte depuis sa conquête par le Sultan Selym Ier, jusqu'à celle du général en chef Bonaparte', in *Description de L'Égypte*, vol. 1, p. 243.
29 See Lancret, 'Imposition territoriale', p. 249.
30 See Estève, 'Finances', p. 311.
31 See Rivlin, *Agricultural policy*, ch. 2.
32 See Lancret, 'Imposition territoriale', p. 249.
33 See *ibid.*, p. 244.
34 Shaw estimates that Egyptian expenditures for the Porte fell 87 per cent from 1596

to 1796 in nominal terms. See *Ottoman Egypt*, p. 151. Hansen estimates that the share of the Porte in land taxes fell from roughly 25 per cent in the sixteenth century to roughly 15 per cent in 1798 ('An economic model, p. 10).

35 'Any victory over the enemy, however decisive, could not make the life of the victorious secure as long as the defeated enemy had the slightest chance of recuperating and gathering strength. The logical conclusion was: the enemy must be wiped out', D. Ayalon, 'Studies in al-Jabarti', *Journal of the Economic and Social History of the Orient*, 3(1960), 306.
36 See Hansen, 'An economic model', p. 16.
37 See Girard, 'Agriculture', p. 529.
38 See S. Shaw, *Financial and administrative organization and development of Ottoman Egypt, 1517–1798* (Princeton, Princeton University Press, 1962), pp. 22–3.
39 See Girard, 'Agriculture', p. 529.
40 See Shaw, *Ottoman Egypt*, pp. 133, 136–9.
41 See Lancret, 'Imposition territoriale', pp. 250–1.
42 Shaw, 'Landholding'.
43 Cited in Fernand Braudel, *Capitalism and material life: 1400–1800*, trans. Miriam Kochan (New York, Harper and Row, 1973), p. 13.
44 M.I. Finley, *The ancient economy* (Berkeley, Univ. of California Press, 1973), p. 31.
45 See Hansen, 'An economic model', pp. 40 ff.
46 'Abd al-Raheim, '*Hazz al-Quhuf*: a new source for the study of the fallahin of Egypt in the XVIIth and XVIIIth centuries', *Journal of the Economic and social History of the Orient*, XVIII, 2(1975), 260.
47 Shaw, 'Landholding', p. 101.
48 Rivlin, *Agricultural policy*, ch. 2.
49 G. Baer, *A history of landownership in Modern Egypt* (London, Oxford University Press, 1962).
50 Rivlin, *Agricultural policy*, ch. 2.
51 *Ibid.*
52 Shaw, 'Landholding'.
53 Lancret, 'Imposition territoriale', p. 236.
54 See E.R.J. Owen, *Cotton and the Egyptian economy, 1820–1914* (London, Oxford University Press, 1969), p. 71.
55 See Gabriel Baer, 'The dissolution of the village community', in *Studies in the Social History of Modern Egypt* (Chicago, Chicago University Press, 1969), pp. 17–29.
56 See H.A.R. Gibb and H. Bowen, *Islamic society and the West, I: Islamic society in the eighteenth century* (London, Oxford University Press, 1950), p. 213.
57 See Charles Singer, *et al.* (eds.), *A history of technology*, vol. 1 (London, Oxford University Press, 1954).
58 See William Willcocks, *Egyptian irrigation*, (2nd edn, London, F. Spon, 1913), pp. 38–9.
59 See Girard, 'Agriculture', pp. 557, 564.
60 See *Ibid.*, p. 497.
61 See Willcocks, *Egyptian irrigation*, pp. 36–8.
62 See Girard, 'Agriculture', p. 497.
63 *Ibid.*, p. 562.
64 See Willcocks, *Egyptian irrigation*, p. 42.
65 See Girard, 'Agriculture', pp. 515–17, 568–9.
66 See de Chabrol de Volvic, 'Essai sur les moeurs des habitants modernes de l'Égypte', in *Description de l'Egypte, état moderne* (Paris, 1822), vol. 2, pt 2, p. 511.
67 See Girard, 'Agriculture', p. 563.

68 See *ibid.*, p. 572.
69 See *ibid.*, p. 545.
70 See *ibid.*, p. 581.
71 See Owen, *Cotton*, p. 9.
72 See Girard, 'Agriculture', pp. 708–9.
73 See P.M. Holt, 'The later Ottoman Empire in Egypt and the Fertile Crescent', in *The Cambridge History of Islam* (2 vols., Cambridge, Cambridge University Press, 1970), vol. 1, p. 381.
74 See Rivlin, *Agricultural policy*, p. 253.
75 See Owen, *Cotton*, p. 169.
76 This was also a Mamluk practice. See Shaw, *Ottoman Egypt*, p. 121. A comparison of the ratio of prices paid to market prices or selling prices given in Shaw for wheat and rice with those of the same crops for Muhammad ʿAli given by ʿAmr indicates that the difference between the two prices was smaller in the case of Muhammad ʿAli:

Crop	p selling/	p purchase
	Mamluks	Muhammad ʿAli
Wheat	3.33	1.35
Rice	1.9	1.56

This helps to explain ʿAmr's assertion that the peasants' position had advanced (*tuqaddamat*) under Muhammad 'Ali relative to Mamluk times. As we shall see, on other grounds precisely the opposite conclusion seems more likely. See Ibrahim ʿAmr, *Al-ard wʾal-fellah: alʾmasʾilah az-ziraʿiyya fi misr* (The land and the peasant: the agricultural problem in Egypt) (Cairo, Dar al-Maarif, 1958), p. 81.
77 See Rivlin, *Agricultural policy*, ch. 10.
78 See S.B. Clough, *France: a history of national economics* (New York, Charles Scribner's Sons, 1939).
79 See *ibid.*, 130. By contrast, wheat exports had been prohibited before the revolution.
80 See J.D. Chambers and G.E. Mingay, *The agricultural revolution, 1750–1880* (London, B.T. Batsford, 1966), ch. 6.
81 Patricia Herlihy, 'Odessa and Europe's grain trade in the first half of the nineteenth century', unpubl. MS, p. 24.
82 See Owen, *Cotton*, p. 29.
83 *Ibid.* Owen also gives the fact that peasants couldn't cheat on the monopoly system by eating cotton or otherwise consuming it locally as a reason for the choice of cotton versus wheat. This argument essentially posits lower enforcement costs to government revenue collection for cotton as opposed to wheat. Now, it is true that, although peasants in various districts had spun cotton, weaving was performed in larger urban areas where it would have been more difficult for 'cheaters' to escape detection by Muhammad ʿAli's officials (see Girard, 'Agriculture'). However, given that the production of cotton on a large scale required huge corvées for irrigation works and considerably increased field labour, it is not clear that such reasoning is valid.
84 See Owen, *Cotton*, p. 47.

85 See *ibid.*, pp. 48–9. He notes, however, that it is not clear that the units of measure are the same in the two cases.
86 *Ibid.*, p. 140.
87 See *ibid.*, p. 34
88 D. Mackenzie Wallace, *Egypt and the Egyptian question* (London, 1883), p. 264.
89 See Rivlin, *Agricultural policy*, p. 141.
90 Export prices in that year were from 356 to 534 piastres per *qantar*.
91 See Owen, *Cotton*, p. 36.
92 See Rivlin, *Agricultural policy*, pp. 138–9.
93 See Ahmad Ahmad Al-Hitta, *Taʾrikh az-ziraʿiyya al-misriyya fiʿahd Muhammad ʿAli al-kabir* (The history of Egyptian agriculture in the age of Muhammad 'Ali the Great) (Cairo, Dar al-Maarif, 1950), p. 126.
94 See Al-Hitta, *Ta'rikh* pp. 244–5; ʿAmr, *Al-ard*, p. 81.
95 See ʿAmr, *Al-ard*, p. 81. Unfortunately, it is unclear from the context whether he means every year or only in certain years, although the latter is almost certainly the case. See Rivlin, *Agricultural policy*, ch. 12.
96 See Rivlin, *Agricultural policy*, ch. 12.
97 See *ibid.*
98 See *ibid.*, ch. 11.
99 *Ibid.*, pp. 21–2.
100 See Jacques Berque, *Egypt: imperialism and revolution*, trans. Jean Stewart (London, Faber, 1972), p. 173.
101 See Rivlin, *Agricultural policy*, ch. 11, and J.A. St John, *Egypt and Nubia* (London, 1845).
102 See Gabriel Baer, 'Submissiveness and revolt of the fellah' in *Studies*, p. 98.
103 See Rivlin, *Agricultural policy*, ch. 11.
104 See *ibid.*, ch. 12.
105 Owen, *Cotton*, p. 60.
106 Baer, *A history*, p. 17.
107 *Ibid.*
108 *Ibid.*, p. 18, fn. 5.
109 See *ibid.*, p. 14.
110 Rivlin, *Agricultural policy*, p. 73.
111 These figures are extremely rough, have somewhat peculiar definitions, include double counting, etc. See Rivlin, *Agricultural policy*, Appendix II for a discussion of these numbers. She notes that, owing to these numerical problems and after many complicated adjustments, the 'increase in peasant holdings was minute', p. 322, fn. 32.
112 ʿAmr, *Al-ard*, p. 78–9.
113 See above, p. 209.
114 The forms of labour supervision on these estates are treated briefly below.
115 See Nadav Safran, *Egypt in search of political community* (Cambridge, Mass., Harvard University Press, 1961).
116 See Rivlin, *Agricultural policy*, p. 83, fn. 17.
117 Gabriel Baer, 'The village shaykh', in *Studies*, p. 38.
118 *Ibid.*
119 See Rivlin, *Agricultural policy*, *passim*.
120 See Baer, *A history*, p. 14.
121 *Ibid.*
122 *Ibid.*
123 See *ibid.*, p. 17.

124 See *ibid.*, pp. 15–18.
125 See *ibid.*, pp. 6–8.
126 See *ibid.*, p. 9; ᶜAmr, *Al-ard*, p. 83.
127 ᶜAmr, *Al-ard*, p. 83.
128 Owen, *Cotton*, pp. 92–3; ᶜAmr, *Al-ard*, pp. 83, 86–7.
129 A.E. Crouchley, *The economic development of modern Egypt* (London, Longmans, Green and Co., 1938), p. 117.
130 *Ibid.*
131 See Owen, *Cotton*, p. 69.
132 See Owen, *Cotton*, p. 80; Clough, *France*, p. 101.
133 See Wallace, *Egypt*, pp. 265–6.
134 See Owen, *Cotton*, p. 82.
135 See Crouchley, *Economic development*, p. 120.
136 See Baer, *A history*, p. 31.
137 See below, p. 232.
138 See Owen, *Cotton*, p. 72.
139 *Ibid.*, p. 75.
140 See *ibid.*, p. 76.
141 *Ibid.*, p. 75.
142 See *ibid.*, pp. 76, 104.
143 *Ibid.*, pp. 76–7.
144 Lozach and Hug, writing in 1928, asserted that the system was 'about one hundred years old', Ayrout, writing in 1938, says the same thing. J. Lozach and G. Hug, *L'habitation rurale en Égypte* (Cairo, Imprimerie de L'Institut Français d'Archéologie Orientale du Caire, 1930); Henry Habib Ayrout, *The Egyptian peasant*, trans. J.A. Williams (Boston, Beacon Press, 1963), p. 111. This is roughly contemporaneous with Muhammed ᶜAli's decentralization of agricultural administration, which began in 1837. See Owen, *Cotton*, pp. 58 ff.
145 The word derives from the root *azaba*, 'to be distant'.
146 Documentation for these assertions can be found in my *Egypt's agricultural development, 1800–1980: technical and social change* (Boulder Colorado, Westview Press, 1982), ch. 3, sect. 3.3. It should be emphasized that the ᶜ*ezbah* system described here is an 'ideal type', since the evidence indicates the existence of many variations.
147 Bayle St John, *Village life in Egypt* (2 vols., London, Chapman and Hall, 1852), vol. 1, p. 190.
148 *Ibid.*
149 See Baer, *A history*, ch. 2.
150 See Kamel Gali, *Essai sur l'agriculture de l'Égypte* (Paris, Henri Jouve, 1889), p. 137; Muhammad Saleh, *La petite propriété rurale en Égypte* (Grenoble, Joseph Allier, 1922), p. 72.
151 See Gali, *Essai*, p. 140.
152 See *ibid.*, p. 138.
153 See *ibid.*, pp. 136–7.
154 See Crouchley, *Economic development*. On economies of scale in supervision, see Mustapha Nahas, *Situation économique et sociale du fellah égyptien* (Paris, 1901), p. 141.
155 Nassau Senior, *Conversations and journals in Egypt and Malta, 1855–6* (London, Low, Marston, Searl, Rivington, 1882), p. 111.
156 See Baer, *A history*, ch. 2.
157 *Ibid.*
158 See Baer, 'The village shaykh'.
159 See Crouchley, *Economic development*, p. 101.

160 See Baer, 'The village shaykh'.
161 Baer, *A history*, p. 52.
162 Senior, *Conversations*, p. 279.
163 Baer, *A history*, p. 53.
164 *Ibid.*, p. 54.
165 *Ibid.*
166 *Ibid.*, p. 53.
167 See Bayle St John, *Village life in Egypt*, vol. 2, pp. 60 ff.
168 See Baer, *A history*, p. 29.
169 *Ibid.*
170 See Owen, *Cotton*, pp. 144–5.
171 See Baer, *A history*, p. 30.
172 See Owen, *Cotton*, p. 93, fn.
173 See Wallace, *Egypt*, p. 337.
174 Baer, *A history*, p. 30; see also Lady Duff Gordon, *Letters from Egypt*, ed. G. Waterfield (London, Routledge and Kegan Paul, 1969), p. 182.
175 See Owen, *Cotton*, p. 105.
176 See Baer, *A history*, p. 35. One might object that if yields were rising, then perhaps the incidence of taxation was steady or even declining. This was almost certainly not the case. Even if we consider average yields (a misleading indicator, as I will argue in a moment), the incidence of taxation rose sharply in certain critical years: from 1865/6 to 1869 there is no evidence of any change even in the average yields of cotton. Yet, during those years, taxes rose by 70 per cent. As I mentioned in the text, this increase coincided with a fall in the price of cotton of 50 per cent (see Table 9.5). At the same time, a cattle plague decimated the peasants' work animals. The peasants were also subjected to a host of other taxes: salt, poll, date palm, not to mention the corvée.

Owen does mention a rise in average yields from two to two and a half *qantar*s per *feddan* in 1869–71, at the same time as the 25 per cent surcharge was levied. But this is really beside the point for two reasons. First, average yields are deceptive. We know that there was a marked difference between the techniques of cultivation of pashas and peasants; we also know that the latter group was losing land to the former. Peasants continued to employ the *balli* method into the 1880s, so it seems very likely that yields on peasant lands changed very little, if at all. There is certainly no testimony that peasant yields were rising, nor any reason to suppose that they might have been. Secondly, the numbers on the tax rates give a most inadequate picture of the incidence of taxation. Owen aptly summarizes this point: 'It is unlikely that such figures [on the land tax] provide any real guide to the amounts of money actually collected at this time. Throughout Ismail's reign taxes continued to be gathered by methods which varied little from those employed under Muhammad 'Ali. Collections were made at all times of the year, often necessitating the sale of standing crops; animals and seed were seized when money was not forthcoming; those with cash were expected to pay for defaulters; and in general the tax gatherers were free to make any sort of demand they wished on any illiterate, unprotected peasant population. When those on the Commission of Inquiry appointed in 1878 tried to find out on what principle taxes were being levied, they were unable to discover whether the sum due each year was the total of all the figures inscribed in the various tax registers or an arbitrary amount decided upon in Cairo and divided up among the different provinces' (Owen, *Cotton*, pp. 146–7). This arbitrariness, as well as the compulsory collection of six years' advance taxes in 1871, is reminiscent of conditions in the Chinese countryside from 1911 to 1949. See Lucien Bianco, *The origins of the Chinese Revolution*, trans. Muriel Bell (Stanford, Stanford University Press, 1967), pp. 88–103.

177 See Owen, *Cotton*, pp. 146 ff.
178 Although apparently a faction of Turco-Egyptians also supported ᶜUrabi. See Alexander Schoelch, *Aegypten den Aegyptern: Die politische und gesellschaftliche Krise der Jahre 1878–1882 in Aegypten* (Zurich, 1972).
179 See R.L. Tignor, *Modernization and British colonial rule in Egypt* (Princeton, Princeton University Press, 1966).
180 Baer, 'The village shaykh', p. 57.
181 *Ibid., passim.*
182 Earl of Cromer, *Modern Egypt* (London, Macmillan, 1908), p. 187; Schoelch, *Aegypten*, p. 243.
183 See Albert Hourani, 'Introduction', in Schoelch, *Aegypten*, p. 11; cf. ᶜAmr, *Al-ard*, p. 87.
184 See ᶜAmr, *Al-ard*, p. 87.
185 See, for example, Earl of Cromer, *Modern Egypt*, p. 187; the report from the British consul, Borg, quoted in Baer, *A history*, p. 53; Wallace, *Egypt*, pp. 222–8. Schoelch points out, however, that the evidence of the first two men may have been intentionally distorted to improve the 'moral position' of the British intervention against ᶜUrabi.
186 See Baer, *A history*, p. 36.
187 *Ibid.*
188 *Ibid.*
189 See Villiers Stuart, *Egypt since the war* (London, John Murray, 1883), pp. 17–21, 39–40, 54–9, 70, 100, 137–9.
190 See *ibid.*, pp. 17–21, 47, 143.
191 See ᶜAmr, *Al-ard*, p. 87.
192 See Wallace, *Egypt*, pp. 290–1.
193 Baer, 'Submissiveness and revolt', p. 101.
194 Eric R. Wolf, *Peasant wars of the twentieth century* (New York, Harper and Row, 1969).
195 *Ibid.*, p. 292.
196 *Ibid.*, p. 291.
197 See Schoelch, *Aegypten*, p. 268.
198 *Ibid.*
199 David Landes, *Bankers and pashas: international finance and economic imperialism in Egypt* (Cambridge, Mass., Harvard University Press, 1958), p. 133.
200 Karl Marx, *Grundrisse*, p. 92.
201 This became even clearer in the twentieth century when the beaches of the Riviera were filled with the multi-lingual, highly sophisticated scions of the pasha class. Their behaviour supports Wallerstein's observation that the 'capitalist farmers of the periphery . . . would gladly have thought of themselves as part of an international gentry class. They willingly sacrificed local cultural roots for participation in "world" cultures.' Immanuel Wallerstein, *World-system*, pp. 352–3.
202 See Mahmoud Abdel-Fadil, *Development, income distribution, and social change in rural Egypt (1952–1970): a study in the political economy of agrarian transition* (Cambridge, Cambridge University Press, 1975), p. 48.
203 Anouar Abdel-Malek, *Egypt: military society*, trans. C.L. Marham (New York, Random House, 1968), p. 401.
204 See my *Technical and social change*, ch. 3, on debt-peonage mechanisms in the countryside.
205 The above is based on my reading of Marx, *Capital*, vol. 1, especially ch. 1, ch. 6, and ch. 10, sect. 2; vol. III, pts. I and II. See also Michio Morishima, *Marx's economics: a dual theory of value and growth* (Cambridge, Cambridge University Press, 1973).
206 See A. Lambert, 'Les salariés dans l'entreprise agricole égyptien', *L'Egypte*

contemporaine, 33(1943), 223–35.

207 See Lancret, 'Imposition territoriale', p. 244.

208 See Owen, *Cotton*, p. 240.

209 See Richards, *Technical and social change*, ch. 3.

210 See Harry Braverman, *Labor and monopoly capital* (New York, Monthly Review Press, 1974).

211 See ʿAmr, *Al-ard*, p. 28, where he contrasts 'capitalist land monopoly' with 'feudal land monopoly': the former is for the purpose of exploitation, for use (*ghard al-istighlal*), the latter for skimming of the product (*ghard tasarruf*).

212 James O'Connor, 'The need for production and the production of needs', in *The corporations and the state* (New York, Harper and Row, 1971), p. 37.

213 See ʿAmr, *Al-ard*, p. 32.

214 Herodotus, *The histories*, trans. Aubrey de Selincourt (Baltimore, Penguin, 1954).

215 de Chabrol de Volvic, 'Moeurs', p. 511.

216 See G. Hamdan, 'Evolution of irrigation agriculture in Egypt', in L. Dudley Stamp (ed.), *A history of land use in arid regions* (Paris, UNESCO, 1961), p. 122 (previously noted in 1926 by V.M. Mosseri).

217 See Eric Wolf, *Peasants* (Englewood Cliffs, NJ, Prentice Hall, 1966), for a taxonomy of 'paleotechnic' agricultural systems and their characteristics. In general, human energy input and yield per acre vary directly.

218 See Clifford Geertz, *Agricultural involution: the process of ecological change in Indonesia* (Berkeley, University of California Press, 1963), ch. 2.

10 Price history and the Bursa silk industry: a study in Ottoman industrial decline, 1550–1650

1 Ömer Lütfi Barkan, 'The price revolution of the sixteenth century: a turning point in the economic history of the Near East', *International Journal of Middle East Studies*, 6(Jan. 1975), 3–28.

2 On the importance of Bursa as the centre of silk industry and trade see the following studies by Halil İnalcık: 'Capital formation in the Ottoman Empire', *The Journal of Economic History*, 29(March 1969), 97–140: 'Harir', *Encyclopaedia of Islam*, 2nd edn (Leiden, 1960); 'Bursa XV. Asır Sanayi ve Ticaret Tarihine Dair Vesikalar' (Documents on the industrial and commercial history of Bursa during the fifteenth century), *Belleten*. 24(1960), 45–102. See also Fahri Dalsar, *Türk Sanayi ve Ticaret Tarihinde Bursa'da İpekçilik* (The place of the Bursa silk industry in the industrial and commercial history of Turkey) (İstanbul, İstanbul Üniversitesi İktisat Fakültesi, 1960).

3 Benjamin Braude, 'International competition and domestic cloth in the Ottoman Empire, 1500–1650: a study in undevelopment', *Review* (Journal of the Fernand Braudel Center, SUNY), II, 3(Winter 1979), 437–61.

4 Maliye Defterleri (Finance Ministry Registers; hereafter *MAD*), *MAD* 2477/18, 90, 131; *MAD* 15988/3, 4; *MAD* 20286/8, Prime Ministry Archives. For more information on the Salonica woollen industry see Halil Sahillioğlu, 'Yeniçeri Çuhası ve II. Beyazid'in Son Yıllarında Yeniçeri Çuha Muhasebesi' (Accounts of the woollen cloth for janissaries during the last years of Bayezid II), *Güney Doğu Avrupa Araştırmaları Dergisi*, 2–3(1974), 415–67.

5 Ömer Lütfi Barkan, 'Research on the Ottoman fiscal surveys', *Studies in the Economic History of the Middle East*, ed. Michael A. Cook (London, Oxford University Press, 1970), pp. 163–71; Ronald C. Jennings, 'Urban population in Anatolia in the sixteenth century: a study of Kayseri, Karaman, Amasya, Trabzon and Erzurum',

International Journal of Middle Eastern Studies, 7(1976), 21–57, and Mustafa Akdağ, *Türk Halkının Dirlik ve Düzenlik Kavgası, Celali İsyanları* (The struggle of Turkish people for peace and order, the Celali uprisings) (İstanbul, Bilgi Yayınevi, 1975), *passim*.

6 Akdağ, *Türk Halkı*, pts. III and IV.

7 Ömer Lütfi Barkan, 'Edirne Askeri Kassamına Ait Tereke Defterleri, 1545–1659' (Inheritance registers of the Edirne Askeri class, 1545–1659), *Türk Tarih Belgeleri Dergisi*, 3(1966), 1–479.

8 Frequency of observation determined the weight given. For more detailed information on the methodology applied the reader is referred to Çizakça 'Inflation and the Bursa silk industry', chs. 2 and 3.

9 This situation, however, does not create a problem, as my purpose is to compare the relative price trends of raw silk and silk cloth, a comparison that can be easily made by using the prevailing nominal prices. The basic source on Ottoman monetary history is the partly unpublished work of Halil Sahillioğlu, 'Kuruluşundan XVII. Asrın Sonlarına Kadar Osmanlı Para Tarihi Hakkında Bir Deneme' (A study of Ottoman monetary history from the beginning to the seventeenth century) (İstanbul University, 1958) Unpublished Ph.D dissertation; *idem, Bir Asırlık Osmanlı Para Tarihi, 1640–1740* (Ottoman monetary history, 1640–1740) (İstanbul, 1965). See also *idem*, 'XVII. Asrın İlk Yarısında İstanbul'da Tedavüldeki Sikkelerin Rayici' (The exchange rate of *sikke* in circulation in İstanbul), *Belgeler Dergisi*, 1(1964), 227–35, and his latest article, 'Osmanlı Para Tarihinde Dünya Para ve Maden Hareketlerinin Yeri (1300–1750)' (The place of worldwide movements of money and precious metals in Ottoman monetary history, 1300–1750), *Gelişme Dergisi* (Middle East Technical University), special issue (1978), pp. 1–38. That converting nominal Ottoman prices into grams of pure silver can be misleading has been explained to me by Sahillioğlu.

10 Barkan, 'Turning Point', p. 15.

11 In this difficult process I consulted Barkan, 'Edirne', and Fahri Dalsar, *Bursa'da İpekçilik*. I also benefited from the comments of Professor Halil Sahillioğlu of İstanbul University, and from long conversations with old silk clothiers of Bursa, who, remarkably enough, knew some of the names.

12 Consider the statement, '1600 tarihlerinden sonra rastgeldiğimiz atlasların hemen hepsi Venedik ve Frenk malı olarak görülmektedir' (After the 1600s almost all of the *atlases* we have found appear to have been of Venetian and European origin). F. Dalsar, *Bursa'da İpekçilik*, p. 38.

13 *Zira*, although widely used, was by no means a standard unit of length. For example, there were twenty different forms of *zira* in the Arab provinces alone; W. Hinz, *Islamische Masse und Gewichte, Handbuch der Orientalistik*, pt. 1, vol. 1, issue 1(Leiden, E.J. Brill, 1970). What expedited this study is the proximity of Bursa to İstanbul. According to Hinz (*ibid.*, p. 58) there was a type of *zira* which Arabs called *Ad-dira*ᶜ*al-İstanbuliyya* (*zira* of İstanbul), ranging from 65 to 68 centimetres. The fact that this form was known in distant Arab provinces suggests that this İstanbul *zira* must have been a fairly standard and widely accepted unit. Furthermore, even if the *zira* of Bursa was not exactly equal to the *zira* of İstanbul, as long as each maintained a constant length throughout our period we would have no formidable problem.

14 On this question see the forthcoming Ph.D. dissertation on the customs of Erzurum by Neşe Erim (University of İstanbul).

15 *MAD* 399/41 and *MAD* 399/51.

16 Huri İslamoğlu and Suraiya Faroqhi, 'Crop patterns and agricultural production trends in sixteenth-century Anatolia', *Review*, II, 3(1979), 413.

17 Paul Masson, *Histoire du commerce français dans le Levant au XVIIIe siècle* (Paris, Hachette, 1911), pp. 445–6.
18 On the production of *orsoglio* and spread of the hydraulic mill, see Carlo Poni, 'All'origine del sistema di fabbrica: Tecnologia e organizzazione produttiva dei mulini da seta nell'Italia settentrionale (Sec. XVII–XVIII)', *Rivista storica italiana*, 3(1967), 445–97, and *idem*, 'Archéologie de la fabrique: la diffusion des moulins à soie "alla bolognese" dans les États vénitiens du XVIe au XVIIIe siècle', *Annales ESC*, 6(1972), 1475–96.
19 Personal correspondence with Carlo Poni dated 17 Dec. 1977. According to Poni the rapid expansion of the hydraulic mill in Italy occurred between 1634 and 1670 (see 'Archéologie de la fabrique', p. 1478). Thus, the Italian influence on price trends must have been more pronounced for these years. But this is not to say that an Italian impact was not felt previously: the production of *organzino* had been increasing since the beginning of the century, and Italians exported this product throughout the period.
20 Ralph Davis, 'English imports from the Middle East, 1580–1780', Studies in the economic history of the Middle East, ed. Michael A. Cook, p. 202. In this context see also Necmi Ülker, 'The rise of İzmir, 1686–1740', (University of Michigan, 1974) Unpublished Ph.D. dissertation, ch. 2.
21 Paul Mantoux, *The industrial revolution in the eighteenth century* (New York, Macmillan, 1965), pp. 193–5.
22 On Ottoman–Dutch trade the reader is referred to K. Heeringa, *Bronnen tot de Geschiedenis van den Levantschen Handel* (vol. I, 2 pts., The Hague, M. Nÿhoff, 1910–17), and A.H.de Groot, *The Ottoman Empire and the Dutch Republic* (Leiden/Istanbul, Nederlands Historisch-Archaeologisch Institut, 1978), *passim*.
23 Herman Van der Wee, 'Konjunktur und Welthandel in den Südlichen Niederlanden (1538–4)', *Wirtschaftskräfte und Wirtschaftswege, Beiträge zur Wirtschaftsgeschichte*, ed. Hermann Kellenbenz and Jürgen Schneider (Bamberg, Klett, Cotta, 1978), p. 144.
24 Wilfrid Brulez, 'The balance of trade of the Netherlands in the middle of the sixteenth century', *Acta Historiae Neerlandica*, 4(1970), 36, and Herman Van der Wee, 'Handel in de Zuidelijke Nederlanden', p. 91.
25 For the English importation, see Ralph Davis, *Aleppo and Devonshire Square* (London, Macmillan, 1967), p. 139; for the Dutch see the unpublished paper by F.S. Gaastra, 'The Dutch East India Co. and the Asian market', presented at the French-Dutch Economic History Conference, Leyden, Oct. 1978, sponsored by the Institute for the History of Overseas Expansion, University of Leyden. Early seventeenth-century English attempts at carrying the Persian silk via the Indian Ocean had failed. Alfred C. Wood, *A history of the Levant Company*, 2nd edn (London, Frank Cass and Co., 1964), pp. 47–9.
26 On the economies achieved in the Italian silk industry, see Poni, 'All'origine del sistema di fabbrica'.
27 Leila Erder, 'The making of industrial Bursa: economic activity and population in a Turkish city, 1835–1975' (Princeton University, 1976) Unpublished Ph.D. dissertation, p. 98.
28 On the low wages in the English textile industry see, Barry E. Supple, *Commercial crisis and change in England, 1600–1642* (Cambridge, Cambridge University Press, 1970), pp. 124, 144, 224. For Switzerland see, Walter Bodmer, *Die Entwicklung der Schweizerischen Textilwirtschaft im Rahmen der Übrigen Industrien und Wirtschaftswege* (Zurich, Verlag Berichthaus, 1960), pt. 11.
29 For the successive debasements of the Ottoman *akçe* see, Sahillioğlu, 'Osmanlı Para Tarihinde', p. 38. For a comparison of the exchange rates between various European

currencies and the *akçe* see Fernand Braudel and Frank Spooner, 'Prices in Europe from 1450 to 1750' in *The Cambridge Economic History of Europe* (Cambridge, Cambridge University Press, 1967), vol. 4, p. 458. This argument is more valid for the Dutch than the English merchants, who were legally prohibited from exporting bullion from their country.

30 The following price histories were consulted without any result: Aldo de Maddalena, *Prezzi e aspetti di mercato in Milano durante il secolo XVII* (Milan, Malfasi, 1949), pp. 172–7; G. Parenti, *Prime recherche sulla rivoluzione dei prezzi in Firenze* (Florence, C. Cya, 1939), p. xvi; M.J. Elsas, *Umrisse einer Geschichte der Preise und Löhne in Deutschland* (Leiden, A. Sythoff, 1936–49), W.H. Beveridge, *Prices and wages in England from the 12th to the 19th century* (London, Frank Cass and Co., 1966), and N.W. Posthumus, *Inquiry into the history of prices in Holland* (2 vols., Leiden, E.J. Brill, 1964), vol. 2. There were two exceptions: Earl J. Hamilton, *American treasure and the price revolution in Spain, 1501–1650* (New York, Octagon Books, 1965), Appendix IV, and Herman Van der Wee, 'Konjunktur und Welthandel', p. 144. The former work concerns Spanish prices, which are of limited importance for our purposes as the Spanish were not particularly involved in Levantine trade: the latter, though more relevant, covers only the period 1538–44.

31 A vigorous policy of import substitution was indeed applied by many European countries in the early seventeenth century. See Van der Wee, 'Konjunktur und Welthandel', p. 139, Alfons K.L. Thijs, *De Zijdennijverheid te Antwerpen in de Zeventiende Eeuw* (Liege, Crédit Communalde Belgique, 1969), pp. 61–3; and Charles W. Cole, *Colbert and a century of French mercantalism* (Hamden, Archon Books, 1964), vol. 2, ch. 10.

32 Ralph Davis, *Aleppo and Devonshire Square*, p. 42; *idem*, 'England and the Mediterranean, 1570–1670', *Essays in the economic and social history of Tudor and Stuart England*, ed. F.J. Fisher (Cambridge, Cambridge University Press, 1961), pp. 120–1; Ülker, 'İzmir', pp. 125–55; and Cole, *Colbert*, ch. 10. Also see, A.H. de Groot, *The Ottoman Empire and the Dutch Republic*, p. 109.

33 Çizakça, 'Inflation and the Bursa silk industry', p. 262.

34 This is no place to give a detailed overview of the Ottoman land system. Suffice it to say that inflation, population growth, and changing political conditions all led to the impoverishment of the peasantry. See Ömer Lütfi Barkan 'The social consequences of economic crisis in later-sixteenth-century Turkey', *The social aspects of economic development* (İstanbul, Boğaziçi Univ., 1964), Michael A. Cook, *Population pressure in rural Anatolia, 1450–1600* (London, Oxford University Press, 1972), and Metin Kunt, *Sancaktan Eyalete* (From Sancak to Eyalet) (İstanbul, Boğaziçi Üniversitesi, 1978), ch. 4.

35 Davis, 'England and the Mediterranean', pp. 120–2; Supple, *Crisis and change in England, passim.*

36 So far we have only preliminary evidence on raw-cotton production; see İslamoğlu and Faroqhi, 'Crop patterns and agricultural trends', pp. 413-14.

37 Wilfrid Brulez, 'L'exportation des Pays-Bas vers l'Italie par voie de terre au milieu du XVIe siècle,' *Annales, ESC*, XIV, 3(1959), 461–91.

38 Peter J. Bowden, 'Movements in wool prices, 1490–1610', *Yorkshire Bulletin of Economic and Social Research*, 4(1977), 116.

39 Beveridge, *Prices and wages in England, passim.*

40 Braude, 'International competition and domestic cloth', p. 442.

41 *Ibid*, p. 442. It may be argued here that faster price increases on the Continent may have induced English merchants to export wool to the main centres of wool consumption. But it is well known that protectionist policies pursued by the English

crown between the fourteenth and seventeenth centuries transformed the structure of English exports; exports of wool declined throughout this period while those of cloth increased; see E.M. Carus-Wilson, *Medieval merchant venturers* (London, Methuen, 1954), p. xviii, and E. Lipson, *The history of the woollen and worsted industries* (London, Barnes and Noble, 1965), pp. 87–8.

42 According to Davis, 'The trade can almost be reduced, in fact, to the exchange of broadcloth for raw silk' ('England and the Mediterranean', p. 125).

43 The main exporters of cloth from England were the Merchant Adventurers' Company and its 'offshoots', the Levant Co. and the Eastland Co. Hanseatic merchants, chief competitors of the London merchants in exporting English cloth, lost their privileges in the latter half of the sixteenth century. Thus English cloth producers who lost a major source of demand now faced a powerful group of merchants who enjoyed the sole right of cloth exportation. This group has often been accused of depressing the cloth market in England. See Richard H. Tawney (ed.), *Studies in economic history: the collected papers of George Unwin*, 3rd edn (London, Frank Cass, 1966), pt. 2.

44 Bruade showed that broadcloth prices in İstanbul were 20 to 30 per cent lower than those in London; 'International competition and domestic cloth', pp. 443–5.

45 For the effects on the Italian woollen industry see Brian Pullan, *Crisis and change in the Venetian economy in the sixteenth and seventeenth centuries* (London, Methuen, 1968), and Richard T. Rapp, 'The unmaking of the Mediterranean trade hegemony: international trade rivalry and the commercial revolution', *The Journal of Economic History*, 35(Sept. 1975), 499–525. For the effects on the Ottoman woollen industry see Braude, 'International competition and domestic cloth', *passim*.

46 Rapp, 'Mediterranean trade hegemony', p. 523.

47 Dalsar, *Bursa' da İpekçilik*, p. 38.

48 Lütfi Güçer, 'Osmanlı imparatorluğu Dahilinde Hububat Ticaretinin Tâbi Olduğu Kayıtlar' (Rules regulating wheat trade within the Ottoman Empire), *İ.Ü. Iktisat Fakültesi Mecmuası*, XIII, 1–4(1951–2), 79–98.

49 Murat Çizakça 'Considerations on the cost structure of the Bursa silk industry', *Acta Historica-Oeconomica Iugoslavia*, forthcoming.

50 Turkish historians are just beginning to enter this field. See Günhan H. Danışman, 'An operational fulling-mill at Kirha-Divan in the center Anatolian plateau of Turkey', *Post-Medieval Archeology*, 2(1977), 80–6.

51 Leila Erder, 'The making of industrial Bursa', ch. 3.

52 The government took elaborate measures to assure the competitiveness of the auctions. See Mehmet Genç, 'Osmanlı Maliyesinde Malikâne Sistemi' (The system of life-term tax farms in Ottoman public finance) *Türkiye İktisat Tarihi Semineri*, ed. Osman Okyar and Ü. Nalbantoğlu (Ankara, Hacettepe Üniversitesi, 1975), pp. 231–92.

53 Of the total value of the silk brought to the *mizan* (scale), 3–4 per cent was collected by the state as *mizan resmi* (scale tax) in 1571 (document A88/103-9B among the Bursa court registers). But this tax based on the total value apparently was not the rule; much more generally taxes were based solely on the weight. We have solid evidence that already in the 1470s silk taxes were based on weight in Eastern Anatolia. The Ottomans weighed silk with *lodra* or *lidre*; thirty *lodras* equalled one *vezne*. On a *vezne* of silk the seller paid 52 *akçes* scale tax (*Mizan resmi*) in 1570 in Bursa. The purchaser paid the same amount, making the total yield to the state 104 *akçe* (Dalsar, *Bursa' da İpekçilik*, pp. 243–5; for additional information on Ottoman weight units see Hinz, *Osmanische Masse und Gewichte*, *passim*). Furthermore, this tax rate of 52 *akçes* from a *vezne* of silk most probably remained constant. On the rigidity of Ottoman tax rates

see Genç, 'Malikâne Sistemi', p. 296, and Ammon Cohen and Bernard Lewis, *Population and revenue in the towns of Palestine in the sixteenth century* (Princeton, Princeton University Press, 1978), pt. 2. Thus there was a positive relationship between the total tax yield of the tax farm and the amount of raw silk brought into it. When the supply of raw silk was continuous and large, the tax-farmer could realize a handsome profit even after paying the state its share. If this profitable situation continued, there would be stiff competition to purchase the tax farm when it was later resold in auction. Consequently, the new price determined in auction would reflect the tax farm's profitability, hence the volume of its raw silk supplies. The same argument holds for cloth production and the cloth-stamping tax farm, *damga-ı akmişe mukataası*.

54 *Damga resmi* was also collected from the quantity of cloth brought to the tax farm. See Dalsar, *Bursa' da İpeçilik*, p. 249; Nejat Göyünç, *XVI. Asırda Mardin Sancağı* (Province of Mardin in the sixteenth century) (İstanbul, İstanbul Üniversitesi, Edebiyat Fakültesi, 1969), p. 137; and Ömer L. Barkan, *Osmanlı İmparatorluğunda Zirai Ekonominin Hukuki ve Mali Esasları* (Legal and financial principles of the Ottoman agricultural economy) (İstanbul, İstanbul Universitesi, 1943), pp. 136–9.

55 The records of some of these cases have been published by Dalsar, *Bursa' da İpekcilik*, pp. 323–5, 328.

56 Quantity based taxes rule out any effect inflation might have had on total yields of the tax farm. The same argument applies to stamp tax where taxes were based on the length or weight of cloth, i.e. quantity of cloth.

57 Çizakça, 'Inflation and the Bursa silk industry', pp. 140–1.

58 Davis, 'English imports from the Middle East'; Ülker, 'The rise of İzmir'.

59 Murat Çizakça, 'A short history of the Bursa silk industry, 1500–1900', *Journal of the Economic and Social History of the Orient*, 23, pts. 1 and 2 (Summer 1980), 142–52.

11 Notes on the production of cotton and cotton cloth in sixteenth- and seventeenth-century Anatolia

1 For the work of Halil İnalcık, compare the bibliographies contained in the articles 'Bursa' and 'Harir' in the *Encyclopedia of Islam*, 2nd edn (EI^2); see particularly 'Bursa and the commerce of the Levant', *Journal of the Economic and Social History of the Orient* (*JESHO*), 3 (1960), 131–47, and 'Bursa: XV. Asır Sanayi ve Ticaret Tarihine dair Vesikalar', (Documents on the industrial and commercial history of Bursa during the fifteenth century), *Belleten*, XXIV, 93 (1960), 45–102; Fahri Dalsar, *Türk Sanayi ve Ticaret Tarihinde Bursa' da İpekçilik* (The place of the Bursa silk industry in the industrial and commercial history of Turkey) (İstanbul, İstanbul Üniversitesi, 1960); Özer Ergenç, '1600–1615 Yılları Arasında Ankara between 1600 and 1615), in Osman Okyar and Ünal Nalbantoğlu (eds.), *Türkiye İktisat Tarihi Semineri, Metinler Tartışmalar* (Seminar on Turkish economic history: Texts and Debates) (Ankara, Hacettepe Üniversitesi, 1975), pp. 145–68, and also Murat Çizakça, 'Sixteenth-seventeenth-century inflation and the Bursa silk industry: a pattern for Ottoman industrial decline?' (University of Pennsylvania, 1978), unpublished Ph.D. dissertation. On the weaving of woollen fabrics in Salonica see Halil Sahillioğlu, 'Yeniçeri Çuha Muhasebesi' (Woollen cloth accounts concerning the janissaries), *Güney-doğu Avrupa Araştırmaları Dergisi*, 2–3 (1974), 415–67.

2 Compare W. Heyd, *Histoire du commerce du Levant au moyen-âge*. (2 vols., Leipzig, Otto Harrasowitz, 1936), vol. 2. pp. 612–14. F.C. Lane, *Venice. A maritime republic* (Baltimore, Johns Hopkins University Press, 1973), pp. 378–9.

3 On the Ottoman tax registers in general see Halil İnalcık, *Suret-i defter-i sancak-ı Arvanid* (Copy of an official register for the province of Arvanid, Hicri Year 815)

(Ankara, Türk Tarih Kurumu, 1954), Ömer Lütfi Barkan, 'Essai sur les données statistiques des registres de recensement dans l'Empire Ottoman aux XVe et XVIe siècles', *Journal of the Economic and Social History of the Orient*, 1(1958), 9–36. Concerning evaluation of the registers as a source for agricultural production see Bruce McGowan, 'Food supply and taxation on the Middle Danube (1568–1579)', *Archivum Ottomanicum* 1(1969), 139–96.

4 Mainly to be found in the section *Maliyeden Müdevver* (*MM*) of the Başbakanlık Arşivi (Archives of the Prime Minister) in İstanbul (BA). For an introduction to this collection compare Mithat Sertoğlu, *Muhteva bakımından Başvekalet Arşivi* (Ankara, Ankara Üniversitesi Dil ve Tarih-Coğrafya Fakültesi, 1955).

5 Sertoğlu, *Başvekalet Arşivi*, pp. 15, ff 23.

6 See the article 'Daftar', in *EI*[2]. For the edition of selected documents see particularly the many publications of Ahmet Refik (Altınay).

7 Halil İnalcık, '15. Asır Türkiye İktisadi ve İçtimâi Tarihi Kaynakları' (Sources for the economic and social history of Turkey during the fifteenth century) *İstanbul Universitesi İktisat Fakültesi Mecmuası*, XV, 1–4(1953–4), 51–75.

8 Compare Ali Tanoğlu, Sırrı Erinç, Erol Tümertekin (eds.), *Türkiye Atlası* (Atlas of Turkey) (İstanbul, Milli Eğitim Basımevi, 1961), map no. 75.

9 On this area compare Himmet Akın, *Aydınoğulları Tarihi Hakkında bir Araştırma* (Research on the Aydınoğulları) 2 edn (Ankara, Ankara Üniversitesi Dil ve Tarih-Coğrafya Fakültesi, 1968).

10 Compare the tax registers nos. 172 (Alanya), 40 (Erzincan), and 142 (Malatya) located in the Tapu Kadastro Genel Müdürlüğü, *Kuyudu Kadime* (*TK*) in Ankara.

11 Compare for instance *TK* 114, fols. 45b, 46a.

12 BA, section *Tapu Tahrir* (*TT*) 252, fol. 15; *TT* 257, fol. 2.

13 For the values of *kantar* and *men*, Walther Hinz, *İslamische Masse und Gewichte umgerechnet ins metrische System* (Leiden, Brill, 1955), pp. 17–22, 24–7.

14 *TK* 142, fol. 1b ff.

15 *Türkiye Atlası*, map no. 75.

16 M. Soysal, *Die Siedlungs- und Landschaftsentwicklung der Çukurova, mit besonderer Berücksichtigung der Yüregir-Ebene*, Erlanger Geographische Arbeiten (Erlangen, Fränkische Geographische Gesellschaft, 1976), pp. 30–2.

17 *TK* 134, fols. 1–105b (980/1572–3).

18 *TK* 134, fol. 1b. According to the anonymous *Ziraat Sayımı Neticeleri* (Agricultural statistics), *Türkiye Cumhuriyeti Başvekalet İstatistiği Umum Müdürlüğü*, No. 371 (Ankara, T.C. Başvekalet İstatistiği Umum Müdürlüğü, 1958), the entire territory of the Turkish Republic in 1950 produced 280,070 metric tons of cotton, of which 152,756 tons or 55 per cent were produced in the provinces (*vilayet*) of İçel and Seyhan, which approximately correspond to the Çukurova.

19 For *bocassino* in Medieval Egypt see Heyd, *Histoire du commerce*, vol. 2, p. 702. For cotton production in İçel and Aydın compare S. Faroqhi, 'Sixteenth-century periodic markets in various Anatolian *sancaks*', *JESHO*, XXII, 1(1979), 32–79, and 'Rural society in Anatolia and the Balkans during the sixteenth century I', *Turcica*, IX, 1(1977), 177, 184–5.

20 BA, *MM* 78, fols. 64b ff. On the stamp or *damga* see Dalsar, *Bursa' da İpeçilik*, p. 118ff. In relation to various types of cotton cloth, an entry in the tax register of the province of İçel provides the following information: Sales were limited to specific markets, and whoever bought or sold unstamped cloth (*boğası*, *kirpas*) was punishable by a fine. On the other hand, only cloth which conformed to certain standards was to receive a stamp. However, this rule was not always enforced: certain officials preferred to collect higher stamp dues and allow sub-standard cloth to pass, an abuse the central

administration tried to correct by entering the value of the stamp tax into the tax register. Compare *TK* 128, fol. 339(992/1584); BA, *MM* 125, fol. 119 (around 960/1552–3); BA, *Şikayet Defteri*, no. 1, fol. 189 (1060/1650).

21 Xavier de Planhol, *De la plaine pamphylienne aux lacs pisidiens, nomadisme et vie paysanne*, Bibliothèque Archéologique et Historique de l'Institut Français d'Archéologie d'Istanbul, III(Istanbul, 1958), p. 123.

22 The *bac-ı keyl* was taken on market sites and proportional to the amount of grain sold: *TK* 68, fol. 11a. For an evaluation of tax-farmers' records compare Mehmed Genç, 'Osmanlı Maliyesinde Malikâne Sistemi' (The system of life-term tax farms in Ottoman public finance), in Osman Okyar and Ünal Nalbantoğlu (eds.), *Türkiye İktisat Tarihi Semineri*, pp. 231–96. See also Özer Ergenç, '1580–1596 Yılları Arasında Ankara ve Konya' (Ankara and Konya between 1580 and 1595) (Ankara University, Dil ve Tarih-Coğrafya Fakültesi, 1973), unpublished Ph.D. dissertation.

23 Such a special market appears to have existed for instance in late sixteenth-century Kayseri and Larende: *TK* 136, fol. 6b ff, *TK* 104, fol. 133b ff. Unfortunately the amount of tax is not documented.

24 Where we have a reasonable amount of information on the development of a given economic activity, recurring arrears in themselves may be an indicator of difficulties. Considerable pressure was put on tax-farmers to settle their accounts on time, sureties were required and bankrupt tax-farmers thrown in jail (for example, see Ankara Kadı Sicilleri, Etnoğrafya Müzesi, Ankara (*AKS*), vol. 3, p. 200, n. 1121). Where all this was of no avail, very likely the problems attending collection must have been considerable. But since non-economic factors such as administrative corruption may also have been responsible for arrears, the whole question needs to be studied in a larger context.

25 *TK* 51, fol. 125b.

26 According to *TK* 51, fol. 114b this little town contained about 600 taxpayers during the reign of Selim II (1566–74).

27 For weaving as a house industry in this area during the 1940s see Orhan Tuna, 'Senirkent Kasabasında El ve Ev Dokumacılığı ve Kasabanın İktisadi Durumuna Umumi bir Bakış' (Handweaving in the town of Senirkent: a view of the town's economic activity), *İ.U. İktisat Fakültesi Mecmuası*, XII, 3–4(1951), 134–45.

28 According to BA, *TT* 166, fol. 575, the town contained about 700 taxpayers in 937/1530–1.

29 This can be understood from the account of the seventeenth-century travelogue Evliya Çelebi, *Seyahatname* (Book of Travels) (10 vols., İstanbul, different publishers, 1896–7/1938), vol. 9, pp. 290–1. Even so, the area seems to have possessed a considerable number of markets.

30 Stamp taxes on cotton cloth in the village of Vakıf near Amasyacık in the province of Aydın amounted to 60,000 *akçes* in 1575–6. In the almost entirely rural province of İçel, stamp taxes were worth 133,333 *akçes* a year throughout the later sixteenth century: BA *Mühimme Defteri* (*MD*), no. 41, fol. 378; for İçel see n. 20.

31 BA, *MD* 6, fol. 330 (972/1564–5); *MD* 84, fols. 23, 28 (1038/1628–9).

32 Ömer Lütfi Barkan, 'XV. Asrın Bazı Büyük Şehirlerinde Eşya ve Yiyecek Fiyatlarının Tesbit ve Teftişi Hususlarını Tanzim Eden Kanunlar' (The laws establishing prices of foods and other goods in certain big cities of the fifteenth century), *Tarih Vesikaları*, I, 5(1942), 326–40; II, 7(1942), 14–40; II, 9(1942), 168–77.

33 On the role of the *muhtesib* compare the literature cited in the article 'iḥtisāb' in *EI*². For a reference to this official in Bursa see Haim Gerber, 'Guilds in seventeenth-century Anatolian Bursa', *Asian and African Studies*, XI, 1(1976), 82.

34 As shown by an investigation of this particular administrative area in *TT* 82, fol. 289ff.
35 *TK* 51, fol. 125ff.
36 *TK* 114, fol. 76. For Aleppo compare *MD* 81, fol. 80.
37 *MD* 80, fol. 471 (1023/1614–5). For the existence of a shop district (*suk*) devoted to the sale of cotton cloth in Tokat see *MD* 96, fol. 126(1089/1678–9).
38 Compare *TK* 161, fol. 22b (982/1574–5).
39 *MD* 90, fol. 111 (1056/1646–7). For similar merchants in the Thracian area of Vize see *MD* 96, fol. 127 (1089/1678–9).
40 *MD* 95, fol. 42 (1075/1664–5). This area was heavily forested and an important source of wood for İstanbul: BA, *MM* 412, fols. 24ff.
41 *MD* 78, fol. 728 (1018/1609–10).
42 Compare Robert Mantran, *Istanbul dans la seconde moitié du XVIIe siècle*, Bibliothèque Archéologique et Historique de l'Institut Français d'Archéologie d'Istanbul (Paris, Maisonneuve, 1962), p. 387.
43 *AKS*, vol. III, fol. 184; vol. IV, fols. 283, 386; vol. V, fol. 48.
44 For cotton trade in Bursa see İnalcık, 'Ticaret Tarihinde', pp. 55–6. For cotton production in rural areas around Bursa, see Halil İnalcık, 'Capital formation in the Ottoman Empire', *Journal of Economic History*, XXIX(1969), 118, and the same author's 'Impact of the Annales School on Ottoman studies and new findings', *Review*, I, 3–4(1978), 89–90, n. 81.
45 Compare for instance the inventories edited by Ö.L. Barkan, 'Edirne Askeri Kassamına Ait Tereke Defterleri (1545–1659)', (Inheritance registers of the Edirne *Askerî* class), *Belgeler*, III, 5–6(1966), *passim*.
46 Ralf Davis, English imports from the Middle East 1580–1780', *Studies in the economic history of the Middle East*, ed. M.A. Cook (London, Oxford University Press, 1970), pp. 193–206.
47 *MD* 74, fol. 247 (1004/1595–6). Compare in this context: Necmi Ülker, 'The rise of İzmir, 1688–1740' (University of Michigan, 1974), Unpublished Ph.D. dissertation.
48 *MD* 73, fol. 523 (1004/1595–6).
49 This becomes apparent if we compare production figures for the adminstrative district of Adana in 943/1536–7 (according to BA, *TT* 177, fols. 7ff.) and *TK* 114, fols. 7b ff. (980/1572–3).
50 Compare references to Englishmen and Venetians in *MD* 76, fol. 141 (1013/1604–5); *MD* 80, fol. 4 (1022/1613–14); *MD* 90, fol. 43–4, 82, 90 (1056/1646–7); *MD* 91, fols. 79, 112 (1056/1646–7).

Reference to French boats *MD* 78, fol. 393 (1018/1609–10); *MD* 80, fol. 4 (1022/1613–14); *MD* 82, fol. 69 (1027/1617–18).

For a reference to exports of raw wool from Manisa see *MD* 80, fol. 406 (1024/1615).

51 *MD* 84, fol. 27 (1038–40/1628–31).

12 The silk-reeling industry of Mount Lebanon, 1840–1914: a study of the possibilities and limitations of factory production in the periphery

1 These and other figures come from the major work on the subject, G. Ducousso, *L'industrie de la soie en Syrie et au Liban* (Beirut, Imprimerie Catholique/Paris, Librairie Maritime et Coloniale, 1913), pp. 142, 155–6, etc. Ducousso's data must be used with care, however, as they contain a number of important inconsistencies, for example, those relating to the numbers of silk factories and their basins where the figures given on p. 132 differ from those in Annexe I. See also the account I give in R. Owen, *The*

Middle East in the world economy (London, Methuen, 1981), especially pp. 154–9, 249–53, which I have amended in important respects in this present paper.

2 Page 123; D. Chevallier, *La société du Mont Liban à l'époque de la Revolution Industrielle en Europe* (Paris, Librairie Orientaliste Paul Geuthner, 1971), pp. 210–14.

3 Ducousso, *L'industrie de la soie*, pp. 130–1.

4 *Ibid*, p. 130; Chevallier, *Mont Liban*, p. 212.

5 For example, L.M.Li, *China's silk trade: traditional industry in the modern world 1842–1937* (Cambridge, Mass., Harvard University Press, 1981), pp. 29–30.

6 Chevallier, *Mont Liban*, pp. 218–19.

7 Ducousso, *L'industrie de la soie*, p. 125.

8 *Ibid.*, pp. 127, 132; V. Cuinet, *Syrie, Liban et Palestine* (Paris, E. Leroux 1896), p. 219. In the early twentieth century there were only three French-owned enterprises but one of them (Veuve-Guerin) contained four separate factories in the same village, Ducousso, *L'industrie de la soie* pp. 127, 135, 228–9.

9 Ducousso, *L'industrie de la soie*, Annexe I; P. Saba, The development and decline of the Lebanese silk industry', B. Litt., Oxford, May 1977, p. 58.

10 Ducousso, *L'industrie de la soie*, p. 142; D. Chevallier, 'Lyon et la Syrie en 1919: Les bases d'une intervention', *Revue Historique*, CCXXIV (Oct.–Dec. 1960), 286; B. Labaki, 'Sériculture et commerce extérieur; deux aspects de l'impact européen du Liban et son environment arabe en fin de période Ottomane (1840–1914)'. Doctorat de 3me cycle, Paris, École Pratique des Hautes Études, 5me Section, June 1974, p. 19.

11 Ismail Haqqi (ed.), *Lubnan: Mabahith ilmiya wa ijtimaiyya* (Beirut, Editions du l'Université Libanaise, 1970 edn), quoted in Labaki, 'Sériculture et commerce exterieur', p. 153. Population in Cuinet, *Syrie, Liban et Palestine*, p. 211.

12 Chevallier, *Mont Liban*, p. 212. Population figures in Cuinet, *Syrie, Liban et Palestine*, pp. 235, 243, 282.

13 Chevallier, *Mont Liban*, p. 212; P. Saba, 'The creation of the Lebanese economic growth in the nineteenth and early twentieth centuries', in R. Owen (ed.), *Essays on the crisis in Lebanon* (London, Ithaca Press, 1976), pp. 13–14; M. Fevret, 'La sériculture au Liban', I, *Revue de Géographie de Lyon*, XXIV, 3(1949), 256–7. For roads, see Cuinet, *Syrie, Liban et Palestine*, p. 225.

14 Li, *China's silk trade*, pp. 167–8, 203.

15 Ducousso, *L'industrie de la soie*, pp. 162–3. Not only was there a harsh system of fines, but at least one owner, the Marquis de Freige at Chemlan, had a prison under his factory in which he locked up recalcitrant workers.

16 A.I. Tannous, 'Social change in an Arab village', *American Sociological Review*, VI, 5(Oct. 1941), 656–7.

17 M.H. Chehab, *Rôle du Liban dans l'histoire de la soie* (Beirut, 1967), pp. 47–8.

18 Ducousso, *L'industrie de la soie*, pp. 159–60.

19 Chevallier, *Mont Liban*, p. 212; Ducousso, *L'industrie de la soie*, p. 151.

20 Tannous provides a good account of the establishment of some of the first factories in the Kura in the early 1880s, 'Social change', pp. 652–4.

21 Ducousso, *L'industrie de la soie*, pp. 117–18.

22 For example, Chevallier, 'Lyon et la Syrie', pp. 278–9.

23 *Ibid.*, p. 280 note; Owen, *Middle East*, pp. 162–4; Ducousso, *L'industrie de la soie* pp. 169–70.

24 Ducousso, *L'industrie de la soie*, pp. 67–70.

25 P. Hobeika, *Le soie libanaise* (Beirut, Imprimerie Catholique, 1930), p. 8.

26 Ducousso, *L'industrie de la soie*, pp. 72–3; Saba, 'Development and decline', pp. 68–9.

27 Ducousso, *L'industrie de la soie*, pp. 74–6; C.J. Huber, *The raw silk industry of Japan* (New York, publ. for the Raw Silk Association of America, 1929), pp. 9–10.

28 See for examples the recommendations put to the first Congrès Libanais de le Sériculture in *Rapports du Ier Congrès Libanais de la Sériculture* (Beirut, 1930?), pp. 158–76.
29 Calculations by Labaki, presumably on the basis of names to be found in Ducousso's list of factory owners, 'Sériculture et commerce extérieur', p. 113.
30 Ducousso, *L'industrie de la soie*, p. 173.
31 *Ibid.*, pp. 172–3.
32 *Ibid.*, pp. 127–8.
33 This is the figure for China but it accords closely with rough calculations on the basis of Ducousso's figures for Mount Lebanon: Li, *China's silk trade*, p. 176.
34 This point is well illustrated by Tannous, 'Social change', pp. 654–6.
35 Ducousso, *L'industrie de la soie*, pp. 126–7. The only major difference between French-owned and local factories was that few of the latter used steam-power to turn their reels.
36 *Ibid.*, pp. 172–3.
37 *Ibid.*, p. 173.
38 *Ibid.*, Annexe IV; Labaki, 'Sériculture et commerce exterieur', pp. 38–45.
39 Copy in *Great Britain. Parl. Papers*, 1912–13, C, p. 487.
40 Chevallier, 'Lyon et la Syrie', p. 291.
41 Ducousso, *L'industrie de la soie*, pp. 160–1; British Commercial Report for Beirut, 1910, *Parl. Papers*, 1911, XCVI, p. 810.
42 C. Issawi, in C. Issawi (ed.) *The economic history of the Middle East, 1800–1914* (Chicago, University of Chicago Press, 1966), p. 269. The British Commercial Report for Beirut for 1912 gives figures of 10,000 migrants each leaving from Beirut and Tripoli, *Parl. Papers*, 1914, XCV, p. 9. I have assumed that half the total population was over 15.
43 E. Pariset, *Histoire de la fabrique Lyonnaise* (Lyon, A. Rey Imprimeur, 1901), pp. 358–60; Ducousso, *L'industrie de la soie*, pp. 133–5.
44 Ducousso, *L'industrie de la soie*, p. 134.
45 *Ibid.*, pp. 158–9.
46 *Ibid.*, pp. 134–5.
47 This assertion is based on an international comparison of the size of factories. In the case of France, for example, the average size of its silk factories in the 1870s was only a little over forty basins, Pariset, *Histoire*, p. 350 note.
48 Figures from Ducousso's list of silk factories, *L'industrie de la soie*, Annexe I.
49 On the qualities of Lebanese silk see Fevret, 'La sériculture', p. 259.
50 Ducousso, *L'industrie de la soie*, pp. 85–90.
51 *Ibid.*, pp. 86–7, 91.
52 *Ibid.*, pp. 105–7.
53 For example, Li, *China's silk trade*, pp. 202–3.
54 Apart from *L'industrie de la soie* see, for example, A. Naccache, *Le soie. Le Liban* (Beirut, Publications du Comité Executif du 1er Congrès Libanais de la Sériculture, 1932), Hobeika, *Le soie libanaise* or E. Bechara, *Les industries en Syrie et au Liban* (Cairo, Société anonyme de presse et d'edition, 1922).
55 Huber, *Raw silk industry*, pp. 7–22.
56 Shichiro Matsui, *The history of the silk industry in the United States* (New York, Howes Publishing Co., 1930), pp. 74–5.
57 Li, *China's silk trade*, pp. 197–206.
58 Chinese factories tended to be many times larger than Lebanese ones in terms of basins but, according to Li, there were many of the same problems in introducing new technology, *Ibid.*, pp. 167–8, 203–5.

59 Fevret, 'La sériculture', II, *Revue de Géographie de Lyon*, XXIV, 4 (1949), 348–50; Saba, 'Development and decline', pp. 64–5; *Rapports du 1er Congrès Libanais de la Sériculture*, pp. 22, 144.
60 *Rapports du 1er Congrès Libanais*, pp. 102–3.
61 *Ibid.*, pp. 4, 205–6; Comité Exécutif du Premier Congrès Libanais de la Sériculture, *Annual Reports*, 1934–5, etc.
62 *Annual Reports.*
63 *Ibid.*, 1936–7, pp. 203; Fevret, 'La sériculture', II, p. 352.
64 Comité Exécutif, *Annual Reports.*

13 The silk industry of Bursa, 1880–1914

1 For Bursa silk in the early Ottoman period see Halil İnalcık, 'Capital formation in the Ottoman Empire', *Journal of Economic History* 29(1969), 97–140, and by the same author, 'Bursa and the commerce of the Levant', *Journal of the Social and Economic History of the Orient*, 3, pt. 2(1960), 131–47. Also, Fahri Dalsar, *Türk sanayi ve ticaret tarihinde Bursa' da ipekçilik* (Bursa silk industry: its place in the commercial and industrial history of Turkey) (İstanbul, Sermat Matbaası, 1960). Brief overviews in Halil İnalcık, 'Bursa', *Encyclopedia of Islam*, (2nd edn, Leiden, 1960), vol. 1, pp. 1333–6; Halil İnalcık, 'Harir', *Encyclopedia of Islam*, 2nd edn, (Leiden, 1971), vol. 3, pp. 211–18; and Besim Darkot, 'Bursa', *Islâm Ansiklopedisi* (İstanbul, 1961), vol. 2, pp. 806–10. Leila Erder, 'Factory districts in Bursa during the 1860s', Middle East Technical University, *Journal of the Faculty of Architecture*, 1, no. 1(Spring, 1975), 85–99, for a more recent account. Reinhard Stewig, *Bursa, Nordwestanatolien. Strukturwandel einer orientalischen Stadt unter dem Einfluss der Industrialisierung* (Kiel, Geographische Institut der Universität, 1970), for a study of modern Bursa. Two studies have appeared since completion of the present article. See Leila Erder, 'Bursa ipek sanayiinde teknolojik değişmeler 1835–1865' (Technological changes in the Bursa silk industry, 1835–1865), Middle East Technical University, *Studies in Development*, special issue, 1978, 111–22; and Murat Çizakça, 'A short history of the Bursa silk industry, 1500–1900', *Journal of the Economic and Social History of the Orient*, 23, pts. 1 and 2(Summer 1980), 142–52).
2 Turkey, Ticaret ve Ziraat Nezareti, *Sanayi istatistiki, 1329, 1331* (Industrial Statistics, 1329, 1331) (İstanbul, Matbaa-ı Amire 1333/1917), p. 125. A. Gündüz Ökçün, *Osmanlı sanayii: 1913, 1915 yılları sanayi istatistiki* (Ottoman industry: industrial statistics for the years 1913, 1915) (Ankara, Sevinç Matbaası, 1970), p. 161, is a modern Turkish transliteration, with some changes, of the Ottoman survey.
3 'Silk', *Encyclopedia Britannica*, 9th edn (1895), vol. 22, p. 59.
4 Turkey, Ministry of Agriculture, *Turk ziraat tarihine bir bakış* (An overview of Turkish agricultural history) (İstanbul, Devlet Basımevi, 1938), p. 188.
5 *Ibid.*; Dalsar, *Bursa'da ipekçilik* (Silk industry in Bursa), pp. 418, 240. Andreas D. Mordtmann, *Anatolien: Skizzen and Reisebriefe aus Kleinasien (1850–1859)*, ed. Franz Babinger (Hannover, Heinz Lafaire, 1925), p. 353.
6 *Le journal de la chambre de commerce de Constantinople*, 2 August 1885 and 12 March 1887, 62. Charles Morawitz, *Les finances de la Turquie* (Paris, Arthur Rousseau, 1902), p. 319.
7 *Türk ziraat tarihine bir bakış*, p. 137, and Turkey, Ministry of Justice, *Düstur* (Regulations), birinci tertib, (İstanbul, Matbaa-ı Amire, 1289/1872), vol. 2, p. 438. Also Başbakanlık Arşivi, İstanbul (hereafter BA), Meclis-i Vala, 1279/1862, p. 21304. *Journal*, 21 May 1887, p. 122.
8 *Journal*, 11 May 1885; Vital Cuinet, *La Turquie d'Asie: géographie administrative*

statistique descriptive et raisonnée de chaque province de l'Asie Mineure (4 vols., Paris, E. Leroux, 1891–4), vol. 4, p. 59.

9 *Journal*, 2 March 1887, p. 58, and 11 May 1885. Cuinet, *La Turquie*, vol. 4, pp. 59–60, and Morawitz, *Les finances*, p. 319.

10 A. Du Velay, *Essai sur l'histoire financière de la Turquie depuis le règne du Sultan Mahmoud II jusqu'à nos jours* (Paris, A. Rousseau, 1903), p. 499. Darkot, 'Bursa', pp. 808–9, states that Turkey exported one million ounces after 1900. Proceeds from the silk tithe (Table 13.4) can be used to measure changes in the value of silk production. Improvements in tithe-collection efficiency, however, account for at least some of the increase, particularly in the 1880s. After that date, standards of collection efficiency were uniform.

11 United States, Bureau of the Census, *Historical statistics of the United States; colonial times to 1957* (Washington, US Government Printing Office, 1960), pp. 548–9; William W. Lockwood, *The economic development of Japan*, expanded edn (Princeton, NJ, Princeton University Press, 1970), pp. 16, 113; Dalsar, *Bursa' da İpekçilik*, p. 446.

12 United States, Department of State, *Consular reports* 1901, 65, no. 244, p. 311 and 1902, 68, no. 256, p. 344; 'Silk', *Encyclopedia Britannica*, 13th edn (1926) new vol. 3, p. 548; *The Manchester Guardian Commercial*, special supplement, 'European textiles', 10 December 1925, 42; Dalsar, *Bursa'da İpekçilik*, p. 473.

13 US *Consular*, 1900, 62, no. 232, p. 78; *ibid.*, 1902, 68, no. 256, p. 344. In the twentieth century, Bursa surpassed France in raw-silk output.

14 *Revue commerciale du Levant, bulletin mensuel de la chambre de commerce française de Constantinople*, 31 May 1907, 846; Zentrales Staatsarchiv, Potsdam, Auswärtiges Amt (hereafter ZstA,AA), Nr 53736, Bl. 107.

15 In 1850, Persia produced one million kg of raw silk; in 1865, *c.* 280,000 kg and, in 1909, 550,000 kg. F. Lafont and H. L. Rabino, *L'industrie séricicole en Perse* (Montpellier, Coulet et fils, 1910), pp. 12–13, 44, and table on pp. 128–9.

16 Article Eight of the Decree of Muharrem, 8 December 1881; Donald C. Blaisdell, *European control in the Ottoman Empire: a study of the establishment, activities, and significance of the Ottoman public debt* (New York, Columbia University Press, 1929) is still a valuable analysis of the organization.

17 L'Administration de la Dette Publique Ottomane, *Compte rendu du conseil d'administration* for the years 1882–6 and 1893–1911 (İstanbul, 1888–1912).

18 *Hudavendigâr vilâyet salnamesi 1325* (1907) (Yearbook for the province of Hudavendigâr), pp. 261, 268; Cuinet, *La Turquie*, vol. 4, p. 60; and sources cited in nn. 16 and 17.

19 *Hudavendigâr* 1325(1907), p. 261; Cuinet, *La Turquie*, vol. 4, pp. 59–61; ZStA, AA, Nr 15073, Bl. 70–2, 86–7r, 98, 112–14, 116–17, 119–20, and Nr 52364, Bl. 70–122. Scholer's recommendations may have stemmed from the 1881 request of the sultan.

20 Kirkor Kömürcan, *Türkiye imparatorluk devri dış borçlar tarihçesi* (History of external debts in the Ottoman period) (İstanbul, Şirketi Mürettiye Basımevi, 1948), pp. 75–6; Cuinet, *La Turquie*, vol. 4, p. 61; *Hüdavendigâr* 1325(1907), pp. 262–3. *Journal*, 24 December 1887, 334.

21 *Düstur*, 1st edn, vol. 6(Ankara, Başvekâlet Matbaası, 1939), pp. 755–7 and 1206–8; *ibid.* (Ankara, 1941), vol. 7, pp. 1027–8. Also *Journal*, 4 March 1893, 103–4; Cuinet, *La Turquie*, vol. 4, pp. 45–65; Morawitz, *Les finances*, p. 321.

22 *Journal*, 30 June 1894, 301–3. This imposition of an import duty, in the era of capitulatory treaties and the Ottoman inability to unilaterally alter tariff schedules, suggests the international influence of the Debt Administration.

23 *Journal*, 30 April 1892 and 30 November 1895, 569; BA, Orman 1318(1900), Şaban no. 1. See above, note 7 for precedents.

24 *Hüdavendigâr*, 1324(1906), p. 597, *Journal*, 18 March 1899 and 17 June 1899.
25 BA, Orman 1319(1902), Zilhicce no. 1; *Journal*, 1 April 1899; 22 April 1899; 30 March 1901, p. 101 and 5 April 1902, p. 108. Vincent Caillard, 'Turkey', *Encyclopedia Britannica*, 11th edn (1911), vol. 27, 437; Du Velay, *Essai*, pp. 497–99.
26 BA, Orman 1316(1899), Zilhicce no. 2.
27 *Journal*, 30 September 1893, 463; 28 July 1894, 350; 15 August 1894, 399; 20 October 1894, 495, and 9 February 1895, 64.
28 Dalsar, *Bursa' da İpekçilik*, p. 429; Kömürcan, *Dış Borçlar* (External debts), pp. 75–6.
29 *Hüdavendigâr*, 1325(1907), pp. 261–3; *ibid.*, 1324(1906), p. 597; *Journal*, 12 August 1893, 379, and 19 May 1894, 234.
30 BA, Orman 1312(1898), Şevval no. 3; *Hüdavendigâr*, various years, enumerate the Institute staff, for example, 1324(1906), p. 269.
31 *Hüdavendigâr*, 1317(1899), p. 331, *ibid.*, 1318(1900), p. 92; *ibid.*, 1325(1907), p. 262; Du Velay, *Essai*, p. 497; *Hüdavendigâr Gazetesi*, 26 Rebiyülevvel 1312(27 September 1894), 1 and 3 Rebiyülâhir 1312(4 October 1894), 3; *Journal* and *Hüdavendigâr* sources cited in note 39 below.
32 ZStA, AA, Nr 53735, Bl. 41–2r; Nr 15073, Bl. 116–17; Nr 53738, Bl. 16; Paul Fesch, *Constantinople aux derniers jours d'Abdul-Hamid* (Paris, M. Rivière, 1907), pp. 571–2. Cuinet, *La Turquie*, vol. 4, pp. 326–7, indicates that, exclusive of egg raising in individual homes, there were 31 nurseries for the purpose in the district (*sancak*) of Bursa.
33 Lucy M.J. Garnet, *The women of Turkey and their folk-lore* (London, D. Nutt, 1893), pp. 58–9, 214–15, also pp. 44, 213, 346; ZStA, AA, Nr 8729, Bl. 119. Mordtmann, *Anatolien*, pp. 289–90, however, states that men, women, and children were active in silk-raising in some Greek villages.
34 Quoted in Dalsar, *Bursa' da İpekçilik*, pp. 406–7.
35 For the role of women in Japanese silk-raising see Lockwood, *Japan*, pp. 45, 27–30.
36 *Revue Commercial du Levant*, 31 May 1908, p. 834; US *Consular*, 1900, 62, no. 232, p. 77; Zentrales Staatsarchiv, His. Abt. II, Merseburg, Rep. 120 C Tit. VI, II, Nr 74, Bd. 1, Bl. 263–4. *Journal*, 9 November 1895, 536, and 5 November 1898, 350, list the names of those receiving awards; Mesdames Varik Papazyan and Rèpéga were among the winners in the October 1898 competition. Members of the minority populations won 59 per cent of the awards granted in two competitions.

The practice of double-cropping so successfully introduced in Japan was not implemented in Turkey, another suggestion that silk-raising at Bursa was a secondary activity for many cultivators.
37 Du Velay, *Essai*, pp. 499–500.
38 *Düstur*, 1st edn, vol. 6, pp. 1433–5, gives the text of the law, dated 8 Rebiyülâhir 1311 (19 October 1893). For the text of four amendments, in 1902 and 1906, see *Düstur*, 1st edn, vol. 7, pp. 854–7, and vol. 8 (Ankara, 1943), pp. 556–9, 559–62. Also, Morawitz, *Les finances*, p. 320, and Cuinet, *La Turquie*, vol. 4, p. 63.
39 Bursa-area residents' share of the total number of graduates and certificate holders derived from *Hüdavendigâr*, 1325(1907), pp. 263–5. The balance of the students came from other areas of Anatolia (15 per cent), European Turkey (10 per cent), and the Arab provinces (2 per cent). Composition of Bursa-area residents derived from lists of graduates, 1893–8, and certificate recipients in 1894 and 1895. This sample contains 195 individuals or 22 per cent of all Bursa residents receiving such recognition between 1888 and 1905.

The sampling for the entire Empire, drawn from the same years as above and also 1891 and 1892, contains 363 individuals or 29 per cent of the 1,234 persons who successfully completed the various programs between 1888 and 1905.

Sources: *Journal*, 17 November 1894, 544; 9 November 1895, 536; 21 November 1896, 470; 20 November 1897, 374; 5 November 1898, 350. In BA, Yıldız 31 76/151 76 139, the government lamented the under-representation of its Muslim population at the Institute, citing statistics with proportions similar to those given above.

40 *Hüdavendigâr*, for example, 1303(1885), p. 68, and 1318(1900), pp. 338–40. Also see Cuinet, *La Turquie*, vol. 4, p. 113, and BA, Yıldız 31 76/151 76 139.

41 See sources cited in note 39, above.

42 Du Velay, *Essai*, p. 499, notes exports of 18,000 ounces of eggs from Bursa.

43 ZStA, AA, Nr 6692, Bl. 87; *Sanayi 1917* (Industry 1917), pp. 23–124, and Ökçün, *Sanayi*, p. 160.

44 *Sanayi 1917*, pp. 103, 123–4 and Ökçün, *Sanayi* (Industry), pp. 134, 160. An excellent account of the silk industry in the Lebanon is Dominique Chevallier, 'Lyon et la Syrie en 1919', *Revue Historique*, 224(October-December 1960), 275–320, esp. 275–305.

45 See sources cited in Table 13.3; Cuinet, *La Turquie*, vol. 4, p. 98, for 1892–3 figures. The relatively minor importance of silk weaving at Bursa suggested its exclusion from the present study.

46 *Sanayi 1917*, pp. 5–7, 13, and Ökçün, *Sanayi*, pp. 4–6, 14.

47 Erder, 'Bursa', pp. 85–99; Enver Ziya Karal, *Osmanlı tarihi, VI: ıslahat fermanı devri, 1856–1861* (Ottoman history, VI: the period of reform, 1856–1861) (Ankara, Türk Tarih Kurumu Basımevi, 1954), p. 243, and 'Broussa', *Encyclopedia Britannica*, 9th edn (1878), vol. 4, p. 382; sources cited in note 48; and, Regis Delbeuf, *Une excursion à Brousse et à Nicée* (İstanbul, 1906), pp. 145–52.

48 For example, Mordtmann (*Anatolien*) is an excellent observer of conditions in Anatolia during the 1840s and 1850s. After discussing the introduction of steam-powered reeling mills, he presents a table giving the number of *spinnerei* in the various areas. He notes that, in 1851, Bursa had 23 *spinnerie* with 1,572 reels and, in 1856, 45 *spinnerei* with 1,674 reels. It is unlikely that all the new *spinnerei* were steam powered. The 22 *spinnerei* founded between 1851 and 1856 collectively contained 102 reels.
Until additional research on this subject is undertaken, the precise number of steam mills, of whatever horsepower, remains uncertain. The statement of Karal, *Tarih* (History), VI, p. 243, that Bursa contained 14 steam- or water-powered silk factories in 1853 may be compared with Mordtmann's figures.

49 *Revue*, 31 May 1907, 846, Delbeuf, *Excursion*, pp. 133–9, for different figures. At this time, only one steam reeling mill was operating in Persia and it apparently failed; Lafont and Rabino, *L'industrie*, pp. 47–8.

50 See note 46; also *Sanayi 1917*, Table VI, p. 20 and Ökçün, *Sanayi*; Table VI following p. 18. The survey surely excluded numbers of small steam-powered reeling mills not meeting the stated criteria.

51 Derived from *Sanayi 1917*, pp. 119–20 and Ökçün, *Sanayi*, pp. 154–6, which also note that five mills were owned by 'the wife of . . .' and Madame Gamet held another in partnership with a male. BA, İrade 1303(1886), Dahiliye 77484.

52 Delbeuf, *Excursion*, pp. 133–9.

53 İnalcık, 'Capital Formation'.

54 For example, Werner Sombart, *Der moderne kapitalismus*, first volume, second half-volume (Munich and Leipzig, Dunken und Humblot, 1924), p. 883; Warren Dean, *The industrialization of Sao Paolo, 1888–1945* (Austin, University of Texas Press, 1969), pp. 48–57; and Thomas R. De Gregori, *Technology and the economic development of the tropical African frontier* (Cleveland, Case Western Reserve University Press, 1969), esp. pp. 14–32, for points of comparison and contrast with the Bursa case.

55 BA, İmtiyaz Defteri, no. 2, p. 140, 1308(1890); Bab-ı Âli Evrak Odası (hereafter BEO) 57834, 1313(1896); BEO 61201, 1314(1896); İmtiyaz Defteri, no. 1, pp. 96–7,

1319(1901); Nafia 1316(1898), Rebiyülevvel no. 3; İrade 1307(1889), Dahiliye 89995; and, Nafia 1318(1901), şevval no. 5. Also see *İştirak*, 20 Şubat 1325(5 March 1910) and Delbeuf, *Excursion*, pp. 133–9.

56 For example, the sources cited in Darkot, 'Bursa', p. 808; also Erder, 'Bursa', p. 80.

57 Mordtmann, *Anatolien*, p. 296.

58 *Sanayi 1917*, Table VIII, p. 23, and Ökçün, *Sanayi*, Table VIII, p. 21. See Lockwood, *Japan*, p. 30, for a similar situation in the Japanese silk industry.

59 *İştirak*, 20 Şubat 1325(5 March 1910) and 27 Mart 1326(9 April 1910); Ökçün, *Sanayi*, p. 157, notes a fourteen-hour work day. A 1905 Berne international agreement, to which states voluntarily could adhere, forbade night work for women.

60 *Sabah*, 18 August 1910, 3.

61 'Turkey', *Encyclopedia Britannica*, 13th edn (1926), vol. 3, p. 853. Great Britain, *Report on the trade and economic conditions of Turkey, dated January, 1921*, (London, HM Stationery Office, 1921), pp. 14–15, states that cocoon production at Bursa fell below 500,000 kg in 1918.

62 *Guardian Commercial* article, 41; Lockwood, *Japan*, p. 45; United States, *Historical Statistics*, pp. 548–9; Dalsar, *Bursa' da İpekçilik*, p. 473.

63 Compare Tables 13.1 and 13.5 above. Dalsar, *Bursa'da İpekçilik*, p. 476, notes the inability of republican Turkey to break into the Japanese-dominated market. The introduction of artificial silk made silk products available at lower cost and, until at least the 1920s, stimulated world consumption of natural raw silk. Here, United States demand again played the crucial role.

14 A provisional report concerning the impact of European capital on Ottoman port workers, 1880–1909

1 Benjamin Braude, 'International competition and domestic cloth in the Ottoman Empire, 1500–1650, a study in underdevelopment', *Review*, II, 3(1979), 437–54.

2 H. Schurtz, 'Türkische basare und zünfte', *Zeitschrift für Socialwissenschaft* 6(Berlin, 1903), 683–706.

3 Osman Nuri (Ergin), *Mecelle-i umur-u belediyye* (Regulations concerning municipalities), (5 vols., İstanbul, 1914–22), vol. 3, pp. 595–610; Edgar Pech, *Manuel des sociétés anonymes fonctionnant en Turquie* (5th edn, Constantinople, Gerard Frérés, 1911), pp. 179–82; Jacques Thobie, *Intérêts et impérialisme français dans l'empire ottoman (1895–1914)* (Paris, Imprimerie nationale, 1977), pp. 162–4, 563.

4 Based on statistical reports in Zentrales Staatsarchiv, Potsdam, Auswärtiges Amt (hereafter ZStA, AA), Nr 53739, Bl.79.

5 W.S. Monroe, *Turkey and the Turks: an account of the lands, the peoples, and the institutions of the Ottoman Empire* (Boston, L.C. Page, 1907), p. 216.

6 Great Britain, Department of Overseas Trade, *General report on the trade and economic conditions of Turkey, dated Jan. 1921*, by C.H. Courthope-Munroe (London, HM Stationery Office, 1921), p. 32.

7 W.J. Childs, *Across Asia Minor on foot* (London, W. Blackwood, 1917), p. 406.

8 *Stamboul*, 26 June 1908.

9 See note 6 above.

10 Lucy M.J. Garnett, *Home life in Turkey* (New York, Macmillan, 1909), pp. 19–20.

11 *Ibid.*

12 H.G. Dwight, 'A Turkish village', *Scribner's Magazine*, 45(June 1909) 709–10.

13 Thobie, *Intérêts et impérialisme*, p. 385.

14 United States, Department of State, Bureau of Foreign Commerce, *Commercial relations of the United States with foreign countries*, 1907, vol. 2, Ozmun at İstanbul, p. 528.

15 Başbakanlık Arşivi, İstanbul (hereafter BA), Babıâli Evrak Odası (hereafter BEO), No. 258370 (21 VIII 1326). For another apparent reference to the firing see BEO, No. 231817 (21 V 1325).
16 BA, BEO, No. 258370 (19 X 1326).
17 *Ibid.*
18 BA, BEO, No. 258370 for the overall correspondence; *Stamboul*, 15 August 1908 for the arbitration.
19 Stefan Velikov, 'Sur le mouvement ouvrier et socialiste en Turquie après la révolution Jeune-Turque de 1908', *Études Balkaniques*, 1(1964), 38, quoting newspapers of 8 and 20 August 1908; compare with *Stamboul* account in note 18 above.
20 *İkdam*, 21 August 1908, 3, and *Stamboul*, 21 August 1908.
21 *Stamboul*, 21 August 1908.
22 BA, BEO, No. 258370 (22 August 1908).
23 *İkdam*, 10 September 1908, 3.
24 BA, BEO, No. 258370 (19 September 1908).
25 BA, BEO, No. 258370 (19 X 1326).
26 ZStA, AA, Nr 6634, Bl. 40–5.
27 ZStA, AA (Merseburg), Rep. 120 C 270, 121, clipping from *Das Handelsministerium*, Wien, 19 November 1908.
28 ZStA, AA, Nr 6635, Bl. 119, 120, 123–123r. My *Social Disintegration* devotes a separate chapter to the boycott against Austria–Hungary.
29 Maxime Rodinson, 'Islam Resurgent?', *Gazelle Review*, 6(1979), 1–17, esp. 4–5.
30 These points and much of the remaining discussion are studied further in the port worker and boycott chapters of my *Social disintegration.*
31 BA, BEO, No. 260923 (15 December 1324).
32 BA, BEO, No. 259012 (21 XI 1326); BEO 261857 (23 February 1324); BEO 255630 (15 March 1324).
33 While the *hamal*s and boatmen were struggling with the state and the company, they were simultaneously engaged in disputes with their *kahya*s: for example, see *İkdam* 13 August 1908, 4, and 21 August 1908, 2, as well as BA, BEO, No. 256143 (23 IX 1326). The two groups retained their respective identities and influence long after the dispute recorded here. For example, the post-World War I source cited in note 6 states the two guilds were the most powerful in İstanbul.

15 The Venetian presence in the Ottoman Empire, 1600–30

1 Frederic C. Lane, *Venice, a maritime republic* (Baltimore, Johns Hopkins University Press, 1973), pp. 400–1. However, during the last quarter of the sixteenth century, the Venetian merchant marine had already dwindled to a fraction of its former strength: Ruggiero Romano, 'La marine marchande vénitienne au XVIe siècle', in Michel Mollat *et al.* (eds.), *Actes du quatrième colloque international d'histoire maritime en Europe, du moyen age au XVIIIe siècle* (Paris, Sevpen, 1962), p. 46.
2 Vitorino Magalhaes Godhino, 'Le repli vénitien et égyptien et la route du cap 1496–1553', in *Éventail d'histoire vivante . . . Hommage a Lucien Febvre* (Paris, 1953), p. 284.
3 Niels Steensgaard, 'Consuls and nations in the Levant from 1570 to 1650', *The Scandinavian Economic History Review*, XV, 1–2(1967), 13–53.
4 Alfred C. Wood, *A history of the Levant Company* (London, Oxford University Press, 1935); Ralph Davis, *Aleppo and Devonshire Square* (London, Macmillan, 1967).
5 Halil İnalcık, 'Capital formation in the Ottoman Empire', *The Journal of Economic History*, 29(1969), 97–140; Halil Sahillioğlu, 'Bursa Kadı Sicillerinde İç ve Dış Ödemeler Aracı Olarak Kitâbu'l kadı ve Süfteceler' (Bills of exchange as a means of

payment in internal trade according to the registers of the *kadı* of Bursa), in Osman Okyar, Ünal Nalbantoğlu (eds.), *Türkiye İktisat Tarihi Semineri: Metinler, Tartışmalar* (Seminar on the economic history of Turkey: Texts, Debates) (Ankara, Hacettepe Üniversitesi, 1975), pp. 103–44.

6 Lütfi Güçer, 'Osmanlı İmparatorluğu Dahilinde Hububat Ticaretinin Tâbi Olduğu Kayıtlar' (The rules to which the grain trade in the Ottoman Empire was expected to conform) *İstanbul Üniversitesi İktisat Fakültesi Mecmuası*, XIII, 1–4(1951–2), 93–5.

7 Robert Paris, *Histoire du commerce de Marseille*, vol. V: *1660 to 1789. Le Levant* (Paris, Plon, 1957), pp. 443–4.

8 Alberto Tenenti, *Piracy and the decline of Venice 1580–1615* (Berkeley, University of California Press, 1967), p. 20.

9 Nicolaas Biegman, *The Turco-Ragusan relationship* (The Hague, Mouton, 1967).

10 For the tendency to stress the continuing strength of the Ottoman Empire down to the second half of the eighteenth and the beginning of the nineteenth century see: A. Raymond, 'La conquête Ottomane et le développement des grandes villes arabes', *Revue de l'Occident Musulman et la Méditerranée*, 1(1979), 117–34; Huri İslamoğlu and Çağlar Keyder, 'Agenda for Ottoman History', *Review*, I, 1(1977), 53; Fernand Braudel, *Civilization matérielle, économie et capitalisme XVe–XVIIIe siècle*, vol. 3: *Le temps du monde* (3 vols., Paris, Colin, 1979), pp. 406–16.

11 On the Ottoman state ideology compare particularly İnalcık, 'Capital formation', pp. 97–103.

12 Majid Khadduri, *War and peace in the law of Islam* (Baltimore, Johns Hopkins Press, 1955), p. 168.

13 On the importance of Holy War in Ottoman 'public opinion', see Halil İnalcık, *The Ottoman Empire, the classical age 1300–1600* (London, Weidenfeld and Nicholson, 1973), pp. 187–8.

14 Tuncer Baykara, *İzmir Şehri ve Tarihi* (The city of İzmir and its history) (Bornova-İzmir, Ege Üniversitesi Arkeoloji Enstitüsü, 1974), pp. 30, 53. Katip Çelebi, referring to the first half of the seventeenth century, mentions İzmir as centre of the *sancaks* of Aydın and Saruhan (*Cihannuma* (İstanbul, İbrahim Müteferrika, 1732), p. 669). However, this information was probably valid only for a short time, if at all.

15 Paris, *Marseille*, pp. 443–4.

16 Khadduri, *War and peace*, pp. 225–6.

17 On Ottoman attitudes toward foreign trade see Halil İnalcık, 'The Ottoman economic mind and aspects of the Ottoman economy', in M.A. Cook (ed.), *Studies in the economic history of the Middle East* (London, Oxford University Press, 1970), pp. 207–18. For an overview of export prohibitions as enforced in different parts of the Ottoman Empire compare Suraiya Faroqhi, 'Die osmanische Handelspolitik des frühen 17. Jahrhunderts zwischen Dubrovnik und Venedig', *Wiener Beiträge zur Geschichte der Neuzeit*, 10(1938), 207–22.

18 Thus the exportation of raw materials necessary to local artisans was often prohibited, especially if the industry in question produced important tax revenues. However, I have not as yet encountered a sixteenth–seventeenth-century rescript forbidding the importation of wares competing with local manufactures.

19 İnalcık, 'Ottoman economic mind', p. 215.

20 Paul Bois, *Paysans de l'Ouest*, abridged version (Paris, Flammarion, 1978), pp. 177 ff, 196.

21 Fernand Braudel, *La Méditerranée et le monde Méditerranéen a l'époque de Philippe II* (2 vols., Paris, Colin, 1966), vol. 2, p. 416.

22 Tenenti, *Piracy*, *passim*.
23 Domenico Sella, 'The rise and fall of the Venetian woollen industry', in Brian Pullan (ed.), *Crisis and change in the Venetian economy in the sixteenth and seventeenth centuries* (London, Methuen, 1968), pp. 106–26.
24 S.J. Woolf, 'Venice and the Terraferma: problems of the change from commercial to landed activities', in Pullan, *Crisis and change*, pp. 175–203.
25 Lane, *Venice*, p. 397.
26 Gunther Rothenberg, 'Venice and the Uskoks of Senj: 1537–1618', *The Journal of Modern History*, XXXIII, 2(1961), 148–56. For the Ottoman point of view compare İstanbul Başbakanlık Arşivi, *Mühimme defterleri* (*MD*) 5, p. 445 (973/1565–6).
27 Tayyip Gökbilgin, 'Venedik Devlet Arşivindeki Vesika Külliyatından Kanuni Süleyman Devri Belgeleri', (Documents from the age of Kanuni Süleyman among the collections of the Venetian State Archives), *Belgeler*, I, 2(1964), 119–220; *idem*, 'Venedik Devlet Arşivindeki Türkçe Belgeler Kolleksiyonu ve Bizimle İlgili Diğer Belgeleri' (The collection of Turkish documents and other documents concerning us, located in the Venetian State Archives) *Belgeler*, V–VIII, 9–12(1968–71), 1–51; *idem*, 'Kanuni Sultan Süleyman devrine ait Bosna ve Hersek ile ilgili Venedik Arşivindeki Türkçe Belgeler' (Documents in the Venetian archives relating to Bosnia and Herzegovina during the reign of Sultan Süleyman the Lawgiver), *Tarih Dergisi*, 32(1979), 319–330; Şerafettin Turan, 'Venedik'te Türk Ticaret Merkezi', (The Turkish trade centre in Venice), *Belleten*, XXXII, 126(1968), 247–83.
28 For examples from these registers, compare Halil İnalcık, 'Osmanlı İdari, Sosyal ve Ekonomik Tarihiyle İlgili Belgeler: Bursa Kadı Sicillerinden Seçmeler' (Documents relating to the administrative, social, and economic history of the Ottoman Empire: selection from the *kadı* registers of Bursa), *Belgeler*, X, 14(1980–1), 1–91.
29 For a guide to the Ottoman archives in İstanbul, see Atilla Çetin, *Başbakanlık Arşivi Kılavuzu* (A guide to the Archives of the Prime Ministry (İstanbul, Enderun Kitapevi, 1979).
30 Çetin, *Kılavuz*, pp. 68–72. However, the two registers upon which this article is largely based are to be found the section *Maliyeden Müdevver* (*MM*) 6004 and 17901. They cover the period AH 1028–37/1618–28.
31 On the capitulations in general, compare the article 'İmtiyazat' by Halil İnalcık in the 2nd edition of the *Encyclopedia of Islam*. Mahmut H. Şakiroğlu has published the text of a capitulation from the reign of Kanunî Süleyman: '1521 tarihli Osmanlı-Venedik andlaşmasının asli metni' (The original text of the 1521 treaty between the Ottomans and the Venetians) *Tarih Enstitüsü Dergisi*, 12(1981–2), 387–404. For the text of the capitulations granted by Mehmet III, which was retained virtually unchanged by his successors, see M. Belin, 'Relations diplomatiques de la République de Venise avec la Turquie', *Journal Asiatique*, VIIe Série, 8(1876), 381–424.
32 Steensgaard, 'Consuls and nations', p. 21.
33 For an example of a register of miscellaneous rescripts see *MM* 9829.
34 Apart from *MM* 6004 and 17901, individual rescripts from the *mühimme* registers have been taken into consideration.
35 Halil İnalcık, 'An outline of Ottoman–Venetian relations', in *Venezia centro di mediazione tra Oriente e Occidente (secoli XV–XVI), aspetti e problemi* (Florence, Leo Olschki, 1977), pp. 83–90.
36 Lane, *Venice*, pp. 408ff.
37 Lane, *Venice*, pp. 393.
38 Brian Pullan, *Rich and poor in Renaissance Venice* (Oxford, Basil Blackwell, 1971), *passim*.

39 For an example see *MM* 6004, p. 2 (1028/1618–19).
40 *MM* 6004, p. 14 (1030/1620–1).
41 *MM* 6004, p. 135 (1037/1627–8).
42 *MM* 6004, p. 5 (no date).
43 Pierre Chaunu, *La civilization de l'Europe classique* (Paris, Arthaud, 1966), p. 100; Geoffrey Parker, *The army of Flanders and the Spanish Road 1567–1659* (Cambridge, Cambridge University Press, 1981), pp. 80–101.
44 *MM* 6004, p. 113 (1034/1624–5).
45 Lane, *Venice*, p. 409.
46 Compare Chaunu, *L'Europe classique*, p. 70.
47 *MM* 6004, p. 125 (1035/1625–6).
48 Chaunu, *L'Europe classique*, p. 71. For a different evaluation of the choices open to the Spanish governments of the seventeenth century, compare however A. Dominguez Ortiz, 'The revolt of Catalonia against Philip IV', *Past and Present*, 29(1964), 105–10.
49 On his account compare Andrew C. Hess, 'The battle of Lepanto and its place in Mediterranean history', *Past and Present*, 57(1972), 53–73.
50 According to Chaunu, *L'Europe classique*, p. 71. See also Parker, *Spanish Road*, pp. 231–68.
51 Over the succession in Mantua, see J.H. Elliot, *Imperial Spain 1469–1716*, (Harmondsworth, Penguin Books, 1970), pp. 334–5.
52 Chaunu, *L'Europe classique*, p. 70. The expression comes from William McNeill, *Venice the hinge of Europe (1081–1797)* (Chicago, The University of Chicago Press, 1974).
53 Nicolaas Biegman, 'Ragusan spying for the Ottoman Empire', *Belleten*, XVII, 106(1963), 237–55.
54 *MM* 6004, p. 53 (1033/1623–4).
55 *MM* 6004, p. 53 (1033/1623–4).
56 *MM* 6004, p. 143 (1030/1620–1).
57 *MM* 6004, p. 41 (1032/1622–3).
58 *MM* 6004, p. 108 (1034/1624–5).
59 Jorjo Tadic, 'Le commerce en Dalmatie et à Raguse et la décadence économique de Venise au XVIIIème siècle', in *Aspetti e cause della decadenza economica veneziana nel secolo XVII* (Venice, 1961), p. 237–74. See also Faroqhi, 'Venedig und Dubrovnik'.
60 Lane, *Venice*, pp. 387–8, and Tenenti, *Piracy*, pp. 16–31, 56–88.
61 Richard Tilden Rapp, *Industry and economic decline in seventeenth-century Venice* (Cambridge, Mass., Harvard University Press, 1976), p. 154.
62 *MM* 6004, p. 80 (1032/1622–3).
63 *MM* 6004, p. 34 (1032/1622–3), p. 35 (1032/1622–3), p. 52 (1032/1622–3), p. 104 (1035/1625–6), p. 105 (1033/1623–4), p. 109 (1034/1624–5), p. 126 (1036/1626–7); *MM* 17901, p. 5 (1028/1618–19).
64 Khadduri, *War and Peace*, p. 220.
65 *MM* 17901, p. 12 (1028/1618–19).
66 *MM* 6004, pp. 109–10 (1034/1624–5).
67 *MM* 6004, p. 26 (1031/1621–2).
68 *MM* 6004, pp. 109–10 (1034/1624–5), p. 111 (1034/1624–5).
69 *MM* 6004, p. 134 (1037/1627–8).
70 Lane, *Venice*, p. 408.
71 *MM* 6004, p. 33 (1032/1622–3).
72 *MM* 17901, p. 15 (1028/1618–19).
73 *MM* 6004, p. 103 (1033/1623–4).

74 *MM* 17901, pp. 6, 15, 17 (all 1028/1618–19).
75 *MM* 6004, p. 20 (1031/1621–2).
76 *MM* 6004, p. 101 (1033/1623–4).
77 *MM* 6004, p. 97 (no date, about 1033/1623–4).
78 Gabriel Efendi Noradounghian, *Recueil des actes internationaux de l'Empire Ottoman* (Paris, 1897–1902), vol. 1, p. 95.
79 For a copy of the *ahidname* of Galata as confirmed in the early seventeenth century, see *MM* 6004, p. 96.
80 *Ad hoc* rescripts were apparently preferred even when a given problem related to commerce was encountered in many ports of the Ottoman Empire. Thus both *MM* 6004 and *MM* 17901 contain a sizeable number of rescripts in which the tax-farmers of ports like İzmir or İskenderun were forbidden to borrow money from Venetian merchants. Apparently many tax farmers had got into the habit of demanding loans from merchants, promising to deduct the money from future customs payments. However, the tax farmers frequently evaded payment under various pretexts, so that the Venetians seem to have demanded, and obtained, the prohibition of this practice. However, at least in the early seventeenth century, this matter was never included in the *ahidname*. Compare *MM* 6004, p. 29 (1032/1022–3), and *MM* 17901, p. 13 (1028/1618–19).
81 Compare *MD* 27, p. 56, no. 142 (983/1575–6).
82 *MM* 6004, p. 101 (1033/1623–4).
83 Halil İnalcık, 'Kanuni Süleyman the Lawgiver and Ottoman law', *Archivum Ottomanicum*, 1(1969), 105–38 particularly 108–10.
84 Khaddouri, *War and peace*, p. 225.
85 On the dues to be paid by foreign merchants, see Steensgaard, 'Consuls and nations', pp. 39–41; *MM* 6004 p. 100 (1033/1623–4).
86 *MD* 6004, p. 21 (1031/1621–2).
87 Belin, 'Relations diplomatiques', p. 417.
88 *MM* 17901, p. 12 (1028/1618–19).
89 Belin, 'Relations diplomatiques', p. 417.
90 *MM* 6004, p. 117 (1034/1624–5).
91 Belin, 'Relations diplomatiques', p. 417.
92 Steensgaard, 'Consuls and nations', p. 14.
93 On the Venetian salt trade compare Jean Claude Hocquet, *Le sel et la fortune de Venise* (2 vols., Villeneuve d'Asq., Publications de l'Université de Lille 3, 1978–9).
94 *MM* 6004, p. 52 (no date).
95 *MM* 6004, p. 115 (1034/1624–5).
96 *MM* 6004, p. 2 (1028/1618–19).
97 *MM* 6004, p. 4 (1028/1618–19); p. 116 (1034/1624–5); p. 38 (1032/1622–3).
98 *MD* 21, p. 123 no. 300 (980/1572–3).
99 *MM* 6004, p. 21 (1031/1621–2).
100 *MD* 7, p. 403 no. 1696 (976/1568–9).
101 *MM* 6004, p. 103 (1033/1623–4), p. 26 (1031/1621–2). As a pretext for his exactions, the official in question had instituted a separate checkpoint of his own.
102 *MM* 17903, p. 5 (1028/1618–19).
103 *MM* 6004, p. 32 (1032/1622–3).
104 Özer Ergenç, '1600–1615 Yılları Arasında Ankara İktisadi Tarihine Ait Araştırmalar' (Research concerning the economic history of Ankara, 1600–1615), in O. Okyar, Ü. Nalbantoğlu (eds.), *Türkiye İktisat Tarihi Semineri*, pp. 145–68.
105 *MM* 7527, p. 69 (1055/1645–6).
106 *MM* 6004, p. 17 (1031/1621–2).

107 *MD* 5, p. 23 no. 60 (972/1564–5).
108 Suraiya Faroqhi, 'The early history of the Balkan fairs', *Südost-Forschungen*, XXXVII (1978), 50–68.
109 *MD* 23, p. 47 no. 96 (981/1573–4).
110 Başbakanlık Arşivi, section Ali Emirî 148.
111 *MD* 73, p. 113, no. 256 (1003/1594–5); *MM* 6004, p. 17 (1031/1621–2).
112 *MM* 6004, p. 8 (1029/1619–20); p. 42 (1032/1622–3).
113 For a general discussion of this matter, see Halil İnalcık, 'The question of the closing of the Black Sea under the Ottomans', *Archeion Pontou*, 35(1979), 74–110.
114 For example *MM* 6004, p. 24 (1031/1621–2).
115 *MM* 6004, p. 86 (1032/1622–3).
116 *MM* 6004, p. 1 (1028/1618–19).
117 *MM* 6004, p. 37 (1032/1622–3), p. 103 (1033/1623–4).
118 Steensgaard, 'Consuls and nations', p. 14.
119 Tapu ve Kadastro Genel Müdürlüğü (Office of the Cadastre), *Kuyudu kadime*, no. 167, fol. 3b ff; Jean Baptiste Tavernier, *Les six voyages . . . en Turquie en Perse et aux Indes* (2 vols., Paris, G. Clouzier, 1681–2), vol. 1, p. 85.
120 Iranian silk, which in the second half of the seventeenth century constituted one of the major items traded in İzmir, is not yet mentioned in *MM* 6004; compare p. 34 (1032/1622–3).
121 *MM* 6004, p. 54 (1033/1623–4).
122 *MM* 6004, p. 47 (1033/1623–4).
123 *MM* 6004, p. 34 (1032/1622–3), p. 47 (1033/1623–4). In fact, the French capitulations of 1604 contained a clause to that effect: Novadounghian, *Recueil*, vol. I, p. 95. According to this text, Selim II and Mehmet III had granted similar permissions.
124 Steengard, 'Consuls and nations', p. 26. See also *MM* 6004, p. 6 (no date).
125 Compare İnalcık, 'Kanuni Sultan Süleyman', pp. 105–6.
126 *MM* 17901, p. 6 (no date).
127 Eliyahu Ashtor, 'The Karimi merchants', *Journal of the Royal Asiatic Society* (1956), 54.
128 *MM* 17901, p. 7 (1028/1618–19). Most of the rescripts in *MM* 17901 were renewed at the same time, and therefore bear the same date.
129 *MD* 27, p. 20, no. 60 (983/1575–6).
130 *MM* 17901, p. 7 (1028/1618–19).
131 Mübahat Kütükoğlu, '1009 (1600) tarihli Narh Defterine göre İstanbul'da çeşitli eşya ve hizmet fiatları' (Prices of various goods and services in İstanbul, according to an official price register dated 1600); *Tarih Enstitüsü Dergisi*, 9(1978), 20.
132 İnalcık, 'Capital formation', p. 98.
133 *MM* 17901, p. 12 (1028/1618–19).
134 *MM* 17901, p. 13 (1028/1618–19).
135 *MM* 6004, p. 16 (1030/1620–1).
136 See also Steensgaard, 'Consuls and nations', p. 39.
137 *MM* 17901, p. 11 (1028/1618–19).
138 Halil Sahillioğlu, 'Osmanlı Para Tarihinde Dünya Para ve Maden Hareketlerinin Yeri (1300–1750)', (The place of world-wide movements of money and precious metals in Ottoman monetary history), *Türkiye İktisat Tarihi Üzerine Araştırmalar* (special issue), *Gelişme Dergisi* (Middle East Technical University) (1978), p. 11.
139 *MM* 17901, p. 9 (1028/1618–19).
140 *MM* 17901, p. 10 (1028/1618–19).
141 *MM* 17901, p. 10 (1028/1618–19).

142 *MM* 17901, p. 10 (1028/1618–19), p. 8 (1028/1618–19).
143 Belin, 'Relations diplomatiques', pp. 416, 421
144 *MM* 17901, p. 14 (1028/1618–19).
145 *MM* 6004, p. 138–9 (1038/1628–9).
146 *MM* 6004, p. 9 (1028/1618–19), p. 17 (same date).
147 *MM* 17901, p. 9; *MD* 62, p. 133, no. 298 (995–6/1586–8).
148 *MM* 17901, p. 9.
149 *Ibid.*
150 Long-term tenants could protect themselves by concluding a contract of so-called 'double rent': a lump sum was paid at the time the contract was first concluded, while the monthly or yearly rent might be so small as to be almost symbolic. In this case, the lease could even be passed on to the heirs. Compare Ömer Lütfi Barkan, 'Edirne Askeri Kassamına Ait Tereke Defterleri (1545–1659)' (Inheritance registers of the Edirne *Askeri* class, 1545–1659), *Belgeler*, III(1966), 36–7.
151 *MM* 17901, p. 9 (1028/1618–19).
152 Biegman, *The Turco-Ragusan relationship*, p. 71.
153 Joseph Schacht, *An introduction to Islamic law* (Oxford, Clarendon Press, 1964), pp. 124–5, 192–4).
154 *MM* 17901, p. 11 (1028/1618–19).
155 Recourse to İstanbul was frequently granted in capitulations. Compare Noradounghian, *Recueil*, vol. 1, pp. 98, 101.
156 See for example *MM* 17901, p. 8 (1028/1618–19).
157 *MM* 17901, p. 13 (1028/1618–19).
158 *MM* 17901, p. 15 (1028/1618–19).
159 *Ibid.*
160 *MM* 6004, pp. 138–43 (about 1028/1618–19). Since the most important provisions of these rescripts have already been discussed in other contexts, no analysis of their contents is necessary here.
161 Steensgaard, 'Consuls and nations', pp. 16–19.
162 Tenenti, *Piracy and the decline of Venice*, p. 51.

16 A study of the feasibility of using eighteenth-century Ottoman financial records as an indicator of economic activity

1 N. Svoronos, *Le commerce de Salonique au XVIIIe siècle* (Paris, PUF, 1956), p. 323.
2 This paper is a continuation of my earlier study 'Osmanlı maliyesinde malikane sistemi' (The *malikane* system in Ottoman finances, *Türkiye iktisat tarihi semineri, metinler/tartışmalar*, ed. Osman Okyar and Ünal Nalbantoğlu (Ankara, Hacettepe Universitesi Yayınevi, 1975), pp. 231–91.
3 The data from which this graph was constructed are derived from individual cases for which I was able to determine the amount of profit accruing to various *malikane* owners from specific *mukataa* in the year in which they deposited the *muaccele*. I did not wish to take up extra room or confuse the issue by including the figures in the text. These figures, which I will be glad to supply to anyone interested, are not normally to be found in the *mukataa* or *ahkam* registers of the Treasury. I located them in the private expense registers of individual *malikane* owners, in the register of the same individual's possessions compiled after his death (*muhallefat*), and in legal documents drawn up in situations in which it seemed likely there would be a conflict over the farming of a *malikane*. Since it is only by chance that one comes across such data in these sources, which are themselves limited in number, it was possible to collect only 150–200 samples. Figure 16.1 was constructed from these samples, dealing with

various *malikanes* in various years between 1700 and 1820. If more data could be accumulated, new graphs could be constructed for shorter periods of time, or for various *malikane* groups in different regions according to separate and differential values, which might reflect more accurately the real situation.

4 Of course this is only valid if the relative proportions of cotton and cotton thread exported remained constant during this period. Otherwise it is clear that the rate of increase would be different.

5 Svoronos, *Le commerce de Salonique*, p. 78.

6 Robert Paris, *L'histoire du commerce de Marseille*, vol. 5: *1660 to 1789. Le Levant* (Paris, Plon, 1957), p. 115.

7 Alfred C. Wood, *A history of the Levant Company* (London, Oxford University Press, 1935), p. 159.

8 Svoronos, *Le commerce de Salonique*, p. 323.

9 This is true of the great majority of the members of these two groups throughout the eighteenth century. There were, however, a small percentage of *malikane* owners who were *ayan-eşraf* and similarly a number of *mültezims* who were part of the central authority. After 1800, there begins to be a recognizable change in the composition of the two groups.

10 As a result, after 1800, when the conflict between the centre and periphery peaked, data of the type we are using here can no longer be relied upon to determine changes in the level of economic activity.

11 The levels at which the bargaining strength of these two groups balanced out may vary from region to region, but they will tend to be similar for *mukataas* of any one region. Therefore, probability of error will decline when comparisons are made between individual *mukataas* located in the same region.

17 When and how British cotton goods invaded the Levant markets

1 Halil İnalcık, 'Osmanlı İdare, Sosyal ve Ekonomik Tarihiyle İlgili Belgeler: Bursa Kadı Sicillerinden Seçmeler' (Documents concerning Ottoman administrative, social, and economic history: selections from Bursa court records), *Belgeler*, 10(1980–1), 1–91; Ömer L. Barkan, 'Edirne Kassamına ait Tereke Defterleri, 1545–1659' (*Tereke* registers concerning *askeri* class in Edirne), *Belgeler*, 3(1966) – in particular see document nos. 4, 18, 30, 31, 38, 52, 56, 60, 66, 68, 84; Halil İnalcık, 'The question of the closing of the Black Sea under the Ottomans', *ARKHEION PONTOU* (Athens), 32(1979), 91–110.

2 Halil İnalcık, 'Bursa: XV. Asır Sanayi ve Ticaret Tarihine Dair Vesikalar' (Bursa: documents concerning commercial and industrial history in the fifteenth century), *Belleten*, 24(1960), document nos. 3, 12, 40.

3 Yaşar Yücel (ed.), *Es'ar Defteri* (Ankara, Dil-Tarih ve Coğrafya Fakültesi Yayınları, 1982), pp. 41–59.

4 Fernand Braudel, *The Mediterranean and the Mediterranean world in the age of Philip II*, vol. 1 (2 vols., New York, Harper and Row Publishers, 1972), pp. 463–6; K.N. Chaudhuri, *The trading world of Asia and the English East India Company* (Cambridge, Cambridge University Press, 1978), pp. 152–89.

5 For the significance of cotton goods in Asian trade, see Chaudhuri, *East India Company*, pp. 49–196; Neils Steensgaard, *Carracks, caravans, and companies* (Copenhagen, 1973), pp. 380–8; W. Flor, *Avvalin-i Sufara-yi Iran-Holland* (Tehran, 1978), p. 20.

6 *Naima Tarihi* (6 vols., Istanbul, Matbaa-ı Amire, AH 1281), vol. 4, p. 293.

7 *Alaca, kutni, bayrami* types of cotton or cotton-and-silk mixture fabrics were manufactured in great quantities in Aleppo, Bursa, and İstanbul. See Yücel, *Es'ar*,

pp. 41–59. Also Halil İnalcık, 'Osmanlı Pamuklu Pazarı, Hindistan, İngiltere: Pazar Rekabetinde Emek Maliyetinin Rolü' (Role of labour costs in market competition: England and India in the Ottoman market for cotton), *Middle East Technical University, Studies in Development*, special issue (1979–80), pp. 21–9, Table IV.

8 For the debate on the importance of changes in the cotton textile industry in the Industrial Revolution see R.M. Hartwell (ed.), *The causes of the Industrial Revolution in England* (London, Methuen, 1967); A.F. Wadsworth and J. de Lacy Mann, *The cotton trade and industrial Lancashire* (Manchester, Manchester University Press, 1931), pp. 111–41, 411–508.

9 A. B. Cunningham, 'The journal of Christophe Aubin: A report on the Levant trade in 1812', *Archivum Ottomanicum*, 8(1983), 5–136.

10 See N.G. Svoronos, *Le commerce de Salonique au XVIIIe siècle* (Paris, PUF, 1956), pp. 245–54.

11 *Ibid.*, pp. 250–3.

12 Evliyâ Çelebi, seventeenth-century Ottoman traveller, described the fabrics used for making clothes by different classes in the cities he visited. *Seyahatname* (Istanbul, AH 1314), vol. 2, p. 91 (Trabzon); vol. 8, p. 197 (Yenişehir).

13 Mübahat Kütükoğlu, *Osmanlı-İngiliz Münasebetleri* (Ottoman–British relations; 2 vols., Ankara, Türk Kültürünü Araştırma Enstitüsü 1974), vol. 1, p. 174.

14 Cunningham, 'The journal'.

15 Osman Nuri (Ergin), *Mecelle-i Umur-ı Belediyye* (Regulations concerning municipalities; 5 vols., Istanbul, 1922), vol. 1, pp. 379–81.

16 Ottoman imports of coarse American cotton cloths were valued at 4,563 dollars in 1829; 29,117 dollars in 1830; 61,587 dollars in 1862; 8,748 dollars in 1872; 111,957 dollars in 1892. See L.J. Gordon, *American relations with Turkey, 1830–1930: an economic interpretation* (Philadelphia, University of Pennsylvania Press, 1932), pp. 43, 51, 52, 66.

17 See M.E. Edwards, *The growth of the British cotton trade* (New York, A.M. Kelley, 1967), pp. 44–8.

18 Clive Emsley, *British society and the French wars, 1793–1815* (London, Rowman, 1979).

19 Cunningham, 'The journal'.

19a A. C. Wood, *A History of the Levant Company* (London, Frank Cass and Co., 1964), p. 192.

20 William J. Hamilton, *Researches in Asia Minor, Pontus, and Armenia* (2 vols., London, J. Murray, 1842), vol. 1, p. 242.

21 Cunningham, 'The journal'; D. Chevallier, 'Les tissus ikatés d'Alep et de Damas', in *Syria*, 39(1962), 300–2.

22 David Urquhart, *Turkey and its resources, its municipal organization and free trade: the prospects of English commerce in the East* (London, Saunders and Otley, 1833), p. 148.

23 *Ibid.*

24 *Ibid.*

25 *Ibid.*, pp. 148–9.

26 *Ibid.*, p. 150.

27 *Ibid.*, p. 151.

28 See Gertrude Robinson, *David Urquhart: some chapters in the life of a Victorian knight-errant of justice and liberty* (Oxford, Kelley, 1920); *Dictionary of National Biography*, vol. LVIII, p. 43; G.H. Bolsover, 'David Urquhart and the Eastern question, 1833–37: a study in publicity and diplomacy', *Journal of Modern History*, vol. 8, no. 4(Dec. 1936), 444–67.

29 Urquhart, *Turkey*, pp. 142–8.

30 See D.G. Barnes, *A history of the English corn laws, 1600–1848* (2nd. edn, New York, Kelley, 1965).

31 Thomas Thornton, *The present state of Turkey* (London, J. Mawman, 1807), and David Urquhart were well aware that the Ottoman or, more accurately, the Islamic economic mind was basically one that favoured freedom of trade. For this point see my 'Capital formation in the Ottoman Empire', *The Journal of Economic History*, 29(1969), 98–108. Mustafa Reşid, initiator of Western inspired reforms in Turkey, claimed to remain within the confines of the Islamic law when he introduced his liberalizing measures, abolishing the guilds, signing the most liberal treaties of commerce with Western nations and extending private property rights on land. He had a firm conviction that free trade would result in an unprecedented expansion of the Empire's economy and enrich the Treasury; for Reşid Paşa's policies, see Halil İnalcık, 'Sened-i İttifak ve Gülhane Hatt-ı Humayunu', (Tanzimat rescript) *Belleten*, 28(1964), 603–22. However, his initial and lasting concern was to secure England's political support against Mehmed Ali of Egypt. See V.J. Puryear, *International economics and diplomacy in the Near East: a study of British commercial policy in the Levant, 1834–1853* (London, Oxford University Press, 1935), pp. 146–79; F.E. Bailey, *British policy and economic growth in England* (Cambridge, Mass., Harvard University Press, 1942), pp. 129–233. See also Barry Gordon, *Economic doctrine and Tory liberalism 1824–1830* (New York, Barnes and Nobles, 1979).

32 For the arduous negotiations between the Ottoman government and England on the issue of customs rates see Kütükoğlu, *Osmanlı-İngiliz*, vol. 1, pp. 78–86; vol. 2, pp. 7–108; Puryear, *International economics*, pp. 117–27; Bailey, *British policy*, pp. 84–128.

33 Urquhart, *Turkey*, p. 134.

34 Bailey, *British policy*, p. 74.

35 Charles Issawi, *The economic history of Turkey, 1800–1914* (Chicago, University of Chicago Press, 1980), p. 79.

36 C. Hamlin, *Among the Turks* (New York, R. Carter and Brothers, 1877), p. 59.

37 Ergin, *Mecelle*, vol. 1, p. 760. The document (dated 1868) is a regulation for the organization of an association of weavers in İstanbul.

38 Chevallier, 'Les tissus', p. 300, n. 1.

39 Ottoman public opinion began to voice its discontent and protested against the disruptive effects of Western capitalism as early as 1860s. See İhsan Sungu, 'Yeni Osmanlılar' (New Ottomans), *Tanzimat*, I (İstanbul, Maarif Matbaası, 1940), pp. 787–94, 837–40.

40 P. Deane and W.A. Cole, *British economic growth, 1688–1859: trends and structure* (London, Cambridge University Press, 1964), pp. 166, 170–1, 185.

41 *Ibid.*, pp. 187–8, 191–2.

42 In a list of market dues at Beypazarı, a small town near Ankara, dated 1836 (İhtisab Defteri, no. 32, p. 6, Başvekalet Arşivi, İstanbul) mention is made of European goods called 'goods of *fatura*' or *mal-ı fatura*, which is obviously a distortion of the Italian word *manifattura*. In Turkish *manifaturacı* became a common designation for traders in textiles of European origin or design. It should also be added that around 1840 Galata or Pera – the market place for European goods – superseded the Grand Bazaar (Kapalı-çarşı) in İstanbul as the area where the well-to-do did their shopping. (Charles White, *Three years in Constantinople* (3 vols., London, H. Colborn, 1846), vol. 2, pp. 54–9.) White also pointed out that the Grand Bazaar was the market where traditional wares were sold; for instance, shawls imported from Iran and India as well as their Turkish imitations. White also observed that the prices of such items were higher than they were in London (vol. 2, p. 45; vol. 3, pp. 217–18). Thus, as a result of changes in tastes and the growing demand for cheaper European-made, cotton or

woollen shawls, there was a decline in the imports of Indian shawls. Middle and lower classes increasingly preferred European shawl materials to make their belts, turbans or garments. Finally, White added that in local district markets cheaper cotton goods were in great demand (vol. 1, p. 27) and gave a list of muslins produced by the local industries. On the other hand, White observed that Europeanization of official costumes resulted in a considerable increase in European woollen imports (vol. 2, pp. 53–4).

43 Kütükoğlu, *Osmanlı-İngiliz*, vol. 1, pp. 117–27; vol. 2, pp. 43–64; Orhan Kurmuş, *Emperyalizmin Türkiye'ye Girişi* (Imperialist penetration of Turkey; İstanbul, Bilim Yayınları, 1974).

44 Issawi, *Turkey*, p. 145; for a list of country fairs in Rumeli see Halil Sahillioglu, 'XVIII. Yüzyılda Edirne'nin Ticari imkanları', (Trade opportunities in Edirne during the 17th century) *Belgelerle Türk Tarihi Dergisi*, 13(1968), 63. For fairs in Anatolia see Suraiya Faroqhi, 'Sixteenth-century periodic markets in various Anatolian sancaks: İçel, Hamid, Karahisar-ı Sahib, Kütahya, Aydın, Menteşe', *Journal of the Economic and Social History of the Orient*, 22, pt. I, 32–80.

45 Lewis Farley, *The resources of Turkey considered with special reference to the profitable investment of capital in the Ottoman empire* (London, Longman, Green, Longman and Roberts, 1862), p. 56; for the dramatic increase in British cotton goods exported to the Ottoman dominions after 1844 see Kütükoğlu, *Osmanlı-İngiliz*, vol. 2, pp. 130–1, Tables 9 and 10; E. Michelsen, *The Ottoman Empire and its resources* (London, Simpkin, Marshall, 1853); A. Rafeq, 'The impact of Europe on a traditional economy: the case of Damascus, 1840–1870', Paper presented at the Second International Conference on the Social and Economic History of Turkey, July 1980, Strasbourg.

46 Farley, *Resources of Turkey*, p. 59.

Index